BEGINNING WOODWORK

7th Edition

BEGINNING WOODWORK

7th Edition

John L. Feirer

New York, New York Columbus, Ohio Woodland Hills, California Peoria, Illinois

Glencoe/McGraw-Hill
A Division of The McGraw-Hill Companies

Previous copyrights 1984 and 1988 by John L. Feirer under title *Beginning Woodwork*, 1978 and 1972 by John L. Feirer under title *Bench Woodwork*, and 1965 and 1959 by John L. Feirer under title *I.A. Bench Woodwork*.

Printed in the United States of America

Send all inquiries to:
Glencoe/McGraw-Hill
3008 W. Willow Knolls Drive
Peoria, IL 61614-1083

ISBN 0-02-677600-6 (Text)
ISBN 0-02-677601-4 (Instructor's Resource Guide)
ISBN 0-02-677602-2 (Student Workbook)

6 7 8 9 10 11 12 026 07 06 05

The publisher acknowledges the assistance of the following reviewers for their help in preparing this revision:

Charles A. Park
Woodworking Instructor
Metamora Township High School, Metamora, IL

Bill Schaaf
Wood Technology Instructor
Jefferson County Schools, Arvada, Colorado

Steven A. Ramsey
Industrial Technology Teacher

You can find plans for these projects in Chapter 57.

The Plan of This Book

Beginning Woodwork, as a part of a modern industrial education program, includes the following as some of its major objectives:

1. It teaches students about the woodworking industry, including sources of lumber, how lumber is made into plywood and other wood materials, how wood projects are designed and produced, and how people earn a living in woodworking. It is a study of one of our most common materials.

2. It teaches students how to design, plan, and carry through a project in woodworking. They are introduced to the need for planning their own projects and making bills of materials for these projects. While most beginning students will not be able to design, they should know how to select well-designed projects and make planning sheets, bills of materials, and stock-cutting lists.

3. It teaches basic hand skills in woodworking that are useful to everyone, regardless of the

aim in life. Many will use these woodworking skills in their hobbies. Others will find them useful around the home. A small number may use these skills in occupations such as carpentry or teaching of industrial education.

4. It teaches students how to work safely with woodworking tools and materials and to protect themselves from accidents.

5. It teaches consumer values. Students learn how to order lumber, plywood, finishing materials, and hardware.

6. It teaches the conservation of natural resources. Students are taught the value of our forests and the importance of preserving them.

This book contains 57 chapters, each of which offers a good learning opportunity. The arrangement of the book makes for great flexibility. Only those chapters need be covered that meet the outline of a particular course. Questions at the end of each chapter focus attention on the important ideas and information.

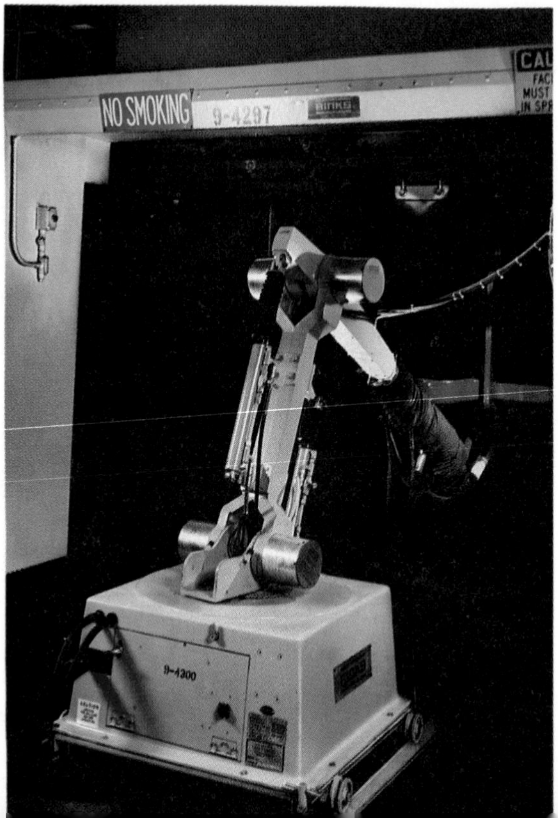

Numerous project ideas are found in the main text and in the project section. If a student needs a detailed drawing, he or she may choose one from the project section. However, as the student grows in ability to work independently, he or she may develop his or her own project drawings, using one of the ideas shown in the text.

This book could be used as a first course in woodwork for any age group, although the illustrations and projects included would probably appeal mostly to early teenagers. To make the book more useful to these age groups, the sentences were checked for length and difficulty. The vocabulary has been confined to the early teenage degree of development. Technical words and other advanced terms are defined the first time they are used. The sentences are short, to keep the reading level well within the ability of the age group. Older students should find the book especially easy to follow in a beginning course in

This 1994 edition incorporates a chapter on the applications of computers, robots, lasers, and other new technology to woodwork as well as a general updating of information and a number of new projects. As before, full-color illustrations of selected woods and prize-winning projects have been included to show the beauty and versatility of wood.

This new edition also includes thirteen new projects. Each of these projects has been designed to challenge students at varying skill levels.

This edition also includes a Glossary, which provides definitions of over two hundred terms commonly used in woodworking.

Acknowledgments

Some of the classroom pictures were taken at South Junior High School in Kalamazoo, Michigan. Pictured are Mr. Wolfgang Lugauer, instructor, and students Edward Hughes, Kenneth Randt, William Erwin Grossnick, Kevin Sutton, and Nina Feirer.

The author would like to express his appreciation to Kerry R. Jackson and Susan M. Hutchings.

Listed below are the companies that were so generous in helping to supply illustrations and other materials. Special assistance was given by those listed in italics.

Adage, Inc.
Adjustable Clamp Company
American Forest Products Industries
American Plywood Association
American Screw Company
Baker Furniture Company
Behr-Manning Company
Bell System News
George B. Bent Company
Better Light Better Sight Bureau
The Black and Decker Manufacturing Company
Boice-Crane Company
Butler Furniture Company
Cadwell Furniture Co.
Calcomp—A Sanders Company
Cascade Graphic Development Company
Cherry Tree Toys, Inc.
The Cincinnati Tool Company
Clausing Corporation
Conant Ball Company
The Cooper Group
Dansk Designs
Dez Company
Docugraphix, Inc.
Dremel Manufacturing Company
Drexel Furniture Company
Dunbar Furniture Corporation of Indiana
Eastman Kodak Company
E.I. duPont de Nemours & Co., Inc.
Ethan Allen, Inc.
The Franklin Glue Company
General Electric Corporation
General Motors Company

Similar projects can be found in Chapter 57.

Georgia-Pacific Corporation
Gold Medal Inc.
Greenlee Tool Company
Gulf Oil Company
The Gunlocke Company
Hardwood Dimension Manufacturers' Association
Harris & Mallow Products, Div. Thomas Industries
Heath Company
Heritage Furniture Company
Inland Steel Company
Iowa Department of Public Instruction
I.P. Hyde Company
Jam Handy Corporation
Jens Risom Design, Inc.
John Stuart Incorporated
Kroehler Furniture Company
Lasercraft
Lockheed Star
Los Angeles Public Schools
Magnum Machine Company
Manpower Magazine
Masonite Corporation
McDonald Products Company
McDonnell Douglas Corporation
Millers Falls Company
Mummert-Dixon Company
National Association of Home Builders
National Lumber Manufacturing Association
Nicholson File Company
Owens Corning Fiberglas Corporation
Frank Paxton Lumber Company
Pennsylvania House
Peter Pepper Products, Inc.
H.K. Porter Company
Precision-Built Homes
Quaker Industries
Reynolds Metals Company
Rockwell Manufacturing Company
Rohm and Haas Corporation
Ryobi Power Tools
Senco Products
Sherwin-Williams Company
Shopsmith, Inc.
D. Simpson
Simpson Timber Company
Skil Corporation
Stanley Tools
Thonet
Triangle Pacific Corporation
U.S. Department of Agriculture
U.S. Department of Labor
U.S. Forest Service
U.S. Steel Corporation
Victorian Millworks
Western Electric Company
Western Wood Products Association
David White Instruments
Woman's Day (The A & P Magazine)
The Woodworker's Store
X-Acto Crescent Products, Inc.
Yates-American Machine Company
Zinc Institute, Inc.

Table of Contents

Look in Chapter 57 for the plans for this cradle.

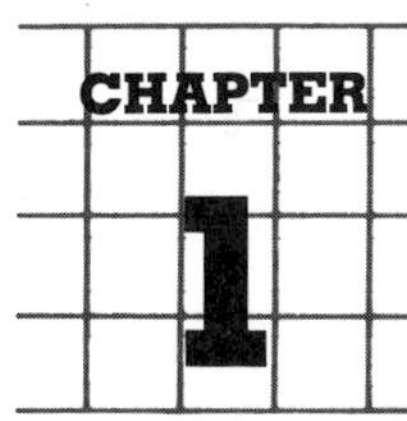

CHAPTER 1

Exploring Woodworking

There's so much to do and learn in woodworking. You can make a project of wood . . . learn to use hand tools safely . . . run a machine . . . find out how a house is built . . . be part of a manufacturing company. In this book you will find ideas about things to make, tools to use, machines to run, and materials to try.

You will learn how important wood is to the way we live. Fig. 1-1. The average person in the United States uses more wood products than the average person in other countries. Almost 90 percent of us live in homes made of wood. Every day we use paper, packaging material, furniture, equipment, and many other things made from wood. Almost everything that is manufactured is first made of wood. Even a jet airplane or a missile is first made of wood as a small model and/or full-size mock-up. These are studied and tested before the real product is built.

Wood comes in many colors, textures, strengths, weights, and costs. Fig. 1-2. The wood to use depends on the item being made. For a baseball bat, the wood used might be hickory or

(cont'd. on p. 21)

1-1. *How many uses for wood do you see in this picture?*

1-2. ***Some common kinds of wood. (Photos courtesy of the Frank Paxton Lumber Company)***

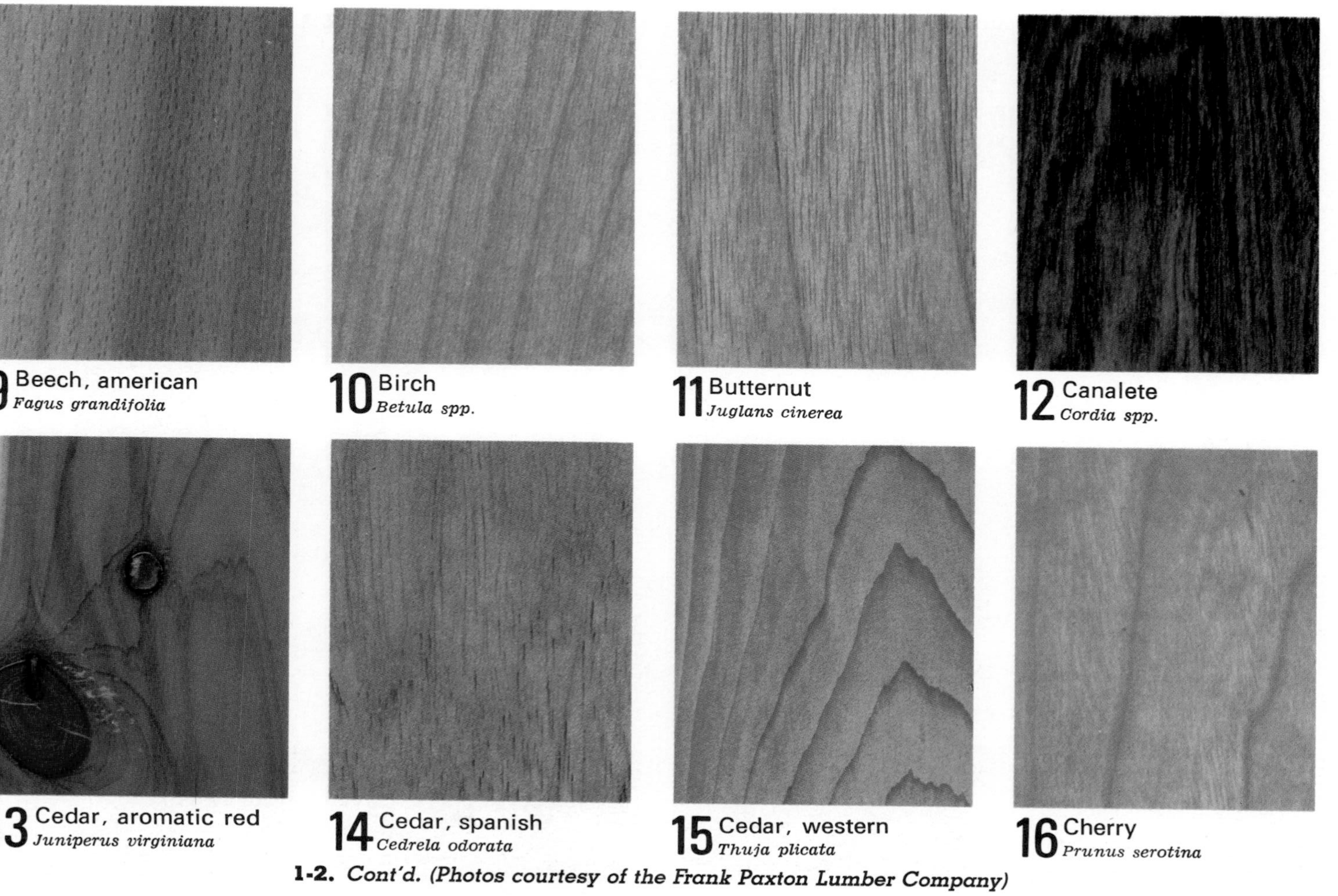

9 Beech, american *Fagus grandifolia*

10 Birch *Betula spp.*

11 Butternut *Juglans cinerea*

12 Canalete *Cordia spp.*

13 Cedar, aromatic red *Juniperus virginiana*

14 Cedar, spanish *Cedrela odorata*

15 Cedar, western *Thuja plicata*

16 Cherry *Prunus serotina*

1-2. ***Cont'd. (Photos courtesy of the Frank Paxton Lumber Company)***

1-2. *Cont'd. (Photos courtesy of the Frank Paxton Lumber Company)*

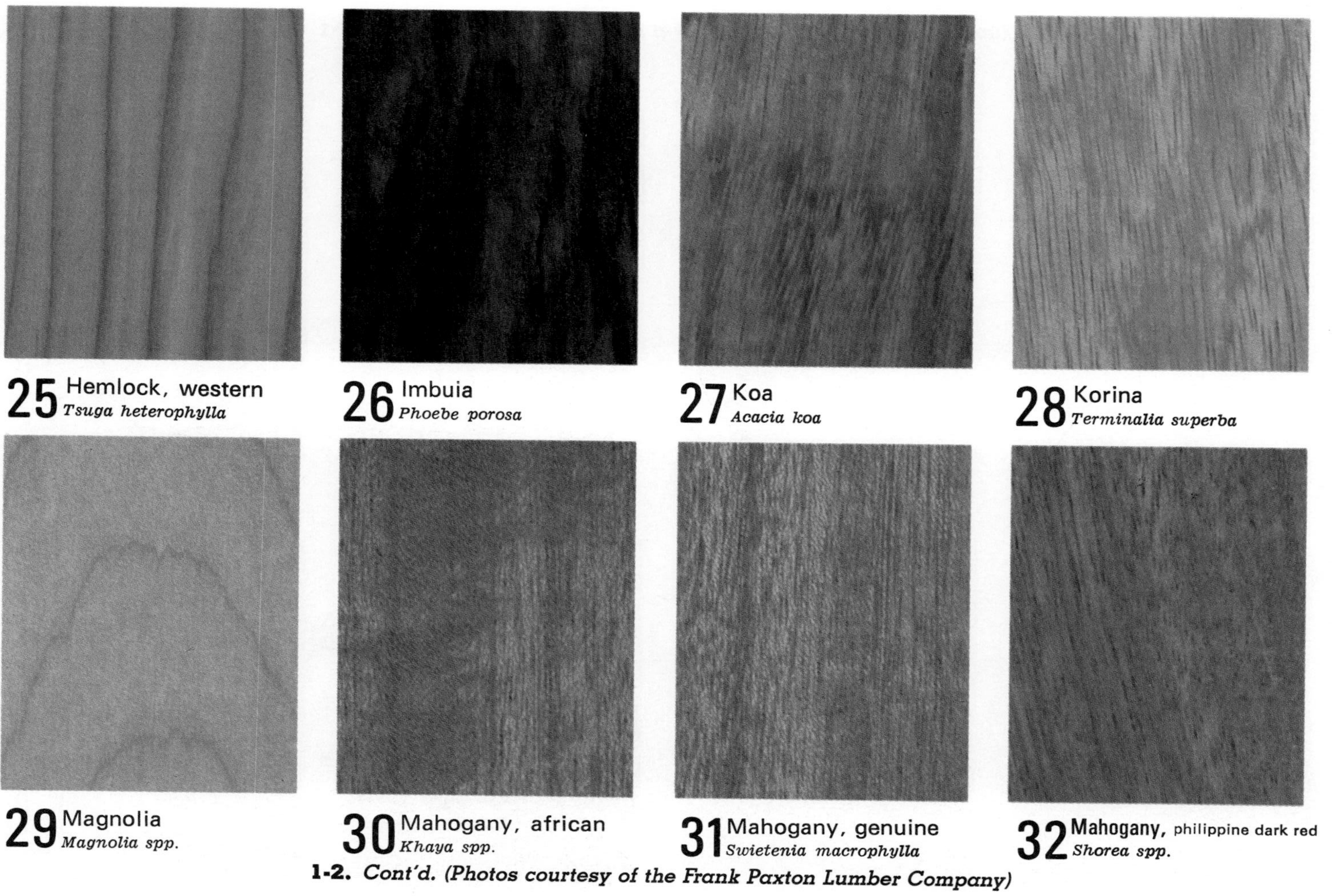

1-2. *Cont'd. (Photos courtesy of the Frank Paxton Lumber Company)*

1-2. ***Cont'd. (Photos courtesy of the Frank Paxton Lumber Company)***

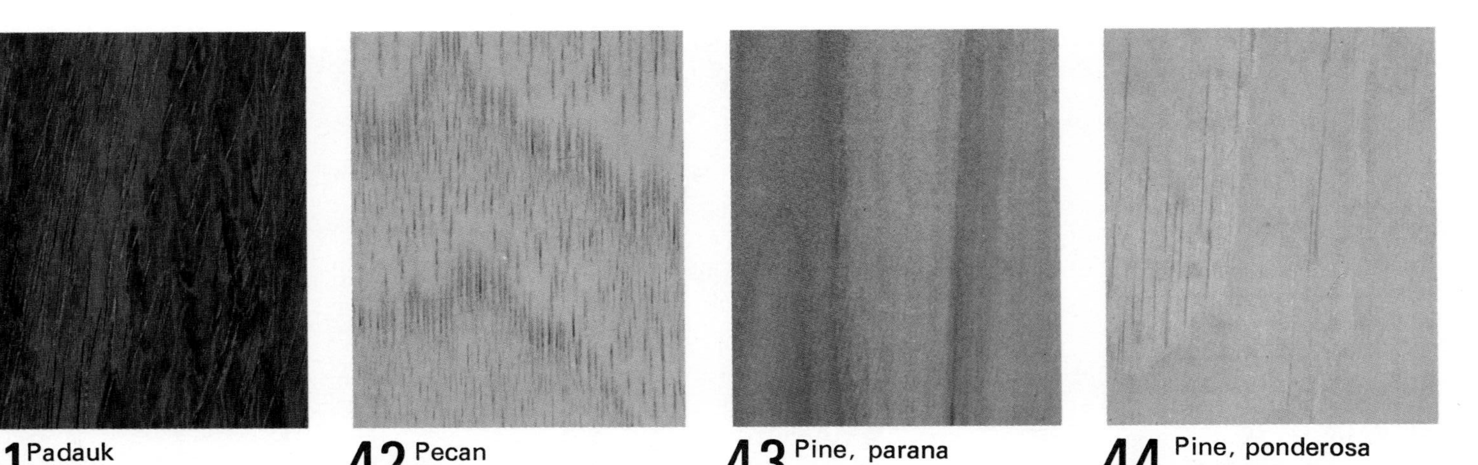

41 Padauk
Pterocarpus soyauxii

42 Pecan
Hicoria spp.

43 Pine, parana
Araucaria spp.

44 Pine, ponderosa
Pinus ponderosa

45 Pine, sugar white
Pinus lambertiana

46 Pine, yellow
Pinus spp.

47 Poplar
Liriodendron tulipifera

48 Pradu
Pterocarpus spp.

1-2. ***Cont'd. (Photos courtesy of the Frank Paxton Lumber Company)***

1-2. *Cont'd. (Photos courtesy of the Frank Paxton Lumber Company)*

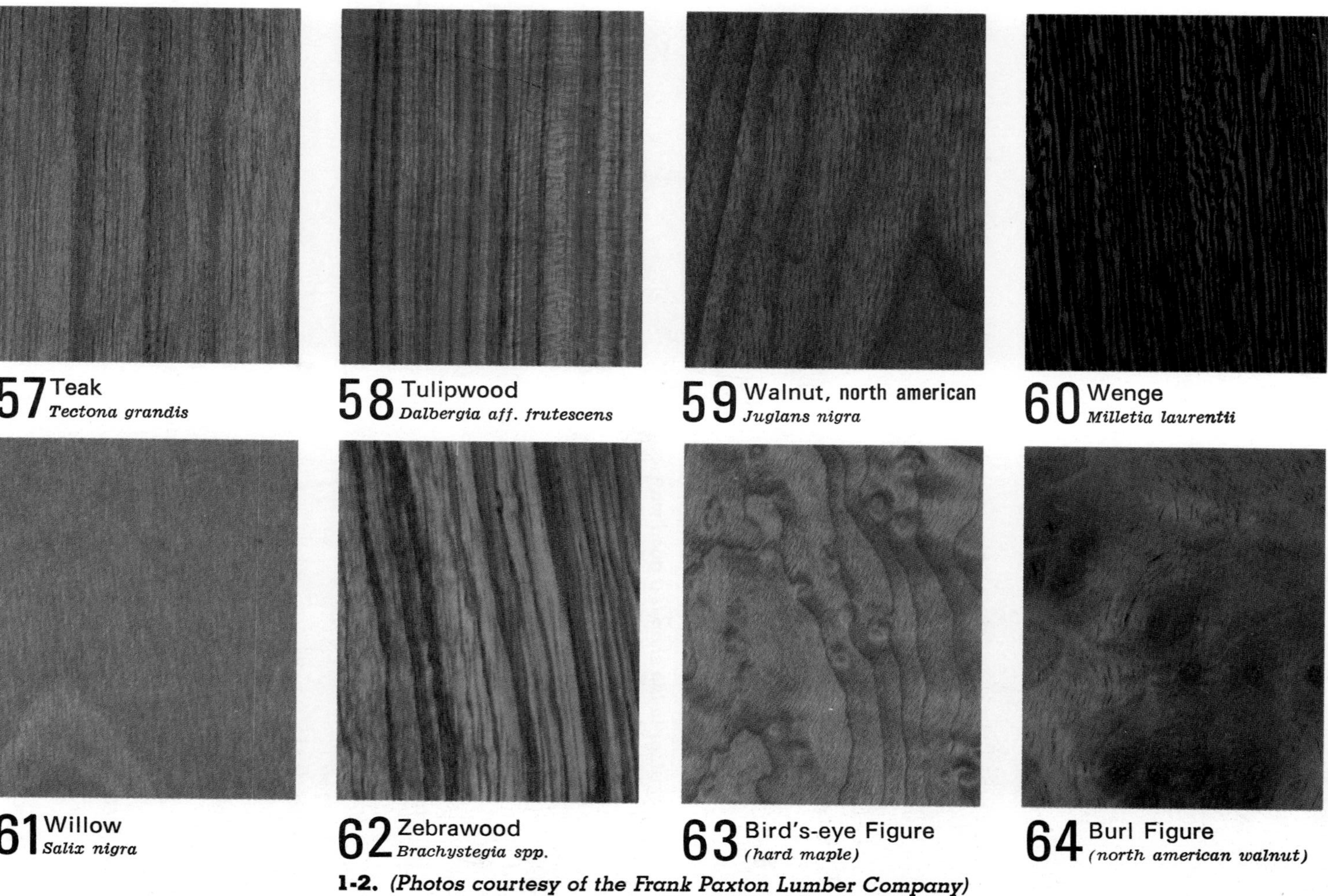

1-2. *(Photos courtesy of the Frank Paxton Lumber Company)*

1-3. *Getting to know tools makes them your servants. (Stanley Tools)*

1-4. *Working together in the shop is a good way to learn how to get along with other people.*

1-5. *It is interesting to make things of wood. Here a group is listening while the instructor evaluates their work.*

ash. For a piece of fine furniture, it might be walnut, cherry, or mahogany. Most of the woods used in building construction are pine, fir, or cedar.

Wood is one of our most important renewable resources. We can grow trees for houses, furniture, sporting goods, musical instruments, and even for fuel. Because wood is plentiful and easy to work, it is a favorite material for many things we use in the home, school, and workplace. It is also the most popular material for hobby and leisure time activities.

You will find woodworking both interesting and useful. Here are some of the things you will learn:

- Where wood and other products of trees come from.
- How lumbering is done.
- How plywood and similar products are manufactured.
- Common kinds of woods and their uses.
- How to buy lumber and other wood supplies.
- How to buy woodworking tools and machines.
- How to work safely with hand tools and simple power tools. Fig. 1-3.

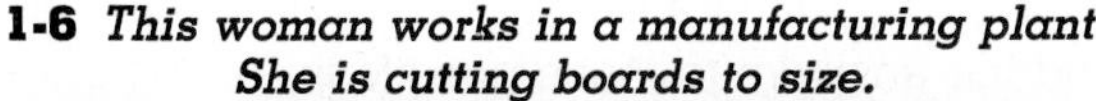

1-6 ***This woman works in a manufacturing plant. She is cutting boards to size.***

1-7. ***You will learn how wood projects are made, from the raw material . . .***

- How to work with others. Fig. 1-4.
- How to design, plan, and construct useful and attractive projects. Fig. 1-5.
- How to apply a finish.
- How people earn a living in woodworking. Fig. 1-6.
- How to begin a lifelong hobby in woods.
- How to take care of the shop or work area so that it's neat, clean, and orderly.
- How houses and other living units are built.
- How wood products are manufactured. Figs. 1-7 and 1-8.

All of these skills and information will come as you make projects with tools and machines.

Let's take a look at what you will do when you make a project:

1. **Selecting or designing the project.** What to make is a big question. Will it be something for yourself or for your room? Will it be a gift for your mother or father or someone else in your family? Maybe you'd like to make a game or build

a piece of sports equipment. Or perhaps you'd like an out-of-doors project for birds or a pet. You, your instructor, and the other students will all help to decide what to make. You may find a drawing of a project in a book or magazine. Maybe you would like to design your own project. Fig. 1-9. Your instructor may want you to build the first project from a design he or she has chosen. The students in the class may decide to vote on what will be the mass production project. Fig. 1-10. After you've learned some of the basic skills, you will probably select and design a project all your own.

1-9. ***Suppose you decide to make a message center. Would you know how to begin?***

1-8. *. . . to the finished product.*

2. **Reading a drawing and making a sketch.** You must be able to read a drawing to find the answers to these questions:

- What is the overall size of the project?
- How big are the pieces?
- What shape are the pieces?

Sometimes it will be necessary to make a *shop sketch* to keep with you all the time you're building the project. A shop sketch is a simple drawing made on squared paper. You always need one when you design your own project. You also need a shop sketch if the project is in a library book or a magazine that you can't keep.

3. **Selecting the materials.** What materials will you use to make the project? For example, will it be pine, cedar, or poplar? Could plywood be used? How would you buy it if you had to go to a lumberyard yourself?

4. **Planning your work.** What is the size of each part? How many parts are alike? How will

1-10. ***These students decided to make house numbers for their manufacturing project.***

you make the project? What steps will you follow? What tools will you need?

5. **Building the project.** Now you are ready to follow the steps for building the project.

6. **Rating the project.** After the project is finished, ask yourself these questions: Am I satisfied with it? What have I done well? What could I have done better? How can I improve on the next project?

QUESTIONS

1. How is a first project in woodworking usually chosen?
2. Why must you be able to read a drawing?
3. Why should you rate a project after building it?

ACTIVITIES

1. Your home probably includes some wood furniture, but what other wood items are there? Make a list of five wood products (besides furniture) that are in your home.
2. Have you ever built a wood project? If so, tell the class about the project. Did you build it from scratch or assemble it from a kit? Do you have the drawings? If so, bring them to class.
3. Make a list of what you expect to learn from woodworking. Show this list to your teacher.

CHAPTER 2 Safety

Safety is important in all types of work. When you get a job in industry or business, you will have to observe federal safety standards. These standards were established when the United States Congress passed the Occupational Safety and Health Act (OSHA). These strict regulations are meant to protect both the employee and the employer in all aspects of work. Many states have passed laws similar to the federal law. More and more, these regulations apply to both industries and schools.

Safety standards established by law are very complete. They include not only the obvious, such as safety glasses or goggles, but also standards for guards, noise and air pollution, electrical hazards, and every other aspect of working conditions. Each employer must establish and maintain conditions of work that are safe and healthy. All employees must follow all safety regulations. No employee may remove, displace, damage, destroy, or carry off any safety device or safety item.

In woodworking you must "be prepared" in order to work safely. When people do not know how to use a tool, machine, or other equipment safely, they put themselves and others in danger. Sometimes one person dares another to do something reckless. Sometimes you may say to yourself, "I'll do it this way just once"—even though you know it is dangerous. If people do something they know is reckless, they are not being brave or smart. They are being foolish. One accident can cause the loss of a finger or an eye.

When accidents happen, people get excited and may not think clearly. You might get excited too, if you don't know what to do. Find out where the nearest medical attention is available. Does your school have a nurse on duty, or must you go to a doctor's office or the emergency room of a hospital? Learn these things now so that you will be prepared if an accident does happen.

Remember:

- Learn the safety rules.
- Follow them at all times.
- Know where and how to get medical help.

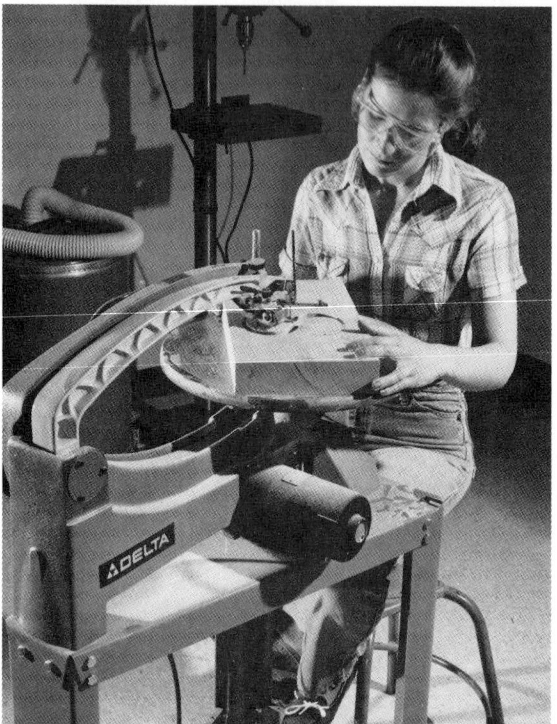

2-1. *When working with power tools and machines, it is best to wear short sleeves. This young woman is using an electronic variable speed scroll saw with speed ranges from 40 to 2000 strokes per minute. You'll learn more about electronic tools in Chapter 56.*

2-2. *If you wear long sleeves, make sure you button the cuffs.*

WORKING SAFELY

- Follow directions. The correct way is the safe way. The safe way is shown in this book.
- Your instructor will show you how to do things correctly and safely.
- Never try to get by "just this once." That's usually the time an accident happens.
- A good slogan to follow is, "It is better to be safe than sorry." The ABCs of safety are Always Be Careful.
- Avoid horseplay. It is the most dangerous thing you can do. Practical jokes in the shop aren't funny. Would you want to cause a friend's accident? Wrestling, pushing, shoving, or tripping usually end in an accident. Your instructor can't allow it, and *you can't afford it.*

PERSONAL PROTECTION

Clothing. Loose clothing can get caught in machinery that is turning. Tuck in any loose clothing. If long sleeves are worn, they must be tightly buttoned at the wrist or rolled up to the elbows. A short-sleeved shirt or sweater is best. Figs. 2-1 and 2-2.

Jewelry. Remove rings, watches, and other jewelry before working with tools and machines.

Eyes. Wear goggles or safety glasses equipped with side shields. These will protect your eyes from flying chips, nails, sawdust, kickbacks, and splashes. Fig. 2-3.

Ears. Wear ear protectors (muffs) when working around machines for long periods of time.

2-3. *You have only one pair of eyes. You can't buy a new pair.* Protect them.

2-4. *Safety rules for using tools and machines will be set off with this stop sign.*

Industry requires this safety equipment. Figure 1-6 in Chapter 1 shows ear protectors being worn.

Hair. Keep long hair away from moving machines. Tie your hair in back or wear a protective hat or net.

USING TOOLS

- Learn to use tools correctly and observe all safety rules. Throughout this book, special safety rules for using a tool or machine are brought to your attention with a stop sign. Fig. 2-4. Whenever you see this sign, read the safety rules next to it. Follow these rules when using the tool or machine.
- A cutting tool must have a sharp edge to do a good job. A sharp tool cuts the wood easily. A dull tool could slip and cut you.
- Never try to test the sharpness of tools on your hand or fingers. Always use wood or paper.
- Keep your hands away from the front of sharp-edged cutting tools and machines. Fig. 2-5.
- Be especially careful when you use your finger or hand as a guide when starting a cutting tool.
- Make sure that your tools are in good condition. Check to see that the handles are not broken or cracked and that they are fastened tightly.
- Remember to use the correct tool for the job every time. Don't misuse tools. For example,

2-5. *These students are following good safety practices for operating machines. They are keeping their hands away from the cutting edge of this shaper. What other good safety practices do you see?*

2-6. *Use the right tool for the job, and use it safely.*

don't use a chisel to open a wooden box or a can of paint. There are openers made for this purpose. Fig. 2-6.

- When carrying tools, always keep the pointed ends down and away from you.

HOUSEKEEPING

- Keep the top of your bench and the floor around it clean and neat.
- Put your tools away after you have used them.
- Wipe up oil and grease spots. Keep rags in a metal container.
- Place scrap stock in scrap boxes immediately.
- Don't wait for someone else to clean up. A clean shop is a safer shop.

REPORTING ACCIDENTS

- Report every accident, no matter how small. Get first aid for every cut or scratch. An infection can start from even the smallest cut. If you get something in your eye, get help from someone who knows what to do.

QUESTIONS

1. Tell how to dress correctly in the wood shop.
2. Why is it important to follow directions?
3. Why is it important to learn how to use tools correctly?
4. What is the most dangerous thing you can do in a shop?
5. Why is it important to report all accidents?

ACTIVITIES

1. Prepare a poster based on one of the safety rules discussed in this chapter.
2. Prepare a housekeeping checklist. This list can be used during the lab clean-up time to help make sure tools and materials have been properly put away and the area has been cleaned.

CHAPTER 3 Measurement

When people first began to measure things, they used parts of their bodies or other natural objects as measuring units. For example, a *cubit* was the distance from the elbow to the fingertips. Since this distance varied from one person to the next, it was not a very accurate way to measure. Fig. 3-1. Gradually, units became standardized. The Egyptians, for example, had a royal cubit made of black granite. All the other cubit sticks in the land were regularly compared to the royal cubit to make sure they were the same length. From such beginnings came many of the world's measuring systems, including our *customary* system. The customary system is based mostly on traditional English measurements such as the foot and the pound. Fig. 3-2.

In the late 1700s, scientists in France developed the *metric* system. It was based on amounts that were believed to remain constant, such as the size of the earth. Fig. 3-3. This system has been improved and is now known as the SI (modernized) metric system. The abbreviation SI stands for System International. Today most countries use the metric system. The United States still uses the customary system, but many of our industries have gone metric. It is a good idea to learn to measure in both systems. Fig 3-4.

THE SI METRIC SYSTEM

Let's look at the measuring system used by most of the world. The modernized metric system of units, SI, consists of seven *base units.* These are the metre[1], kilogram, kelvin, second, ampere, candela, and mole. Fig. 3-5 (page 32). Other units are derived from these base units. For example, the unit for liquid capacity, the litre[1], is derived from the unit of length, the metre. A litre is the amount of liquid that can be contained in a cube which measures ten centimetres (one-tenth of a metre) on each side.

In everyday life, only four units are used:

- The *metre,* the unit of length, is a little longer than a yard (about 39.37 inches).
- The *kilogram,* the unit of weight (mass), is a little more than two pounds (actually 2.2 pounds).
- The *litre,* the unit of liquid capacity or volume, is a little more than a quart (about 1.06 quarts).
- The *degree Celsius* is the everyday unit for measuring temperature. On the Celsius scale, water freezes at 0°C and boils at 100°C. Degrees Fahrenheit can be converted to degrees Celsius. Subtract 32 from the degrees Fahrenheit and divide by 1.8. If the Fahrenheit temperature is above 50 degrees, there is a faster way to convert. Start with 50°F and 10°C. For every 9 degrees increase in Fahrenheit temperature, add 5 degrees to the Celsius temperature. For example, 59°F is equal to 15°C. A pleasant spring day with a temperature of 68°F (50 + 9 + 9) would be 20°C (10 + 5 + 5).

The metric system is a decimal system. All larger and smaller units are based on multiples of ten, with no fractions. To indicate these larger and smaller units, prefixes are added to the unit words. For example, larger and smaller units of length are indicated by adding such prefixes as *kilo-, centi-,* and *milli-* to the word *metre.* A kilometre is 1000 times larger than a metre. A centimetre is 100 times smaller than a metre (one-hundredth of a metre). A millimetre is 1000

[1]The words *metre* and *litre* can also be spelled *meter* and *liter.*

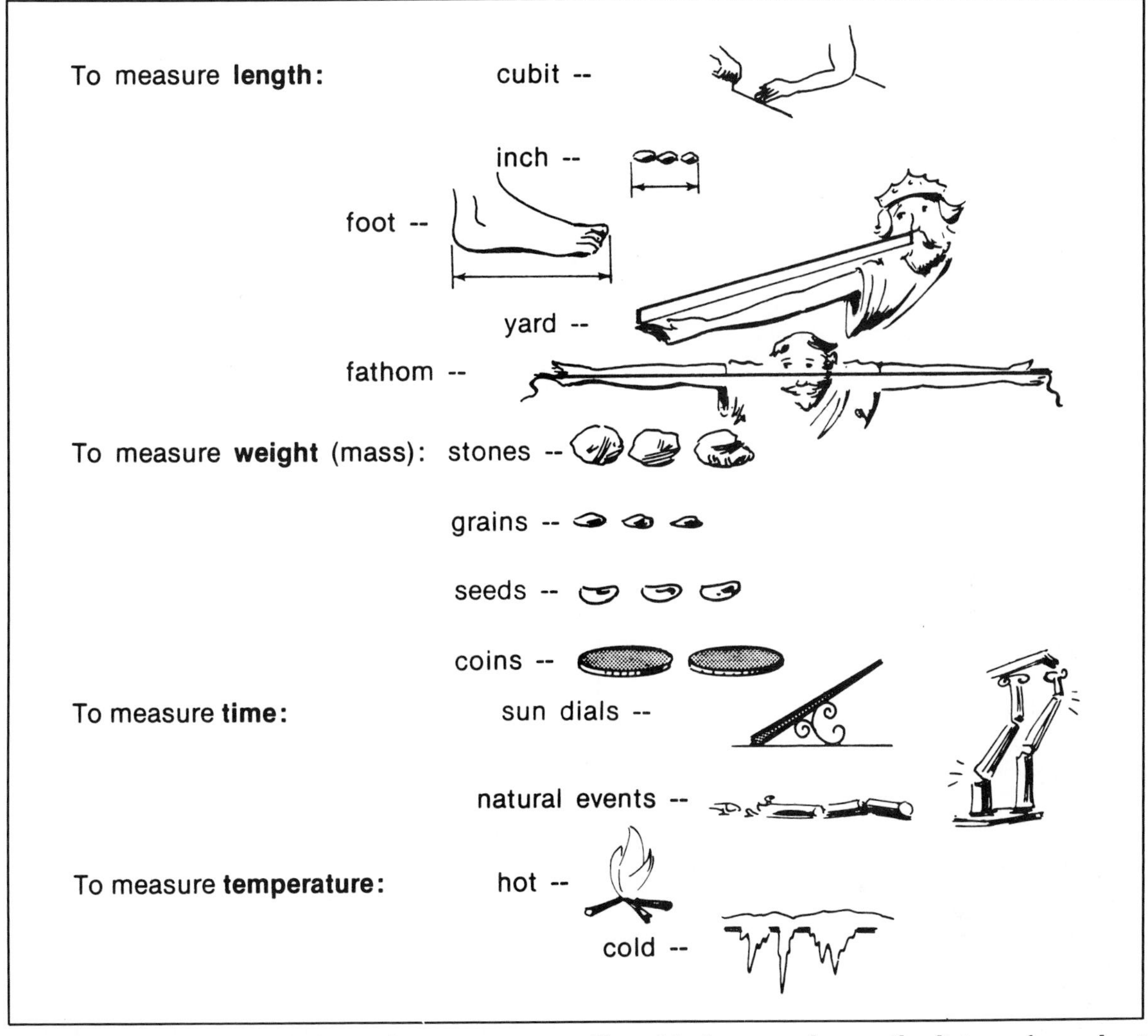

3-1. *Here's how people used to make measurements. The* cubit, *for example, was the distance from a bent elbow to the tip of a finger. The* fathom *was the distance between the fingers of outstretched arms. Can you see why these measuring instruments are not very accurate?*

times smaller than a metre (one-thousandth of a metre). These three prefixes are the most common and are used for nearly all units of measurement.

Both the prefixes and the names of the units can be shortened into symbols. Figures 3-6 and 3-7 show the symbols for the most common units and prefixes.

Other Metric Measurements

Speed. Machine speeds are shown in metres per minute (m/min). Highway speed is in kilometres per hour (km/h).

Power. All power is measured in kilowatts (kW). For example, a two-horsepower motor on a saw would be listed as 1.5 kilowatts. One horsepower equals about 0.75 kW.

The customary (English) system used in the United States is called the Imperial system in England.

King Edward I and his successor, Edward II, established legal standards for trading purposes.

Their yard, a metal bar, the unit of length, was called the "iron ulna."

The standard was described as follows:

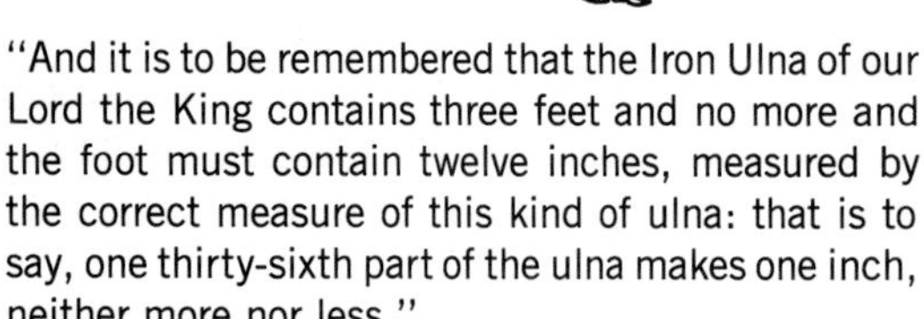

"And it is to be remembered that the Iron Ulna of our Lord the King contains three feet and no more and the foot must contain twelve inches, measured by the correct measure of this kind of ulna: that is to say, one thirty-sixth part of the ulna makes one inch, neither more nor less."

Another definition from early history:

"It is ordained that three grains of barley, dry and round, make an inch; twelve inches make a foot; three feet make an ulna."

From this early beginning, there developed over 80 standards of weights and measures, most of them with no rhyme or reason. This is why most of the world is changing to the metric system

3-2. ***The customary system developed in England. Today England uses the metric system.***

THE METRIC SYSTEM

During the time of Napoleon, French scientists developed a more accurate system based on earth measurements. It was called the **metric system.** The base unit, the metre, was one ten-millionth (1/10 000 000) of the distance from the North Pole to the equator when measured on a straight line running along the surface of the earth through Paris.

There was a small error in this definition so scientists later defined the metre as the distance between two lines engraved on a special platinum-iridium bar. This bar is kept at the International Bureau of Weights and Measures near Paris.

Still later, the metre was defined in terms of the wavelength of light given off by the krypton-86 atom.

3-3. ***The metric system developed in France. Today most of the world uses a modernized version called SI metric. The SI stands for*** **Système International,** ***the French term for international system.***

The alarm rings in the morning to wake you. The **time** is 7:30 a.m.

You get up and step on the bathroom scale. Your **weight** (mass) is 60 kilograms (132 pounds).

You look at the outdoor thermometer. The **temperature** is a cool 15 degrees Celsius (59 degrees Fahrenheit).

You walk to the door to get the morning paper—a **distance** of 10 metres (33 feet).

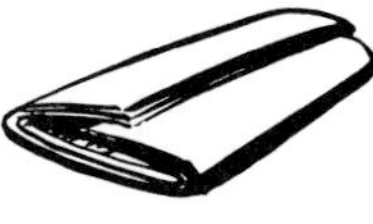

Now you're ready for breakfast. Out comes a box of cereal—the big size. The **weight** (mass) is printed on the front as 397 grams (14 ounces).

You open the refrigerator and take out a carton of milk. Its **liquid capacity** is 1 litre (1.06 quarts).

After breakfast you ride to school at a **speed** of 60 kilometres per hour (about 35 miles per hour).

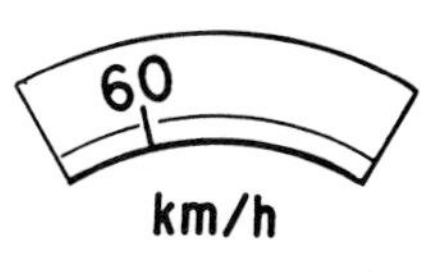

3-4(a). ***All day long you are taking measurements.***

COMPARISON OF CUSTOMARY AND METRIC RULES

Woodworking rules with customary markings include the 6″, 12″ (foot), and 36″ (yard). Similar rules in the metric system are 150 mm (15 cm), 300 mm (30 cm), and 1 m long. Fig. 3-8.

Let's compare the common 12″ rule with the 300-mm metric rule. Fig. 3-9 (page 34). As you saw in Fig. 3-8(a), the 300-mm (30-cm) rule is slightly shorter than the 12″ rule. The customary rule is divided into twelve inches, and each inch is

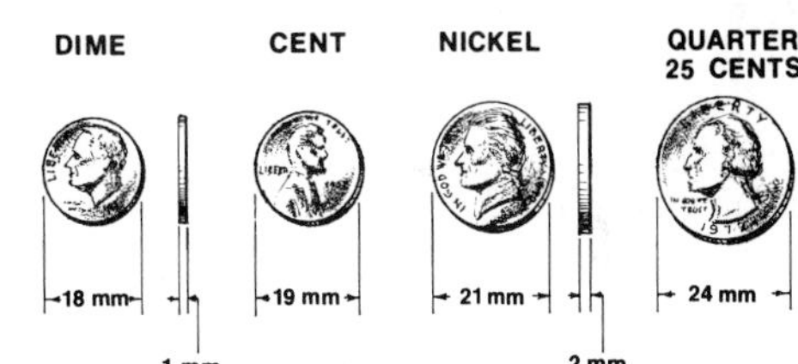

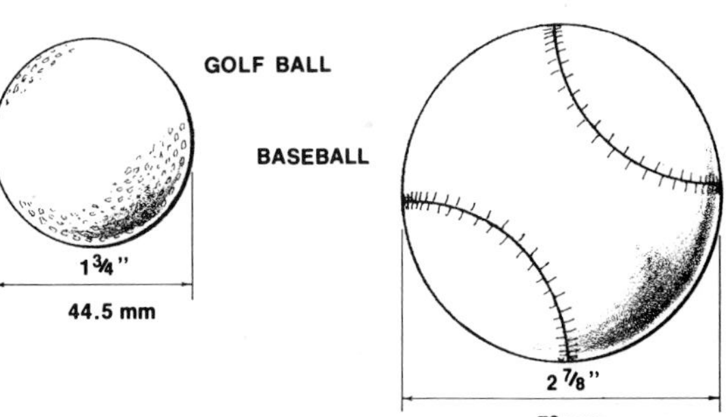

3-4(b). ***You can get a "feel" for metric sizes by remembering the sizes of common things in metric units.***

	Physical Quantity	**SI METRIC SYSTEM** Base Unit (word and symbol)	**Customary (English) or Inch-Pound System** Unit (word and abbreviation)
m	Length	metre—m	inch, foot, or yard—in, ft, or yd
kg	Weight (mass)	kilogram—kg	pound—lb
K	Tempera-ture	kelvin—K. Used for scientific measurements. Degrees Celsius—°C—is for everyday use.	Fahrenheit—°F
		SAME IN BOTH SYSTEMS	
s	Time	second—s	second—s
A	Electrical Current	ampere—A	ampere—A
cd	Luminous Intensity	candela—cd	candela—cd
mol	Amount of Substance	mole—mol	mole—mol

3-5. ***The base units of the metric system. Note that some units are the same in both the metric and customary systems.***

COMMON METRIC UNITS

Unit	Symbol	Quantity
ampere	A	Electric current
candela	cd	Luminous intensity
degree Celsius	°C	Temperature
gram	g	Weight (mass)
kelvin	K	Temperature (for scientific use)
litre	L	Liquid capacity (volume of fluids)
metre	m	Length
metric ton	t	Weight (mass)—1 t = 1000 kg
second	s	Time
volt	V	Electric potential
watt	W	Power

NOTE: If a unit was named after a person (for example, watt for Scottish inventor James Watt), then the *symbol* for that unit is capitalized. Otherwise, the symbol is lower case. An exception is the symbol for litre, L, which is capitalized so that it won't be confused with the numeral 1.

3-6. Some common metric units and their symbols. Note that there is no period after a metric symbol.

COMMON METRIC PREFIXES

Prefix	Symbol	Meaning
giga	G	one billion times
mega	M	one million times
kilo	k	one thousand times
centi	c	one-hundredth of
milli	m	one-thousandth of
micro	μ	one-millionth of
nano	n	one-billionth of

NOTE: Some prefixes are capitalized so that they won't be confused with metric units. For example, G = giga, but g = gram.

3-7. These are the most commonly used metric prefixes. Some examples of how they are used: km = kilometre; cm = centimetre; and mm = millimetre.

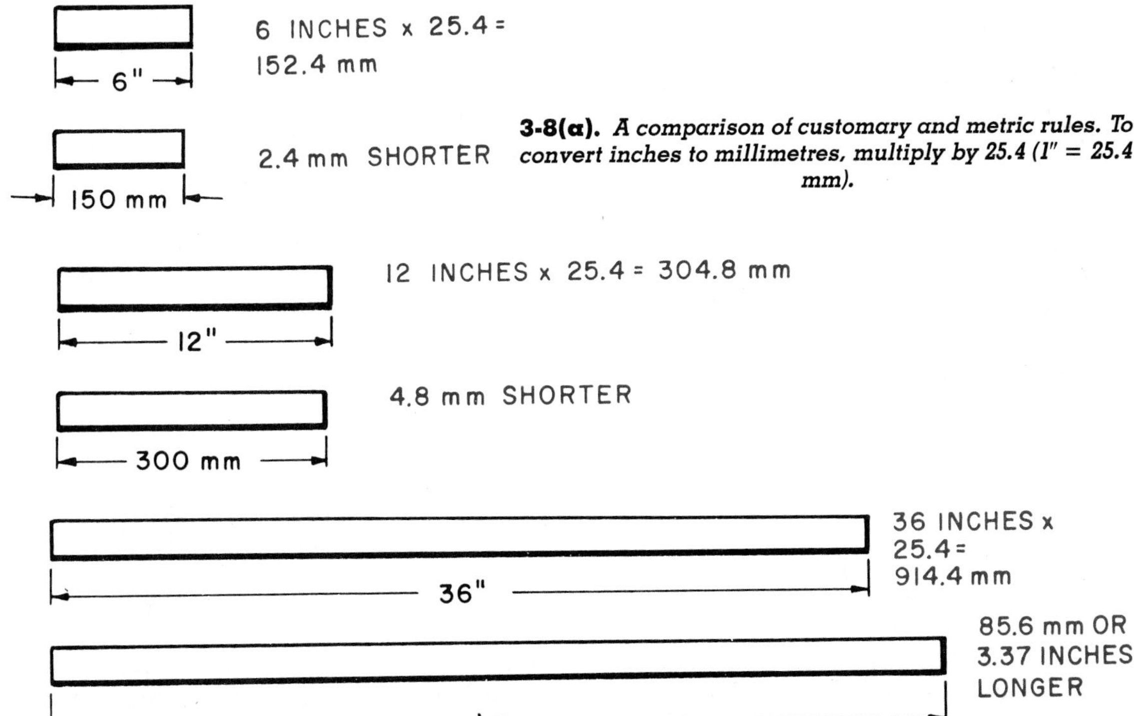

3-8(a). A comparison of customary and metric rules. To convert inches to millimetres, multiply by 25.4 (1" = 25.4 mm).

3-8(b). *This sight-impaired student is comparing a yardstick with a metre rule. Which is longer?*

divided into fractions of either eighths (1/8″) or sixteenths (1/16″). The metric rule is divided into millimetres. Every tenth line is marked 1, 2, 3, etc., or 10, 20, 30, etc. If the numbers are 1, 2, 3, and so forth, these are centimetre divisions (10 mm = 1 cm). If the rule is marked 10, 20, 30, and so on, these numbered lines represent millimetres. In either case, each of the small divisions is 1 mm.

The centimetre rule is harder to use because you often have to change centimetres into millimetres. For example, if there are 3 small divisions beyond the 2, you must think of the 2 cm as 20 mm. Then you must add the 3 small divisions, for a total of 23 mm. On the millimetre rule, you do not have to change units. You simply read three small divisions beyond the 20 as 23 mm. Fig. 3-10.

Note that on the metric rule the smallest division is 1 mm, which is about 1/25″. The smallest division on the customary woodworking rule is 1/16″. The 1-mm division is smaller than the 1/16″ but larger than the 1/32″ division found on many tape measures and metal rules. For most woodworking using metric dimensions you should measure to the nearest millimetre. This will be more accurate than if you measure to the nearest 1/16″ in customary dimensions.

Rules are available with three kinds of markings: customary, metric, and metric-customary combination. The metric-customary rule is usually divided into inches and fractions of an inch on one half of the rule and into millimetres and centimetres on the other half.

READING A CUSTOMARY RULE

Before using measuring tools, you must be sure that you can use the rule correctly. It isn't hard to measure in feet and exact inches. If the measurement is in feet, you place a single mark (′) after the number. If the measurement is in inches, you place a double mark (″) after the

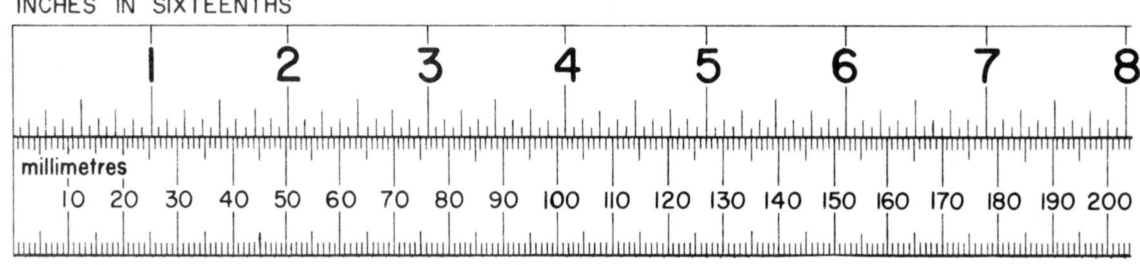

3-9. *Customary rules are divided into inches and fractions of an inch. Metric rules are divided into centimetres and millimetres.*

3-10(a). *Measuring with a metric rule that is graduated in centimetres.*

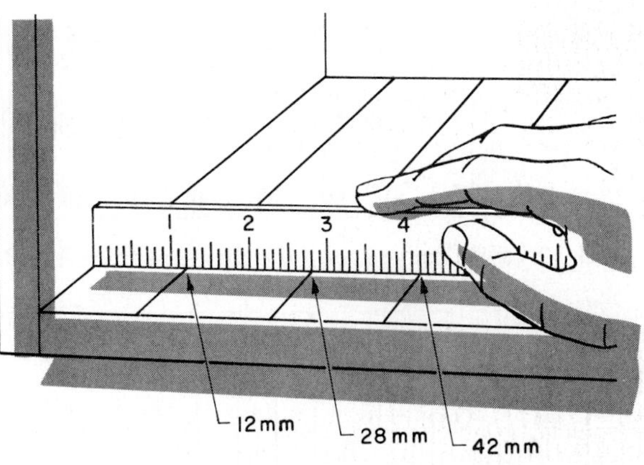

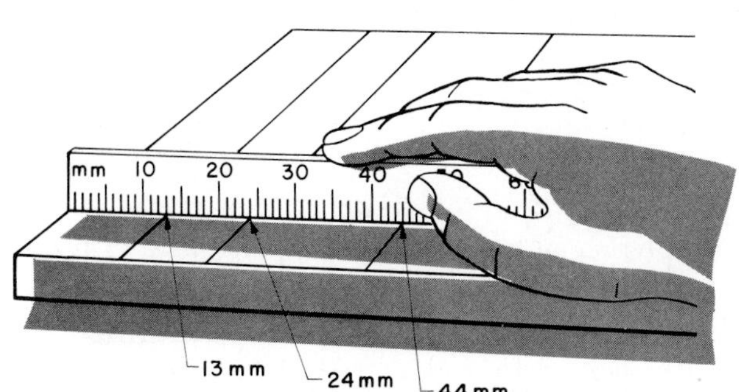

3-10(b). *It is easier to measure with a metric rule graduated in millimetres.*

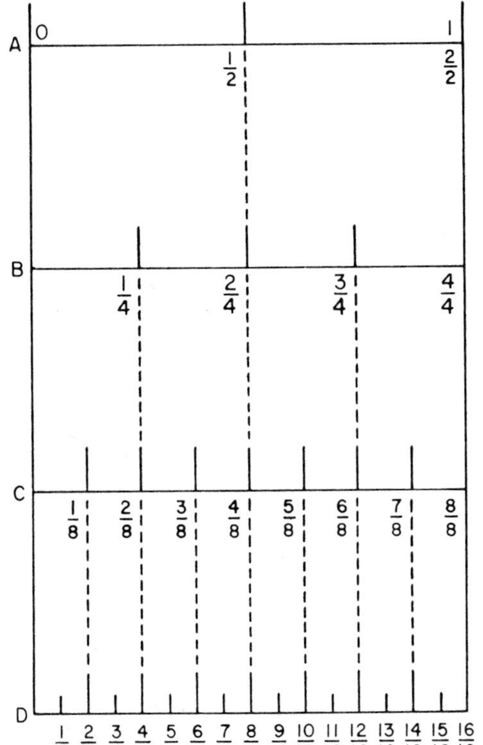

3-11. *Study this chart. It will help you to read a rule to 1/16″.*

number. You already know that there are 12 inches in a foot and 3 feet (or 36 inches) in a yard.

Measuring in parts (fractions) of an inch takes a little more care.

- Look at the enlarged inch shown in Fig. 3-11. Notice that the distance between 0 and 1 is 1 inch.
- Look at Line A. You see that the inch is divided in half. Each half is 1/2 inch (1/2″). This half-inch division line is the longest line between the inch marks on a rule.
- Look at Line B. Here the inch is divided into four equal parts. Each part is 1/4″. The distance to the first line is 1/4″, to the second is 2/4″, or 1/2″, and to the third is 3/4″.
- Look at Line C. Here the inch is divided into eight equal parts. Each small division is therefore 1/8″. Two of these divisions make 2/8″, or 1/4″, as shown on Line B. Four of these divisions make 4/8″, or 2/4″, or 1/2″. Some rules used in woodworking are divided into only eight parts, making the smallest division 1/8″.
- Look at Line D. Here the inch is divided into sixteen parts. This is usually the smallest division on rules in woodworking. Notice again that 4/16″ is equal to 2/8″, or 1/4″. One line past 1/4″ would be 5/16″. On your rule or square, the half-inch mark is the longest line between the inch marks. The 1/4″ is the next longest, the 1/8″ is next, and the 1/16″ mark is the shortest.

A B C D E F G H I J K L M
mm
10 20 30 40 50 60 70 80 90 100 110 120 130 140 150 1

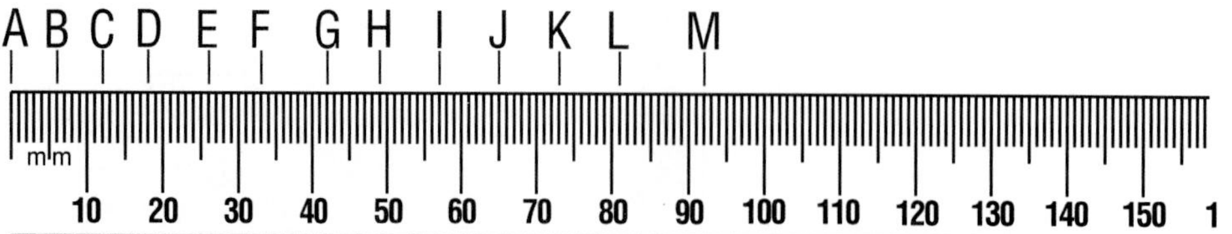

3-12 (a). *Can you read the distance from A to B, A to C, A to D, etc.? Answers are on page 39.*

1 2 3 4 5 6 7
A B C D E F G H I J K L M

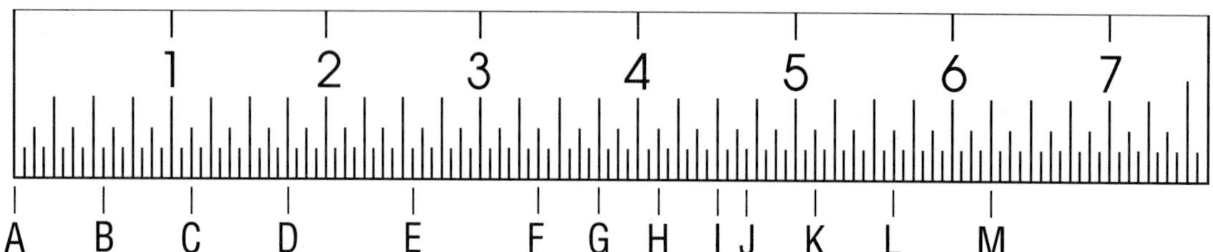

3-12 (b). *Can you read the distance between A and the other lettered points? Answers are on page 39.*

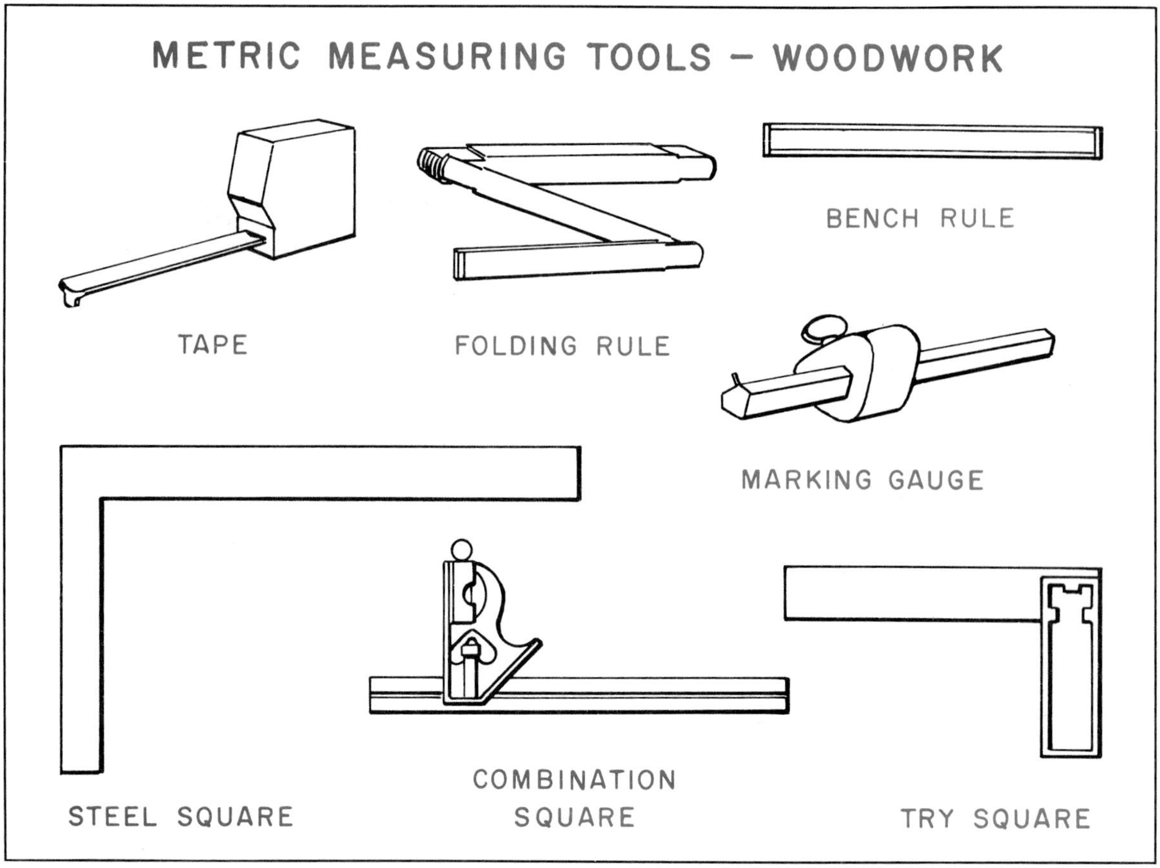

METRIC MEASURING TOOLS – WOODWORK
TAPE
FOLDING RULE
BENCH RULE
MARKING GAUGE
STEEL SQUARE
COMBINATION SQUARE
TRY SQUARE

3-13. *Common measuring tools that need to be replaced to work in metrics.*

TOOLS WHICH WILL NOT NEED REPLACEMENT

METRIC EQUIVALENTS SHOWN ARE THE EXPECTED REPLACEMENT SIZES TO BE AVAILABLE IN THE FUTURE.

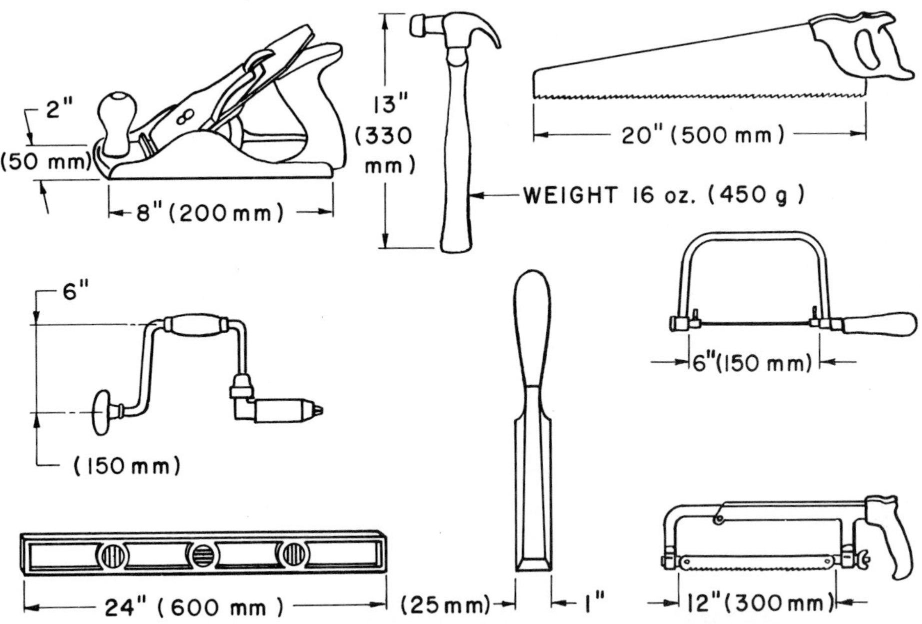

3-14. *Most woodworking tools do* not *have to be replaced to work in metrics.*

• To read a part, or fraction, of an inch, count the number of small divisions beyond the inch mark. Then see how many divisions there are in the inch on the rule you are using. If there are only eight, for example, and you count five divisions, the measurement is 5/8". If there are sixteen divisions in the inch and you count five, then the measurement is 5/16".

• On scrap paper, draw a line 2 1/4" long. If your rule is divided into eighths, then the line measures 2 inches plus two small divisions (2/8"). If your rule is divided into sixteenths, then this extra section is 4/16", which is the same as 2/8", or 1/4".

READING A METRIC RULE

Like reading the customary rule, this is done by counting the markings. To read the metric rule, count the number of millimetre spaces for a given length. For example, in Fig. 3-12 the length from A to B is 6 mm. The length from A to C is 12 mm. Practice your rule reading by figuring the distances AD, AE, AF, etc. You should also practice measuring nails, screws, lumber, and other common shop objects. Remember to round your measurements to the nearest millimetre.

CONVERTING TOOLS AND MACHINES

It is fairly simple to convert to the metric system in woodworking. The only hand tools that need replacement are rules and other measuring instruments. Fig. 3-13. It is not necessary to replace such tools as planes, drills, or boring bits. Fig. 3-14. Even in countries now going metric,

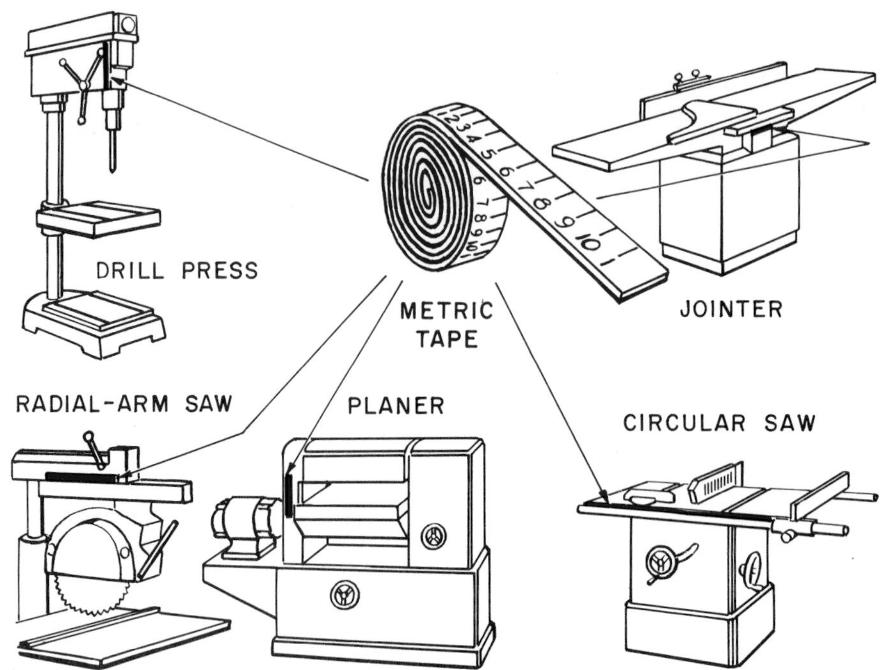

3-15. *Gauges and scales on woodworking machines can be converted by pasting metric tape next to or over the customary gauges and scales.*

METRIC CHANGES FOR WOODWORKING

Units of Measurement	millimetre (about 1/25 in.) for all dimensions on drawings —for thickness and width of lumber —for size of panel stock metre (about 10 percent longer than a yard) —for lengths of lumber —for large commercial building litre (about 6 percent more) to replace the quart kilogram (about 2.2 times) to replace the pound
Tool Replacement	All measuring tools—No change in other tools
Machine Changes	Add a metric *scale* (rule) next to the customary scale
Lumber Thickness	1/4 inch becomes 6 millimetres 1/2 inch becomes 12 millimetres 1 inch becomes 25 millimetres
Lumber Lengths	6 feet become 1.8 metres 8 feet become 2.4 metres
Panel Sizes	4 × 8 feet become 1220 × 2440 millimetres
Fasteners	No actual change in size —1-inch nail becomes 25-millimetre nail —2-inch screw becomes 50-millimetre screw
Drills	Metric sizes are available. However, customary sizes are close enough for metric use.

3-16. *These are the major changes that must be made in woodworking to use the metric system.*

ANSWERS TO FIG. 3-12(a)

A to B = 6 mm
A to C = 12 mm
A to D = 18 mm
A to E = 26 mm
A to F = 33 mm
A to G = 42 mm
A to H = 49 mm
A to I = 57 mm
A to J = 65 mm
A to K = 73 mm
A to L = 81 mm
A to M = 92 mm

ANSWERS TO FIG. 3-12(b)

A to B = 9/16"
A to C = 1-1/8"
A to D = 1-3/4"
A to E = 2-9/16"
A to F = 3-3/8"
A to G = 3-3/4"
A to H = 4-1/8"
A to I = 4-1/2"
A to J = 4-11/16"
A to K = 5-1/8"
A to L = 5-5/8"
A to M = 6-1/4"

such items as dowels and wood screws are not being changed in actual size. These countries are merely using the metric measurement to identify the tools. For example, a 2" plane becomes a 50-mm plane, and a 1" boring bit becomes a 25-mm tool.

Converting woodworking machines is simple. A piece of plastic paste-on metric tape is placed next to or over the customary scale. Fig. 3-15. Figure 3-16 summarizes the changes that need to be made in order to do woodworking in the metric system.

QUESTIONS

1. Which measuring system is more widely used, the metric or the customary?
2. What is the base unit of length in the metric system? The base unit of weight (mass)? The base unit of time?
3. Which is longer, the metre or the yard? Explain.
4. On a 300-mm rule, what is the smallest unit?
5. On customary woodworking rules, what is usually the smallest unit?
6. Do saws, planes, and other hand tools need to be replaced to do work in the metric system? Explain.
7. How can woodworking machines be converted to the metric system?

ACTIVITIES

1. Ask your teacher for a metric ruler or measuring tape. What is your height in centimetres?
2. Check some products in your home, such as canned goods or soda bottles. How many have both metric and customary amounts listed on the label?
3. What examples of metric measurements (road signs, weather reports, etc.) can you find in your community? Prepare a brief report.

CHAPTER 4

Design

What would you look for if you were going to buy a new bicycle? How would you choose among the different makes and models? Would you think about the color, size, and construction? Would you test the seat and the angle of the handlebars? Look at the tires and wheels? Check to see if the brakes work? You would certainly consider most of these things. Actually, what you'd be doing would be deciding *which design you liked the best.*

In the wood shop you also decide on the *design you like best.* When you choose a project, you must think not only about how it looks but also how well it works. A stereo cabinet, for example, ought to look good, but it's just as important that it hold the records well. Fig. 4-1. Sometimes a thing looks pretty good but isn't useful. Or it might do the job quite well but be made so poorly that it is ugly to look at. People choose the design they like best, that best meets their needs. If you don't like a design, you won't pick it.

Design, then, is what a thing looks like and how useful it is. In order to have good design, an object must be useful and beautiful. Design is a part of everything we make and use. It is not something you just study about. Houses, cars, bridges, and all other things that are built must first be designed by someone.

Choosing and making well-designed wood projects is not easy. However, studying this unit and looking at well-designed wood objects in magazines, books, and stores will be a big help to you. Soon you will begin to get a "feeling" for what is good and be able to discard what is poor.

4-1. ***This small stereo cabinet is designed for efficient use of space.***

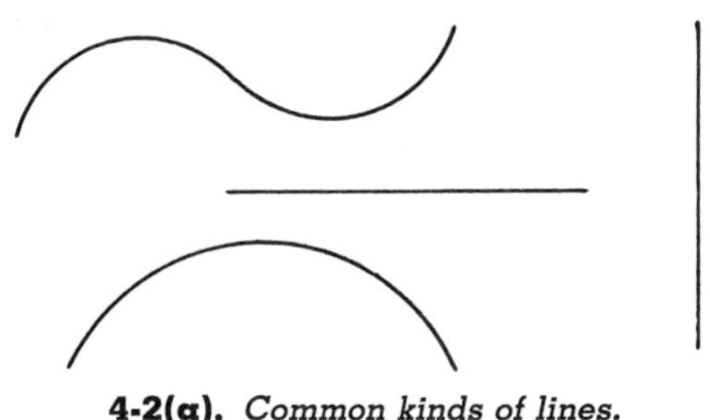

4-2(a). *Common kinds of lines.*

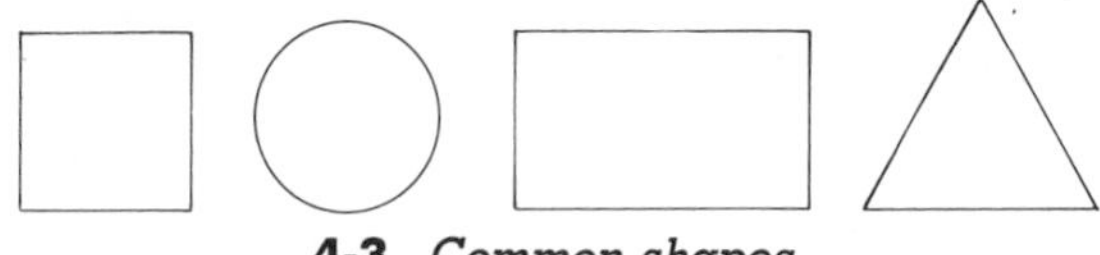

4-3. *Common shapes.*

WHAT MAKES UP DESIGN?

Design is made up of certain elements. Every object has these elements. The way they are put together makes up the design of the object.

Line

Lines enclose space to create shape. Lines can express feelings. For example, horizontal (across) lines appear restful. Vertical (up and down) lines appear to reach upward, and slanted lines seem aggressive. Wavy lines can express motion or rhythm. Lines can also imitate texture, light, or shade. Fig. 4-2.

Shape

Shape is the space enclosed by lines. Some common shapes are the square, circle, rectangle, triangle, hexagon, and octagon. Fig. 4-3. You see shapes or parts of them wherever you look. Fig. 4-4.

Form

Shapes are combined to make up forms like cubes, pyramids, or spheres. These forms, or solids, are three-dimensional; that is, they have height, width, and depth. Fig. 4-5.

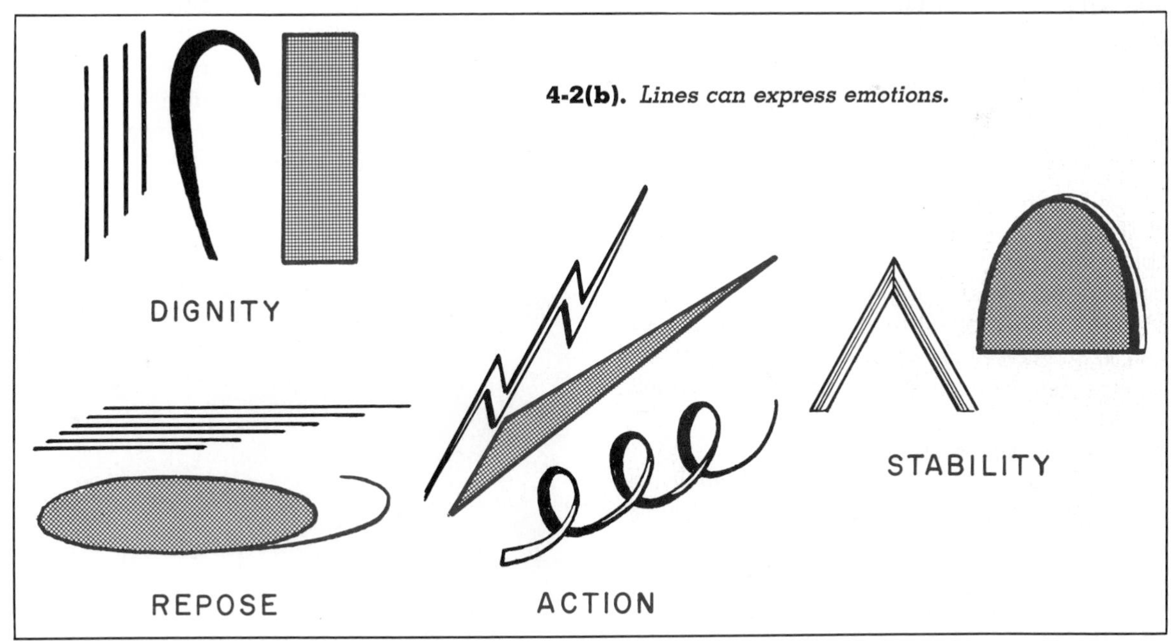

4-2(b). *Lines can express emotions.*

4-4. *What kinds of shapes can you see in these tables?*

Color

Color is an important element of design. Some colors give a warm feeling. Examples of warm colors are red, yellow, and orange. Green and blue are cool colors. Fig. 4-6. Woods have their own, natural colors. When you build a project, you can leave the wood natural or you can change the color with stains, paints, or enamels.

Tone and Texture

Tone is the light and dark, the shadow and brightness of an object. Texture is the makeup or grain of the material. Each wood has a different texture. Texture gives interest to a surface. There are many ways of adding or increasing texture. Fig. 4-7.

WHAT MAKES A DESIGN GOOD OR PLEASING?

It is hard to say exactly what makes one project attractive while another is not. There are many rules about this, but rules by themselves don't make good design. Well-designed modern furniture often doesn't follow all the rules. However, ugly objects are those that violate (break) the principles (basic rules) of good design. These are the principles:

Proportion

Proportion is the way areas or parts of an object are related to each other. Some shapes have better proportion than others. For example, the rectangle has better proportion than the square. This is because the exact relationship between the height and width of a rectangle is not easily seen by the eye. The golden oblong is an example of good proportion. This is a rectangle with a proportion of about five to eight. For every five units of height, there are eight units of width. Fig. 4-8. Objects such as serving trays, bulletin boards, or picture frames with this proportion are pleasing to look at.

To divide this rectangle horizontally into three or four parts, place the largest at the bottom and make each of the next areas smaller. To divide the rectangle into three parts vertically, make the center area largest and the other two of equal size and shape. Fig. 4-9.

4-5. *These trunks are perfect cubes.*

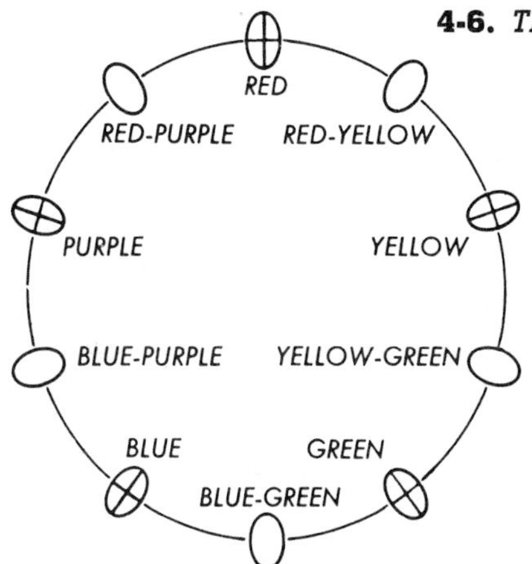

4-6. *This color wheel shows the relationships of different colors.*

4-7. *The bold grain of this oak telephone cabinet gives it an interesting texture.*

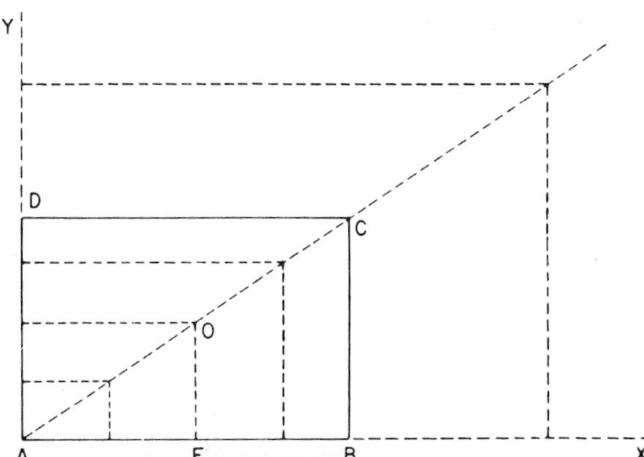

4-8. *Here is a way to enlarge a 5 × 8 proportion to whatever size you want. Make AB eight units long and BC five units high. Then lay off along the line AX any length you want, for example, AE. The distance for height, then, would be EO.*

4-9. *This mirror is a rectangle divided into three parts.*

4-10. *A well-proportioned lampshade and base.*

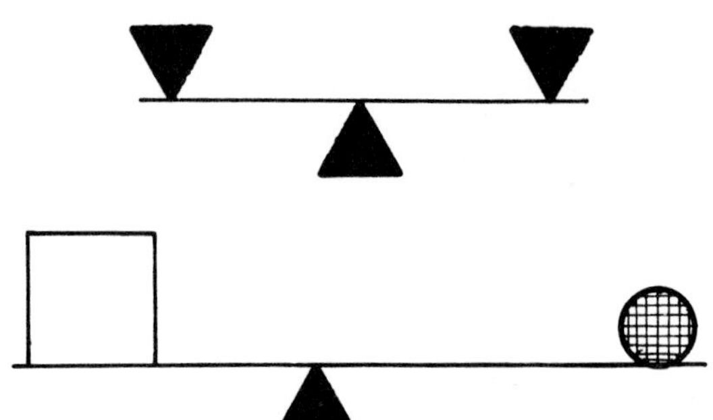

4-11. *Formal balance (top) and informal balance (bottom).*

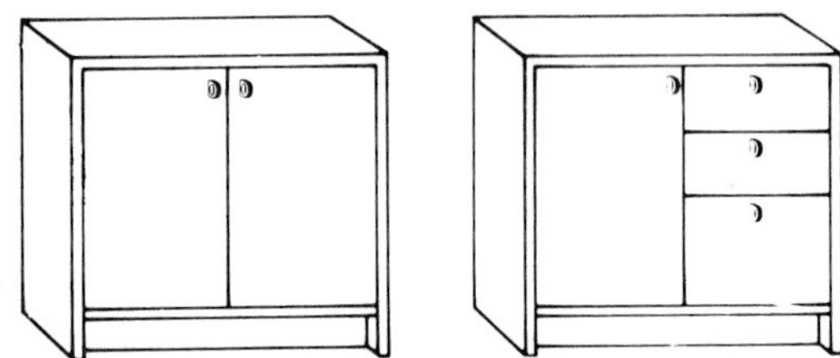

4-12. *The cabinet on the left shows formal balance. The one on the right shows informal balance.*

Proportion is important when planning a project. For example, the shade for a lamp must be in good proportion to the base. Fig. 4-10. A large shade on a small base would look top-heavy.

Balance

Balance makes an article appear equal in weight on both sides. There are two kinds of balance: formal and informal. Fig. 4-11. An example of formal balance is a seesaw with two children of equal size using it. Two identical lamps on either end of a chest are in formal balance. In informal balance things appear to be balanced, or at rest, but they are actually not equal. Fig. 4-12.

Rhythm

The repetition of such things as shape, color, or line is rhythm. Fig. 4-13.

Harmony

Harmony is the way the parts of an object get along together. For example, an Early American leg on a Modern table would be out of harmony. A lacy lampshade would not be in harmony with a heavy base. When the parts go together well, the object has harmony. Fig. 4-14.

Emphasis

The point of emphasis catches your eye the first time you look. It is the center of interest or the

4-13. ***The tops of these tables illustrate rhythm.***

point of greatest importance. Sometimes an unusual shape provides the emphasis. At other times a beautiful piece of hardware or simply a fine finish is the point of emphasis. In Fig. 4-5, for example, your eyes are drawn to the hardware.

DESIGNING A PROJECT

It would be impossible to tell you everything you need to know in order to design good wood projects. Some people have more of a flair for design than others, but everyone can learn to appreciate a well-designed wood project. You will also learn to recognize poor design. Here are some guides to selecting and designing projects:

- Make sure the project meets a real need in your life. If it is a stool, for instance, it should be both sturdy and comfortable.
- The design should be up to date. Sometimes old designs are popular and therefore still up to date.
- The object should be made of the best materials for its construction, use, and appearance.
- The design should carry out the real purpose of the article. Look at the tools used in woodworking. See how well they have been designed to do their jobs.
- Use really beautiful woods as they are. Don't cover them with paint or a poor finish. Don't try to make woods seem to be what they are not. Pine can never look like mahogany.

4-14. ***This mirror and shelf make a set. Their designs are in harmony with each other.***

4-15. *Even a simple project must be well constructed.*

• Take time for good construction in making your projects. Make sure your project is assembled with the best methods. Fig. 4-15.
• Keep your project simple. Don't add a lot of frills.

HOW TO TELL IF A PROJECT IS WELL DESIGNED

Check your project with the following points in mind:

4-16(a). *These clocks are attractive novelty projects.*

• **Does it do its job well?** A birdhouse must attract the kind of birds for which it has been built. A shoe rack must be a good shoe holder. If your project is functional (really does its job), then it is worthwhile.
• **Is it interesting?** A table lamp might give the proper light for reading but be uninteresting to look at. Give your project "personality" and style.
• **Is it well made?** A chair may be comfortable and attractive but have such poor joints that it comes apart in a short time. Many wood articles have the joint construction exposed to show how well they are made.
• **Does it make the best use of materials?** Most woods have a beautiful grain pattern and attractive natural color. Apply a finish that brings out the beauty of the wood. Of course, when a project is made of inexpensive wood, painting or enameling it a bright color adds to its appearance.

KINDS OF DESIGNS

The things you make in a wood shop can be grouped in this way:

4-16(b). *These designs could be used for wall plaques or cutting boards.*

• Novelty items. These projects may be clever and popular without showing good design. For example, you could make bookends, a door stop, or a funny wall plaque. Fig. 4-16. Such projects don't have lasting value. You would probably use them for a while and then say, "Well, that was sure a lot of fun to make, but I'm tired of it now." Some of the plans in this book are novelties.

• Utility projects. These do a useful job. If they do it well, they are well designed. A fishing lure must be made of the right material and be the correct shape. So must a bicycle stand or a workbench. This kind of project must be strong and serviceable. Fig. 4-17.

• Artistic or decorative projects. These are such projects as chairs, tables, lamps, and cases. They should be a certain style. The most common styles are Modern (Contemporary), Early American, Colonial, and Traditional. Fig. 4-18. The design, the kind of wood, the finish, and the hardware make the differences in styles.

STEPS FOR DESIGNING A PROJECT IN WOODWORK

Let's suppose you decide to build something to hold books. You must first ask yourself how the books can be kept neatly arranged. Books can lie flat, stand upright, or lean at an angle. What kinds of things will hold books in these ways? There are book troughs, bookends, bookracks, book holders, and bookcases. Perhaps you can think of some others.

Next you should know how many and what size books you want to store. Most books are about 6½″ × 9½″ in size, although they vary from 5″ × 8″ to 10″ × 12″ and even larger.

Let us say you decide to build a bookcase.

1. You can make the shelves various distances apart to hold books of different heights. It is a

4-17. *This workbench and stand are very practical utility projects.*

4-18(a). *A Modern table.*

4-18(b). *This end table is Early American.*

mistake in design to have the shelves equally spaced.

2. Next you must decide on the appearance of the bookcase and the shape and size of each part.

3. You need to decide how the parts go together and make a sketch of your project.

4. You might at this point want to build a model.

5. Next comes a working drawing.

6. Last, prepare a bill of materials and write a plan sheet.

The next five chapters will explain how to draw and plan a project and how to get the materials for it.

QUESTIONS

1. Name the elements of design.
2. Name four common shapes.
3. How can you add color to a wood article?
4. What are the proportions of the golden oblong?
5. What is the difference between formal and informal balance?
6. Why shouldn't you put a lacy lampshade on a nautical (sea and ships) lamp? What principle of design would it violate?

ACTIVITIES

1. Select a product that has a design you like. Tell what pleases you about the design.
2. Select a product whose design you dislike. What makes the design seem bad to you?
3. People have been designing furniture and other wood products for a long time. In encyclopedias or other reference sources, find examples of good design from the past or from other cultures. Are any of these designs found in products we use today?

CHAPTER 5 Ordering Materials

You don't have to be an expert to start making something in the shop. As you work with woods, you'll learn more and more about the materials you are using. One thing you will learn is how to buy materials from a lumberyard. This will save you money. Materials are expensive and you won't want to waste them by buying too much or buying the wrong thing. Here are some things you should know about lumber and other building materials.

LUMBER

Lumber is wood that comes from trees. Fig. 5-1. *Wood* is the hard substance under the bark of trees and shrubs. If you could look at a piece of wood through a microscope, you would see that it is made up of long, narrow tubes. Each tube is as small as a hair on your head. These tubes, or wood fibers, usually grow straight up and down. This makes wood straight-grained. You can see from looking at Fig. 5-2 that it is easier to cut with the grain than across it. When you cut across the grain, you must cut through the packed fibers.

The tree trunk is cut lengthwise into lumber. Some of the fibers are cut off at an angle. This makes the grain surface look something like Fig. 5-3.

How Lumber Is Classified

Lumber is classified as either softwood or hardwood. *Softwoods* come from evergreen, or needle-bearing, trees. Fig. 5-4. Common softwoods are pine, cedar, fir, and redwood. *Hardwoods* come from broad-leaved trees that shed their leaves in the fall. Fig. 5-5. Some of these are birch, maple, oak, walnut, cherry, poplar, and mahogany.

You will soon find that these terms don't tell how hard the wood really is. Some softwoods are actually harder than some hardwoods! Hard-

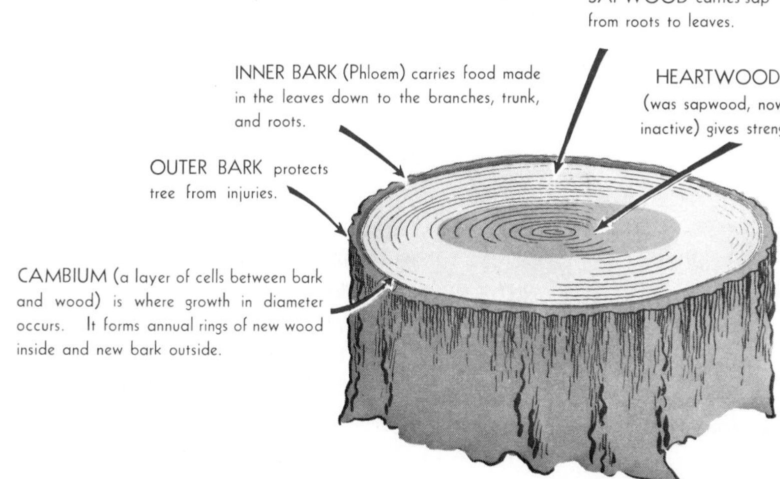

5-1. ***Parts of a tree trunk. Lumber comes from the sapwood and heartwood.***

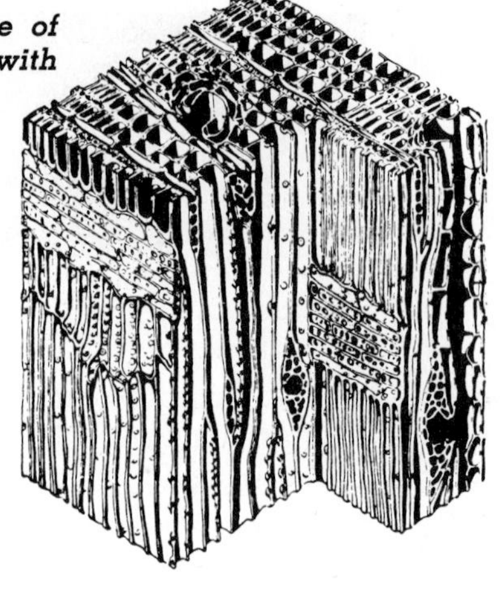

5-2. *This drawing shows the tube structure of wood. It is easy to see why wood can be cut with the grain more easily than across it.*

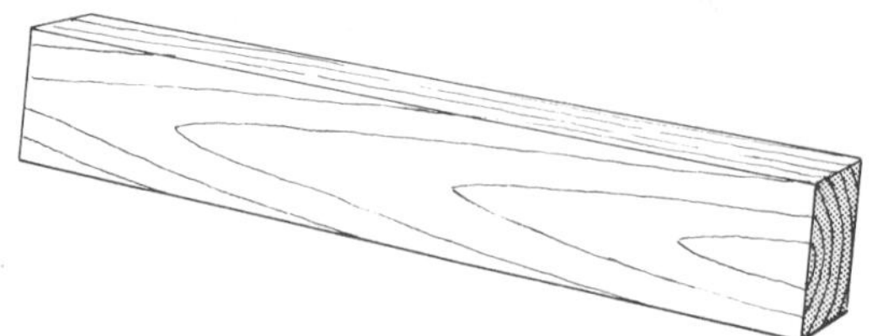

5-3. *The surface of lumber looks like this when it is cut.*

woods usually (but not always) cost more than softwoods.

How Boards Are Cut from Logs

Boards are cut from logs in two major ways. The cheapest and most economical way is called *plainsawed* (when it is a hardwood tree) or *flat-grained* (when it is a softwood tree). The log is squared and sawed lengthwise from one side to the other. Fig. 5-6. *Quartersawed* (for hardwood) or *edge-grained* (for softwood) is a more expensive method of cutting. It shows a better grain pattern, especially in oak and other hardwoods. Fig. 5-7.

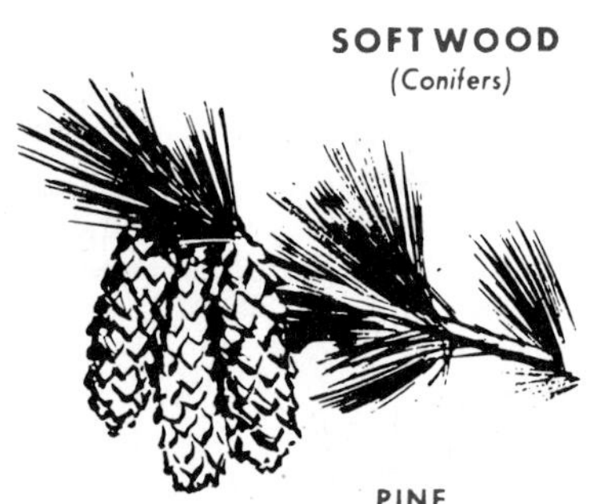

5-4. *Softwoods come from evergreen trees such as pine.*

How Lumber Is Worked

Some lumber is purchased just as it comes from the sawmill. The surface of the lumber is rough ("Rgh"). It must be smoothed by running it through a machine called a surfacer, or planer, before it can be used in the shop.

Most lumber comes from the lumberyard already smoothed (surfaced, or dressed). Lumber can be purchased surfaced on two sides (S2S) or surfaced on four sides (S4S). You would purchase surfaced, or dressed, lumber if you wanted to build something at home.

How Lumber Is Dried

When a tree is first cut down, the wood contains a lot of moisture. Most lumber is dried before it is used. *Softwood* lumber is cut into logs and placed in the open air to dry. Lumber made this way is called air-dried lumber (AD). If this lumber is sold with a moisture content of more than 19 percent, it is considered green lumber. If the lumber has a moisture content of 19 percent or less, it is classified as dry lumber. Most *hardwoods* are dried in special drying rooms called kilns (often pronounced "kills"). Hardwood lumber used for furniture and interiors is kiln-dried (KD) to about 6 to 12 percent moisture. This is the only kind to buy for furniture and other fine projects.

5-5. *Hardwoods come from broad-leaved trees such as maple.*

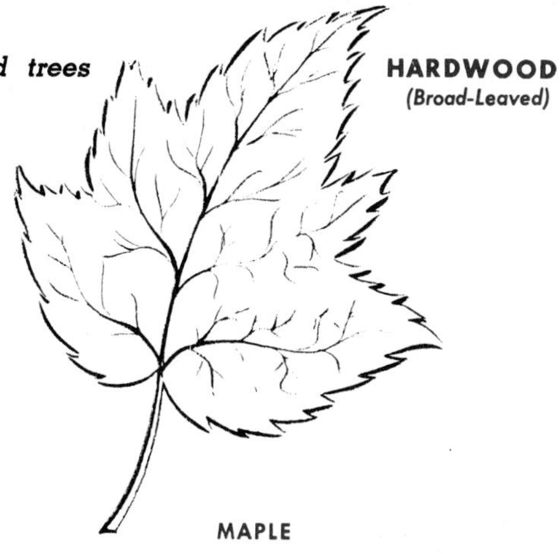

Lumber Sizes

The nominal, or stock, size of lumber is always larger than the actual size. The actual size is smaller because the lumber is seasoned (dried) and surfaced (run through a machine to smooth it). The actual size of softwood is determined by whether it is green or dry. For example, a 2 × 4 (2 inches by 4 inches) will actually measure only 1½ inches × 3½ inches if dry or 1⁹⁄₁₆ inches × 3⁹⁄₁₆ inches if green. The actual size of 1-inch hardwood that has been surfaced on two sides (S2S) is ¹³⁄₁₆ of an inch.

Lumber Grades

The *select,* or best, grades of softwood lumber are *Grade A* and *Grade B.* These are often sold as "B and better." B-and-better lumber is used for trim on the inside of a house and for projects you make in the school shop. The *C* and *D* grades of lumber are less expensive but can be used for the same things as Grades A and B. *Common lumber* is used only for rough purposes such as in house framing.

The best grade of hardwood is *FAS.* This means "firsts and seconds." It is the best grade for making furniture. *Number 1* and *Number 2* have some defects and are poorer quality than FAS.

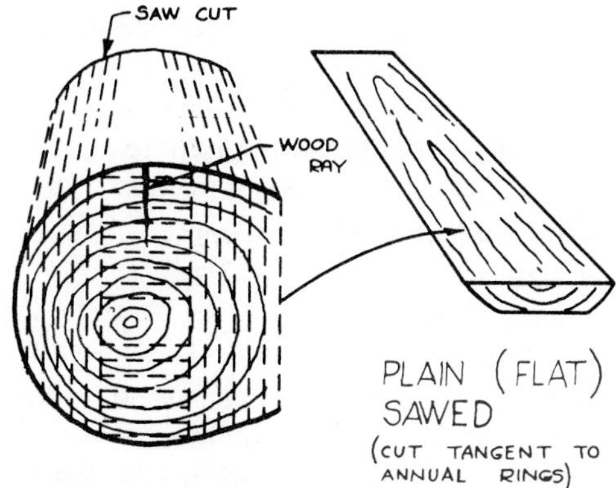

5-6. *Plainsawed or flat-grained lumber.*

How Lumber Is Sold

Lumber is sold by the board foot. A *board foot* of lumber is a piece 1 inch thick, 12 inches wide, and 12 inches long. The board foot is the standard unit of measurement used in lumberyards. Lumber less than 1 inch thick is figured as 1 inch. Here is one way to figure board feet: multiply the thickness in inches by the width in feet by the length in feet.

$$BF = T\ (\text{in.}) \times W\ (\text{ft.}) \times L\ (\text{ft.})$$

For example, a 2 by 4 inch piece that is 12 feet long would be 8 board feet:

$$2 \times \tfrac{4}{12} \times 12 = 8$$

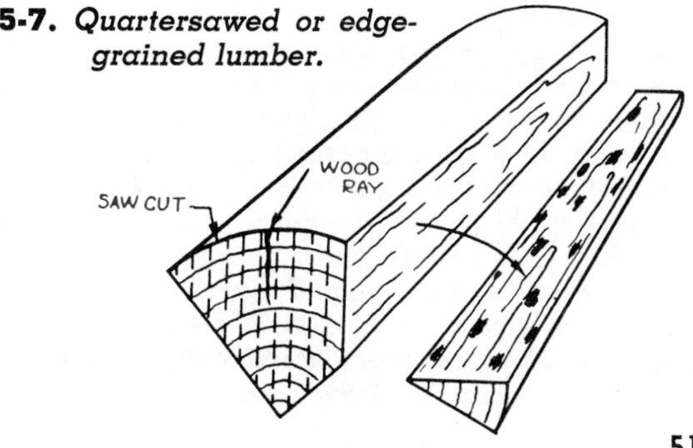

5-7. *Quartersawed or edge-grained lumber.*

The width (4 inches) is divided by 12 to change it to feet.

A simpler way to figure board feet for small projects is as follows: Board feet equals the thickness in inches times the width in inches times the length in feet, all divided by 12.

$$BF = \frac{T\ (in.) \times W\ (in.) \times L\ (ft.)}{12}$$

For example: How many board feet are there in a piece of white pine 1 inch by 7 inches by 6 feet?

$$BF = \frac{1 \times 7 \times 6}{12}, \text{ or } 3\tfrac{1}{2}$$

For very small pieces found in many smaller projects, you can figure board feet this way: Board feet equals the thickness in inches times the width in inches times the length in inches divided by 144. There are 144 cubic inches in one board foot.

$$BF = \frac{T \times W \times L\ (\text{all in inches})}{144}$$

For example: How many board feet are there in a piece of walnut ½ inch thick, 9 inches wide, and 28 inches long? (Remember that stock less than 1 inch thick is figured as 1 inch).

$$BF = \frac{1 \times 9 \times 28}{144}, \text{ or } 1\tfrac{3}{4}$$

Lumber is sold by the board foot, by the hundred board feet, or by the thousand board feet (M). For example, if lumber sells for $600.00 per M, it would cost you $60.00 for 100 board feet and 60 cents for one board foot. If you purchased one board foot, the piece would be about ¾ to 13/16 inch thick, 11½ to 11⅝ inches wide, and 12 inches long.

In the metric system lumber is always dimensioned in millimetres for thickness and width and in metres for length. Lumber is sold in bulk by the cubic metre—a very large amount of about 424 board feet. Panel stock is dimensioned in millimetres for thickness, width, and length. Fig. 5-8.

COMMON THICKNESSES

in.	mm
¼	6
½	12 or 13
¾	19
1	25

COMMON LENGTHS

ft.	m
6	1.8
8	2.4
10	3.0
12	3.6
14	4.2
16	4.8

COMMON LUMBER SIZES FOR HOME CONSTRUCTION

Nominal Size (in.)	Actual Dry Size (in.)	Dry Size (mm)
1 × 2	¾ × 1½	19 × 38
1 × 4	¾ × 3½	19 × 89
1 × 6	¾ × 5½	19 × 140
1 × 10	¾ × 9¼	19 × 235
1 × 12	¾ × 11¼	19 × 285
2 × 4	1½ × 3½	38 × 89
2 × 6	1½ × 5½	38 × 140
2 × 10	1½ × 9¼	38 × 235
2 × 12	1½ × 11¼	38 × 285
3 × 6	2½ × 5½	75 × 140
4 × 4	3½ × 3½	89 × 89
4 × 6	3½ × 5½	89 × 140

5-8. *Metric equivalents for common lumber sizes. These are* soft conversions—*merely a change in the measuring language, not in the real size of the material. In a* hard conversion, *all building construction would be based on a module of 100 millimetres with the preferred multiples of 300, 600, 900, 1200, and so forth. This would mean an actual change in the size of materials. For example, panel stock that is 4′ × 8′ measures 1220 × 2440 mm. This size would be reduced to 1200 × 2400 mm in hard conversion.*

How to Order Lumber

To order lumber you must specify:

- The number of pieces you want.
- The size of the pieces.
- The kind of wood.
- The grade of lumber.
- The surface (whether it is to be rough or surfaced).
- Whether it is to be air-dried or kiln-dried. Fig. 5-9.

YOUR GUIDE IN SELECTING LUMBER

<table>
<tr><th colspan="3">Standard Sizes of Softwood</th><th colspan="2">Standard Thickness of Hardwoods</th><th colspan="2">Grade</th></tr>
<tr><th rowspan="2">Nominal or Stock Size</th><th colspan="2">Actual Size</th><th rowspan="2">Rough</th><th rowspan="2">S2S</th><th rowspan="2">Softwood</th><th rowspan="2">Hardwood</th></tr>
<tr><th>Green</th><th>Dry</th></tr>
<tr><td>1″
2″
3″
4″
5″
6″
7″
8″
9″
10″</td><td>25/32″
1 9/16″
2 9/16″
3 9/16″
4 5/8″
5 5/8″
6 5/8″
7 1/2″
8 1/2″
9 1/2″</td><td>3/4″
1 1/2″
2 1/2″
3 1/2″
4 1/2″
5 1/2″
6 1/2″
7 1/4″
8 1/4″
9 1/4″</td><td>3/8″
1/2″
5/8″
3/4″
1″
1 1/4″</td><td>3/16″
5/16″
7/16″
9/16″
13/16″
1 1/16″</td><td rowspan="3">1. Yard Lumber
Select—Good appearance and finishing quality. Includes:
Grade A—Clear.
Grade B—High Quality.
Grade C—For best paint finishes.
Grade D—Lowest Select.

Common—General utility. Not of finishing quality. Includes:
Construction or No. 1—Best Grade.
Standard or No. 2—Good Grade.
Utility or No. 3—Fair Grade.
Economy or No. 4—Poor.
No. 5—Lowest.

2. Shop Lumber—For manufacturing purposes. Equal to Grade B Select or better of Yard Lumber. Includes:
No. 1—Average 8″ wide.
No. 2—Average 7″ wide.

3. Structural Lumber.</td><td rowspan="3">FAS—Firsts and Seconds. Highest Grade.

No. 1 Common and Select. Some defects.

No. 2 Common. For small cuttings.</td></tr>
<tr><th colspan="2">Surface</th><th>Method of Drying</th><th colspan="2">Method of Cutting</th></tr>
<tr><td colspan="2">Rgh. or Rough—as it comes from the sawmill.

S2S—surfaced on two sides.

S4S—surfaced all four sides.</td><td>AD—Air dried.

KD—Kiln dried</td><td colspan="2">Plainsawed or Flat-grained

Quartersawed or Edge-grained</td></tr>
</table>

5-9. ***This chart shows the choices you have when ordering lumber.***

5-10. *This simple work-play desk is made of softwood plywood.*

5-11. *The tray tops are of hardwood plywood trimmed with solid hardwood.*

PLYWOOD

Plywood consists of panels made by gluing layers of wood together. The outside layers are single plies (thin sheets) of wood. They are called *faces* or *face* and *back.* The center layer, or *core,* may be one or more plies of wood, or it may be glued-up lumber or particle board. The plies between the faces and the core are called *cross-bands.*

The layers are placed so that the grain of one runs at right angles to the grain of the next. When the core consists of more than one ply, these plies may be glued with their grains parallel. The entire core is considered one layer, and it is glued with the grain at right angles to the adjoining layers. There are usually three, five, or seven layers.

Softwood plywoods (also called "construction and industrial" plywoods) are divided into exterior (waterproof) and interior (not waterproof) types. For projects that are to be painted or enameled, interior plywood should be used. The more common grades of softwood plywood are A-A (both sides with a smooth surface), A-B (the face side smooth and the back side with a solid surface), and A-C (the back side of poor quality). Fig. 5-10.

On hardwood plywoods, the outside ply is a good hardwood such as birch, mahogany, walnut, cherry, or gum. The grade of the entire panel is determined by the quality of the face and back. Grades in order of quality are: (1) premium, (2) good, (3) sound, and (4) utility. Fig. 5-11.

Plywood comes in standard thicknesses such as ¼, ⅜, ½ inch, etc. The most common size plywood sheet is 4 feet by 8 feet. Plywood is sold by the square foot. A piece 2 feet wide and 4 feet long has 8 square feet. Fig. 5-12.

HARDBOARD

Hardboard is made by "exploding" wood chips into wood fibers and then forming them into

YOUR GUIDE IN SELECTING PLYWOOD

Hardwoods		Construction and Industrial (Softwoods)	
Grade	**Uses**	**Grade**	**Uses**
Premium Grade	Best quality for very high-grade natural finish. Too expensive except for best cabinet work or paneling.	A–A	Best grade for all uses where both sides will show. Exterior or interior.
Good Grade (1)	For good natural finish. Excellent for cabinets, built-ins, paneling, and furniture.	A–B	An alternate for A–A grade for high-quality uses where only one side will show. Exterior or interior. The back side is less important.
Sound Grade (2)	For simple natural finishes and high-grade painted surfaces.	A–D	A good all-purpose "good-one-side" panel for lesser quality interior work.
Utility Grade (3)	Not used for project work.	B–D	Utility grade. Used for backing, cabinet sides, etc.
Reject Grade (4)	Not used for project work.		
Widths from 24″ to 48″ in 6″ multiples. Lengths from 36″ to 96″. Veneer-core panels in plies of 3, 5, 7, and 9 are available as follows: 3 ply—1/8″, 3/16″, 1/4″; 5 ply—5/16″, 3/8″, 1/2″; 5 and 7 ply—5/8″; 7 and 9 ply—3/4″. There are three types: Type 1 is fully waterproof, Type II is water resistant, and Type III is dry bond.		Many other grades for special uses in home construction are available in thicknesses of 1/2″, 3/8″, 5/8″, and 3/4″; both exterior and interior; 1″ is also available in exterior grades. Common widths 3′4″, or 4′; common length is 8′. Be sure to specify exterior grade for outside work (including boats) and interior grade for interior construction.	

5-12. ***This chart shows the grades, uses, and sizes of plywood.***

panels under heat and pressure. There are two types: standard, or untreated, and tempered, or treated. In the tempering, the board is dipped in drying oils and baked.

On some hardboard one face is smooth and the other is rough and looks like screening. Other hardboard has two smooth surfaces.

Tempered hardboard can be purchased with evenly spaced holes drilled all over the surface. This type of board is used for hanging tools, displays, and many other items.

The standard sizes of hardboard are 4 × 6 feet (1/8 inch thick) and 2 × 12 feet (1/4 inch thick).

PARTICLE BOARD

Particle board is a type of composition board made from wood chips. The pieces of wood are bonded together under heat and pressure with an adhesive or other binder. This material is something like hardboard except that it is thicker and whole chips are used in making it. Shavings from lumber planing mills are an abundant and cheap source of chips, flakes, shavings, and splinters that go into the making of particle board.

Particle board is available in common thicknesses of 3/8, 1/2, and 3/4 inch and in sheets of 4 × 8 feet. Both particle board and hardboard can be worked with regular woodworking tools and machines.

CHOOSING LUMBER FOR PROJECTS

Which wood to choose for a project depends on three things:

- The type of project. For example, for outdoor furniture, you would want a wood that resists decay.
- The price of the wood.
- The appearance of the wood.

This section describes some of the woods that can be used for beginning, intermediate, and advanced projects. Pictures of these woods can be found on pages 12-19.

Beginning Projects

For beginning projects, the wood should be easy to work with hand tools. The grain should not become ragged when hand planed. The wood should not be expensive. Some good woods for beginning projects include:

Willow. This is the best wood for beginning projects. It is low-priced, lightweight, strong, and tough. Willow is easy to work, glue, and finish. It has interesting grain patterns. If care is used in finishing, willow is a very handsome wood. It can be stained to resemble walnut, but it is also pleasing in its natural colors. There is a wide color range in willow; so pieces should be sorted for color harmony. A filler may be used for the best work, but it isn't necessary as a rule. Willow grows in the eastern United States.

Basswood. This wood is soft and easy to work. It sands smoothly and is easy to glue. Basswood holds its shape well. It will not twist or warp if properly seasoned (dried). The texture is fine and even. Basswood is light in weight and strong enough for most projects. Simple finishes are suggested. Strong stains should not be used because basswood is porous and does not stain evenly. It does take paint well and is often used in place of pine for shop projects. Basswood grows in the eastern United States.

Poplar grows in the northeastern part of the United States from Rhode Island to Michigan and as far south as Georgia and Arkansas. It is sometimes called the tulip tree because it bears tuliplike flowers. Poplar is classified as a hardwood but is rather soft and easy to work. However, tools should be sharp. Poplar has a very straight grain and uniform texture. It is light in weight. It tends to be slightly fuzzy when sanded. Poplar takes a very good finish and is used in house building for both inside and outside trim. In commercial furniture making, parts are sometimes made of poplar and stained to look like mahogany.

Pine. There are many trees in the pine family. Some of the most common are ponderosa, red, sugar, white, and Idaho. All of these are similar in general appearance, but they vary in color, texture, hardness, and working qualities. Most are medium-soft and easy to work. They have a light color and a fairly straight grain. Pine is used in building construction for making doors, frames, siding, paneling, and many other things. It is also used for interior woodwork. You will probably use white or ponderosa pine for simple projects. The western soft pines—sugar pine and ponderosa pine—do not take a finish as well as some of the other woods and are often painted. Pine forests are found in many areas of the United States.

Intermediate Projects

For intermediate projects the wood should be fairly easy to work with hand tools and simple power tools. It should be reasonable in price. The wood should take a good finish. Recommended woods include poplar, willow, and western soft pines (already described) plus the following.

Northern soft elm has a prominent grain and light color. It is a good wood for natural finishes. The coloring is generally even, with some mineral spots or streaks. Elm can be an economical substitute for more expensive hardwoods in some projects. However, it is not always available, so make sure you can get it before designing your project. Elm is harvested in the eastern United States and southeastern Canada.

Philippine mahogany (lauan) comes from the Philippine Islands. It is reasonable in price, not too hard to handle, and can be used for almost anything you would choose to build. It machines well and finishes well. Philippine mahogany runs from very light red to deep red in color. The color and grain pattern often vary a great deal from board to board.

Advanced Projects

The following woods are valued for their decorative and finishing qualities and their great worth as cabinet woods.

Genuine mahoganies include Honduras (American) and African mahogany. Honduras mahogany is found in Mexico and Central America. African mahogany comes from Western Africa. Genuine mahogany is the ideal cabinet wood. It is tough, strong, easy to work, and takes a good polish. It is also quite expensive. Genuine mahogany has a deep reddish-brown color which darkens with age.

Black walnut is the most valuable cabinet wood which grows in the United States. Most black walnut comes from the central states of Missouri, Kansas, Iowa, Illinois, Indiana, Ohio, Kentucky, and Tennessee. Although fairly hard and dense, walnut works well with both hand tools and machines. This wood takes a beautiful polish. It varies in color from rich chocolate brown in the heartwood to creamy white in the sapwood. It has a very attractive grain that takes almost any kind of finish. Besides fine furniture, walnut is used for veneer, interior finish, and cabinets. Because the upper grades are expensive, consider using a lower grade of walnut for your project.

Cherry is very good for furniture because, once dried, it doesn't warp. This hardwood machines well and takes a beautiful finish. It is strong, stiff, and relatively hard. It varies in color from reddish brown in the heartwood to yellow in the sapwood. Cherry has a fairly uniform texture. The cherry used for woodworking does *not* come from the cultivated fruit tree. It grows wild in the forests of the eastern United States.

White ash is one of the finest hardwoods. It has a beautiful grain and a firm texture. White ash turns well on a lathe and is therefore popular for woodworking and furniture making. It is found in the northern and eastern United States.

Hard maple is excellent for many advanced projects. It is a hard, dense, and beautiful wood that resists shock and wear. Be sure to buy "selected white" hard maple. "Selected white" is not a grade but refers only to color. Maple lumber comes mostly from the Middle Atlantic and Lake states. It is a hard, strong wood that resists shock and wear.

Oak is an open-grained wood that has been widely used in furniture and interiors. It is quartersawed to show its broad rays, which add to its beauty. Oak is somewhat hard on machinery blades and knives, but it finishes well. Red oak has a slightly reddish tinge and a rather coarse grain. It is used in furniture, paneling, moldings, and flooring. Most red oak lumber comes from the southern states, southern mountain regions, and Atlantic coastal plain. White oak has a better color, finer texture, and more interesting grain pattern than red oak. It is considered the better choice for fine furniture. White oak is also more resistant to rot, moisture, and weathering. The heartwood is grayish brown, and the sapwood is nearly white. White oak grows throughout the eastern half of the United States and Canada.

QUESTIONS

1. What is lumber?
2. What is the difference between softwood and hardwood?
3. Are all softwoods softer than hardwoods? Explain.
4. What does the expression "dressed lumber" mean?
5. Why is the actual size of lumber always smaller than the nominal size?
6. What is the best grade of hardwood lumber?
7. What information should be included to order lumber correctly?
8. What is plywood?

ACTIVITIES

1. Calculate the number of board feet in a piece of lumber 1 inch by 10 inches by 8 feet. If you are not sure how to do this, review "How Lumber is Sold" on pages 51-52.
2. Find out more about the sources of the woods described on pages 56-58. What do the trees look like? Where do they grow? How long does it take before the trees are ready to harvest? Prepare a report on your findings.
3. Check a local lumberyard or building supply center. What types of lumber and plywood are available? Make a chart of the types and their prices.

Reading a Drawing and Making a Shop Sketch

A drawing can say many things. It can tell you how to find someone's house or where a city is located. A drawing can also tell you how to build a project. The drawing will tell you how big each part is, what the material is, what shape each part is, and how the parts go together. When you make your own design, it shows how the finished article should look; so there is no guessing to do. Before you can use a drawing though, you will have to know how to read it. The drawing is your guide. It tells you everything you need to know about the project. Fig. 6-1.

This chapter will tell you how to read a drawing. It will also explain how to make a sketch. If you have already taken drawing and sketching, the following will be a review.

6-1. ***Learn to make and use a drawing to build a project.***

DRAWINGS USED IN WOODWORKING

As you look through this book, you'll see that most drawings are *working drawings.* These are also called *view drawings.* They have two or more views (usually three) of the project. Figs. 6-2 and 6-3. The most common views are the front, top, and the right side (end). Many drawings found in magazines are *pictorial drawings.* Pictorial drawings look more like a picture of the object. The two most common pictorial drawings are *isometric* and *cabinet drawings.* Figs. 6-4 and 6-5. Notice that both of these drawings show how the project will look when it is completed and the size and shape of each part. Sometimes even a *perspective drawing* is used. Fig. 6-2.

Woodworking drawings differ. A drawing of a project will often be made partly as a view drawing and partly as a pictorial drawing. Then, too, when view drawings are used, the views are not always placed correctly. That is, the right side, or end, view isn't always to the right of the

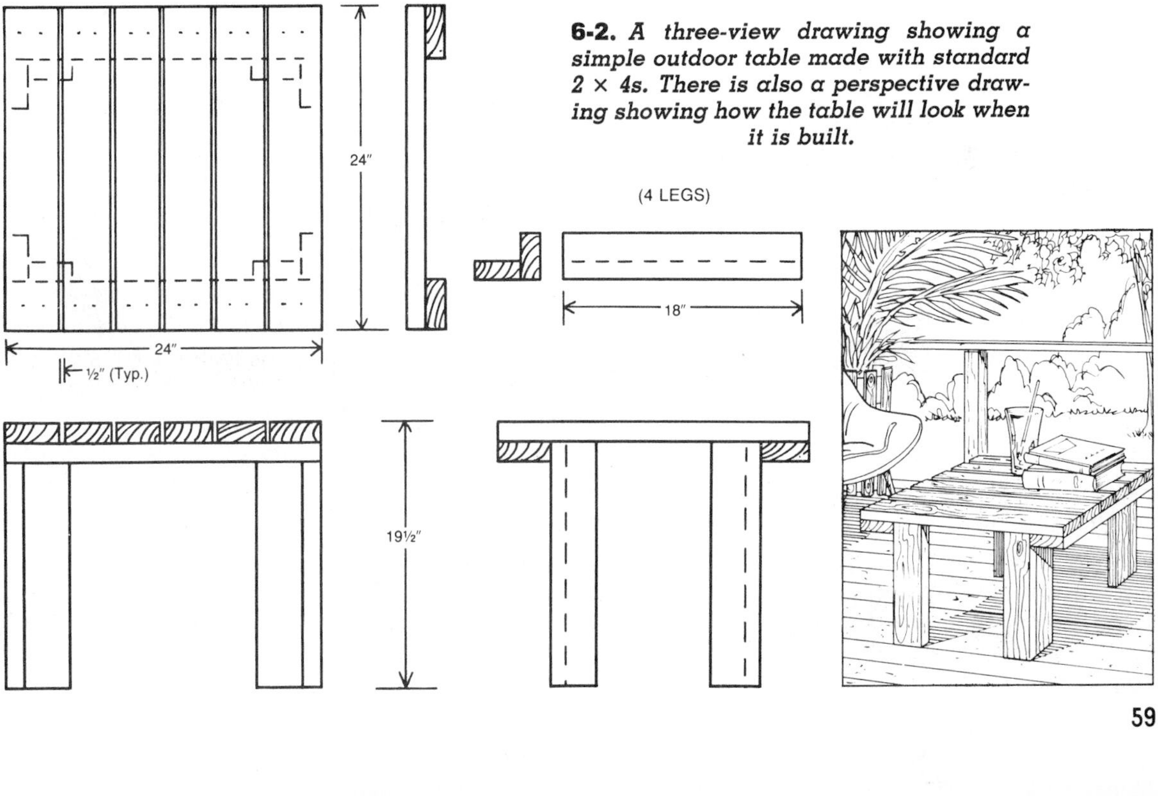

24"

24"

½" (Typ.)

(4 LEGS)

18"

19½"

6-2. ***A three-view drawing showing a simple outdoor table made with standard 2 × 4s. There is also a perspective drawing showing how the table will look when it is built.***

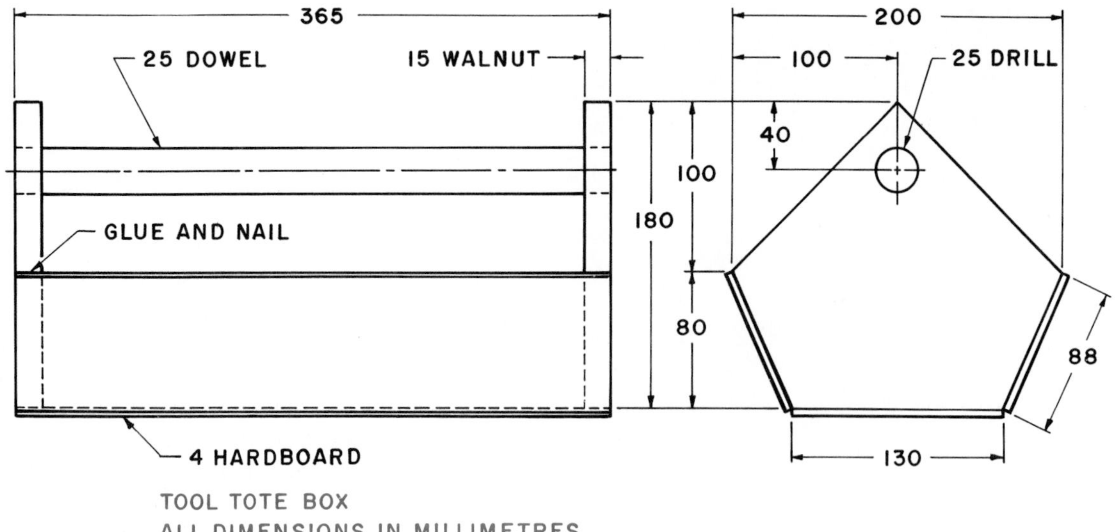

6-3. *Only two views are needed of this tool box. Note that the sizes are metric.*

front view. You'll also find many drawings made as *exploded* (taken apart) views. This kind shows each part more clearly and also shows how the parts fit together. Fig. 6-6.

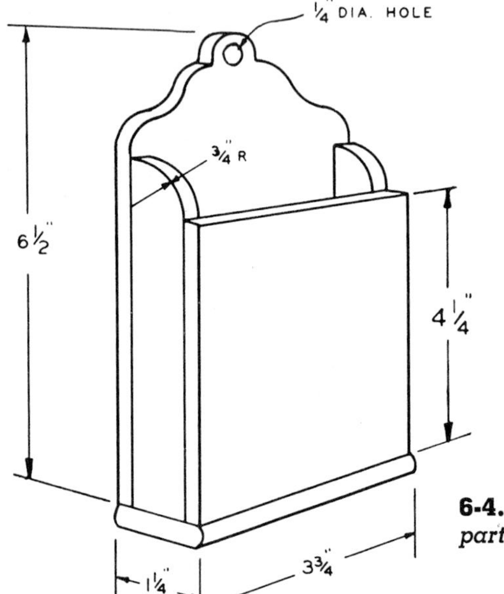

6-4. *An isometric drawing of a card holder. All parts are 1/4" thick except the bottom, which is 3/8".*

KINDS OF LINES

Lines show the shape of each part. Different kinds of lines have different meanings. Fig. 6-7.

- *Visible (object) lines* show all edges or surfaces that can be seen. They are solid, heavy lines.
- *Hidden (invisible) lines* show hidden edges. These are broken lines.
- *Center lines* are used to show the centers of arcs and circles and to divide an object into two equal parts.
- *Extension lines* stick out from the drawing. Between these lines the sizes of each part can be shown.
- *Dimension lines* usually have arrowheads at one or both ends and are broken in the center. The dimension figure (size of the part) is written in the gap of the dimension line. The dimension lines and figure are usually placed between the extension lines. Sometimes there is not enough room within the extension lines. Then the dimen-

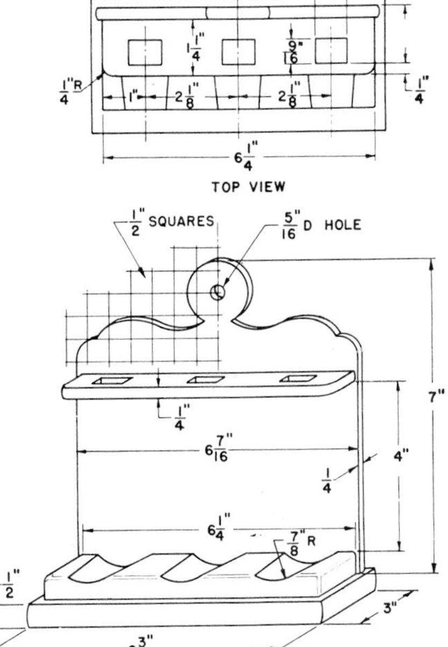

6-5. *A cabinet drawing of a pipe rack.*

sion lines and the figure are placed outside the extension lines. See Fig. 6-5.

DIMENSIONS

Dimensions tell you the sizes of things. These dimensions must be followed in writing a bill of materials and in building the project. There are four common ways by which dimensions are added to drawings:

1. **Customary (inch) drawings** are dimensioned in inches and fractions (parts) of an inch. Sometimes the inch marks (″) are placed after the dimensions to show that the sizes are in inches.
2. **Metric drawings** are dimensioned in millimetres. Fig. 6-3.
3. **Dual-dimensioned drawings** show both the inch and millimetre dimensions. Sometimes the inch dimensions are first and sometimes the millimetre dimensions are. Figs. 6-8 and 6-9.
4. A **readout chart** can be used. Either metric or inch dimensions are shown on the drawing. A readout chart is added showing the dimensions in the other system. Fig. 6-10 (page 64).

SCALE

Nearly always a woodworking project is too big to be drawn full size on a piece of paper. Very large projects must be drawn smaller so that they can fit on standard-size paper. Drawings made larger or smaller than full size are called *scale drawings.* For example, if the part is 8 inches long and you draw it 4 inches long, you are using a scale that is *half size* (6 inches equal 1 foot). Other common scales are: *one-fourth size* (3 inches equal 1 foot) and *one-eighth size* (1½ inches equal 1 foot). If even larger projects must be drawn, a scale such as ¼ inch to the foot (¼″ = 1′0″) may be followed, as in house plans.

On metric drawings, the common scales for reducing the size are 1:2 (half size), 1:5 (one-fifth size), 1:10 (one-tenth size), and 1:20 (one-twentieth size). In drawings of buildings, a scale of 1:50 or 1:100 is often used.

READING A DRAWING

In Fig. 6-11 you see the kind of project you might make in the wood shop. Find the answers to these questions by reading the drawing in Fig. 6-11(a).

- How many parts are there in this project? (Count the dowels, too.)
- What is the thickness of the back?
- What is the length of the back?
- What is the diameter of the dowels?
- At what angle are the dowels attached to the back?
- What is the diameter of the holes for mounting the rack?
- How far in are the dowels placed from the ends?
- What is the distance between the dowels?

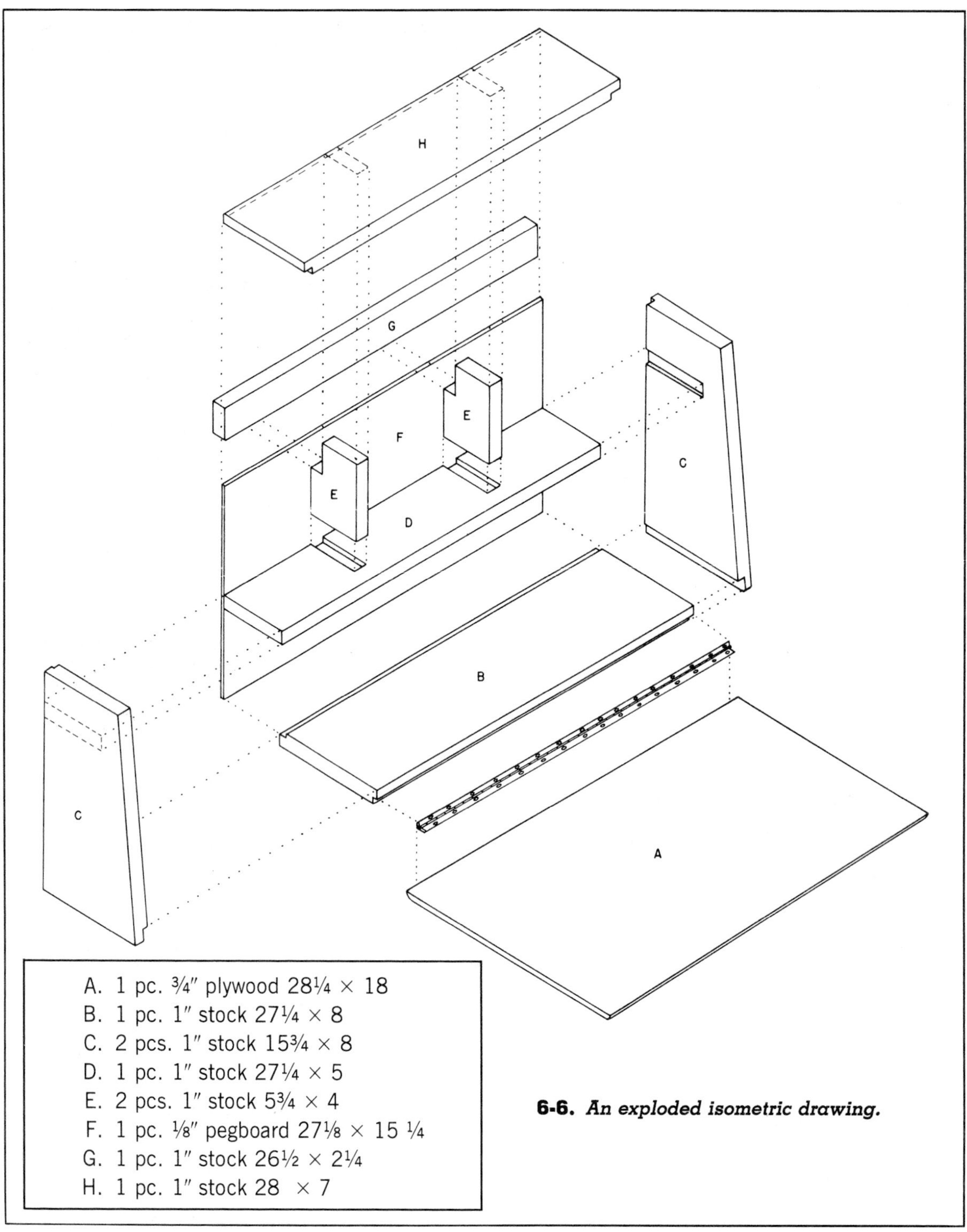

6-6. *An exploded isometric drawing.*

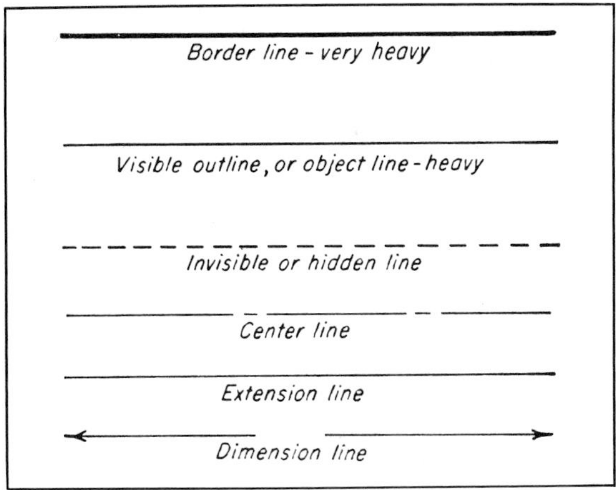

6-7. *These are some of the lines used in drawing. The border line is used around the drawing to "frame" it.*

6-8. *Cracker tray.*

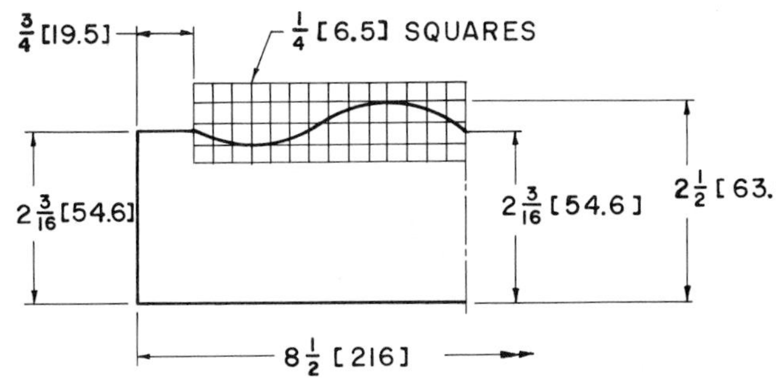

6-9. *The drawings for the cracker tray are dual dimensioned. The inch measurements are given first, and the millimetre measurements are in brackets.*

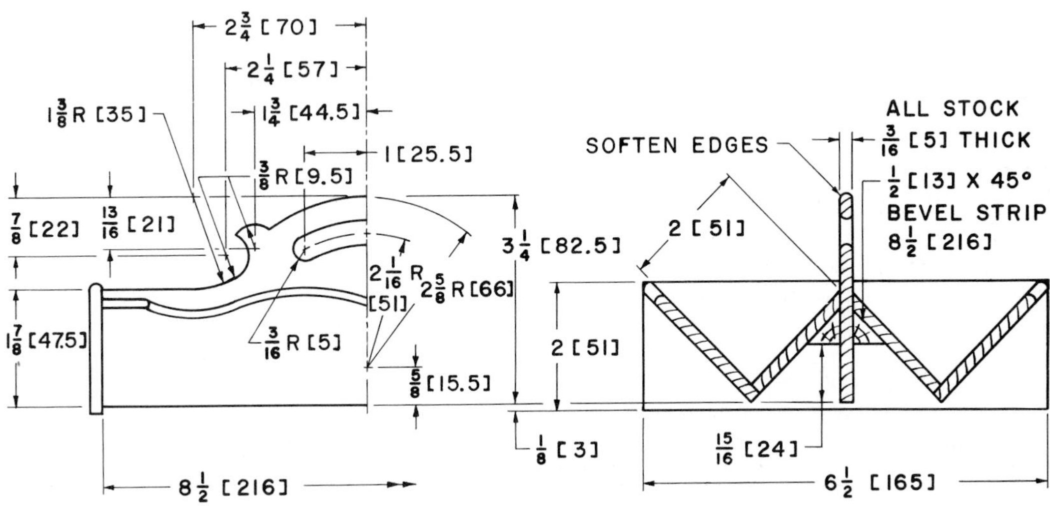

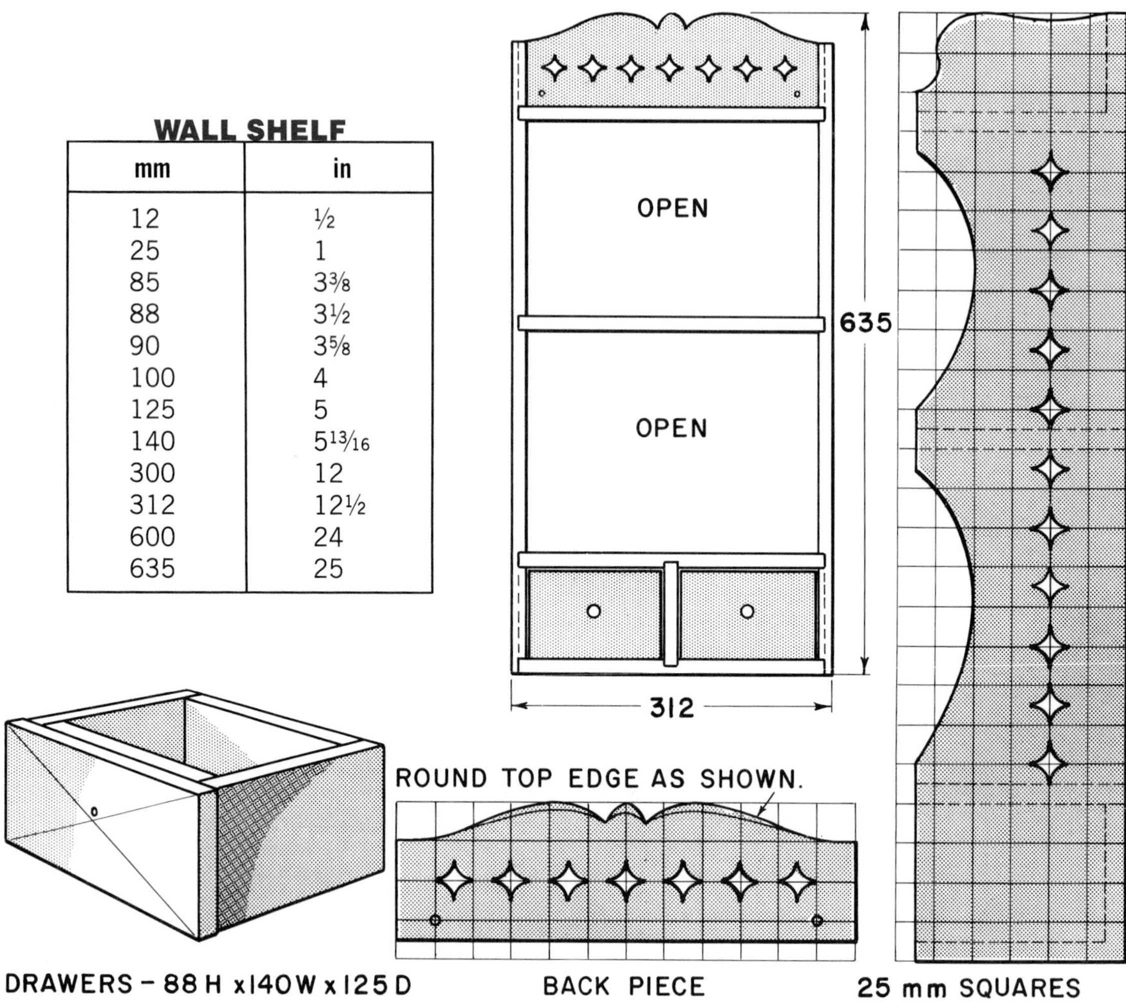

WALL SHELF

mm	in
12	$\frac{1}{2}$
25	1
85	$3\frac{3}{8}$
88	$3\frac{1}{2}$
90	$3\frac{5}{8}$
100	4
125	5
140	$5\frac{13}{16}$
300	12
312	$12\frac{1}{2}$
600	24
635	25

6-10. *This wall shelf is dimensioned in millimetres. A customary readout chart makes it easy to convert from millimetres to inches.*

MAKING A SHOP SKETCH

A *shop sketch* is just a very simple drawing of a project made on ruled drawing paper. Sometimes you will find an idea you want to use in a book or magazine in the library. Perhaps you'll find a suggestion in your own book that you like but want to change a little. You might want to use an idea of your own also or sketch something you have seen. Whatever its source, you will need to get the idea "on paper" so that you can see what it will look like. A shop sketch is needed for planning and building anything.

For making the shop sketch, you need the following materials.

- A No. 2 writing pencil or an HB drawing pencil.
- Squared or cross-sectioned paper that is lined

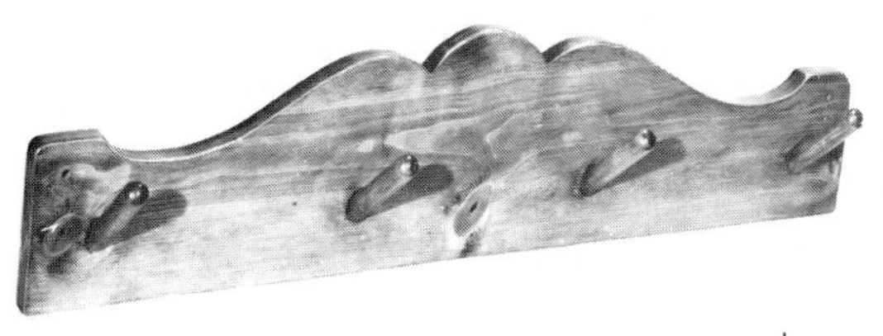

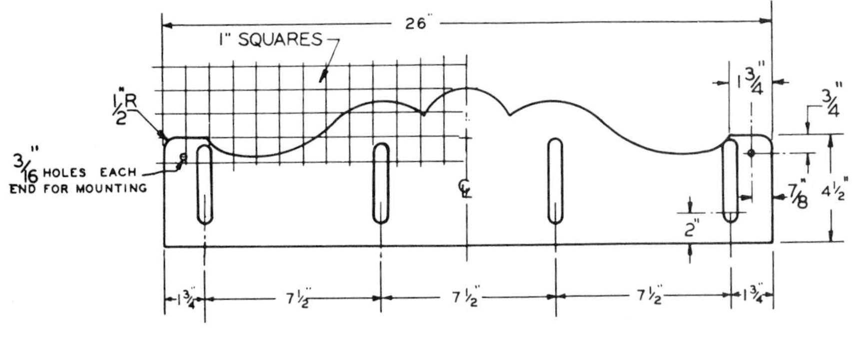

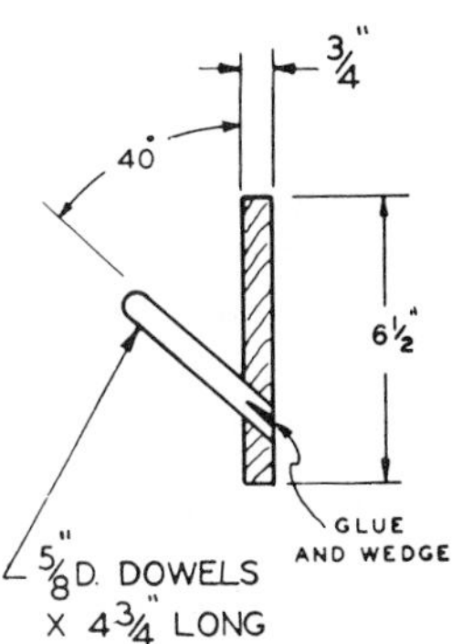

6-11(a). *A photograph and working drawing of a hat and coat hanger. Can you answer the questions by reading the drawing?*

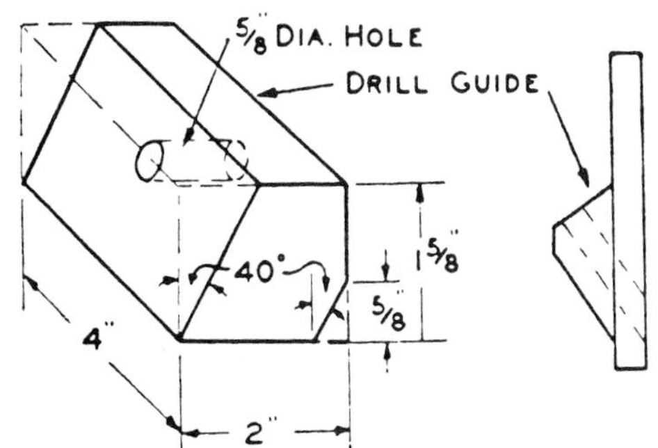

6-11(b). *A drill jig (guide) used for drilling the angle holes in the hanger.*

PLAN OF PROCEDURE

1. Cut back to size on circular saw.
2. Lay out irregular surface and cut out on band saw or jigsaw. Sand edges with drill press drum sander.
3. Drill mounting holes.
4. From a scrap piece of 2 × 4, make guide for drilling holes in hanger back. Dimensions for guide are shown in Fig. 6–11(b). Clamp guide to hanger back, and drill the peg holes.
5. Smooth back and soften edges with sandpaper.
6. Purchase 5/8-inch dowel or turn pine on lathe to 5/8-inch diameter. Cut four pegs to length of 4 3/4 inches. Cut 3/4-inch deep slot in base end of pegs to receive wedges. Round top end of pegs.
7. Cut four wedges to size.
8. Glue and wedge pegs into back.
9. Trim projecting pegs and wedges and sand even with rear of back.
10. Finish sand entire project.
11. Apply antique pine finish.

6-11(d). *The steps for making the project.*

BILL OF MATERIALS
Stock: Pine

IMPORTANT: All dimensions listed below are FINISHED size.

No. of Pieces	Part Name	Thickness	Width	Length
1	Back	3/4"	6 1/2"	26"
4	Pegs	5/8" dia.		4 3/4"
4	Wedges	0"-1/8"	5/8"	3/4"

6-11(c). *Materials needed for the hanger.*

in squares or dots, eight to the inch. These squares or dots help you to draw the plan to the correct size and to keep your lines straight.

- A pencil compass may be used for drawing circles and arcs (parts of circles). However, you can sketch these *freehand* (with no instruments, just a pencil).
- A shop rule or a straightedge for drawing straight lines.

Here's how to make a shop sketch:

1. Decide on the views you'll need to build the project. Sometimes one view is enough. For example, if it's a one-piece project, such as a cutting board, only the top view is needed. A little note on the sketch can tell you the thickness of the *stock* (wood). At other times, you'll have to make two or three views.

2. Decide on the scale to use. In your first attempt, make the drawing full size, if possible. This is simplest. Maybe you'll need to use more than one piece of cross-sectioned paper to do this. But for all needs, with paper having eight squares to the inch, the following scales are easiest:

- Full size. Each small square represents (stands for) ⅛ inch, and so each large, dark-lined square represents 1 inch.
- Half size. Each small square represents ¼ inch and each large square equals 2 inches.
- Quarter size. Each small square represents ½ inch and each large square equals 4 inches.
- Eighth size. Each small square represents 1 inch and each large square represents 8 inches.

For example, suppose you want to draw the house numbers shown in Fig. 6-12. Notice that the back is 6 inches wide and 16 inches long. You couldn't make this full size, so half size would be best. Always make the drawing as large as possible. Each small square in this case will represent ¼ inch.

3. Start in the lower left-hand corner of the paper about 1 inch up and 1 inch in. Mark a dot.

4. Count off eight large squares from left to right. (Each large square equals 2 inches.) Mark a dot.

5. Count off three large squares up. Mark a dot.

6. Notice that the ends are irregular. Mark off three large squares from the lower right-hand corner. Draw any free (irregular) line to the upper right-hand corner. Also draw an irregular line on the other end.

7. Then draw the lines to complete the outline.

8. Now draw in the numbers of your house.

9. Add a note for the size of stock.

To make a sketch with metric dimensions, use metric cross-sectioned paper. Metric cross-sectioned paper has 1 mm squares covering the surface, with every five squares in slightly darker lines. It is easy to use any scale. For example, each square can represent 1 mm for a full-size sketch or 2 mm for half size. You can also use cross-sectioned paper with 20-mm or 25-mm squares. Fig. 6-13.

DESIGNING IN THE METRIC SYSTEM

A soft conversion to metric dimensions can yield some awkward numbers. Since the soft conversion is only a mathematical change, the metric sizes may be very odd. For example, if the original dimension is 1″, then the exact metric equivalent is 25.4 mm. This is hard to measure on most metric rules. To be truly metric, a project should be designed in the metric system, using the more common full numbers like 5, 10, 15, 20, and 25 mm.

When designing a product to metric measurements, it is handy to have a dual-reading metric rule. Begin to think about replacement sizes, not soft conversions. For example, if you are designing bookends, you will find that a 5″ customary width is about right. But suppose you are designing metric bookends. What do you do? Look at the dual-reading rule. You will see that 5″ converts to about 127 mm. That size could be rounded off to 125 mm. Because 125 mm is easier to read on your rule and more convenient to use, it's called a "rational" size. Fig. 6-14.

789
6
16
1/2 X6X16 BACK
1/4 PLYWOOD NUMBERS

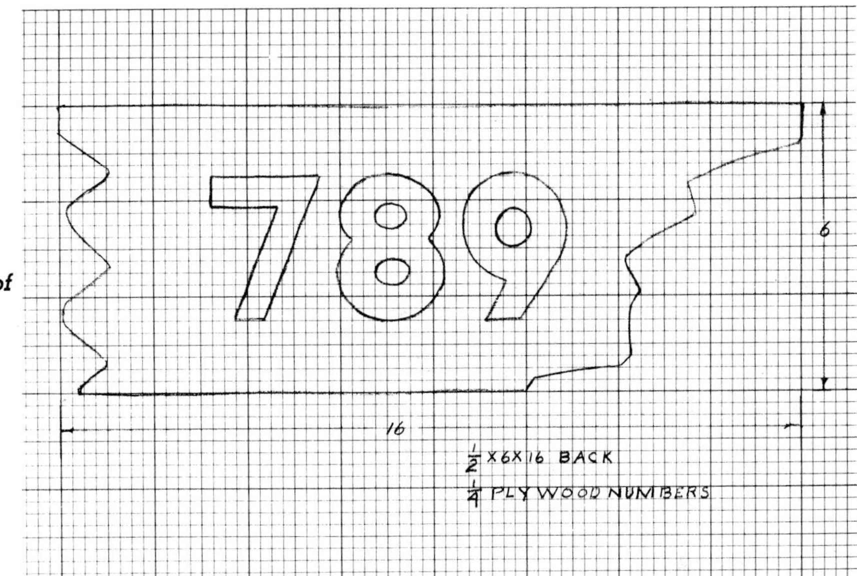

6-12. *A shop sketch of house numbers.*

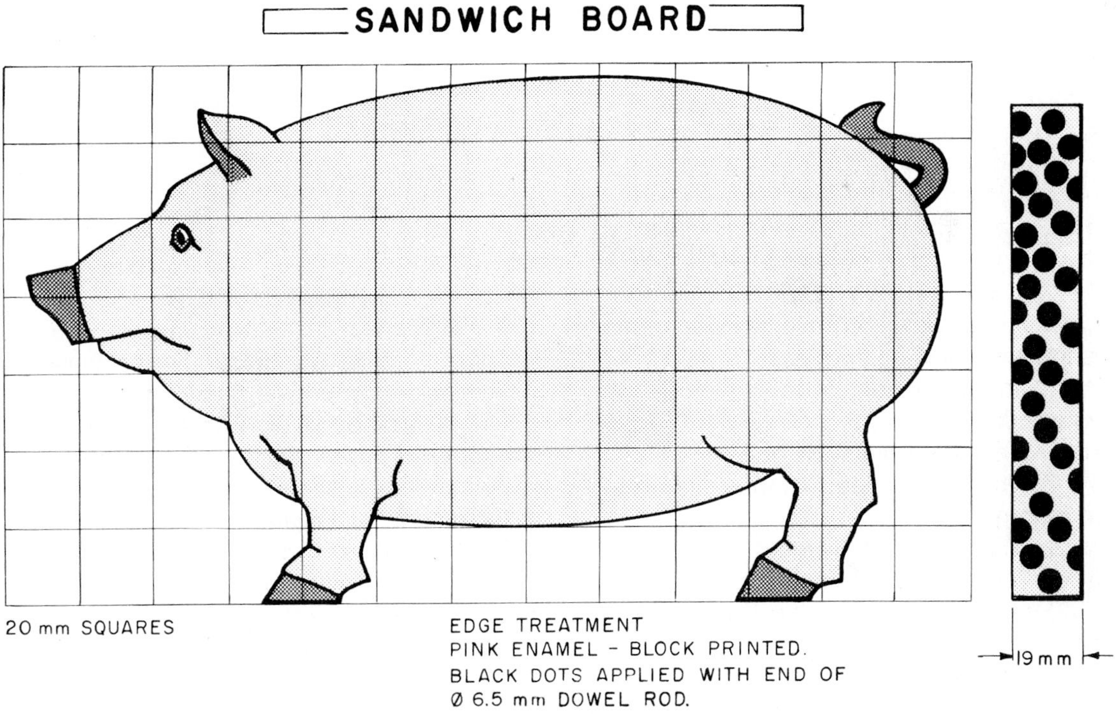

SANDWICH BOARD
20 mm SQUARES
EDGE TREATMENT
PINK ENAMEL - BLOCK PRINTED.
BLACK DOTS APPLIED WITH END OF
Ø 6.5 mm DOWEL ROD.
19 mm

6-13. *This sandwich board is designed in metric measurements.*

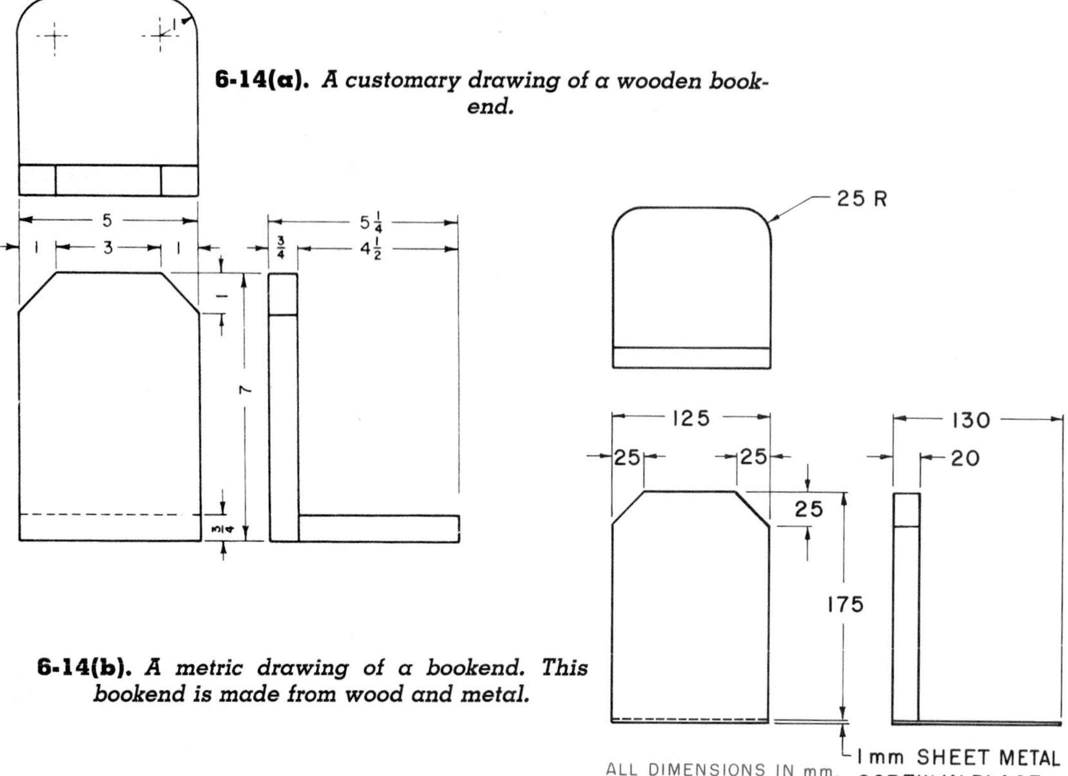

6-14(a). *A customary drawing of a wooden bookend.*

6-14(b). *A metric drawing of a bookend. This bookend is made from wood and metal.*

QUESTIONS

1. What are the three views usually shown in a working drawing?
2. Name three kinds of pictorial drawings.
3. What are dimensions?
4. Why do you need dimensions on a drawing?
5. What is a scale drawing?
6. Tell how to make a shop sketch.

ACTIVITIES

1. Figure 6-4 shows an isometric drawing of a card holder. Dimensions are given on the drawing and in the caption. Make a shop sketch of this product on squared paper. Since the card holder is larger than a sheet of paper, you will need to determine a scale.
2. Look at home for examples of drawings. Newspapers and hobby magazines are good sources. Label the drawings to tell what kind they are (pictorial, exploded, or working drawing).

Planning Your Work

What are you going to do next summer? Is your family going to take a trip? Will you work for your dad or some of your neighbors? Are you going to camp? Will you go to the beach or the mountains? If your summer is to be successful, whether it's work or play, you have to make plans. Before you can do anythhing that is interesting and worthwhile, you have to get ready for it.

In the working world where people are paid for their ideas and efforts, planning is a most important part of the job. Without planning, there wouldn't be much of a chance of building bridges, roads, houses, cars, or any of the thousands of products we depend on.

Plans must be made not only for the big things like buildings but also for small things. Planning is especially important when you are going to use tools and materials to make things. In fact, the job is already half done when it is well planned. A good slogan to follow is *"Plan your work; then work your plan."* Sure, you can start right out "butchering wood." But if you do, you'll waste a lot of material, do poor work, and end up with something nobody wants.

WHAT YOU WILL NEED FOR PLANNING

How do you plan in wood? Suppose all of you in the class and your instructor have decided on the first project. Fig. 7-1. In making your plans, you will need the following items.

Drawing of the Project

You will need a drawing of the project or a shop sketch that you have made yourself. This drawing or sketch must have the dimensions on it. Fig. 7-2.

7-1. *Your first project could be this mirror.*

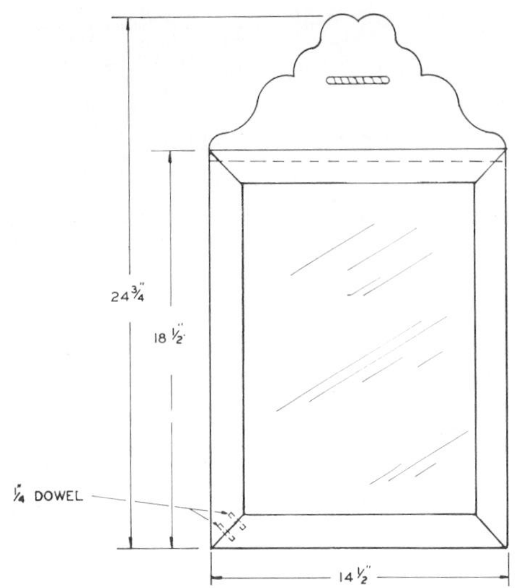

7-2. A drawing of the mirror shown in Fig. 7-1.

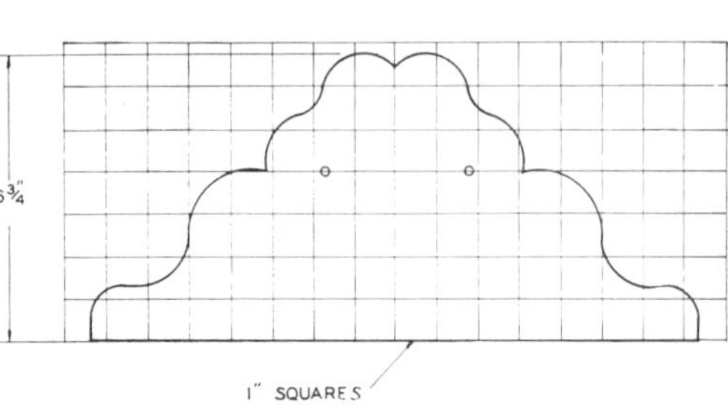

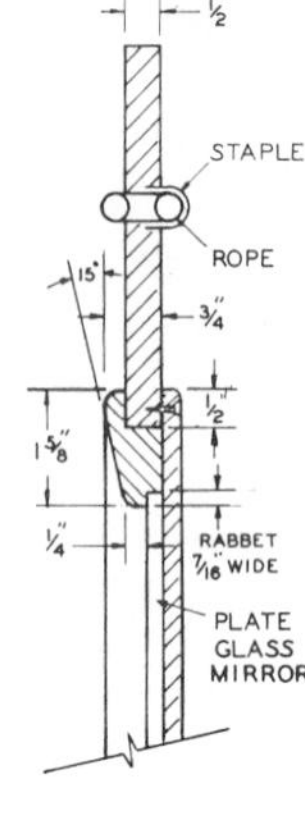

Bill of Materials

This is a list of all the things you will need to build the project. Fig. 7-3. Always make out the bill of materials before you start because:

- It tells you exactly what size and kind of lumber and other materials you need.
- It helps you find out the cost of the project.
- It makes a good list to take with you if you must buy your own materials.
- It is a good checklist to use when you are getting the materials together in the shop.

A complete bill of materials includes *everything* you need to build the project. The list includes:

- Number of pieces needed.

BILL OF MATERIALS

IMPORTANT: All dimensions listed below, except for length of dowel, are FINISHED size.					
No. of Pieces	Part Name	Thickness	Width	Length	Material
1	Top	½"	6¾"	14½"	Knotty Pine
2	Top and Bottom Rails	¾"	1⅝"	14½"	Knotty Pine
2	Side Rails	¾"	1⅝"	18½"	Knotty Pine
1	Back	¼"	14¼"	18¼"	Plywood or Hardboard
1	Mirror	¼"	12"	16"	Glass
1	Dowel	¼"		20"	
2	Small Screw Eyes				
As needed:	¾" #6 Flathead Wood Screws				
1	Piece Twisted Rope 6" long				
1	Small Staple				

7-3. Bill of materials for the mirror.

PROCEDURES

1. Lay out the pattern for the top on paper. Trace the design on the stock and cut on a band or scroll (jig-) saw.
2. Drill the two holes for the rope.
3. Cut the four rails and miter the ends. Cut a rabbet on the back of each rail for the mirror and cut a large rabbet in the top rail to receive the top piece.
4. Bevel the rails on a circular saw and round the edges with the router.
5. Cut the back.
6. Assemble the rails with dowels and glue.
7. Sand all parts and apply the finish.
8. Insert mirror and fasten the back to the rails and top with wood screws.
9. Insert ornamental rope and staple to the back. Mirror should be hung with picture wire fastened to two screw eyes in the back.

7-4. ***These are the steps to follow in building the mirror.***

- Thickness, width, and length of each piece.
- Name of each part.
- Kind of lumber or other building material.
- Cost.

The size of each part listed in the bill of materials is the exact, final dimension. Before you get out your materials, you can make a *stock-cutting list.* This list gives the size of each piece that you cut out of the lumber, before the finished size. To the sizes in the bill of materials you must add about 1/16 to 1/8 inch for thickness, 1/8 to 1/4 inch for width, and 1/2 inch for length. (Of course, plywood is cut from the exact thickness and as close to finished size as possible.)

Procedures List

This is a list of the steps you will follow in making each part, putting the project together, and applying a finish. Fig. 7-4. Each chapter in this book describes a step in making a project.

List of Tools and Machines

You should also make a list of the tools you will use and any power machines you may need. Then you can make sure that the tools are available and that you will be allowed to operate the machines. Fig. 7-5.

PLANNING SHEET

To help with your planning, use a form like the one shown in Fig. 7-6. Fill out the form as carefully as you can. Check it. Did you forget anything? When your plan is approved, you can begin to draw the project. Check off each step as you do it.

In your planning, follow the example shown in Fig. 7-6. Notice that:

(1) There is a clear, easy-to-read drawing.

(2) The bill of materials tells exactly what you need.

(3) The steps in making the project are clear and easy to follow.

(4) The list of tools includes only those really needed.

TOOLS AND MACHINES

Pencil
Rule
Try square
Band or scroll saw
Drill press or hand drill
Circular saw
Router
Screwdriver
Clamps

7-5. ***These are the tools and machines you would need to make the mirror.***

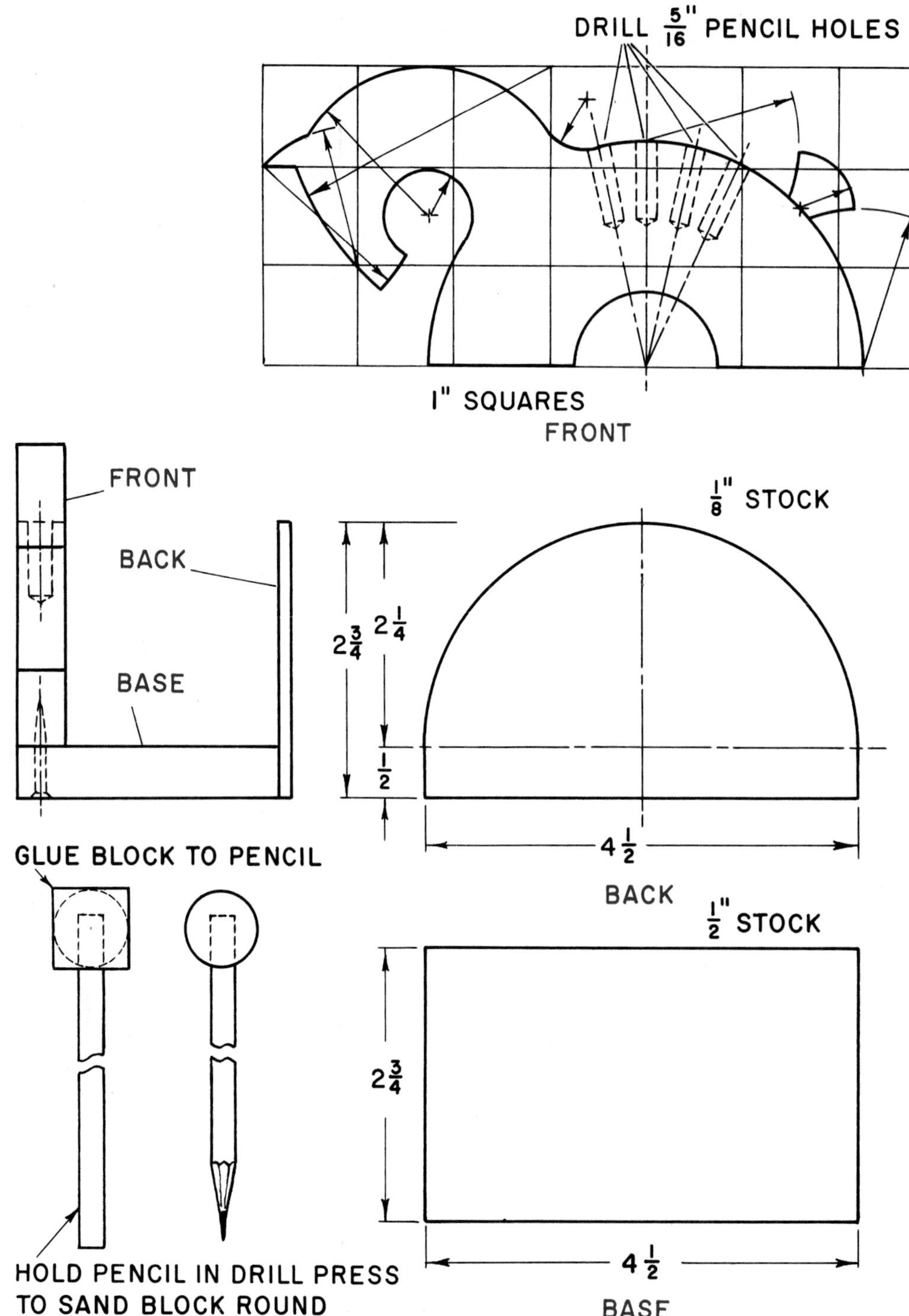

7-6(a). *Drawing for a note holder.*

PLANNING SHEET

Name Note Holder Grade

Name of the Project Date Started Date Completed

Bill of Materials:

No.	T	W	L	Name of Part	Material	Unit Cost	Total Cost
1	½″	3″	7″	Front	Pine		
1	⅛″	2¾″	4½″	Back	Pine		
1	½″	2¾″	4½″	Base	Pine		
1	⅝″	⅝″	⅝″	Pencil top	Pine		

TOOLS AND MACHINES:

Crosscut saw, coping saw or jigsaw, backsaw, rule, try square, pencil, jack plane, twist drill, hand drill, sandpaper, drill press, hammer, screwdriver.

PROCEDURES OR STEPS:

1. Make a stock-cutting list.
2. Lay out and cut all pieces to size.
3. Complete the front:
   - Enlarge the design.
   - Transfer the design to the wood.
   - Cut out design with coping saw or jigsaw.
   - Smooth the edges.
   - Drill the holes for the pencils.
4. Square up the base.
5. Lay out and cut the back to shape.
6. Assemble the parts with screws and nails.
7. Make the ball for the end of the pencil.
8. Apply the finish.

7-6(b). ***A planning sheet for the note holder.***

QUESTIONS

1. Why is it important to plan your work?

2. Name the four important parts of a plan. Describe each one.

3. Is a stock-cutting list the same as a bill of materials? Explain.

4. How can a plan help you do your work faster and better?

ACTIVITIES

1. What could happen if you failed to plan your work? List some of the mistakes you could make.

2. Suppose you were going to build the mirror that is described in this chapter. From the bill of materials on page 70, you learn that you will need ½-inch thick pine, ¾-inch thick pine, and ¼-inch thick plywood or hardboard. These materials come in standard lengths and widths. Go to a lumberyard or home improvement center to find out what sizes are available and how much they cost.

Using Measuring and Marking Tools

You must learn to measure accurately in both systems of measurement. Remember the motto, "Measure twice; cut once." No project will turn out well if you measure incorrectly.

TOOLS FOR MEASURING

Rules

A *bench rule* is a wood rule with brass tips on the ends. The brass tips protect the ends from damage. A damaged rule does not measure accurately. One side is graduated (divided) into eighths of an inch along both edges. The other side is graduated in sixteenths. Bench rules are made in 1-foot (12 inch), 2-foot (24 inch), and 3-foot (36 inch) lengths. Sometimes the 3-foot rule is called a yardstick. Metric bench rules are also available. Fig. 8-1.

The *zigzag rule,* or *folding rule,* is used to measure longer stock when very exact measurements are not too important. Fig. 8-2.

The *push-pull, steel tape,* or *tape rule* is a metal rule that rolls up into a case. Fig. 8-3. There is a hook at the end to slip over the edge of the board. Fig. 8-4. Since it is flexible (bends easily) it can measure curved surfaces. It is also very good for measuring the inside diameter of things. Fig. 8-5.

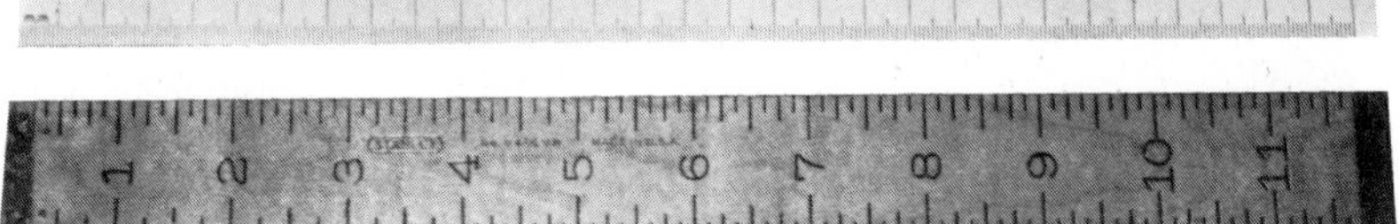

8-1. *One side of this 12" bench rule has been covered by a 300 mm metric rule.*

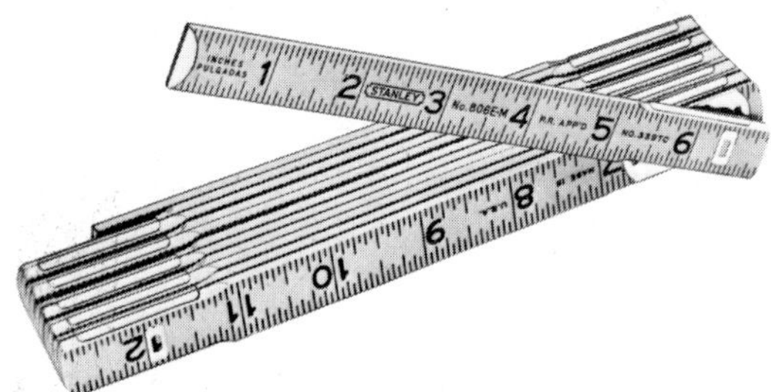

8-2(a). *A zigzag rule with inch measurements.*

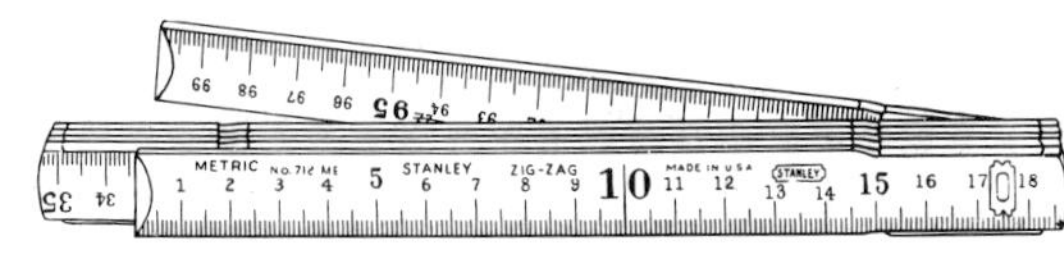

8-2(b). *A metric zigzag rule.*

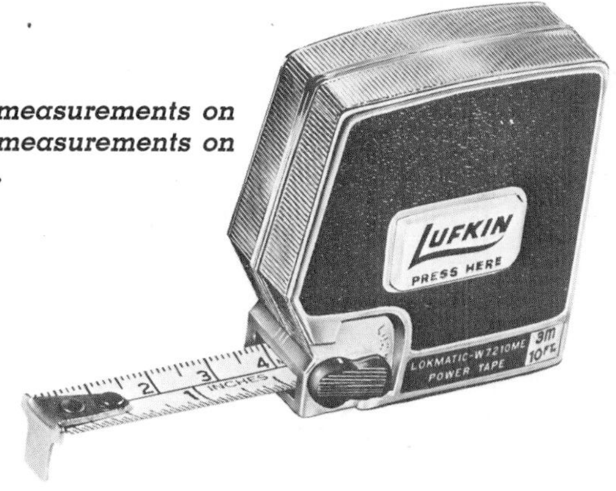

8-3. *This tape rule has metric measurements on the upper edge and customary measurements on the lower edge.*

8-4. *Using a steel tape to check the length of material.*

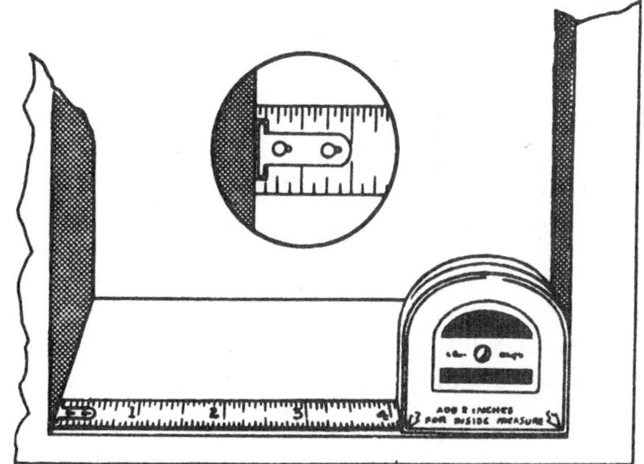

8-5. *Checking an inside measurement with a steel tape. You must add two inches to the amount shown on the tape to allow for the size of the tape's case.*

Squares

The *try square* is used for squaring, measuring, and testing. Fig. 8-6. The blade and handle are at right angles (90 degrees) to each other. The try square is used:

- To test whether a surface is flat.
- To check a face and edge surface for squareness.
- To mark lines across the face or edge of stock.

Fig. 8-7. There are graduations along the edge for measuring. *Never use this tool for pounding or hammering.*

The *combination square* is being used more and more by woodworkers because it can do so many things. This tool has a blade and a head. The blade has a groove cut along its length so that it can slide into the head. One side of the

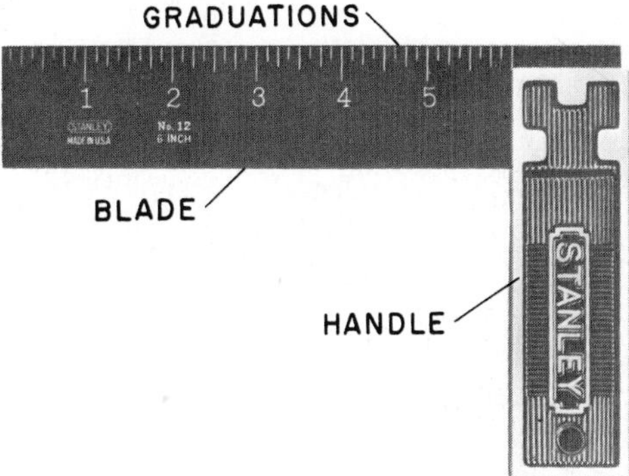

8-6. *Parts of a try square. (Stanley Tools)*

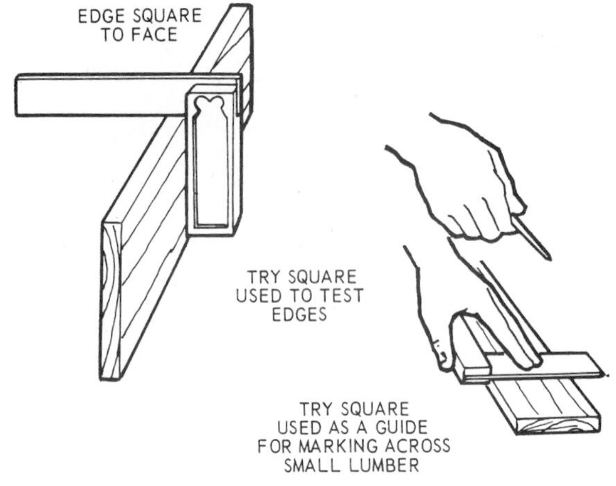

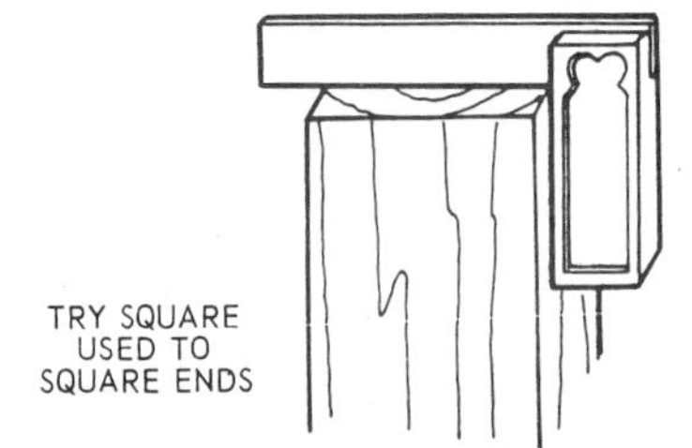

8-7. *Some uses of the try square.*

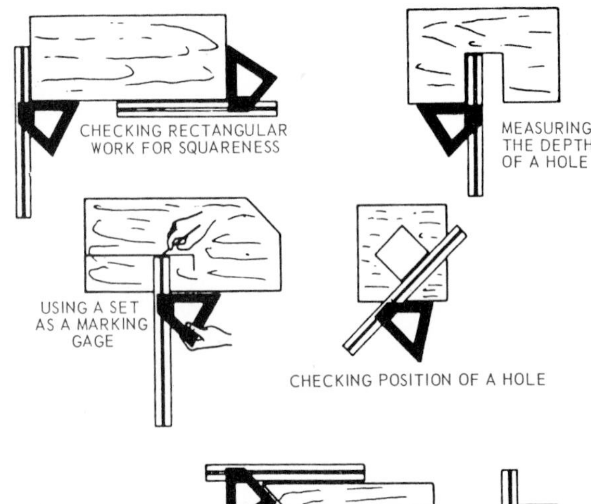

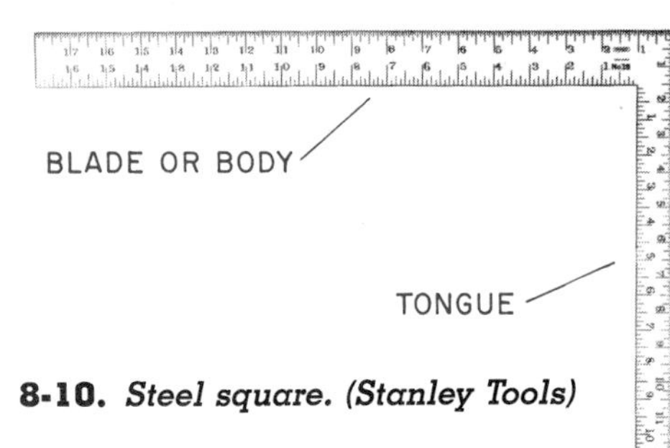

8-9. *Using a combination square.*

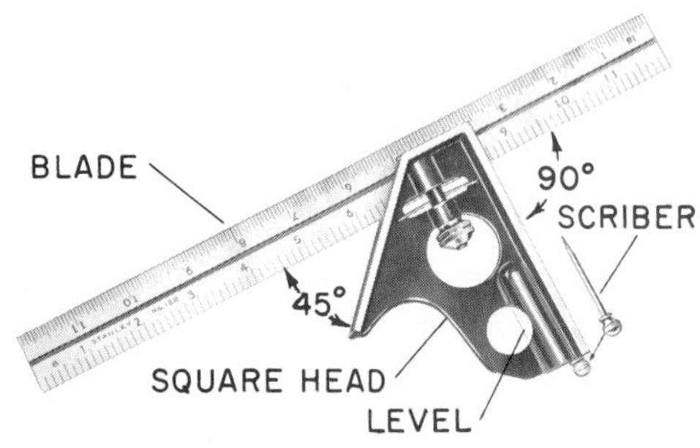

8-8. *Parts of a combination square. (Stanley Tools)*

BLADE OR BODY

TONGUE

8-10. *Steel square. (Stanley Tools)*

head makes a 90-degree angle with the blade and the other side a 45-degree angle. There is a *level* (a tool for testing for a flat, horizontal surface) in the head. Fig. 8-8. The combination square can be used as:

- A try square.
- A miter square to lay out 45° angles and check them.
- A depth gauge.
- A level.
- A marking gauge. Fig. 8-9.

The *steel square* is L-shaped like the try square but larger. It has a body (the longer part)

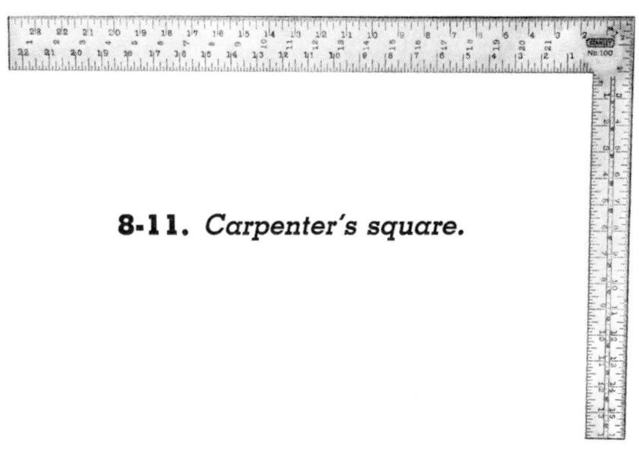
8-11. *Carpenter's square.*

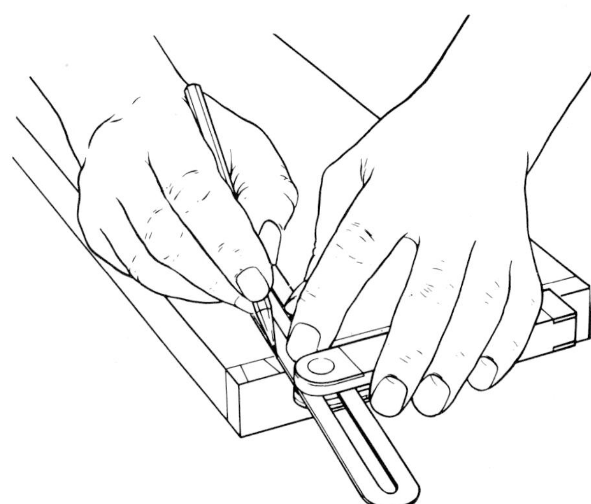
8-12(b). *Using a sliding T bevel.*

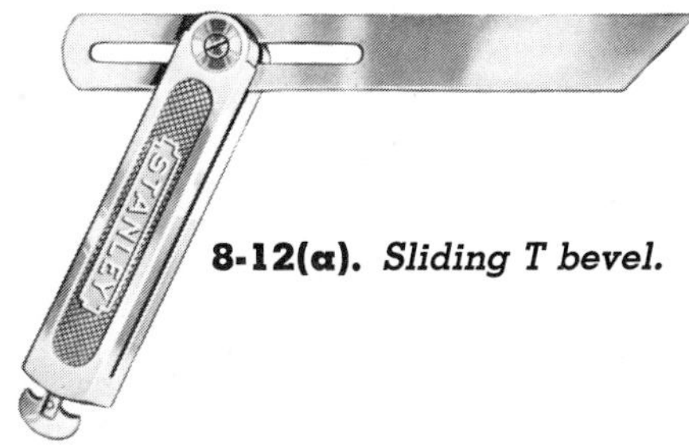
8-12(a). *Sliding T bevel.*

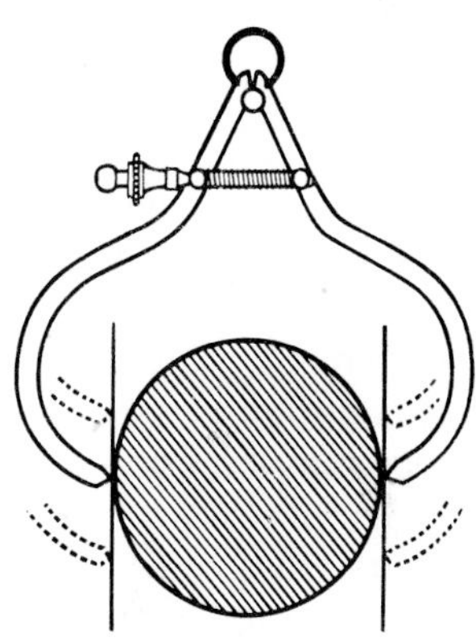
8-13. *Using calipers to measure the outside diameter of a cylinder.*

and a tongue (the shorter part). The steel square is used for measuring and checking. Fig. 8-10.

The *carpenter's square* (also called a *framing square)* is a large steel square used for measuring and laying out. The body is 2 × 24 inches and the tongue is 1½ × 16 inches. There are tables of figures on this square to help the carpenter while working on a house. Fig. 8-11.

Other Common Measuring Tools

The *T bevel (sliding T bevel)* consists of a handle and an adjustable blade. It is used to lay out and check all angles other than 45 and 90 degrees. Fig. 8-12.

Outside calipers have two curved legs hinged at the end so that the distance between them is adjustable. Outside calipers are used to measure the outside diameter of round pieces. Fig. 8-13.

The *all-purpose measuring tool* has many uses. It can function as a square, marking gauge, protractor, depth gauge, dowel gauge, nail gauge, and other types of measuring tools. Fig. 8-14.

TOOLS FOR MARKING

An ordinary *lead pencil* is the most common marking tool. A pencil mark is easy to see and can be quickly removed. Use a hard lead (such as No. 2) and mark lightly. When working with dark woods like walnut, a white or yellow artist's

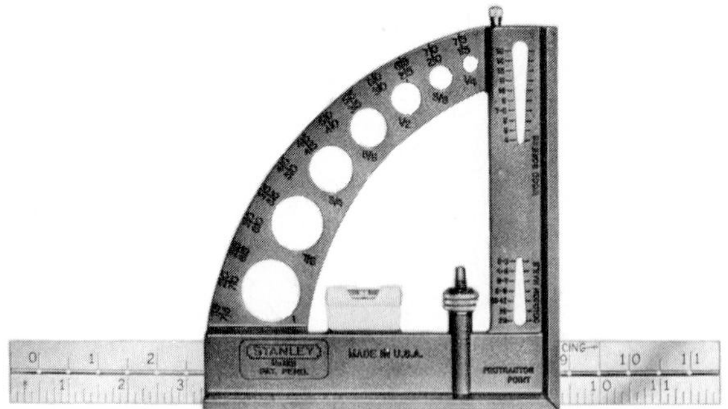

8-14. *This all-purpose measuring tool can be used in many ways.*

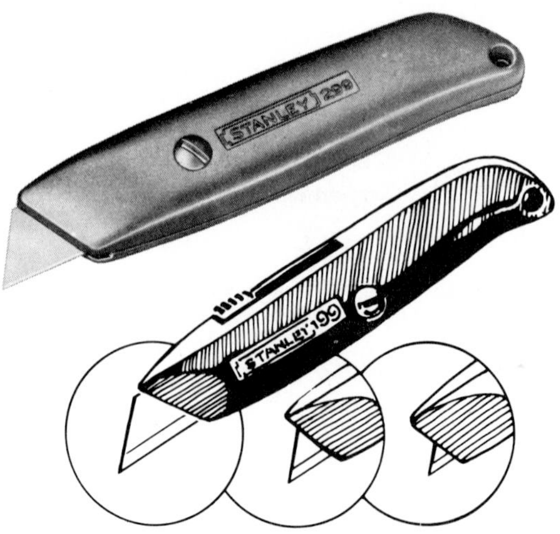

8-16. *Utility knife.*

pencil will show up better. *Never sand off pencil lines.* Doing so forces the lead (actually graphite) into the wood grain. The marks will show after the finish has been applied. Either plane or scrape off the lines.

A short-bladed *knife* (like the sloyd knife) is used for very accurate marking and for cutting and whittling. It should be used only when sawing to (on) the line. Then the saw will remove the mark. Fig. 8-15.

The *utility knife* has a sharp blade that extends from a handle. Use it only when you know the mark will disappear as the wood is cut, formed, or shaped. Fig. 8-16.

The *marking gauge* is used for marking a line parallel with the edge or face, especially when the distance is 6 inches or less. Fig. 8-17.

The *combination square* is used often for marking as well as for measuring. Fig. 8-9.

A *scratch awl* is used for marking the center of holes to be drilled or bored. It can also serve as a punch to make a small dent for starting nails, screws, brads, and cup hooks. It is handy for scribing (drawing) lines on wood to show where it will be cut. Fig. 8-18.

MEASURING STOCK

Length

To check length, place the left end of the rule directly over one end of the stock, with the rule on edge. At the other end of the stock, read the measurement on the rule. (Chapter 3 tells how to read both inch and millimetre rules.) For longer

8-15. *Sloyd knife.*

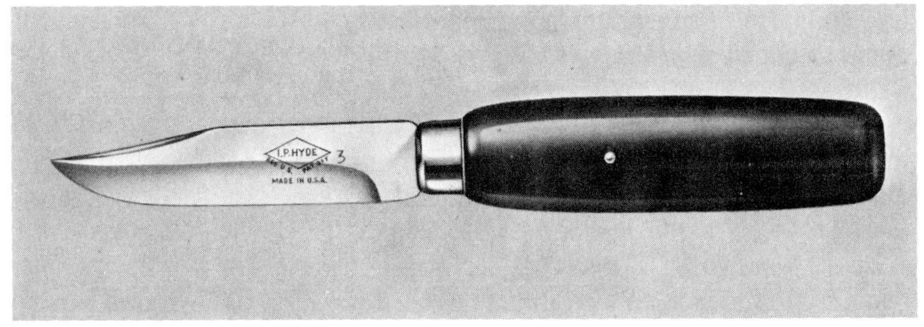

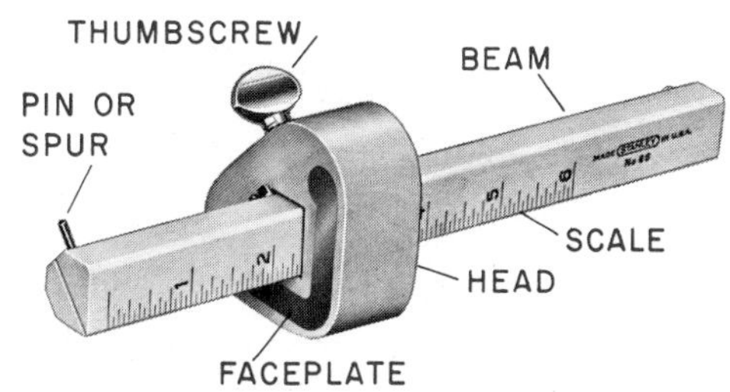

8-17. *Parts of a marking gauge.*

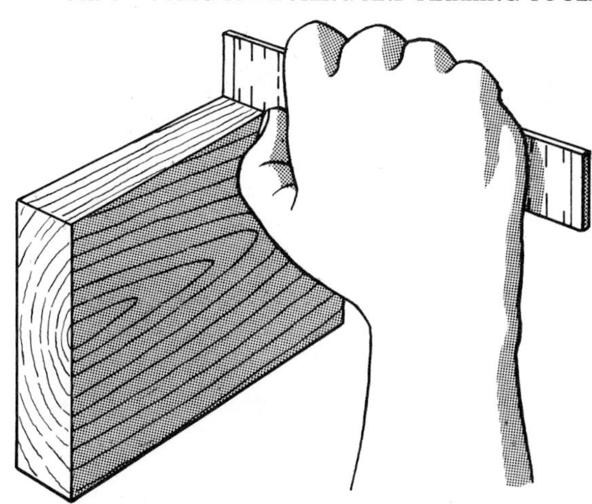

8-20. *Checking the thickness of stock. Notice that one end of the rule is held over one edge of the board. The thumb slides along until you can read the thickness.*

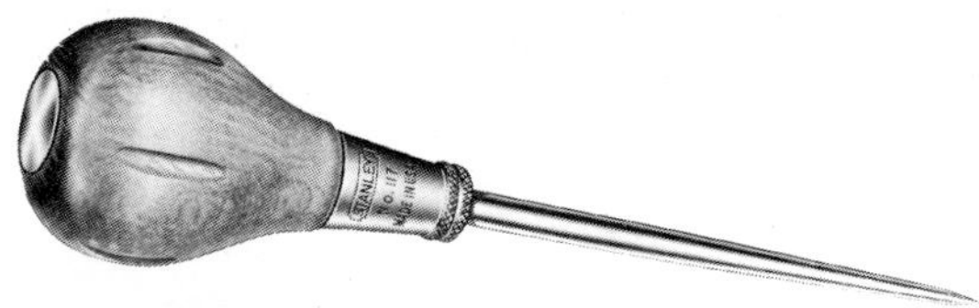

8-18. *Scratch awl. (Stanley Tools)*

lengths, use a zigzag rule or a steel tape. This will avoid measuring errors that come from moving a short rule several times.

Width

Measure the width by holding the left end of the rule on one edge of the stock. Slide your right thumb along the rule until you can read the correct width. Fig. 8-19.

Thickness

To check thickness, hold the rule as shown in Fig. 8-20. You can read the thickness by looking at the graduation mark directly over the corner.

MARKING STOCK

Length

1. Look at the end of the board. Make sure it is square and doesn't have a split, check (slight separation) or other flaw. If it is not square, trim the end. (Find out from the drawing how long the board must be and then add about ½ inch for trimming and squaring up. Use the try square to test for squareness.)

2. Hold the rule on edge and parallel with the edge of the board. Place the end of the rule exactly even with the end of the board. The rule must not be at an angle. It is held on edge so that the graduation marks are right next to the surface of the wood. Fig. 8-21.

8-19. *Checking the width of stock. One finger acts as a guide to hold the end of the rule even with the edge of stock. Slide the other finger along until you can read the correct width.*

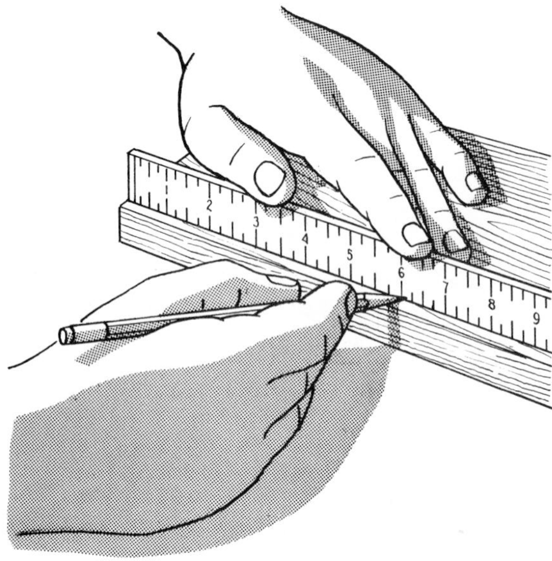

***8-21.** Marking to length. Note that the rule is held on edge for more accurate measurement.*

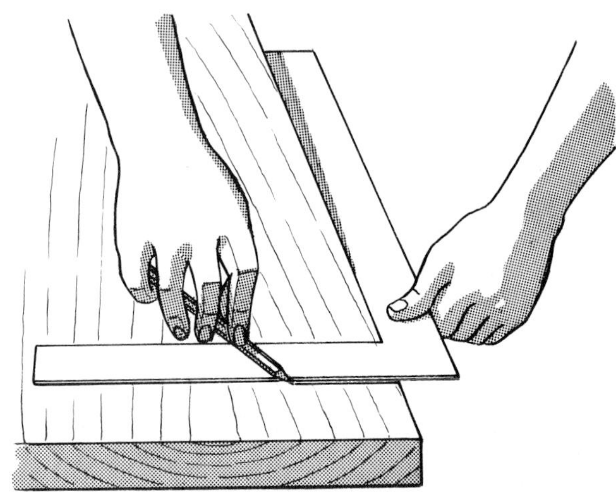

***8-22.** Drawing a line across the board using a steel, or carpenter's, square.*

3. Mark the wood at the correct length with a sharp pencil or knife. Make a small point right at the mark on the rule.
4. Place a try square so that the handle is against the edge of the board. Slide the blade along until the pencil mark just barely shows.
5. Rule a line along the board.

If it is a wide board, use a steel or carpenter's square instead. Fig. 8-22. Tilt the blade slightly and then hold it firmly against the edge. For long boards, use a zigzag rule or a tape rule.

Width

1. Find out from the drawing how wide the board must be. Allow about ¼ to ⅜ inch extra for squaring up.
2. Hold a rule at right angles to the edge and mark this width at several points. Fig. 8-23.

***8-23.** Marking for width. Several marks should be made at various points along the board.*

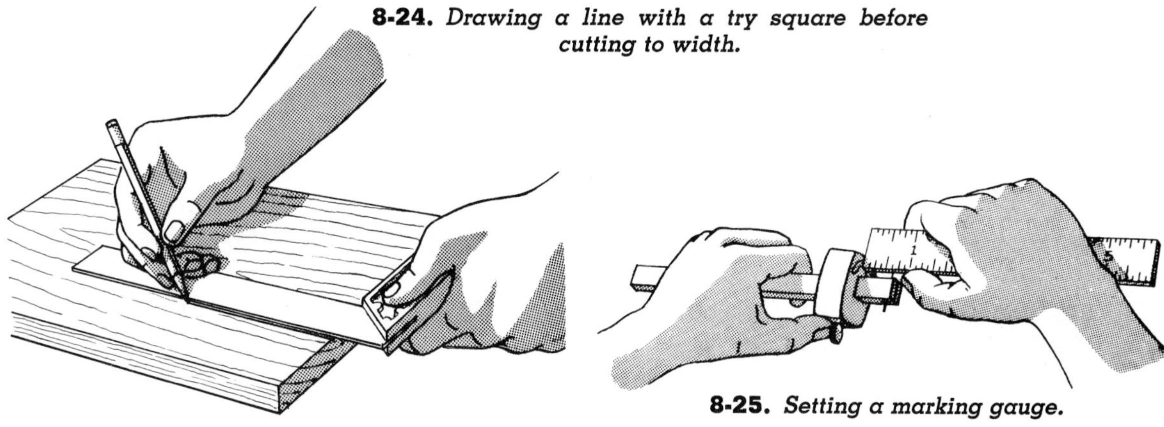

8-24. *Drawing a line with a try square before cutting to width.*

8-25. *Setting a marking gauge.*

3. Hold a try square or carpenter's square along these points and draw the line. Fig. 8-24.

Using a Marking Gauge

1. Check the marking gauge to make sure the spur, or pin, is a sharp wedge shape. If dull, this must be sharpened.

Some types have a wheel at the end of the beam.

2. Adjust to the correct length. Notice the rule on the side of the beam. This can be used to set the distance. It will not be accurate, however, after you have sharpened the pin, or spur. To adjust again:

- Adjust to the distance as shown on the beam and tighten the thumbscrew lightly.
- Hold the gauge in your left hand with the spur up.
- Hold a rule on edge in your right hand. Place the end of the rule against the head of the gauge. Fig. 8-25.
- Check the distance. A slight movement of the head in either direction will adjust it to the correct amount. Tighten the thumbscrew.

3. Try the gauge on a piece of scrap stock. Get the "feel" of the tool. It is better to push the tool than to pull it.

4. Tilt the gauge at a slight angle. Hold the head gently, but firmly, against the surface or edge. Fig. 8-26. Push the tool away from you. Make a shallow groove. If you push too hard, the point may jump out of place and scratch the surface.

5. Never mark across the grain. Do not use the gauge to mark for a bevel or chamfer (slanted cut).

Marking with a Combination Square

1. Adjust the blade to the correct length measured from the right-angle side of the head.

2. Hold the head against the work and a pencil against the end of the blade. Fig. 8-27.

3. Slide both along the board to mark the line.

You can also use a rule and pencil for gauge-marking. This is a little more difficult because you must keep the rule square with the edge as you slide it along.

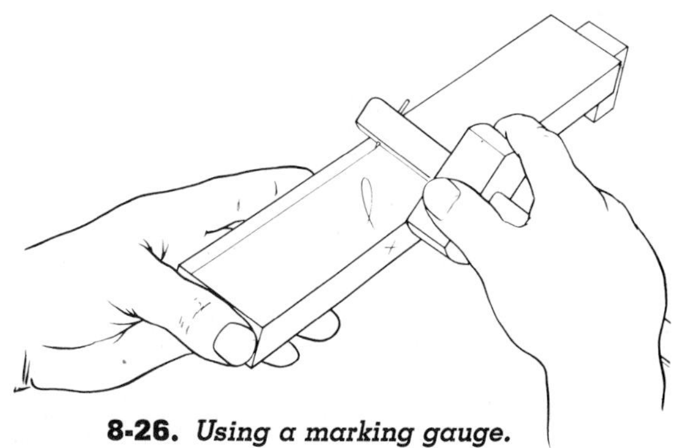

8-26. *Using a marking gauge.*

8-27. *Using a combination square and pencil for marking. This is one of the simplest ways for marking to width.*

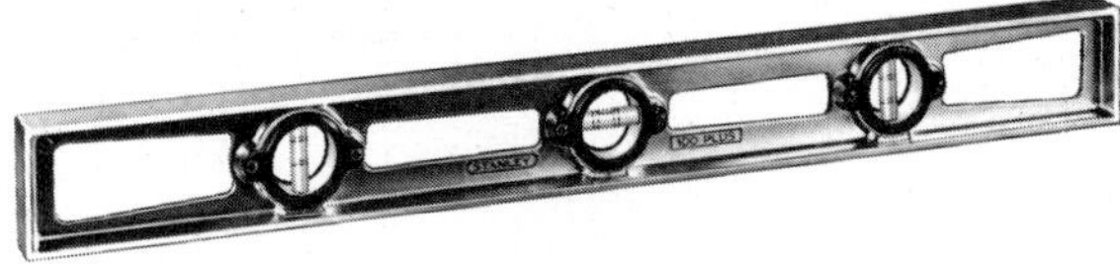

8-28. *A level is used to make sure the work is level or plumb (straight up and down).*

Using a Carpenter's Level

A carpenter's level is a wood, metal or plastic frame. It has several small liquid-filled tubes set into it. It is used to check the true horizontal or vertical surfaces of stock.

1. Place the level on the stock you want to check.
2. Look at the small liquid-filled tubes to see if the bubble is between the lines.
3. If the bubble is not between the lines, make the necessary adjustments to the stock.

QUESTIONS

1. Name three common kinds of rules.
2. What kind of rule is good for measuring curved surfaces?
3. Name four kinds of squares found in the wood shop.
4. Name three things that can be done with a try square.
5. Which kind of square has a blade that can be removed from the handle or head?
6. What is the purpose of outside calipers?
7. Why must the end of a board be square before you can mark to length?
8. What would happen if the rule were not parallel to the edge of the board when you measured for length?
9. When marking a wide board for length, what kind of square should be used to mark a line across it?
10. About how much material must be allowed for squaring up stock?

ACTIVITIES

1. Select a measuring or marking tool. Demonstrate to the class how to use it. Be sure to observe all safety precautions.
2. Here's an experiment to try. Hold this book about 12 inches in front of you. Hold your left thumb about 6 inches above the book. Now close your left eye and move your left thumb until it blocks your view of the page number (82). Don't move the book or your thumb, but open your left eye and close your right eye. Does the page number appear to have moved? This effect is called parallax. It is caused by the fact that one eye sees things from a slightly different angle than the other eye. When making measurements, try to position yourself directly above the endpoint of the line. If you move to the right or left, you may not measure accurately.

Making a Layout

A *layout* is a guide, or pattern, that can be drawn or traced directly on the wood for each part. The layout shows shape and size, location of holes and other openings, and all the things to be worked. For irregular shapes and designs, a *template* is often used.

On some parts, the layout may be made one step at a time as you work the wood.

POINTS TO CONSIDER IN MAKING A LAYOUT

Lumber Defects

Most lumber has some defects. Bad defects such as a crack or hole must be avoided. Get the most out of the lumber by first checking the sizes of each part of the project. Then lay out the pieces around these defects. Sometimes defects such as knots are left in the pieces to add interest. For example, most knotty pine furniture has some exposed but tight knots.

Allowance for Cutting, Planing, and Shaping

Make sure you allow some extra material for working the wood to size. However, keep this waste to a minimum. If rough lumber is used, usually ⅛″ in thickness, ¼″ in width, and ½″ in length are allowed for cutting, planing and shaping to size.

Grain

Grain direction is the way in which the pores of the wood are arranged. Wood is stronger when pressure is applied "with the grain"; that is, in the same direction as the grain. Wood is weaker when the force is across the grain. Therefore, make the layout for legs and other support parts so that the length is *with* the grain.

Using Sheet Stock

Sheet materials such as plywood, particle board, and hardboard are accurately cut to a rectangular shape during manufacturing. Always start a layout at the corners since these first two edges will not have to be reworked.

LAYOUT TOOLS

All the tools used for measuring and marking are used in making a layout: rules, marking gauge, squares, pencil, knife. In addition, you will need dividers or a pencil compass.

A *dividers* is a tool with two pointed metal legs. Fig. 9-1. It is used to lay out circles and arcs and for stepping off equal distances. To set a dividers, place one leg over an inch mark of the rule and open the other leg to the measurement you want. To use a dividers, place one leg over the starting point, tilt the dividers slightly, and turn it clockwise (the direction clock hands move). Be careful not to change the setting of the dividers.

A *pencil compass* can be used in place of a dividers in the wood shop. Fig. 9-2. It has one metal leg and one pencil leg.

DRAWING A CIRCLE

1. Locate the center of the circle.
2. Adjust the dividers or compass to equal the radius of the circle. The *radius* is half the diameter. The *diameter* is the distance across the middle of the circle. The *circumference* of a circle is the distance completely around it. It is equal to the diameter times 3.1416.
3. Place one leg at the center mark. Tilt the

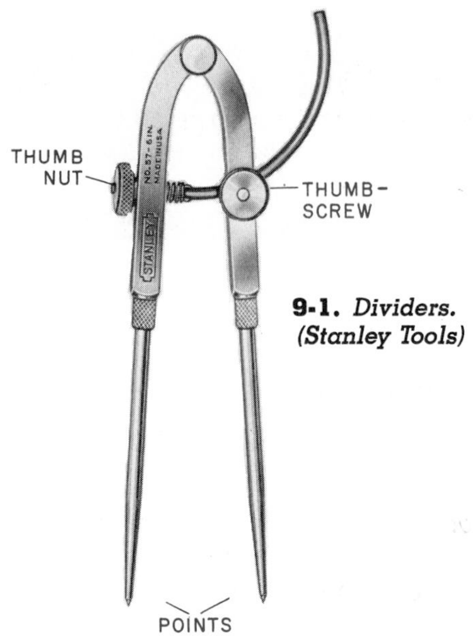

9-1. *Dividers. (Stanley Tools)*

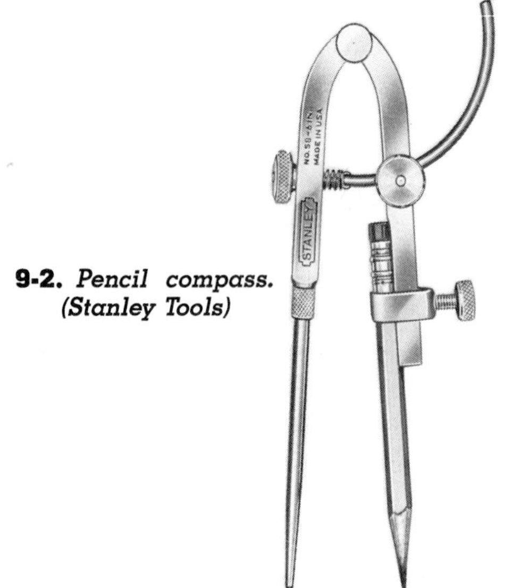

9-2. *Pencil compass. (Stanley Tools)*

compass or dividers slightly and swing it clockwise to draw the line or sharp groove. An *arc* (a part of a circle) is drawn the same way. Fig. 9-3.

4. To keep from scratching the wood surface at the center, place a small rubber eraser over the sharp point of the dividers or compass. A piece of masking tape can also be placed at the center to protect the wood.

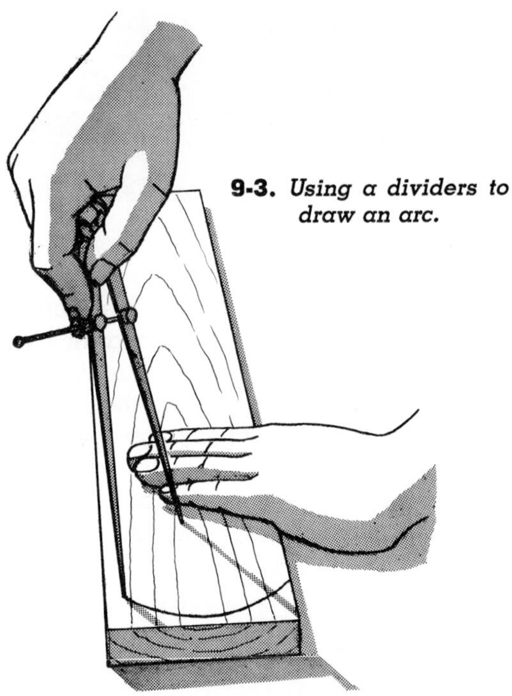

9-3. *Using a dividers to draw an arc.*

DRAWING A ROUNDED CORNER

Many things are made with rounded corners to improve their appearance.

1. Find the radius of the corner.
2. Mark this distance from the corner on one side and end.
3. Hold a try square against the side and end and draw two lines to mark the center. Fig. 9-4.
4. Set the dividers to the correct radius.
5. Swing the dividers from the left to the right, clockwise, to mark the rounded corner.

LAYOUT OF DUPLICATE PARTS

Many articles have two or more parts that are exactly alike. Lay out these duplicate parts together to save time.

1. Place the pieces on edge and side by side on a bench top.

2. Make sure the working ends are even by holding a try square over them. Hold the pieces together firmly in a vise or with a clamp.

3. Measure the correct length along one edge.

4. Mark a line across all the pieces at the same time. Fig. 9-5.

DIVIDING A BOARD INTO EQUAL PARTS

If a board is an odd width and you want to divide it into any number of equal parts, follow this simple procedure:

1. Hold a rule at an angle across the face of the board until the inch marks divide the space evenly. For example, if the board you need to divide is 5 inches wide and you want to divide it into three equal parts, hold the rule at an angle with the 6-inch mark on one edge. Then make a mark at the 2-, 4-, and 6-inch marks. Fig. 9-6.

2. Draw lines through these marks. The lines should be parallel with the edge of the board.

DRAWING A HEXAGON

A *hexagon* is a six-sided figure with equal sides and angles. This figure might be used for the bottom of a wastepaper basket, a hot dish holder, or similar article.

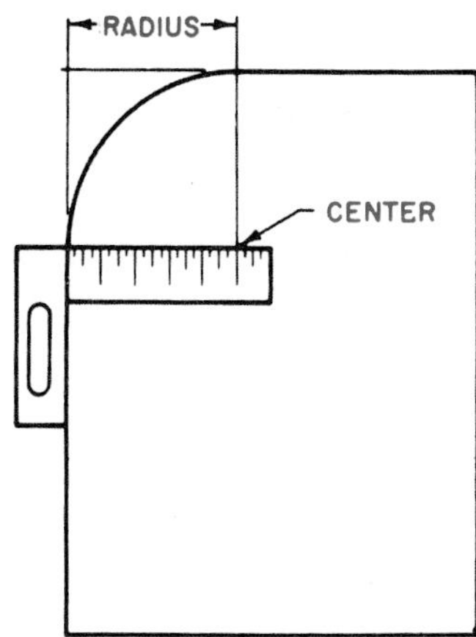

9-4. *Finding the center for drawing a rounded corner.*

1. Determine the maximum (greatest) distance across the corners. Then use half this distance as the radius, or use a radius equal to one side of the hexagon.

2. Draw a circle with this radius.

3. Start at any spot on the circle and draw an arc that crosses the circle.

4. Move the point of the dividers or compass to this point and draw another arc.

5. Continue to draw arcs, dividing the circle into six equal parts.

6. Connect these points. Fig. 9-7.

DRAWING AN OCTAGON

An *octagon* has eight equal sides and angles. It might be used as the shape of a wall decoration, a stool, or a tabletop.

9-5. *Laying out duplicate parts. Mark all pieces at the same time.*

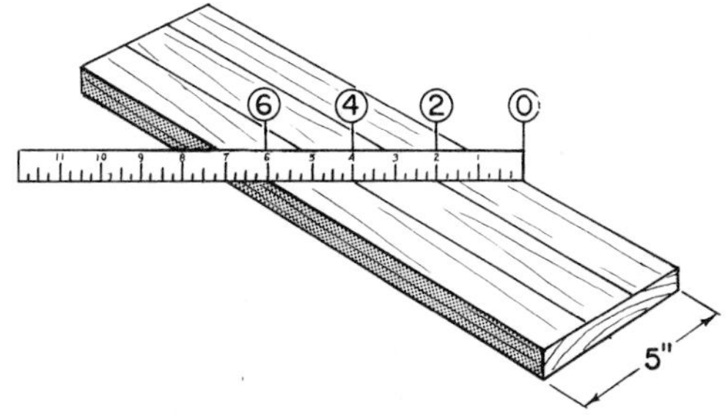

9-6. *Dividing a board into three equal parts.*

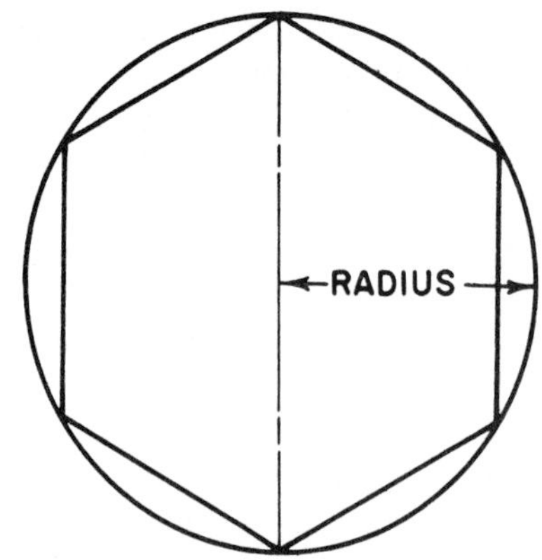

9-7. *Laying out a hexagon. This shape might be used for the base of a wastepaper basket.*

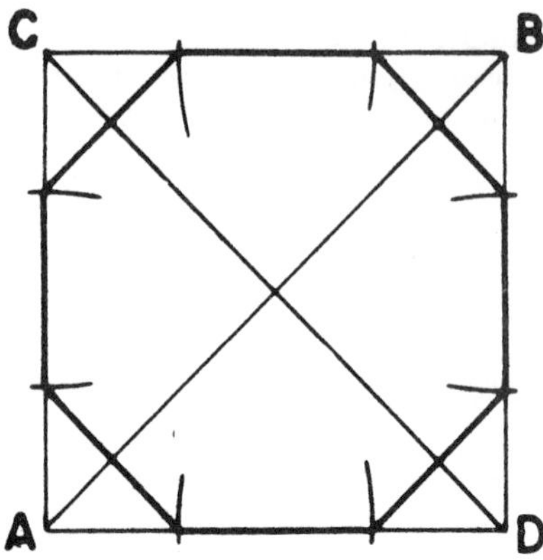

9-8. *Laying out an octagon.*

1. Draw a square equal to the width of the octagon.
2. Draw diagonal lines (lines across the corners). These are lines AB and CD in Fig. 9-8.
3. Adjust the dividers or compass to half the length of one of the diagonal lines.
4. Using points A, B, C, and D as centers, strike arcs intersecting (cutting across) the sides.
5. Connect the points where the arcs intersect (cross) the sides of the square.

DRAWING AN ELLIPSE BY THE SHOP METHOD

An *ellipse* is an oval having both halves alike. It might be used as the shape of a tabletop, a plaque (wall decoration), or the back of a wall lamp.

1. An ellipse has a long and a short diameter. Lay out the two diameters at right angles to each other. Fig. 9-9.
2. Set the dividers equal to half the longest diameter.
3. Using D as center, strike arcs intersecting AB at X and Y.
4. Place brads (small nails) at X, Y, and D. Tie a string around these three brads.
5. Take the brad at D away, and put a pencil in its place.
6. Hold the pencil tight against the string and carefully draw the ellipse.

STEPPING OFF EQUAL DISTANCES

To step off equal distances or to divide a space into equal parts, the dividers or compass can be used. This is especially good for dividing a curved line.

1. Adjust the dividers to the correct amount (usually a small, even part of the total distance).
2. Place one leg on the starting point and then turn the dividers from side to side as shown in Fig. 9-10.

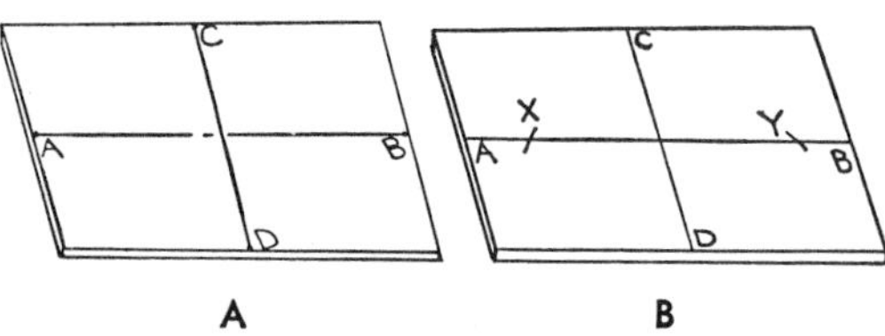

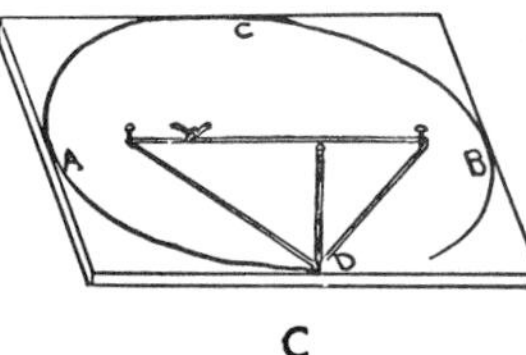

9-9. *Drawing an ellipse (oval) using the shop method.*

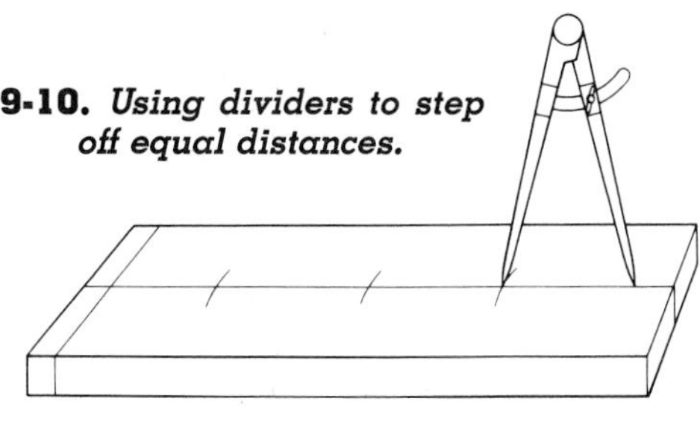

9-10. *Using dividers to step off equal distances.*

ENLARGING A DESIGN AND USING A TEMPLATE

Often you will find the plan for a project you like in a book or magazine. The only problem is that it's less than full size. Your first job is to enlarge this pattern so that you can transfer it to the wood. This is something you'll be doing often in woodworking. The steps are simple, but you need to follow them carefully to make the full-size pattern exactly like the small one.

Suppose you saw the design in Fig. 9-11 in a book. In most books and magazines the drawing is laid out in squares. A note tells you what size the full-size squares must be. Sometimes, however, you find a drawing or photograph that has no squares. If the design is about ¼ the size you would like to have it, first cover it with ¼-inch squares. If the design is in a book, draw the squares on transparent paper (you can see through it) and clip the paper over the page. Now proceed as follows:

1. On a large piece of paper, draw squares the full size. (You can also use cross-sectioned paper.) For example, if the drawing says, "one-inch squares," make your squares this size. Start in the lower left-hand corner of both the original drawing and the full-size sheet. Letter up the left side A, B, C, etc. Number across the bottom, 1, 2, 3, etc. Fig. 9-12.

2. Locate points on the drawing. Transfer them to the full-size pattern. Continue to locate enough points to make the outline take shape.

3. After enough points are located, use a French curve (also called an irregular curve) to trace the outline. You can also bend a piece of

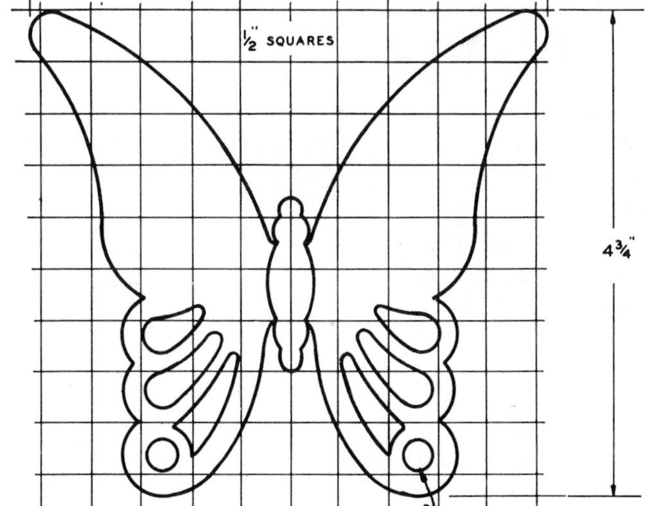

9-11. *A pattern for a napkin holder. The pattern must be enlarged before it can be used. Make two and assemble with dowels.*

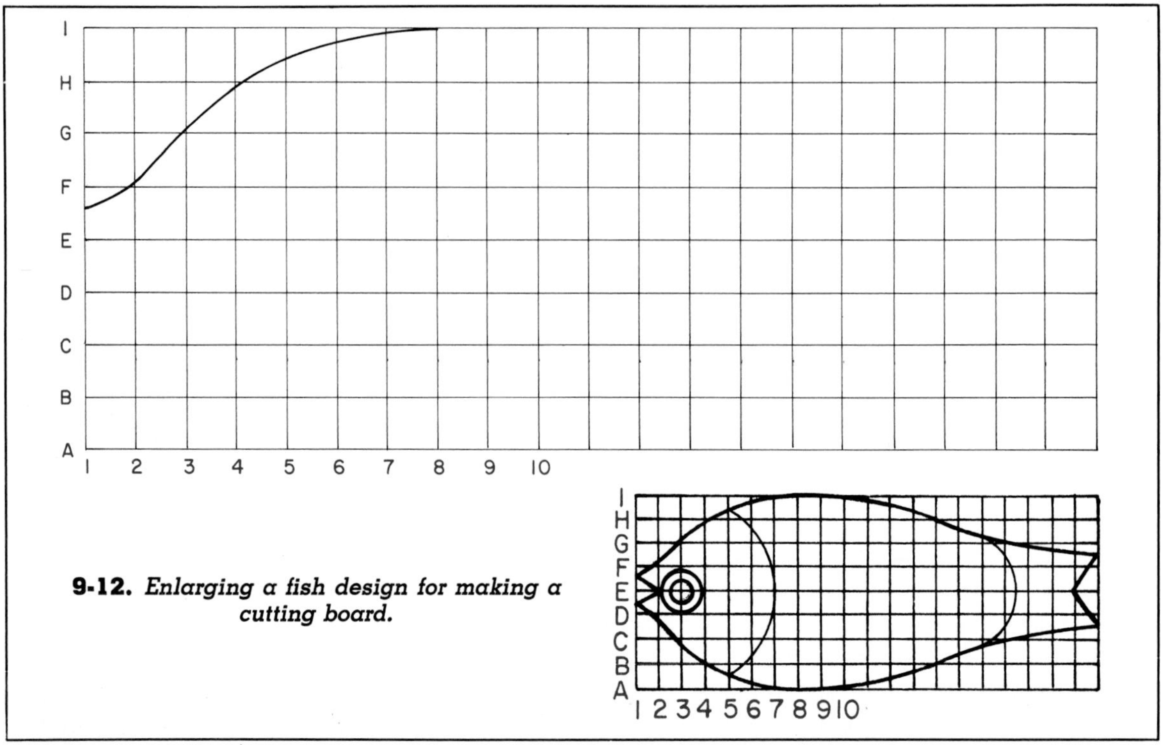

9-12. *Enlarging a fish design for making a cutting board.*

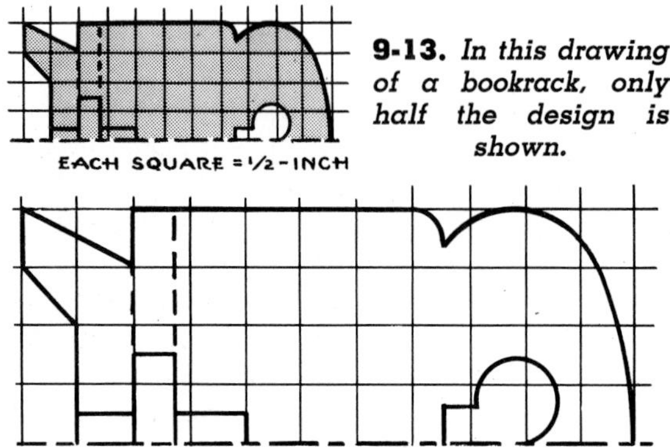

9-13. *In this drawing of a bookrack, only half the design is shown.*

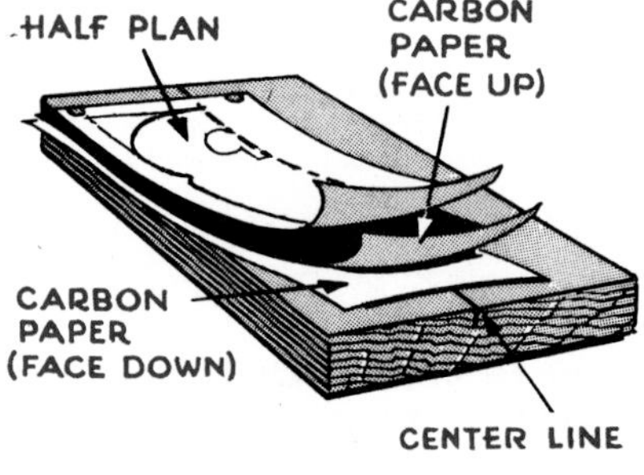

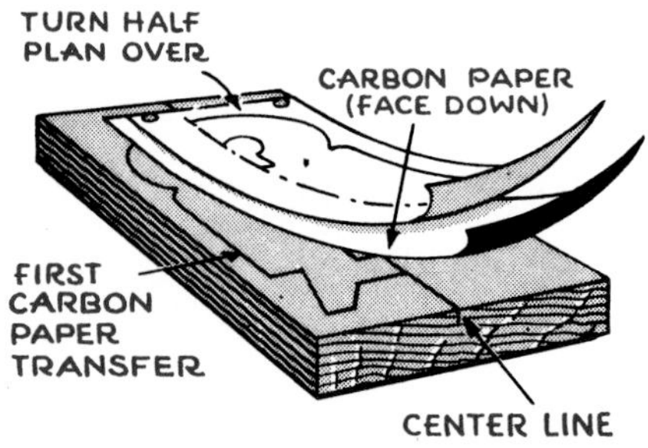

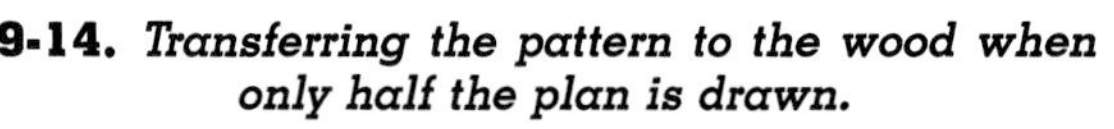

9-14. *Transferring the pattern to the wood when only half the plan is drawn.*

soft wire (such as solder) to follow the various points. Trace the line.

4. If the design is the same on both sides (a symmetrical plan), you need to trace only half the pattern. Fig. 9-13. Then fold the paper down the center. Cut out the full pattern or trace the full pattern by placing carbon paper between the folds, carbon side facing toward the blank half.

5. A design can be made smaller by using smaller squares. For example, if the original is on ¼-inch squares, you can make the design half-size by drawing it on ⅛-inch squares.

6. You can use the full-size plan in one of several ways:

- Cut out the plan with scissors, fasten corners with transparent tape, and trace around it on the wood. Then remove.
- Cut out the pattern with scissors and paste or glue it on the wood. It stays on while the wood is trimmed to size.
- Place carbon paper between the pattern and the wood and trace the design. Then remove.

7. If the drawing shows only half the plan, you can transfer the pattern to the wood as shown in Fig. 9-14.

8. When many parts of the same design are to be made, a *template* (a pattern that can be used many times) is made of thin wood or metal. Hold the template firmly on the wood and trace around it.

QUESTIONS

1. What is a layout?
2. What is a divider?
3. Describe the way to adjust dividers to draw a circle that is 3 inches in diameter.
4. How can you divide a 9-inch board into four equal parts?
5. How many sides are there in a hexagon? An octagon?
6. Tell three ways to use a pattern in making a layout on wood.
7. What is a template?
8. When is a template used?

ACTIVITIES

1. Suppose you are writing a training manual. You want to describe how to make the layout for a rounded corner. Review the steps listed on page 84. Then, in your own words, write how to do the procedure.
2. Suppose a product you are building will need four parts that are the same length. Demonstrate to the class how to lay out these duplicate parts.
3. Show your classmates the shop method of drawing an ellipse.
4. Suppose you wanted to enlarge a design to full size. If the plan is ⅓ as large as you want it and it is covered with ¼-inch squares, how large must the full-size squares be?

CHAPTER 10 Machines in Woodworking

You probably know that complicated devices such as the drill press and jigsaw are machines. However, you might be surprised to learn that the hand tools you will use in the shop are also machines. Chisels, hammers—even things like a nail or screw—are machines, operated with hand power. Each of these simple items is just as truly a machine as the more complicated ones. As a matter of fact, machines such as the jigsaw are made up of several very simple machines fitted together in different ways.

WHAT IS A MACHINE?

A *machine* is a device used to make work easier. As you use hand tools, materials, and machines in woodwork you will be doing work. What do we mean by work? *Work* is done when a force moves through a distance to make something move or stop moving. You are "working" when you strike a ball with a bat or when you ride a bicycle. You are also doing work when you pound a nail or saw a board. *Force* is the push or pull that can do work. A machine helps you work by multiplying the force you use. Such a gain of force is obtained by "trading" distance. Work accomplished over a short distance requires more force than the same work done over a long distance. For example, try turning a screw into wood with your fingers. Can you do it? Now use a screwdriver. How can such a simple machine help you do work? Easy. You apply force to the handle. The outside of the handle moves a *greater distance* with less force so that the tip of the blade moves a *shorter distance* with more force.

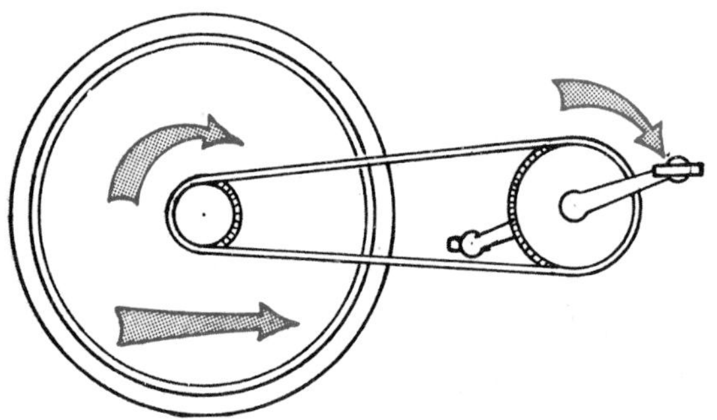

10-1. *Force applied to the pedals of a bicycle is changed from rotary motion to forward motion.*

By exerting a force on a machine in one place, the machine can exert a force at another place and, in some cases, in another direction. Consider the bicycle. You apply an up-and-down force with your thighs while your feet go around in a circle. The force applied to the pedals turns the large gear wheel. The large gear wheel is connected to the small gear wheel with a chain. The small gear wheel turns the rear wheel to move the bicycle forward. The bicycle gears change the direction of the force that you apply with your legs to a forward motion. Fig. 10-1.

You can never get more out of a machine than you put in. In fact, some force is lost through the friction of the machine itself. *Friction* is the resistance caused by the rubbing together of machine parts. No machine can increase both force and distance at the same time. The screwdriver tip has the greater force but moves through less distance than the handle. The rear wheel of the

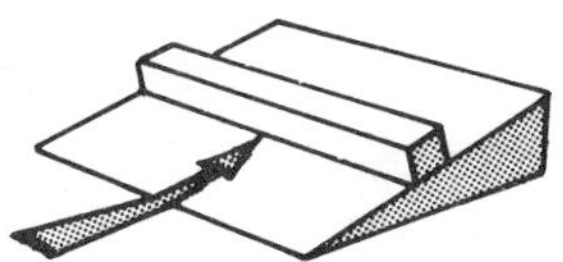

10-2. *Inclined plane.*

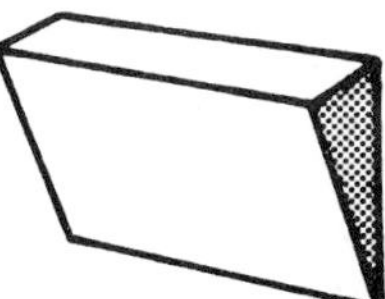

10-3. *Wedge. You will find the wedge shape on the cutting edge of a chisel, knife, or gouge, on the teeth of a saw or file, and on a nail.*

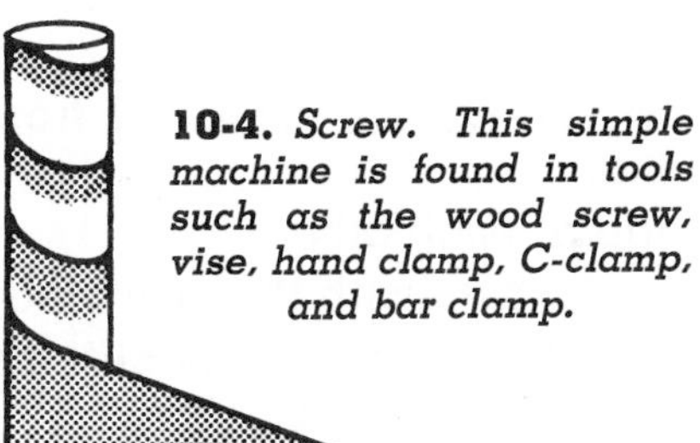

10-4. *Screw. This simple machine is found in tools such as the wood screw, vise, hand clamp, C-clamp, and bar clamp.*

bicycle moves through greater distance but has less force than that applied to the pedals.

THE SIX SIMPLE MACHINES

There are six simple machines. All complicated woodworking machines are made up of a combination of these.

1. The **inclined plane** makes work easier, since a smaller effort (the force exerted) can lift a heavy weight. However, the effort must move farther (along the incline) than when a weight is lifted directly. Inclined planes are found, for example, on a woodworking plane. Fig. 10-2.

2. A **wedge** has one or two sloping sides. All knives, chisels, saws, and axes have wedges. Fig. 10-3.

3. A **screw** is actually a spiral-shaped inclined plane. A wood screw clamp or vise is a good example of the screw. Fig. 10-4.

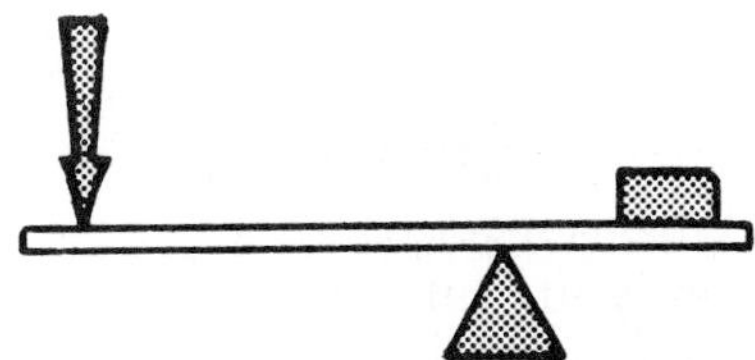

10-5. *Lever. Hammers, pliers, hinges, and paintbrushes make use of the lever.*

4. A **lever** is a long, rigid bar supported at one point. The support point is called the fulcrum. The hammer and axe are levers. Fig. 10-5.

5. The **wheel and axle** has a wheel connected firmly to an axle. When one turns, the other turns too. A screwdriver, a door handle, and a brace are examples of the wheel and axle. Fig. 10-6.

6. A **pulley** is a wheel that turns around an axle. Fig. 10-7.

Remember these six machines. As you look through this book you'll see how woodworking tools are based on them.

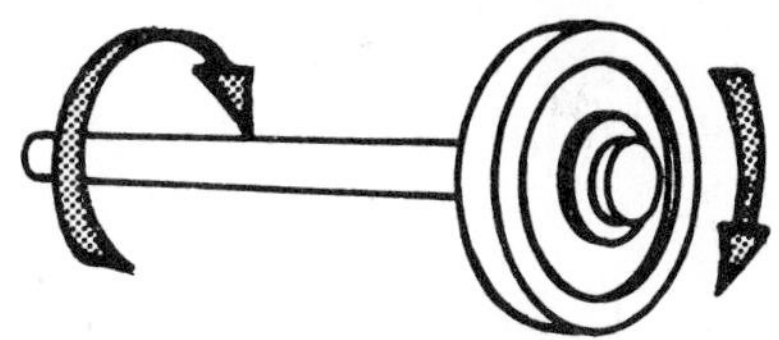

10-6. *Wheel and axle. This is found in braces, screwdrivers, and hand drills.*

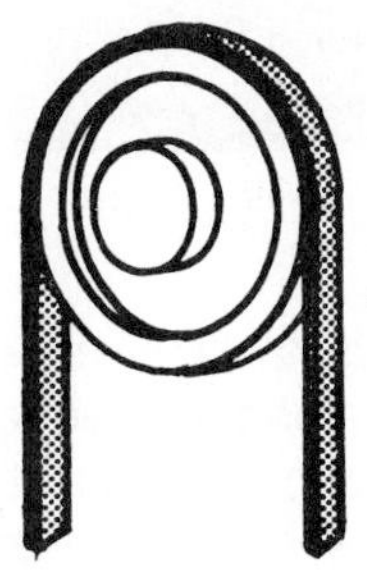

10-7. *Pulley. The pulley can be seen on a band saw, belt sander, or jigsaw.*

QUESTIONS

1. What is a machine?
2. Do you get as much out of a machine as you put in? Why or why not?
3. A machine gains force by "trading" distance. Explain.
4. Name the six simple machines.

ACTIVITIES

1. Find examples of the six simple machines in your lab's tools.
2. Use a simple lever to demonstrate that work accomplished over a short distance requires more force than the same work done over a long distance.

LEARN THESE SAFETY RULES BEFORE USING THE HANDSAW

- **Never strike the teeth of the blade on a metal surface, such as the edge of a metal vise.**
- **Make sure nails and screws are removed from old material before sawing.**
- **Never pile tools on top of each other.**
- **Never twist off strips of waste with the saw blade.**
- **When finishing a cut, support the waste side to prevent splitting work on the underside.**
- **Raise the workpiece enough to prevent the saw blade from striking the floor.**
- **Fasten the work securely before cutting.**
- **Carry the saw with the toe towards the floor.**

Sawing to a Line with Handsaws

A *saw* is a woodcutting tool that has a thin steel blade with small sharp teeth along the edge. Handsaws are hand tools used to cut wood to different sizes and shapes. They are also used for making the joints that hold parts together. Your skill in using handsaws is important because it shows in the final appearance of the project. Fig. 11-1.

11-1. *Sawing a board. Remember the six simple machines. The teeth of a handsaw are wedges. The saw itself is a lever in your hand. Notice that the wedges are shaped to cut mostly on the down, or forward, stroke. Here again the force applied to the handle is divided into smaller forces that make each tooth (wedge) do the cutting.*

TOOLS AND EQUIPMENT FOR SAWING

The **crosscut saw** is used to saw across grain. The parts are shown in Fig. 11-2. The teeth of the crosscut saw are knife-shaped and bent alternately to the right and left. This is called *set.* It makes the saw cut wider than the blade. The saw cut is called the *kerf.* Since the kerf is wider than the blade, the blade will not bind (stick) as the sawing is done. Fig. 11-3. The saw teeth may be coarse (with only six or eight teeth per inch) or fine (with as many as ten or twelve per inch). A saw for general-purpose cutting should have about eight or nine *points* per inch. There is always one more point than teeth per inch. The length of the saw should be about 20 to 26 inches.

The **ripsaw** is used for sawing with the grain. The teeth are chisel-shaped and are set alternately to the right and left. Fig. 11-4. A 26-inch, 5½-point saw is a good one for most work.

A **workbench** is needed to do all kinds of operations. Some benches are designed to be used by one or two people, while others have room for four workers. Fig. 11-5.

A **wood vise** is a clamping device for holding wood to the workbench for sawing and other work. The metal vise is lined with wood to protect the work. Fig. 11-6 (page 96). One type of vise has movable jaws on a continuous thread so that the jaws can be opened or closed by turning the

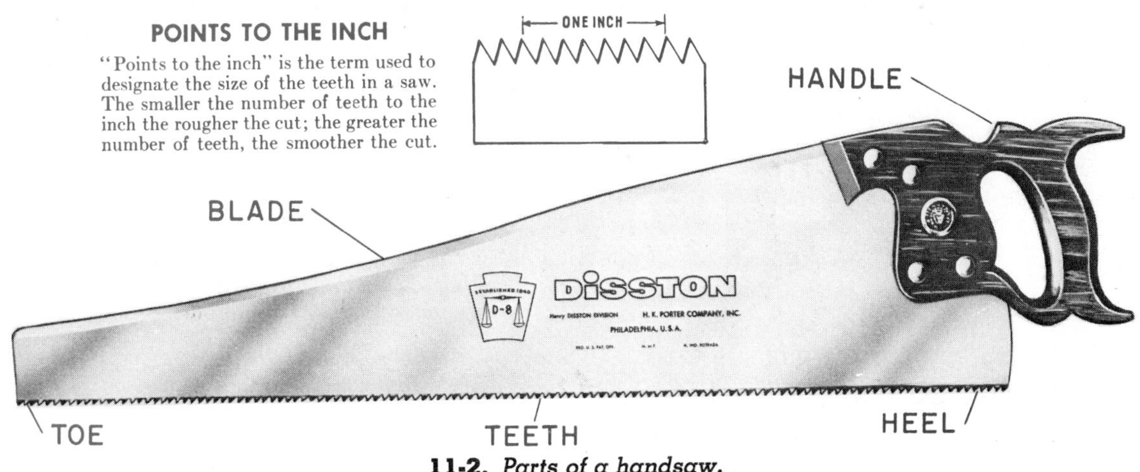

11-2. *Parts of a handsaw.*

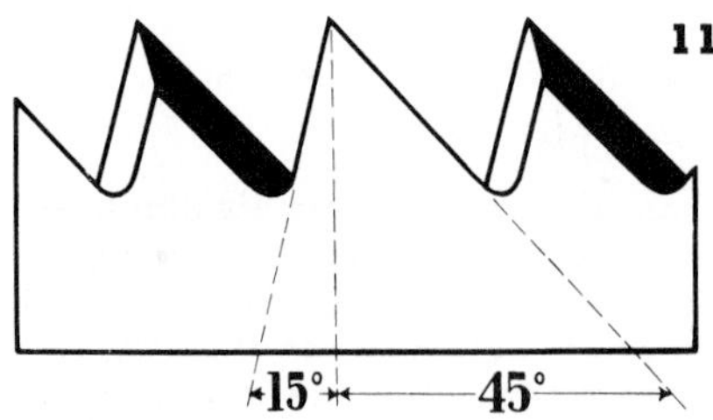

11-3(a). *This enlarged view of a crosscut saw blade section shows the knifelike teeth.*

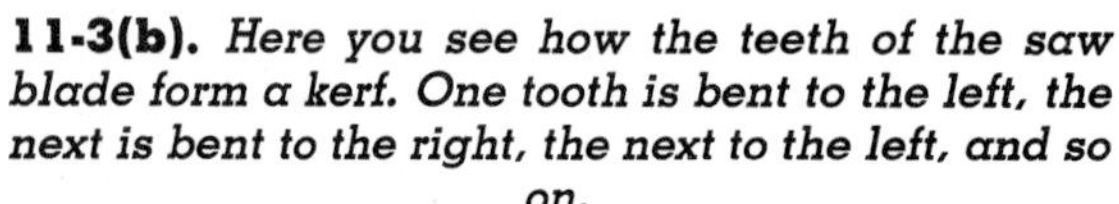

11-3(b). *Here you see how the teeth of the saw blade form a kerf. One tooth is bent to the left, the next is bent to the right, the next to the left, and so on.*

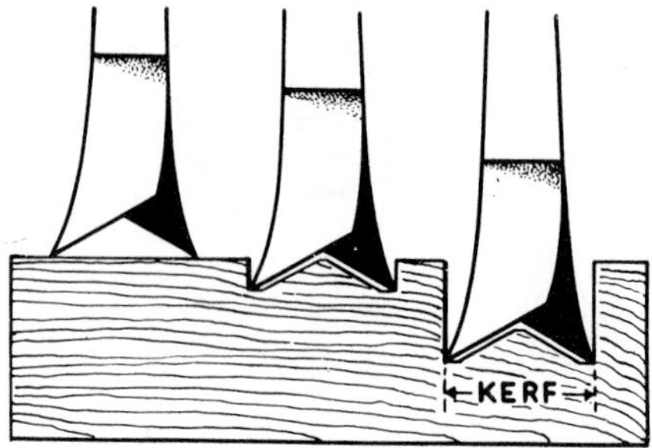

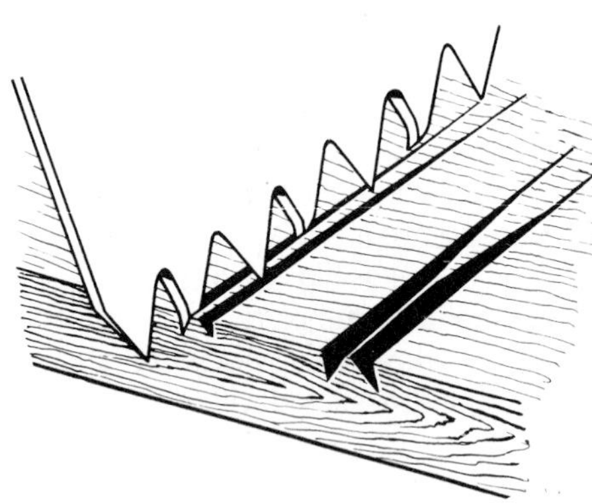

11-3(c). *An example of how a crosscut saw does its cutting. The beginning cut makes two grooves if drawn lightly over the surface.*

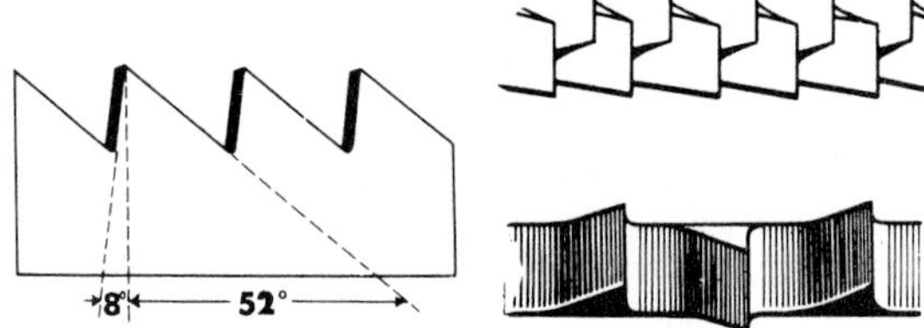

11-4(a). *The teeth of the ripsaw are shaped like small chisels. They are designed to cut with the grain.*

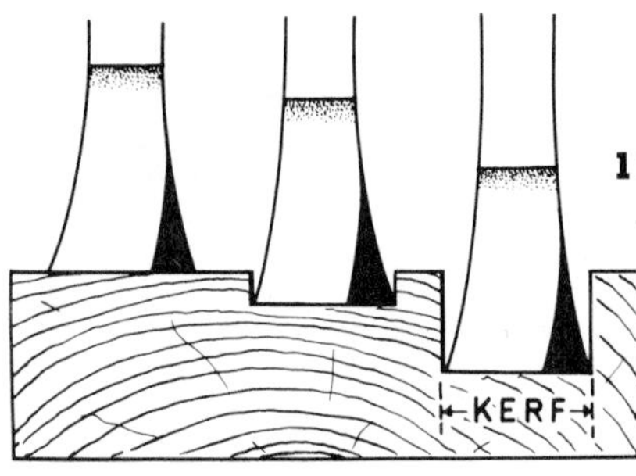

11-4(b). *This drawing shows the cutting action of the ripsaw teeth.*

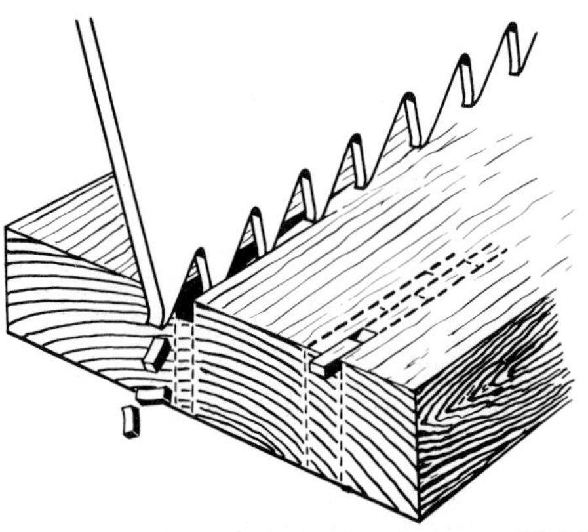

11-4(c). *The ripsaw cuts with many small chisels. First a tooth on one side cuts a small piece free and then the tooth on the other side cuts a similar piece.*

11-5(a). *A workbench designed to be used by one person.*

handle. A quick-action vise has movable jaws that can be pushed closed on the work. A short turn of the handle tightens the jaws. There is a dog (section) in the movable jaw that can be raised. A bench stop can be inserted in holes along the top of the bench. The work is held between the dog and the bench stop when cutting or planing.

A **sawhorse** supports the lumber for cutting. One or two are needed. Fig. 11-7.

CUTTING STOCK TO LENGTH WITH A CROSSCUT SAW

1. Lay out the cutoff line across the board with a pencil. Chapter 8 explains how to do this.
2. Place the board in a vise or over sawhorses. The cutoff line must be outside the supports, never between them.
3. Hold the saw handle in your right hand with your index finger extended to support it. If left-handed, reverse.

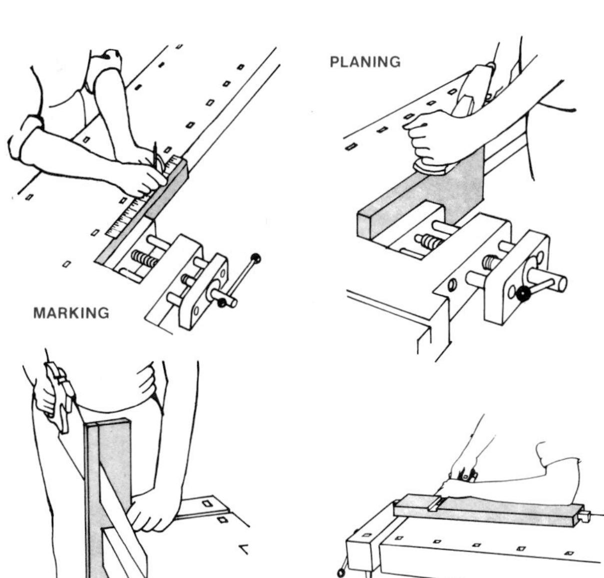

11-5(b). *Some uses of the workbench.*

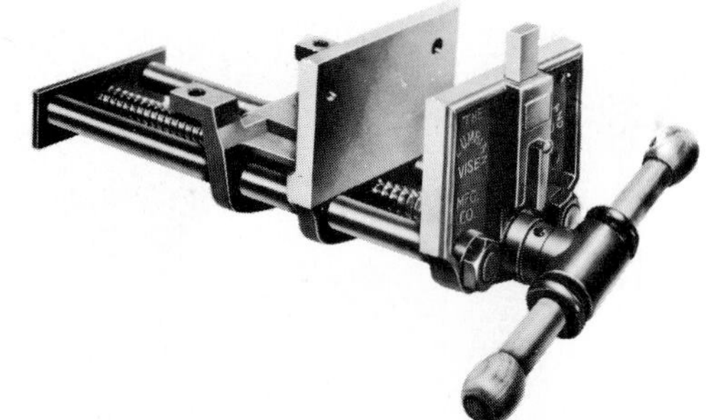

11-6. ***A wood vise made of metal is used to hold the stock when cutting short pieces. The vise is mounted on a sturdy bench.***

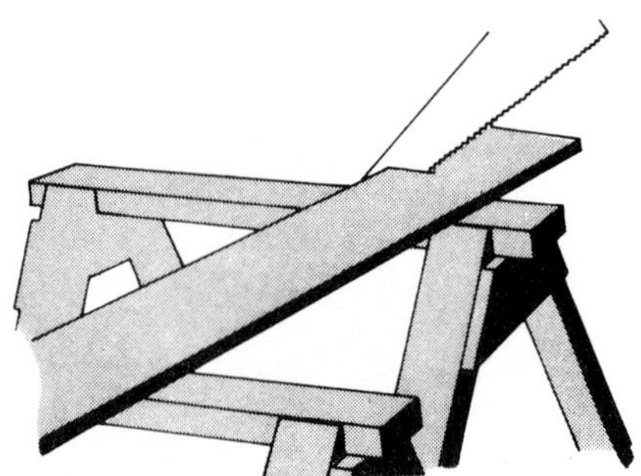

11-7. ***When cutting large pieces, place the lumber over one or two sawhorses.***

4. Place your free hand on the board using your thumb as a guide to start the cut. Fig. 11-8. Remember: The kerf must be in the waste stock. Don't try to saw on the line or "saw out" the line. If you do, the piece may be too short. Fig. 11-9.

5. Start the cut by pulling back on the saw once or twice. Be careful that the saw doesn't jump and cut your thumb.

6. After the kerf is started, hold the saw at an angle of 45 degrees to the surface. Fig. 11-10. Move your hand away from the blade. Take long, even strokes. The correct position for cutting is shown in Fig. 11-11. Sawing goes easier, truer, and faster when full-length strokes are made. Unlike the ripsaw, the crosscut saw cuts both on the forward and back strokes.

7. Sight along the saw or check with the try square to make sure you are making a square cut. Fig. 11-12.

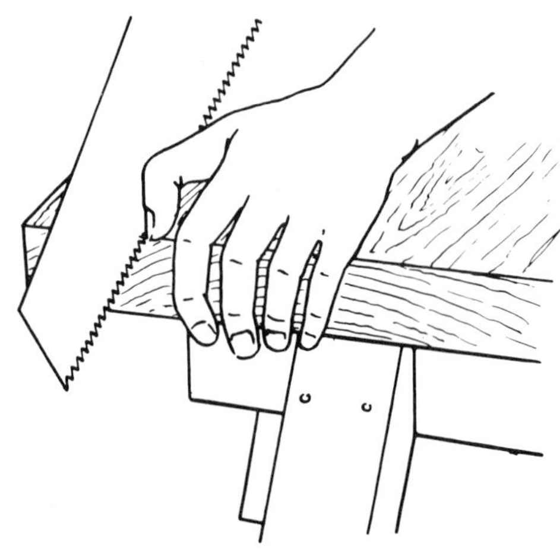

11-8. ***Use your thumb as a guide to get the saw started.***

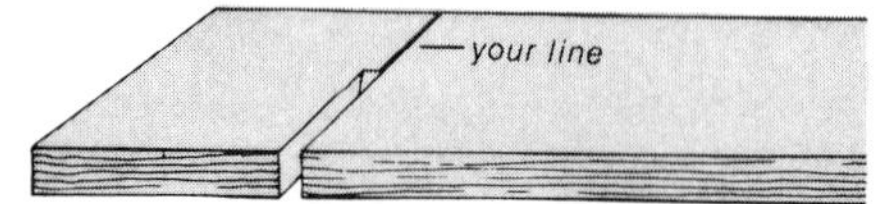

11-9(a). ***Saw just outside the layout line. The kerf must be in the waste stock.***

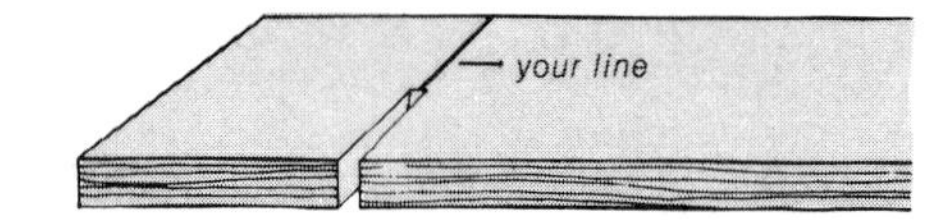

11-9(b). ***Do*** not ***saw directly on the layout line.***

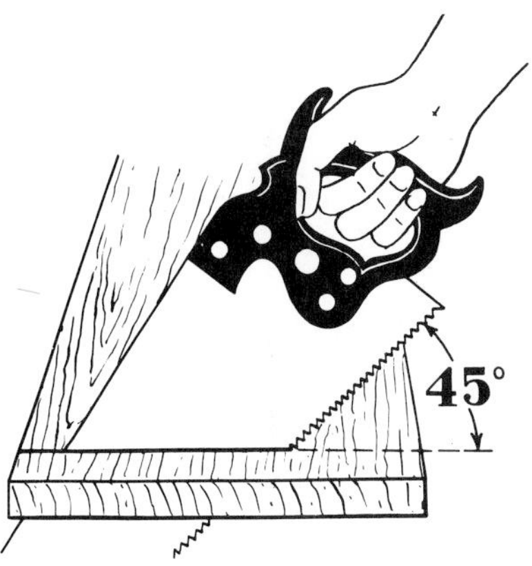

11-10. *Angle for crosscutting.*

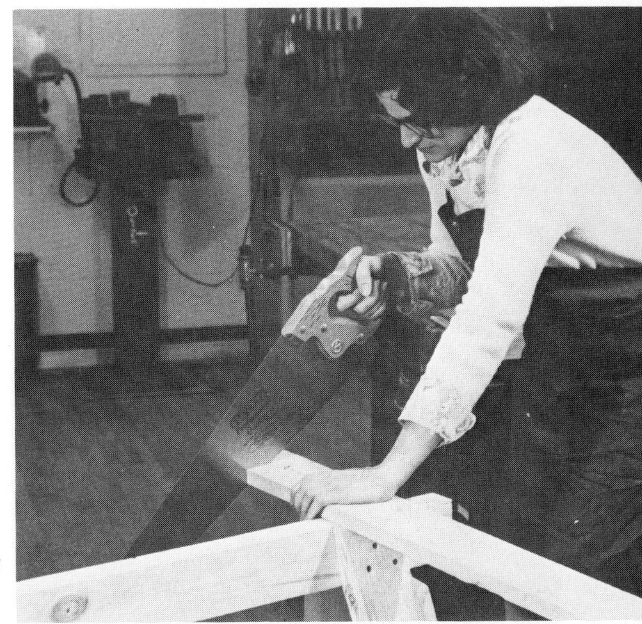

11-11. *Cutting a board to length with a crosscut saw.*

8. As you cut, watch the layout line, not the saw. Blow the sawdust away.

9. If the saw is moving into or away from the line, twist the handle slightly to bring it back.

10. As the final strokes are made, hold the end to be cut off. If you don't do this, the corner will split out as the piece drops. Never twist off thin strips of wood with the saw blade.

CUTTING STOCK TO WIDTH WITH A RIPSAW

1. Mark the cutting line along the length of the board. Be sure to measure accurately before starting. For a very long cut you might want to fasten a guide board just outside the layout line to help keep the cut straight.

2. Place the board over two sawhorses so that your cut will be at knee height. If you are right-handed, put your right knee on the board and your left hand a few inches to the left of the cutting line. If you are left-handed, do the opposite. Start by taking short strokes, backward only. Use the teeth at the heel of the blade. Don't put pressure on the saw until the kerf is well started.

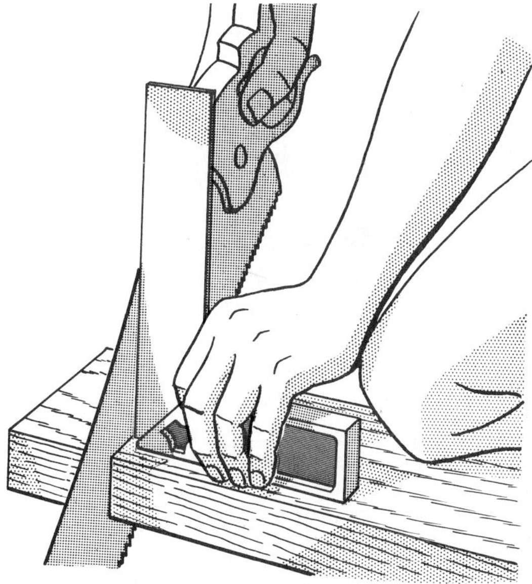

11-12. *A way to keep the saw cut square with the face of the board. Place the handle of the try square firmly on the face of the wood and then slide it along until the blade of the try square comes in contact with the blade of the saw, to check it for squareness.*

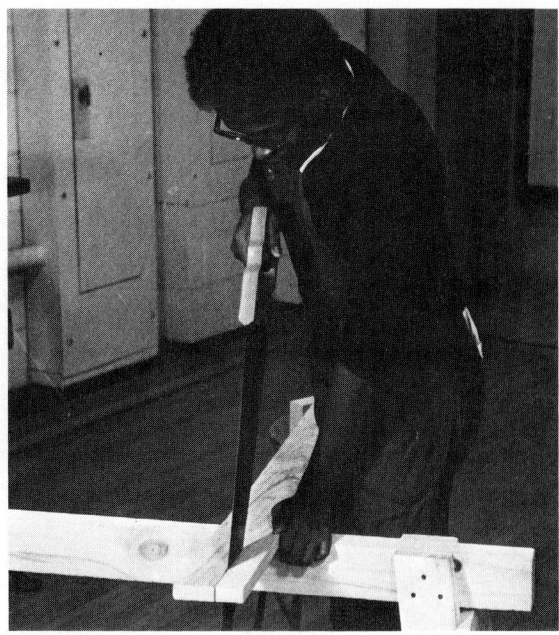

11-13. *Sight along the saw to keep it cutting straight.*

11-16. *A commercial device for holding the kerf open.*

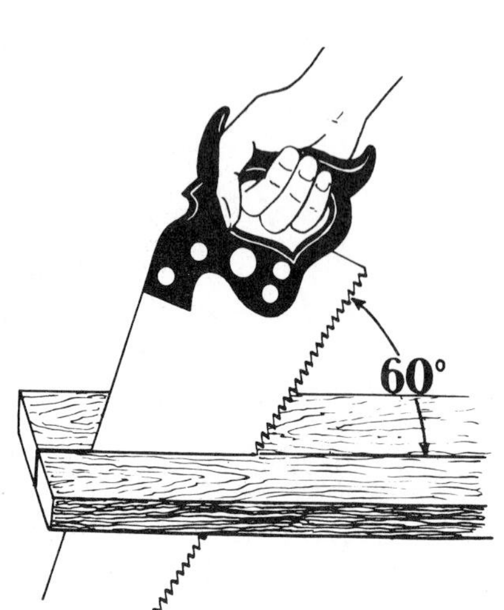

11-14. *Angle for ripping.*

11-17. *Ripping with the stock held in a vise.*

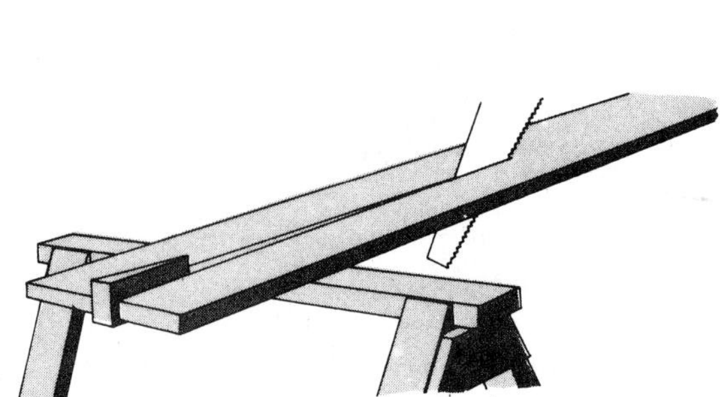

11-15. *You can use a wedge of wood to hold the kerf open during sawing.*

3. As you saw, watch the layout line so that you keep the saw cut straight. Fig. 11-13. Hold the saw at an angle of 60 degrees. Fig. 11-14.

4. Sometimes on a long cut, the kerf may close enough to cause the saw to bind. To avoid this, insert a wooden wedge into the kerf to keep it open. Fig. 11-15. There are also commercial devices that do this. Fig. 11-16.

5. Fasten shorter boards in the vise with the layout line vertical (up and down) and slightly left of the vise jaw. If the board is quite long, clamp it near the top at first and move it up as you cut. Fig. 11-17.

6. When cutting plywood to width, use a crosscut saw. Keep the saw at a very low angle of about 30 degrees.

SAWING TIPS

① WHEN WORK IS COMPLETE, HANG UP THE SAW.

② DO NOT PILE TOOLS ON TOP OF THE BENCH SO AS TO DISTORT BLADE.

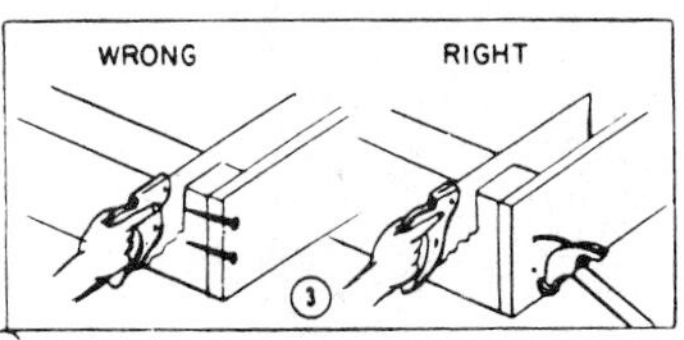

③ LOOK CAREFULLY OVER REPAIR OR ALTERATION WORK; SEE THAT ALL NAILS ARE REMOVED TO AVOID CUTTING INTO METAL.

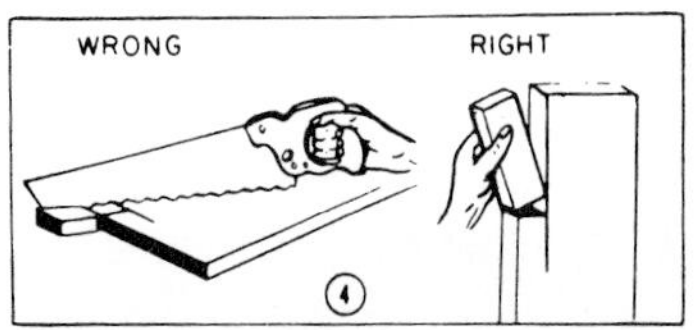

④ STRIPS OF WASTE SHOULD NOT BE TWISTED OFF WITH BLADE, BUT BROKEN OFF WITH HAND OR MALLET.

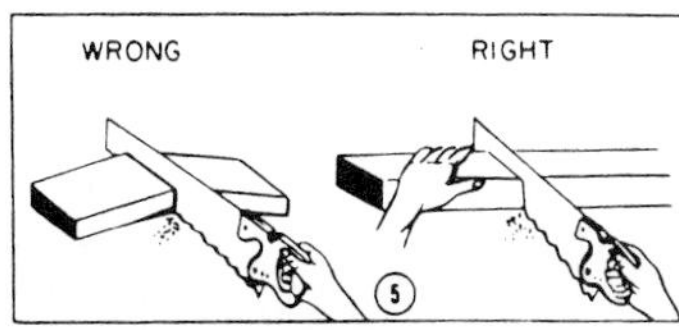

⑤ SUPPORTING THE WASTE SIDE OF WORK WILL PREVENT SPLITTING OFF.

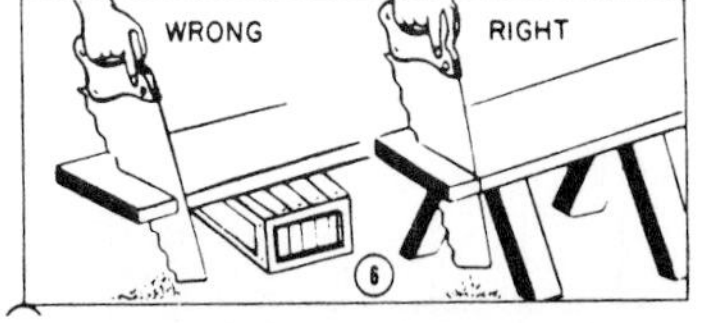

⑥ RAISE THE WORK TO A HEIGHT SUFFICIENT TO KEEP THE BLADE FROM STRIKING THE FLOOR. IF THE WORK CANNOT BE RAISED, LIMIT THE STROKE.

QUESTIONS

1. What kind of saw must be used to cut across grain? With the grain?
2. Why are the teeth of the saw wider than the saw itself?
3. Is the saw cut started by pushing or pulling?
4. How should you guide the saw when starting a cut?
5. Which should you watch when the cutting is done, the layout line or the saw?

ACTIVITIES

1. Use a magnifying glass to examine the teeth of the saws in your lab. Which are crosscut saws? Which are ripsaws?
2. Describe the kind of saw you might buy for general use in a home workshop. Check hardware stores or home improvement centers to find out the cost of such a saw.
3. Prepare a poster to remind people how to use a saw safely.

LEARN THESE SAFETY RULES BEFORE USING THE PLANE

* Make sure the cutting edge is sharp.
* Clamp the stock firmly on the workbench or in a vise.
* Never slide the plane iron cap over the cutting edge of the blade.
* Always place the plane on its side when it is not in use.
* Never plane over a nail, screw, or other metal surface. Doing so will ruin the cutting edge of the blade. A dull blade is dangerous.
* Don't use a plane with a dull blade; it may jam and stick.
* Never grasp the underside of the plane at or near the cutting edge. You may cut your finger.
* Stand properly balanced on both feet when using a plane.
* Don't try to cut too thick a shaving at one time.
* Raise the plane above the work on the backward stroke to protect the blade from dulling.

Assembling and Adjusting a Plane

A *plane* is a special tool with a blade for smoothing and removing wood as shavings. The modern plane developed from the chisel. The plane is nothing more than a chisel held in a block of metal so that it can be controlled to take an even cut. This is one tool you'll use a lot.

It takes patience to learn to adjust and use the plane correctly. Even more skill is needed to sharpen the blade correctly, yet a plane works well only if the blade is sharp and adjusted correctly. Even then it will smooth a surface only if it is used in the right way.

KINDS OF BENCH PLANES

The **jack plane** ("Jack of all trades") is the most common plane. It is either 14 or 15 inches long, with a 2-inch blade. It is ideal for rough surfaces that require a heavier chip. It is also good for obtaining a smooth, flat surface. Fig. 12-1.

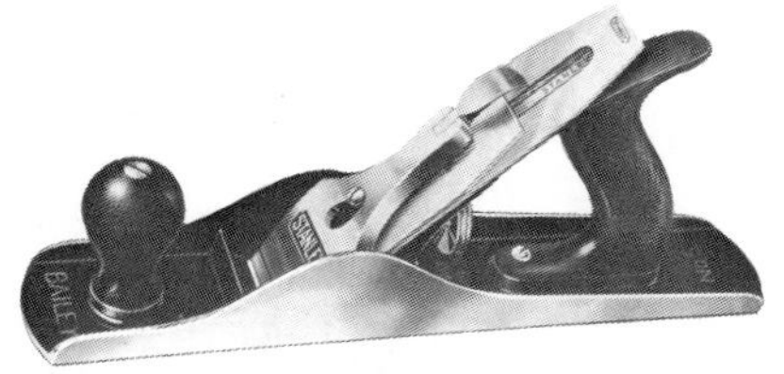

12-1. *The jack plane is the most useful, all-around tool for both rough planing and final smoothing. (Stanley Tools)*

A slightly narrower and shorter plane is the **junior jack plane.** It is 11½ inches long with a 1¾-inch blade.

A **smooth plane** is 9¼ or 9¾ inches long and is used for smaller work. It is a good plane for general use around the home.

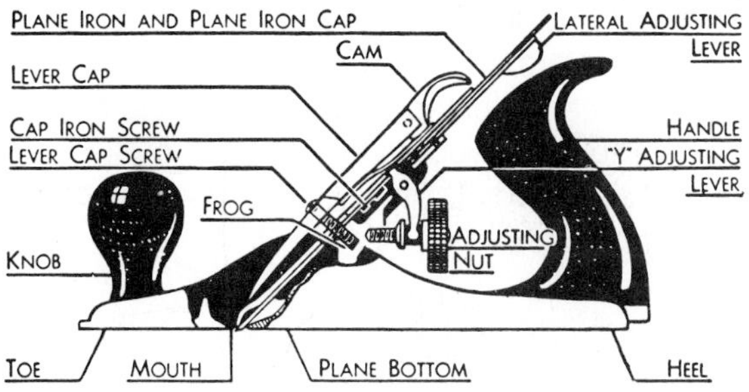

12-2(a). *Parts of a plane. (Stanley Tools)*

A **fore plane** is longer (18 inches) and has a 2¾-inch cutter. It is used to plane long surfaces and edges.

The largest plane is called a **jointer plane.** It is 22 inches long with a 2¾-inch cutter. It is used by carpenters for planing long boards such as the edges of doors.

PARTS OF THE PLANE

The plane is the most complicated hand tool you will use. You should learn the major parts and how to adjust it. Let's look at the hand plane in Fig. 12-2. The main part is called the *body,* or *bed,* and the wide flat part is called the *bottom.* The back of the bottom is the *heel* and the front is the *toe.* The opening across the bottom is called the *mouth,* or *throat.* The *knob* (in front) is held in one hand and the *handle* (in back) in the other hand. Lift up on the *cam lever* to release the *lever cap.* Then slide the lever cap up and it will come off over the *lever cap screw.* Now carefully lift the *double plane iron* out of the plane. Notice that this is made in two parts. The top one is called the *plane iron cap.* It breaks the chips and forces the chips or shavings up and out. The lower edge of the plane iron cap is called the *chip break.* The lower part of the double plane iron is the actual cutting edge. It is called a *single plane iron.* It must be kept sharp as described in Chapter 18. The part that supports the double plane iron is called the *frog.* There is an *adjusting nut* for

LATERAL ADJUSTING LEVER SETS CUTTING EDGE PARALLEL TO BOTTOM
PLANE IRON BLADE DOES THE CUTTING
PLANE IRON CAP STIFFENS PLANE IRON BLADE, AND CURLS SHAVINGS
ADJUSTING NUT FOR DEPTH OF CUT
LEVER CAP
FROG SUPPORTS PLANE IRON BLADE AND PLANE IRON CAP
LEVER CAP ADJUSTING SCREW SETS LEVER FOR CORRECT TENSION

12-2(b). *Uses of the working parts. (Stanley Tools)*

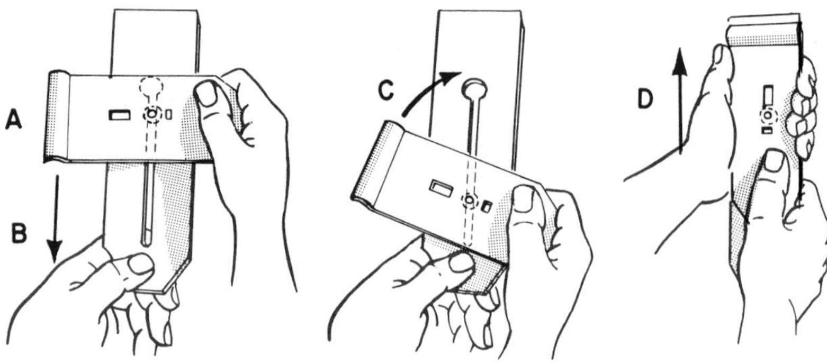

12-3. *The steps in assembling a double plane iron. (Stanley Tools)*

changing the depth of the cut. A *lateral adjusting lever* can be moved to the right or left so that the cutting edge will be straight (parallel with the bottom).

HOW TO PUT THE DOUBLE PLANE IRON TOGETHER

1. Hold the single plane iron in your left hand with the bevel side of the blade down. Hold the plane iron cap crosswise and drop the cap screw through the hole. Fig. 12-3(A).

2. Slide the plane iron cap away from the cutting edge. Fig. 12-3(B).

3. Rotate it 1/4 turn so that it is straight with the plane iron. Fig. 12-3(C).

4. Carefully slide the cap forward, guiding it with your left thumb and forefinger. Fig. 12-3(D). Be careful not to slip the cap over the cutting edge, as this might nick it. The cap should be about 1/16 inch from the cutting edge for most work. For very fine planing, about 1/32 inch is better.

5. Hold the two parts together and then tighten the cap screw with a screwdriver or with the lever cap. Be sure the two parts are good and tight. If chips get between the plane iron and the cap, you'll have trouble planing. Fig. 12-4.

PUTTING THE DOUBLE PLANE IRON IN THE PLANE

1. Place the plane upright on the bench with a small scrap of wood under the toe to raise one end of the bottom. This is done to protect the cutting edge.

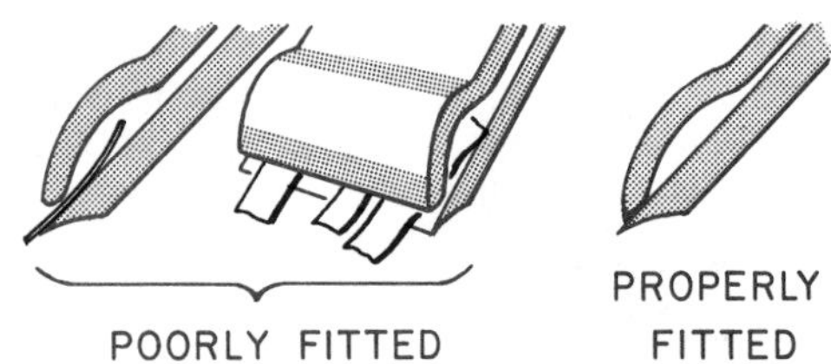

12-4. *The plane iron cap must fit the plane iron tightly. If it doesn't, chips get between the two parts and cause poor planing action. (Stanley Tools)*

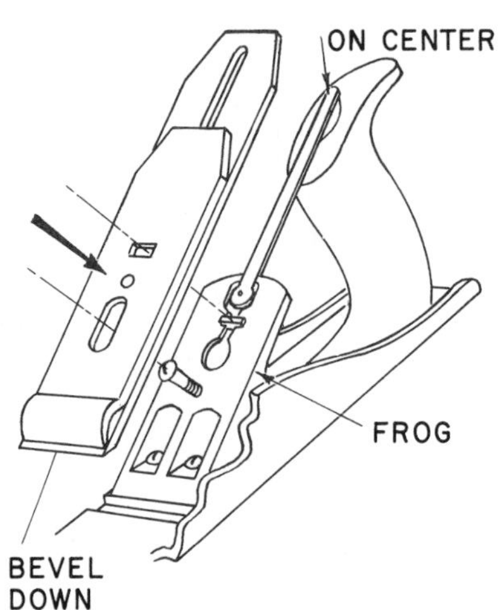

12-5. *The assembled double plane iron is placed over the frog.*

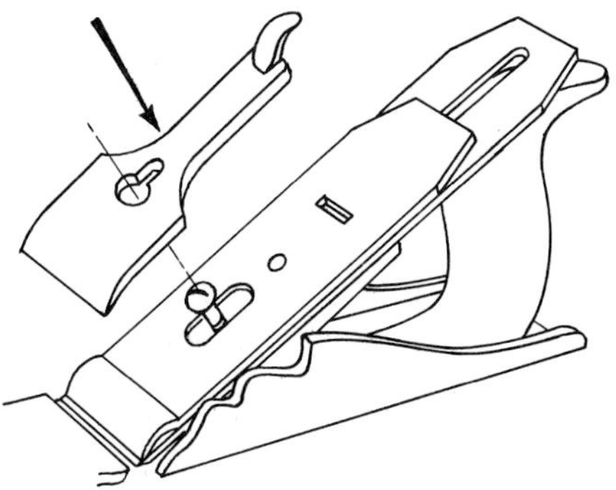

12-6. *The lever cap is placed over the double plane iron.*

12-7. *Push the cam down to lock the assembly in place.*

2. Hold the double plane iron with the cap up. Carefully guide the cutter into the plane and over the lever cap screw. Be careful not to hit the cutting edge on the side of the plane. Fig. 12-5.

3. Now make sure that (a) the long slot in the plane iron fits over the roller of the lateral adjusting lever and (b) the small slot in the plane iron cap fits over the depth-of-cut or Y adjusting lever. Both must be in place before you can adjust the plane. Fig. 12-6.

4. Slip the lever cap in place and push the cam down. Fig. 12-7. The cap should hold the double plane iron snugly. If the cap is too tight, it will be hard to adjust the plane. If it is too loose, the plane won't stay in adjustment. You can tighten or loosen the lever cap screw (with a screwdriver) until the cam lever will close with a little push.

ADJUSTING THE PLANE

1. Turn the plane upside down, holding the knob in your left hand.

2. Look along the bottom. It's a good idea to face a window. Fig. 12-8.

3. Turn the adjusting nut with your right hand until the cutting edge appears. It should stick out about the thickness of a hair.

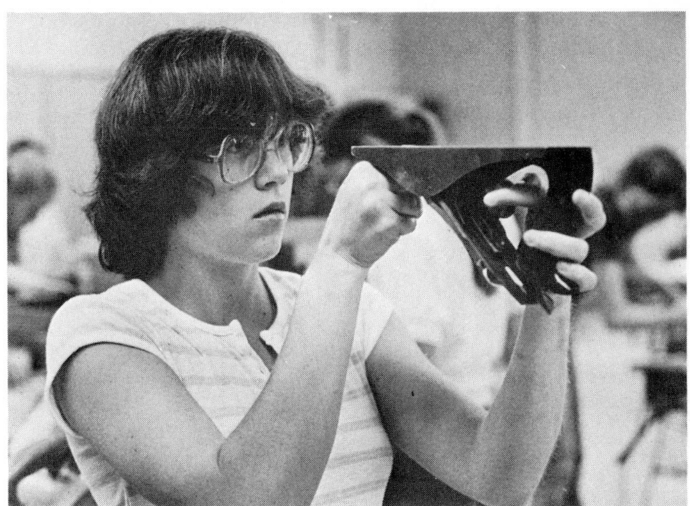

12-8. *Sighting along the bottom of the plane to make sure the cutting edge is parallel with the bottom.*

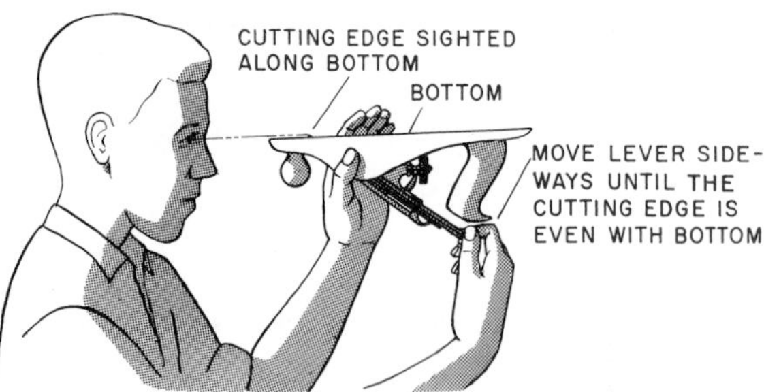

12-9. *Adjusting the plane.*

4. Now move the lateral adjusting lever to the left or right until the cutting edge is parallel with the bottom. Figs. 12-9 and 12-10.

5. Turn the adjusting nut again until the blade just appears above the bottom.

6. Try the plane on a piece of scrap stock. Continue to adjust it until you are satisfied with the appearance of the shavings. They should be smooth, silky, and of uniform (even) thickness. Fig. 12-11.

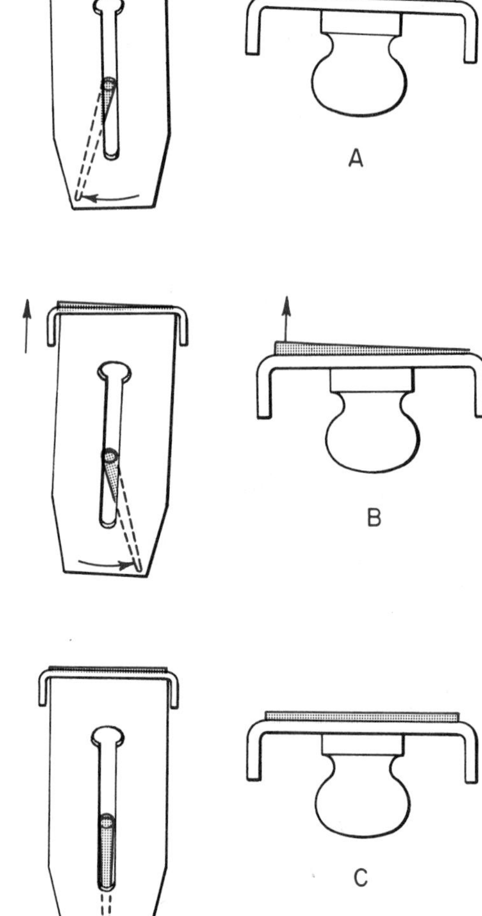

12-10. *(A) Moving the lateral adjusting lever to the left raises the right side of the plane iron. (B) Moving the lever to the right raises the left side of the plane iron. (C) The plane iron is parallel with the bottom.*

12-11. *You will get shavings like these when you use a good plane that is correctly adjusted.*

12-12. *Always place the plane on its side when it is not in use.*

POINTS TO REMEMBER

1. Always plane with the grain to get a smooth surface. Planing against the grain roughens the wood.

2. If possible, clamp the stock to the workbench to hold it steady.

3. Check often to make sure the plane's cutting edge is sharp. A blade which is sharp will not reflect much light. A dull blade appears shiny. Test the blade by planing a piece of scrap stock.

4. Do not let the cutting edge contact metal. Scraping metal can ruin the blade.

5. When you stop planing, always rest the tool on its side, never on its bottom. Fig. 12-12. The cutting edge will be damaged if you put the tool down in an upright position. Even worse is to place it in a pile with other hand tools.

QUESTIONS

1. Which are the largest and smallest planes found in the wood shop?

2. Which is the most common type of plane for general work?

3. Why should you learn the main parts of the plane?

4. How do you change the depth of cut?

5. Which adjustment changes the blade so that it is parallel with the bottom?

6. For most work about how far should the cap be set from the cutting edge?

7. Why should one end of the bottom of a plane be kept off the bench surface when installing the double plane iron?

ACTIVITIES

1. In your own words, write the directions for installing the double plane iron in the plane.

2. With your teacher's help, prepare a display of planes. Label each plane with its name and length.

CHAPTER 13

Planing the First Surface

In squaring up stock, the best face should be planed first. Usually this is the widest surface that requires the least amount of planing. Fig. 13-1.

TOOLS

You will need a jack plane, try square or straightedge (rule), vise, bench, and bench stop.

PROCEDURE

1. Check the stock and choose the better of the two largest surfaces. Check the board for three things:

• *Bow.* Bow (rhymes with *low*) means that one side of the board is concave (dished in) and the other side is convex (rounded outward). With a pencil, mark the high spots that must be planed. Fig. 13-2.

• *Wind* (rhymes with *kind).* A board has wind if it twists along its length. You can check this by placing two broad sticks on the board and sighting along them. Fig. 13-3. Another way is to place the board on a flat surface. If it has wind, it will rock on two corners.

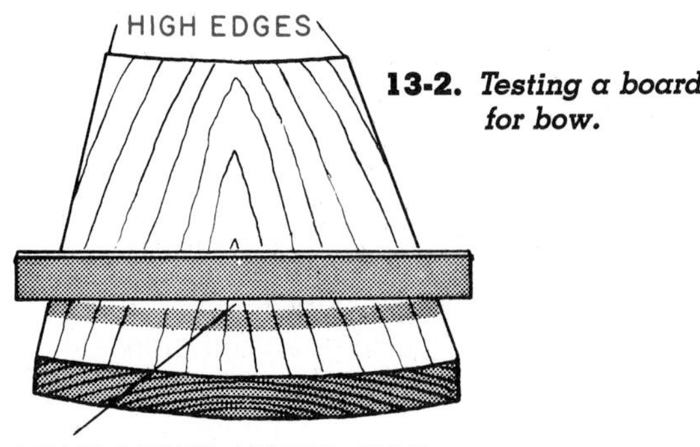

13-2. *Testing a board for bow.*

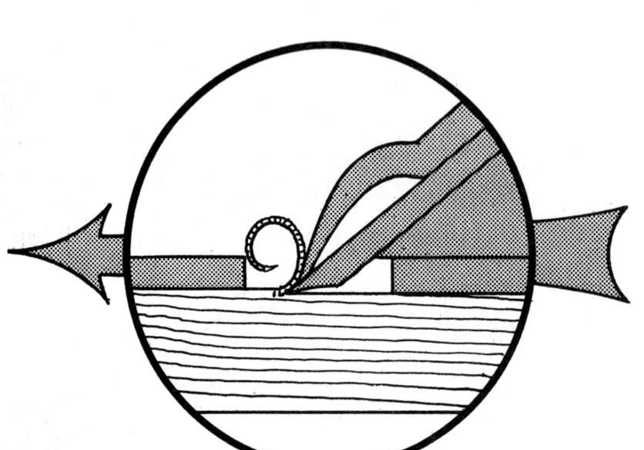

13-1. *Planing wood. Remember the six simple machines. The plane is made up of several simple machines. Here, the plane blade (a wedge) is cutting the chip. The cap is an inclined plane to help the chip slide out of the way. Look at the plane. You'll find a* wheel and axle, *several* levers, *and some* screws. *The plane is the most complicated hand tool.*

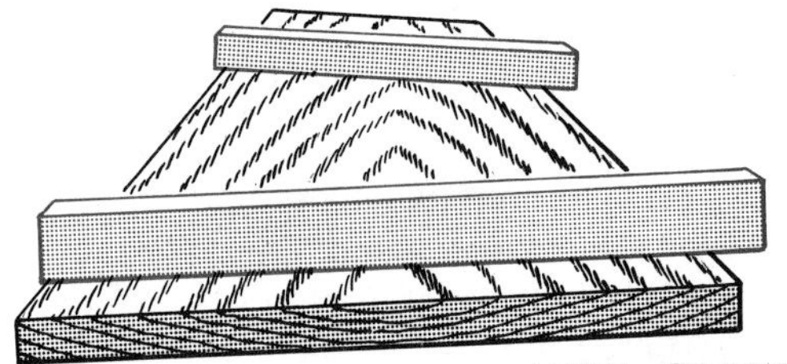

13-3. *Two sticks placed across either end of the board show wind, or twist.*

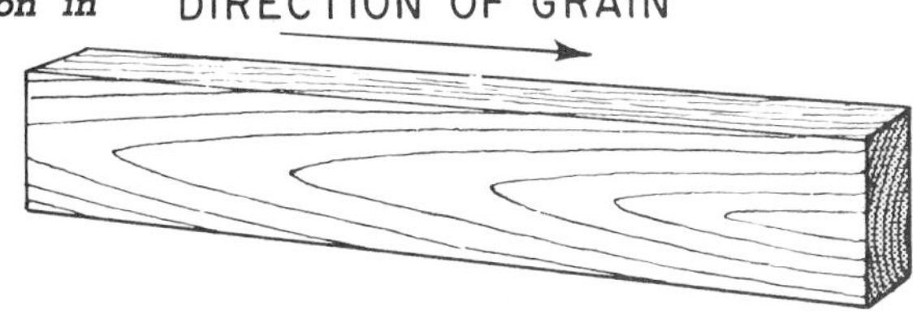

13-4. *Grain direction. This is the direction in which the planing should be done.*

13-5. *The board is clamped between the vise dog and a bench stop (or pin).*

• *Grain direction.* If possible, decide the direction of the grain. Always plane with the grain, never against it. Fig. 13-4. Planing against the grain roughens the wood. It is difficult to see grain direction on a rough board.

2. Clamp the work so that it is held securely. Two ways to do this are:

   a. Place a bench stop in a hole in the bench and place the work on the bench with the end grain against it. The work must be centered or it will slip as you begin to plane. Clamp the work between the bench stop and the vise dog. Fig. 13-5.

   b. Place the work against a board fastened to the end of the bench.

3. Stand with your feet apart (left foot forward) and your right side near the bench. *Left-handed persons reverse the procedure.*

4. Hold the knob firmly in your left hand and the handle in your right. Fig. 13-6.

5. Place the toe of the plane over the end of the board. Push down on the knob as you start the stroke.

6. As the whole plane comes onto the board, apply equal pressure on both the knob and handle. As the toe of the plane leaves the board, apply more pressure to the handle. This kind of stroke will keep the surface level from one end to the other. Fig. 13-7.

7. Lift the plane on the return stroke. Dragging it back will roughen the surface and dull the cutting edge.

8. After the first few strokes, you'll be able to tell for sure if you're planing with the grain.

9. Start at one edge of the board and make a series of strokes until you reach the other side.

13-6. *Correct way to hold the plane.*

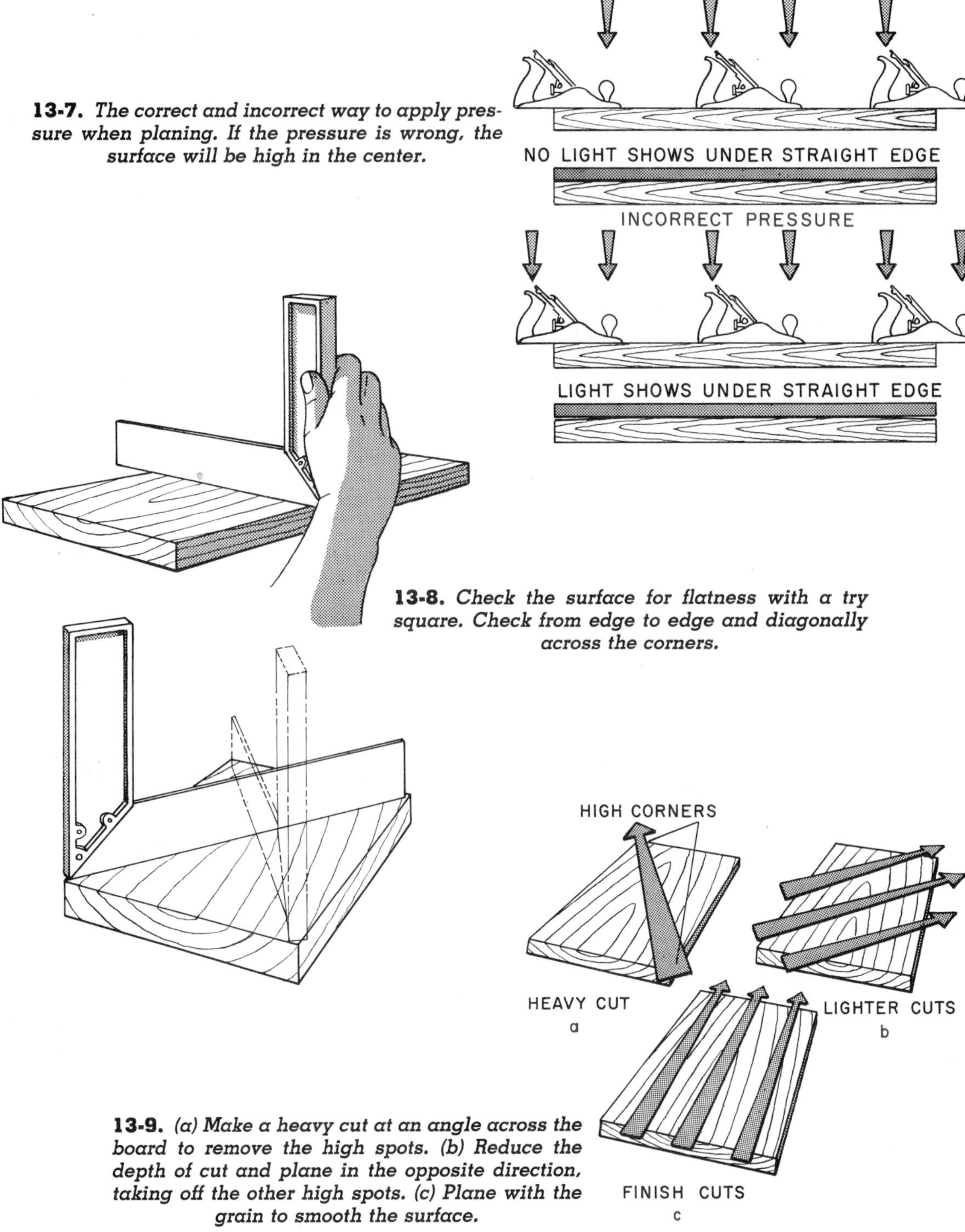

13-7. *The correct and incorrect way to apply pressure when planing. If the pressure is wrong, the surface will be high in the center.*

13-8. *Check the surface for flatness with a try square. Check from edge to edge and diagonally across the corners.*

13-9. *(a) Make a heavy cut at an angle across the board to remove the high spots. (b) Reduce the depth of cut and plane in the opposite direction, taking off the other high spots. (c) Plane with the grain to smooth the surface.*

Always place the plane on its side when not in use.

10. Test the surface with the try square or straightedge in several directions as shown in Fig. 13-8.

11. If there are high spots, mark these with a pencil. Then make heavy cuts diagonally across the board. Reduce the depth of cut and plane in the opposite direction until the high points are removed. Then plane straight along the board. Fig. 13-9.

12. If only the end towards you must be planed, start the stroke as before. Then, as you near the end of the area, slowly lift up on the handle to stop the shaving gradually.

13. If the end away from you must be planed, start the stroke with the toe of the plane against the surface and the heel held high. Gradually lower the plane as the stroke is made.

14. Decide which edge should be planed first. Mark the face surface near this edge.

QUESTIONS

1. Which surface should you plane first?
2. Describe bow.
3. What is wind in a board?
4. Why must the pressure on a plane change from the start to the end of the stroke?

ACTIVITIES

1. Demonstrate how to stand when planing a board. Show how a left-handed person should stand and how a right-handed person should stand.
2. Demonstrate how to test a surface to make sure it is flat.

Planing the First Edge

The *first,* or *face, edge* must be planed straight and smooth. It must be at right angles (square) to the face surface. Always choose the best edge to plane first. You'll be measuring from this edge for all of the other steps.

TOOLS

You will need a jack plane or jointer plane, try square, vise, and hand clamp. Fig. 14-1.

PROCEDURE

1. Clamp the work in the vise with the edge about 2 or 3 inches above the jaw. If the piece is long, support the other end with a hand clamp. Also, use a jointer plane on long boards. Notice how a long plane bridges (reaches across) the low spots. Fig. 14-2.

2. Hold the plane at right angles to the face surface and make a long, even stroke. Fig. 14-3.

14-1. *Select a plane and adjust it for a fine cut.*

14-3. *Hold the plane at right angles to the face surface. Here the smooth plane is being used to remove the rough surface. The fore plane will be used to smooth-plane the edge.*

It is very important to keep the plane square with the face surface. To help guide the plane, you may hold the toe end as shown in Fig. 14-4. Curl your thumb around the back of the knob and place your fingers against the bottom. Take a light cut.

3. Continue to plane until a uniform shaving comes off the edge. To get the edge square and the surface smooth, remove as little stock as possible.

4. Remove the board from the vise. Hold the handle of a try square against the face surface to check for squareness at several places along the entire edge. Fig. 14-5.

5. It is also a good idea to test for straightness. Hold a straightedge along the edge from one end to the other. Fig. 14-6.

6. Mark the *face surface* and *face edge* with a face mark as shown in Fig. 14-5. This mark will be your guide in making measurements to square up stock.

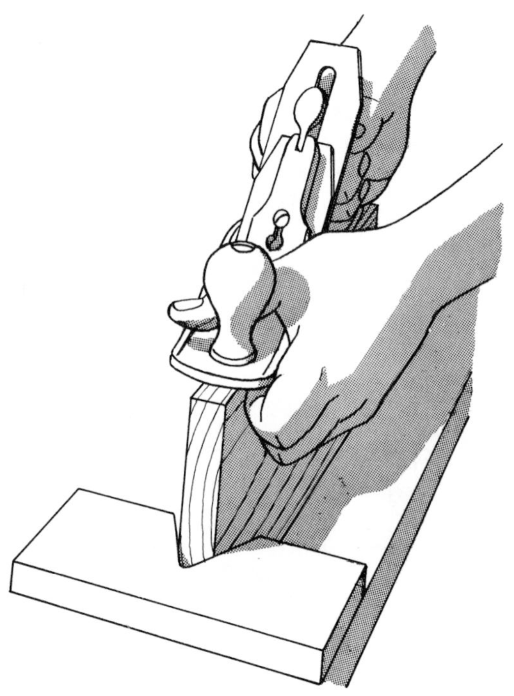

14-4(a). *One method of holding the plane to keep it square with the face surface. The board is held against a V block.*

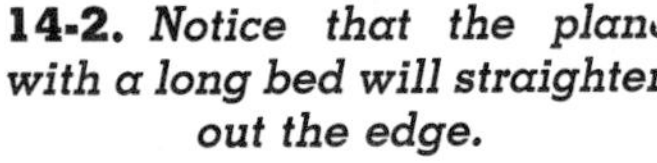

14-2. *Notice that the plane with a long bed will straighten out the edge.*

14-4(b). *If you're planing the edge of a door or other large object, clamp the work as shown here. Be sure to use scrap stock under the clamps to protect the surface of the workpiece. (Note: To plane the edge of a door, you'll need a fore plane, as shown here.)*

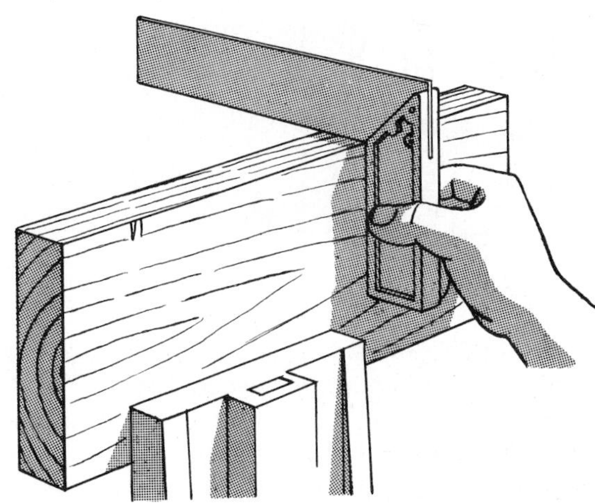

14-5. *Testing the edge for squareness. Notice also the face mark used to show which is the face surface and which is the face edge.*

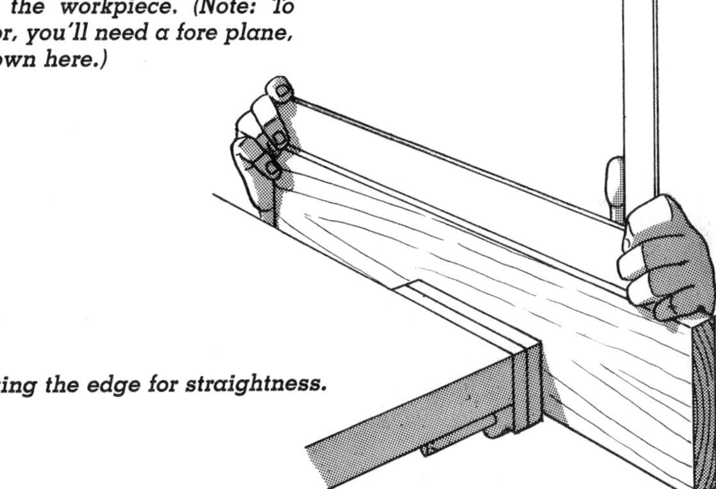

14-6. *Testing the edge for straightness.*

QUESTIONS

1. The first edge should be at what angle to the face surface?
2. Which edge should you choose to plane first?

ACTIVITIES

1. Demonstrate how to hold a plane for planing an edge.
2. Suppose you are writing a how-to book for woodworkers. Write the instructions for testing an edge for squareness and straightness.

Planing End Grain

End grain is more difficult to plane because you are shearing through the wood fibers. Planing end grain is like shaving off whiskers. End grain requires planing because sawing has left it very rough. However, it doesn't have to be planed if the end of the board won't show in the finished project.

TOOLS

A *block plane* is a small plane that has a low-angle cutter. Fig. 15-1. Because the blade is held at a low angle to the surface, it works well on end grain. Because of its low angle, the cutter is set bevel up. The cutter is a single plane iron with no chip breaker. The block plane can be held with one or both hands.

Besides cutting end grain, the block plane is also useful for general-purpose planing. For example, it is a good plane for shaping a ship-model hull or for planing a chamfer. Fig. 15-2.

To adjust the cutter for thickness, sight along the plane bottom. Turn the adjusting screw to push the cutter out or to pull it in. To adjust the cutter for evenness of shaving, sight along the bottom. Move the lateral adjusting lever to the right or left as necessary.

If you don't have a block plane, use a jack plane or smooth plane. You will also need a try square to check the edge after planing.

PROCEDURE

1. Choose the end that needs the least amount of planing. Mark a sharp line across the face surface and edge as a guide to show how much stock is to be removed.
2. Clamp the work in the vise with about 1 inch of the end grain showing. Don't plane end grain with the board sticking out too far from the vise. The work will vibrate and the cutting tool will jump.
3. The plane must be very sharp and the cap set close to the cutting edge. Adjust the depth of cut as thin as possible.
4. If you plane completely across end grain, the back edge will split off. There are three ways to avoid this:
   a. Plane halfway across the end; then lift the heel. This will feather the shaving (thin it out). Then plane from the other edge. Fig. 15-3.
   b. Select a piece of waste stock the same thickness as the board. Place it behind the board. Fig. 15-4.
   c. Plane a short chamfer in the waste stock on the opposite edge. Then you can plane all the way in one direction.
5. Readjust the plane to a very light cut. Hold the plane at a slight angle and take a shearing cut. Try to plane an even surface that will look good when a finish is applied.
6. Check the end with a try square from both the face surface and edge. Fig. 15-5. Put an "X" in pencil on the end so that you know it has been planed.

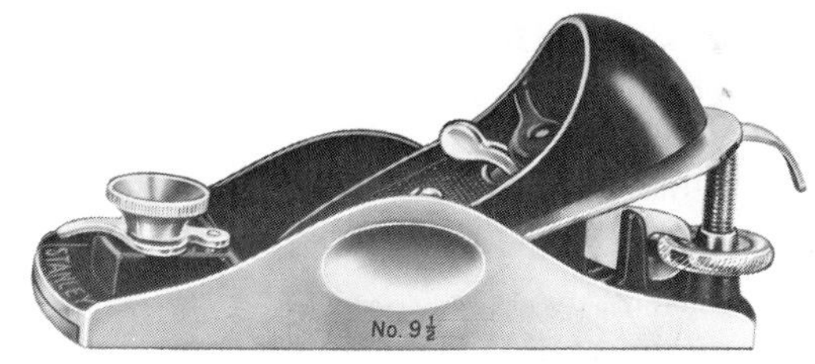

15-1(a). ***A block plane. (Stanley Tools)***

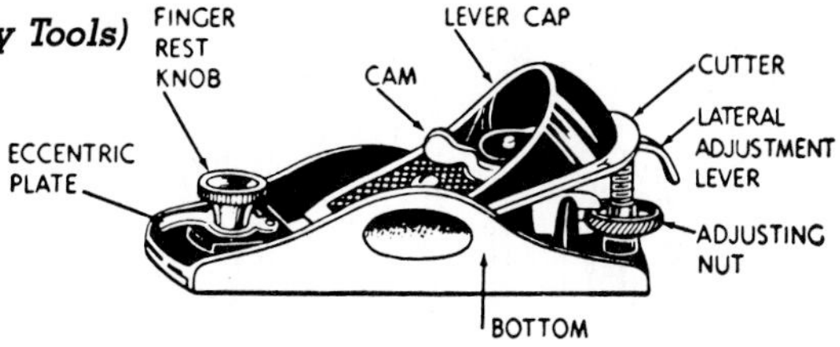

15-1(b). *Parts of a block plane. (Stanley Tools)*

15-2. *Using a block plane to plane a chamfer.*

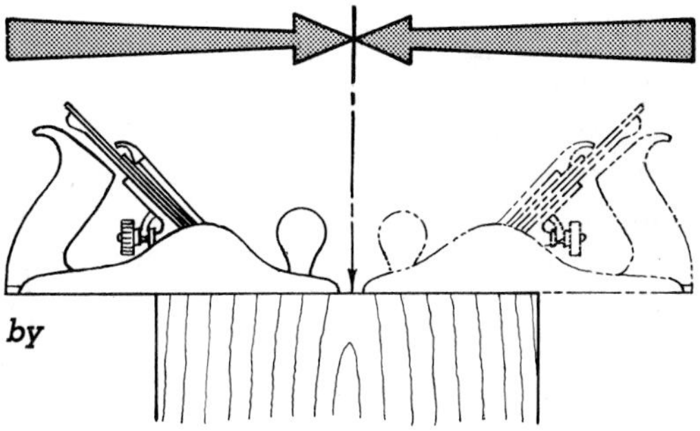

15-3(a). *The correct way to plane end grain by planing halfway across the stock.*

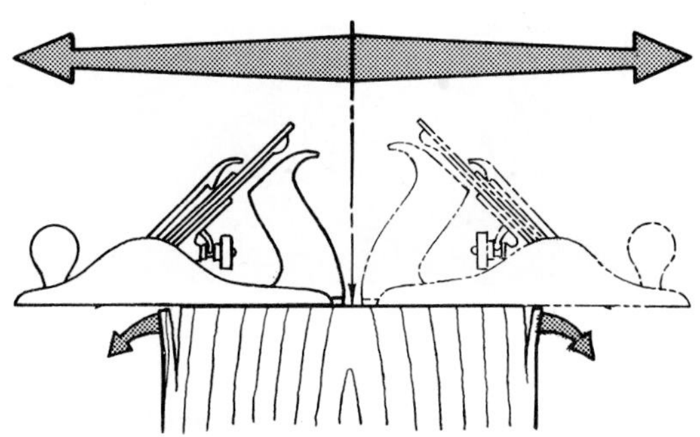

15-3(b). *This is what happens if you plane toward the outer edge.*

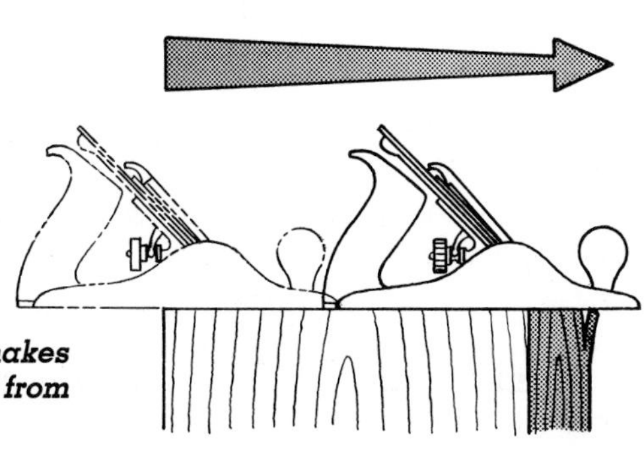

15-4. *Notice the piece of waste stock. This makes it possible to plane all the way across the end from one direction.*

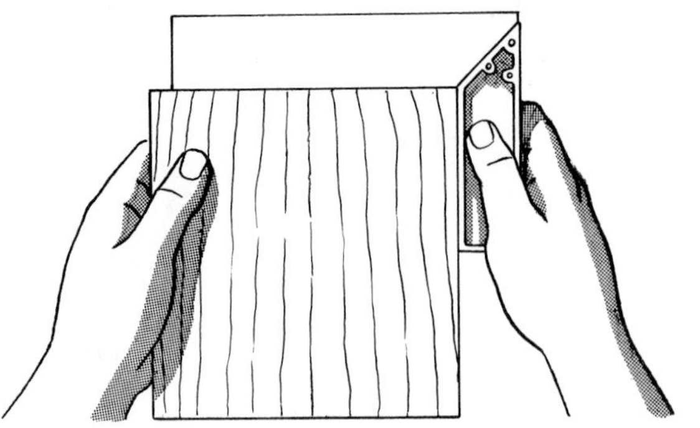

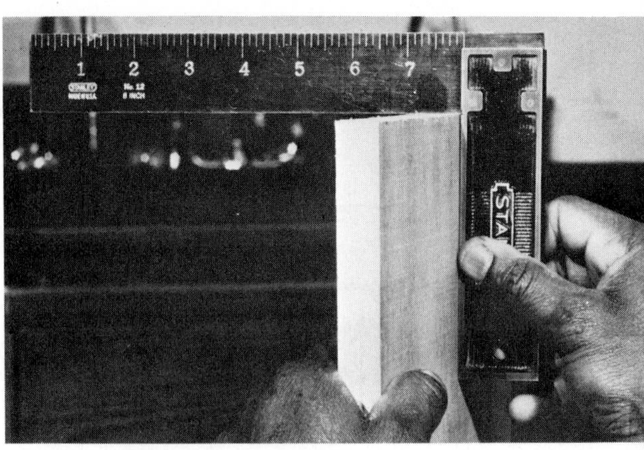

15-5. ***Testing the end from the face surface and face edge to make sure it is square.***

QUESTIONS

1. Why is end grain more difficult to plane?
2. Why is a block plane a good tool for planing end grain?
3. Does end grain always have to be planed? Explain.
4. Which end should be planed first?
5. Why must a light cut be made when planing end grain?

ACTIVITIES

1. In a written or oral report, describe three ways to avoid splitting off the back edge of the wood when planing end grain.
2. With a magnifying glass, examine end grain before and after it has been planed. Make a drawing of what you see.

Using a Backsaw

A backsaw is used for fine sawing, especially when making joints or squaring up stock. The thin blade and fine teeth make a narrow kerf and leave a smooth surface.

TOOLS

The backsaw is a fine-tooth crosscut saw. It got its name because it has a heavy metal band along the back that supports the thin blade. Fig. 16-1.

A bench hook is a wooden board with a cleat slightly shorter than the width of the board across the ends, one on each side. It is used on the bench top for such jobs as cutting and chiseling, to give support to the work, and to protect the bench. Fig. 16-2.

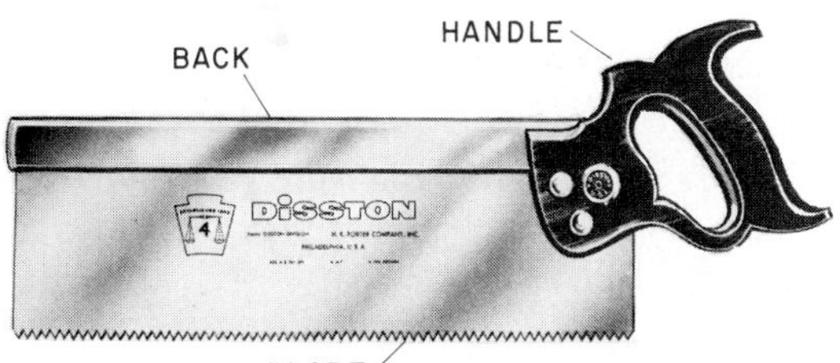

16-1. *Parts of a backsaw.*

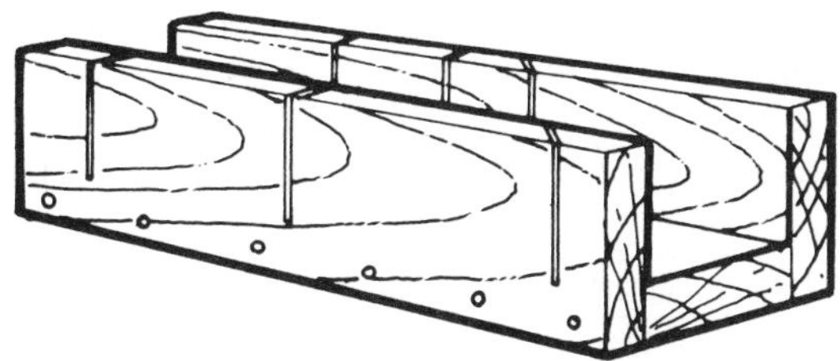

16-3. *This miter box has slots to guide the backsaw in cutting 45- and 90-degree angles.*

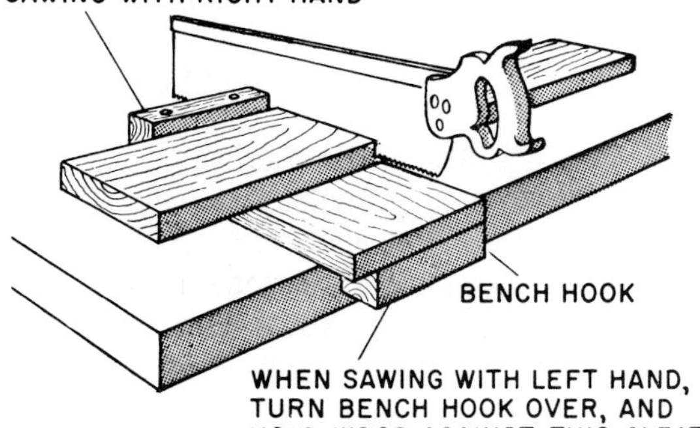

16-2. *A bench hook in use.*

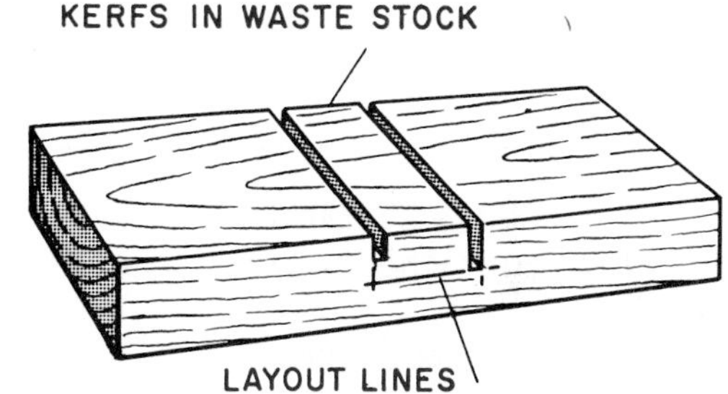

16-4. *Make the cuts at the layout line but in the waste stock.*

A miter box, Fig. 16-3, can be used for cutting 45- and 90-degree angles.

CUTTING WITH A BACKSAW

1. Carefully mark the location of the cut.
2. Place the bench hook over the top of the bench.
3. Hold the saw in your right hand and the work against the bench hook with the layout line to the right. If left-handed, reverse. Make sure the kerf will be in the waste stock. Fig. 16-4.
4. Use your thumb as a guide and start the cut with the handle held high.
5. As the cut is started, lower the blade a little at a time until the saw is parallel with the surface. Fig. 16-5.

16-5. *Cutting with a backsaw.*

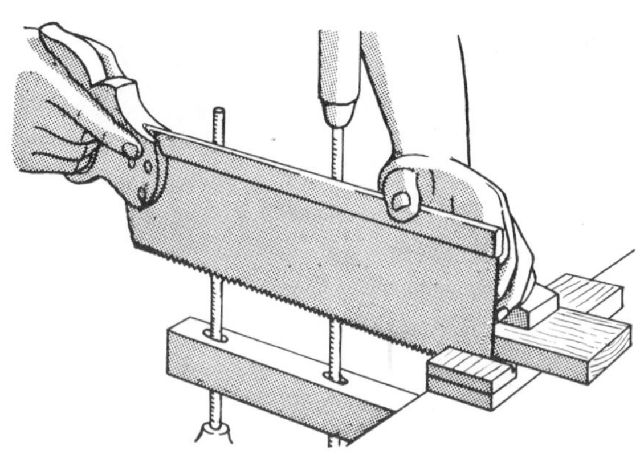

16-6. *A guide board has been clamped next to the layout line. Remember that the saw kerf must be in the waste stock.*

6. Continue to cut until the correct depth is reached or the waste stock is cut off.

7. To help the saw make an accurate cut, clamp a smooth piece of scrap stock right next to the layout line. Fig. 16-6. Then you can hold the saw with both hands to start the cut. Don't start with the handle held high. By keeping the blade flat against the guide board, the cut will be in the correct location and square with the surface.

QUESTIONS

1. How does the backsaw get its name?
2. What is a bench hook?
3. Where should the kerf be made in the wood?
4. When holding the saw with one hand, how should the handle of the saw be held to start a cut?
5. Describe the way to make a more accurate cut with the backsaw.

ACTIVITIES

1. A miter box is useful for guiding the saw when cutting a 45- or 90-degree angle. Draw a shop sketch for building a miter box. How will you make sure the slots are at the correct angles?
2. Find out what materials are in a backsaw and how much the saw costs.

Squaring Up Stock

Rough lumber is sometimes used in building construction and repair work but never for small articles. Most of the lumber you use will be S2S—surfaced two sides. This lumber will have to be planed very little on the surface. At other times you might have to plane two surfaces and one edge; for example, when cutting out a design. In other cases, when the ends don't show, the surfaces and edges are planed and the ends simply cut to length with a saw. There will be many times, however, when you must completely square up stock. To *square up* stock means to

17-1. *The top of this table is a good example of a part that must be planed on all four sides.*

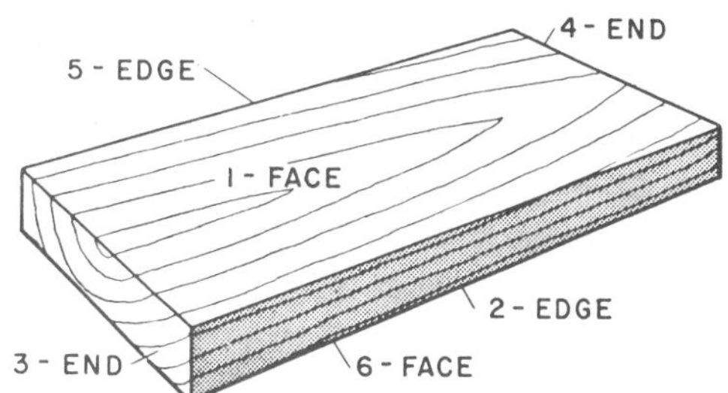

17-2. *Steps in squaring up stock.*

make all surfaces flat, all corners square, and all opposite sides parallel. The top of a stool or small table is a good example of a part that must be completely squared up. Fig. 17-1.

On plywood, you only have to plane the edges. The edges and ends are all the same in plywood.

TOOLS

You will need a jack or smooth plane, fore plane, and block plane, a try square, rule, pencil, marking gauge, and straightedge.

PROCEDURE

Squaring up stock is something every good woodworker must learn to do well. There are six steps. Fig. 17-2.

1. Plane the first, or face, surface true and smooth.
2. Plane the first, or face, edge. Mark the face surface and edge.
3. Plane the first end.
4. Measure the correct length and mark a line across the face surface and end. With a backsaw cut about 1/16 inch longer than the finished length. Plane the second end to correct length.
5. Plane to correct width. If the board is rather narrow, adjust the marking gauge to the correct width and mark a line along the face surface and the second surface. You can also use the other methods of gauging as described in Chapter 8. If the board is quite wide, mark the width at several points and then use a straightedge to draw a line showing the width. Saw to about 1/8 inch of the layout line. Now plane the second edge smooth, straight, and square.
6. Plane the second face. Adjust the marking gauge to correct thickness and mark a line from the face surface along the edges and ends. Plane to correct thickness. It is easy to remember the steps—face, edge, end; then reverse: end, edge, and face. Steps can be marked on the wood.

Some woodworkers like to square the stock in a different order. They plane the face surface, then the face edge, then the first end. Next, they plane the second edge, the second face, and finally the second end.

After squaring up stock, a cornering tool may be used to remove the sharp corners. Fig. 17-3.

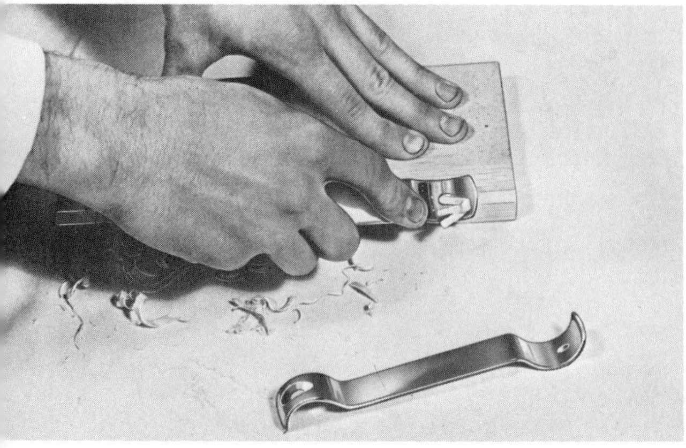

17-3. *Using a cornering tool to remove the sharp edge and to round the corner. (Stanley Tools)*

QUESTIONS

1. What does S2S mean?
2. Does stock always have to be completely squared up in order to use it for a project?
3. Is it better to plane the face edge before planing the face surface true and smooth?
4. How much material should be allowed for planing end grain?

ACTIVITIES

1. Prepare a checklist for the lab. The list should include all the steps for squaring up stock.
2. Across a sheet of paper, list the tools used for squaring up stock. Under each tool, list safety rules for using that tool.

LEARN THESE SAFETY RULES BEFORE SHARPENING TOOLS

* **Wear eye protection when using the grinder.**
* **Make sure the wheel guards are in place.**
* **Make sure the edge of the grinding wheel is straight and clean.**
* **Keep the tool rest on the grinder about 1/8″ from the wheel.**
* **Don't grind on the side of the wheel unless that machine is designed for it.**
* **Test for sharpness with a piece of paper or wood—not your finger.**

CHAPTER 18 Sharpening Planes and Chisels

Planes and chisels cut well only if they are sharp. Dull tools make woodworking difficult and results poor. Tools stay sharp a lot longer if handled correctly. The time you spend putting your tools in condition is rewarded in better work.

Two kinds of operations are done to sharpen tools. *Grinding* reshapes the cutting edge of the tool. It should be done only when the tool needs a new bevel or when the edge of the cutter is nicked. Otherwise, *honing*—sharpening the tip of the cutting edge—is enough.

TOOLS AND MATERIALS

Several kinds of power-driven grinders can be used to sharpen tools. A *slow-speed grinder* is good because there is little danger of overheating the tool blade. On a *fast-speed grinder* you must be careful not to hold the tool blade on the wheel too long. Fig. 18-1. Many grinders have a plane iron grinding attachment to guide the blade. Fig. 18-2. A *grinder hone* can be used for both grinding and honing cutting edges.

An *oilstone* is a fine-grained stone used to hone cutting edges. Fig. 18-3. Many oilstones are made from synthetic abrasives. The best type has a medium-coarse stone on one side and a finer abrasive on the other side. A natural stone is preferred by some woodworkers.

Oil is needed to do a faster sharpening job, to get a finer edge, and to keep the stone free of

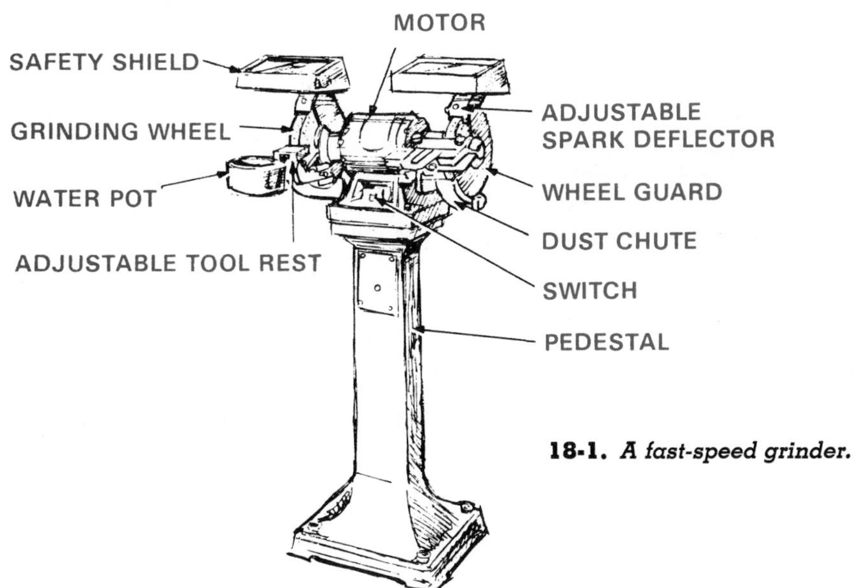

18-1. *A fast-speed grinder.*

18-2. *A plane iron grinding attachment. (Stanley Tools)*

18-3. *Oilstones like these are used to hone cutting edges.*

chips. A good mineral oil is recommended. The oil floats away metal particles and prevents wear on the stone.

A *sharpening holder* can be used to keep the tool at the correct angle. The holder can be adjusted to the correct bevel angle. Fig. 18-4.

18-4. *A sharpening holder controls the angle of the tool for honing.*

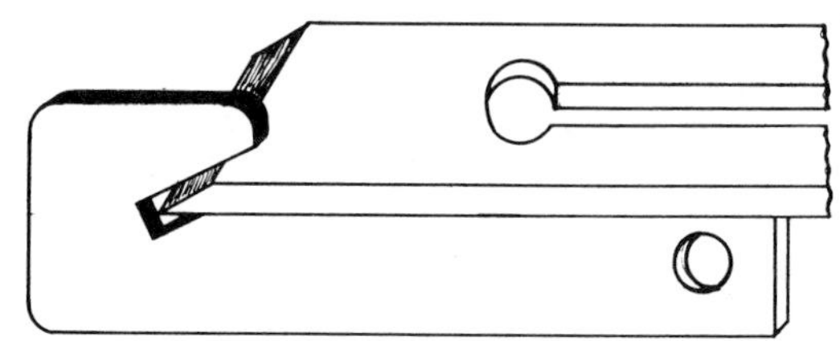

18-5. *Checking the angle of a plane iron blade with a gauge.*

A *bevel-grinding gauge* is needed to check the bevel after grinding. Fig. 18-5.

GRINDING A PLANE IRON BLADE

1. Loosen the screw that holds the plane iron cap to the plane iron. Separate the two parts.

2. Check the cutting edge of the plane iron under a light. If the cutting edge reflects light, it needs sharpening (honing). Are there nicks along the edge? Is the bevel rounded? If so, you must both grind and hone.

3. Hold a try square on the edge of the blade and check to see if the cutting edge is square with the sides. Fig. 18-6. A blade sharpened correctly for general work will have a straight cutting edge and the corners slightly rounded off. If it does not, grind off the old edge at right angles to the sides until any nicks are removed and the edge straightened. Fig. 18-7.

4. If a plane iron grinding attachment is available, fasten the blade in it with the bevel side

down. The bevel should be about twice the thickness of the blade. This will give a 30-degree angle to the cutting edge. Fig. 18-8.

5. If the grinder does not have an attachment, reverse the plane iron cap on the plane iron. Set the cap at right angles to the plane iron. Check this with a try square. Then hold the cap against the front edge of the tool rest. It may be necessary to move the cap toward or away from the cutting edge until the blade just touches the grinding wheel. Fig. 18-9.

6. Move the blade back and forth across the wheel face. Fig. 18-10. Remove the blade quite often and dip the edge in water to keep it cool. If the blade turns blue, it is overheating. If the edge

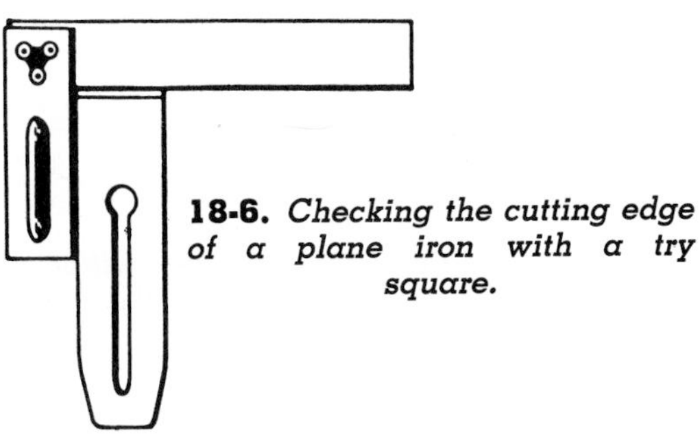

18-6. *Checking the cutting edge of a plane iron with a try square.*

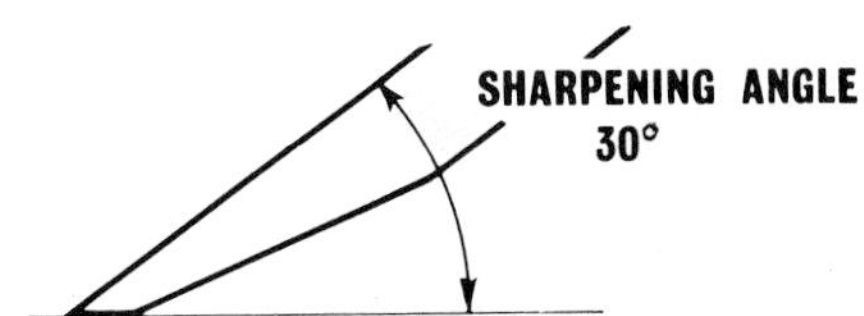

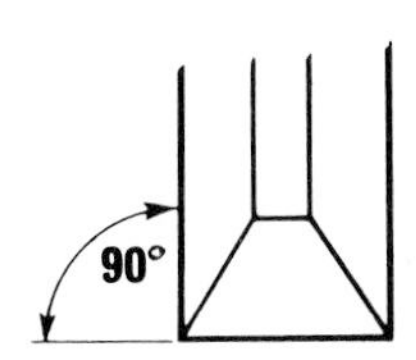

18-8. *The bevel should be about two times the thickness of the plane iron blade, or at an angle of 30 degrees. The cutting edge should be at right angles to the sides.*

18-7. *One way to square the edge is to move it back and forth across a coarse oilstone, holding it so that the edges are at right angles to the stone. This can also be done on the grinder.*

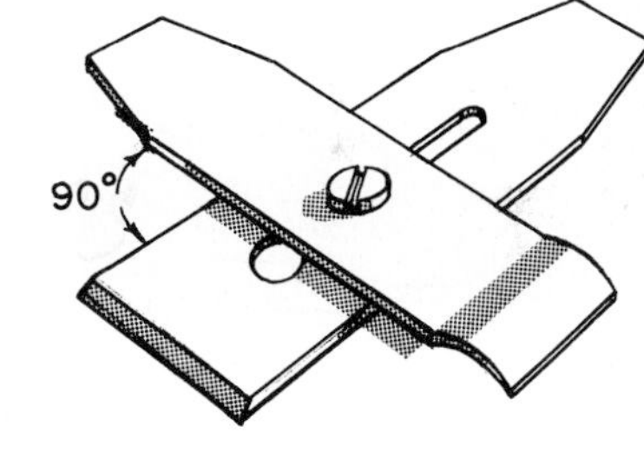

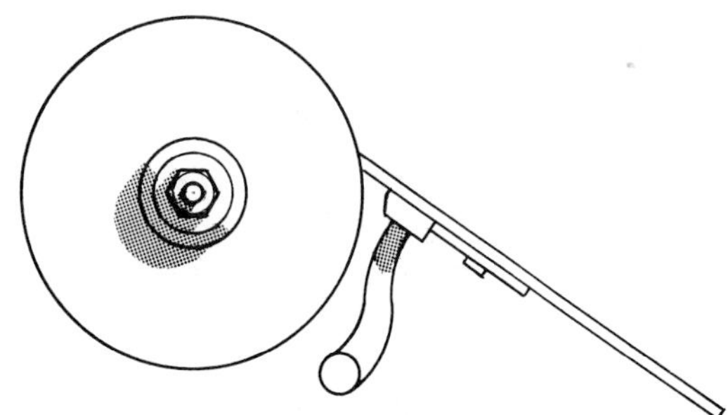

18-9. *Using the plane iron cap as a guide in grinding.*

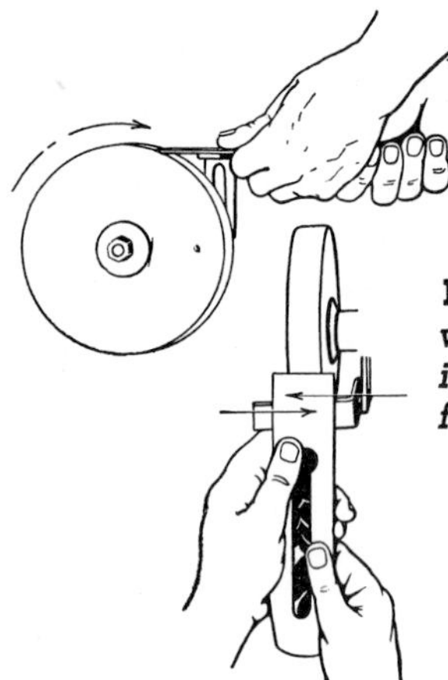

18-10. *The correct way to hold the plane iron. Move it back and forth as it is being ground.*

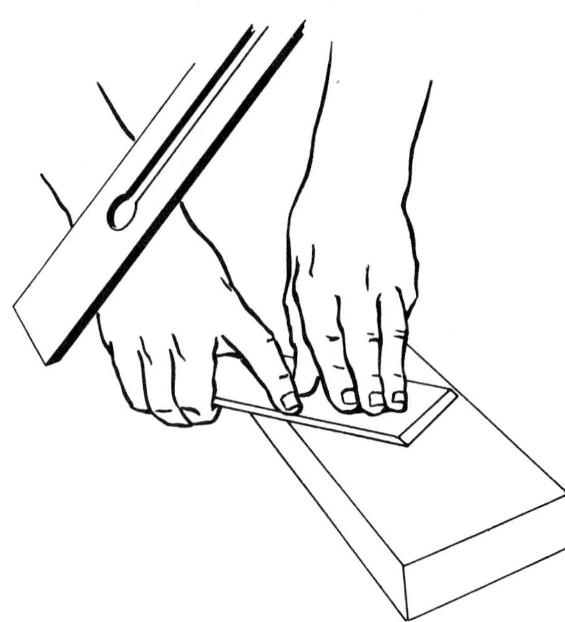

18-12. *Removing the burr from the cutting edge by holding the plane iron flat on the stone.*

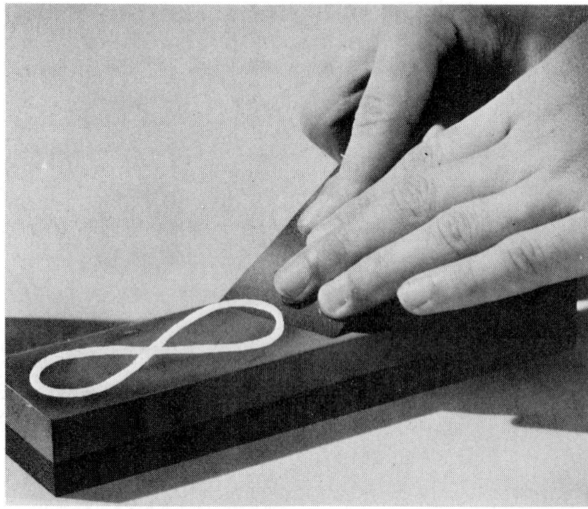

18-11. *Hold the plane iron at the same angle and move it in a figure 8. You could also move it back and forth in a straight line.*

is burned often, the blade will never hold a cutting edge again.

7. If you're grinding the blade "freehand," grind as close as possible to the same angle each time the blade is returned to the wheel. You must get the feel of the grinding. The beginner makes the mistake of holding the blade at different angles, making the bevel very uneven.

8. Continue to grind the blade until a wire edge (a very thin burr) appears.

HONING (WHETTING) THE BLADE

1. Apply a few drops of mineral oil to the face of the oilstone.

2. Place the blade at a very low angle to the surface, bevel side down. Now raise the end slowly until the blade makes an angle of about 30 to 35 degrees to the stone. Keep the blade at this angle.

3. To hone the edge, move the blade back and forth in a straight line or in a figure eight. Fig. 18-11. Be sure your hands move parallel to the stone so that the angle stays the same throughout the stroke.

4. Now turn the blade over and place it flat against the stone. Move it back and forth to remove the wire edge. Fig. 18-12. To help remove this wire edge, draw the cutting edge across a corner of a soft piece of wood.

5. To test for sharpness, try slicing a piece of paper with the blade. It should cut the paper easily.

6. A chisel is sharpened in the same way.

QUESTIONS

1. Why should planes and chisels be kept sharp?
2. Name three kinds of grinders.
3. At about what angle should the bevel be on a plane iron?
4. Why should the plane iron be kept cool when grinding it?
5. How should you test the sharpness of a plane iron blade?

ACTIVITIES

1. Check the plane irons in your lab. Do any of them need honing? Do any need both grinding and honing?
2. Demonstrate how to hone a plane iron blade. Be sure to observe safety rules.

Cutting Curves and Inside Openings

Many cutout designs and projects have curved edges, very sharp corners, or angles that must be cut with a thin saw blade. Fig. 19-1. Inside openings also must be cut with a narrow blade.

19-1. ***The curved shapes on this magazine rack can be cut with a coping saw. Of course, it would be faster to do the cutting with a power tool.***

TOOLS

The *coping saw* has a U-shaped frame which holds a replaceable blade. The blade can be adjusted to any angle to the frame. For example, it can be turned so that the teeth point in, toward the frame. Fig. 19-2.

The *compass saw* has a tapered blade that fits into a handle. It is really a fine-tooth crosscut saw. Sometimes several sizes of blades are furnished with the same handle. The compass saw is used to cut curves and inside openings. Fig. 19-3.

A *keyhole saw* is much like a compass saw except that it is smaller and has a shorter blade.

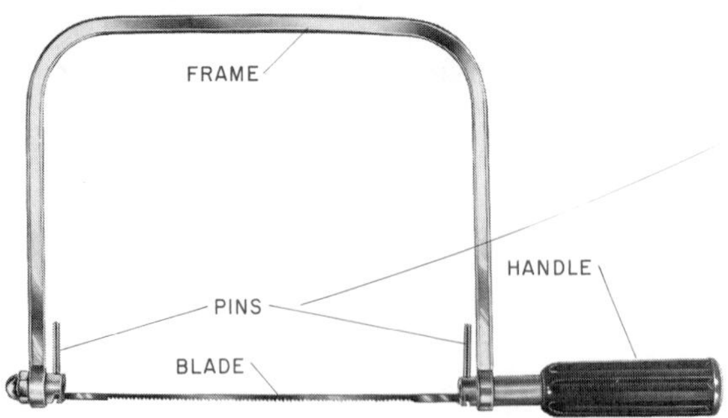

19-2. *Parts of a coping saw.*

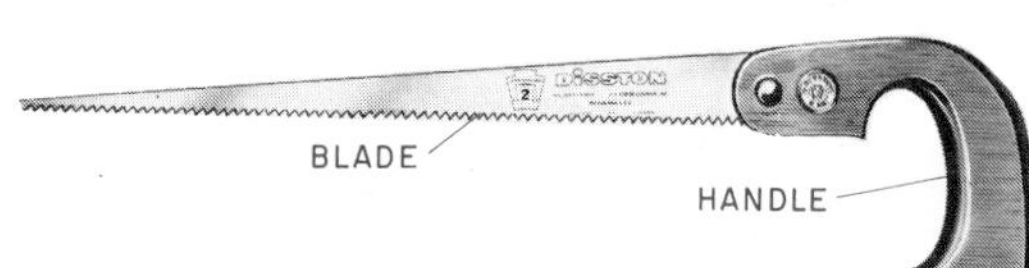

19-3. *Compass saw.*

"V"-BRACKET

USE 3/4" PLYWOOD FOR ALL PARTS

19-4. *Here's how to build a saw bracket that can be used with the coping saw.*

A *saw V bracket,* or *jack,* is a wooden support used with a coping saw. One type is a rectangular piece of wood with a V cut out of the end. This is clamped to the top of the table. The other type is clamped in a vise so that you can stand up to do the cutting. Fig. 19-4.

Coping saw blades are made in different widths with teeth similar to a ripsaw. Blades with ten to fifteen teeth to the inch are used for wood, while those with twenty and thirty-two teeth are for cutting metal. Another type of blade has spiral-shaped teeth that will saw up or down, right or left, or in circles.

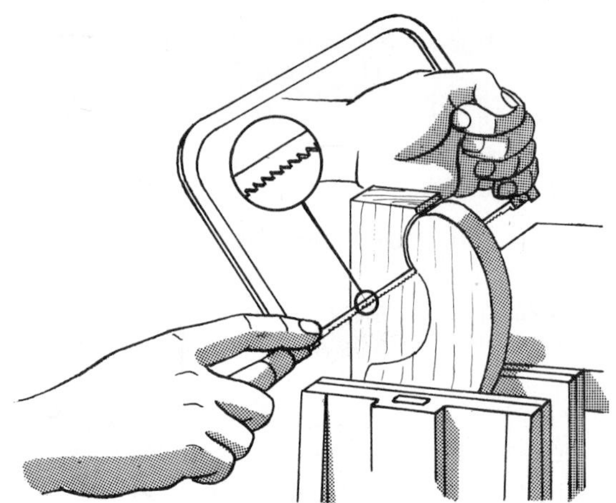

19-5. *Sawing a curve with the work held in a vise. The teeth must be pointed away from the handle.*

USING A COPING SAW WITH THE WORK HELD IN THE VISE

1. Fasten the work in the vise with the start of the layout line just above the vise jaws. Move the work away from the top of the vise a little at a time as the cutting proceeds. If the sawing is done too far away from the vise, the work vibrates and makes the cutting difficult.

2. Install a blade in the frame with the teeth pointing *away from the handle.*

3. Hold the saw in both hands as shown in Fig. 19-5. Cut just outside the layout line, using even strokes. Apply a little pressure as you push forward. Release the pressure as you pull back.

4. Guide the saw frame so that the saw follows the line. At sharp curves, move the saw

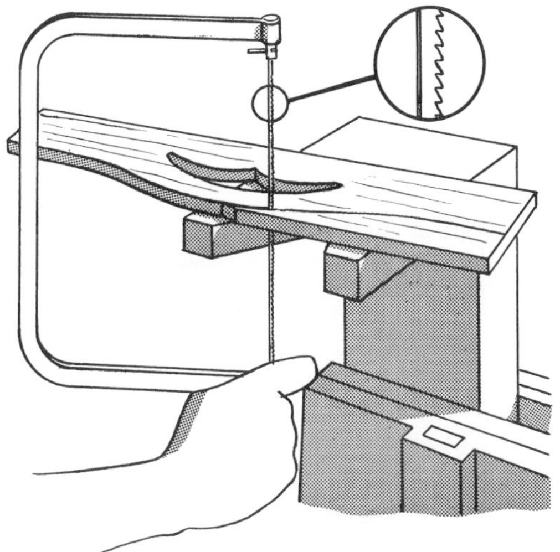

19-6. *The teeth must be pointed toward the handle.*

19-7. *Using a coping saw with the work held over a saw bracket or jack.*

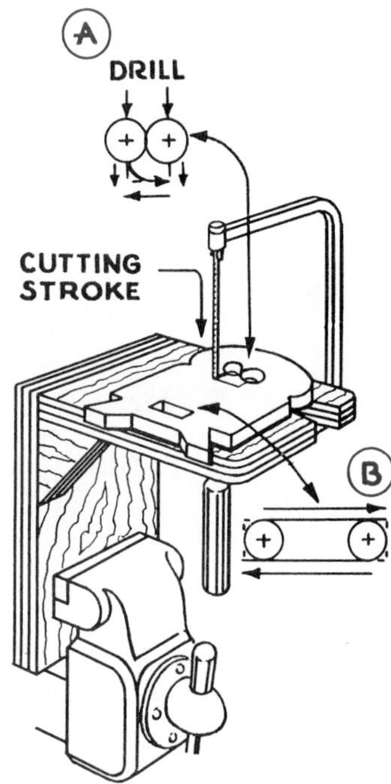

19-8. *In cutting an inside opening, drill or bore holes in the waste stock. You could also make them part of the design.*

back and forth as you slowly turn the frame without applying much pressure. *Do not twist the saw,* as this will break the blade.

5. The blade can be turned at any angle to the frame. Make sure both pins are turned the same amount. For example, to make a long cut, adjust the blade at a right angle to the frame.

USING A COPING SAW WITH THE WORK HELD OVER A SAW JACK OR V BRACKET

1. Clamp the bracket to the bench or in the vise.

2. Fasten a blade in the frame with the teeth pointing *toward the handle.* The cutting is done on the down stroke. Fig. 19-6.

3. Hold the work firmly on the bracket, with the area to be cut near the bottom of the V. Fig. 19-7.

4. Draw down on the saw to cut. Move the work so that the cutting is always near the bottom of the V.

5. For inside cutting, drill or bore a hole in the waste stock. Fig. 19-8. Remove the blade from the frame. Then slip the blade through the hole

19-9. ***Cutting an inside curve with the compass saw. Note that a hole has been bored in the waste stock close to the layout line.***

and fasten it in the frame again. Cut up to and around the design. Then remove the blade.

USING A COMPASS SAW

This saw is best for sawing gentle curves in heavy stock.

1. For outside curves, use short strokes. Twist the handle slightly to follow the curve. Do not force the saw, as it may bend or buckle.

2. For inside curves, bore a hole in the waste stock to start the cutting. Fig. 19-9. Sometimes a hole is part of the design. Start the saw, using short strokes. Work slowly. For very small openings, use the keyhole saw, which is like a miniature compass saw.

QUESTIONS

1. List three kinds of saws for cutting curves and irregular shapes.
2. In using a coping saw with the work held in a vise, how should the blade be installed in the frame?
3. Why must the work be held securely when using a coping saw?
4. How should the blade be placed in a coping saw when cutting with the work held over a V bracket?
5. What must you do before you can cut an inside opening?
6. What is the difference between a keyhole saw and a compass saw?

ACTIVITIES

1. Look around your home and find examples of furniture or other products that have curved edges, sharp corners, or angles that might have been cut with a narrow saw blade. Describe these examples to the class.
2. Suppose you are preparing a tool catalog. Write descriptions of a coping saw, compass saw, and keyhole saw. Put pictures or drawings next to your descriptions.

CHAPTER 20

Cutting a Chamfer, Bevel, or Taper

Three angle surfaces cut in the same way are the chamfer, bevel, and taper. A *chamfer* is a slanted surface made by cutting off an edge, end, or corner. The chamfer is cut only partway down, usually at an angle of 45 degrees. Fig. 20-1. A chamfer is cut in order to remove the sharp edge and improve appearance. A *bevel* is a sloping edge or end. Fig. 20-2. It is used, for example, to fit two pieces together to form a V shape. A *taper* is a cut that becomes gradually smaller toward one end. Fig. 20-3. For example, tent pegs and the legs of tables, chairs, and stools are often tapered. Sometimes all four sides of a leg are tapered. At other times only the two inside sides may be tapered.

TOOLS

The *sliding T bevel* is used to lay out and check angles, especially those other than 45 or 90 degrees. Fig. 20-4. It consists of a handle with an adjustable blade. A clamping screw at one end of the handle locks the blade. To set a bevel, use a protractor or carpenter's square. A protractor is used if you must set the bevel at an "odd" angle, such as 62 degrees. Fig. 20-5. To set a sliding T bevel to a 45-degree angle, hold the blade of the bevel across the corner of a carpenter's square until there is equal distance on the body and

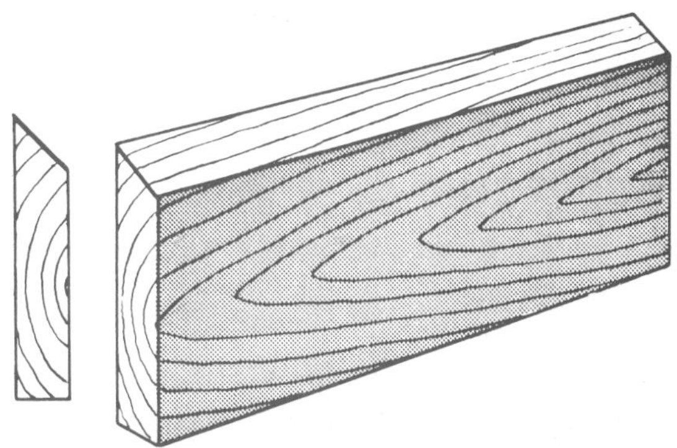

20-2. ***A bevel. Note that it is cut all the way across the edge.***

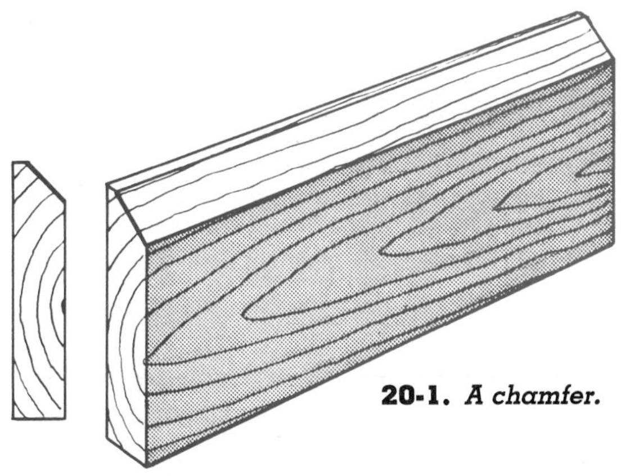

20-1. ***A chamfer.***

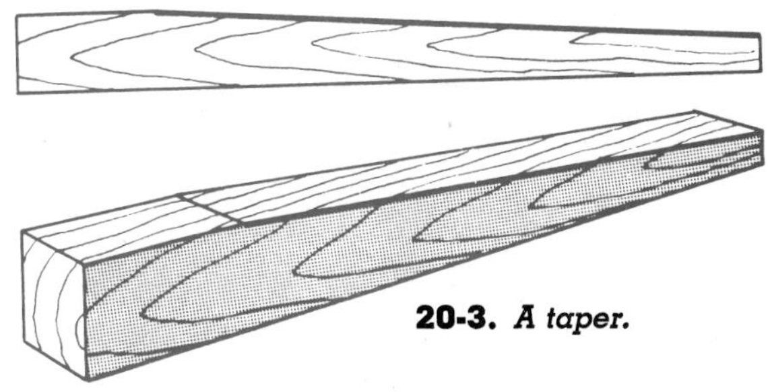

20-3. ***A taper.***

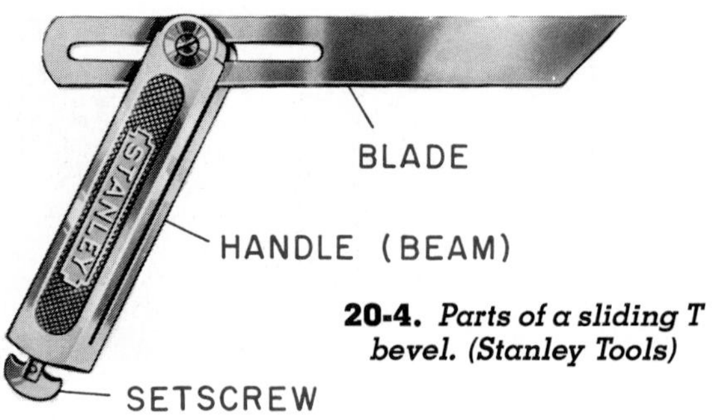

20-4. *Parts of a sliding T bevel. (Stanley Tools)*

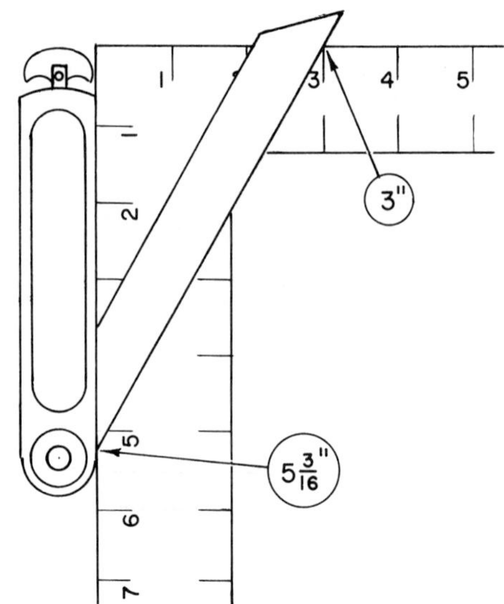

20-6. *Setting the blade to 3 inches on the tongue and 5³⁄16 inches on the blade of the carpenter's square. This setting gives angles of 30 and 60 degrees.*

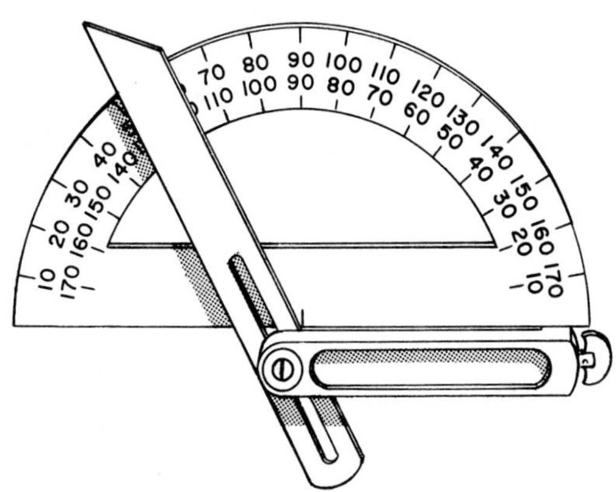

20-5. *Using a metal protractor to adjust the sliding T bevel. Loosen the nut slightly, so that the blade will just move, and set the blade to the correct angle. Then retighten the nut.*

tongue. To set a 30- or 60-degree angle, set the blade to 3 inches on the tongue and 5³⁄16 inches on the body. Fig. 20-6.

Other tools you need for making chamfers, bevels, and tapers are a plane, pencil, rule, and try square.

CUTTING A CHAMFER

1. Decide on the amount of the chamfer. For example, on ¾-inch stock, the chamfer usually is made ³⁄16 to ¼ inch.

2. Lay out the lines for all chamfers with a pencil. *Never use a marking gauge.* The spur of the marking gauge will cut a groove that never comes out.

3. Clamp the work in a vise with the chamfer side toward you and somewhat above the top of the vise.

4. Tilt the plane at about a 45-degree angle and begin to plane. Fig. 20-7. You may guide the plane by curling the fingers of your left hand under the bottom of the plane. Make the movements of the plane even and long.

5. After you have planed partway, check the chamfer with a try square. Fig. 20-8. Is there about an equal amount to be removed to bring it to the layout lines? If not, you might have to tilt the plane more in the direction where the most stock must be removed. You can also check the chamfer with a sliding T bevel.

6. Always plane the chamfer *with the grain* (along the edges) first.

7. To plane end grain, clamp the work rather high in a vise. Make a shearing cut to plane the chamfer. This is done by holding the plane at an angle as well as at a tilt. Fig. 20-9.

8. For small work a block plane is a good tool to use.

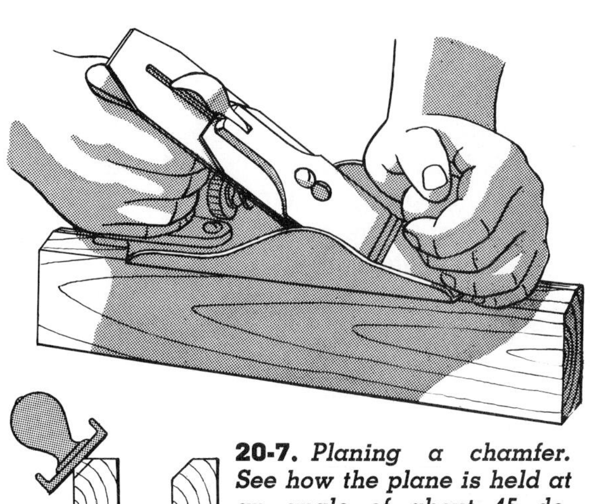

20-7. *Planing a chamfer. See how the plane is held at an angle of about 45 degrees.*

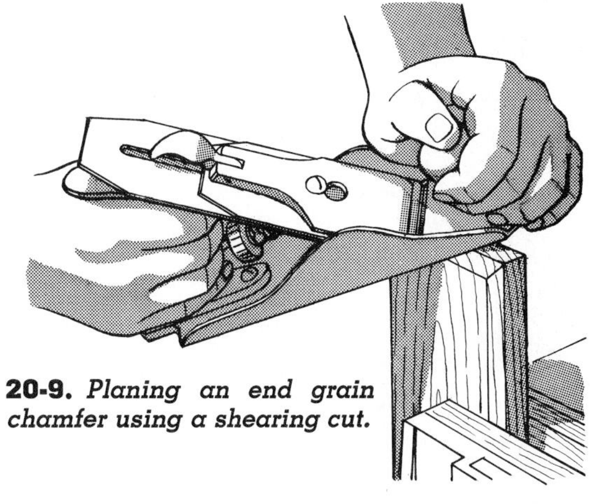

20-9. *Planing an end grain chamfer using a shearing cut.*

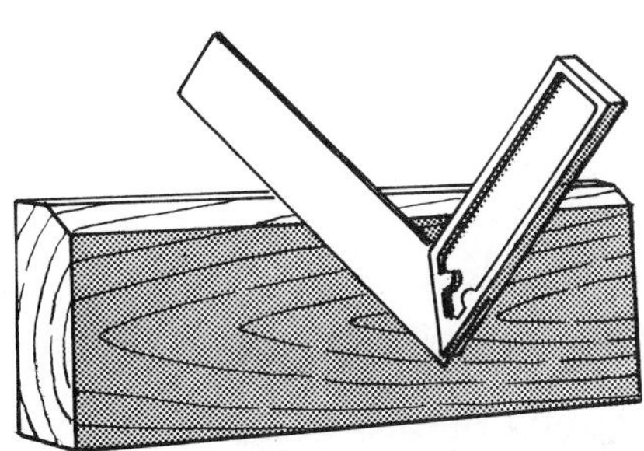

20-8. *Checking a chamfer to make sure it is even.*

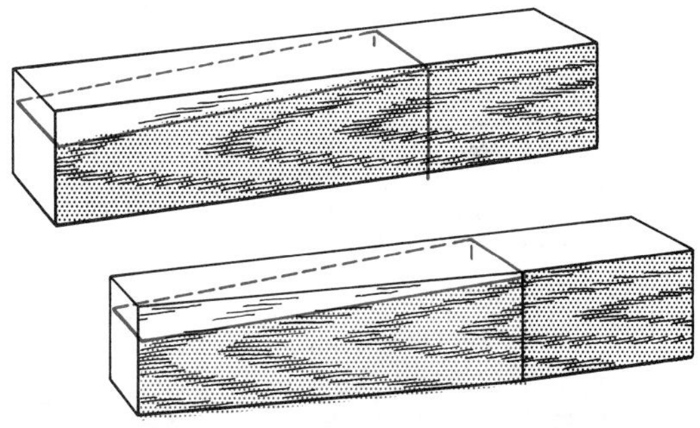

20-10. ***When the taper is to be cut on two adjoining surfaces, one side should be laid out and cut before the second layout is made.***

CUTTING A BEVEL

1. Determine the angle of the bevel and adjust the sliding T bevel to that angle.

2. Mark a line across the ends of the stock to show the bevel angle. Then draw a line across the second surface of the board as a guide.

3. Plane the bevel as you did a chamfer. Check frequently with the T bevel to be sure you are cutting it at the correct angle.

CUTTING A TAPER

1. Mark a line around the leg to show how far the taper will go.

2. If the leg is to be tapered on all four sides, first mark the two opposite sides on one end to show the amount of the taper. Draw lines along the legs to show the stock to be removed. If the leg is tapered only on two adjoining sides, mark the taper on one side only. Fig. 20-10.

3. If it is a rather sharp taper, saw away some of the waste stock. Planing is usually enough, however.

4. Clamp the work in a vise with the taper line parallel with the top.

5. Start planing near the end of the leg. Each cut will be a little longer until you have reached the taper line.

6. After you have planed both sides (or one side if only two are to be tapered), lay out and cut the taper on the other sides (or side).

QUESTIONS

1. Describe a chamfer.
2. How is a bevel different from a chamfer?
3. What is a taper?
4. What is the usual size of a chamfer on ¾-inch stock?
5. Why should a marking gauge never be used in laying out a chamfer?
6. What tool do you need to lay out a bevel?
7. Where is a taper most commonly used?

ACTIVITIES

1. Look around your home for furniture or other products that have chamfers, bevels or tapers. Write a description of the examples you find.
2. Demonstrate how to set a sliding T bevel to an angle of 75 degrees.

LEARN THESE SAFETY RULES BEFORE USING CHISELS AND KNIVES

✻ Clamp the work securely before using a chisel.

✻ Use mallets only with socket or solid tang chisels. If a mallet is used with a pointed tang chisel, the tang may split the handle.

✻ Always use a wood or plastic mallet—never a metal hammer—to strike the handle of the chisel.

✻ Keep your hands away from the front of the cutting edge when working.

✻ Chisel away from your body—not toward it.

✻ Never strike the cutting edge of the tool on metal, such as the edge of a vise, a nail or wood screw, or other metal objects.

✻ Keep the edge of the chisel sharp.

✻ Never file the edges of a chisel.

✻ Never use a chisel for prying open a paint can or similar jobs.

Cutting with Chisels

A *chisel* is a strong, steel cutting tool with a sharp bevel edge at one end. Chisels are used to shape and fit parts. Fig. 21-1. It is important to know how to choose a sharp chisel and how to handle it correctly. It is easy to cut yourself because the chisel has a sharp, exposed blade. Keep your fingers clear of the cutting edge while working.

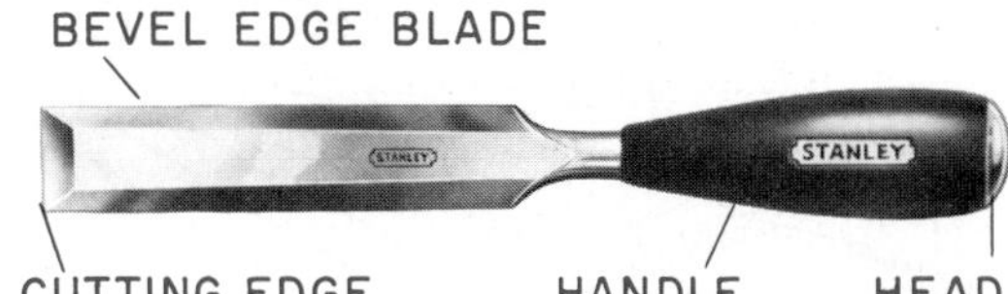

***21-2(a).** A solid tang chisel. The tang, or shank, extends all the way through the handle and is attached to a steel head. (Stanley Tools)*

TOOLS

There are three types of chisels: the *pointed tang* (also called *shank*), the *solid tang*, and the *socket* type. Fig. 21-2. The pointed tang chisel has a short point, or tang, that extends into the wood handle. Present-day solid tang chisels have the blade and tang in one piece. The tang extends all the way through the handle to a metal cap. The socket chisel has a socket (cup shape) at the end of the blade into which the handle fits.

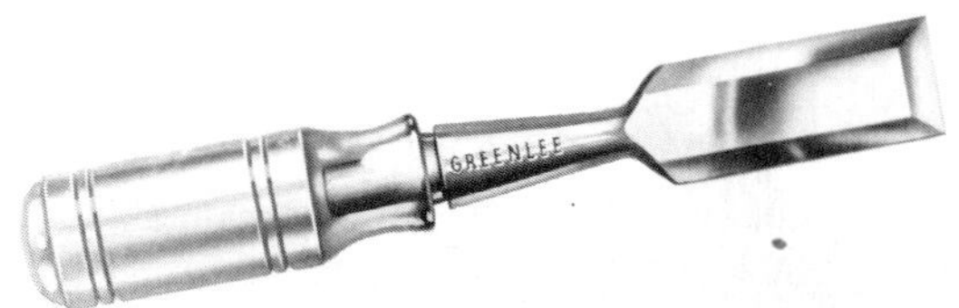

***21-2(b).** A socket chisel. The handle fits into the socket (the cup-shaped part of the blade).*

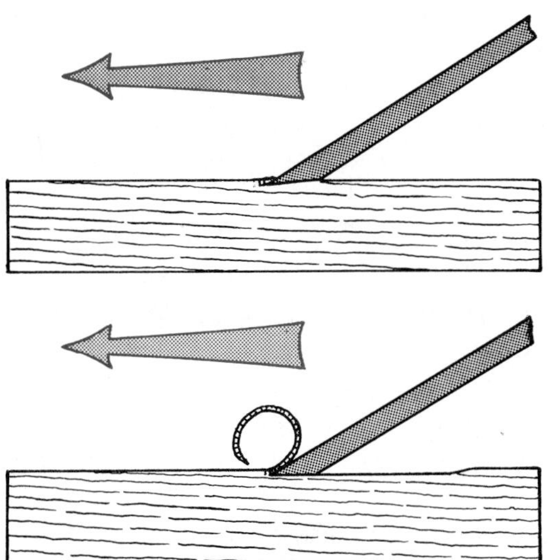

21-1. *Using a chisel. Remember the six simple machines. The cutting edge of a chisel is half a* **wedge.** *The sharper the wedge, the better the machine. That is why sharp cutting tools are so important. The handle is a* **lever.** *The upper side of the blade acts as an* **inclined plane** *to allow the chip to move more easily up the machine.*

Chisel size is shown by blade widths. The widths range from ⅛ to 1 inch, in ⅛-inch intervals, and from 1 inch to 2 inches in ¼-inch intervals. The most common sizes are ¼, ½, ¾, 1, 1¼, and 1½ inch.

A *mallet* is a short-handled hammer with a large head made of wood, rawhide, or plastic. It is used to strike a socket or solid tang chisel for heavy cutting. Fig. 21-3.

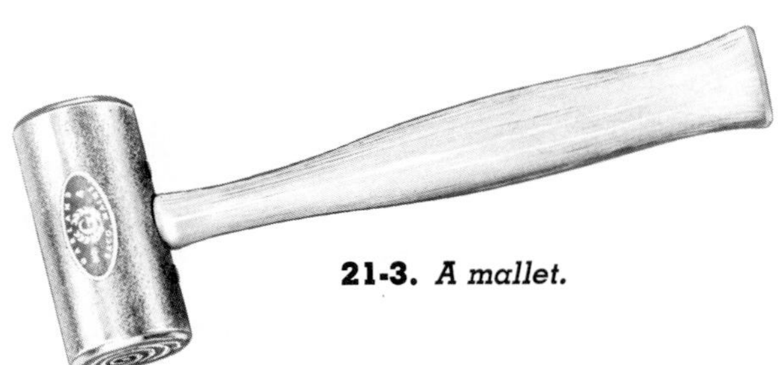

21-3. *A mallet.*

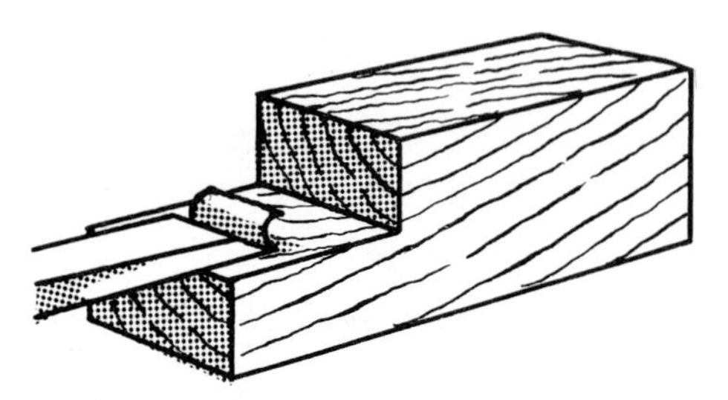

21-4. ***Always cut with the grain or across it. Avoid cutting against the grain.***

HORIZONTAL CUTTING ACROSS GRAIN

1. Select a socket or solid tang chisel. Make sure it is sharp and free of nicks.

2. Clamp the work in a vise or fasten it to the top of the bench. Cut across grain or with the grain, never against it. Fig. 21-4. "Against the grain" means that the chisel slopes down into the wood. When you cut against the grain, the chisel tends to dig into the wood and split it rather than cut it.

3. To remove large amounts of wood, turn the chisel with the *bevel side down.*

4. Hold the chisel in one hand. Use your other hand to strike the chisel with a mallet. Cut from both sides towards the center. Fig. 21-5. Cutting from one side will chip out the opposite edge.

5. When the cutting is within about 1/8 inch of the layout line, continue the cutting by hand rather than with the mallet.

6. For light trimming, turn the chisel with the *bevel up.* Fig. 21-6. Guide the blade by pressing the hand that holds the chisel against the edge of the wood. Work at a slight angle to the grain.

21-5. ***Making rough cuts with the bevel side down. Strike the chisel with a mallet. Cut from both sides toward the center.***

7. Apply pressure with your other hand, cutting a little at a time. Sometimes you must swing the handle from side to side to do the cutting.

8. Be sure to hold the flat side parallel with the work but at an angle to the grain.

HORIZONTAL CUTTING WITH THE GRAIN

1. Clamp the work in a vise in such a way that you can cut with the grain.

2. For heavy cutting, hold the chisel with the bevel side down. For light paring cuts, hold the chisel with the bevel side up.

3. Grasp the blade in your left hand and the handle in your right hand. Reverse if left-handed.

4. Press forward as you push the cutting edge into the wood.

5. Guide the chisel so that the cut isn't too deep.

21-6. ***For light chiseling (trimming), hold the bevel side up. For heavier cutting, place the bevel side down.***

21-7. *Cutting vertically across the grain. Notice how the left hand guides the chisel as the right hand applies pressure.*

6. Sometimes it is better to move the handle back and forth in a short arc as you push.

VERTICAL CUTTING ACROSS GRAIN

1. Place the work over a bench hook or scrap stock.

2. Hold the chisel with the flat side against the wood.

3. Rest one hand on the wood to guide the chisel and use your other hand to apply pressure. Fig. 21-7.

4. Take a light cut. Apply pressure and move the handle in an arc from an angle to a vertical position. This makes a shearing cut.

5. To cut a chamfer across the grain, fasten the stock in a vise. Hold the chisel at an angle of 45 degrees. Swing the handle back and forth, making a slicing cut. Fig. 21-8.

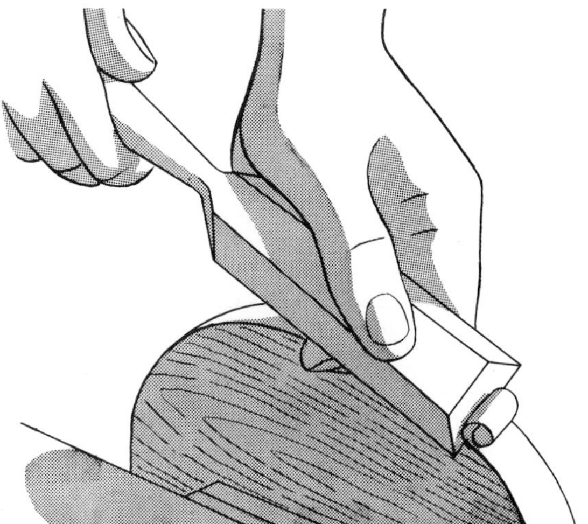

21-9. *Cutting a convex curve. Raise the handle a little at a time to follow the curve.*

CUTTING A CONVEX (CURVED-OUT) SURFACE

1. Clamp the work in a vise so that the cutting can be done with the grain (towards the end grain).

2. Hold the chisel with the flat side down. Fig. 21-9.

3. Guide the chisel with one hand and press forward with the other. Move the handle in an arc that is the same as the convex surface.

21-8. *Chamfering across the grain. Chisel at 45°, producing a slicing cut.*

CUTTING A CONCAVE (CURVED-IN) SURFACE

1. Hold the chisel with the bevel side down. Cut with the grain. Fig. 21-10.
2. Move the handle toward you as you press forward.

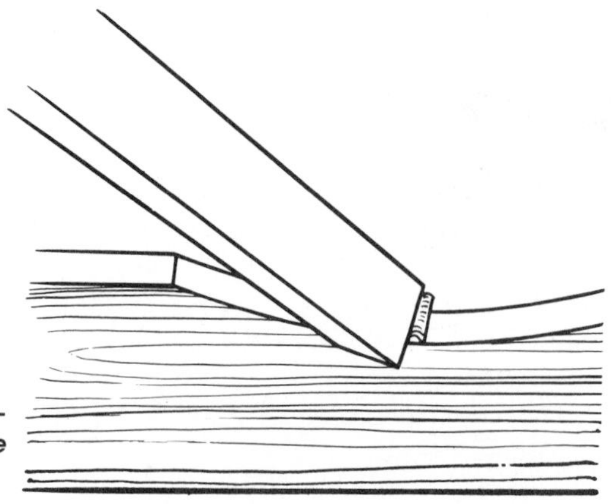

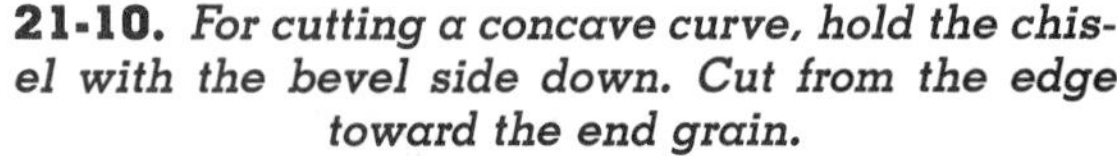

21-10. *For cutting a concave curve, hold the chisel with the bevel side down. Cut from the edge toward the end grain.*

QUESTIONS

1. Name the parts of a chisel.
2. Describe two types of chisels.
3. What is a mallet? How does it differ from a hammer?
4. What is meant by convex? Concave?
5. In which direction should you cut when chiseling a convex surface?

ACTIVITIES

1. The caption for Fig. 21-1 explains that a chisel includes three simple machines. Make a drawing of a chisel and label the parts that act as a wedge, a lever, and an inclined plane.
2. Demonstrate how to hold a chisel for horizontal cutting across the grain. Explain safety rules as you demonstrate.

Shaping with Gouges, Carving Tools, and Knives

To shape such things as the inside of a fruit tray, model boat hull, or carved animal figure you need sharp gouges and carving tools. Fig. 22-1. Tools are made in many different shapes and sizes to do all kinds of shaping, carving, and whittling. Fig. 22-2.

TOOLS

A *gouge* is a chisel with a curved blade. It is used to cut grooves and holes and to shape openings in wood. Gouges come in common blade sizes from ⅛ inch to 2 inches. The size is measured between corners. The blade may be

22-1(a). ***This attractive fruit bowl is the kind of project that can be made by shaping the wood with gouges.***

sharpened or ground on the inside or the outside. The outside-ground gouge is more common. The inside gouge is needed for cutting a curve that runs vertically. Fig. 22-3.

A *carving-tool set* is a group of gouges, each with a different shape of blade. These are used for detailed carving and shaping. Fig. 22-4.

A *carving set* has replaceable blades of different shapes for model making, hand carving, and whittling. Fig. 22-5.

Another carving tool is the *sloyd knife.* Fig. 22-6. You may also use a utility knife.

A regular mallet or a *carver's mallet* may be used. Fig. 22-7.

WOODS FOR WHITTLING AND CARVING

The kind of wood to use depends on what you want to make. For example, balsawood, a light, soft wood, is suitable for most model parts. Softwoods such as white pine, cedar, and redwood are good for less expensive projects. For very fine carvings, woods such as walnut, cherry, or mahogany are good choices. All woods selected should be free of knots, checks, and other defects.

USING A GOUGE

1. Mark the area to be removed by the gouge.

2. Fasten the work in a vise or clamp it to the bench top with a hand clamp. Fig. 22-8.

3. Rest the blade of the gouge in your left hand and the handle in your right. (If left-handed, reverse these procedures.)

4. Start near the center of the waste area. Hold the gouge at an angle of about 30 degrees and make long strokes with the grain. Guide the blade with your left hand. (If left-handed, guide the blade with your right hand.)

5. Force the gouge into the wood only enough to remove a long, thin shaving. To cut end grain, move the cutting edge in a circular motion.

6. To remove a great amount of waste stock, strike the end of the gouge with a mallet to drive the blade into the wood. Fig. 22-9.

22-1(b). ***The figure on this clock is hand carved.***

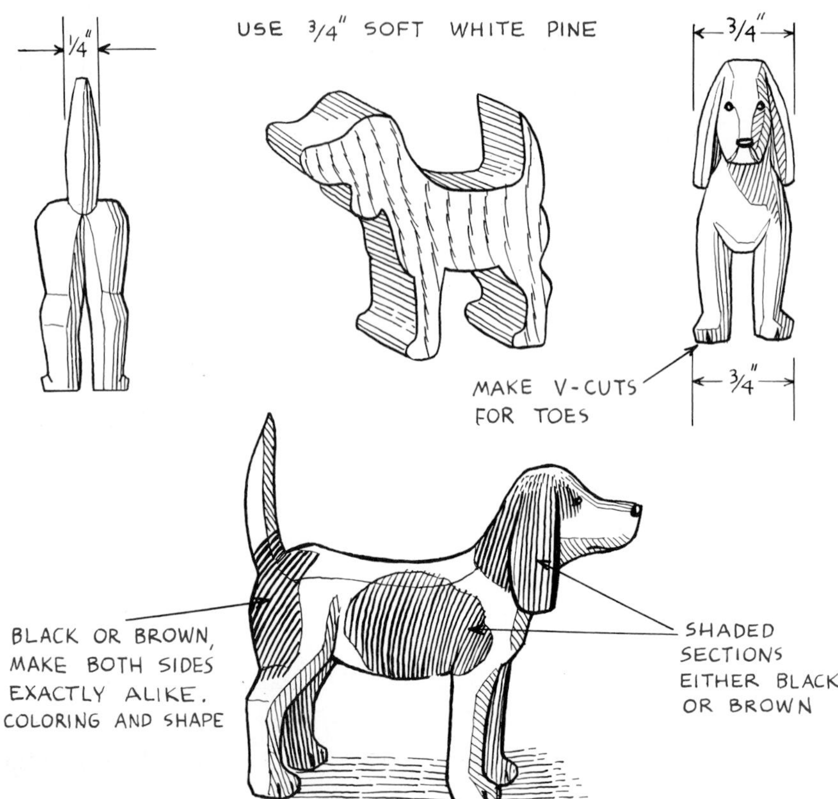

22-2. *A project made by whittling.*

22-3. *Notice the difference in shape between an outside and an inside gouge.*

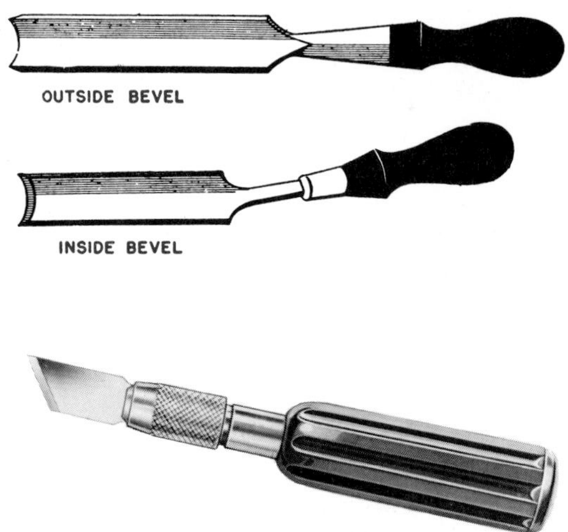

22-5. *A carving set comes with a handle and replaceable blades.*

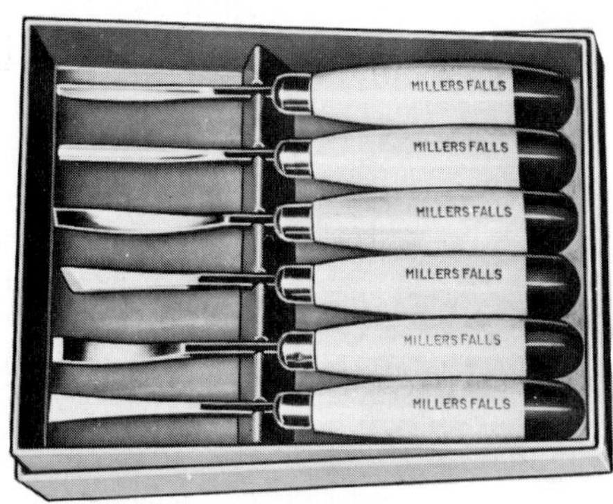

22-4. *A carving-tool set.*

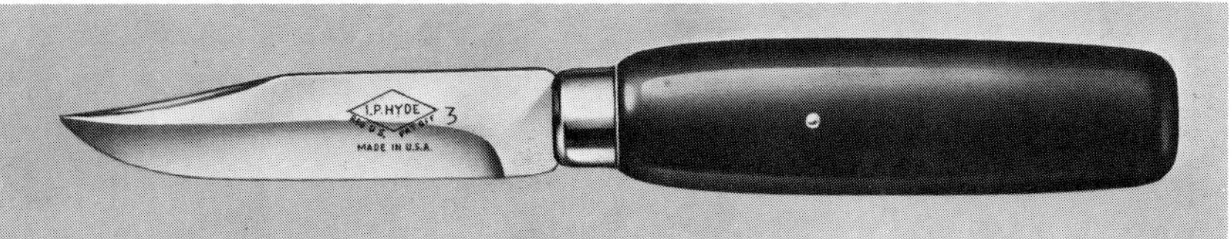

22-6. *Sloyd knife.*

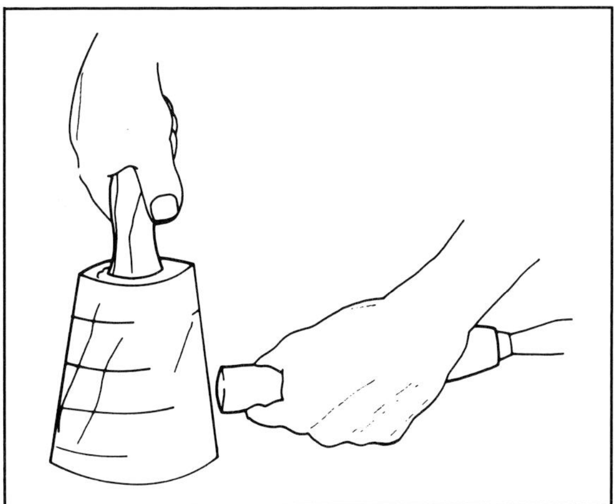

22-7. ***A carver's mallet has a different shape from a standard mallet. It is made of a very hard and dense wood.***

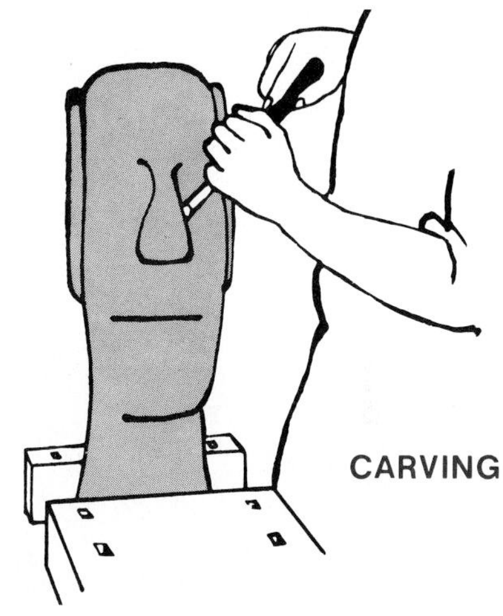

22-8. ***For a larger object, carving can be done with the piece held in a vise.***

7. As you approach the layout line, take thin shavings in all directions from the layout line toward the center. Fig. 22-10.

8. Sand the surface to remove small irregularities.

USING CARVING TOOLS

Carving tools are used in the same general manner as gouges. Roughly shape the work with a gouge and with the large blades of the carving tools. For detail work, use the specially shaped tools.

WOOD CARVING OR WHITTLING

1. Lay out the general shape of the model on stock of the correct size.

2. Cut out the rough shape with a jigsaw and/or a coping saw.

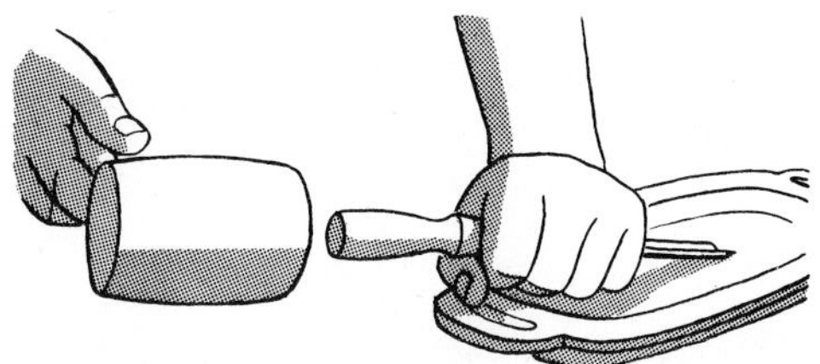

22-9. ***Removing waste stock by striking the gouge with the mallet.***

3. Using a sharp knife, start the whittling in the corners or where the detail is greatest. Cut with the grain.

4. Always cut away from yourself if possible. Fig. 22-11. Sometimes you'll need to cut toward yourself. At all times be especially careful that the knife doesn't slip. Fig. 22-12.

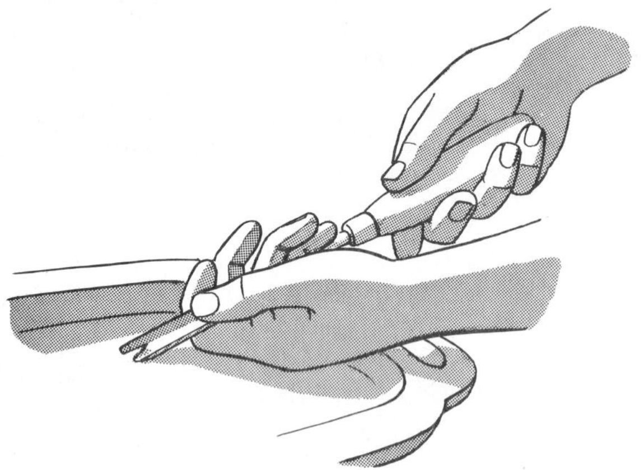

22-10. *Final shaping of a tray.*

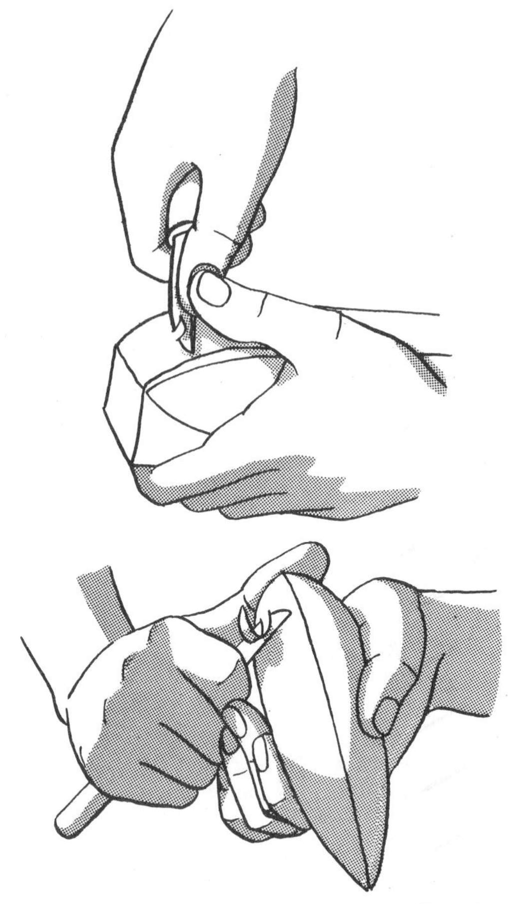

22-12. *Two methods of whittling: pull and push. When pulling the knife, keep your thumb below and out of the way of the cutting edge.*

22-11. *A safe way to use a knife.*

5. Shape both sides the same, cutting a little at a time. Fig. 22-13.

USING POWER CARVING TOOLS

Several models of high-speed power carving tools are available. These power tools usually come in a kit with a variety of cutter shapes. The shapes range from ball shapes to cones to circular cutters like miniature saw blades. These tools are used to cut and shape hardwoods, softwoods, and plastics. With a little practice you can do all kinds of internal and external carving. Fig. 22-14.

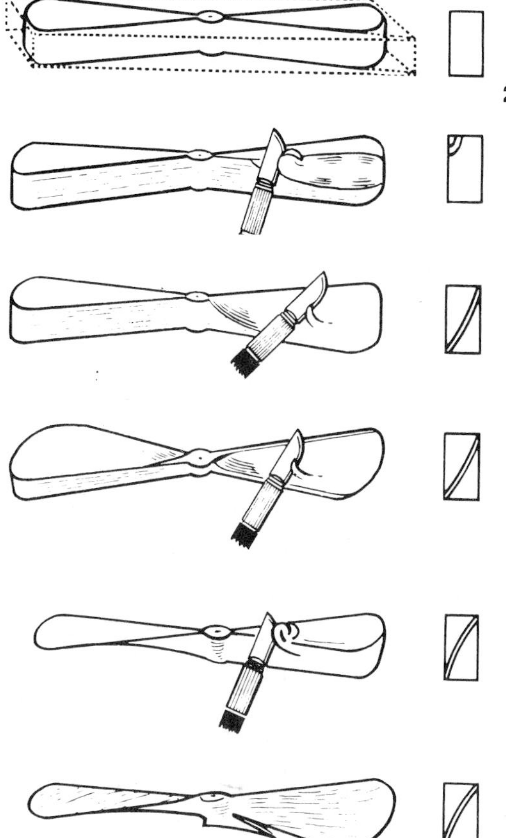

22-13. *Steps in shaping a balsawood propeller for a model airplane.*

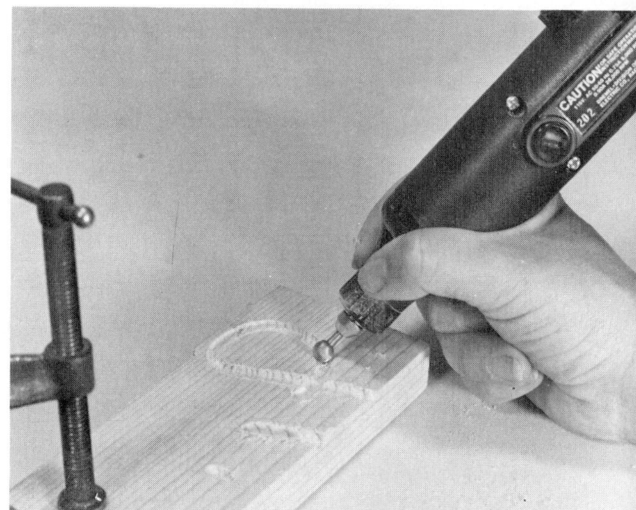

22-14. *When carving with a power tool, rest the heel of your hand on the table as a pivot point. Guide the tool with your fingers. It is a good idea to practice on a piece of scrap wood.*

QUESTIONS

1. What is a gouge?
2. What are the uses of carving tools?
3. Name two types of gouges.
4. Describe the way to use a gouge for removing a large amount of material.
5. When should a mallet be used with a gouge?
6. Name at least two safety rules for doing wood carving or whittling.

ACTIVITIES

1. In your home, find wooden items that have been shaped by carving or whittling. With your parents' permission, bring one item to class.
2. You can practice whittling on a bar of soap. Try making a car or some other simple shape. Be sure to follow safety rules.

LEARN THESE SAFETY RULES BEFORE USING RASPS AND FILES

* Make sure the tool has a handle.
* Keep files and rasps clean; use a file card. Never strike the tool on the edge of the bench to loosen chips.
* Never use a file or rasp as a pry bar. It is brittle and will break.
* Hold the work firmly in a vise or on a workbench.

Other Shaping Tools

To form irregularly shaped objects such as carved figures, models, and parts for projects, several different shaping tools are used. The most common are the *spokeshave, files, rasps,* and the *multi-tooth (Surform) tools.*

TOOLS

The *spokeshave* is a small cutting tool much like a simple plane. It has a handle on each side. It was named the spokeshave because it was originally used to shape the spokes of wagon wheels. It has a frame about 10 to 12 inches long, a blade, and a cap. The blade can be adjusted with two small thumb nuts. It is a very safe tool to use. Fig. 23-1.

There are many shapes of files, but the most common ones for woodworking are *half-round cabinet* and *flat wood* files in lengths of 8, 10, or 12 inches. Figs. 23-2 and 23-3. Wood files usually have double-cut teeth. That is, there are two rows of teeth cut diagonally across the face. The file is not as rough as the wood rasp.

The *rasp* is a tool with individual cutting teeth. Fig. 23-4. It removes material faster than a file but leaves a rougher surface.

A *file cleaner,* or *file card,* is needed to keep the teeth of the file or rasp clean and free of wood, resin, or finishing materials. Fig. 23-5.

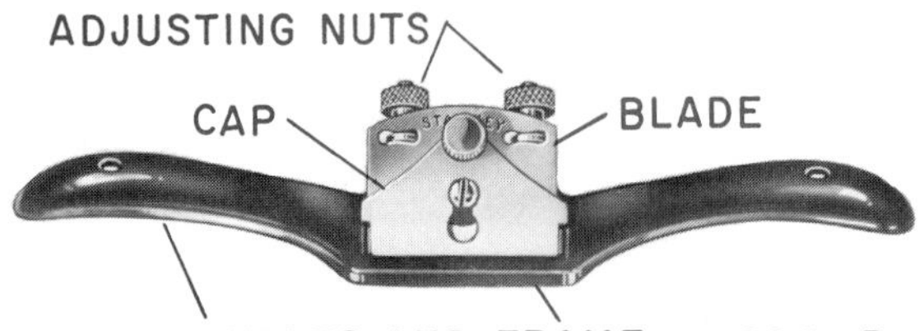

23-1. *Parts of a spokeshave. (Stanley Tools)*

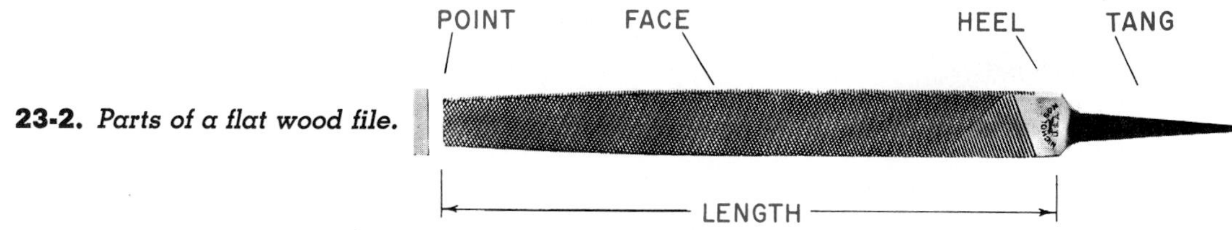

23-2. *Parts of a flat wood file.*

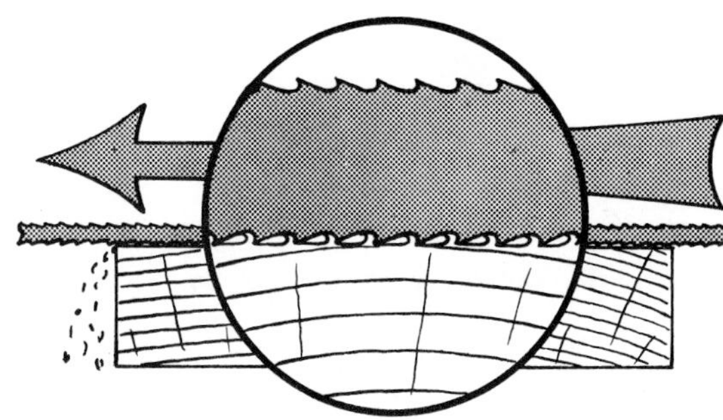

23-3. ***Cutting with a file. Remember the six simple machines. A file or rasp is made up of many small wedges. The force you apply to the handle is divided among the many teeth so that there is a smaller force at each wedge to do the cutting.***

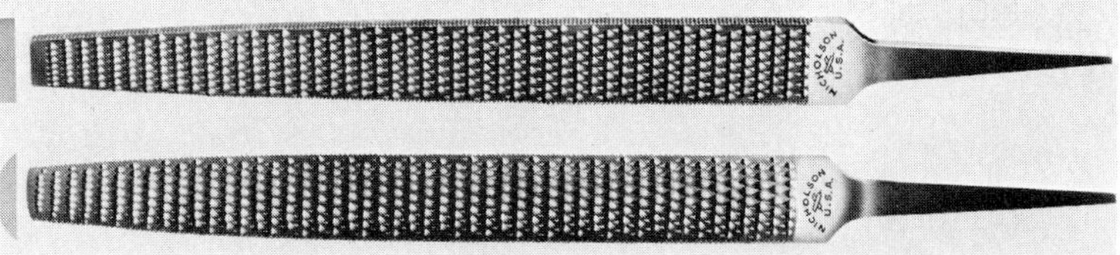

23-4. *A flat and a half-round rasp.*

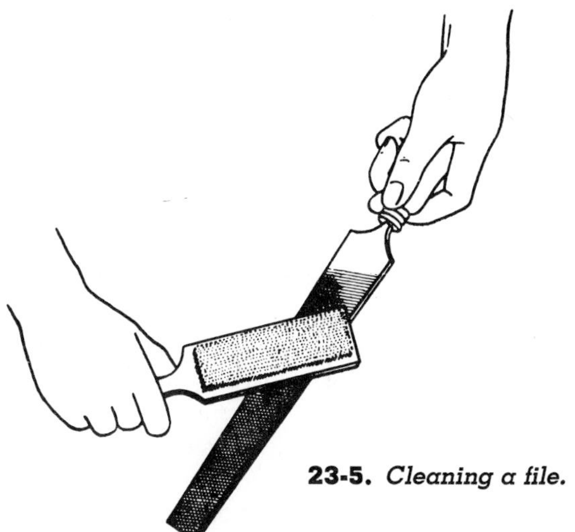

23-5. *Cleaning a file.*

The *multi-tooth (Surform)* tool has a hardened and tempered tool-steel cutting blade. Fig. 23-6. The blade has 45-degree cutting edges that easily cut wood, plastic, or soft metals. The teeth of this tool never become clogged because there are small openings between the teeth. The wood shavings go through these openings. The tool has a replaceable blade which fits into a holder.

USING A SPOKESHAVE

1. Adjust the blade (cutter) until it can just be seen through the mouth of the frame. Don't have it exposed too far. If you do, the tool will chatter

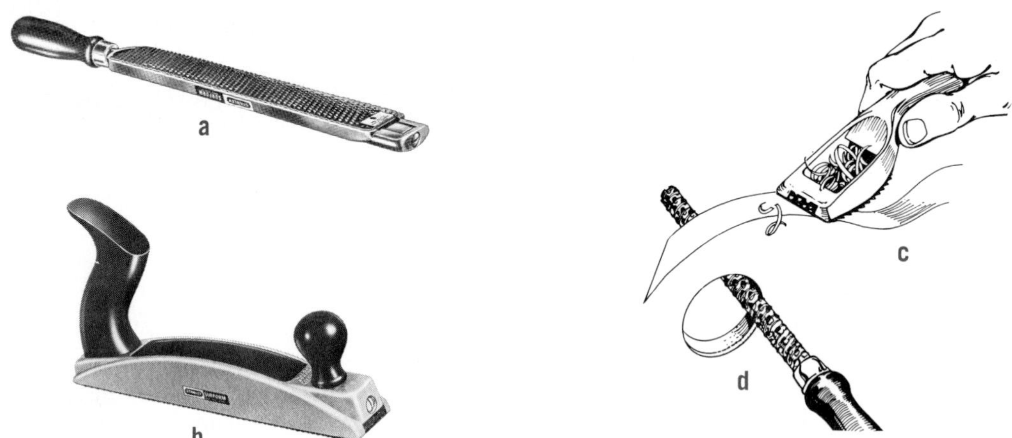

23-6. *Surform tools: (a) File type. (b) Plane type. (c) Shaver. (d) Another file type.*

(jump away) as you use it and make small ridges in the wood.

2. Fasten the work in a vise so that you can push or pull the tool across the surface. Work with the grain.

3. To push the spokeshave, grasp the handles with your thumbs just behind the blade on each side of the frame. Fig. 23-7.

4. Hold the bottom of the frame firmly against the wood and push evenly. Try it a few times. You should produce a long, thin shaving. Make the tool follow the shape of the work.

5. To pull the tool, draw it toward you in long, even strokes.

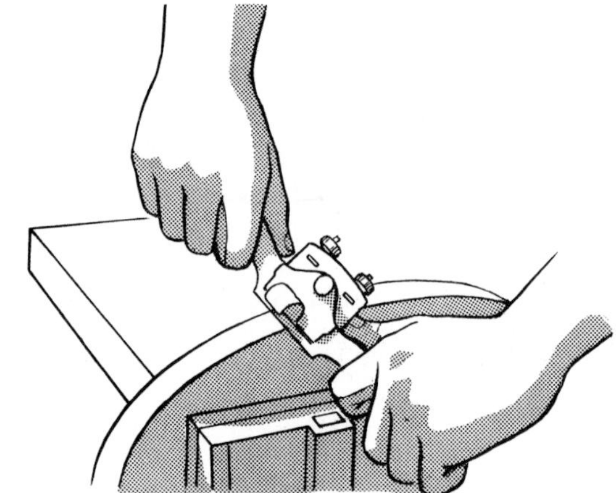

23-7. *Pushing the spokeshave to shape a curved edge. Your thumbs are placed on each side near the blade.*

USING A FILE OR RASP

1. Files or rasps are never to be used without handles. *The tang can puncture your hand* and cause a serious injury. Always fit a handle to the tool before using it.

2. Clamp the work in a vise.

3. Select the finest tool possible. A tool too coarse will splinter the wood.

4. Hold the handle of the tool in your right hand and the point in your left. (If left-handed, reverse this.)

5. Apply moderate (a medium amount of) pressure on the forward stroke. Make a shearing cut at a slight angle. Lift the file slightly on the return stroke.

6. To shape a curved edge, use the round side of the tool. Twist the tool slightly as you push.

7. Always keep the teeth clean with the file card or cleaner.

8. A piece of sandpaper of the correct grade can be wrapped around the file to smooth the

surface or edge of stock after a file or rasp has been used. A round file may be used to shape an inside opening.

USING A MULTI-TOOTH (SURFORM) TOOL

1. Use this tool as you would a rasp.

2. To get best results, apply light, even pressure against the wood. Fig. 23-8.

3. The Surform produces a smooth, even surface. As a repair tool it is excellent for smoothing an edge or end that has been chipped or splintered. The Surform is ideal for shaping a gun stock, canoe paddle, wooden handle for a tool, or other odd-shaped pieces.

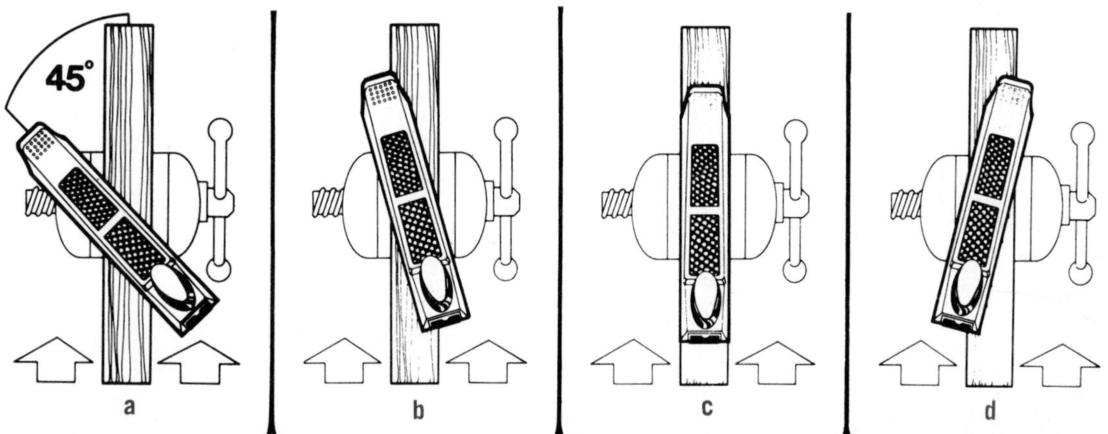

23-8. *Using a Surform tool: (a) To remove a maximum amount of material, simply hold the tool at 45° to the direction of the stroke. (b) To remove less material and obtain a smoother surface, reduce the angle. (c) To finely smooth the work surface, simply direct the tool parallel to it. (d) You can achieve an almost polishing effect by directing the tool at a slightly reversed angle.*

QUESTIONS

1. How should the blade of a spokeshave be adjusted?
2. Name the most common kinds of files used in woodworking.
3. How does a rasp differ from a file?
4. What is a Surform tool? Describe how it operates.
5. How do you shape a curve or edge with a file?

ACTIVITIES

1. Examine a file with a magnifying glass. Note the wedge-shaped teeth. With the magnifying glass, examine a piece of wood before and after filing. Describe what you see.
2. Demonstrate how to clean a file.

LEARN THESE SAFETY RULES BEFORE USING HAND DRILLING AND BORING TOOLS

- **Fasten the work securely in a vise or to the bench top. When fastening work to the bench top, always use scrap wood under the work so that you don't cut holes in the bench.**
- **Make sure the drill is in the chuck straight and then tighten it firmly.**
- **Make sure the square shank auger bit is installed correctly between the two jaws of the brace.**
- **Never carry the hand drill or brace with the cutting tool in it.**
- **Don't bend the hand drill after it is started. Smaller sizes of drills will break easily.**

Drilling Holes

Small holes are needed to install screws, nails, and small bolts. Small holes are also part of the construction of many projects. The holes in a cribbage board are a good example. These holes are *drilled* with twist drills. Fig. 24-1.

TOOLS

Twist drills come in fractional-sized sets from 1/64 to 1/2 inch, in steps of 1/64 inch. Fig. 24-2. These drills can be used for both metal and wood. Sizes 3/8 inch and smaller can be held in a hand drill. Larger sizes can be used in a drill press. See Chapter 48.

The parts of a *hand drill* are shown in Fig. 24-3. Most hand drills are made to hold twist drills up to 3/8 inch in diameter.

USING THE HAND DRILL

1. Mark the locations for the holes with a scratch awl or sharp-pointed nail. The drill starts a lot easier when the location is punched.

2. Fasten the work in a vise so that you can drill either vertically (up and down) or horizontally. Fig. 24-4.

3. Grasp the shell of the chuck in your left hand and turn the crank counterclockwise (opposite of clockwise) until the shank of the drill will slip in. Then turn the crank in the other direction to tighten. Make sure the drill is in the chuck straight so that it doesn't wobble.

4. If holes of a certain depth are needed (holes for screws, for example), make a *depth gauge* from a piece of scrap wood. Fig. 24-5.

24-1. *Drilling a hole. Remember the six simple machines. A drill or auger bit is a combination of several simple machines. The cutting edge is a wedge and the body is a screw. The brace you use on an auger bit is a good example of a* wheel and axle. *The brace handle is like one spoke of a* wheel.

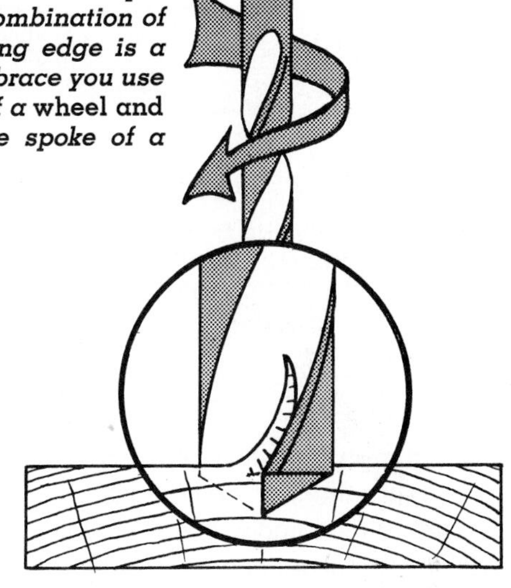

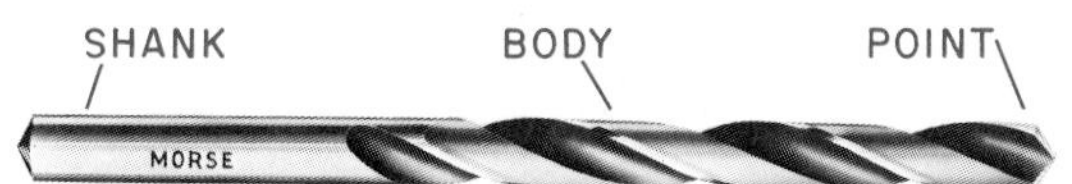

24-2. *Parts of a twist drill. The size is stamped on the shank.*

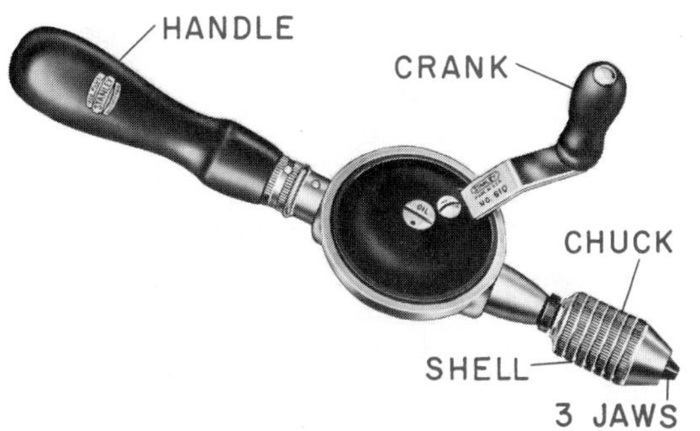

24-3. *Parts of a hand drill.*

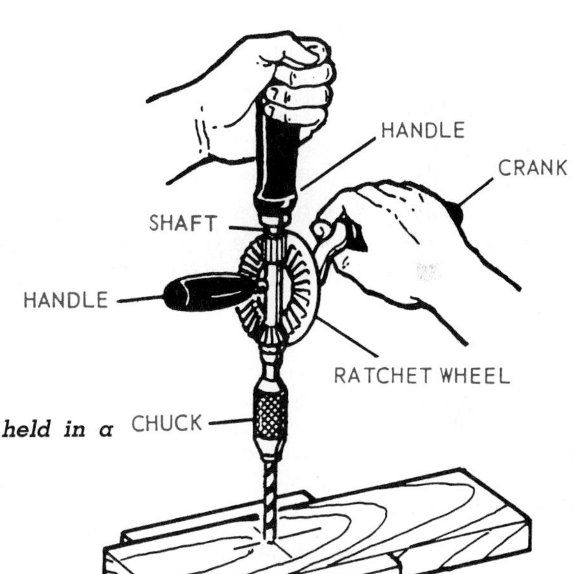

24-4(a). *Drilling with the hand drill held in a vertical position.*

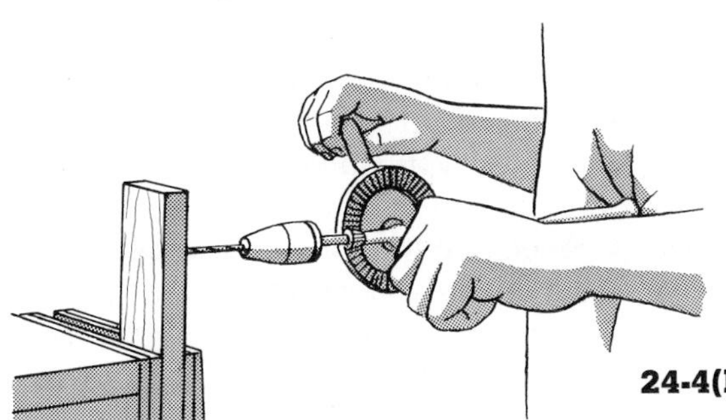

24-4(b). *Drilling a horizontal hole with a hand drill.*

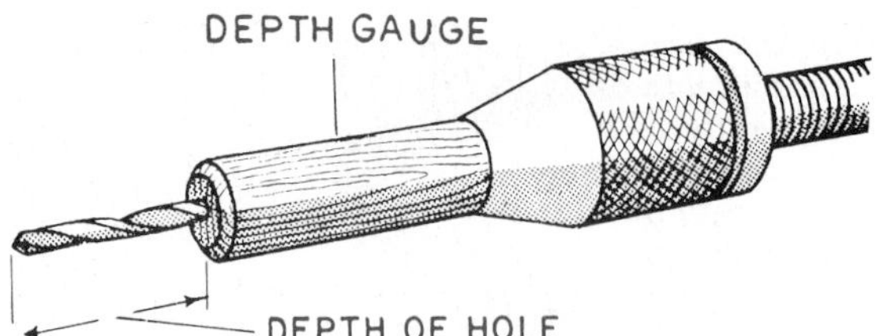

***24-5.** A depth gauge made from a piece of dowel rod covering a part of the drill like a sleeve. Cut the piece until the drill sticks out the right amount.*

5. Place the point of the drill where you want the hole and turn the crank evenly as you apply light pressure to the handle. Press straight down or ahead. *Be careful not to tip the hand drill after it is started.* This will break the drill.

6. Continue to turn the handle in the same direction as you pull the drill out of the hole.

7. Always return the drill to the correct holder.

USING THE PUSH (YANKEE) DRILL

The push drill provides an easy and quick way to drill small holes. The drill can be used with one hand. Fig. 24-6. It takes special bits which are inserted in the chuck. These bits range in size from 1/16 to 11/64 inch. These special bits are stored in the handle of the drill.

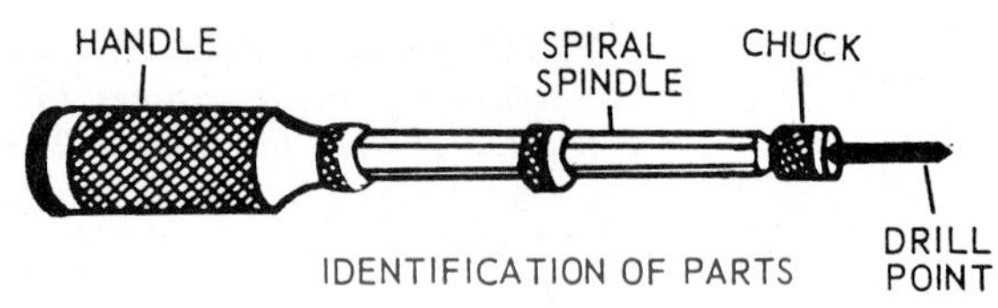

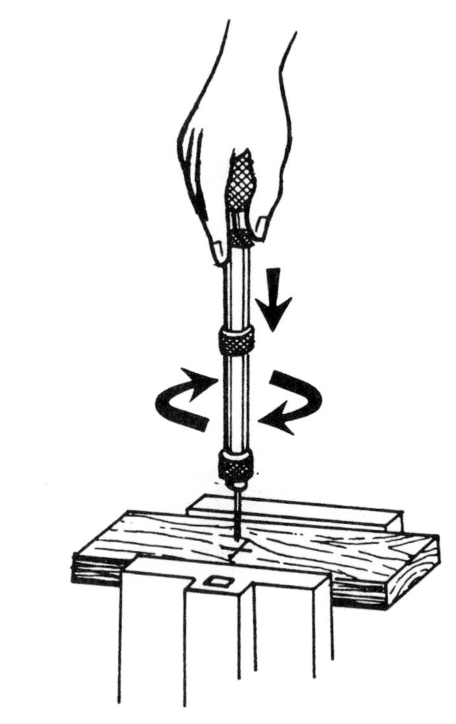

***24-6.** The push (Yankee) drill. When using this tool, keep the drill point straight. The drill bits are brittle and will break easily.*

QUESTIONS

1. Why is drilling small holes necessary?
2. Describe the parts of a hand drill.

ACTIVITIES

1. Demonstrate how to fasten a twist drill in a hand drill.
2. Suppose you wanted to drill a hole that was 1/8 inch in diameter and 1/2 inch deep. Select the twist drill you would use. Tell what length you would set the depth gauge.

CHAPTER 25

Boring Holes

Boring is cutting a hole that is larger than ¼ inch in diameter. (Holes ¼ inch or smaller are drilled.) Boring is also the first step in making a rectangular-shaped opening, such as for a mortise-and-tenon joint.

TOOLS

A *brace* holds the auger bit when the holes are bored. Fig. 25-1. The auger bit goes into the wood as you turn the handle of the brace. The two most common braces are the *plain,* or *common,* and the *ratchet.* The plain brace is used when you can make a full swing of the handle. If you have the problem of boring in a corner or in close quarters, you need a ratchet brace. To use it, turn the ratchet control to the right (clockwise). The brace can then turn the bit to the right. The ratchet slips when the brace is rotated to the left. In this way a half turn or less at a time will bore the hole. If the ratchet is turned to the left, the bit can be rotated out of the hole. To use the ratchet brace as a plain brace, set the ratchet in the center position.

The *auger bit* is the most common cutting tool for boring holes. Fig. 25-2. It ranges in size from ¼ inch (No. 4) to 1 inch (No. 16), by sixteenths. A number stamped on the shank of the bit tells the size in sixteenths. For example, size 8 is 8⁄16, or ½ inch, while a size 9 bores a 9⁄16-inch hole. The screw on the end of the bit pulls the bit into the wood.

A *depth gauge (bit gauge)* is a device that is attached to the auger bit to limit the depth of the hole. You can make a depth gauge by boring a hole through a piece of dowel rod and cutting it until the correct bit length is exposed. See Fig. 24-5. Two commercial bit gauges are shown in Fig. 25-3.

HORIZONTAL (FLAT OR LEVEL) BORING

1. Choose the correct size bit. For example, if the drawing calls for a ¾-inch hole, choose a No. 12 bit (12⁄16 equals ¾).

2. Insert the bit in the brace. Grasp the shell firmly in one hand. Rotate the handle to the left until the jaws are open enough to receive the shank. Then turn the handle to the right to tighten the bit.

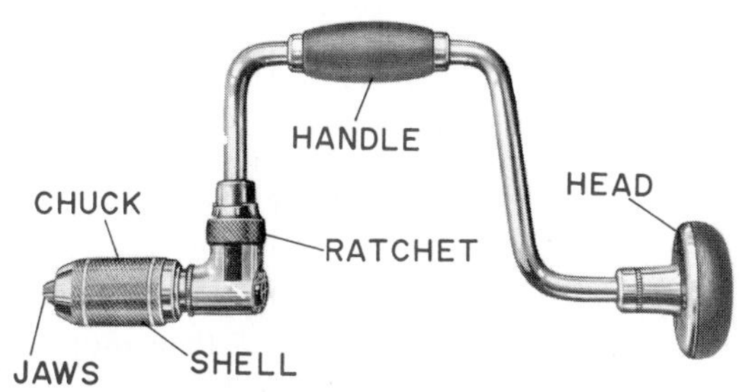

25-1. *Parts of a brace. (Stanley Tools)*

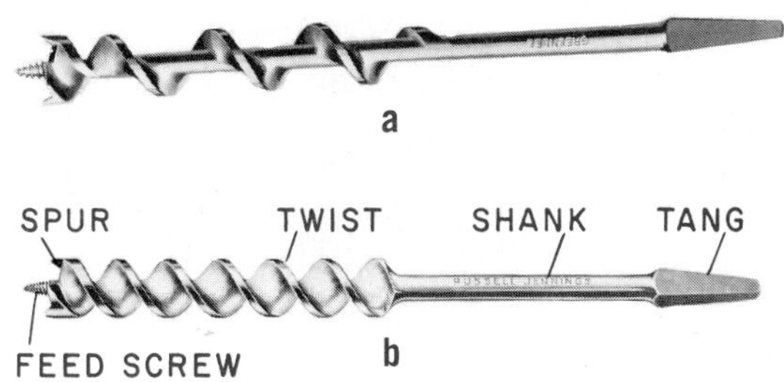

25-2. *(a) A single-twist auger bit. (b) Parts of a double-twist auger bit. (Stanley Tools)*

3. Mark the location of the hole with two intersecting (crossing) lines. Center punch with a scratch awl or the point of a nail.

4. Fasten the work in a vise with the punch mark near the top or side of the vise jaw.

5. Guide the bit with your left hand until the screw point is exactly on the punch mark. Hold the head in your left hand braced against your stomach. Grasp the handle in your right hand. (If left-handed, reverse these instructions.)

6. Now you should ask a friend to help you "sight" the tool so that the hole will be square with the wood surface. You sight it right and left. Have your friend sight it up and down.

7. Turn the handle steadily. Fig. 25-4. In softwood, little pressure is needed because the screw easily draws the point into the wood. For hardwood, press a little harder on the head.

8. Watch carefully for the feed screw to start coming out the opposite side. Stop. Turn the handle in the opposite direction to remove the bit. If you don't stop, the wood will split out. Fig. 25-5.

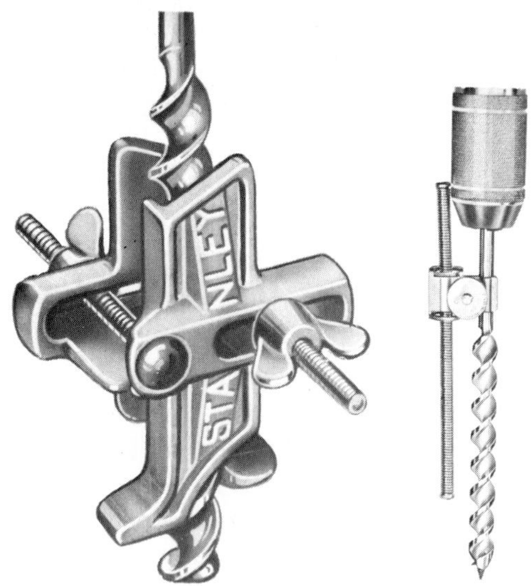

25-3. *Bit or depth gauges: (left) Solid type; (right) Spring type. (Stanley Tools)*

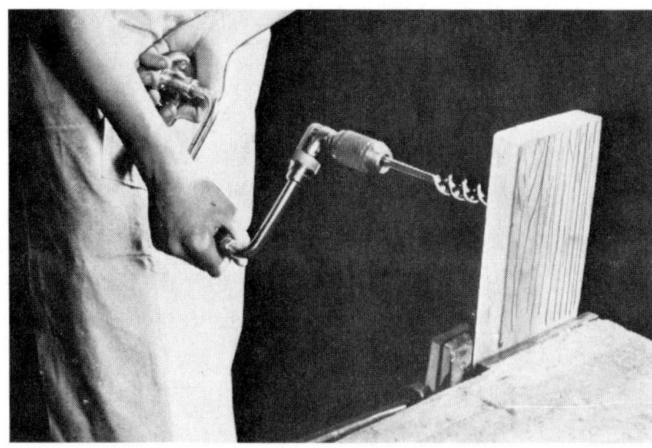

25-4. *Horizontal boring. Remember to keep the auger bit at right angles to the work.*

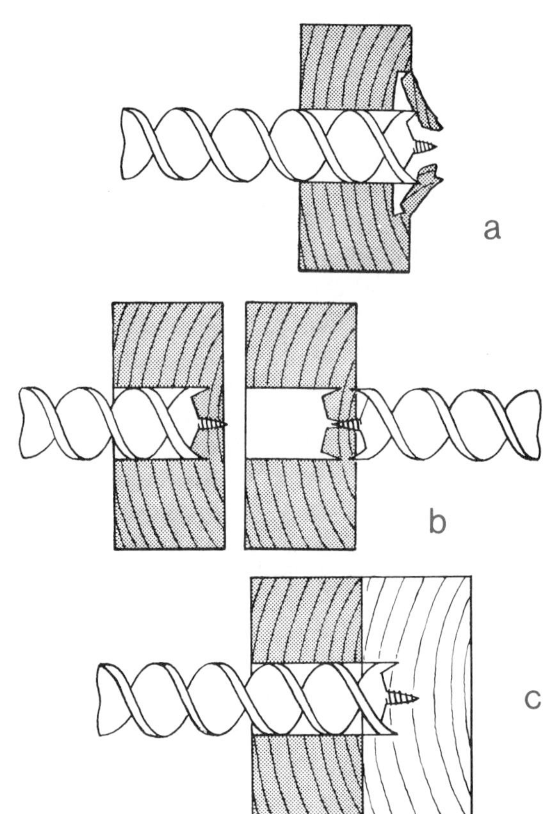

25-5. *(a) This shows what happens when you continue to bore from one side. (b) Boring from one side until the screw appears and then reversing the auger bit. (c) Using a piece of scrap stock to bore directly through the work.*

25-6. *Vertical boring. Hold the tool exactly vertical all the time.*

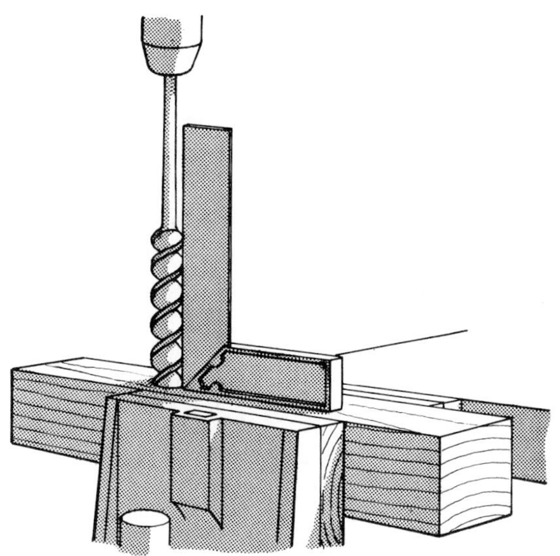

25-7. *Checking to make sure the auger bit is square with the work.*

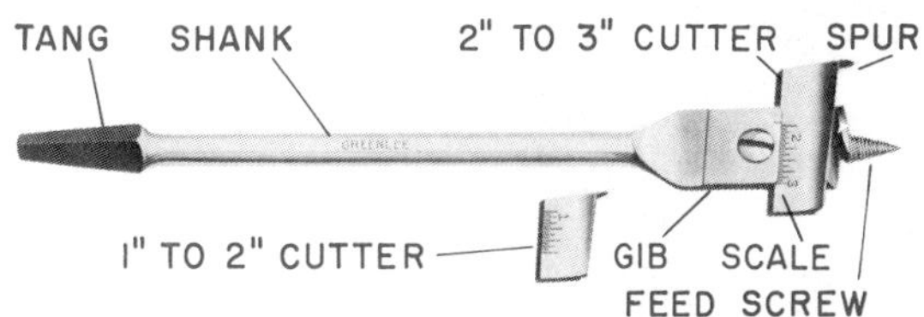

25-8. *Parts of an expansion bit. (Stanley Tools)*

9. Turn the work around and finish the hole by boring from the other side.

10. You can bore the hole completely through from one side if you place a piece of scrap stock on the back of your work.

VERTICAL BORING

1. Mark the hole. Clamp the work with the marked surface up.
2. Start the auger bit by turning it clockwise. Fig. 25-6.
3. Use a square or a block of wood to make sure the bit enters the wood straight. Fig. 25-7.
4. Continue the boring as described in the section on horizontal boring.

STOP BORING, OR BORING TO DEPTH

1. Attach a depth or bit gauge to the bit, with the right length of the cutting tool showing.
2. Bore the hole until the gauge touches the surface.

USING AN EXPANSION BIT

An *expansion (expansive) bit* is used to bore a hole larger than 1 inch. Most expansion bits have two cutters, each a different size; so a wide range of hole sizes can be bored. Fig. 25-8.

1. Choose a cutter of the correct size and slip it into the bit. Adjust the cutter until the distance from the spur to the feed screw equals the radius of the hole. The *radius* is one-half the diameter. A scale on the cutter helps set it. This scale shows the hole diameter. Fig. 25-9. On some types there is an adjusting screw for moving the cutter. Lock the cutter by tightening the lock screw.
2. Fasten the bit in a brace.

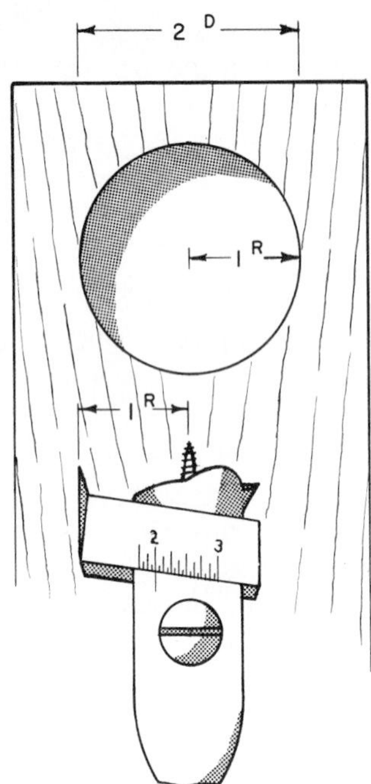

25-9. *Notice that the expansion bit is set to "2" on the cutter graduations in line with the index mark. This will cut a 2-inch hole.*

25-10. *A Foerstner bit.*

3. Clamp a piece of scrap stock in the vise or to the bench top and make a test cut. Is the hole size correct?

4. Mark the location of the hole on the work-piece.

5. *It is very important to have the work held tightly.* Since the bit has only one cutter, it will twist the work if it isn't clamped. It's a good idea to put a piece of scrap stock behind the work. Thin wood tends to crack or split.

6. As you rotate the tool, use just enough pressure to make it cut.

7. When the spur shows through, reverse the work and cut from the other side.

8. Rock the bit from side to side to cut through the last of the hole.

USING A FOERSTNER BIT

A *Foerstner bit* can be used when an auger bit will not work well. Fig. 25-10. Some examples are:

- Boring a shallow hole that has a flat bottom. Fig. 25-11.
- Boring a hole in thin stock near the end or ends where the wood might split with an auger bit.
- Boring holes in end grain. Fig. 25-12.
- Enlarging an existing hole. (This can't be done with an auger bit.)

Foerstner bits are numbered the same as auger bits. The sizes range from ¼ inch to 2 inches.

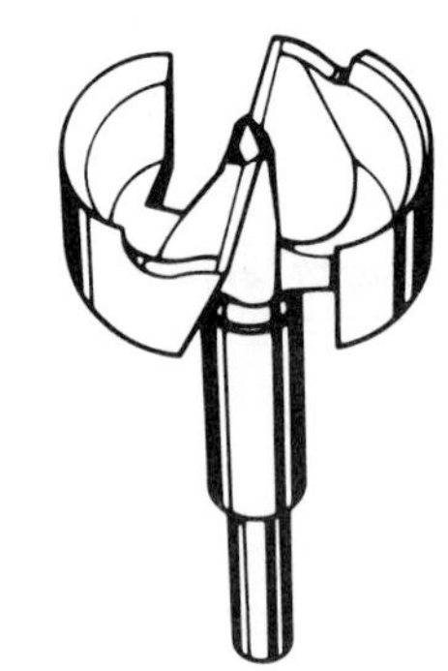

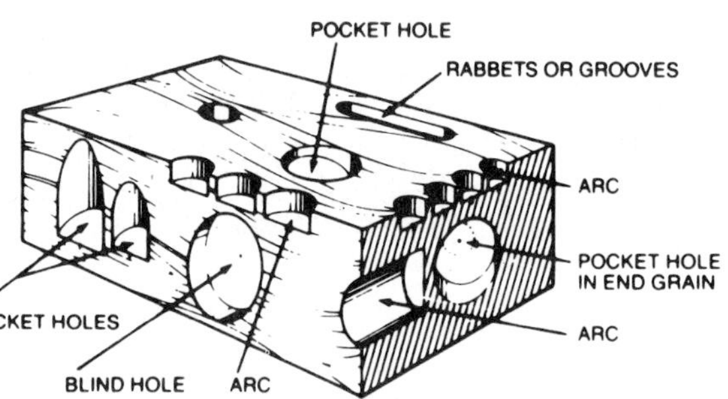

25-12. *Other uses for the Foerstner bit.*

1. Locate the center of the hole. With dividers draw a circle the same size as the hole.

2. If the hole is to go all the way through the work, it's better to place a piece of scrap stock underneath and bore from only one side.

3. Clamp the work securely.

4. Carefully guide the bit over the circle to start the boring.

5. Use a bit gauge if the hole must be bored to a certain depth.

QUESTIONS

1. Describe an auger bit.
2. Name the two kinds of braces.
3. How is the size of an auger bit shown?
4. What size hole will a No. 7 bit cut?
5. For what is a bit or depth gauge used?
6. How do you keep the auger bit square with the work surface?
7. What happens if you bore a hole through a piece of wood from one side and don't support it with scrap stock on the other side?
8. What is the purpose of an expansion bit?
9. Name four uses for a Foerstner bit.

ACTIVITIES

1. Demonstrate how to install a bit in a brace.
2. Working with a partner, demonstrate how to sight the tool when boring a hole.
3. Suppose you wanted to bore a hole that was 2½ inches in diameter. What size of cutter would you need for the expansion bit? What would be the radius of the hole? Demonstrate how to adjust the cutter to the correct setting.

Common Joints and Their Uses

Furniture, houses, and the items you make in the shop are all assembled with *joints.* While there are over one hundred different kinds of joints, most of them are somewhat alike. Only eight are really different from each other. You will use the simpler ones when you build the projects shown in this book. The more difficult joints are found in fine furniture and are usually made with machines. When you take an advanced course in woodworking, you will have a chance to make some of these. Fig. 26-1.

MAKING JOINTS STRONGER

Joints are held together with glue or with glue plus nails or screws. Sometimes a joint is made stronger by adding dowels or a spline. See

COMMON WOOD JOINTS

Kinds	Uses	How Made	Similar Kinds
Edge	For tops of tables, chairs, desks, and other furniture needing large surfaces.	Plane a square edge on both pieces. Add dowels or spline for strength. Glue.	Dowel, tongue-and-groove, or rabbet.
Butt	For simple boxes, cases, cheap drawers, frames, and chairs.	Cut corners square in a miter box. Fasten with nails or screws and/or glue. Use doweling jig for corner dowel joint.	Glued and blocked or doweled corner for greater strength.
Rabbet	For corners of modern furniture, simple drawer construction, and boxes.	Cut rabbet with backsaw. Glue, nail, or fasten with long screws.	Dado and rabbet for good drawer corners.
Dado	For shelves, steps, drawers, and bookcases.	Cut with backsaw and trim out with router plane or chisel. Fit second piece into dado. Glue.	Blind dado (gain) for front edge that doesn't show joint.
Miter	For frames of pictures, boxes, molding around doors or furniture.	Cut with miter box. Fit corners carefully. Fasten with glue, nails, or corrugated fasteners.	Dowel or spline for greater strength.
Cross-Lap	For legs of furniture, doors, frames, and braces.	Make like two dadoes. Assemble with glue.	Half-lap to lengthen material. End-lap for frames. Middle-lap for doors.
Mortise-and-tenon	For best chair, table, and chest construction.	Cut tenon with backsaw. Drill out mortise on drill press. Trim out with chisel.	Open mortise-and-tenon for frames. Haunched mortise-and-tenon for panel construction.
Dovetail	For best drawer and box construction. Furniture corners.	Cut dovetail with jigsaw. Glue.	Blind dovetail for quality furniture.

26-1. *Common woodworking joints.*

Chapter 27. A *spline* is a thin piece of wood inserted in a groove between the two parts of a joint. Fig. 26-2.

EDGE JOINT

In an *edge joint* boards are fastened together to make a larger piece. Fig. 26-3. For instance, the top of a table can be made in this way. The simplest is a plain edge joint in which the edges are planed and then glued together. Often a spline or dowels are added for strength. Fig. 26-4. A *rabbet* (recess) cut on both pieces also strengthens the joint. The *tongue-and-groove joint* has a groove cut along one edge and a tongue along the other. The floorboards in many homes are put together with tongue-and-groove joints.

BUTT JOINT

A *butt joint* is very simple. The end of one piece is fastened to the surface or edge of the other. Fig. 26-5. It is used to make a simple box

26-2. *A* spline *is a good device for joining two pieces of wood without nails. A groove, or slot, is cut in each piece and then a thin piece of wood is inserted and glued in place. This strengthens the joint.*

26-5. *At the left is a simple butt joint. At the right is a butt joint that has been glued and blocked. Adding this triangular corner block to the wood strengthens the joint.*

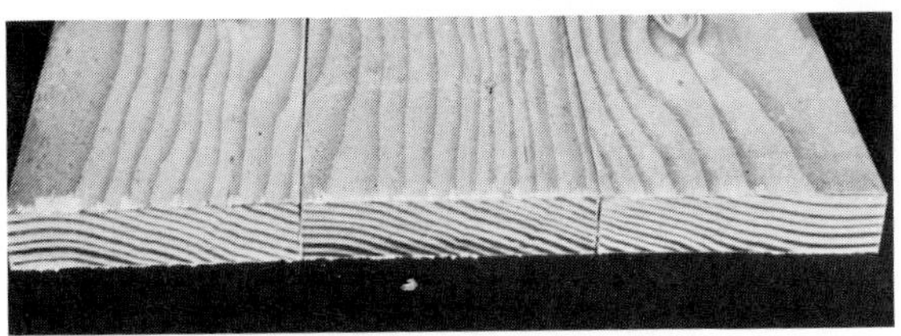

26-3. *A simple edge joint.*

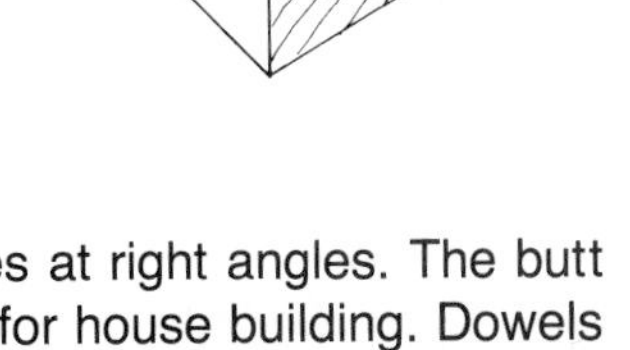

26-4. *An edge joint can be strengthened with a spline.*

26-6. *Rabbet joints are often used in making boxes and drawers. This joint can be made with or across the grain.*

or to fasten two pieces at right angles. The butt joint is a popular one for house building. Dowels or a corner block may be added to make the joint stronger.

RABBET JOINT

In a *rabbet joint* the first piece fits into a channel cut across the end or edge of the second piece. Fig. 26-6. It is found in simple furniture and in some box construction.

DADO JOINT

A *dado joint* is a good one for shelves, steps, bookcases, bookracks, chests and other types of cabinets. Fig. 26-7. A *blind dado,* or *gain,* is one in which the dado is cut only partway across the board. A notch must then be cut out of the second piece. This makes it look better from the front edge because the dado doesn't show. The *dado and rabbet* is a good joint for drawers.

26-7. *The dado joint is shown at the right. The dado-and-rabbet joint at the left is used on better drawer construction.*

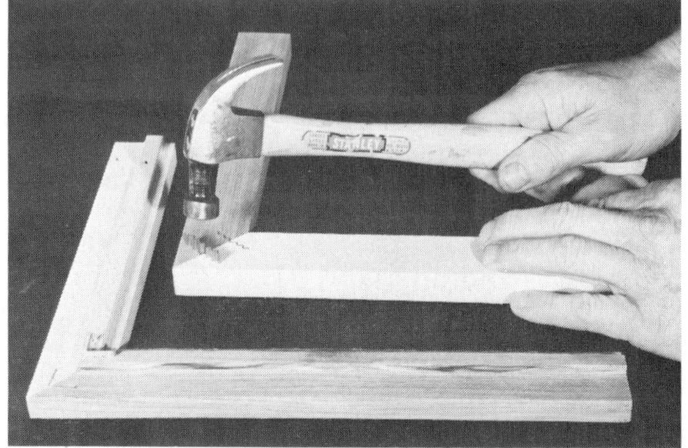

26-8. *The miter joint is used to make frames, moldings, and corners on modern furniture. This window screen frame is being fastened with corrugated fasteners.*

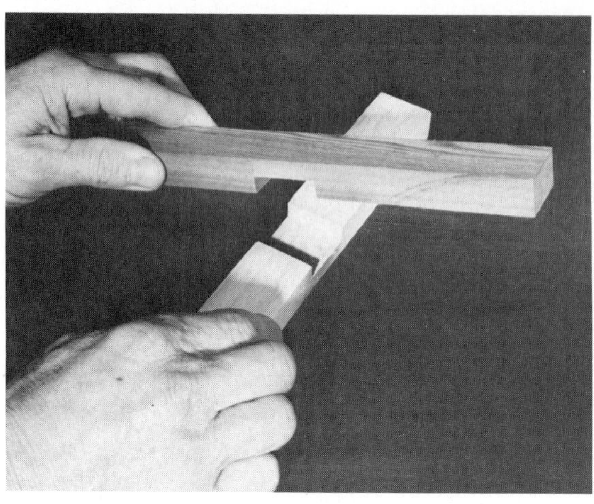

26-9. *Cross-lap joint. Outdoor furniture frequently has this kind of joint.*

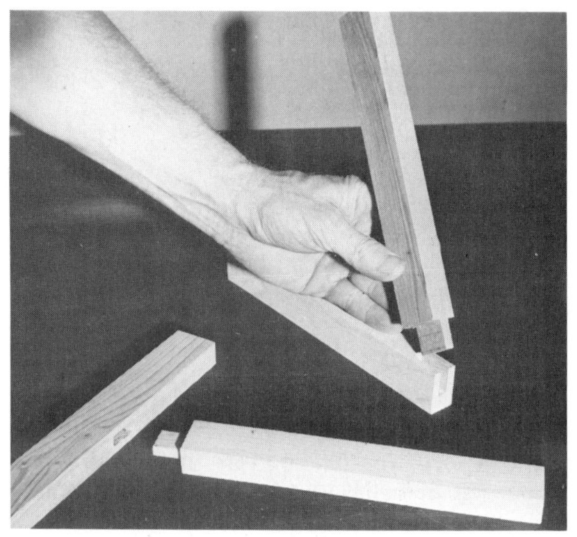

26-10. *The mortise-and-tenon joint is found in the best furniture. The blind mortise-and-tenon joint (at the left) is used to fasten rails to legs on tables, chairs, and similar furniture. The one on the right is called an open mortise-and-tenon joint.*

MITER JOINT

In a *miter joint* the corners are cut at an angle, usually 45 degrees. When the two pieces are joined, they form a right angle. A picture frame is a good example. Trim around doors and windows is also made with a miter joint. A way to strengthen this joint is to use a dowel, spline, or key (a thin piece of wood inserted across the corner). Fig. 26-8.

LAP JOINT

The *cross-lap joint* is made when two pieces of wood must cross. You find it on frames, table legs, and some kinds of chairs (especially outdoor furniture). Fig. 26-9. The carpenter often uses it to strengthen the frame of a house. The pieces may cross at any angle. Other common kinds are the *half-lap,* the *middle-lap,* and the *end-lap.* Lap joints are made in the same way as rabbet or dado joints.

MORTISE-AND-TENON JOINT

The *mortise-and-tenon joint* is one of the strongest. It is found on better-quality chairs, tables, and benches. Fig. 26-10. The *mortise* is the rectangular opening and the *tenon* is the part that fits into the opening. Mortise-and-tenon joints take a lot of time and experience when made by hand. With power tools they can be made quickly.

26-11. ***The dovetail joint is found in fine box and drawer construction. The most difficult joint to make, it is found only in highest quality furniture.***

DOVETAIL JOINT

The *dovetail joint* is used on the corners of the best drawers and boxes. Fig. 26-11. Look at a drawer on a well-made chest or cabinet. The front and sides almost always have dovetail joints. This joint is very difficult to make by hand. Today, power tools are used.

QUESTIONS

1. How many basic joints are there?
2. How can joints be strengthened?
3. Name the main uses for the dado joint.
4. At what angle is the corner of a miter joint usually cut?
5. Where are lap joints used?
6. What kind of joint is found in better-quality chairs and tables?
7. What is a mortise?
8. What is a tenon?
9. Where are dovetail joints usually found in furniture?

ACTIVITIES

1. Sketch an edge joint, butt joint, and rabbet joint. Tell what they are used for.
2. In your home, examine the joints used in drawers. Make a list of the different types.

CHAPTER 27

Using Dowels and Biscuits

Dowels and biscuits are small pieces of wood used to reinforce and strengthen joints. A *dowel* is a peg or pin of wood that fits into two matching holes. Fig. 27-1. A *biscuit* is a football-shaped piece of wood that fits into two slots. Fig. 27-2.

TOOLS AND MATERIALS

Dowel rod is usually made of birch in 36-inch lengths. The common diameters range from 1/8 to 1 inch, in intervals of 1/16 inch. Sometimes a groove is cut along the dowel so that glue holds better. Small *dowel pins* are made with a spiral groove and chamfered ends. The spiral helps the piece go in easier and the glue to flow. Fig. 27-3.

A *dowel sharpener* points the ends of dowels. Fig. 27-4.

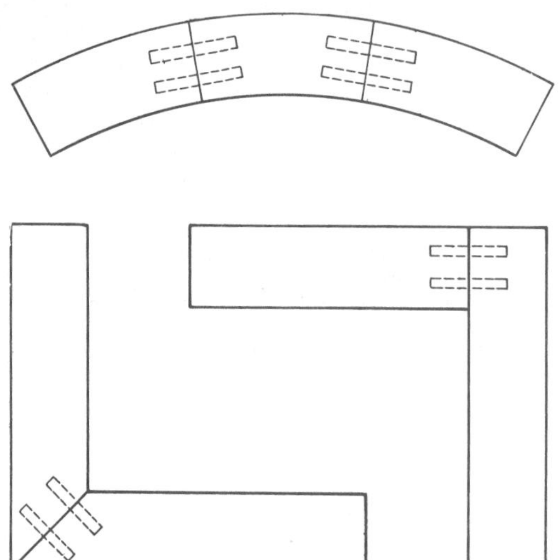

27-1. *Some common uses of dowels.*

A *doweling jig* will help locate the position of the holes and guide the auger bit for boring. This jig comes with several metal guides in sizes of 3/16, 1/4, 5/16, 3/8, 7/16, and 1/2 inch. Fig. 27-5.

Dowel centers are small metal pins used for marking the location of holes on two parts of a joint. They come in sizes of 1/4, 5/16, 3/8, and 1/2 inch. Fig. 27-6.

Dowel bits are auger bits for boring dowel holes. These bits are shorter than regular auger

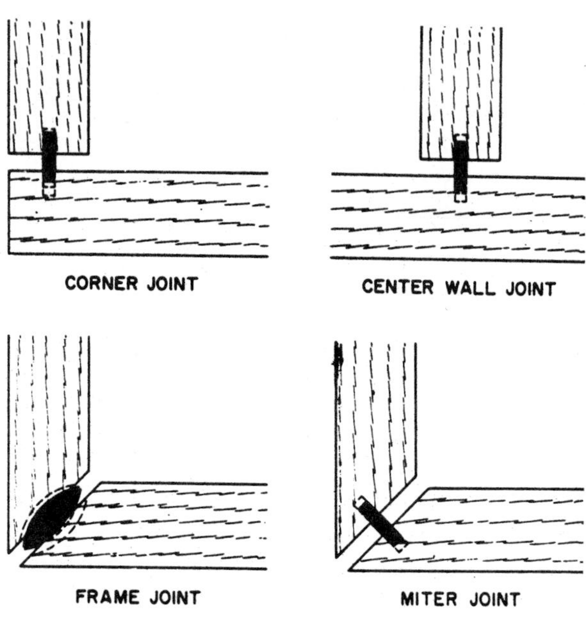

27-2. *Many types of joints, including butt and miter, can be made using biscuits.*

27-3. *A dowel pin with a spiral groove.*

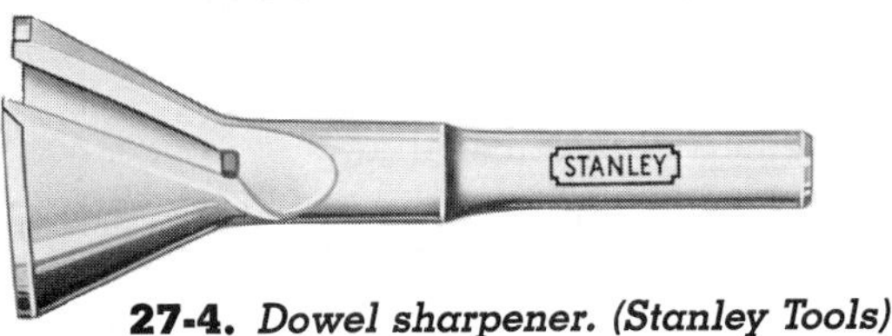

27-4. *Dowel sharpener. (Stanley Tools)*

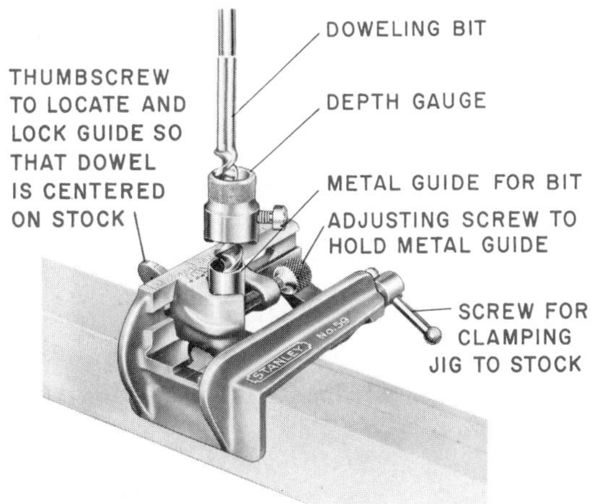

27-5(a). *Doweling jig. (Stanley Tools)*

bits. Fig. 27-7. Other tools for making dowel joints include a marking gauge, try square, rule, and pencil.

MAKING A DOWEL EDGE JOINT

1. Square up the pieces to be joined.
2. Place the pieces on the bench side by side. Arrange them with their grain running in the same direction and their growth rings turned in opposite directions. Fig. 27-8. This will help to prevent warping.
3. Mark the face surface with matching numbers at each joint: 1-1, 2-2, etc.

27-5(b). *Another type of doweling jig. The top part can be rotated and locked in place. Select the correct size hole for the dowel drill. Rotate the top part until the correct hole is directly over the center of the edge. Clamp the guide to the workpiece.*

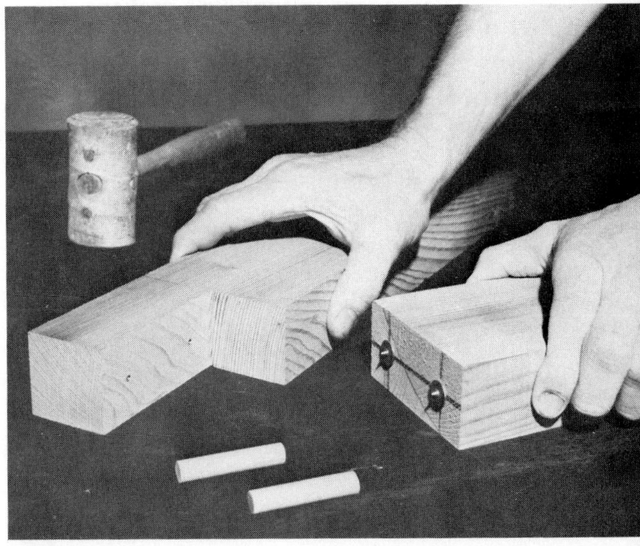

27-6. *The location of the dowels has been marked on one piece, and dowel centers have been fastened in place. When the two pieces are held together and tapped with a mallet, the dowel centers will mark the location of the holes in the second piece.*

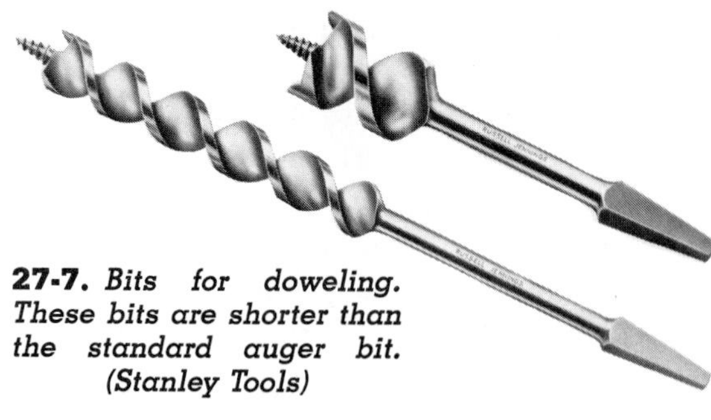

27-7. *Bits for doweling. These bits are shorter than the standard auger bit. (Stanley Tools)*

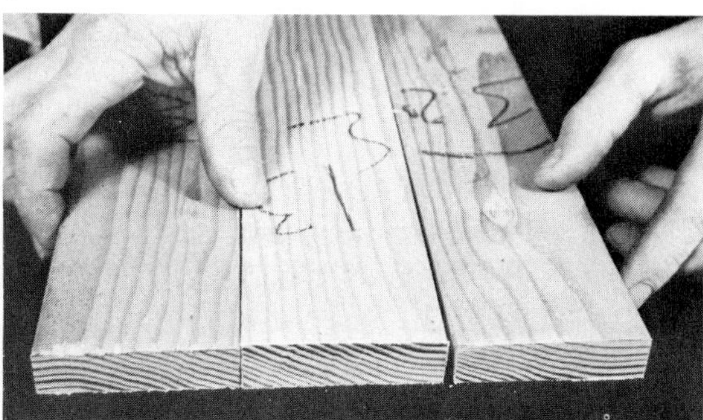

27-8. *Turn the pieces so that the growth rings on the ends face in opposite directions.*

4. Check the edges to be joined. They should be:

- Square with the face surface.
- Straight along the length. Use a large framing or carpenter's square to test them.
- Planed with a slight opening in the center and the ends fitting tightly.

5. Clamp the first two pieces in a vise with the face surfaces out.

6. Mark lines for the position of dowels across the edges. There should be a dowel every 12 to 18 inches. If three dowels are used, locate one in the center and the others about 2 or 3 inches in from each end. These are the only layout lines needed if a doweling jig is used.

7. If a doweling jig isn't used, mark centers for the holes. Use a marking gauge set at half the thickness of the stock and mark from the face surfaces. Fig. 27-9.

8. Choose a dowel rod equal in diameter to about half the thickness of the stock.

9. If a doweling jig is used, proceed as follows:

a. After you choose the dowel rod, select a metal guide of the same size for the doweling jig. Suppose the rod is ¼ inch. Select a guide this size and slip it into the clamp of the jig. Adjust the guide so that it is centered on the thickness of stock.

b. Clamp the jig over the stock so that it is lined up with the cross line.

27-9. *Mark the location of the dowel holes with a marking gauge.*

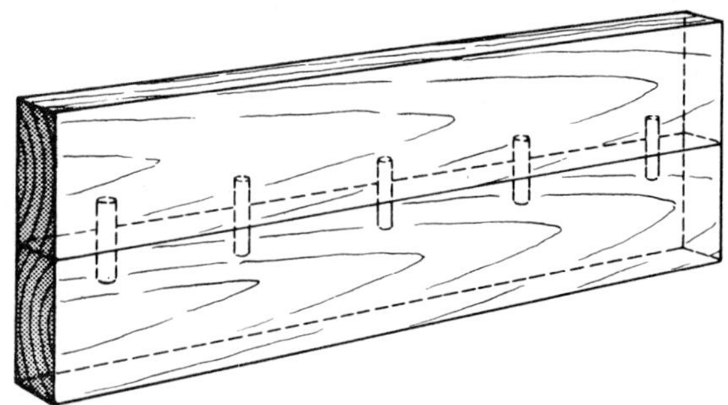

27-10. *Edge joint with the dowels installed.*

c. Place the jig with the solid side against the face surface. Clamp a stop to the bit for the correct depth of hole.

10. Choose an auger bit equal to the size of the dowel. Attach a bit gauge so that the depth of holes will be about 1½ to 2 inches.

11. Use a square to line up the bit. Bore the holes to the correct depth. Make sure the holes are bored squarely and on center. If they aren't, the two parts of the joint won't fit together right.

12. Bore all the holes on both parts of the joint. Countersink the holes so that the dowels will start easily.

13. Cut the dowels about ⅛ to ¼ inch shorter than the combined depth of the two holes. Chamfer or point the ends.

14. Insert the dowels in one edge and then assemble the joint to check if it fits. Fig. 27-10.

15. Take the assembly apart. Remove the dowels. Dip the dowels one-third of the way into glue and drive them into one edge with a mallet.

16. Apply glue to this edge and to the exposed dowels.

17. Put the two edges together and clamp them. (Clamping is discussed in Chapter 32.)

MAKING A RAIL-TO-LEG BUTT DOWEL JOINT

This joint can be used in place of a mortise-and-tenon joint on tables and chairs.

1. Locate the position of the dowels on the leg and in the ends of the rails. The rail may be flush with the outside of the leg or set back some distance. Remember, the dowels are centered in the ends of the *rails*. The position of the dowel holes in the *leg* depends on how far back the rail will be from the edge of the leg.

2. After the holes are located, the joint is made the same way as described above.

MAKING A FRAME WITH DOWELS

1. Cut all pieces to the same thickness and width. If the frame is square, all pieces are the same length. If not, the two pairs of matching pieces must be equal.

2. Locate the position of the dowels in the ends of two pieces and the edges of the other two pieces.

3. Complete the joint as described above.

PLATE JOINERY

Plate joinery is an ideal way to strengthen many kinds of joints. The system consists of a machine that cuts the slots and biscuits (or plates) that fit into the slots. The joiner is a portable machine that cuts crescent-shaped grooves (or slots) in the two adjoining pieces of wood. Fig. 27-11. The joining materials are small flat (5/32 inch thick) football-shaped pieces of compressed beech. The grain runs diagonally to provide strength. Biscuits come in three sizes: small (1¼ inch long); medium (2⅛ inches long) and large (2½ inches long). Biscuits have an advantage over dowels because the slots are slightly longer than the biscuits so that the boards can be shifted slightly to make an accurate joint. The biscuits absorb moisture from the glue and expand to make a tight joint.

To make the joint, follow the three steps shown in Fig. 27-12.

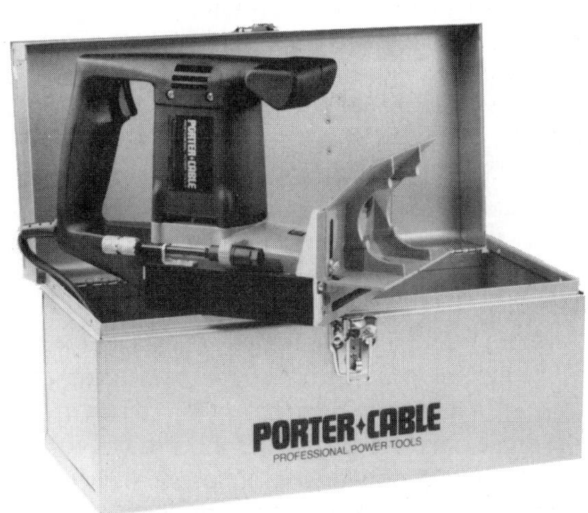

27-11. *A plate joiner.*

27-12. *Steps in making a biscuit joint.*

1

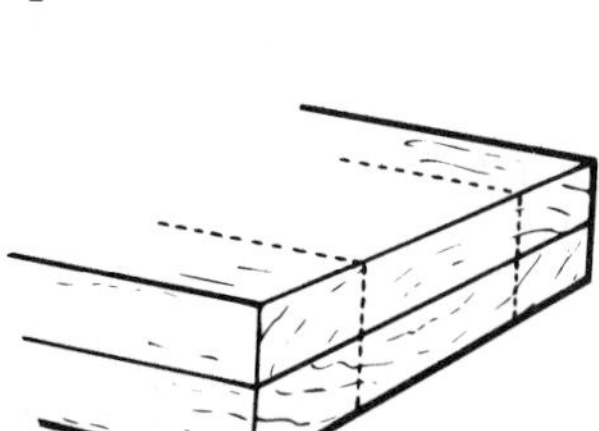

Mark boards at points where biscuits are to be placed.

2

Align center mark on front fence of plate joiner with pencil line. Turn unit on and press into wood. In seconds, you have perfectly cut biscuit slots in all pieces to be joined.

3

Apply glue on inside of biscuit slots. Insert biscuit into one slot and press the two pieces of wood to be joined together.

QUESTIONS

1. What is a dowel?
2. Of what is a dowel usually made?
3. What is the difference between dowel bits and auger bits?
4. What diameter dowel would you use on ¾-inch stock?
5. How long should the dowels be?
6. Tell how to make a dowel edge joint.

ACTIVITIES

1. Check a local building supply center. What sizes and types of dowel rod are available? What do they cost?
2. Suppose you were making a dowel edge joint. The thickness of the stock is ¾ inch. What should the diameter of the dowel rod be? What should be the size of the auger bit?

CHAPTER 28 Making a Rabbet Joint

A *rabbet* is a slot cut at the end or edge of a board. The end or edge of another piece is made to fit into this slot to make a rabbet joint. Fig. 28-1. This joint is one of the simplest. It is used in making a box or to put together parts of furniture such as a table or case. Fig. 28-2.

TOOLS AND MATERIALS

You will need a marking gauge, try square, backsaw, pencil or knife, vise, hammer, nail set, screwdriver, nails, screws, or dowels, and glue.

Four steps are required in all *joinery* (joint making): layout, cutting, fitting, and assembling.

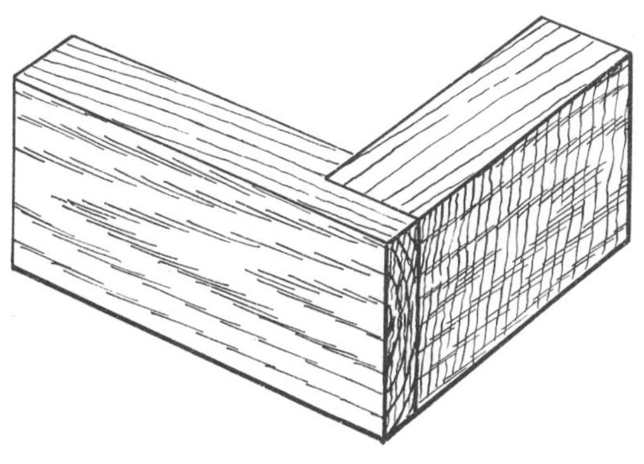

28-1. *A rabbet joint.*

28-2(a). *This wall shelf has rabbet joints.*

LAYOUT

1. Square up stock to the correct dimensions: thickness, width, and length.

2. Mark the shape of the rabbet on the end or edge of one piece.

- One way to do this is to measure from the end or edge a distance equal to the thickness of stock. This is the shoulder line. Mark a line across the stock with a try square and a pencil or knife.
- Another method is to place one piece of stock over the other as shown in Fig. 28-3 and mark a line across. Square the lines across both edges of the first piece.

3. Adjust a marking gauge for a depth of ½ to ⅔ the thickness of the stock. Mark a line across the edges and end to outline the rabbet.

CUTTING

1. Fasten the marked piece in a vise, or clamp it to the top of the bench.

2. Make the shoulder cut to correct depth with a backsaw. It might be a good idea to use a *guide board* for this. Fig. 28-4.

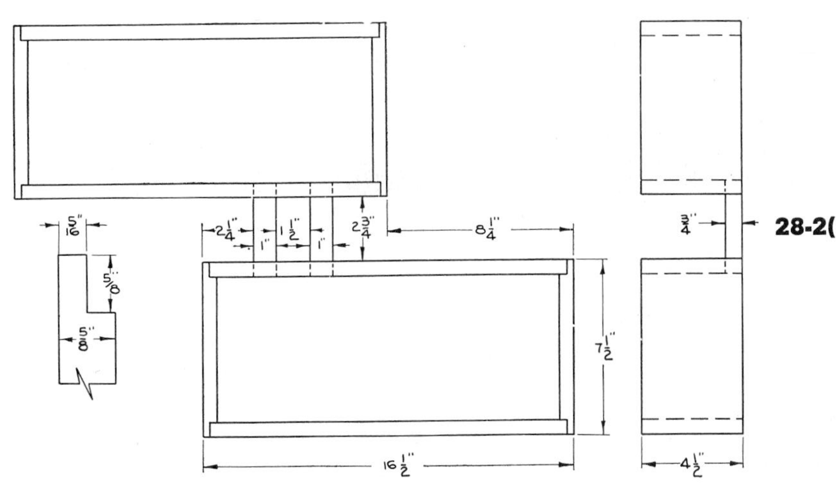

28-2(b). *A working drawing of the wall shelf.*

28-3. *Lay out the width of the rabbet by holding one piece over the other. Mark the width with a pencil or knife.*

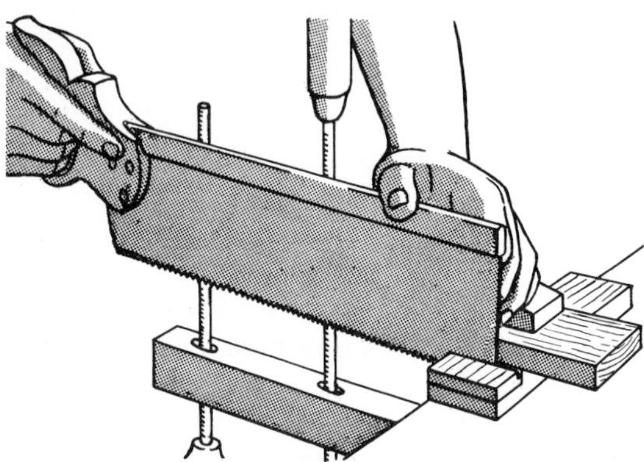

28-4. *Making the shoulder cut. Notice that a guide board is clamped next to the layout line. Carefully cut the shoulder with a backsaw. The saw kerf must be in the waste stock.*

28-5. *Trimming the rabbet after it has been cut.*

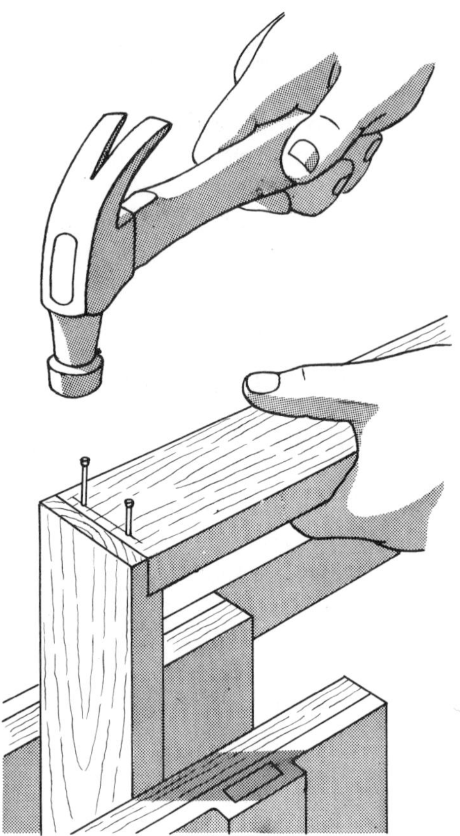

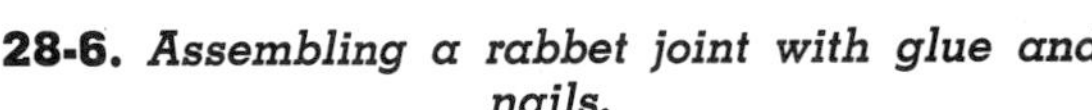

28-6. *Assembling a rabbet joint with glue and nails.*

3. Clamp the work vertically in a vise and make the second cut to form the rabbet.

FITTING

1. Place the end of the second piece in the rabbet and see if it fits tightly. The end of the first piece and the surface of the second piece should be flush.

2. Trim with a sharp chisel until the pieces fit snugly. Fig. 28-5.

ASSEMBLING

1. The rabbet joint is assembled with nails and glue or screws and glue. Apply glue to the rabbet. Fit the second piece in the rabbet and hold or clamp it securely.

2. Install several nails or screws to fasten the two pieces permanently. Fig. 28-6.

3. Rabbet joints can also be fastened with dowels and glue.

QUESTIONS

1. Describe a rabbet.
2. What should be the depth of a rabbet?
3. Why is it a good idea to use a guide board in cutting a rabbet?
4. Name some ways of assembling a rabbet joint.

ACTIVITIES

1. Demonstrate two ways to mark stock for a rabbet joint.
2. Find examples of rabbet joints in your home or school. Make a list of these.

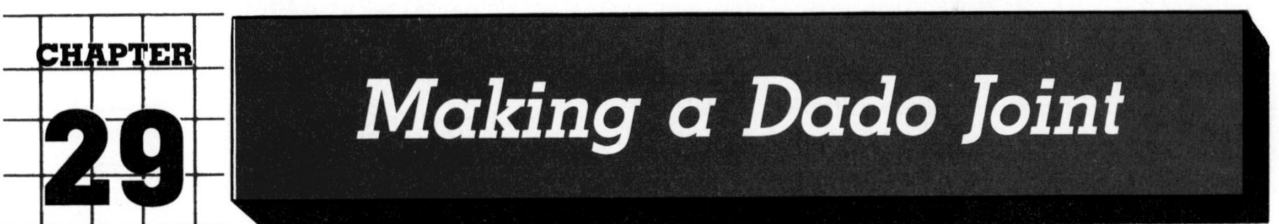

CHAPTER 29 Making a Dado Joint

A *dado* is a slot cut **across** the grain of wood. By contrast, a *groove* is a slot cut **with** the grain.

Dado joints are strong. Figs. 29-1 and 29-2. Bookcase shelves are often assembled with dado joints. Because one piece fits into a slot in another piece, the dado joint is strong enough even for stair steps.

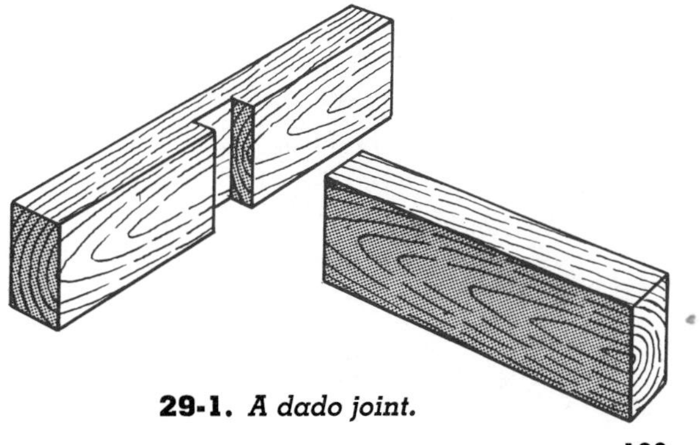

29-1. *A dado joint.*

TOOLS

A *router plane* is a cutting tool made for surfacing the bottom of grooves and dadoes. Fig.

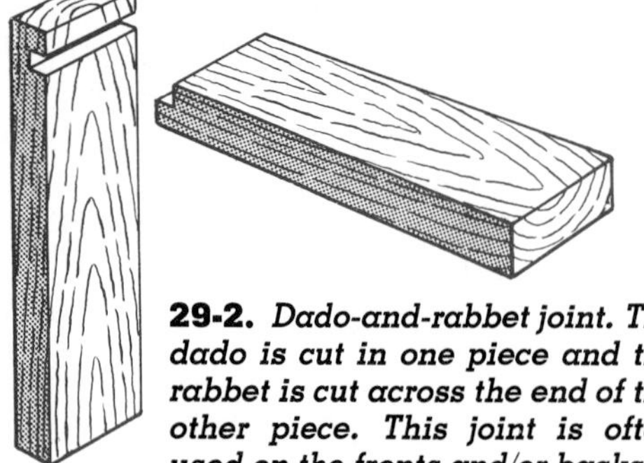

29-2. *Dado-and-rabbet joint. The dado is cut in one piece and the rabbet is cut across the end of the other piece. This joint is often used on the fronts and/or backs of drawers.*

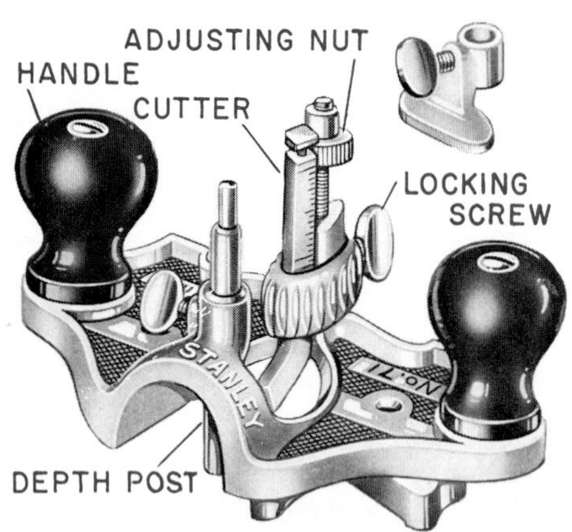

29-3. *Parts of a router plane. (Stanley Tools)*

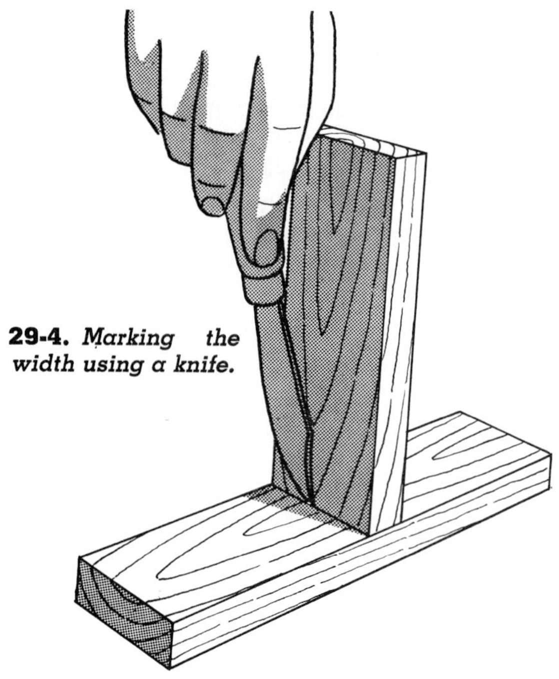

29-4. *Marking the width using a knife.*

29-5. *Marking lines down the edges of the stock.*

29-3. It consists of a bed with two handles. There are three cutters: two straight cutters (¼ inch and ½ inch) and one V cutter. The cutters can be adjusted to different depths.

Other tools needed include the try square, pencil or knife, backsaw, chisel, marking gauge, and hand clamps.

LAYOUT

1. Square up the stock. The end not exposed can be cut to length.

2. To locate one side of the dado, mark a line across one piece with a try square and a pencil or knife.

3. Place the end of the second piece across the first at this line.

4. Mark the width of the dado with a pencil or knife. Fig. 29-4.

5. Continue the lines down the edges of the first piece. Fig. 29-5.

29-6. *Gauging for the depth of the dado.*

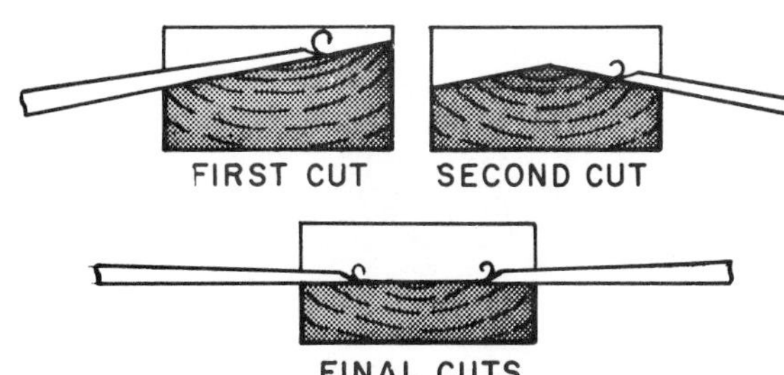

29-8. *Steps in trimming a dado. Work first from one side and then the other.*

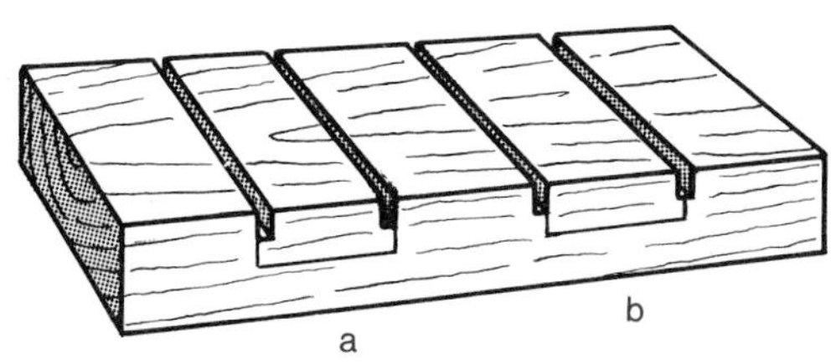

29-7. *(a) The correct way to make the cuts. The saw kerfs are inside the layout line, in the waste stock. (b) The incorrect way. The saw kerfs are on or outside the layout line.*

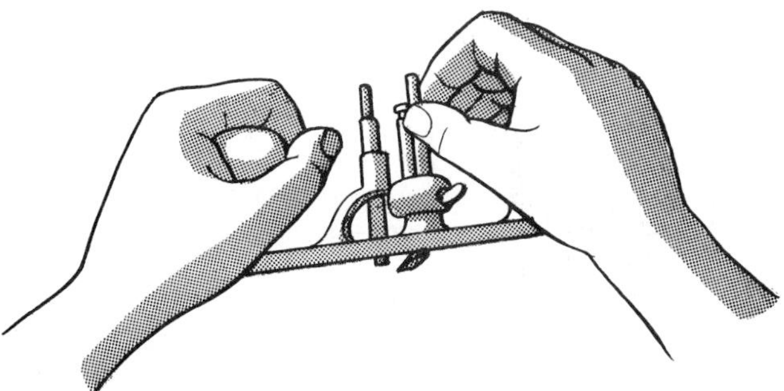

29-9. *Adjusting the router plane for the depth of cut.*

6. Adjust the marking gauge to the depth of the dado. Usually the dado is cut half the thickness of the stock.

7. Draw lines along the edges to show the depth. Fig. 29-6.

CUTTING

1. Fasten the wood in a vise or to the bench top.

2. With a backsaw make cuts just inside the layout line in the waste stock. Fig. 29-7. If you cut outside the line, the joint will be poor. You can do a better job with a guide board.

3. Now make several more saw cuts in the waste stock to the correct depth.

4. Remove the waste stock with a chisel. Chisel from both sides to the center. Fig. 29-8. Another method is to remove the waste stock with a router plane. Fasten the stock securely to the top of the bench with a good clamp. Select the widest cutter that will fit into the dado. Adjust for a light cut. Fig. 29-9. Hold the plane in both hands and work across the stock with short, jerky strokes. Fig. 29-10. Don't try to make the cut too deep at one time. Adjust the plane each time to a slightly deeper cut until the correct depth is reached. Trim out the corners with a chisel.

5. Check the depth of the dado with a combination square (see Chapter 8) or handmade depth gauge as shown in Fig. 29-11.

FITTING

1. Hold the second piece over the dado and press the end in. Fig. 29-12. It should go in with hand pressure.

2. If it is too tight, plane a little off the sides of the second piece until it fits snugly.

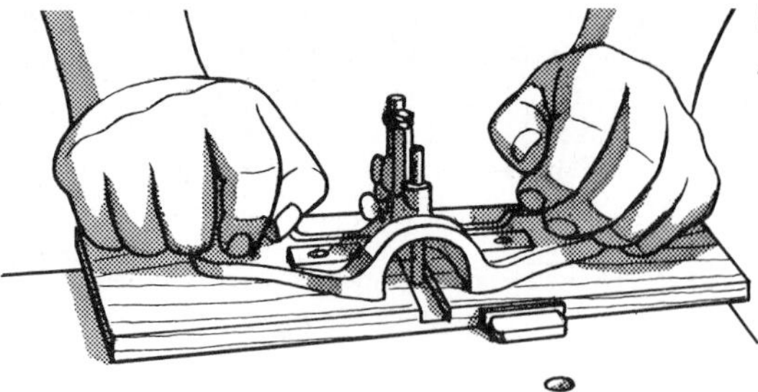

29-10. *Removing the waste stock with a router plane. The work is clamped between the bench stop and the vise dog.*

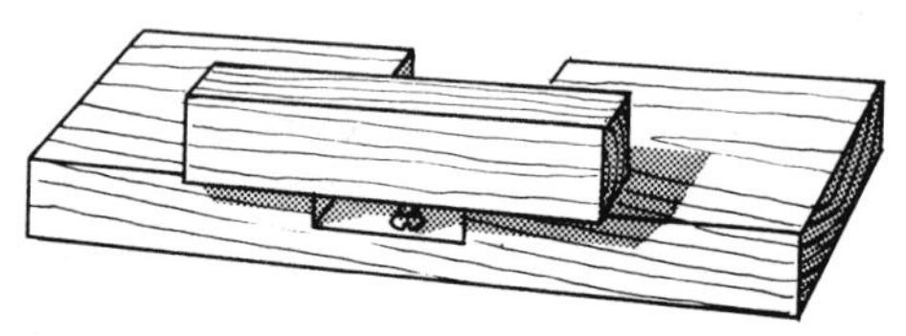

29-11. *Using a block of wood with a screw in it as a depth gauge for testing a dado.*

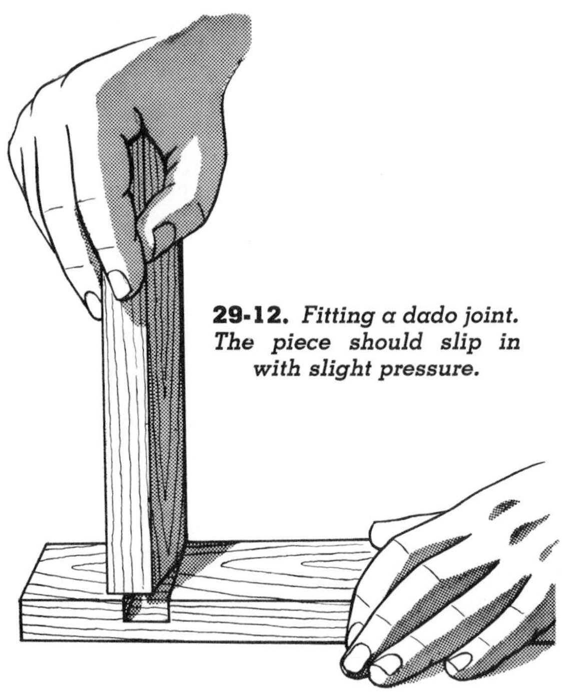

29-12. *Fitting a dado joint. The piece should slip in with slight pressure.*

ASSEMBLING

Use glue alone or glue and screws or nails. In a fine piece of furniture, only glue is needed. Sometimes screws are added for extra strength. In carpentry, such as for building steps, the joint can be nailed.

QUESTIONS

1. What is a dado?
2. How does it differ from a groove?
3. Where is a dado joint used?
4. Describe a router plane.
5. Why should you make several cuts in the waste stock?
6. How can the depth of a dado be checked?

ACTIVITIES

1. On a piece of scrap wood, lay out a dado joint. Show exactly where the cuts should be made.
2. Make a depth gauge like the one shown in Fig. 29-11.

Making Lap Joints

Lap joints are made by overlapping the ends or edges of two boards. Half the thickness of both boards is cut away so that, when joined, the surfaces of the wood are flush. Lap joints tend to be stronger than many other joints because of their shape and because they offer more gluing surface. They are also neat and look nice. As with other joints, they can be reinforced with dowels, nails, or screws.

KINDS OF LAP JOINTS

There are several different kinds of lap joints, each for a different purpose. In the *cross-lap* joint, the two pieces cross. They usually cross at right angles, but it may be at some other angle. This joint is used to make the base for stands or to make furniture parts that cross. Fig. 30-1. The *corner-lap* is used for many types of frames. Fig. 30-2. The *half-lap* is used to extend the length of material. Fig. 30-3. The *middle-lap* is used to make a T-shaped joint, such as for a crosspiece in a frame. Fig. 30-4.

MAKING LAP JOINTS

- The *cross-lap* joint is made exactly like two dadoes except that each is usually wider than a dado. Fig. 30-5.

30-1(a). *The cross-lap joint is used to make the base for this ring game. This joint isn't glued; it can be taken apart for storage.*

30-1(b). *The stretchers (lower crosspieces) of this table have a cross-lap joint cut at an angle.*

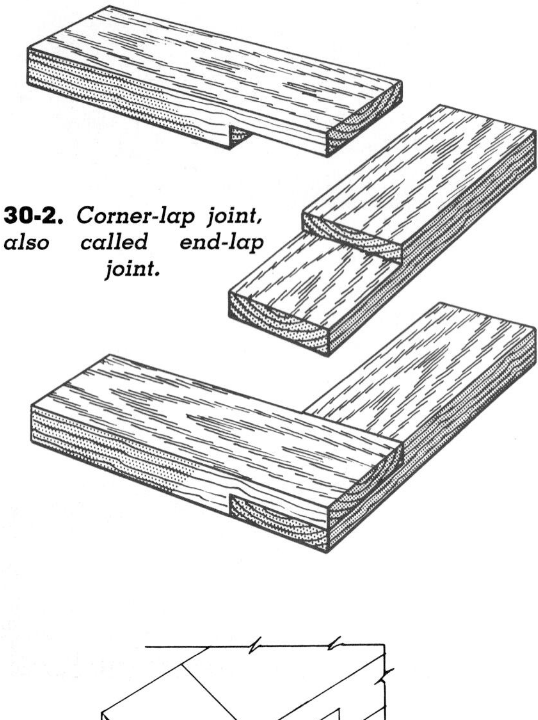

30-2. *Corner-lap joint, also called end-lap joint.*

30-3. *Half-lap joint.*

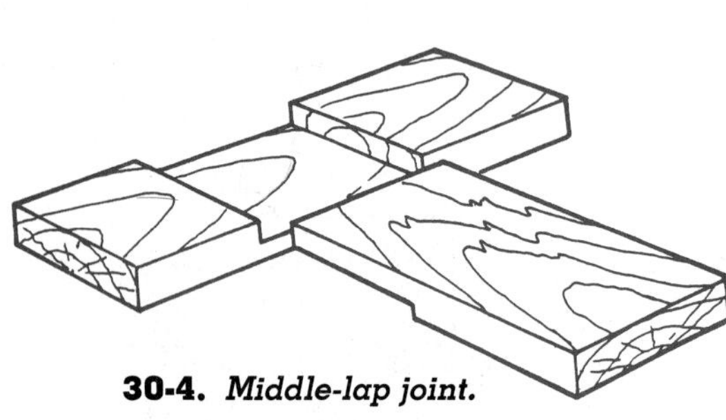

30-4. *Middle-lap joint.*

30-5. *A cross-lap joint. This can be made the same way as a dado joint. Just cut two equal-size dadoes.*

● Make corner- and half-lap joints as follows:

1. Lay out the cut on each piece just as you would for a wide rabbet.
2. Make the shoulder cut with a backsaw.
3. Clamp the stock in a vise at an angle and start sawing across the corner down to the shoulder cut. Then clamp the piece upright and cut straight down to the shoulder cut. Fig. 30-6.
4. Trim each part with a chisel and assemble.

● The middle-lap joint consists of a wide dado on one piece and a wide rabbet on the other.

30-6. ***It is easier to start the cut across the corners. Then place the board upright to complete the cut.***

QUESTIONS

1. Name four common kinds of lap joints.
2. Which type of lap joint is used when pieces must cross?
3. Which type of lap joint forms a T-shaped joint?
4. Are all lap joints cut in the same way? Explain.

ACTIVITIES

1. If you wanted to make a lap joint in 1-inch boards, how much stock would be cut away from each board? What if the boards were 1½ inches thick?
2. Make sketches of corner-lap, half-lap, middle-lap, and cross-lap joints.

Making a Miter Joint

A *miter joint* is an angle joint made by cutting the ends of two pieces of stock at equal slants. The most common miter joint is made by cutting each piece at an angle of 45 degrees. When put together, the two pieces make a right angle. Fig. 31-1. A miter joint is used where no end grain should show. For example, it is used for making picture frames, box and tray corners, bulletin or display boards, and trim for cabinets and chests. Fig. 31-2. A miter joint is found at the upper corners of the trim around the doors and windows

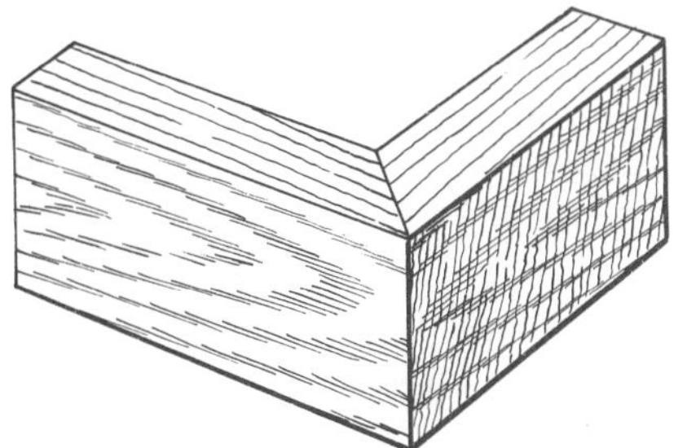

31-1. *A miter joint.*

31-2. *Miter joints are used in many wood products, such as the frame for this clock.*

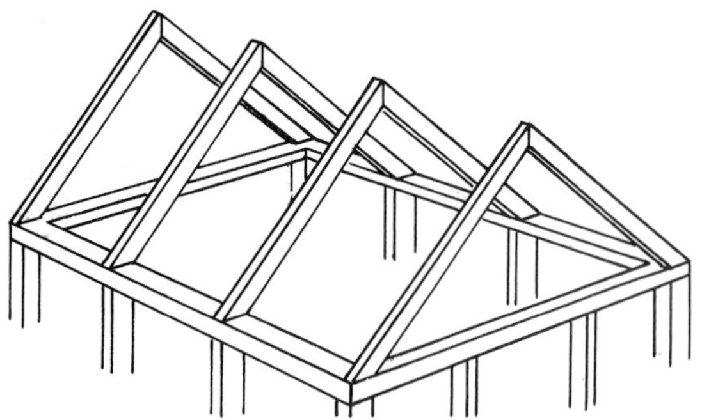

31-3. *Miter joints in roof framing.*

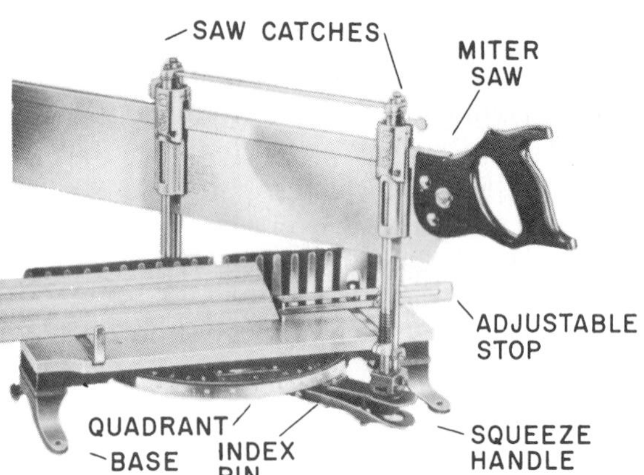

31-5. *Parts of a metal miter box. (Stanley Tools)*

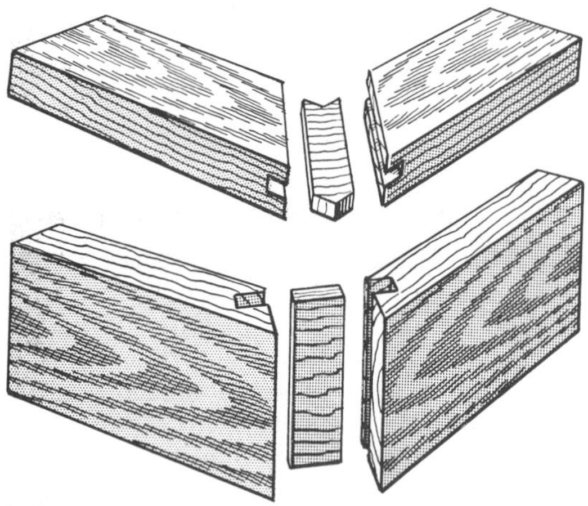

31-4. *Miter joints can be strengthened with splines. A spline is a thin piece of wood, plywood, hardboard, or metal that is inserted in a slot between two parts of a joint.*

31-6. *A miter box can be made by nailing three boards together. Here you see a method of laying out the miter cuts for a 45-degree angle. Measure equal distance from a point to lay out a square. Each rule measures 4⅛ inch.*

in some homes. It is also used in house framing. Fig. 31-3. A plain miter joint is not strong, but it can be reinforced with a spline, key, or dowel. Fig. 31-4.

TOOLS

Most shops have a *metal miter box* for cutting angles. Fig. 31-5. The *miter saw* is a large backsaw. The base and frame of the miter box hold the saw in position. You don't have to guide the saw as you move it back and forth. The quadrant is divided in degrees. An index pin drops into a hole for sawing at angles of 12, 22½, 30, 36, and 45 degrees. To cut a four-piece frame, use the saw with the angle set at 45 degrees. If a frame has eight sides, the miters are cut at 22½ degrees.

A *handmade miter box* is good to have in a home workshop for making a square or 45-

degree cut. To make a miter box, choose three pieces of wood about ¾″ × 4″ × 6″. Fasten them together to make a trough (a U shape). Make one cut at right angles to the sides and two 45-degree angle cuts, one in each direction. The distance between the 45-degree angle cuts on the outside must equal the width of the box. These cuts can be made on a metal miter box if one is available. Fig. 31-6.

A *miter-and-corner clamp* is ideal for assembling frames. This clamp allows you to fasten the corner with the two pieces held firmly in place. Fig. 31-7. If the joint is glued, you can wipe away extra glue easily. If the joint isn't quite perfect, you can true it up with a backsaw. A four-corner miter-frame clamp holds all four corners at the same time. Fig. 31-8.

Other tools needed for making miter joints are the backsaw, combination square, and pencil.

LAYOUT

1. Mark the length of the stock along the edge away from you (the back edge).

2. If you are using picture-framing material with a rabbet edge, make the layout as follows:

a. Measure the overall size of the glass or the board that will go inside the frame.

b. Measure the width of the framing material from the rabbet edge to the outside. Add twice

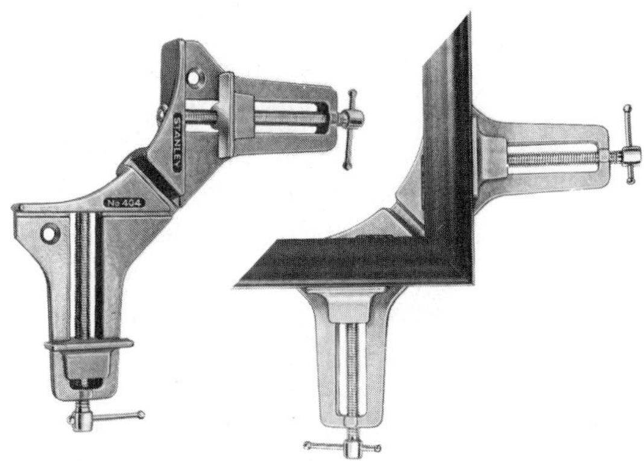

31-7. ***This miter-and-corner clamp is good for making picture frames because it holds the corners firmly in place as they are fastened together.***

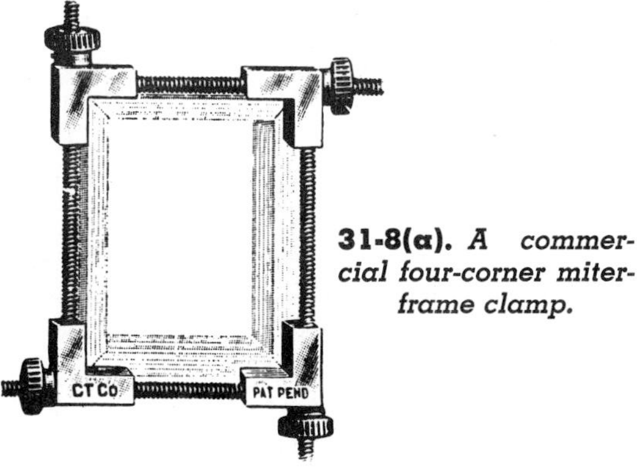

31-8(a). ***A commercial four-corner miter-frame clamp.***

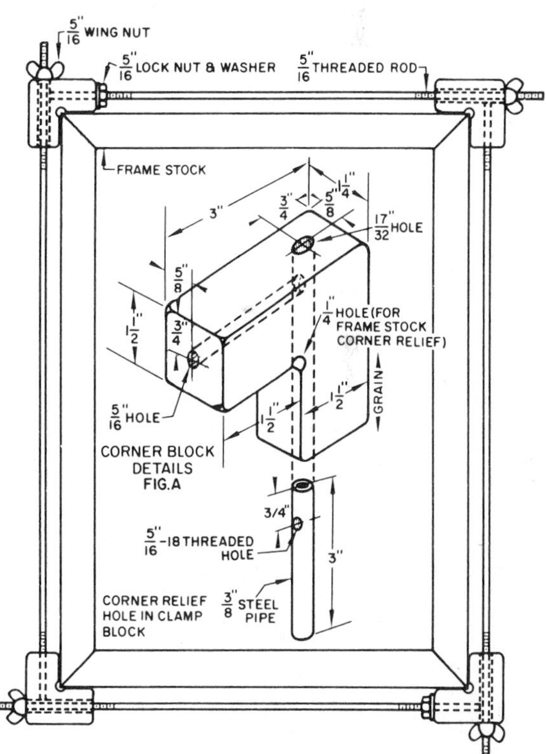

31-8(b). ***This miter-frame clamp can be made in the shop. The four clamp blocks are made of hardwoods such as maple, birch, hickory, or oak. The sides are 5⁄16″ threaded rod. A 3⁄8″ steel pipe acts as a bushing that allows the rods easy movement for making adjustments.***

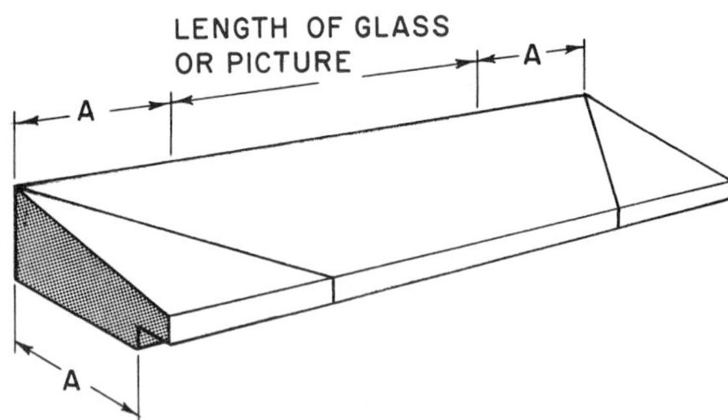

31-9. *Laying out a picture frame. The length marked on the outside of the frame is equal to the length of the glass plus twice the width of the stock measured from the rabbet to the outside edge.*

31-10. *Using a homemade miter box to cut a 45-degree angle. Notice that a handsaw with fine teeth is being used. A backsaw could also be used. This is very satisfactory for doing small jobs around the home.*

this measurement to the length of the glass or board. Fig. 31-9.

c. Mark the length of all pieces on the back edge.

d. If the frame is rectangular in shape, remember to measure the two sides and then the two ends. Make sure both matching pieces are the same length.

3. If no miter box is used, mark the angle of the joint with a combination square.

31-11. *Using a metal miter box.*

CUTTING

1. Hold the stock in the miter box. The back edge of the work should be against the back of the saw. Turn the saw 45 degrees to the left and cut the right end. Fig. 31-10. Cut the right end of all pieces. When using a metal miter box, put a piece of scrap stock under the work. This will keep the saw from marring the base. Hold the saw firmly and then release the catches that hold the saw up. Lower the saw slowly until the blade is just outside the layout line. Hold the stock firmly against the back with one hand. Saw with uniform strokes. Fig. 31-11.

2. Shift the stock. Turn the saw 45 degrees to the right and cut the left end. Remember, *reverse the saw, not the material.* Cut all pieces.

FITTING

1. Place the parts of the frame on a flat bench.

2. Check across the corners with a try square to see that they fit properly.

3. Measure with a rule across the diagonals. Both measurements must be the same.

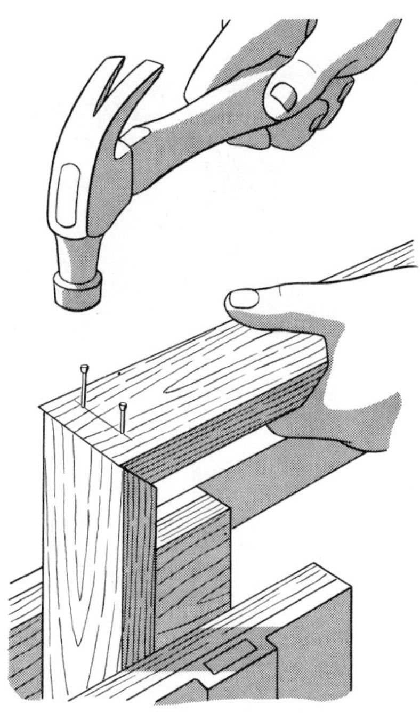

31-12. ***Assembling a miter joint by nailing.***

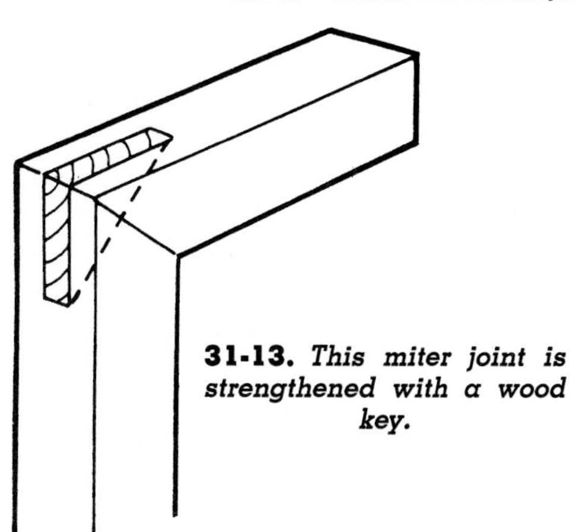

31-13. ***This miter joint is strengthened with a wood key.***

4. If the corner is slightly off, clamp the two pieces in a miter or corner clamp. Then saw through the joint with a very fine backsaw.

5. Another method is to plane or sand any high spots to make the corner fit snugly.

ASSEMBLING

1. There are several ways of fastening a miter joint. The simplest is to nail the corner. Fig. 31-12. Drive a nail into the first piece until the point just comes through the wood. Clamp the second piece in a vertical position in a vise. Hold the first piece with the corner slightly over the edge of the second piece. Drive the nail. The second piece will slip into place as the nail is set.

2. Clamp the two pieces in a miter-and-corner clamp. Nail or glue them.

3. Drill or bore a hole at right angles to each miter cut and fit a dowel across the corners.

4. The joint can also be strengthened by adding a key or spline. Fig. 31-13.

5. For rough work, the joint can be fastened with corrugated fasteners (wiggle nails) across each corner. See Fig. 33-11.

QUESTIONS

1. What are the advantages and disadvantages of a miter joint?

2. What is a metal miter box?

3. Tell how to make a miter box.

4. Describe making a layout for a picture frame that is 10 by 12 inches. The width of the frame from the rabbet edge is 2 inches.

5. Tell how mitered corners can be strengthened.

ACTIVITIES

1. In your home, find examples of items with miter joints. With your parents' permission bring one item to class.

2. Most miter joints are made to form a 90-degree angle. Therefore each piece is cut at 45 degrees. Suppose you wanted to make a 60-degree angle. How would you cut each piece? Try out your solution with strips of paper.

CHAPTER 32

Clamping and Gluing Up Stock

If a project is small or made of plywood, you probably won't need clamps and glue until you assemble it. However, for larger projects you will have to glue pieces together as you go. For example, you might have to glue stock edge to edge to make the top for a table or chair. Stock may have to be glued face to face to make legs. Parts must also be glued in final assembly. Fig. 32-1.

TOOLS AND MATERIALS

Clamps are used to hold pieces together:

- To find out how they fit.
- To hold them as the glue dries.
- For installing nails or screws.
- To do chiseling or planing on them. Fig. 32-2.

Hand screws are used for gluing face to face, for clamping small parts, and for holding work as it is cut or formed. This clamp can be used on finished surfaces without clamp blocks. The best size has a jaw length of 8 to 12 inches. Fig. 32-3.

32-1. *Parts of this project are being assembled with glue and screws.*

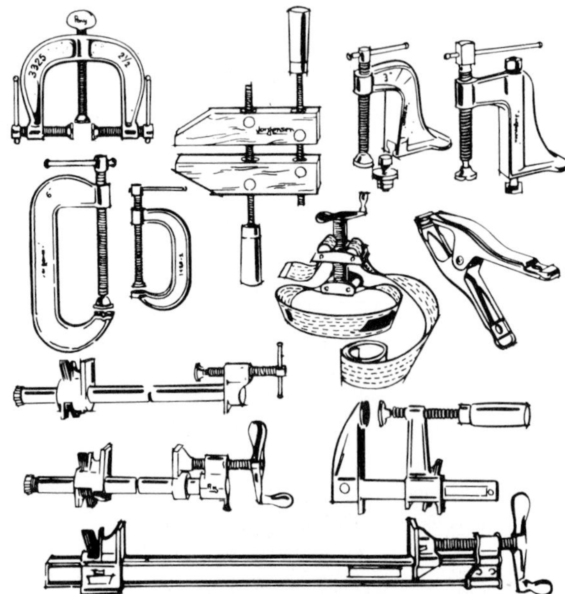

32-2. *A variety of clamps is used in woodworking.*

The *C-clamp* is used for clamping face to face, for repair work, and for holding parts together. The 6- to 10-inch size is for general use. Fig. 32-4.

The *bar clamp* is used for large work such as gluing stock edge to edge or assembling projects. The common lengths are 3 to 5 feet. Fig. 32-5.

The *pipe clamp* is similar to the bar clamp except that the clamping devices attach to steel

32-3. ***Using hand screws in assembling a project.***

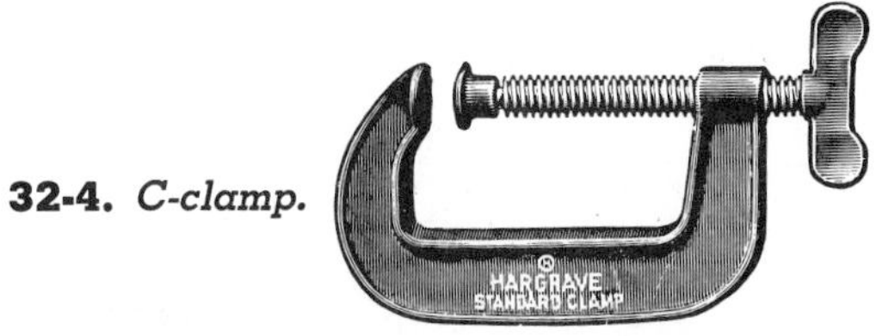

32-4. ***C-clamp.***

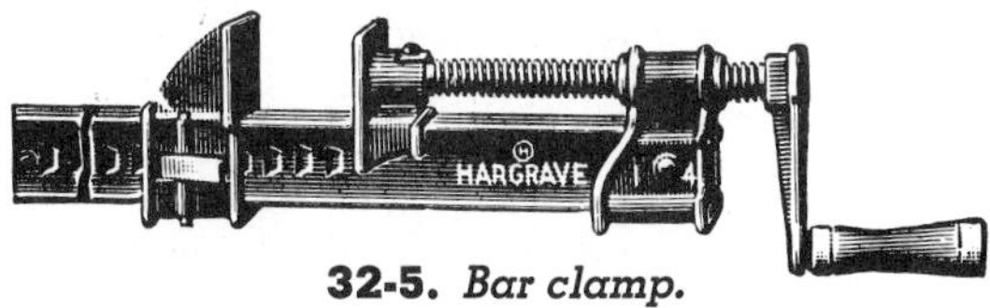

32-5. ***Bar clamp.***

pipe. This tool can be made as long as needed by using different lengths of pipe. Fig. 32-6.

Spring clamps can be applied quickly without turning a handle. Some spring clamps have plastic tips to protect the wood from the metal. Fig. 32-7.

Three-way edging clamps apply "right-angle" pressure to the edge or side of work. Fig. 32-8.

A *rubber* or *wooden mallet* is used to strike the wood when assembling projects.

Glues are used to fasten pieces permanently. Figure 32-9 shows the best kinds of glue for various jobs. The table in Fig. 32-10 describes the common types of glue. A very good all-purpose glue is liquid resin. It comes in tubes, squeeze bottles, and cans. The squeeze bottle is best for most projects because it is neat and there is little waste. This glue dries fast.

Clamp blocks are small pieces of scrap wood used with bar, pipe, and C-clamps to protect the finished parts of a project.

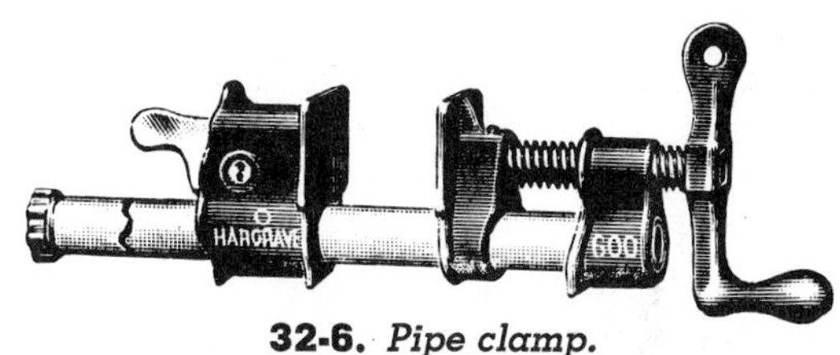

32-6. ***Pipe clamp.***

32-7. ***Spring clamps are useful when making repairs.***

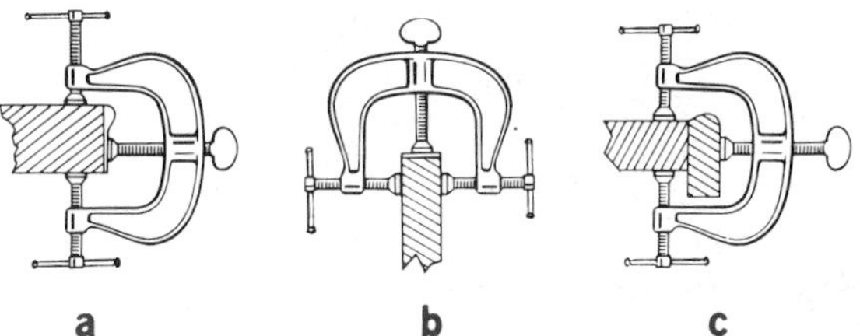

32-8. ***Some ways of using three-way edging clamps: (a) With the right-angle screw off-center. (b) With the right-angle screw centered. (c) Clamping around an edge.***

WHICH GLUE FOR THE JOB?

	Liquid Hide Glue	White (Polyvinyl) Liquid Resin Glue	Resorcinol	Powdered Resin	Powdered Casein	Flake Animal
Especially good for:	First choice for furniture work and wherever a tough, lasting wood-to-wood bond is needed. A favorite for cabinetwork and general wood gluing.	A fine all-around household glue for mending and furniture making and repair. Excellent for model work, paper, leather, and small assemblies.	This is the glue for any work that may be exposed to soaking: outdoor furniture, boats, wooden sinks.	Use it for woodworking and general gluing where considerable moisture resistance is wanted.	Will do most woodworking jobs and is especially desirable with oily woods: teak, lemon, yew.	Good for quantity woodworking jobs that justify the time and trouble of mixing and heating the glue.
Not so good for:	Because it is not waterproof, do not use it for outdoor furniture or for boat building.	Not sufficiently moisture-resistant for anything to be exposed to weather. Not so strong and lasting as liquid hide glue for fine furniture work.	Not good for work that must be done at temperatures below 70°F. Because of dark color and mixing, not often used unless waterproof quality is needed.	Do not use with oily woods or with joints that are not closely fitted and tightly clamped. Must be mixed for each use.	Not moisture-resistant enough for outdoor furniture. Will stain acid woods such as redwood. Must be mixed for each use.	Too much trouble to use for small jobs or most home shop work. Not waterproof.
Advantages:	Very strong because it is rawhide-tough and does not become brittle. It is easy to use, light in color, resists heat and mold. It has good filling qualities, so gives strength even in poorly fitted joints.	Always ready to use at any temperature. Nonstaining, clean, and white. Quick-setting qualities recommend it for work where good clamping is not possible.	Very strong, as well as waterproof. It works better with poor joints than many glues do.	Very strong, although brittle if joint fits poorly. Light-colored, almost waterproof.	Strong, fairly water-resistant, works in cool locations, fills poor joints well.	Same advantages as liquid hide glue but must be mixed, heated, kept hot, used at high temperatures.
Source:	From animal hides and bones.	From chemicals.	From chemicals.	From chemicals.	From milk curd.	From animal hides and bones.

32-9. ***The type of glue to use depends on the project. Here are some guidelines for choosing the right glue.***

FASTENING WOOD WITH ALL TYPES OF GLUE

Glue Type	Room Temperature	How to Prepare	How to Apply	70°F Clamping Time	
				Hardwood	Softwood
Liquid Hide	Sets best above 70°F. Can be used in colder room if glue is warmer.	Ready to use.	Apply thin coat on both surfaces; let get tacky before joining.	2 hours	3 hours
White Liquid Resin	Any temperature above 60°F, but the warmer the better.	Ready to use.	Spread on and clamp at once.	1 hour	1½ hours
Resorcinol	Must be 70°F or warmer. Will set faster at 90°F.	Mix 3 parts powder to 4 parts liquid catalyst.	Apply thin coat to both surfaces. Use within 8 hours after mixing.	16 hours	16 hours
Powdered Resin	Must be 70°F or warmer. Will set faster at 90°F.	Mix 2 parts powder with ½ to 1 part water.	Apply thin coat to both surfaces. Use within 4 hours after mixing.	16 hours	16 hours
Powdered Casein	Any temperature above freezing, but the warmer the better.	Stir together equal parts by volume glue and water. Wait 10–15 minutes and stir again.	Apply thin coat to both surfaces. Use within 8 hours after mixing.	2 hours	3 hours
Flaked or Powdered Animal	Must be 70° or warmer. Keep work warm.	For each ounce glue add 1½ ounces water (softwood) or 2 ounces water (hardwood).	Apply heavy coat at 140°F to both surfaces. Assemble rapidly.	1 hour	1½ hours

32-10. *This table tells how to prepare and apply common types of glue.*

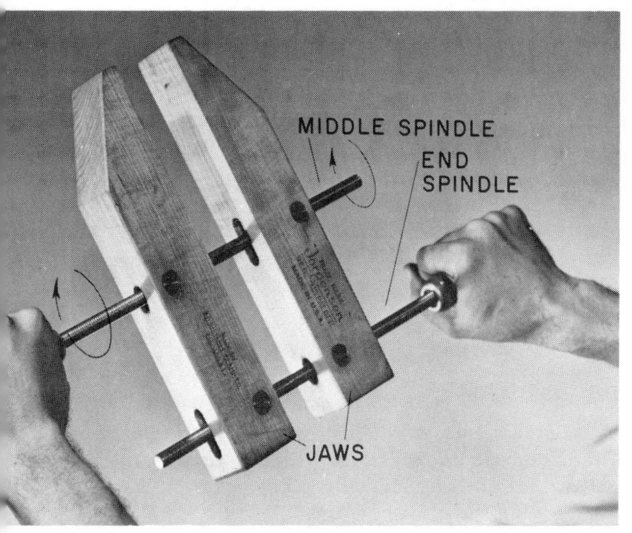

32-11. *Parts of a hand screw.*

CLAMPING

Using Hand Screws

The parts of a hand screw are shown in Fig. 32-11. To adjust a hand screw, grasp the handle of the middle spindle in one hand and the handle of the end spindle in the other. Revolve the spindles at the same time—in one direction to open and in the other to close. If the jaws aren't parallel, adjust one spindle until they are. Always tighten the middle spindle first and then the end spindle. Reverse to remove.

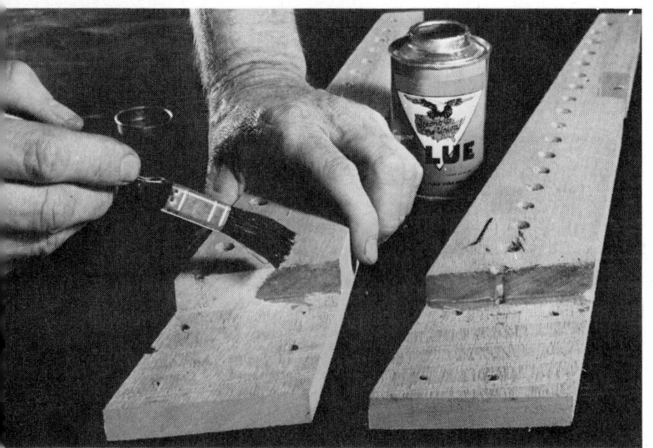

32-12. When gluing end grain it is a good idea to apply a thin coat of glue first. The end grain will absorb the glue. When applying glue to the rest of the joint, apply a second coat to the end grain. Notice that a brush is used to apply the liquid glue.

Tips on Clamping

- Dry-clamp all pieces before gluing to make sure that the joints fit properly and that you have enough clamps to do the job.
- For easy and accurate assembly, mark all pieces before gluing.
- Use small pieces of scrap wood or plastic to protect the wood from metal clamp jaws.
- Don't apply too much pressure. This would force the glue out of the joints, causing a weak, "starved" joint.

GLUING

Mixing Powdered Resin or Casein Glues

1. Follow directions on the can carefully. Never mix more glue than you can use at one time.
2. Many powdered glues are mixed with an equal amount of water.
3. Stir the glue briskly. Then allow it to stand about 10 to 15 minutes.
4. Mix again for about one minute. The glue should be about as thick as whipping cream.
5. Apply the glue with a brush or stick.

Mixing Resorcinol Glue

1. This glue comes in two separate cans. One contains the liquid resin and the other the powdered catalyst. The catalyst makes the glue work better and helps it to harden.
2. Mix the liquid and the powder in the exact amounts stated on the label. Never mix more than you need for one job.

Applying Glue

Follow these tips in applying all glues:

- Work at correct temperature.
- Apply two coats of glue to end grain. End grain tends to soak up glue. Fig. 32-12.
- Find the most convenient way to apply the glue (tube, squeeze bottle, etc.).
- Cover surfaces evenly.

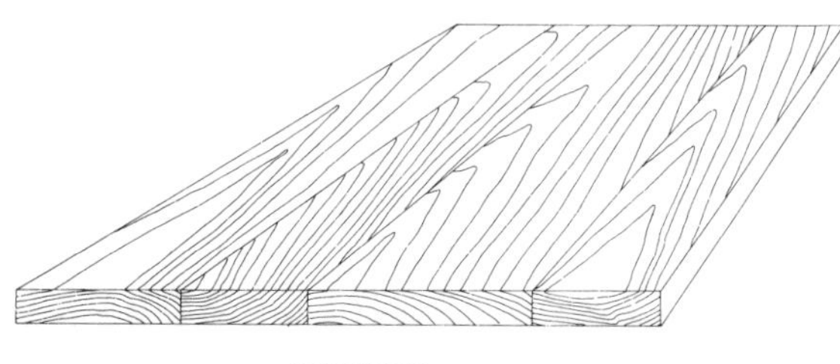

CORRECT

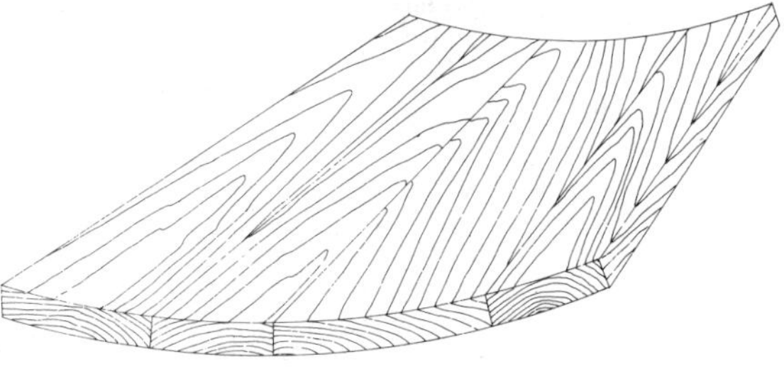

INCORRECT

32-13. Correct and incorrect way to assemble stock edge to edge. If assembled with growth rings all in same direction, the piece is more likely to warp.

Gluing Stock Edge to Edge

1. Choose the number of pieces needed to make the larger surface. Use pieces not more than 5 to 6 inches wide.
2. Square up each piece.
3. Arrange the pieces so that:

- The grain matches.
- The grain runs in the same direction.
- The growth rings at the ends of boards are in opposite directions. Fig. 32-13.

4. Mark the matching joints 1-1, 2-2, etc.
5. Test the edge joints to make sure the ends are tight. On long pieces the edges are planed so that there is a little opening (about the thickness of paper) near the center.
6. Add dowels or splines if you want a stronger joint.
7. Choose at least three bar clamps to hold the parts together. There should be a clamp every 10 to 12 inches along the assembly.
8. If the outer edges must be protected, use clamp blocks.
9. If the assembly is wide, put cleats across the ends to keep the surface level. Fig. 32-14.
10. Make a trial assembly to see that everything is all right. Open the bar clamps slightly wider than the assembly. Alternate the clamps—one above, the next below. Fig. 32-15. Tighten the clamps with moderate pressure. Check to make sure the surface is level and the joints are closed.

32-14. ***Cleats can be placed across the assembly to keep it level.***

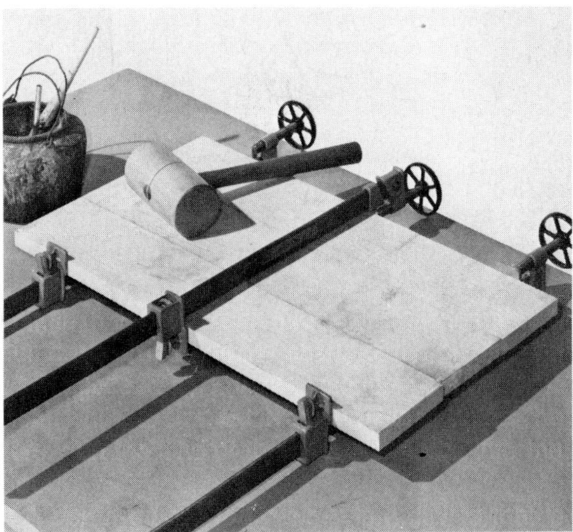

32-15. ***Note that the clamps are fastened from opposite sides.***

11. Take the assembly apart.
12. Apply glue to the edges and dowels or splines. Cover the edges but do not put on so much glue that it will squeeze out.
13. Put the joints together quickly.
14. Tighten the clamps a little at a time. If necessary, force the parts together with a rubber mallet.
15. If necessary put cleats across the ends. Wax paper under the cleats will keep them from sticking.

Gluing Stock Face to Face

1. Choose pieces to make the correct thickness. For most furniture legs, two pieces glued together are enough.
2. Square up the stock to rough size. This is done so that you can see the grain and know how to match the parts.
3. Assemble with the growth rings in opposite directions. Check to make sure the grain match-

32-16. *When gluing face to face with C-clamps, always use clamp blocks.*

es. Don't put a very light and a very dark piece side by side.

4. Use glue blocks and C-clamps or hand screws to hold the parts together. Fig. 32-16.

5. Apply the glue evenly over the surfaces. Clamp together.

ASSEMBLING A PROJECT

The steps in gluing up a project depend on how difficult it is. For a simple project of two or three pieces, all the gluing is done at the same time. For a more advanced project, such as a small table, the assembling is done in the following stages:

1. Get all the parts together and check to see that everything is complete.

2. Decide on how the project is to be assembled. Some projects of this kind have four legs

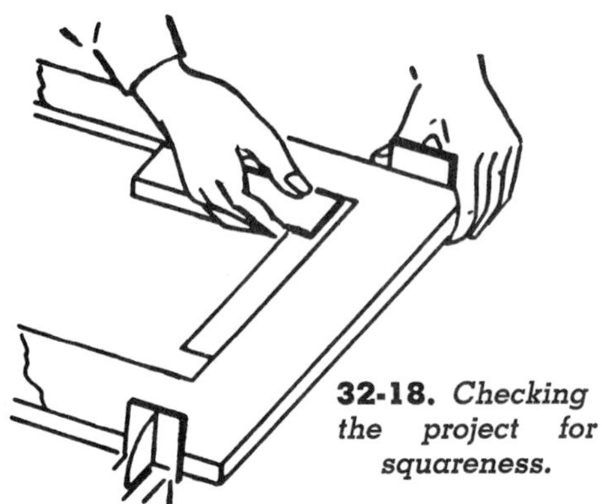

32-18. *Checking the project for squareness.*

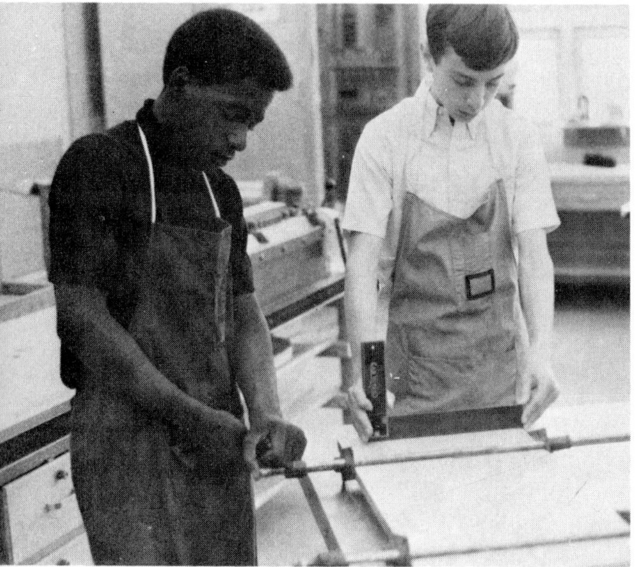

32-17. *Gluing up a frame may be one step in making a larger project.*

32-19. *Checking the project for levelness.*

and four rails. The best way is to glue the ends together first and then the complete project. Fig. 32-17.

3. Cut clamp blocks to protect the finished wood surface.

4. Select the correct kind and number of clamps.

5. Clamp the parts together to see if they fit. Make sure the parts are square and level. Figs. 32-18 and 32-19. Then take the project apart.

6. Mix the correct kind and amount of glue.

7. Apply the glue with a brush or squeeze bottle. Don't put on too much. Put a little extra glue on end grain.

8. Assemble the first part of the project. Clamp lightly. Then recheck to make sure the parts are square and level. Sometimes you have to shift a clamp or strike a joint with a rubber mallet to bring it into place.

9. Remove excess glue with a wet rag or sponge.

10. Allow the first section to dry.

11. Follow these steps for each section. Then assemble the complete project.

LEARN THESE SAFETY RULES BEFORE CLAMPING AND GLUING

* **Long bar and pipe clamps are heavy and hard to handle. Take special care when lifting the clamps from the rack. Be careful so you don't hit yourself or another student.**
* **Make sure you know where your helper's hands are when moving and tightening large clamps.**
* **Always position glued up stock out of the way so that the clamps aren't in the aisle.**
* **Keep glue off metal clamps and wooden hand screws. If metal clamps have glue on them and touch wood, they will stain the wood. If hand screws with glue on them touch the workpiece, they will stick together.**

QUESTIONS

1. Which glues are waterproof?
2. Why is liquid resin a good all-around glue to use in a school shop?
3. What three things must you check for when gluing stock edge to edge?
4. What can be used on the edge of stock to make a stronger joint?
5. Should a small table be glued up all at once? Explain.

ACTIVITIES

1. Refer to the tables on pages 176 and 177 and answer the following questions. (a) Which glue is a good all-around adhesive for household use? (b) Which glue should be used for outdoor furniture and boats? (c) Which glues require the longest clamping time?
2. Demonstrate how to use C-clamps.

LEARN THESE SAFETY RULES BEFORE USING HAMMERS

- Strike the surface squarely.
- Never use a claw hammer on hardened metal (chisels, punches).
- Never use a hammer to strike another hammer.
- Always wear safety goggles to protect your eyes.
- The greatest danger is to miss the head of the nail and strike your fingers. Watch the nailhead, not the hammer.
- Don't put nails in your mouth.
- When nailing together pieces of very hard wood, such as oak or maple, drill a small pilot hole in the first piece. This makes it easier to drive the nail into the wood.
- Make sure the hammer is in good condition so that the handle will not splinter or the head fly off.
- Keep the hammer's face free of grease and oil to keep it from slipping while being used.
- To drive a nail safely, hold the nail near its head with your thumb and forefinger. Position the hammer on the nailhead. Draw the hammer back and give the nail one or two light taps to start. Then let go of the nail and finish hammering.

Using Nails

Nails are used to hold wood pieces together. Nailing is one of the most common ways of assembling projects. Although it seems very simple, nailing takes a good deal of skill. Just watch an experienced carpenter or cabinetmaker drive nails and you'll appreciate this skill.

Remember the six simple machines in Chapter 10? The hammer is a *lever.* As you see in Fig. 33-1, it is used as an extension of the lever that is your arm. By using the hammer, you increase the speed and distance the force moves. This force drives the nail into the wood. Here, less force over longer distance gives greater force over shorter distance (the amount the nail moves with each blow). The nail goes in easier when it has a sharp point (wedge). Try starting a nail that has

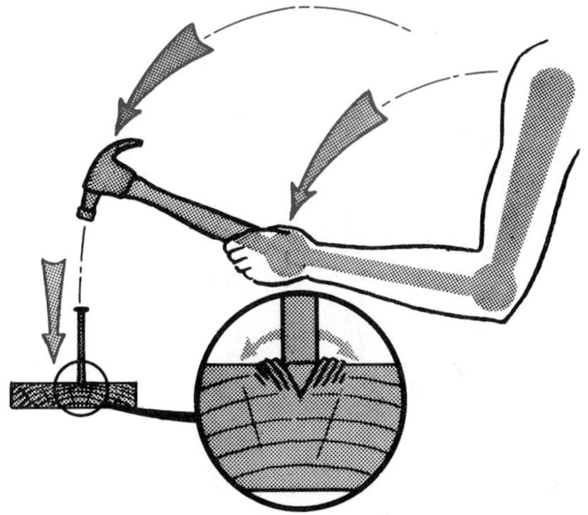

33-1. *Driving a nail.*

no point. As the nail is driven, wood fibers are pressed down or broken off. They are jammed between the nail and other, unbroken fibers. Thus the nail is wedged into the wood.

TOOLS AND MATERIALS

The *claw hammer* has a wood, metal, or fiberglass handle. Fig. 33-2. Some workers like the metal handle. Others prefer the wood or fiberglass because these don't vibrate so much. Hammer size is shown by weight and varies from 7 to 28 ounces. A 16-ounce hammer is good for average work.

There are many kinds of nails. The four used the most are the common, box, casing, and finishing. Most nails are made of mild steel or aluminum. Aluminum nails have the advantage of not rusting when used out-of-doors. *Common nails* are for rough construction such as home building. *Box nails* are somewhat smaller and are used where the common nails might split out the wood, such as in building boxes or crates. *Casing nails* have a smaller head and are used in interior trim in houses and in cabinetmaking. *Finishing nails* have small heads and are ideal for project making, cabinetwork, and finish carpentry. Fig. 33-3.

There are also many special nails used in construction. Fig. 33-4. These are available with different kinds of shanks, heads, points, and finishes or coatings. Fig. 33-5 (page 186). If you have a special nailing problem, ask your building supply dealer to suggest the correct kind of nails to use.

Nail size is given by the term *penny,* which is shown by the letter *d.* No one knows exactly where this term came from. Some people think it meant the cost of nails in pence (English money), while others think it meant the weight per thousand. In either case, the term is still used. For example, a 3d nail is 1¼ inches long; a 6d nail is 2 inches long. A 6d common and a 6d finishing nail are both 2 inches long, but the common nail is larger in diameter. That is because the nails are made from different gauge wire—11½ gauge for common, 13 gauge for finishing. (The higher the gauge number of the nail, the smaller the diameter.) Fig. 33-6.

Two other small nails are escutcheon pins and wire brads. They are used in making novelties and small articles. *Escutcheon pins* are small brass nails with round heads. They come in lengths from ¼ inch to 1¼ inches and in diameters from 20 gauge to 16 gauge. *Wire brads* are small, flatheaded, mild steel nails with sharp points. They come in lengths from ½ inch to 1½ inches, in gauge numbers from 20 to 14. You can get these fasteners at a given length in several gauges.

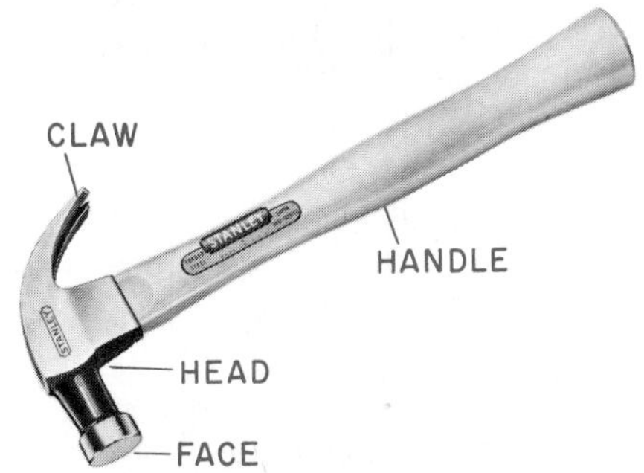

33-2. *Parts of a claw hammer. The handle is hickory. (Stanley Tools)*

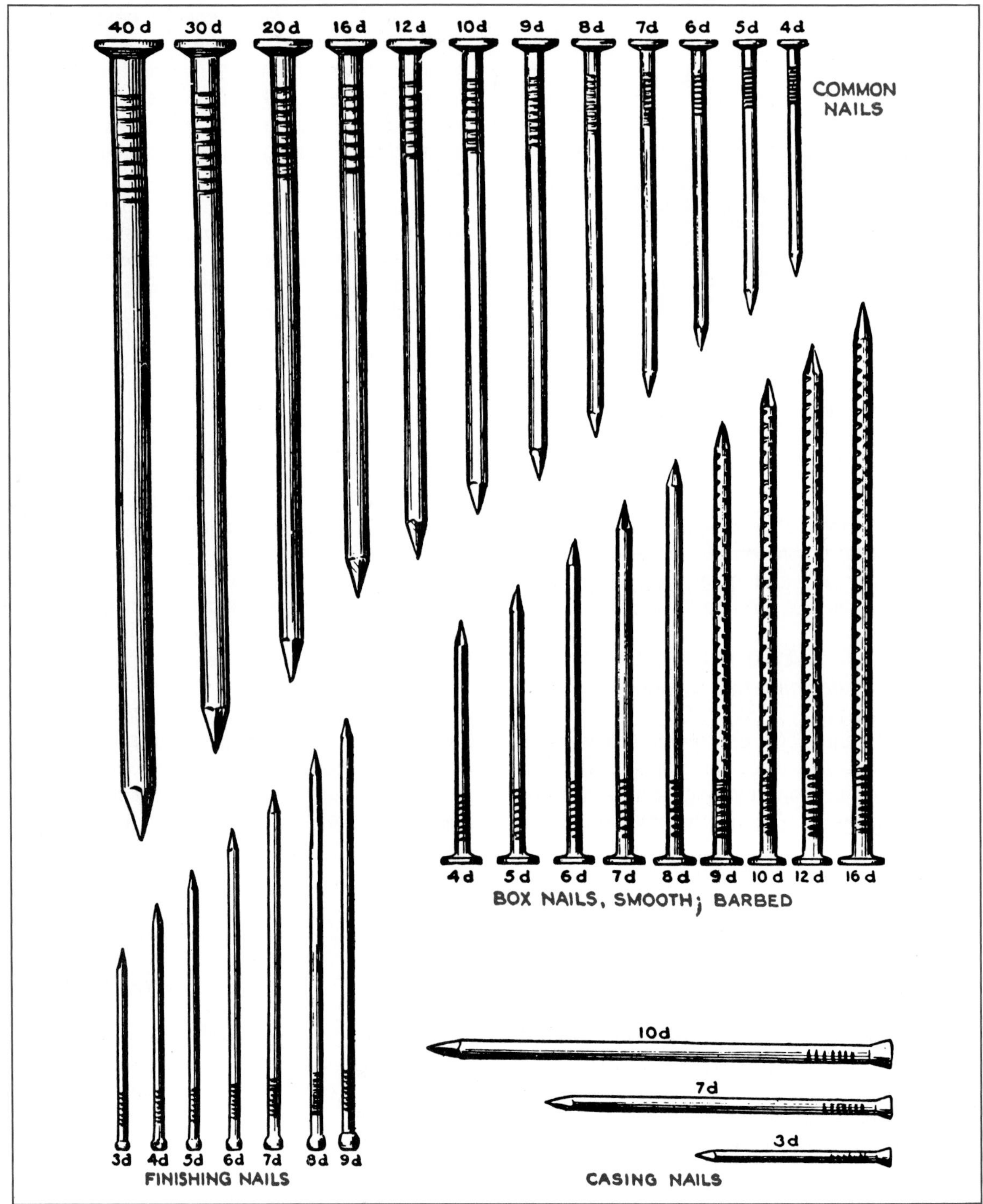

33-3. *Kinds and sizes of commonly used nails. These nails are shown full size.*

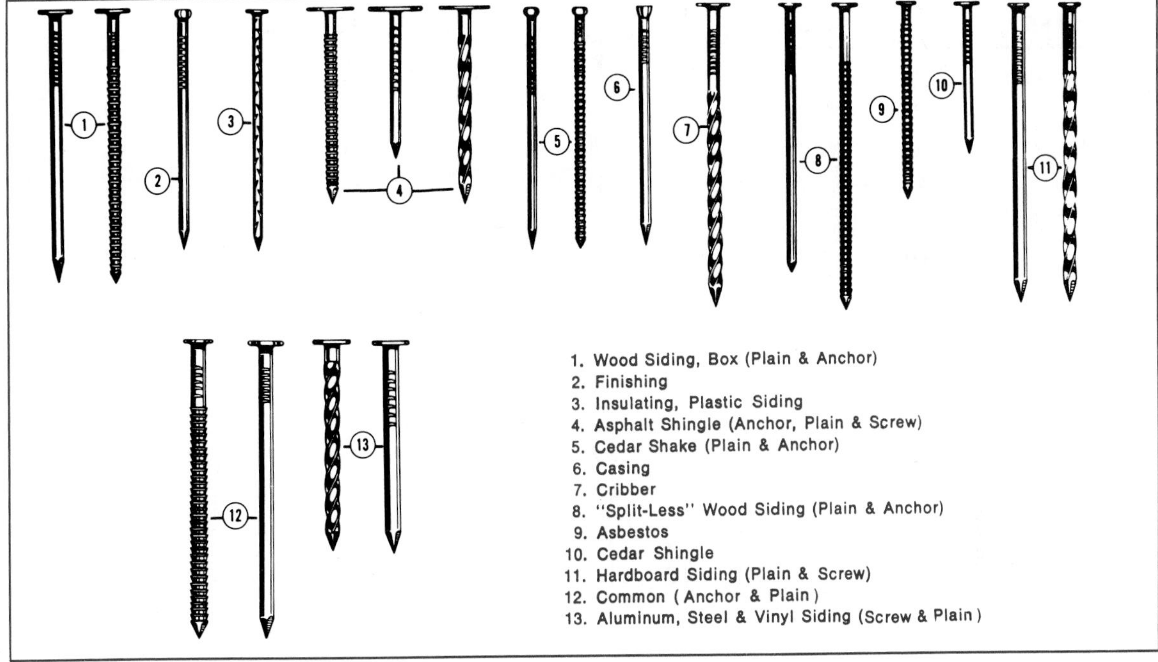

33-4. *A few of the special nails used in construction.*

A *nail set* is a small metal punch with a cupped end. The cupped end prevents it from slipping off the head of the nail. The tool is used to sink the heads of casing or finishing nails below the wood surface. Fig. 33-7.

DRIVING NAILS

1. Decide on the size and kind of nails you need. Choose the smallest diameter that will do the job. A nail too large will split the wood. Nails should be a little shorter than the thickness of the pieces being nailed. In some cases nails are driven through and the points stick out the other side. Then the points are *clinched* (bent over) with the grain.

2. Decide on the number and location of the nails. The nails should be evenly spaced but *staggered* (not in a straight line). Putting several nails along the same grain line will split the wood. When nailing hardwood, put a little wax or soap on the point of the nail so that it goes in easier. If you think there is danger of splitting the wood, first drill a hole that is smaller than the nail (about three-fourths the diameter of the nail).

3. Hold the nail between your thumb and forefinger. Grasp the hammer handle near its end. Tap the nail lightly to start it. Take your hand away from the nail.

4. Drive the nail by swinging the hammer and your arm as a unit. Use just a little wrist movement. Strike the nail with a few good blows, keeping your eye on the nail.

5. If the nail bends, don't try to straighten it by striking it on the side. Remove the nail and use a new one. Nails driven at an angle have better holding power. When nailing into end grain, drive the first nail in straight and the other nails at an angle.

6. If the nail is a casing or finishing nail, drive it until the head still shows. Then use a nail set

	TYPE	REMARKS	ILLUSTRATION
SHANKS	Smooth	For normal holding power; temporary fastener.	
	Spiral	For greater holding power; permanent fastener.	
	Ringed	For highest holding power; permanent fastener.	
HEADS	Flat Counter-Sink	For nail concealment; light construction, flooring, and interior trim.	
	Drywall	For gypsum wallboard.	
	Finishing	For nail concealment; cabinetwork, furniture.	
	Flat	For general construction.	
	Large Flat	For tear resistance; roofing paper.	
	Oval	For special effects; siding and clapboard.	
POINTS	Diamond	For general use, 35° angle; length about 1.5 x diameter.	
	Blunt Diamond	For harder wood species to reduce splitting, 45° angle.	
	Long Diamond	For fast driving, 25° angle; may tend to split harder species.	
	Duckbill	For clinching small nails.	

33-5. ***Nails are made with various kinds of shanks, heads, and points. They can be made of aluminum, mild steel, or high-carbon steel. Nails may have a bright finish, be blued (for better holding power), or be coated with plastic or metal (such as zinc).***

with a point slightly smaller than the head of the nail. Place the point of the nail set over the head of the nail, guiding it with your fingers. Drive the head a little below the surface (about 1/16 inch). Fig. 33-8.

REMOVING NAILS

1. To remove nails from a board, use the claw of the hammerhead. Slip the claw under the nailhead and pull the handle down.

2. On finished surfaces, place a thin board or

NAIL SIZES

Size	Length in Inches	American Steel Wire Gauge Number		
		Common	Box and Casing	Finishing
2d	1	15*	15½	16½
3d	1¼	14	14½	15½
4d	1½	12½	14	15
5d	1¾	12½	14	15
6d	2	11½	12½	13
7d	2¼	11½	12½	13
8d	2½	10¼	11½	12½
9d	2¾	10¼	11½	12½
10d	3	9	10½	11½
12d	3¼	9	10½	11½
16d	3½	8	10	11
20d	4	6	9	10
30d	4½	5	9	
40d	5	4	8	

*Note: The decimal inch equivalent of common gauge numbers is:

15 = 0.072	12 = 0.106	9 = 0.148	6 = 0.192
14 = 0.080	11 = 0.121	8 = 0.162	5 = 0.207
13 = 0.092	10 = 0.135	7 = 0.177	4 = 0.225

33-6. ***Typical sizes of common, box, casing, and finishing nails.***

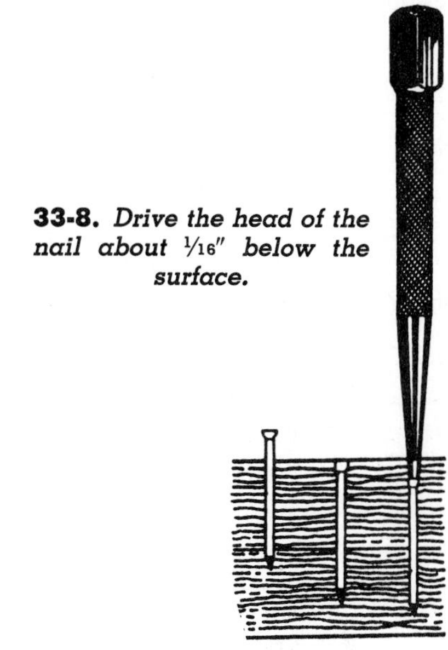

33-8. ***Drive the head of the nail about 1/16" below the surface.***

33-7. ***Nail set. (Stanley Tools)***

33-9. ***Using a piece of scrap wood under the head of the hammer to increase leverage.***

piece of plywood under the claw to protect the surface. If the nail is quite long, put a thick block under the claw after the nail is partway out. This helps to keep the nail straight and gives you better leverage. Fig. 33-9.

TOENAILING

This is a way of fastening the end of one board to the edge or face of another. The nails are driven at an angle from both sides of the first board. This helps to hold the boards tightly together. Fig. 33-10.

USING CORRUGATED FASTENERS

These are a kind of wiggle nail used in general construction and repair work. They are often used, for example, in holding the corners of window screens together. These fasteners hold best when placed at an angle to the grain, but this is not always possible. Fig. 33-11.

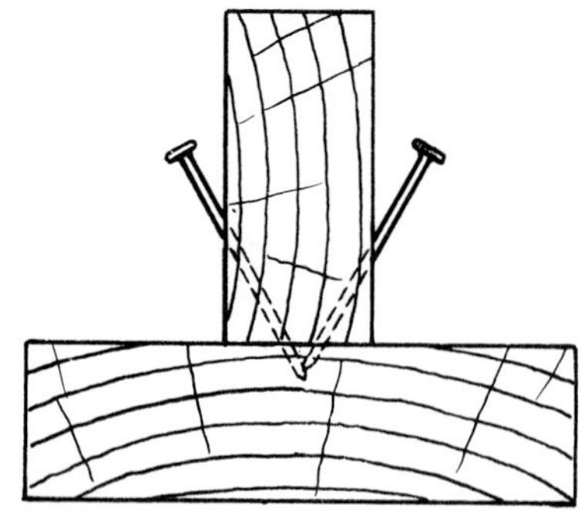

33-10. *The correct method of toenailing.*

33-11(a). *Using a corrugated fastener to reinforce a miter joint. This fastener has greater strength than an ordinary nail.*

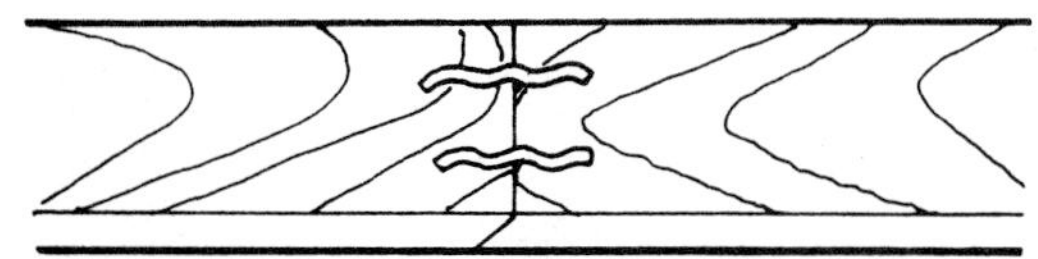

33-11(b). *Another use for corrugated fasteners.*

QUESTIONS

1. Name the parts of a claw hammer.
2. What is a nail set and how is it used?
3. Name the four kinds of nails used most often.
4. What are the uses for a finishing nail?
5. Describe an escutcheon pin.
6. Why should nails be staggered?
7. What is the difference between a brad and a finishing nail?
8. How do you remove a nail?
9. What is toenailing?
10. Describe the way to use corrugated fasteners.

ACTIVITIES

1. Visit a hardware store or building supply center. List the kinds of nails available.
2. Demonstrate how to start a nail. Be sure to observe safety rules. What can be put on a nail to make it easier to drive into hardwood?

Installing Screws

A *screw* is a fastener with a groove twisting around part of its length. It is one of the best wood fasteners. A screw is strong. It does not come out easily. It can be tightened and later loosened to take an article apart. Fig. 34-1.

TOOLS AND MATERIALS

Wood screws are made of mild steel, brass, aluminum, or copper. Brass screws are used for boats, water skis, or other projects used around water. The most common head shapes are *round, flat,* and *oval.* Fig. 34-2. Roundhead screws of mild steel are made with a blue finish. Flathead screws of mild steel have a bright finish. Ovalhead screws are usually plated with cadmium or chromium and are used most often to install hinges, hooks, and other hardware. Most screws have a plain *slotted* head. However, the *recessed* (Phillips) head is becoming more popular.

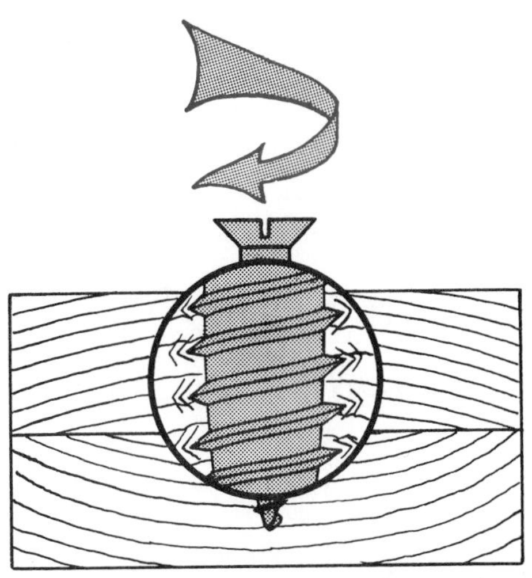

34-1. *A wood screw is the most efficient device for holding pieces together. A force applied to the head causes the screw to move into the wood. One complete turn of the screw moves it straight into the wood by an amount equal to the distance from the top of one thread to the top of the next. The thread itself is an inclined plane.*

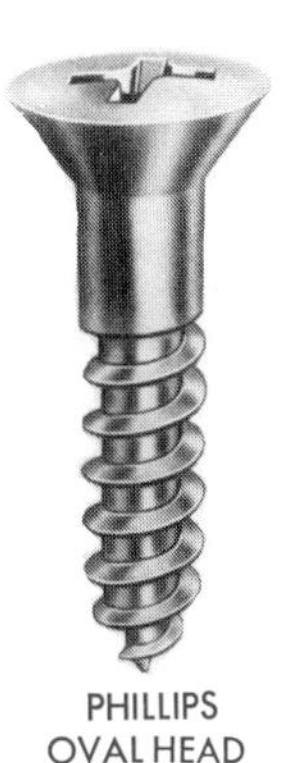

PHILLIPS OVAL HEAD WOOD SCREW

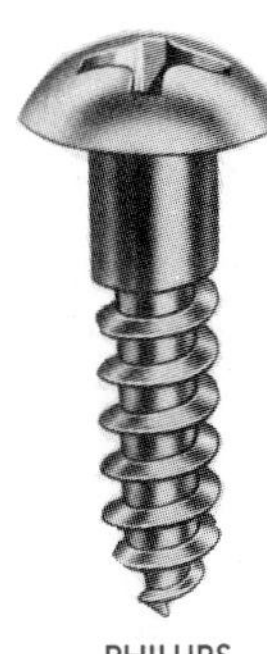

PHILLIPS ROUND HEAD WOOD SCREW

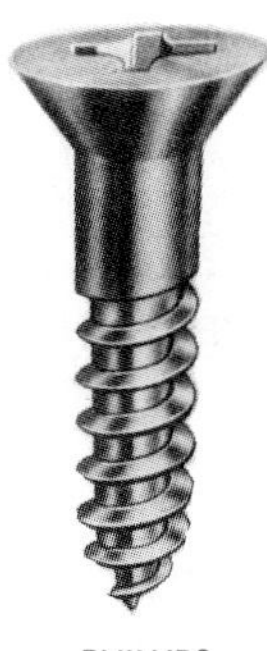

PHILLIPS FLAT HEAD WOOD SCREW

SLOTTED OVAL HEAD WOOD SCREW

SLOTTED FLAT HEAD WOOD SCREW

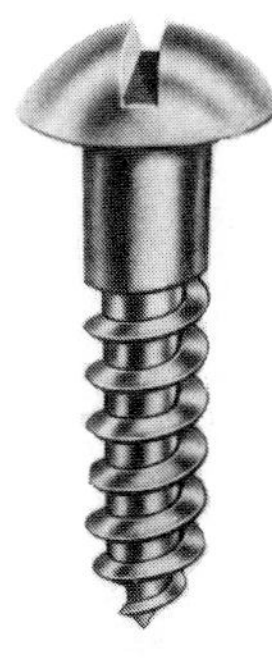

SLOTTED ROUND HEAD WOOD SCREW

34-2. *Common head shapes and types of slots.*

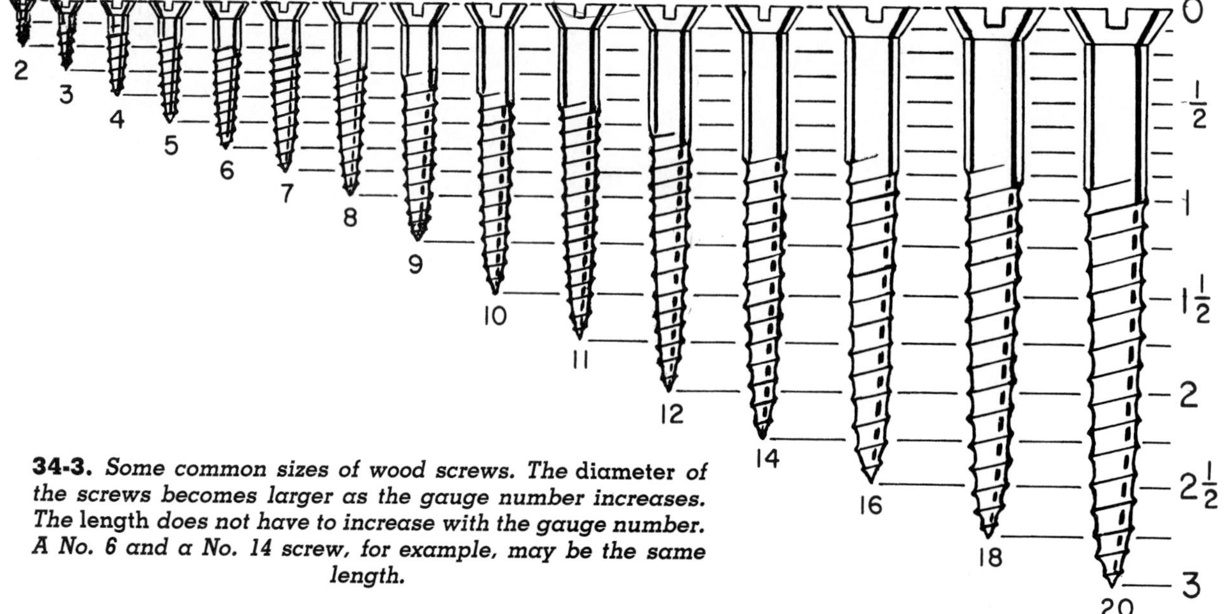

34-3. *Some common sizes of wood screws. The diameter of the screws becomes larger as the gauge number increases. The length does not have to increase with the gauge number. A No. 6 and a No. 14 screw, for example, may be the same length.*

Screws come in different lengths from ¼ inch to 6 inches. They also come in different gauge sizes from 0 to 24. The gauge tells the diameter. The larger the gauge number, the greater the diameter of the screw. Screws of the same length come in different gauge sizes. For example, a No. 6 screw, 1½ inches long, is a very slim screw, while a No. 14 screw, 1½ inches long, is a fat screw. Fig. 34-3. Generally the lower gauge numbers are used for thin wood and the higher numbers for heavy wood.

Screws are sold by the dozen or by the hundred in hardware stores. They are packed in factories by the pound.

The five most common sizes of flathead screws are:

- No. 7: ¾ inch long.
- No. 8: 1 inch long.
- No. 8: 1¼ inch long.
- No. 10: 1¼ inch long.
- No. 12: 1½ inch long.

There are two types of screwdrivers. The *plain* screwdriver is used to install slotted-head screws. The size depends on the length and diameter of the blade. Fig. 34-4. The *Phillips-head* screwdriver is also made in different diameters and lengths. It is used to install Phillips-head screws. Fig. 34-5. Its tip cannot be reshaped.

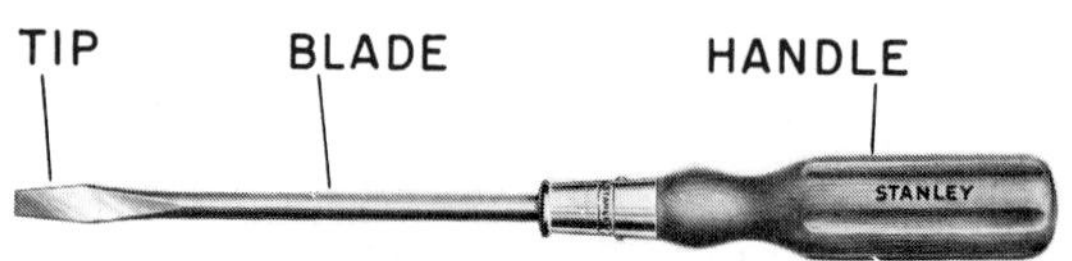

34-4. *A plain screwdriver.*

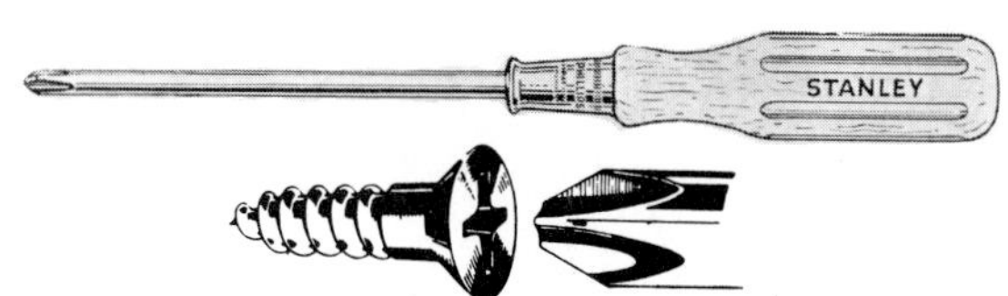

34-5. *A Phillips-head screwdriver. (Stanley Tools)*

An *82-degree countersink* is needed for flathead screws that must be flush with the surface. This tool makes a cone-shaped hole for the head of the screw to go into. Fig. 34-6.

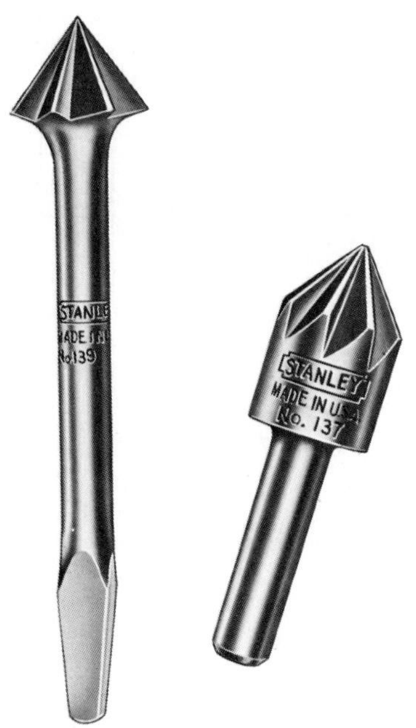

34-6. ***A countersink for a brace (left) and for a hand drill or drill press (right). (Stanley Tools)***

34-7. ***Screwdriver bit to be used in a brace. (Stanley Tools)***

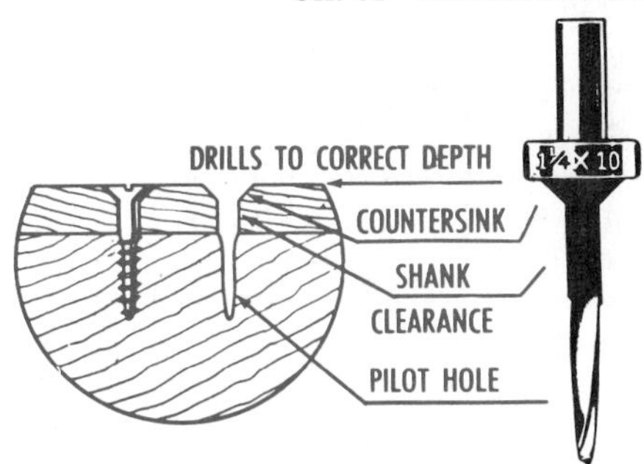

34-8. ***A screw-mate drill and countersink to use with flathead screws. (Stanley Tools)***

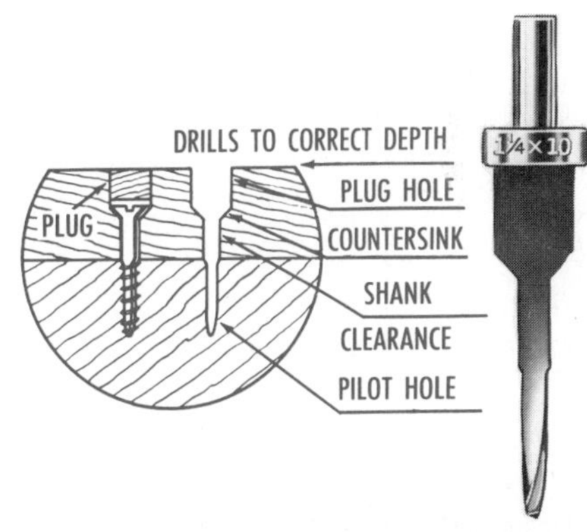

34-9. ***A screw-mate counterbore which does five things at once. A wood plug can be used to cover the screwhead. (Stanley Tools)***

A *screwdriver bit* can be used in a brace for setting screws. Fig. 34-7.

A *screw-mate drill and countersink* is a tool for installing flathead screws. Fig. 34-8. It will do four things at once: drill the hole to correct depth, countersink, make the correct shank clearance, and make the correct pilot hole. This tool is stamped with the length and gauge number. For example, a ¾″ × #6 is used for a flathead screw ¾ inch long and No. 6 gauge size.

A *counterbore* will do all the operations performed by the screw mate, plus drilling plug holes for wooden plugs. Fig. 34-9.

INSTALLING SCREWS

1. Choose a screw long enough to go two-thirds its length into the second piece of wood. Another rule to follow is to make sure that all the threaded part of the screw will go into the second piece. The diameter of the screw should be chosen according to the thickness of the wood.

2. Mark the location of the screw hole in the first piece of wood. Make a punch mark with a center punch or scratch awl.

3. Select a drill that will be equal in diameter to the shank of the screw and drill a shank hole in the first piece. The table in Fig. 34-10 shows the correct drill size. You can also hold the drill behind the screw shank and sight for size.

DRILL SIZES FOR WOOD SCREWS

Screw Gauge No.	0	1	2	3	4	5	6	7	8	9	10	11	12	14	16	18	20
Shank Hole Hard & Soft Wood	1/16	5/64	3/32	7/64	7/64	1/8	9/64	5/32	11/64	3/16	3/16	13/64	7/32	1/4	17/64	19/64	21/64
Pilot Hole Soft Wood	1/64	1/32	1/32	3/64	3/64	1/16	1/16	1/16	5/64	5/64	3/32	3/32	7/64	7/64	9/64	9/64	11/64
Pilot Hole Hard Wood	1/32	1/32	3/64	1/16	1/16	5/64	5/64	3/32	3/32	7/64	7/64	1/8	1/8	9/64	5/32	3/16	13/64
Auger Bit Sizes for Plug Hole			3	4	4	4	5	5	6	6	6	7	7	8	9	10	11

34-10. *This table shows the drill sizes to use for various gauges of screws.*

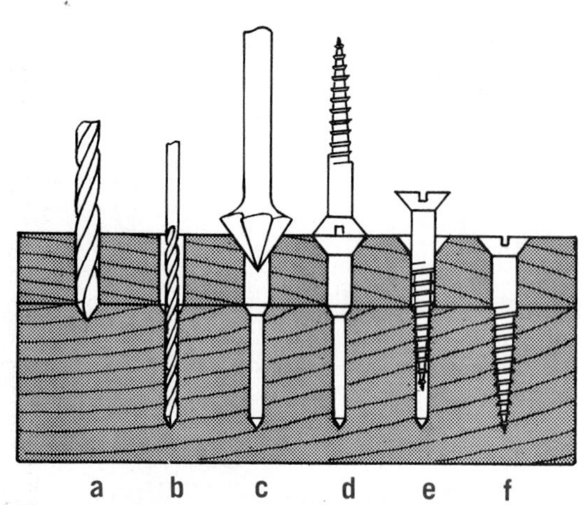

34-11. *Steps in installing a flathead screw: (a) Drill the shank hole. (b) Drill the pilot, or anchor, hole. (c) Countersink. (d) Check the amount of countersink with the screwhead. (e) Install the flathead screw. (f) Screw properly installed.*

4. Place the first piece of wood over the second. Mark the location of the screw hole in the second piece.

5. Drill a pilot hole (anchor hole) to the depth the screw will go. If the wood is very soft, this hole may not be needed. The drill for the pilot hole must be about equal to the smallest diameter of the threaded part of the screw. Here again you can use a chart or sight for size. Use a depth or bit gauge if several screws must be installed.

6. When using flathead screws, cut a conical (cone-shaped) hole with a countersink so that the head of the screw will be flush with the surface. To check, turn the screw upside down and see if the hole is just right. Fig. 34-11. If you are installing many screws of the same size, put a depth or bit gauge on the countersink.

7. The blade of a plain screwdriver should be equal to the width of the screwhead. A screwdriver that is too small will slip and make a *burr* (a rough edge) on the screwhead. A screwdriver that is too large will mar the wood as you finish tightening the screw. The tool should be ground so that it has a straight, square blade. Fig. 34-12.

8. Hold the screw between your thumb and forefinger. Hold the handle of the screwdriver lightly in your other hand. Start the screw. Then slip the hand holding the screw up behind the tip of the screwdriver to guide the tool as you tighten the screw. Fig. 34-13.

9. Don't try to tighten the screw too much. You may break the screw or strip the threads in the wood, and the fastener won't hold. You must be especially careful with aluminum or brass screws.

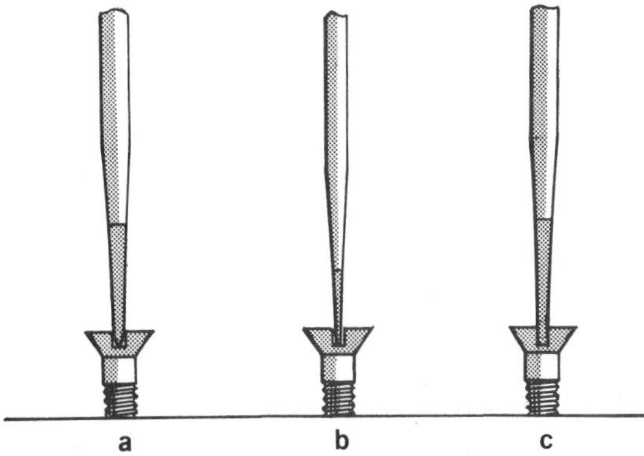

34-12. *Incorrect and correct way of grinding a screwdriver for slotted-head screws: (a) Tip rounded. (b) Tip too thin. (c) Tip properly fitted.*

34-13. *Starting to drive a screw. Note that the screwdriver is guided with the thumb and forefinger.*

10. If several screws are used to fasten two parts together, it is a good idea first to drill all the shank holes (and countersink). Then drill one pilot hole and install the screw before drilling the other pilot holes. This makes it easier to line up the parts to be put together.

11. In driving a large number of screws, a screwdriver bit may be used in a brace to speed the work.

CONCEALING THE SCREWHEAD

On some projects you don't want the screwhead to show. As a first step, bore a shallow hole with an auger bit that is the same diameter as the screwhead. Then, after the screw is set, you can cover the screw with plastic wood or a plug. Figs. 34-14 and 34-15. A plain plug or button (small wood covering) can be cut on the drill press, or a decorative plug can be bought. Fig. 34-16.

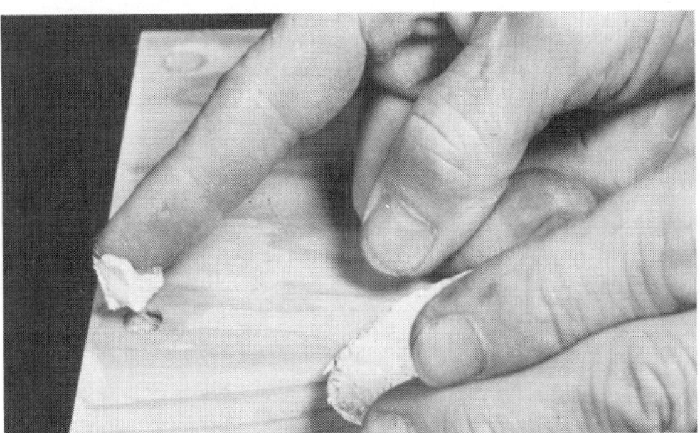

34-14. *Screws can be countersunk and the hole filled with plastic wood. Remember when adding a filler to apply it so that it is slightly higher than the wood. Sand it off level after it is dry.*

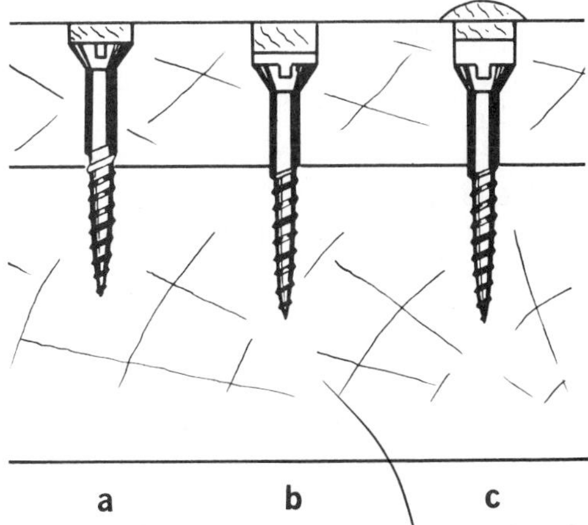

34-15. *Three methods of covering the heads of screws: (a) Plastic wood. (b) A plain wood plug. (c) A fancy wood plug.*

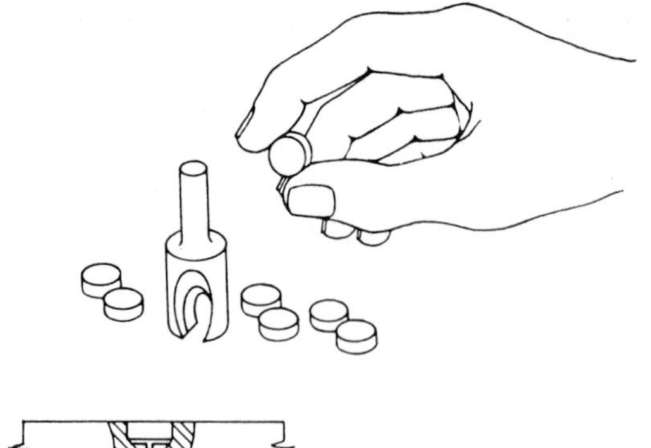

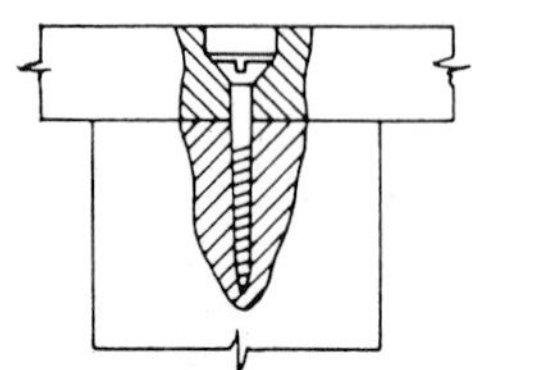

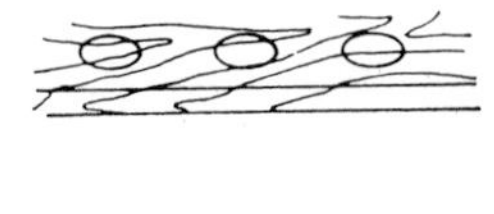

34-16. ***If you make a project where screws are countersunk or counterbored, it will pay to use a plug cutter. This tool cuts perfect plugs from the same stock used for the project. Plug cutters are made in sizes 6, 8, 10, and 12 to match the commonly used screw sizes. The plugs are a snug fit in the counterbored holes.***

HOUSEHOLD SCREW DEVICES

Figure 34-17 shows some of the common household screw devices. Common sizes of *cup hooks* (usually made of brass) are 1/2, 5/8, 3/4, 1, 1 1/4 and 1 1/2 inch. *Screw hooks* are made in lengths from 1 1/4 to 2 1/2 inches. *"L" (square-bent) screw hooks* are available in lengths from 1 inch to 2 1/4 inches. *Screw eyes* are made with either small or medium eyes in many different sizes.

34-17. ***These devices are often used around the home. For example, cup hooks are installed under kitchen cabinet shelves to hold cups.***

QUESTIONS

1. Why is a screw better than a nail?
2. Name three of the materials from which screws are made.
3. What are the three most common head shapes?
4. Which is larger in diameter, a No. 4 or a No. 10 screw?
5. Name the most common sizes of flathead screws.
6. When is an 82-degree countersink needed?
7. How do you choose the correct size screw?
8. What is a shank hole?
9. What is a pilot, or anchor, hole?
10. How can you hide the heads of screws?

ACTIVITIES

1. This chapter describes slotted and Phillips head screws. Visit a hardware store or building supply center. Can you find other varieties of screws?
2. Demonstrate how to install a screw. Be sure to follow all safety rules.

Installing Hardware

Two kinds of hardware are used in constructing certain projects. *Cabinet* hardware (such as hinges, handles, and catches) is needed to complete a project that has doors and drawers. Fig. 35-1. *Structural* hardware (such as repair plates) is used to strengthen wood joints and hold unseen parts of a project together.

Hardware that is part of the final trim should be the proper style. For example, don't put an Early American drawer pull on a modern chest. Hardware stores carry a wide variety of these items. You should choose hardware carefully; know what kind you want before you go to the store. Large catalogs are available that show every different type of hardware item. Some of the more common ones are discussed here.

35-1. ***This small dry sink has surface hinges on the doors and metal knobs for handles. Note the wood plugs. They cover screws used to fasten the parts together.***

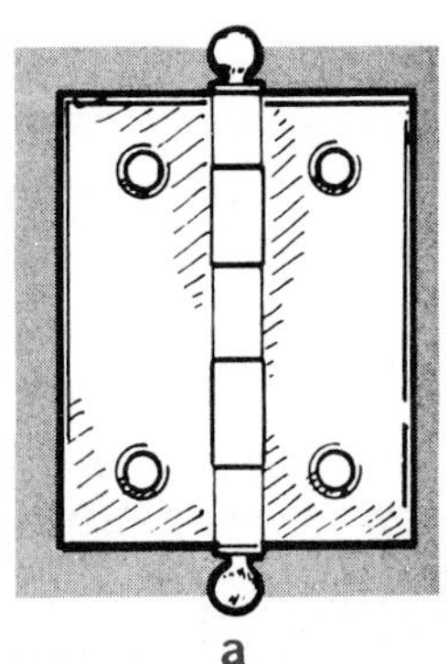

a

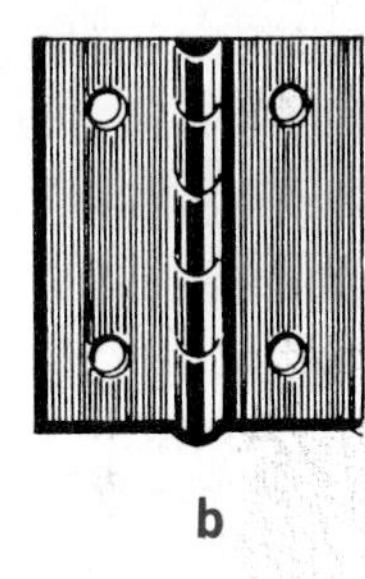

b

35-2. ***Common butt hinges: (a) Loose pin hinge. (b) Solid pin hinge.***

HINGES

The *butt hinge* is the most common. Fig. 35-2. It is used for hanging most kinds of doors. You can buy this hinge with either a loose or a solid pin. If a loose pin is used, be sure that the hinge is mounted so that the pin won't fall out. One leaf of the butt hinge is fastened to the edge of the door and the other to the edge of the frame. A *gain* (a large groove) must be chiseled out in both the door edge and the edge of the frame. The number of hinges and their size depend on the size of the door. A small door of about 18 inches, for example, would probably require only two hinges about 1½ to 2 inches long.

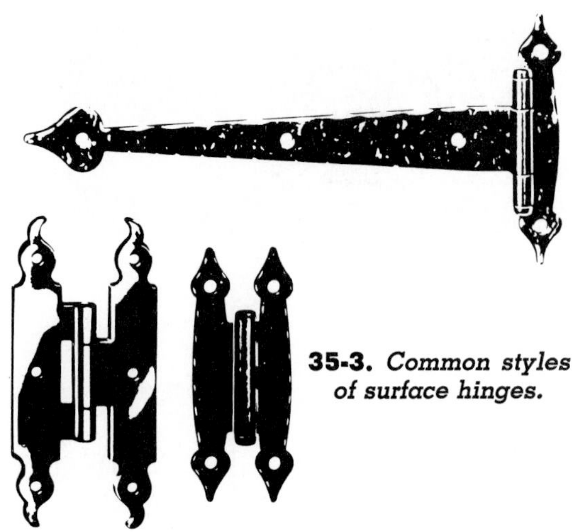

35-3. *Common styles of surface hinges.*

The *surface hinge* is the easiest to use. Fig. 35-3. It can be bought in many different styles, such as Early American, Modern, and Traditional. The surface hinge is fastened directly to the front of both door and frame.

Other *cabinet hinges* are used for installing flush or overlay doors or for a door with a lip. Fig. 35-4. A semi-concealed (partly hidden) cabinet hinge is the most common. To install this, first mark the location for the hinge on the inside of the door and fasten the hinge to the door itself. Then hold the door with the hinge against the frame. Mark the location of the screws, do the drilling, and install the hinge.

DRAWER PULLS AND HANDLES

Drawer pulls and handles are made in a wide variety of designs. Fig. 35-5. You can find a good-looking handle to meet every need, such as a hammered black handle for Early American, a stamped shield and medallion for a Traditional design, or a polished brass handle for a Modern project. Drawer handles and pulls are sold with screws for installing them, and they come with instructions.

CATCHES

The most common catches are the *friction catch* for simple kitchen cabinets and the *magnetic catch* often found on fine furniture. Fig. 35-6. There is also a *roller catch.* Fig. 35-7.

OTHER HARDWARE

Some other common items of hardware are cabinet and chest locks and special types of hooks and braces.

INSTALLING A BUTT HINGE

1. A door is hung with two or three hinges. Select the size and number of hinges according to the size of the door.

2. Fit the door in the opening. If the hinges will be on the left side, insert small wedges at the bottom and to the right of the door itself. If the hinges will be on the right, put the wedges at the bottom and the left.

3. Measure up from the bottom and down from the top, and mark a line showing the location of the hinges.

4. Draw a line across the edges of both door and frame to show the location of the hinges.

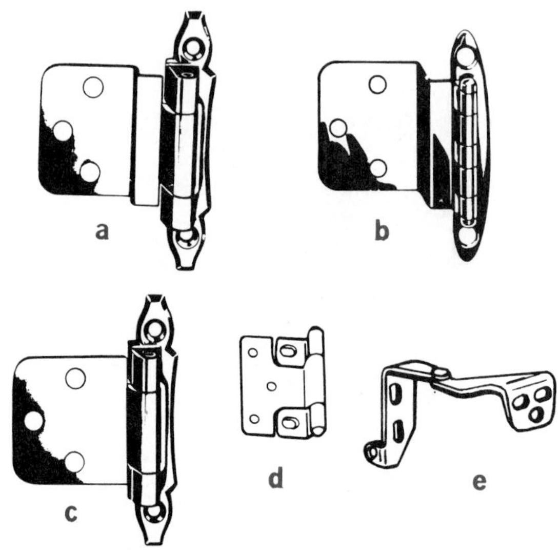

35-4. *Some common kinds of cabinet hinges: (a) Semi-concealed with inset for a lip door. (b) Semi-concealed with offset for an overlay door. (c) Semi-concealed with straight hinge for an overlay door. (d) Another type of semi-concealed hinge for overlay doors. (e) Pivot hinge for doors.*

5. Place one hinge over the edge of the door and mark how far it extends into the door.

6. Measure the thickness of one leaf of the hinge and set a marking gauge to this amount.

7. Draw lines on the door and the frame to show this thickness.

8. Cut the gains for both hinges by hand with a chisel. Figs. 35-8 and 35-9.

9. Place the hinges in the gains of the door and drill the pilot holes for the screws. Fasten the hinges in place.

10. Hold the door against the frame and mark the position of one hole in each hinge. Drill the pilot hole and insert one screw in each hinge.

11. Check to see if the door operates correctly. If it does, install the other screws.

INSTALLING A SURFACE HINGE

1. Place the door in the opening.

2. Put wedges at the bottom and at the right (or left) of the door.

3. Mark the location of the hinges.

4. Place the door on the bench top. Fasten the hinges to the door itself.

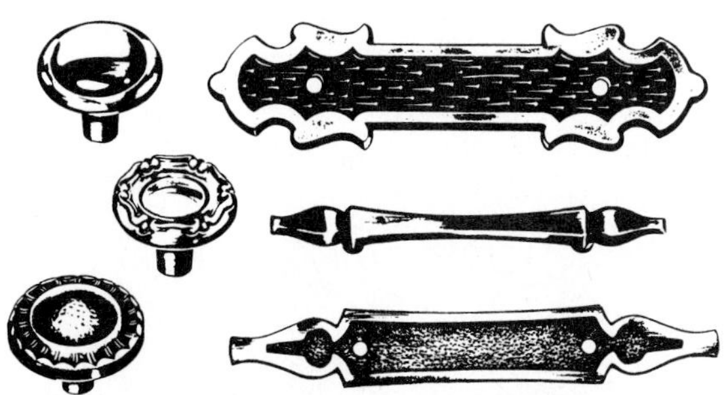

35-5. *Drawer pulls and handles.*

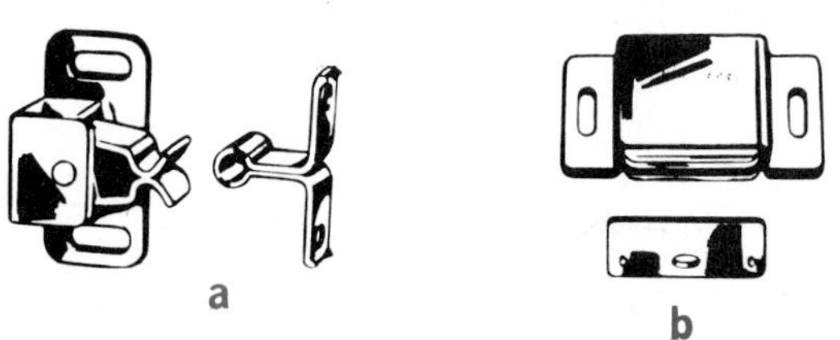

35-6. *Catches: (a) Friction. (b) Magnetic.*

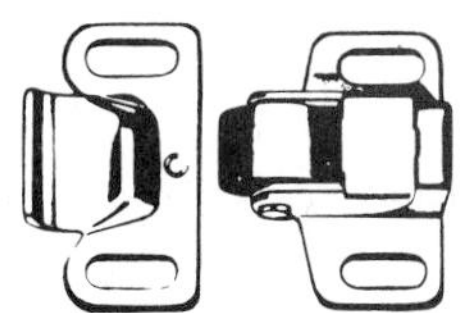

35-7. *A roller catch.*

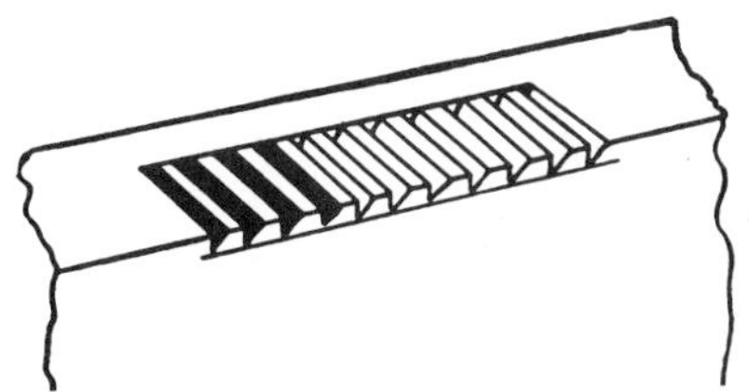

35-8. *Gain notches cut with a chisel.*

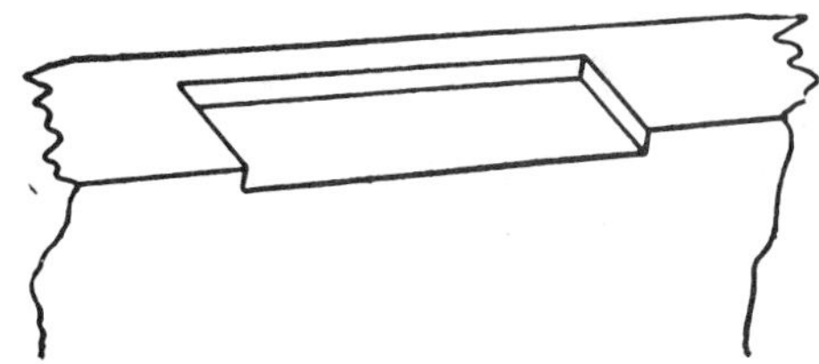

35-9. *The gain cut and ready for the hinge.*

5. Place the door in the opening again with the wedge in its place and install one screw in each hinge.

6. Try the door to see if it works correctly. If it doesn't work right, remove one of the screws and adjust the door until it does.

STRUCTURAL HARDWARE

Repair and mending plates come in many sizes and shapes. Fig. 35-10. *Mending* plates are used to strengthen a butt or lap joint. The *flat corner* iron is used to strengthen corners of frames such as a screen door or window frames. The *bent corner* iron can be applied to shelves and the inside corners of tables, chairs, and cabinets. It can also be used to hang cabinets and shelves. *T plates* are used to strengthen the center rail of a frame. Many other metal devices, such as tabletop fasteners, chair braces, and similar hardware, are also available.

35-10. *Four types of repair plates: mending, flat corner, bent corner, and T plate.*

QUESTIONS

1. What are the two kinds of hardware used in constructing projects?
2. Where can you get the cabinet hardware for your project?
3. Name two kinds of butt hinges.
4. Describe a gain.

ACTIVITIES

1. In your own words, explain how to install a surface hinge.
2. Demonstrate how to mark a door and frame for the location of hinges.

Sanding Stock

Sanding is a way of smoothing the surface of stock with an *abrasive* (a hard, sharp material that wears away a softer surface). Fig. 36-1. Abrasive grains are found on sandpaper and in grinding wheels and are used also as a powder.

Sanding is done (1) on each part after it is cut to final shape and (2) on the whole project after it is put together. Sanding should never be done in place of cutting. Only a poor or careless worker would try to make abrasive paper (sandpaper) do what a plane or chisel should do.

Never use sharp tools on a surface after it has been sanded. The fine abrasive grains left by the sandpaper would dull the tools.

36-1. ***Sanding with a handmade sandpaper block.***

TOOLS AND MATERIALS

Sandpaper is a strong paper with abrasive grains glued on it. The abrasives used most often in the wood shop are:

- *Flint.* This is made of quartz. The paper looks light tan on the abrasive side. It is used for hand sanding. It is cheap but does not last long.
- *Garnet* is a reddish brown, hard mineral that is excellent for hand sanding. It is also used on power sanders. It will last much longer than flint but costs more.
- *Aluminum oxide* is a synthetic abrasive with a brown color. It is used for both hand and power sanding on hardwoods.

Abrasive coarseness is shown in one of two ways. A mesh number, such as 100, shows the size of screen through which the abrasive particles can pass. The larger the mesh number, the finer the abrasive. The older method uses a numbering system; for example, 2/0 is the same as 100. Fig. 36-2.

The following common sizes of garnet paper are used: 1 or 1½ (40 to 50) for sanding parts with deep tool marks; ½ (60) for all general sanding; 1/0 (80) for sanding after the project is assembled; 2/0 or 3/0 (100 to 120) for sanding before applying a finish; 4/0 to 6/0 (150 to 220) for sanding finishes.

A *sandpaper block* is very helpful. A rectangular block like the one in Fig. 36-1 is a good one. A piece of leather or heavy felt glued to the base makes a good backing. Putting the sandpaper right over the block is not good. If a sliver of wood gets between the paper and the block, the hard spot can tear the paper or make the sanding uneven. A commercial sandpaper holder is shown in Fig. 36-3.

GRIT SIZES

	Grit. No.	0 Grade	Uses
VERY FINE	400 360 320 280 240 220	10/0 — 9/0 8/0 7/0 6/0	For polishing and finishing after stain, varnish, etc., has been applied.
FINE	180 150 120	5/0 4/0 3/0	For finish sanding just before staining or sealing.
MEDIUM	100 80 60	2/0 1/0 ½	For sanding to remove final rough texture.
COARSE	50 40 36	1 1½ 2	For sanding after very rough texture is removed.
VERY COARSE	30 24 20 16	2½ 3 3½ 4	For very rough, unfinished wood surfaces.

36-2. ***Grades and uses of abrasive paper.***

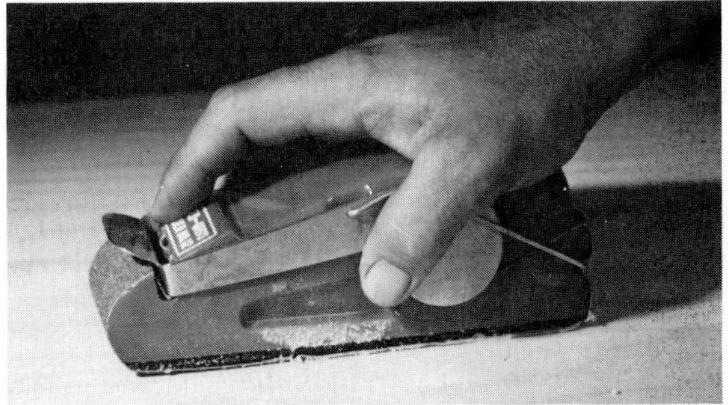

36-3. ***Using a commercial sandpaper holder.***

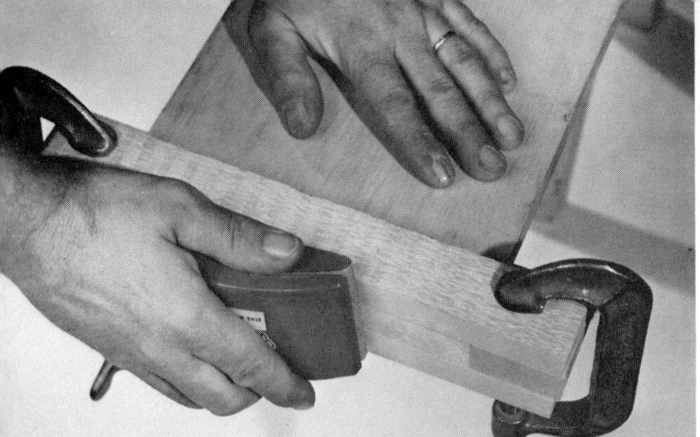

36-4. *Sand end grain in one direction. Notice the guide boards clamped over the end to keep the sanding square with the face surface.*

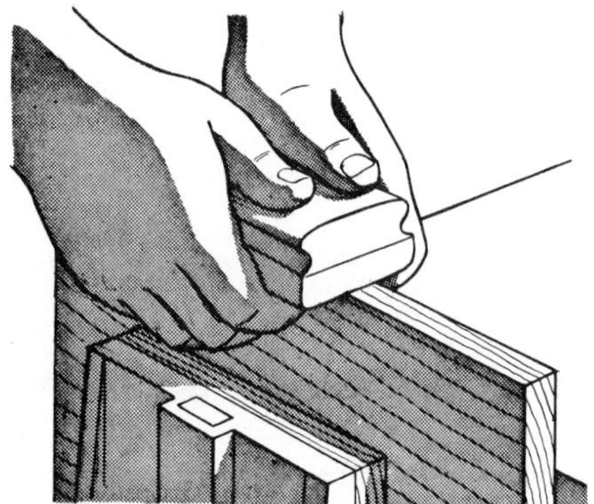

36-5. *Sanding an edge. Notice how the sandpaper block is held.*

CUTTING OR TEARING SANDPAPER

Sandpaper can be bought in sizes to fit sandpaper holders and power sanders. You can also get larger sheets and cut or tear them to the size you need. To cut or tear the paper:

1. Grasp the opposite corners of the paper with the paper side down. Soften the paper by drawing it across the edge of the bench.

2. Fold the paper, abrasive side in. Then hold the folded edge over the corner of a bench and tear with a quick jerk.

3. To cut sandpaper, place the paper with the abrasive side down on a bench. Place the cutting edge of a saw on the paper and tear.

4. Always use a piece of sandpaper as small as possible to do the job.

GENERAL SUGGESTIONS

- Make sure that all cutting is finished before you start sanding. Sanding is done to finish the surface, not to shape it.
- Always sand *with the grain*—never across it. Sanding across grain scratches the wood.
- When sanding end grain, always sand in one direction. Fig. 36-4.
- Apply just enough pressure to make the sandpaper cut. Pressing too hard makes scratches.
- Clean off the sandpaper and the surface often with a brush.
- Don't sand surfaces that are to be glued.
- Don't try to sand off pencil or knife marks. Remove them with a plane or scraper.
- Always brush off the surface after sanding.
- When you are finished sanding, use a tack cloth (a rag lightly moistened with varnish and turpentine) to remove dust before going on to the next step.

SANDING A SURFACE

1. Clamp the stock to the bench or hold it firmly with one hand.

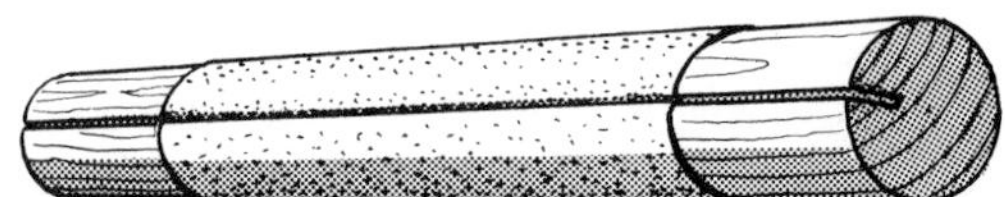

36-6. *A dowel rod with sandpaper attached.*

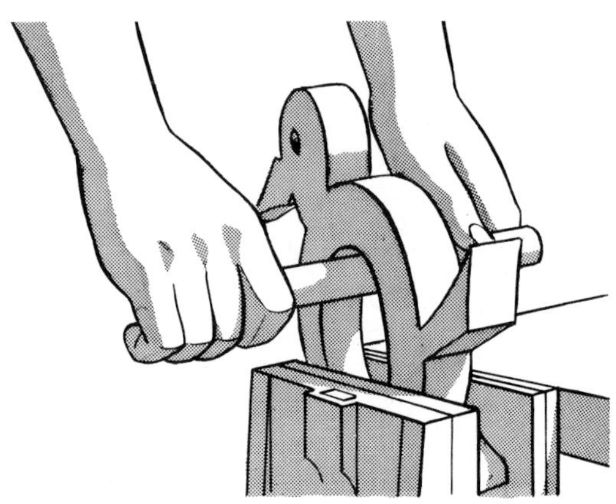

36-7. *Sanding an inside edge.*

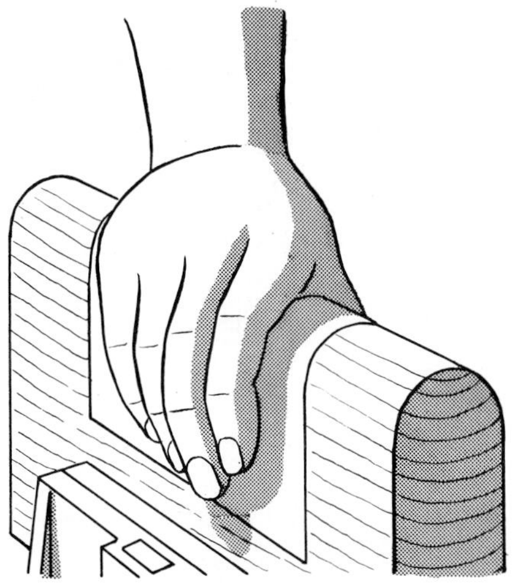

36-8. *Sanding a convex surface.*

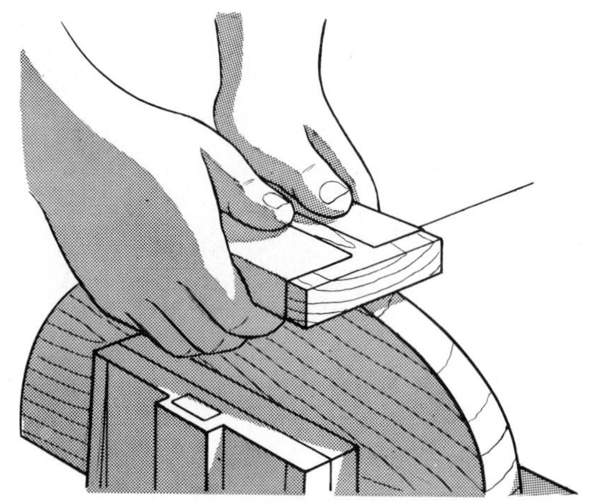

36-9. *Sanding an outside curve with a sanding block.*

2. Place the sandpaper on a block.

3. Take long strokes, sanding with the grain. Sand evenly from one side to the other. Always hold the block flat on the surface, especially as you near the end.

SANDING AN EDGE

1. Clamp the stock in a vise.

2. Hold the block as shown in Fig. 36-5. Your fingers guide the block and keep it from rocking. Remember that you must sand surfaces square. Unless you are careful you will tend to round all edges.

3. "Break" all edges slightly to prevent splintering. This is done by holding a piece of fine sandpaper in your hand and going over all the sharp edges lightly.

SANDING CURVED SURFACES

1. To sand a concave (inside) curve, wrap a piece of sandpaper around a piece of large dowel rod or a round file. Fig. 36-6. Twist the tool a little as you sand the surface. Fig. 36-7.

2. For convex (outside) curves, hold a piece of sandpaper in the palm of your hand. Fig. 36-8. Another method is shown in Fig. 36-9.

QUESTIONS

1. Should you use a chisel on a piece of wood after it has been sanded? Explain.

2. Name three kinds of sandpaper or abrasives.

3. What grade of sandpaper would you use for general sanding?

4. Should you sand across grain? Why or why not?

5. What must you watch for when sanding an edge?

6. How do you sand an inside curve?

ACTIVITIES

1. Demonstrate how to cut a piece of sandpaper into equal parts.

2. Make a sandpaper block.

Preparing for Wood Finishing

Before applying a finish, make sure your project is really ready for it. A finish will not cover up mistakes. In fact, it tends to show them up! Time spent in preparing the project for finishing is well worth it.

TOOLS AND MATERIALS

Shellac sticks are hard, colored pieces of shellac that become soft when heated. They come in these colors: oak tones of natural, light, medium, golden, and dark; walnut tones of light and dark; mahogany tones of light, medium, and dark. Other colors are transparent (clear), old ivory, white, and cedar. Shellac sticks are used to repair cracks and dents.

Plastic wood is a wood paste that comes in such colors as natural, light mahogany, oak, walnut, and mahogany. It is used to fill holes and cracks.

Wood patch is a synthetic (artificial) wood that also can be used for filling holes and cracks. It comes in cedar, walnut, pine, mahogany, fir, and oak as well as a neutral color.

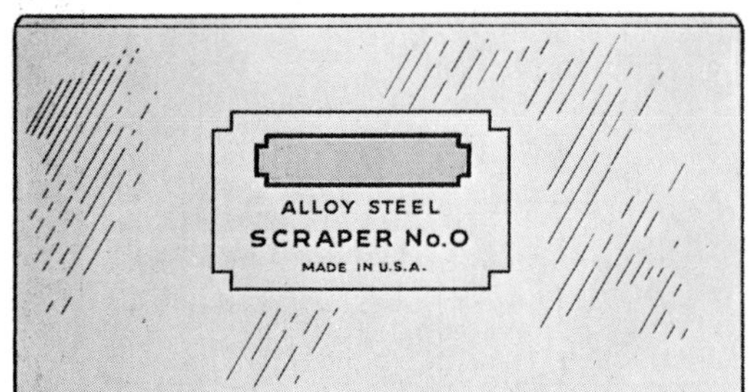

37-1. *A hand scraper.*

37-2. *A cabinet scraper.*

Wood sawdust mixed with powdered resin glue makes a good crack filler. Don't use sawdust from the power sander because this contains abrasive grains that would darken the mixture. Use sawdust from white pine or basswood for lighter wood filler. Mix the sawdust half and half with glue and then add water to make a thick paste.

A *hand* or *cabinet scraper* is sometimes used on open-grained wood to get a fine finish. Figs. 37-1 and 37-2.

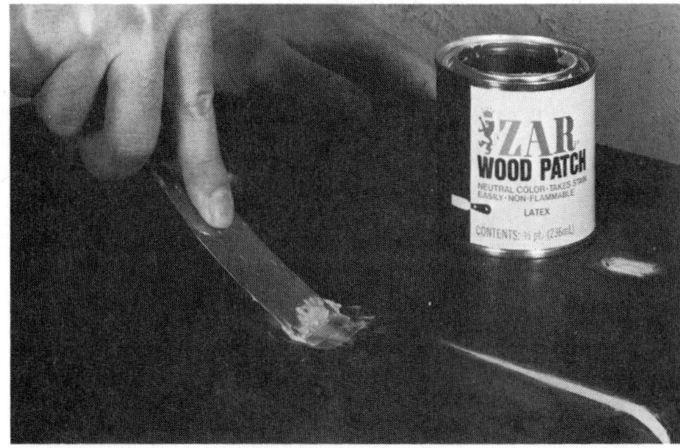

37-3(a). *Using wood patch to fill cracks. This is a neutral color that takes stain easily.*

37-3(b). ***Filling a crack with stick shellac. The alcohol burner is used to heat the end of the stick shellac and the blade of the putty knife. This is a good way to repair dents. It is easy to match the color of the wood.***

Oxalic acid crystals for bleaching can be purchased in any drugstore.

Commercial acid bleaches come from paint or hardware stores.

You will also need a putty knife, Bunsen or alcohol burner, chisel, and scraper.

REPAIRING DENTS, CRACKS, AND HOLES

1. If there is a small dent in the wood, allow a wet cloth to cover it for several hours. This will raise the grain. Then sand the surface.

2. For deeper dents, put a heavy, wet cloth over the dent and apply a hot soldering copper or iron to the cloth.

37-4. ***Scraping the surface of wood with a hand scraper. This is usually done on open-grained woods such as oak, mahogany, or walnut. Hold the scraper with both hands, at an angle of 50 to 60 degrees to the surface. Turn the blade a little toward the direction of the stroke. Then push or pull the blade.***

3. Fill all cracks, dents, and nail and screw holes with plastic wood, wood patch, or stick shellac. Fig. 37-3. Clean out the crack or hole carefully. Make sure the wood is dry. To use stick shellac, heat the end over a Bunsen or alcohol burner until it is soft. Also heat the blade of a putty knife. Then press the shellac into the dent or crack with the knife.

Apply enough filler to make it slightly higher than the surface. Sand off when dry until it is smooth and level.

SCRAPING AND/OR SANDING THE SURFACE

1. Use a chisel to remove excess glue that has squeezed out around joints. This must be done because glue will not take stain.

2. On a large piece of furniture made of open-grained wood, scrape the surface with a hand or cabinet scraper. Fig. 37-4. This must be done before any sanding.

3. Finish sand your project with 3/0 to 6/0 garnet paper. The finer the grit you finish up with, the more prominent the grain pattern and glossier the final finish will be. Check for any rough areas that may need further sanding by running a nylon stocking over the wood. If it snags, you've got some more sanding to do. Soften all sharp edges and corners by lightly sanding them.

37-5. ***Using a two-step commercial bleach. Rubber gloves must be worn to protect the hands.***

4. Remove most of the sawdust from the project with a bench brush or shop vacuum. Then give it a thorough rubdown with a tack cloth to remove any dirt, dust, or abrasive particles and leave a perfectly clean, smooth surface.

BLEACHING WOOD

To get a very light finish, wood must first be bleached. For small projects, use a solution of oxalic acid crystals mixed in hot water. For larger projects, apply a commercial acid bleach. Always follow the directions given on the container. Fig. 37-5. Bleaching raises wood grain. You must sand again after the wood has dried.

QUESTIONS

1. Will a finish cover up any mistakes made in cutting and sanding? What does it do?
2. What can you use to fill holes?
3. How can you raise a small dent in wood?
4. Why is stick shellac good for filling dents, nail holes, and screw holes?
5. How should you remove excess glue around joints?
6. How is bleaching done?

ACTIVITIES

1. In your own words, describe how to scrape and sand a surface to prepare it for finishing.
2. Tack cloths for removing dust can be bought, but you can easily make your own. Use a soft, lint-free cloth, such as cheesecloth or a cotton handkerchief. Dampen the cloth with water. Sprinkle liberally with turpentine. Pour 2 or 3 tablespoons of varnish on the cloth and squeeze it fairly dry.

Wood Finishes

Finishes are applied to wood to protect and beautify the surface. It is important to choose a finish that will suit the project and be easy to apply. Figure 38-1 lists some clear finishes that bring out the natural beauty of wood.

HOW TO SELECT A FINISH

1. For simple outdoor items such as birdhouses and rabbit hutches, apply exterior paint or enamel.
2. For outdoor sports items such as gun

TRANSPARENT (SEE-THROUGH) FINISHES

Finish (solvent)	Application	Drying Time	Durability	Color	Appearance	Notes
Wax (none)	Hand rub with soft cloth.	½ hour	Good moisture resistance.	Tends to yellow with age.	Soft sheen	Paste wax can be used for sealer.
Shellac (alcohol)	Wide brush or hand wipe.	30–60 min.	Poor. Water turns shellac white. No outdoor use.	Orange shellac dries honey-colored. White shellac dries clear.	Sheen to gloss	Good as a liquid wood filler on some woods. Better as a sealer.
Oil: Boiled Linseed (turpentine or mineral spirits)	Rub with soft cloth.	Indefinite	Won't peel or crack.	Darkens quickly.	Soft sheen	Driers can be added to increase hardness.
Oils: Sealacell, Watco, Tung (mineral spirits)	Rub with soft cloth.	2 days	Won't peel or crack. Better moisture resistance.	Dull, but shines to satin luster when steel wool is used between coats.	Soft sheen	Finish is more durable than boiled linseed oil.
Varnish (turpentine or mineral spirits)	Bristle brush or foam poly-brush.	1–1½ days	Good weather and wear resistance.	Spar varnish tends to darken.	Sheen to gloss	Avoid shaking varnish. Apply several thin coats. Finish in dust-free place.
Lacquer brushing (lacquer thinner)	Brush (sable or camel).	4 hours	Fair moisture resistance, good durability.	Won't discolor wood.	High gloss	Foam polybrush can be used.

38-1. ***Characteristics and uses of transparent finishes.***

38-2 *For wood projects to be used with food, such as these cheese cutting boards, rub on light mineral oil as a finish.*

stocks, baseball stands, and other game equipment, use a simple penetrating finish (one that soaks into the wood).

3. For indoor novelties, use a simple transparent finish or interior paint or enamel.

4. For furniture and accessories, apply a penetrating finish for simpler pieces or a standard finish (described in this chapter) for larger furniture.

5. For kitchen items that come in contact with foods, such as cutting boards or salad bowls, use an oil that will not become rancid (spoiled). Light mineral oil is a good choice. Fig. 38-2.

SIMPLE FINISHES

Wax Finish

Repair any cracks, dents, or holes. Sand the surface of the project. Then apply one of the finishes described here.

1. Apply a coat of shellac to the surface. See Chapter 42.

2. Rub down with fine steel wool.

3. Apply a coat of paste wax. Let it dry about ten minutes. Rub in with a soft wool rag.

Natural Finish

1. Apply a thin coat of oil mixture (1 part boiled linseed oil, 1 part solvent, and 1 part varnish). Use a rag to apply. Allow to dry for 15 minutes. Wipe with a clean, dry cloth.

2. Brush on a coat of thin white shellac (two parts shellac and one part alcohol). Allow the surface to dry about 24 hours. Rub down with fine steel wool.

3. Apply a second coat of shellac.

4. After the shellac is dry, cover the surface with paste wax.

STANDARD FINISH

While the finishing material may vary, all finishing is done about the same way. These are the major steps:

1. *Bleaching.* This step is done only if very light finishes are to be applied. For natural and darker finishes, you may skip it.

2. *Staining.* Staining adds the desired color to wood or improves the natural color. For a completely natural finish, staining may not be required. See Chapter 40.

3. *Sealing.* It is usually a good idea to seal the stain to prevent bleeding of the stain into the topcoat. A *wash coat* (one part shellac to seven parts alcohol) is good for most stains. If the topcoat will be lacquer, apply a lacquer sealer.

4. *Filling.* Paste filler is used on open-grained woods and a liquid filler on other woods. See Chapter 41.

5. *Sealing.* A sealer should again be applied over the filler. It should be a commercial sealer, a wash coat of shellac, or a lacquer sealer.

6. *Applying a standard finish.* A shellac, varnish, or lacquer topcoat is applied after sealing. Usually two or more coats are required. Always sand the surface with 5/0 sandpaper after each

coat is dry. To give a rubbed finish to varnish, rub on pumice or rottenstone after the second and third coats. (See Chapter 39.) After the second and the final coat, all finishes can be made smoother by first rubbing with pumice in oil and then rottenstone in oil, using a felt pad. Always apply a coat of paste wax to protect the final finish.

There are also many wax and penetrating finishes on the market that you can use. These can be bought at hardware stores and home improvement centers.

QUESTIONS

1. What kind of finish should you choose for a birdhouse?
2. What should be chosen for projects to be used in the kitchen?
3. Describe the way to apply a wax finish.
4. Tell how to apply a natural finish using boiled linseed oil.
5. Describe the steps for applying a standard finish.
6. Is bleaching done for all standard finishes?

ACTIVITIES

1. New, "environmentally friendly" finishes are now available. Research magazines, visit a local hardware store or home improvement center, and prepare a report about these finishes.
2. Refer to Fig. 38-1. Which finish(es) would you use (a) for a tabletop that might be exposed to moisture? (b) for fine furniture whose color you don't want to darken?

Care of Finishing Supplies

Many different materials are used in finishing. The kinds you will use on a particular project depend on the finish you will apply. Finishing supplies must be taken care of so that you will get good use from them.

GENERAL SUGGESTIONS

- Most finishing supplies catch fire easily. This is one of the great dangers in the shop. Always keep covers on tight. Store damp rags in a metal container. There should be a fire extinguisher in the finishing area or room.
- Work only in a well-ventilated area.
- Open the covers of cans carefully so that they will not become bent. A tight cover is important if the material is to be kept in good condition.
- Pour out only what you need into a metal or glass container. Certain kinds of paper cups can also be used. Stir the material with a scrap stick of wood.

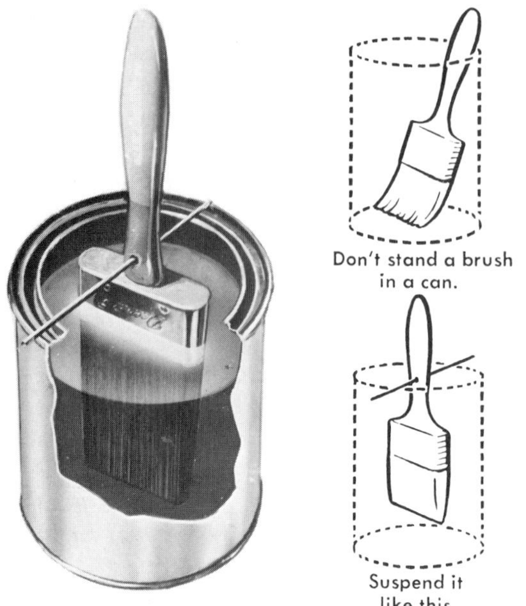

39-1. ***A method of keeping a brush in good condition.***

- Clean out the ridge around the rim of the can and close it tightly. Store the can upside down.
- With plain wrapping or wax paper, cover the table or surface on which you are going to do the finishing.
- Never pour thinned or mixed finishes back into the original container.
- Use the correct *solvents* (liquids that can dissolve other substances) for the finishing material.
- Clean your brushes after you use them.
- Store the brushes in the correct solvent.

BRUSHES AND THEIR CARE

- There are many kinds, styles, grades, and sizes of brushes. Select the best one for the finish to be applied. Brushes are made either from natural hair such as ox, camel, or sable or with some kind of plastic bristles. For some finishes a foam polybrush can be used. This brush looks like a small sponge attached to a handle.
- Store brushes in a solvent if you are going to use them again the next day.

Keep varnish brushes in a solution of half turpentine and half varnish.

Paint and stain brushes are kept in one part turpentine and two parts linseed oil.

Shellac brushes are stored in alcohol.

Enamel brushes are kept in a 50/50 mixture of varnish and turpentine.

Keep lacquer brushes in a lacquer thinner.

- Always suspend (hang) brushes in solvent. Never allow the end to rest on the bottom of the container. Fig. 39-1. Drill a hole in the handle and run a wire through it so that the brush hangs in the solvent. Another way is to cut a short slit in the plastic lid of a coffee can and then push the handle through this opening. Put just enough of the correct solvent in the can to cover the bristles of the brush.
- To clean a brush, follow these steps:

1. Choose the correct solvent. Slosh the brush around in the solvent to remove most of the loose material.
2. Use your fingers to open the hairs and clean out the waste material. Work the solvent into the area around the handle.
3. Wipe the brush dry.

39-2. ***Washing a brush. Use a commercial cleaning solvent or a good grade of detergent.***

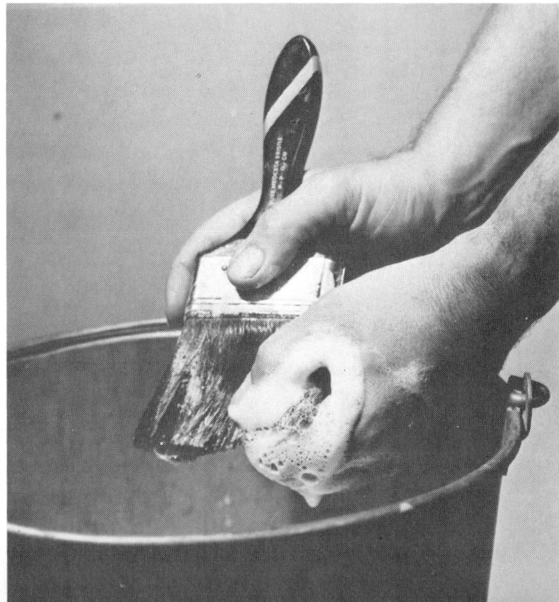

4. Use a commercial cleaning solvent mixed in water or a good grade of detergent. Wash the brush thoroughly. Fig. 39-2.

5. Dry the brush. Apply a thin coat of petroleum jelly or wrap the brush in wax paper.

FINISHING MATERIALS

Benzine is a colorless liquid made from petroleum. It is used as a solvent and cleaning fluid.

Alcohol is a colorless liquid made from wood drippings or chemicals. It is used as a thinner and solvent for shellac.

Turpentine is made from the resin drippings of pine trees. It is used as a solvent and thinner for varnish, paint, and enamel.

Linseed oil is a yellowish oil pressed from flaxseed. It is available both raw and boiled. Boiling improves the drying qualities. It is used in paints, fillers, and stains.

Pumice is a white powder that comes from lava. It is used as a buffing and polishing compound. Use No. 1 for coarse rubbing and No. FF or FFF for fine rubbing.

Rottenstone is a reddish brown or greyish black limestone used for smoothing and rubbing. It is finer than pumice.

Rubbing oil is a good grade of petroleum or paraffin oil used with pumice or rottenstone for rubbing down a finish.

Steel wool is very fine steel shavings. It is used in place of sandpaper for certain finishing operations. Common grades are 000 and 00—very fine; 0—fine; 1 and 2—medium; and 3—coarse.

Wet-dry abrasive paper is waterproof aluminum oxide paper. Grades 240 to 400 are used with water for sanding between finish coats.

QUESTIONS

1. In what ways can finishing supplies be dangerous?
2. What solvent should you use for shellac brushes?
3. What is pumice?
4. What is steel wool used for?

ACTIVITIES

1. Make a poster listing safety rules for handling and storing finishing supplies.
2. Pretend you are writing a report for a consumer's magazine. Compare bristle and foam brushes. Consider cost, durability, and uses for each kind.

Staining Woods

Staining is done to color a surface and to bring out the natural beauty of fine woods such as walnut and mahogany. It is also done to change the tone or shade of woods, such as making oak a darker color. Staining can make less expensive pines or gums look like hardwood. Gum, for example, can be made to look like mahogany. Staining is the first step in applying most finishes.

KINDS OF STAINS

There are three common kinds of stains. They are named according to the solvent used: *oil, water,* and *spirit* (alcohol). Oil and water stains are easiest to use.

Oil stains come in many different colors. The simplest way to buy them is in ready-mixed colors in cans. Some common colors are light oak, golden oak, dark oak, light maple, dark maple, brown maple, red maple, red mahogany, light walnut, and dark walnut. Oil stains can also be made by mixing ground-in-oil pigment or colored powder in a solvent. The solvent can be turpentine, linseed oil, or other light oil. Figure 40-1 shows the colors to add to the solvent to make your own stain. Mix the stain in a glass container or a can. Oil stains are easy to apply and have good color. Their chief disadvantages are that they dry slowly and are quite expensive.

Water stains are made by mixing a powder in water. Usually one ounce of powder will make a quart of water stain. Some good things about water stains are that they are cheap, easy to use, give good clear colors, and penetrate (soak into the wood) very well. However, they do raise the grain.

GENERAL SUGGESTIONS

- Mix enough stain to cover the entire project.
- Try the stain on a piece of scrap wood of the same kind.
- It is better to put on two light coats of stain than one heavy one. It is easier to darken wood than it is to lighten it.
- Wear gloves when using stain.

APPLYING WATER STAIN

1. Sponge the surface lightly with water, let it dry, and then sand slightly with 5/0 sandpaper. This will keep the water stain from raising the grain.
2. Sponge or brush end grain with water or boiled linseed oil to keep it from darkening too much. Fig. 40-2.
3. Use a large brush or sponge to apply the stain.
4. Apply the stain evenly. Wring out the brush or sponge and wipe off excess stain.
5. Using a clean cloth, wipe the surface in the direction of the grain.

USING COLORS IN OIL FOR FINISHING

White	Use zinc oxide ground in oil
Golden Oak	Use white zinc tinted with yellow ochre and raw sienna
Medium Oak	Use raw sienna and burnt sienna
Light Brown	Use Vandyke brown
Dark Brown	Use Vandyke brown and drop black
Walnut	Use half Vandyke brown and half burnt umber
Black	Use drop black

40-1. ***This table shows how to mix some of the common colors of oil stains.***

APPLYING OIL STAIN

1. Choose a good brush to apply the stain.
2. Apply a thin coat of boiled linseed oil to end grain first so that it won't soak up too much stain.
3. Dip the brush about one-third into the stain. Start at the corners or lower surface of the project and work in and up.

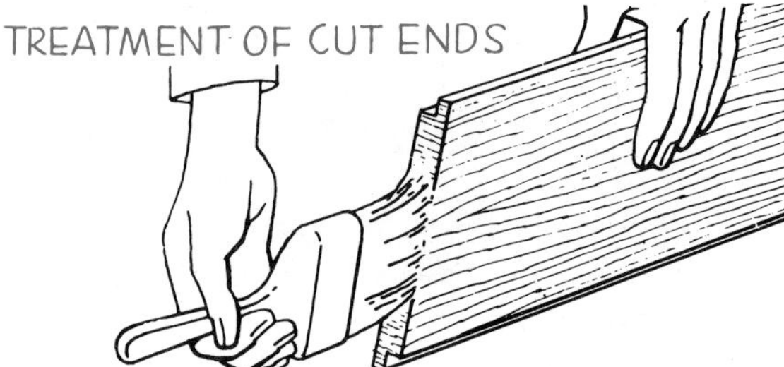

40-2. ***Brush a little water or boiled linseed oil on the end grain before staining. This will keep the surface from absorbing too much stain. If you don't do this, the end grain will appear darker than the rest of the project.***

40-3. *Applying an oil stain.*

40-4. *Wiping the oil stain lightly with a clean cloth.*

4. Keep the strokes light, brushing the stain evenly. Work with the grain. Fig. 40-3.

5. Begin at an unfinished area and work toward the finished part.

6. Wipe softly with a clean cloth. Fig. 40-4.

7 Allow 24 hours to dry before proceeding further.

SEALING

After the stain is dry, apply a wash coat of one part shellac and seven parts alcohol. This will keep the stain from bleeding into the finish. If you use lacquer as your final finish, use lacquer sealer for a wash coat. Sand the dry coat with 6/0-7/0 sandpaper and wipe clean.

QUESTIONS

1. What does staining do?
2. Name three common kinds of stain.
3. What are the advantages of oil stain?
4. What are the advantages of water stain?
5. Tell how to apply water stain.
6. What should you do to end grain before applying stain?

ACTIVITIES

1. The color of stain can change when applied to different woods. Obtain several samples of scrap wood, such as pine, basswood, and oak. Apply the same stain to each. Describe the results.
2. Prepare a table listing the advantages and disadvantages of oil and water stains.

Applying Wood Fillers

Wood fillers are used to fill the pores of most woods and to add beauty to the surface. When the pores are filled, the wood surface is smooth, hard, and ready for any finish you want to apply. Some woods such as ash, hickory, oak, mahogany, and walnut need a paste filler because the surface has millions of small, open pores. Fig. 41-1. Birch, gum, maple, and cherry need only a liquid filler. Fig. 41-2. No filler is required on such woods as pine, poplar, fir, and basswood.

41-2. ***A liquid filler was used in finishing this birch beverage holder.***

TOOLS AND MATERIALS

Paste fillers are made from ground silicon (sand), linseed oil, turpentine, drier, and coloring. Fillers can be purchased in a natural color or in various wood colors. Colors in oil (tinting colors) can be added to the natural color filler to get any effect. See Fig. 40-1 for the correct colors to add to fillers.

Liquid fillers can be made by thinning paste fillers with turpentine. There are also ready-made liquid fillers. A coat of shellac makes a good filler for some woods.

41-1. ***A paste filler was used to produce the finish on this oak clock case.***

A stiff brush is needed to apply the paste filler.

Burlap or coarse rags are needed for removing excess filler.

A fine cloth is needed for the final wiping.

APPLYING PASTE FILLER

1. Mix the paste filler with turpentine or naphtha until it is like heavy cream.
2. Mix the oil color with a little turpentine. Then add this to the filler until you get the color you want.
3. Apply the filler with a stiff brush, rubbing it into the pores. Brush both with and across the

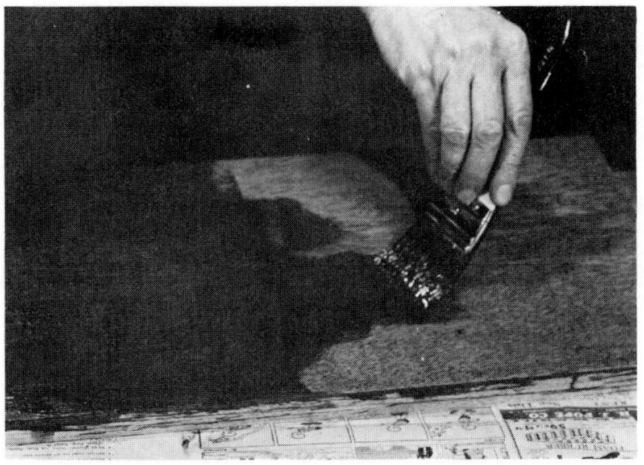

41-3. ***Applying a wood filler with a stiff brush. Brush both with and across the grain.***

grain. Fig. 41-3. Sometimes it works well to rub the filler in with the palm of the hand. Apply a little more filler to end grain.

4. Allow the filler to dry until the gloss disappears. This may take as long as 20 minutes.

5. Rub across the grain with burlap or coarse cloth to remove excess filler. Fig. 41-4.

6. Using a fine cloth, wipe very lightly with the grain to make sure the filler is evenly applied. Do not rub hard, as this removes the filler from the pores.

7. Allow the filler to dry for 24 hours. Apply a sealer.

APPLYING LIQUID FILLER

1. If the filler is made from paste, add turpentine until it is very thin.

2. Apply with a brush and follow the same general procedure described for paste fillers.

3. If shellac is used, apply a coat as described in the next chapter.

41-4. ***Rubbing across grain with burlap or coarse cloth to remove excess filler.***

QUESTIONS

1. Why are fillers used on wood?
2. Name one kind of wood that requires a paste filler. Name another that requires a liquid filler.
3. Which woods do not require a filler?
4. From what are paste fillers made?
5. How can a paste filler be thinned?
6. How should excess filler be removed from the surface?

ACTIVITIES

1. Obtain two samples of a wood that has many pores, such as oak. Finish one with filler and one without. Compare the results.
2. Prepare a table listing that woods that require paste filler, those that require liquid filler, and those that do not need filler at all.

CHAPTER 42 Applying a Shellac Finish

Shellac is an easy finish to apply. Fig. 42-1. It dries quickly and is durable (lasts a long time). Because of its drying speed, you can complete the finish in a short time. Shellac is not good if the project will get damp when used. The shellac would become cloudy. Shellac can be used both as the final finish and as a sealer over stain and/or filler. When shellac is used as the finish, it is better over a water stain. Shellac should be applied to knots before painting a project. Fig. 42-2.

TOOLS AND MATERIALS

Shellac is a thick, yellow material that comes from the lac bug. Most of our shellac comes from India and Thailand. The standard shellac is called a "four-pound cut." This means that there are four pounds of shellac mixed with a gallon of alcohol. Orange shellac is tough and durable, but it leaves a yellowish cast on light finishes. White shellac is bleached. It is used on light finishes.

Alcohol is used to thin the shellac and to clean the brushes. Shellac is thinned as follows:

- For a wash coat: one part shellac (four-pound cut) to seven parts alcohol.
- For first coat: one part shellac to one part alcohol.
- For second coat: one part shellac to three-fourths part alcohol.

You also need a good 1- to 1½-inch brush, a can, and a lintfree cloth.

APPLYING THE FIRST COAT

In working with shellac, it is always better to put on several thin coats than one heavy coat.

1. Pour a small amount of shellac into a container. Add an equal amount of alcohol. Stir with a small stick. Don't get the shellac so thin that it runs like water.
2. Dampen a rag with alcohol and lightly wipe the surface to be finished.
3. Dip the brush about one-third in the shellac and wipe the sides of the brush on the container.

42-1. *This early American sewing cabinet has a shellac finish.*

***42-2.** Applying shellac over knots. This prevents the resin in the wood from leaking out and discoloring the paint or enamel.*

4. Begin at the center or near the top of a vertical surface and brush toward the edges.

5. Use long, even strokes. *Don't go over the same area twice.* Also, don't use so much shellac that it runs and piles up in small drops.

6. Allow the shellac to dry at least an hour. Four to six hours is better.

7. Clean the brush in alcohol immediately after each use.

APPLYING THE SECOND COAT

1. Sand the surface with fine steel wool or 5/0 garnet paper. Rub with the grain.

2. Wipe the surface with a clean cloth.

3. Mix and apply the second coat the same way as the first. Remember to *use less alcohol* for the second coat.

4. Allow the shellac to dry. Clean your brush.

COMPLETING THE SHELLAC FINISH

1. Two coats are usually enough, but, if necessary, sand the surface lightly and apply a third coat. Use slightly less alcohol. Allow to dry.

2. Rub the surface with fine sandpaper.

3. Clean the surface with a dry cloth.

4. Allow to dry for one-half hour.

5. Apply a coat of good paste wax.

QUESTIONS

1. What are the advantages of shellac?

2. Where does shellac come from?

3. Describe what is meant by a four-pound cut.

4. What is the difference between white shellac and orange shellac?

5. What is the solvent for shellac?

6. List the common mistakes made in applying a shellac finish.

7. Name some other uses for shellac.

ACTIVITIES

1. Demonstrate how to apply the first coat of shellac. Pay special attention to the brushing technique.

2. Visit a paint store or home improvement center. What kinds of shellac are available?

CHAPTER 43

Applying a Varnish Finish

Varnish is an excellent clear finish. Fig. 43-1. It is sometimes used on high-quality furniture. Varnish is tough and hard. Except for special dull varnish, it dries to a high, mirrorlike gloss. The chief problem is that you can't get a good varnish finish unless conditions are ideal. Varnish dries slowly and collects dust and lint while it dries. A poor varnish finish can ruin otherwise good furniture. A good varnish finish, on the other hand, is one of the best.

TOOLS AND MATERIALS

Varnishes are made from various materials. Old-time spirit varnish was made from gum, natural resins, and oils. Today, most standard varnishes are made from synthetic resins (certain types of plastic) and oils. Thinners are added to make varnish thin enough to be brushed out. *Alkyd* resin varnish is a synthetic resin combined with some type of alcohol. Oils such as tung, linseed, or soya are also added. *Phenolic* resin varnish is made from special synthetic resins that dry to a tougher, more moisture-resistant film than alkyd resins. *Polyurethane* varnish is a coating that is closer to a true plastic than the others. It dries to a very hard, tough, but somewhat brittle coating.

43-1. ***A varnish finish is an excellent choice for this small table.***

Varnishes are usually sold by some descriptive name such as:

- *Spar varnish* (exterior), an extremely tough, hard varnish. It is very good for tabletops or other surfaces that may become damp. It is pale golden and colors the wood slightly.
- *Clear rubbing and polishing varnishes,* a variety of clear varnishes used mostly for finishing furniture. They are lighter in color than spar or floor varnishes.
- *Satin, or dull, varnish* which dries dull rather than shiny. It can be used on furniture when you don't want a high gloss.
- *Varnish stain,* a finishing material that stains and varnishes a surface at the same time.

You will need a good, clean 2- to 3-inch varnish brush, a clean glass or porcelain container, solvents, and a tack rag. A tack rag is a clean cloth dampened with turpentine to which two or three tablespoons of varnish have been added. The cloth is used to remove dust particles and specks.

43-2. *Applying varnish. Brush in the direction of the wood grain.*

43-3. *Brush crisscross to level out the varnish.*

You'll find complete directions for applying each type of varnish on the can. Follow those directions carefully.

GENERAL SUGGESTIONS

- For the first coat, stir the varnish in the can and then pour out a small amount into another container. Never use varnish right from the can for the first coat. Thin with solvent.
- Wipe the surface with a tack rag.
- Dip the brush about one-third into the varnish.
- Start at a corner or edge and work toward the center. Apply with smooth, even strokes. Fig. 43-2.
- After one surface is varnished, go over it with the tip of the brush to even the coverage. Crisscross with the brush to level it out. Fig. 43-3.
- Each coat of finish should be left to dry overnight before going to the next step.

APPLYING A RUBBED VARNISH FINISH

Follow the directions in Chapters 36-40 for sanding, staining, and sealing. If necessary, apply a wood filler (see Chapter 41) and seal again. Sand the surface smooth with steel wool.

1. Brush on a diluted coat of varnish (50% varnish, 50% thinner). Allow to dry.
2. Lightly sand with 400-grit sandpaper, using water as the lubricant. Allow to dry.
3. Brush on a second coat of varnish direct from the can. Allow it to dry.
4. Sand high spots with wet-dry sandpaper (400 grit or 10/0) using water as a lubricant.
5. Brush on a third coat of varnish direct from the can. Allow it to dry.
6. After sanding, if the finish is not even, a fourth coat may be applied. Let dry and then sand.
7. Rub the finish with pumice, using water as a lubricant.
8. Rub with rottenstone, using water as a lubricant.
9. Wash the surface of the project with water and allow to dry.
10. Apply a thin coat of lemon oil or wax. Buff.

QUESTIONS

1. What is the chief problem in applying a good varnish finish?
2. Name three kinds of varnishes.
3. What are the conditions for good varnishing?
4. How long must the first varnish coat dry?

ACTIVITIES

1. Demonstrate the technique for applying varnish with a brush.
2. Visit a paint store or home improvement center. Prepare a report on the types of varnish that are available.

CHAPTER 44

Applying a Lacquer Finish

Lacquer is a finishing material that dries quickly and leaves a hard, protective, and durable film on the surface of the wood. Fig. 44-1. Most of the lacquers used on furniture are made from nitrocellulose, resins, and solvents. Lacquers are available both clear and in colors. In furniture factories, lacquer is sprayed on with special equipment. In small shops, lacquer is usually brushed on. Sometimes, lacquer is applied from a spray can.

When applying a lacquer finish, be sure to use *lacquer thinner* for thinning the materials and for cleaning brushes.

USING AEROSOL PRODUCTS

Many finishing materials—including lacquers, paints, and enamels—are available in aerosol (spray) cans. Read the directions on the can carefully. Some aerosols require shaking while others do not. Most are held upright when using the product, but some are not. Fig. 44-2.

44-1. ***Most furniture bought in stores has a lacquer finish.***

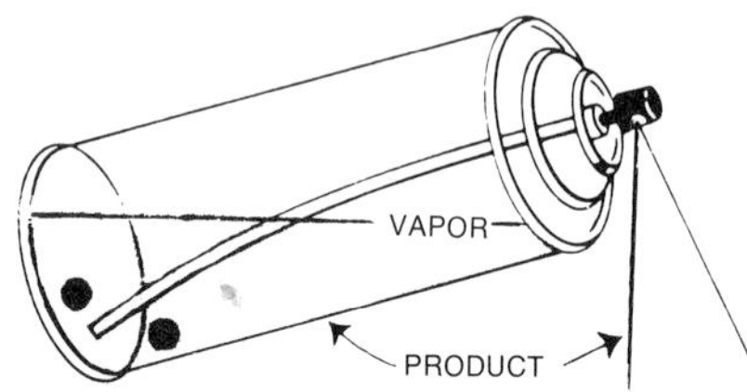

44-2. ***Don't hold this spray can in a horizontal position since the tube must always be in the liquid.***

General Suggestions

- Place the item to be sprayed on a bench that has been covered with newspapers.
- Do the spraying in a well-ventilated room or outdoors.
- Start at the front (side nearest you) and spray back and forth, moving towards the rear.
- Overlap each stroke. Turn the project a quarter of a turn and spray again. Spray several light coats rather than one heavy one. Fig. 44-3.
- When finished, turn the can upside down and press the spray head for a few seconds to clean out the line. Fig. 44-4. If the spray head becomes clogged, remove it. Use a pin to clean out the small opening and a knife to clean out the small slot at the bottom. Fig. 44-5.

LACQUER FINISH

1. After sanding, dust all parts with a clean cloth.

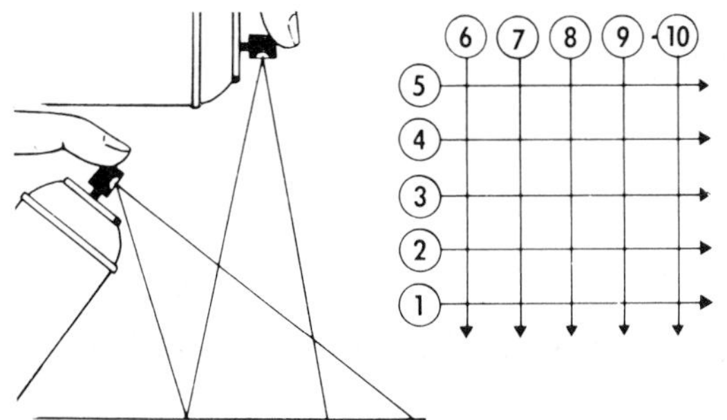

44-3. *Here are the steps in spraying. Start with number one and go to number five. Then turn the work one-quarter turn to the left and repeat.*

44-4. *Hold the can upside down and push the spray head to clean the tube.*

2. Apply stain if desired.
3. Seal with lacquer sealer.
4. Sand lightly with fine steel wool.
5. Apply filler of the desired color. Apply about one square foot at a time and then wipe clean.
6. Seal with lacquer sanding sealer.
7. Sand lightly with steel wool.
8. Brush or spray on 3 to 5 coats of lacquer. No sanding is needed between coats since they dissolve into one another. Allow at least 30 minutes drying time between coats. To brush on lacquer, select a brushing lacquer and use a brush with soft bristles such as a camel's hair or sable brush. A foam polybrush is also good. Dip the brush about one-third of the way into the lacquer but do not wipe any off on the side of the container. Load the brush heavily. Flow on the lacquer with long, rapid strokes. Lap the sides of each stroke. Do not attempt to brush it in as you would paint or varnish.
9. After the last coat has dried overnight, sand with 400 grit (10/0) wet-dry sandpaper using water as the lubricant.
10. Rub with rubbing compound.
11. Wash the surface with water and allow to dry.
12. Polish with lemon oil or wax.

44-5. *Cleaning the spray head. Another method is to soak it in the proper solvent.*

QUESTIONS

1. What is lacquer?
2. How is lacquer most often applied commercially?
3. How many coats of lacquer are usually needed to obtain a good finish?

ACTIVITIES

1. In your own words describe the correct brushing technique for lacquer.
2. Compare the advantages and disadvantages of a lacquer finish.

CHAPTER 45

Applying Penetrating and Wipe-On Finishes

There are many modern commercial finishes that can be used in the shop. These include finishes that soak into the wood (penetrating and wipe-on finishes). Fig. 45-1. Most can be applied with a small cloth or pad, eliminating the need for spray equipment or brushes. These finishes also do away with the dust problem that is so bothersome when using varnish. Penetrating and wipe-on finishes are synthetic, chemical materials. Fig. 45-2.

SEALACELL

This is a three-step process involving three different materials to complete the finish. Each can be applied with a rag or cloth. The materials are as follows:

1. *Sealacell* is a moisture-repellent, penetrating wood sealer that is applied over the raw wood. Ground-in-oil pigments can be mixed with the Sealacell to serve as a stain. Stain and filler can be applied in one step by mixing paste filler into the Sealacell and then adding ground-in-oil pigment to get the desired color. Apply Sealacell very liberally with a cloth. The depth of penetration depends upon the amount applied. Let dry overnight. Buff lightly with fine steel wool.

2. *Varno wax* is a blend of gums and waxes. To apply, make a small cloth pad about 1 x 2 inches. Coat the wood with wax, rubbing first with a circular motion and then wiping out with the grain. Buff lightly with 3/0 steel wool.

3. *Royal finish* is the final coat. It is applied in the same way as the Varno wax. Two or more applications of Royal finish increase the depth and luster. A soft, eggshell (slightly glossy) finish can be obtained by buffing with fine steel wool.

MINWAX

Minwax is a penetrating wood seal and wax that is applied directly to raw wood. Two coats will complete the job. The natural beauty of the wood is preserved because this finish penetrates and seals. The finish is *in* the wood, with very little on the surface. Minwax is available natural and in colors. It dries rapidly. This makes it possible to apply more than one coat in a day. It is not

45-1. *Modern furniture is often given a penetrating finish.*

necessary that this finish be rubbed after each coat. However, by rubbing with 4/0 steel wool, a very fine finish can be obtained.

DEFT

Deft is a semigloss, clear, interior wood finish. It is easy to use, requires no thinning, will not show brush marks, and will not darken. This material seals, primes, finishes the wood, and dries in 30 minutes. Three coats are recommended. The first coat seals the wood. The second coat adds depth. The third coat results in a mirror-smooth, fine finish. The third coat can be sanded with 6/0 wet-or-dry sandpaper or rubbed mirror-smooth with pumice and rottenstone. All three coats can be applied in a few hours. Deft can also be applied from a spray can.

DANISH OIL FINISH

Penetrating oil finishes like linseed oil have long been used to beautify and preserve gun stocks and other fine woods. To produce a Danish oil finish, penetrating resin-oil is needed. This finish actually improves the wood and does not require hours of hand rubbing. Danish oil is long lasting, seldom needs replenishing, and never needs resanding. One of its big advantages is that a surface that has become marred from hard usage is fairly easy to refinish.

Danish oil finish is applied as follows:

1. After sanding, apply a quick-dry alcohol or water-base wood stain with a clean cloth or brush.
2. Let dry for about 45 minutes.
3. Apply liberal amounts of the penetrating resin-oil finish.

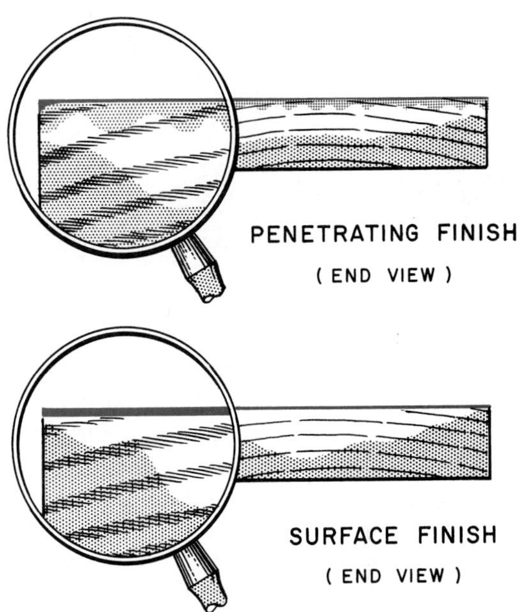

45-2. ***Here you see the difference between a penetrating finish and a surface finish.***

4. Allow the oil to soak into the wood for about 30 minutes or until penetration stops. Keep the surface uniformly wet with the finish.
5. Wipe the surface completely dry with a soft, absorbent cloth.
6. For more luster, let the surface dry for 4 hours.
7. Wet-sand lightly with a small amount of resin-oil finish.
8. Dry the wood thoroughly with a clean cloth.
9. Polish briskly with another cloth.

QUESTIONS

1. How many steps are needed to apply a Sealacell finish?
2. How many coats are usually needed for a Minwax finish?
3. What kind of finish is Deft?
4. How long does it take for Deft to dry?

ACTIVITIES

1. In your own words, describe how to apply a Danish oil finish.
2. Visit a paint store or home improvement center. What kinds of wipe-on finishes are available?

CHAPTER 46

Applying Paint and Enamel

If you use inexpensive wood, a paint or colored enamel is often best to decorate and finish it. Fig. 46-1. Paint and enamel are both opaque (can't be seen through). Enamel is more difficult to apply but will give a hard, glossy surface. Remember always to follow the directions on the can for mixing, thinning, and drying.

TOOLS AND MATERIALS

Paints are made of two basic materials: *pigment* to color and cover the surface and a *vehicle,* or liquid portion. Most paints are water-based *latex* (a kind of plastic). Latex paints are easy to use, dry quickly, and clean up with water. Latex paints can be self-priming; that is, you can use the same paint for the undercoat and the topcoats. However, using a separate primer as the first coat makes for a smoother finish. Some paints are oil-based and require a thinner of turpentine and/or mineral spirits. Paints are made to produce a flat, semigloss, or high-gloss finish.

Enamel paints are often preferred for semi-gloss or high-gloss finishes. They are made from polyester plastics, usually with an oil base. Two coats are enough to cover a wood surface. A suitable primer or enamel undercoat should be used before topcoating.

To apply paint or enamel, use a 1- to 1½-inch brush for small projects and a 2- or 3-inch brush for large areas.

APPLYING ENAMEL

1. Check the surface of the wood to see if it is sanded thoroughly. Fill any holes with wood putty. If there are any knots or streaks of sap, cover these with a wash coat of shellac.

2. Open a can of undercoat (primer) and mix it well.

3. Brush on the undercoat, applying it much like varnish. The undercoat will make the finish smoother.

4. Allow it to dry thoroughly. Sand lightly and dust clean.

46-1. ***This medicine cabinet was constructed of inexpensive softwood and then painted.***

5. Apply the final coat of enamel as it comes from the can.

6. Clean the brush in turpentine.

APPLYING PAINT

1. Make sure the surface of the wood is sanded carefully. Also fill any holes with wood putty. Apply a coat of shellac to knots.

2. Select a can of undercoat (primer). Shake it well. Open the can and mix the undercoat with a stick. If necessary, thin it.

3. Apply a thin coat of undercoat with a good brush. Don't make it too heavy. The undercoat will not completely hide the wood.

4. Allow to dry and then sand lightly with 6/0 sandpaper.

5. Apply the final coat just as it comes from the can. Brush out the paint thoroughly on the surface.

QUESTIONS

1. What is the difference between enamel and paint?
2. Which is more difficult to apply?
3. Why should an undercoat be applied before enamel?
4. Will a primer coat cover the wood surface?
5. How should the final coat of paint be applied to a wood surface?

ACTIVITIES

1. Check the labels on oil-based and latex paints. What instructions are given for cleanup?
2. Did you know that the American colonists made paint from milk or that some types of old paint contain lead? Research the history of paint and prepare a report.

CHAPTER 47 Decorating the Surface of Wood

The grain of most woods is beautiful. On many articles you won't want to do anything except apply a good finish. For novelty items, however, some other surface decoration may be applied. There are many simple ways of adding decorations. Fig. 47-1. Here are four you might like to try.

WOOD BURNING

A design can be burned into the wood with a *burning tool.* This tool looks like a small soldering iron. An electric unit heats the point of the tool. This hot point will burn a groove. Basswood and poplar are good woods for this because they are light in color and the burning shows up clearly.

47-1(a). *These bookends illustrate three of the ways to decorate the surface of wood. The bookend on the left has an overlay of tooled copper. The one at the right has the letter outlined by burning, while the interior of the letter is finished with color pencils.*

Most burning tools come with several different points so that the design can be varied.

1. Transfer the design to the wood surface.
2. Heat the burning tool and try it on a scrap piece of wood. Practice burning straight and curved lines.
3. Place the wood on a bench and sit in a comfortable position.
4. Hold the burning tool like a pencil. Fig. 47-2.
5. Start the burning near yourself and work away.
6. For straight lines, use a straightedge to guide the tool.
7. Steady your hand as you burn a curved line. A little practice is necessary.
8. Work carefully. Make corner lines meet neatly. Try to make the curves smooth.

After the design is completed, the inside or outside can be stained a darker color. The stain won't run because the burning tool has closed the wood pores. However, if you think there is danger of the stain's "bleeding," first apply a thin coat of shellac to the area you don't want darkened. Fig. 47-3.

NOTES: INCLUDE SHEET METAL BASE

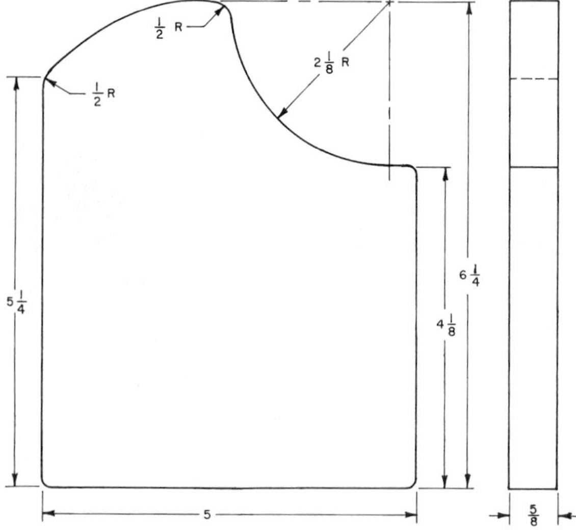

NOTES: INCLUDE SHEET METAL BASE

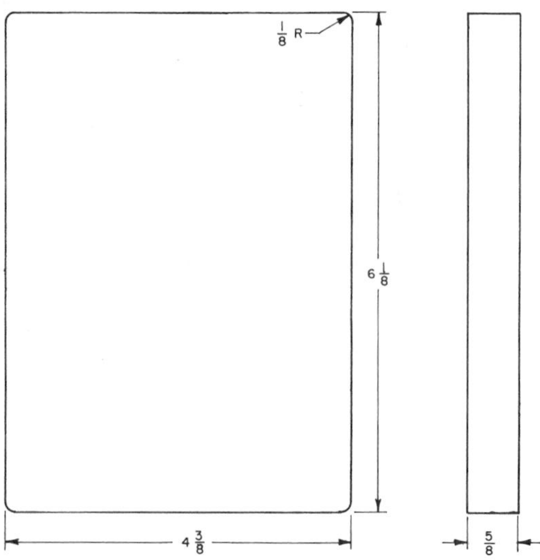

47-1(b). *Plans for the bookends.*

47-2. *Using a burning tool to decorate the wood surface or apply a design.*

APPLYING A DECAL

A *decal* is a design or picture on paper that will stick to a surface. You can buy decals in all sizes, shapes, and designs from most hardware, paint, or variety stores. They should be chosen after the project is completed in order to be the right size and shape. Fig. 47-4.

1. Apply a thin coat of shellac to the wood surface.
2. Smooth the shellacked surface with fine steel wool.
3. Place the decal in a pan of warm water about 30 seconds.
4. Remove the decal and allow the water to soak into the protective paper. This takes about one minute.
5. Slip about one-third of the decal off the protective paper onto the project.
6. Pull the rest of the protective paper off as you hold the decal in place.
7. Use a clean cloth to smooth out the decal. Work from the center out to remove any air bubbles.
8. Cover the decal with varnish or wax. *Never use shellac.*

USING COLOR PENCILS ON WOOD

Certain types of color pencils work well on woods. They can be used to make fine lines, light shadings, or solid masses of color. These color pencils are excellent for applying designs to wooden articles such as plates and trays.

1. Sand the surface of the wood with 3/0 sandpaper. Wipe the surface clean.
2. Transfer the design to the wood as described in Chapter 9.
3. Color the design with different color pencils or with one color, whichever you prefer. Carefully add the color to each area. Begin to color around the lines and then fill in the large areas.
4. Apply a coat of clear varnish. Buff with 3/0 steel wool.
5. Add a second coat of varnish.
6. Buff and then apply a coat of wax.

METAL TOOLING

Thin copper can be shaped by placing it over a pile of newspapers about ½ inch thick. Use a small wooden dowel to press the shape into the metal. The copper can then be used to decorate a wood project, as shown in Fig. 47-1.

47-3. *The designs on these items were made with a burning tool.*

47-4(a). *This key holder has been decorated with decals.*

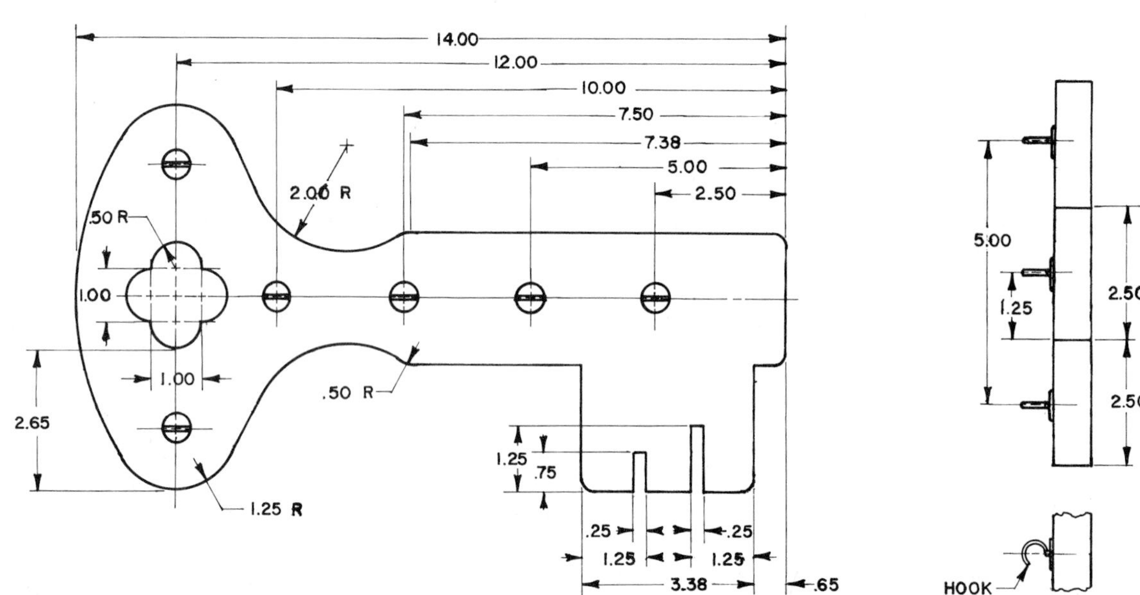

47-4(b). *A working drawing of the key holder. The dimensions are in decimals, as they would be if industry mass-produced this item. For example, 2½ inches is written as 2.5.*

QUESTIONS

1. What is a burning tool? How is it used?
2. Where can you obtain decals?
3. How can color pencils be used on woods?

ACTIVITIES

1. On graph paper, draw one of the patterns for bookends (Fig. 47-1b) and sketch a decorative design on it. To transfer the design to wood, place carbon paper under the graph paper and trace over your design. (See Fig. 9-14.)

Drill Press, Scroll Saw, and Band Saw

LEARN THESE SAFETY RULES BEFORE USING THE DRILL PRESS

- **Operate the drill press only *after your teacher has shown you how.***
- **Remove jewelry, tuck in loose clothing, and confine long hair.**
- **Make sure all guards are in place and operating correctly.**
- **Use proper eye protection.**
- **Hold material securely with a vise or clamps.**
- **Be sure the key is removed from the chuck.**
- **Select a properly sharpened bit.**
- **If a workpiece gets caught in the drill, turn off the power. Do not try to stop the movement with your hand.**
- **Adjust the table or depth stop to avoid drilling into the table.**
- **Select the correct speed. Usually it is slower for metal, faster for wood. The larger the bit, the slower the speed.**

The first three power tools you are likely to use are the drill press, the scroll saw (also called the jigsaw), and the band saw. Each is easy and safe to use when you follow directions.

DRILL PRESS

A *drill press* is a machine for drilling and boring holes. (Holes 1/4 inch or less in diameter are said to be drilled. Holes larger than 1/4 inch are bored.) The drill press can also do sanding, planing, shaping, and many other operations.

Tools

A *bench-type drill press* is the most common. Fig. 48-1. The size is shown by the diameter of the largest workpiece that can be drilled on center. For example, a 15-inch drill press will bore a hole through the center of a round tabletop 15 inches in diameter. A key chuck holds the cutting tools.

A *drill-press vise* holds small pieces of work. Fig. 48-2. Larger pieces can be held in the hand or clamped to the table.

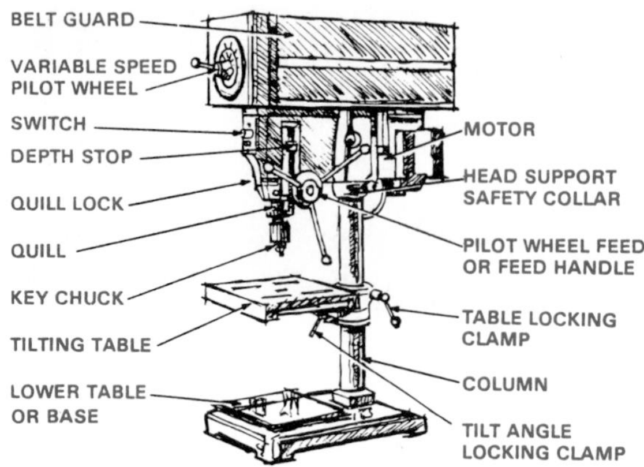

48-1. *Parts of a drill press.*

48-3(a). *Using a machine auger bit to bore a hole. Be sure to lower your face shield before starting the drill press.*

Machine and power *auger bits* have a straight shank and a brad point. Never try to use hand auger bits in the drill press, since only a straight shank will fit into the chuck. *Spade bits* work well in a drill press or electric hand drill. Machine *Foerstner bits* are also available. Fig. 48-3.

Twist drills like those used in a hand drill are best for drilling small holes. Fig. 48-4.

Drilling or Boring Holes

1. Select the correct cutting tool and fasten it in the chuck. Rotate the drill by hand to make sure it runs straight. *Always remember to remove the chuck key.* Never try to fasten a square shank in a chuck.

2. Place the work on the table over a piece of scrap stock. Adjust the table up or down until the work just clears under the cutting tool.

3. Adjust the speed according to the cutting tool size and the kind of wood. Speed adjustment is of two types—the variable speed drive and the step pulley. Adjust the speed of the variable speed drill press *with the machine running.* Adjust the speed on the step pulley machine *with the switch off.* You get the fastest speed by using the *largest pulley on the motor* and the *smallest pulley on the drill.* Fast speed is for small-

48-2. *Holding the work in a vise for drilling.*

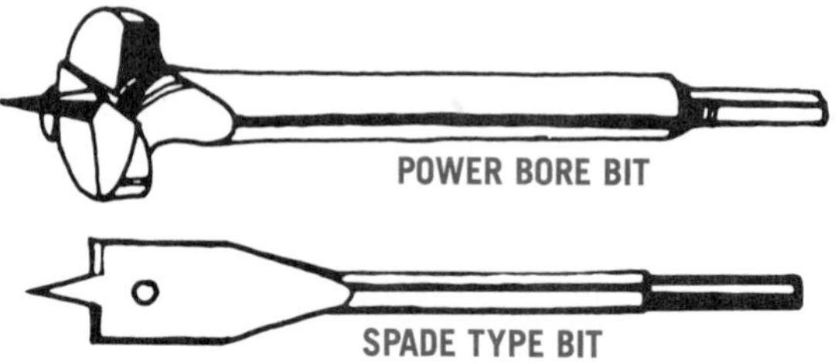

48-3(b). *Two of the bits that can be used in a drill press.*

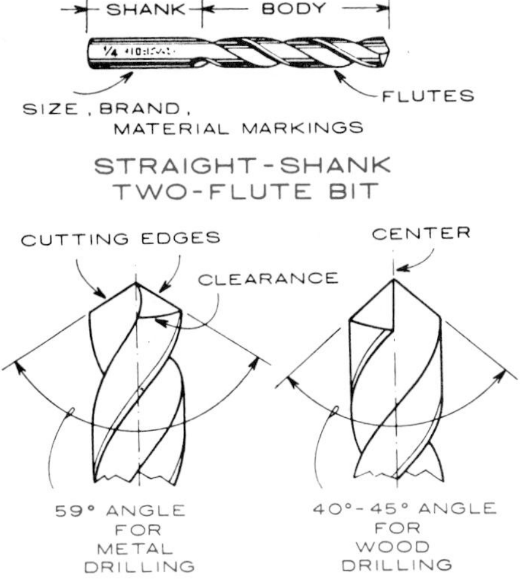

48-4. *Parts of a twist drill.*

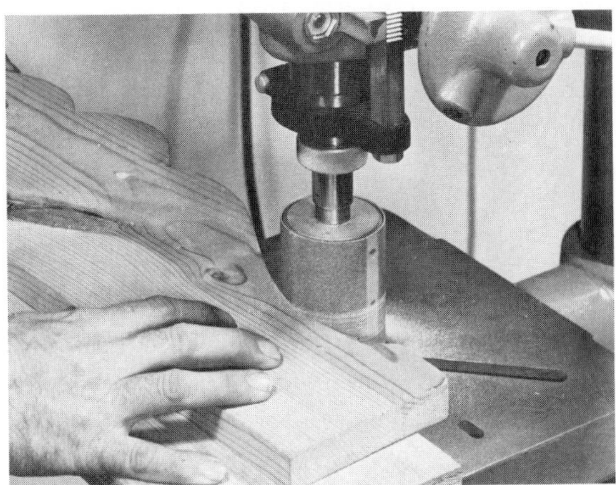

48-5. *Sanding an edge on a drill press.*

diameter cutting tools and softwoods. Speeds should be slow for large bits and hardwoods.

4. Turn on the power. Hold the work firmly with your left hand. If the piece is small or the bit large, clamp the work in a vise or to the table with hand screws or C-clamps.

5. Apply light pressure on the feed handle to cut the hole. Fig. 48-3(a).

6. Release the pressure slightly as the tool cuts through the bottom of the work.

7. A *sanding disk* can be fastened to the spindle to sand the ends and edges of the wood. Fig. 48-5.

LEARN THESE SAFETY RULES BEFORE USING THE SCROLL (JIG) SAW

- **Follow the general safety rules (eye protection, guards, sharp tools, clean work area, etc.) for all machines.**
- **Operate the saw only *after your teacher has shown you how.***
- **Operate the saw at the correct speed. Use a slow speed for thick work and a faster speed for thin materials.**
- **Make sure the saw blade is properly installed.**
- **Don't force or twist the work into the blade. Blades break very easily.**
- **Don't use the machine for materials thicker than 1″.**
- **Keep your fingers away from the saw line; this is the danger area.**

***48-6.** A rocker-action scroll saw. This is a 15-inch saw that will cut wood up to $1\frac{3}{4}$ inches thick and plywood up to 1 inch thick. It can also be used to cut plastic, light metal, and other materials.*

OVERARM
BLADE LOCKING LEVER
HOLD-DOWN AND GUARD
TABLE
SWITCH
MOTOR
BASE

SCROLL SAW (JIGSAW)

The *scroll saw (jigsaw)* has a narrow blade held in a frame. The blade cuts by moving up and down. The scroll saw is used to cut inside and outside curves and irregular shapes. It is a simple, safe power tool.

Tools

There are many kinds and sizes of scroll saws. The least expensive is a *vibrator.* This type moves rapidly up and down. It uses the same blades as the coping saw. That is, the blades have little pins at either end. The vibrator scroll saw will cut only thin wood and plastic. The *rocker-action saw* has a motor that rocks the whole inside frame. The cutting action is smooth and even. This type reduces vibration and blade breakage. Fig. 48-6. It is an excellent machine for most work. The *belt-driven scroll saw* has a belt and pulley arrangement that controls its speed. The blade has no pins and is mounted in the upper and lower chucks. Fig. 48-7. Scroll saw size is determined by the distance from the blade to the inside of the frame. A 15-inch saw, for example, will cut to the center of a 30-inch circle.

Power scroll saw blades are made with either a blank end for larger machines or with pin or bent ends for smaller ones. Blades are 3, 5, or 6 inches long and have from seven to twenty teeth per inch. The thinner the work to be sawed, the more teeth the blade should have. A good rule to follow is to make sure that three teeth touch the

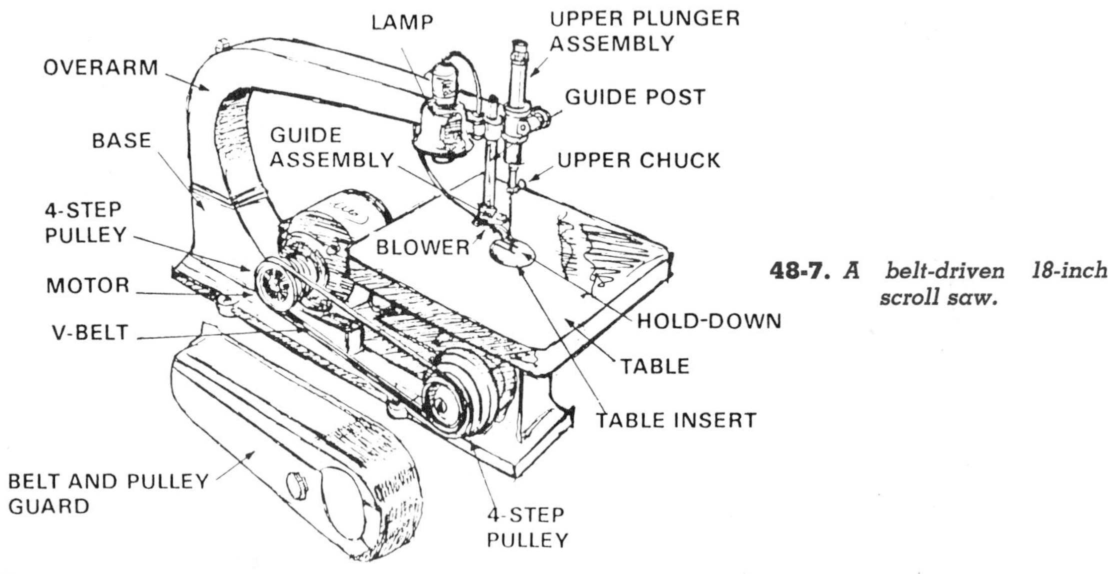

***48-7.** A belt-driven 18-inch scroll saw.*

work at all times. *Jeweler's piercing-saw blades* can be used in power scroll saws to cut metal. These come in widths from very fine (6/0 is about 1/16 inch wide) to rather wide blades (about 3/16 inch).

Installing a Blade in a Belt-Driven Scroll Saw

1. Remove the insert (throat plate) from the table.
2. Loosen the knob that tilts the table and pull the right side of the table up. Turn the belt until the lower chuck is at the highest point.
3. Loosen the jaws in the lower chuck. Either a thumbscrew or an Allen wrench placed in the setscrew is used to do this.
4. Fasten a blade of the correct size in the lower chuck. *The teeth must point down.*
5. Loosen the screw that releases the tension sleeve and lower it.
6. Fasten the other end of the blade in the upper chuck.
7. Now lift up on the tension sleeve about 1 inch to get the correct tension (tightness). Tighten the screw.
8. Adjust the blade guide until the blade just clears on the side and the roller just touches the back of the blade.
9. Replace the throat plate. Level the table and tighten it.
10. Place the work on the table. Lower the guide until the hold-down holds the work firmly on the table.
11. Turn the saw over by hand once to see if it runs freely.
12. Adjust the speed. For the fastest speed, place the belt on the largest motor pulley and the smallest machine pulley. Use this speed with a very fine blade and thin material. Set the machine to a slower speed for a wider blade and thicker stock. Fig. 48-8.

Installing a Blade in a Rocker-Action Machine

1. Select a blade of the correct width and length (3 inches) with pin ends.
2. Release the blade-locking lever. Fig. 48-9.
3. Hold the blade *with the teeth pointing down.*
4. Slip the lower end into the V opening.
5. Pull down the upper end and slip the other end of the blade into this V opening.
6. Tighten the blade-locking lever.
7. For sawing long lengths, the blade can be put in sideways.

Cutting with a Scroll Saw

1. Stand directly in front of the saw so that you can guide the work with both hands.

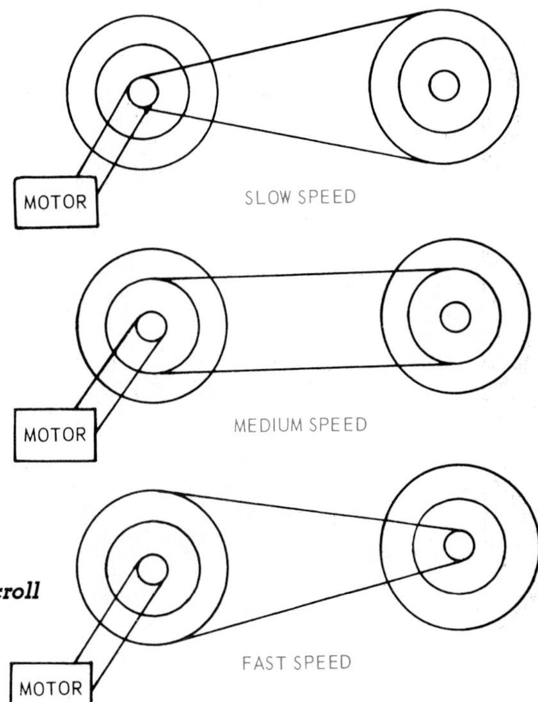

48-8. ***Adjusting the speed on a belt-driven scroll saw.***

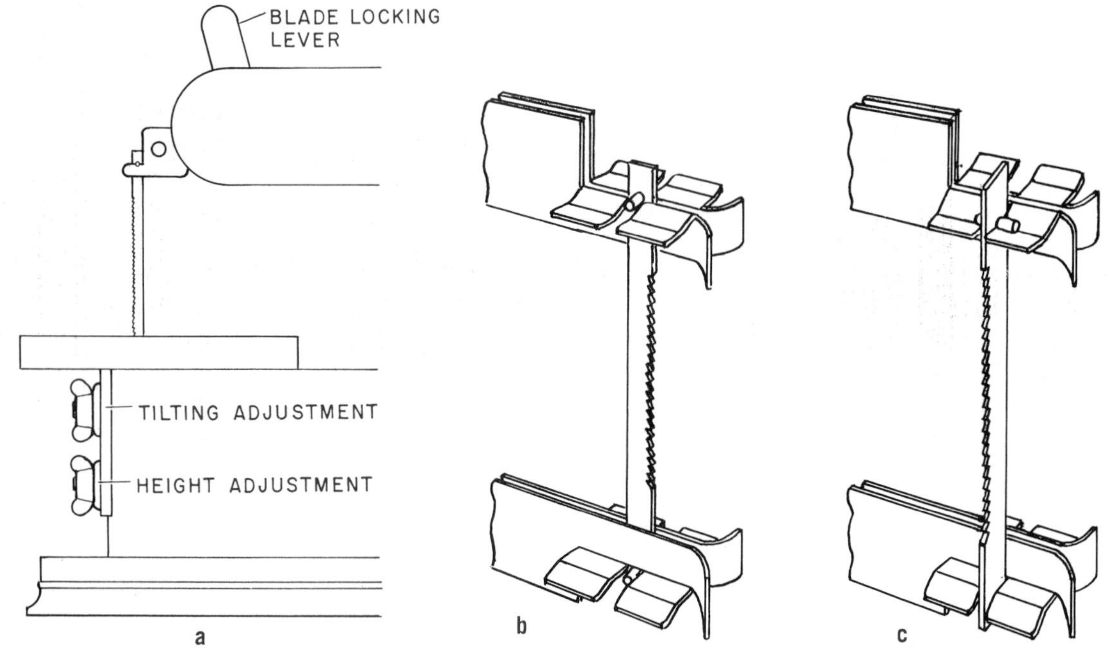

48-9. *Installing a scroll saw blade in a rocker-action saw. (a) Blade-locking lever and table adjustments. (b) Blade installed for cutting from the front. (c) Blade installed for long cutting from the side.*

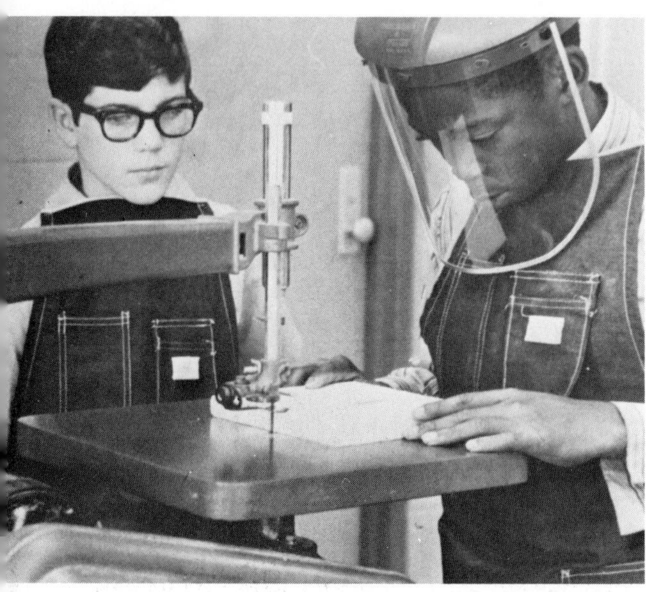

48-10. *Cutting with the scroll saw. It is important to cut slowly and follow the layout line carefully. Avoid "crowding" the work into the blade, especially on sharp curves.*

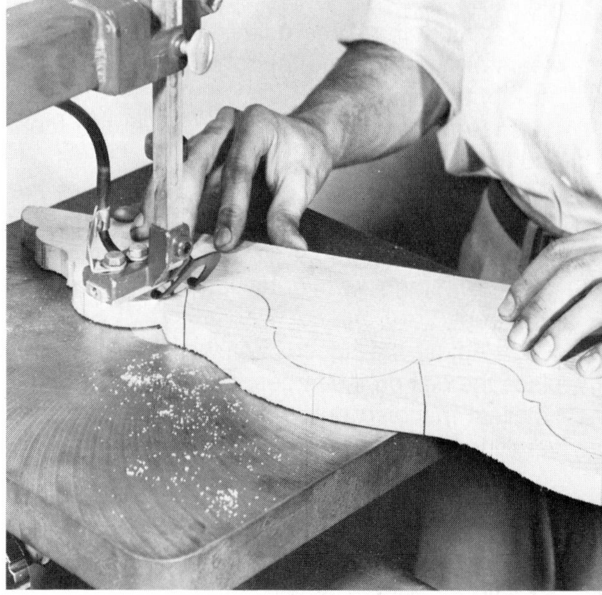

48-11. *Cutting a complicated curve. Saw kerfs made up to the layout line free the blade at sharp curves.*

2. Apply forward pressure with your thumbs and guide the work with your other fingers.

3. Start in the waste stock and cut up to the layout line.

4. Carefully guide the work so that the saw stays just outside the line. Never force the work into the blade. Fig. 48-10.

5. At sharp corners turn the work slowly without pressing forward. If you turn the work too fast, the blade will break. Never twist the blade.

6. For inside cutting, first drill or bore a hole in the waste stock. Loosen the upper end of the blade and slip it through the hole. Fasten the upper end again in the chuck. Cut from the waste stock up to the layout line and then around the line to make the opening or design.

7. For angle sawing, the table on many machines can be tilted as much as 45 degrees.

8. When cutting a complicated part, first make relief cuts up to the layout line. Then start in the waste stock and come up to the layout line at a slight angle. As the cut is made, each piece of scrap stock falls away. Fig. 48-11.

LEARN THESE SAFETY RULES BEFORE USING THE BAND SAW

- **Operate the saw only *after your teacher has shown you how.***
- **Remove jewelry, tuck in loose clothing, and confine long hair.**
- **Make sure all guards are in place and operating correctly.**
- **Use proper eye protection.**
- **Make sure all adjustments are tight and secure and blade guides are properly adjusted.**
- **Upper blade guides should be about 1/8″ above the workpiece.**
- **Guide the work slowly, letting the blade do the work. Do not force the work into the blade.**
- **Do not attempt to cut a smaller radius than the blade will allow.**
- **Avoid backing out of a cut.**
- **Place hands or fingers on each side of the cut line, never on the line. Use a push block if necessary.**
- **Never leave the machine until it has come to a full stop.**

BAND SAW

The band saw is used primarily for cutting exterior curved edges. Although it can do straight cutting, it cannot do internal cutting as the scroll saw does, nor will it cut so sharp a curve. The size of the machine is determined by the diameter of the wheels. Fig. 48-12. The most common of the small machines is the 14-inch band saw. The blade lengths are made to fit the particular size machine and come in widths from 1/8 inch to

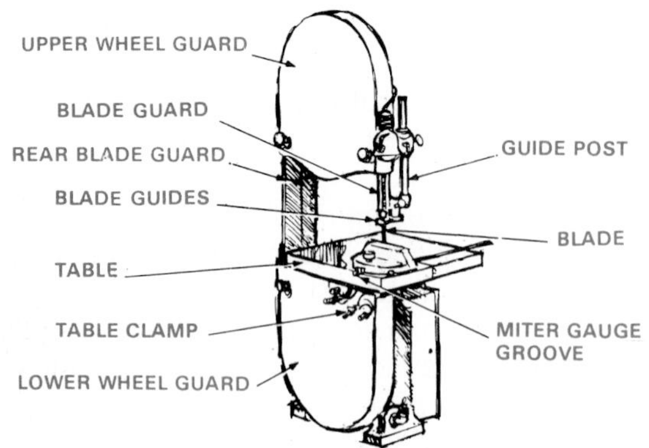

48-12. *Parts of a band saw.*

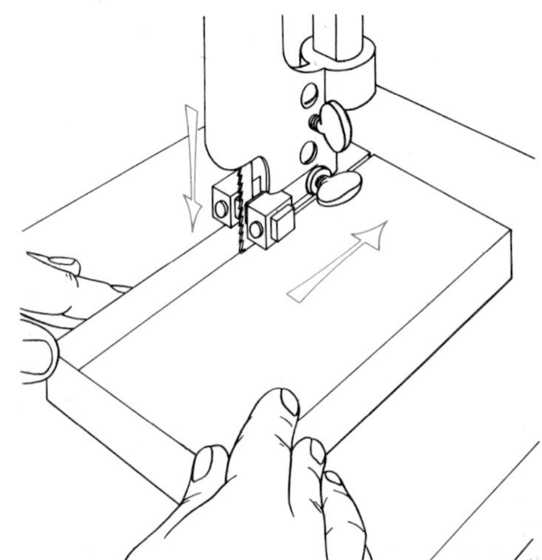

48-14. *Cutting a straight line. Your fingers should be on either side of the cutting line, not directly behind the saw blade.*

½ inch. Sharp curves are better cut with narrow blades than with wide blades. Fig. 48-13.

Follow these guidelines when using the band saw:

- Maintain proper belt tension. Keep the belt just tight enough to prevent slipping.
- Use the correct blade. Choose the largest one with the coarsest teeth that will cut the stock cleanly and will follow the sharpest curve in the pattern.
- Always move the blade guide close to the work to insure accurate cutting and to prevent the blade from twisting.
- Before operating the saw, check the blade for proper tension and proper mounting. The teeth should point down on the downward stroke.
- Examine the stock carefully before sawing to make sure it is free of nails.

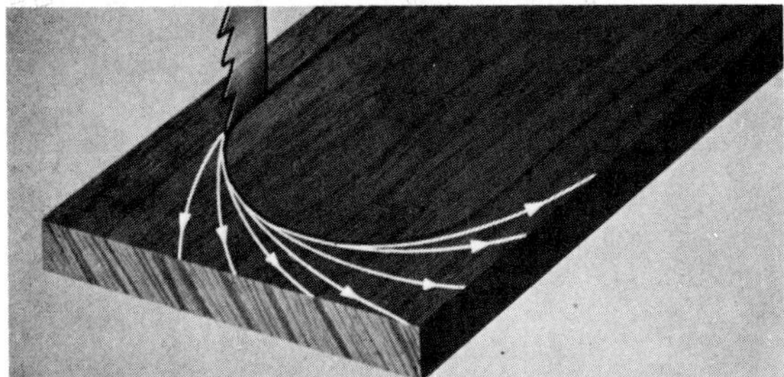

48-13. *Cutting a curve. If the blade is too wide, make a series of cuts as shown.*

- Feed the stock evenly and slowly to keep from twisting the blade or crowding it beyond its cutting capacity. Fig. 48-14.
- Clean sawdust from the table frequently.
- Be sure the wheels turn clockwise as viewed from the front of the saw. The arrow on the motor pulley indicates the direction of rotation.
- Make sure the blade is sharp and in good condition. A clicking noise may indicate a crack in the blade.

Using the Band Saw

1. Choosing the proper blade for each job is of great importance. Always use the widest blade possible to cut the sharpest contours of your pattern. A ⅜-inch blade should cut a circle 3 inches in diameter; a ¼-inch blade, a 2-inch circle; a 3/16-inch blade, a 1-inch circle; and a ⅛-inch blade, a ½-inch circle. For all straight and general cutting, a ⅜-inch blade is recommended.
2. Adjust the top blade guide so that it clears the work by about ¼ inch.
3. Start the machine and allow it to come to full speed. Stand to one side, not directly in front of the blade.
4. Feed the stock slowly through the blade.

48-15(a). *Make short cuts first.*

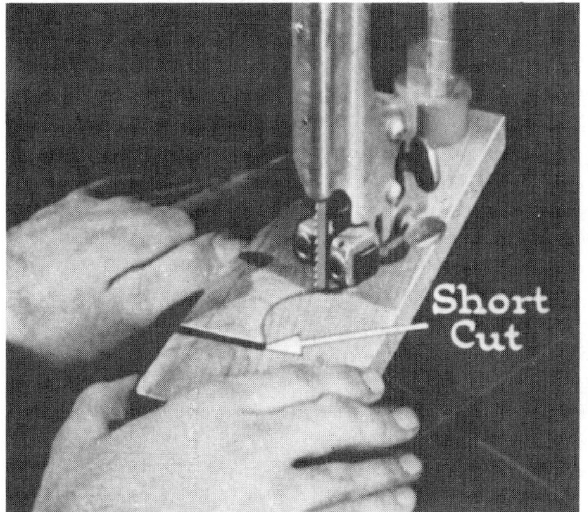

48-15(b). *Then make the long cuts.*

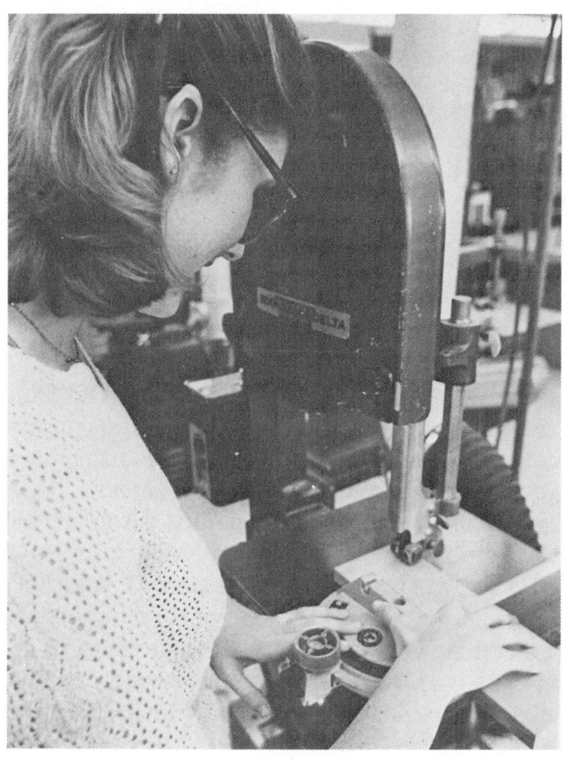

5. Cut to the outside of the layout line in the waste stock. "Back out" only as a last resort, drawing the work very slowly away from the saw blade and making sure the blade follows the saw cut. Failure to do this may force the blade off the wheels.

6. Make short cuts before long ones. Fig. 48-15.

7. If the pattern to be cut has a number of sharp curves, it is best to make a series of saw kerfs in the waste stock opposite each curve before starting the cut.

8. A miter gauge attachment which slides in the table slot can be used to hold the work when doing straight cutting. The work should be held firmly against the gauge. Fig. 48-16.

48-16. *Using a miter gauge to cut stock to length.*

QUESTIONS

1. What kind of shank must auger bits for a drill press have?
2. What kind of cutting tool is usually used for drilling small holes?
3. How do you adjust the speed on a drill press?
4. How do you choose the correct blade for a scroll saw?
5. What kind of blade should you use to saw metal on the scroll saw?
6. What are the common causes of blade breakage on the scroll saw?
7. How is the size of the band saw determined?
8. How can a sharp curve be cut on the band saw?

ACTIVITIES

1. Obtain pictures of a drill press, scroll saw, and band saw. (You can copy them from a tool catalog.) Label the parts. Below each picture, list the main uses for the tool.
2. Suppose you are writing an owner's manual. Explain how to install a blade in a belt-driven scroll saw.
3. Design a safety poster that can be placed in your school lab near the drill press, scroll saw, or band saw.

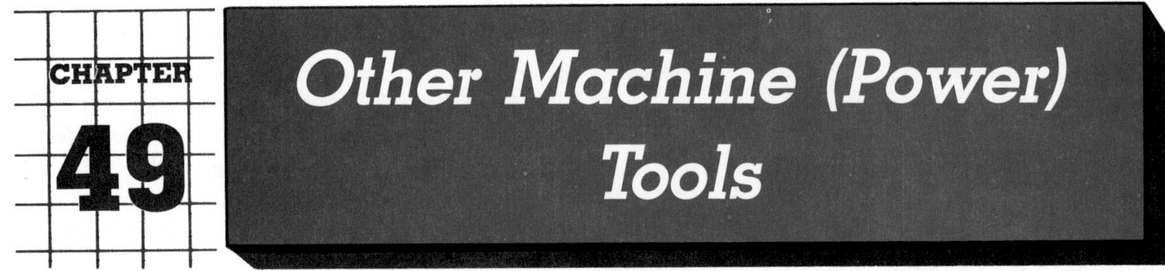

CHAPTER 49 Other Machine (Power) Tools

Have you enjoyed working with the drill press, scroll saw, and band saw? If so, you will want to find out what other machines are used by woodworkers. So far, most of your projects have been built with hand tools plus a few simple machines. For example, you have had a chance to see how much easier it is to cut out a shape with a scroll saw than with a coping saw. You have found that drilling is simple on the drill press.

In more advanced woodwork, however, much of the cutting and shaping of wood is done with power tools which eliminate much of the hard handwork. In industry, machines process lumber from the first step of cutting down the trees to making the finished products, such as furniture and homes. Using these machines requires different skills from those needed when using hand tools. Yet even if you learn to handle these woodworking machines, you must still be able to use hand tools skillfully.

Power tools can be very dangerous, especially if they are used by an inexperienced or careless person. Anyone who uses them incorrectly usually gets hurt. That is why your instructor will not allow you to use even the simplest power tool without safety instruction.

LEARN THESE SAFETY RULES BEFORE USING THE JOINTER

* **Follow the general safety rules (eye protection, guards, sharp tools, clean work area, etc.) for all machines.**
* **Get your instructor's permission before using the machine.**
* **Make sure the guard is in place.**
* **Keep the fence locked securely.**
* **Stop the machine when making adjustments.**
* **Examine the stock carefully to make sure it is free of loose knots and nails.**
* **Make sure the stock is longer than 12 inches.**
* **Use a push block when planing the face of a board.**
* **Do not attempt to plane end grain. Only the very experienced woodworker can do this safely.**
* **Always plane a board *with* the grain. If the direction of the grain changes, feed the stock slowly.**
* **When a very smooth finish is required, take cuts of 1/32 inch or less and feed the stock slowly. On edge jointing, a 1/8-inch cut will remove most irregularities.**

JOINTER

The jointer is a machine that does the work of a hand plane, except that the cutting is done by revolving cutterheads with three or more knives. Fig. 49-1. The size is determined by the widest cut that can be made. There is a table in front and in back of the cutterhead. The front, or infeed, table can be adjusted up and down to vary the

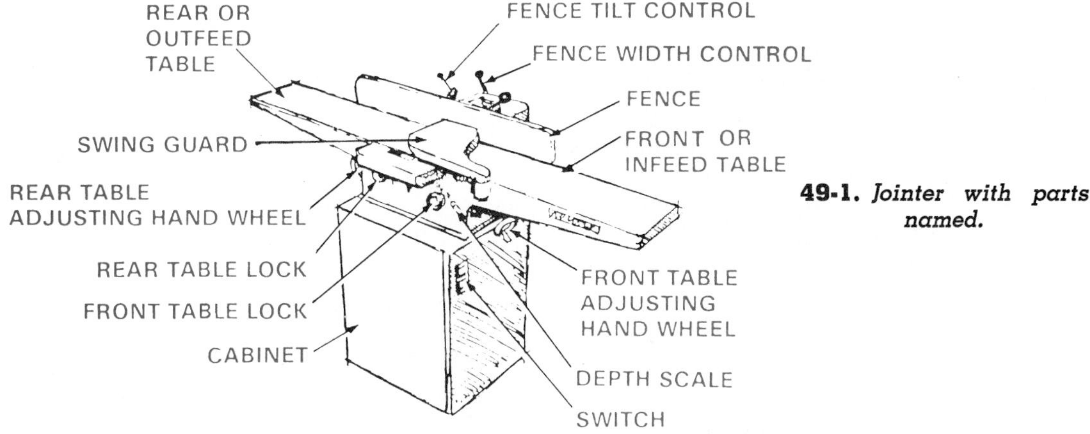

49-1. *Jointer with parts named.*

49-2(a). *In starting a cut, as the stock advances and your left hand nears the cutterhead, stop pushing. Use the right hand to hold the stock down. Shift the left hand back to its original position, and shove the stock ahead again.*

49-2(b). *Continue moving the stock forward until the end of the board is on the infeed (front) table. Then place the left hand on the stock on the other side of the revolving knives. Keep your hands out of the area just over the cutterhead.*

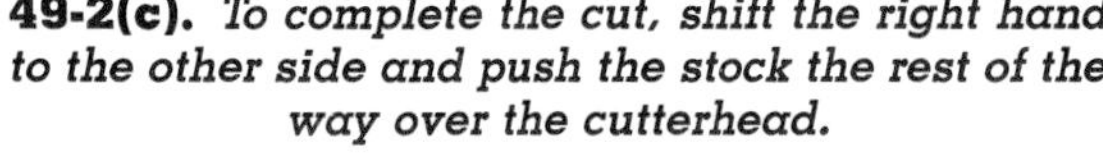

49-2(c). *To complete the cut, shift the right hand to the other side and push the stock the rest of the way over the cutterhead.*

49-3. *Using a push block to complete the surfacing.*

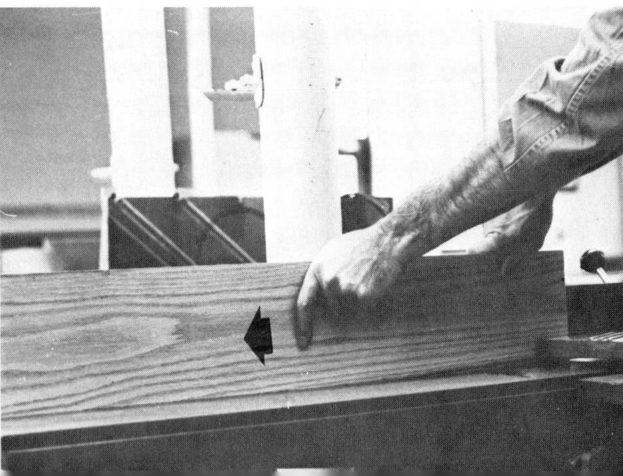

depth of cut. The rear, or outfeed, table is adjusted to the height of the cutterhead.

Jointing an Edge

Check the stock to determine grain direction. (Always plane with the grain.) Adjust the infeed table to cut about 1/16 inch for rough cuts and about 1/32 inch for finish cuts. The kind of wood helps to determine the depth of the cut. For example, you can take a deeper cut on pine or basswood than you can on harder woods such as walnut or birch.

Check the fence with a square to make sure it is at right angles to the table. Make sure the guard is in place. Turn on the machine. Apply uniform pressure to the work to hold it securely against the fence and table. Feed the stock at a uniform speed. Fig. 49-2.

Face Planing

Place the stock flat on the front table. Turn on the power. Start the planing by first holding the work with both hands over the front table. Place your left hand on the front portion of the stock over the outfeed (rear) table as soon as it rests solidly on this table. As your right hand approaches the cutterhead, use a push block to feed the stock past the blades. Fig. 49-3. *Never allow your hands to move above the revolving blades.*

LEARN THESE SAFETY RULES BEFORE USING THE PLANER-SURFACER

* **Follow the general safety rules (eye protection, guards, sharp tools, clean work area, etc.) for all machines.**
* **Be sure to check all material for loose knots, nails, and other foreign objects.**
* **Do not force stock through the planer. Keep hands off the material and let the power feed operate.**
* **Select the proper depth of cut and the rate of speed according to the stock being planed.**
* **Thin stock should be properly supported by a jig or backup board. Check with the instructor for minimum thickness and length.**
* **Never look directly into the throat of a planer at table level while it is running or in operation.**
* **Remove shavings or chips when the power is turned off. Keep hands away from the chip guard and the point of operation.**
* **Do not stand directly in front of the machine in line with a possible kickback.**

49-4. *Feeding stock into a planer.*

PLANER

The planer, or surfacer, is used to plane the surface of stock and to bring it to proper thickness. Most of the wood you will use has been surfaced at the lumber mill. However, if the stock is rough, you or your instructor will run it through a planer. Fig. 49-4. If you look closely at the surface of the wood after it comes from the surfacer or planer, you will find that it has small mill or knife marks made by the rotating cutter. These must be removed with a hand plane.

LEARN THESE SAFETY RULES BEFORE USING THE CIRCULAR SAW

- **Follow the general safety rules (eye protection, guards, sharp tools, etc.) for all machines.**
- **Be sure to use the correct blade: a ripsaw for cutting with the grain, a crosscut for cutting across grain, or a combination blade for both.**
- **Keep saw blades properly sharpened. A dull blade is extremely hard on the machine and motor, and it will not produce clean work.**
- **Stop the saw before making adjustments, removing short stock, or cleaning the table.**
- **The guard should cover the blade at all times.**
- **When ripping thin strips, use a push stick to feed the work past the blade.**
- **Examine the stock carefully before sawing to make sure it is free of nails.**
- ***With the power off*, clean saw mechanism often.**
- **Do not stand directly in front of the saw blade. Take a position a little to either side. This will keep sawdust away from your face and prevent injury in case of kickback.**
- **Use the splitter provided to keep the saw kerf open.**
- ***Never attempt to saw freehand*. Always be sure the fence or miter gauge is used.**
- **Anti-kickback fingers behind the saw blade resist the tendency of the saw to throw stock up and toward the operator. Make sure these are always in place.**

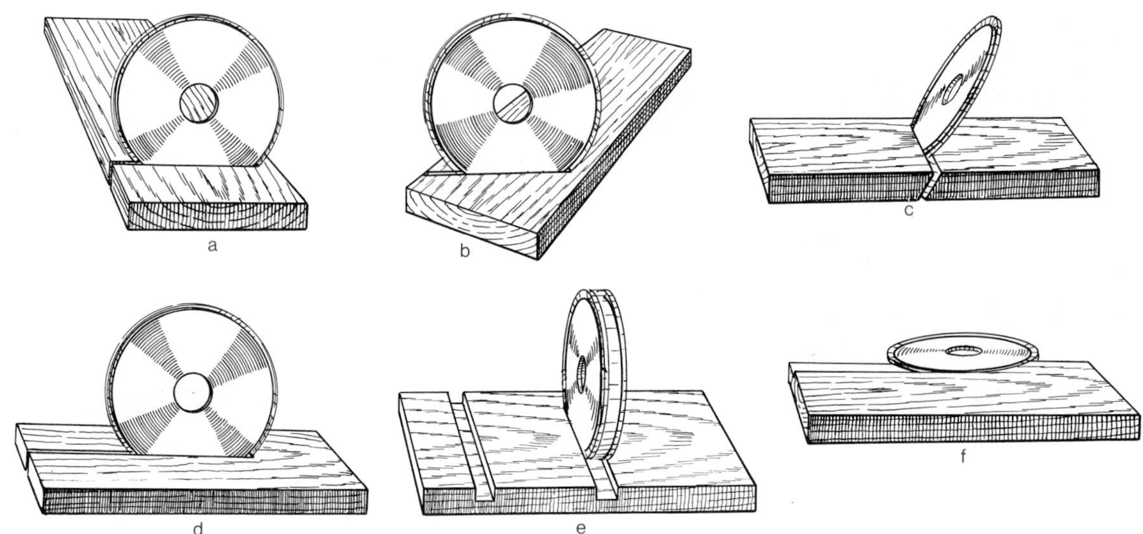

49-5. ***Common cuts that can be made with a circular saw: (a) Crosscutting. (b) Miter cutting. (c) Bevel cutting. (d) Ripping. (e) Cutting a dado with the dado head. (f) Cutting a rabbet.***

CIRCULAR SAW

The circular saw is used for making all types of straight cuts, such as ripping, crosscutting, mitering, and beveling. Fig. 49-5. The size of the saw is determined by the size of blade used, usually from 8 to 10 inches. Fig. 49-6.

The principal blades are shown in Fig. 49-7.

- The *crosscut* blade is for cutting across the grain. This blade is used for sawing all types of wood.
- The teeth of the *combination* blade are designed for both crosscutting and ripping. This blade is ideal for general use.
- The *ripsaw* blade has specially designed hook-type teeth for sawing with the grain of the wood. This saw blade runs free of sawdust accumulation.
- The *chisel combination* blade has a new tooth design made for both crosscutting and ripping. It is adaptable for sawing all types of wood.
- The *fine-tooth crosscut* blade is designed to produce a minimum amount of tearing when sawing fiberboard, plywood, and similar materials.

A fence is needed for all types of ripping operations, and a miter gauge is needed for crosscutting. The fence is a metal guide clamped parallel with the saw blade. The miter gauge slides in the grooves of the table. To keep the operator from getting his or her fingers too near the blade, a guard is used. Circular saws are

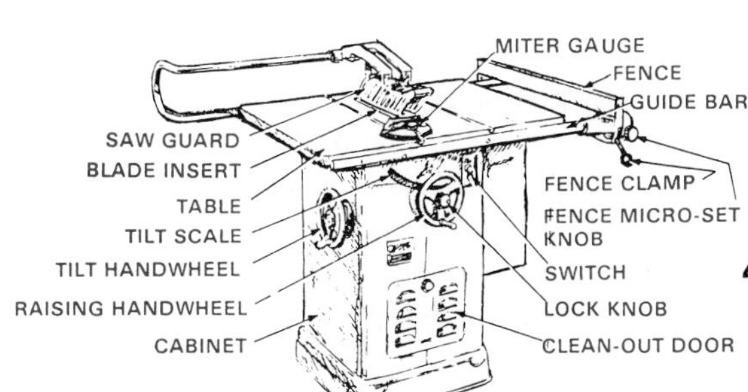

49-6. ***A 10-inch circular saw with parts named.***

49-7. *Kinds of saw blades.*

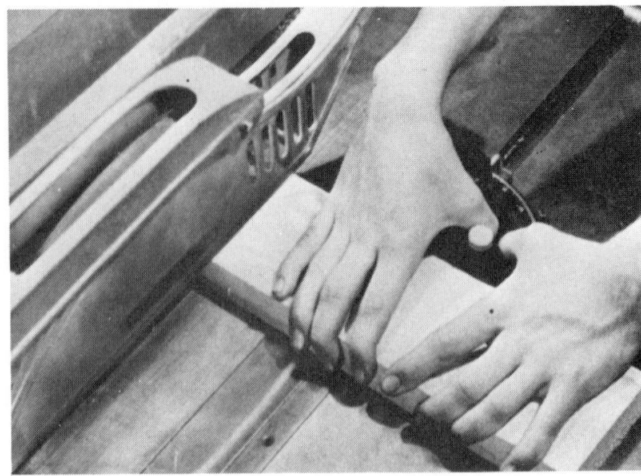

49-9. *Crosscutting.*

responsible for a large number of accidents in woodworking shops, so be careful.

Crosscutting

Crosscutting is sawing across the grain. Follow these steps:

1. Adjust the height of the blade so that it will just cut through the stock. Several teeth should be above the stock to permit the blade to free itself of sawdust.
2. Place the stock on the table and against the miter gauge. Line up the cutoff mark with the saw blade. Fig. 49-8. Make sure the guard is in place.

49-8. *A pencil line on the table of the saw indicates the position of the blade. You can line up the cutoff line on the stock with this line on the table.*

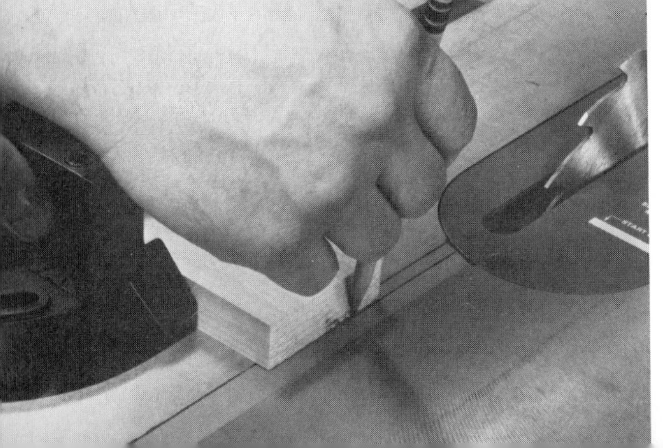

3. Turn on the machine.
4. Hold the stock firmly against the gauge with both hands and push the miter gauge along the groove, feeding it slowly into the saw. Fig. 49-9. Stand behind and to the left side of the miter gauge, not in line with the blade.
5. After the cut is completed, do not attempt to remove the scrap stock with your fingers.
6. Turn off the machine. Wait for the blade to stop. Push the scrap stock out of the way with a push stick.

Ripping

Ripping is sawing in the direction of the grain. Follow these steps:

1. Remove the miter gauge. Place the fence in correct position by measuring the desired distance from the right edge of the blade to the fence. This is the amount that will be cut off.
2. Place the guard in position.
3. Start the machine.
4. Hold the board firmly against the fence and push it slowly into the blade. When three-fourths of the cutting is completed, finish the cutting with a push stick. Push the board completely past the blades. Figs. 49-10 and 49-11.
5. Turn off the machine. Do not pick up any of the pieces until the blade has stopped completely.

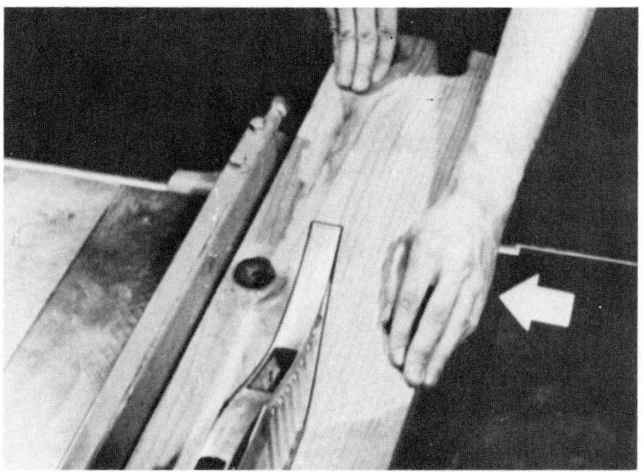

49-10. *Starting a ripping cut. With your left hand, hold the work firmly against the table and fence. Place your left hand near the left edge of the board and as far as possible from the blade.*

49-11. *Completing a ripping cut. Use a push stick to complete the cut. This makes it unnecessary to place your hand between the blade and the fence.*

LEARN THESE SAFETY RULES BEFORE USING THE RADIAL-ARM SAW

* Operate the radial-arm saw only *after your teacher has shown you how.*
* Remove jewelry, tuck in loose clothing, and confine long hair.
* Make sure all guards are in place and operating correctly.
* Use proper eye protection.
* Make all adjustments with the power off.
* Be sure the guards are operating properly and the blade will not extend beyond the table edge.
* When crosscutting, hold the material securely against the fence.
* Always pull the blade through the work and return the cutterhead behind the fence before removing material or starting the next cut.
* Make sure the blade guard and kickback fingers are properly adjusted before ripping.
* Always rip into the blade, never in the same direction as the rotation.
* Make sure the blade has stopped before leaving the machine.

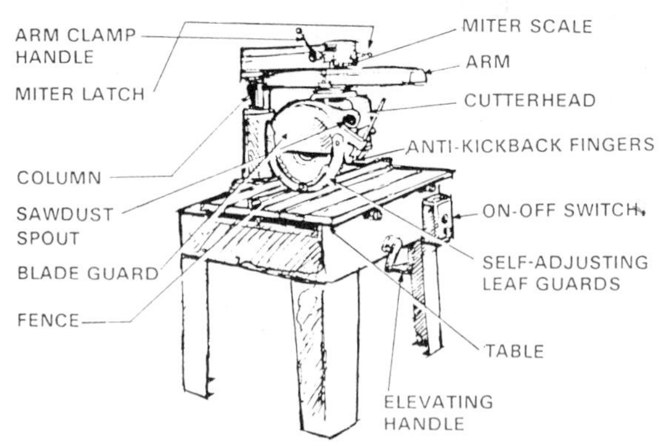

49-12. *A radial-arm saw with the parts named.*

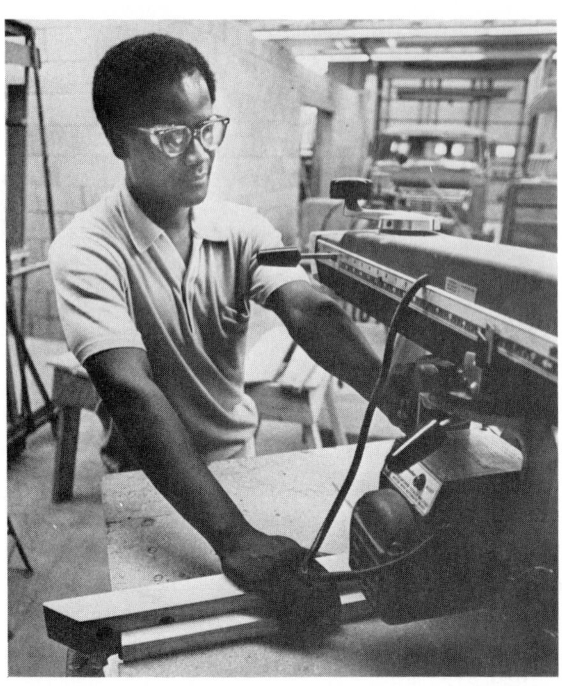

49-13. *You can easily watch the cutting action of a radial-arm saw.*

RADIAL-ARM SAW

The radial-arm saw is an upside-down saw that can be used for the same kind of cutting as the circular saw. Fig. 49-12. This machine is popular with carpenters when building houses because the cutting action is more easily seen. Fig. 49-13.

LEARN THESE SAFETY RULES BEFORE USING THE LATHE

* **Follow the general safety rules (eye protection, guards, sharp tools, clean work area, etc.) for all machines.**
* **Make sure that the setup has been checked by your instructor before turning on the machine.**
* **Maintain proper belt tension. Keep the belt just tight enough to prevent slipping.**
* **Keep the spindle and tailstock centers and tapers clean.**
* **Always examine the stock before you start turning to make sure it is not split and is free of nails.**

✻ Apply beeswax to the tailstock center point when turning stock between centers. This will prevent burning the wood.

✻ When stock is mounted between centers, be sure the tailstock and tailstock ram are locked securely.

✻ When using the faceplate for turning, be sure the work is solidly mounted.

✻ Use a wood wedge between the spindle pulley and headstock to remove the faceplate. *Never use the pulley index pin to lock the pulley.*

✻ To remove a live center, slide a rod through the rear of the spindle and tap it gently against the center. Catch the center as it is loosened.

✻ Keep the tool slide and rest locked securely.

✻ Never adjust the tool rest while the lathe is running.

✻ Hold woodturning chisels firmly to prevent them from "hogging" into the wood or flying out of your hand.

✻ Remove the tool rest before sanding or polishing operations.

✻ Keep the bed ways covered with oil when the lathe is not in use. This will keep the ways from rusting.

✻ Keep the tools sharp.

✻ Wear goggles or face shields for all turning.

WOOD LATHE

The wood lathe is used to shape round and cylindrical parts, such as turned chair and table legs, lamp bases, and bowls. Fig. 49-14. The size of the wood lathe is indicated by the swing (the largest diameter that can be turned) and the distance between centers. When the work is mounted between centers, the operation is called *spindle turning.* When the work is mounted on a faceplate, it is called *faceplate turning.*

While few wood lathes are used in industry, many craftspeople make use of this machine. It is fascinating to watch a piece of wood take shape under the capable hands of a woodcrafter. Many people find that woodturning is a fascinating hobby.

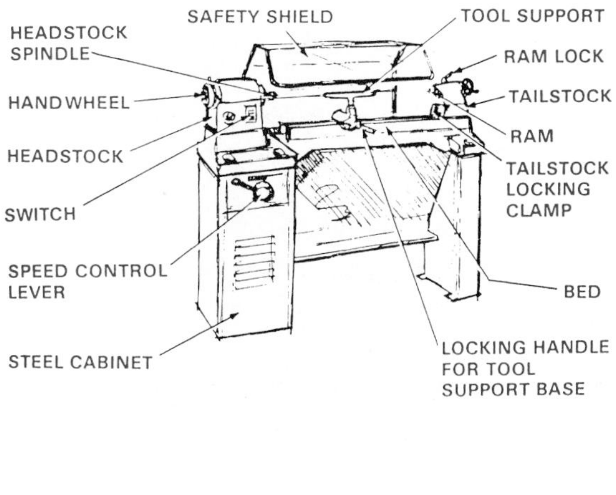

49-14. *A lathe for woodturning.*

LEARN THESE SAFETY RULES BEFORE USING THE SANDER

- **Be sure the sanding belt is mounted properly. The arrow on the belt indicates the direction of rotation.**
- **Maintain proper motor-belt tension. Keep the belt just tight enough to prevent slipping.**
- **Use only light pressure, just enough to hold the work.**
- **When disk sanding, keep the work moving. Holding it still will burn the wood and ruin the abrasive.**
- **Sand parallel with the grain whenever possible to obtain a smooth finish.**
- **Sand only dry wood.**
- **Use a fixture to hold small pieces of stock.**
- **Wear goggles and a filter mask when sanding.**
- **Keep the table of the disk sander covered with a film of oil when the sander is not in use. This will keep the table from rusting.**

SANDERS

The most common sanding machine is a combination belt and disk sander. Fig. 49-15. These may also be separate machines. Fig. 49-16.

Disk Sander

The disk sander is used primarily for edging operations, and, except for squaring and chamfering, such work is done freehand. The work should be held lightly against the disk and moved smoothly back and forth across the half of the disk revolving downward. The sanding disk should rotate counterclockwise. On the downstroke, the friction of the disk helps you hold the stock against the table. Fig. 49-17. *Caution: Keep the work moving.* If it is held in one spot, the wood will be burned and the abrasive ruined.

For angle and chamfer sanding, tilt the disk table to the desired angle. The table tilts to 45 degrees below the horizontal position. A miter-

49-15. *A combination belt and disk sander.*

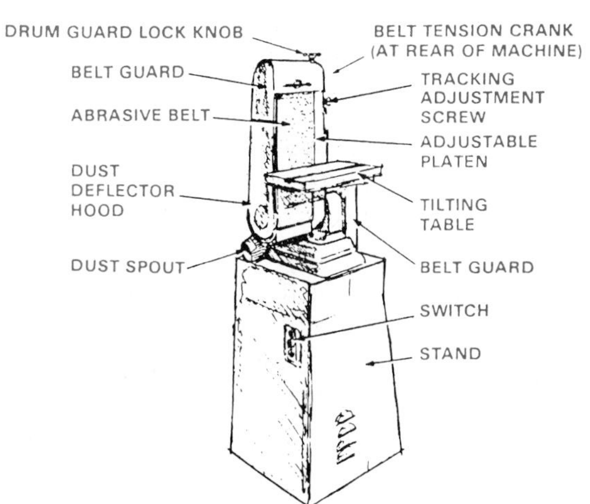

49-16(a). *A belt sander with parts named.*

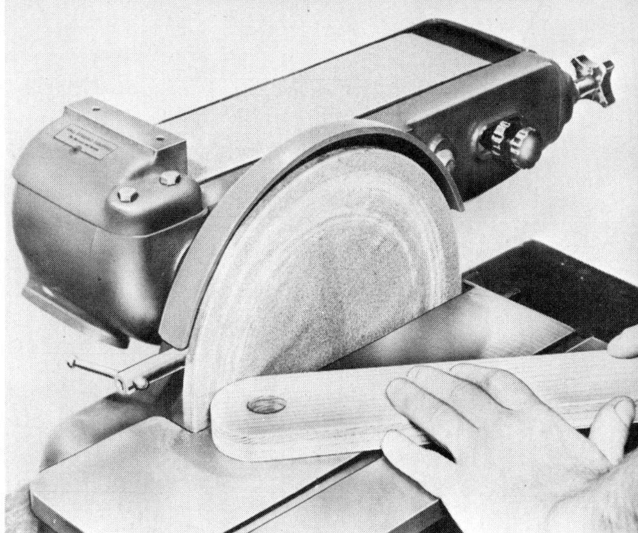

49-17(a). *Always sand on the down stroke.*

gauge attachment, which slides in the table slot, should be used to hold the work when squaring, burring, or chamfering the ends of stock. Fig. 49-18.

The abrasive used on the disk sander depends upon the type of work to be sanded. Garnet is used for wood and plastics, while aluminum oxide and silicon carbide abrasives are used for wood and metal. Since the disk sander is usually used for edge work, the abrasive can be more coarse than for surfacing. When sanding wood, a 1/2 or 1/0 abrasive can be used for fast cutting, and a 2/0 or 3/0 for finish sanding.

To remove old abrasive from the disk, soak it in hot water. Remove the loose abrasive with a putty knife. Be sure the disk is dry before mounting the new abrasive. It can be glued to the disk with water glass or a heavy grade of rubber cement. Hold the abrasive in place with a flat piece of wood and clamps to prevent wrinkles.

Belt Sander

The belt sander is used mainly for surface sanding and is more often operated in a horizon-

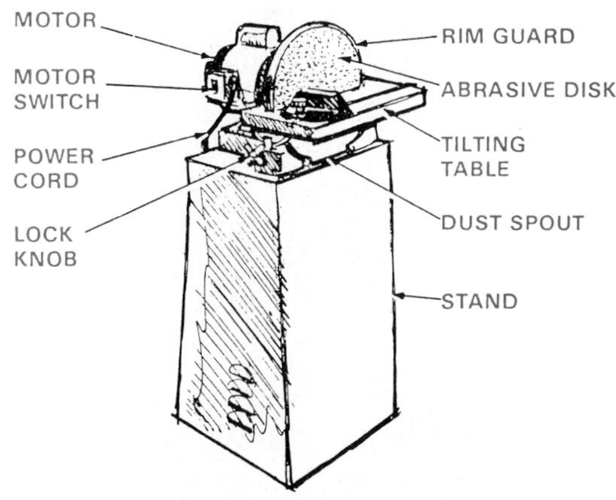

49-16(b). *A disk sander with parts named.*

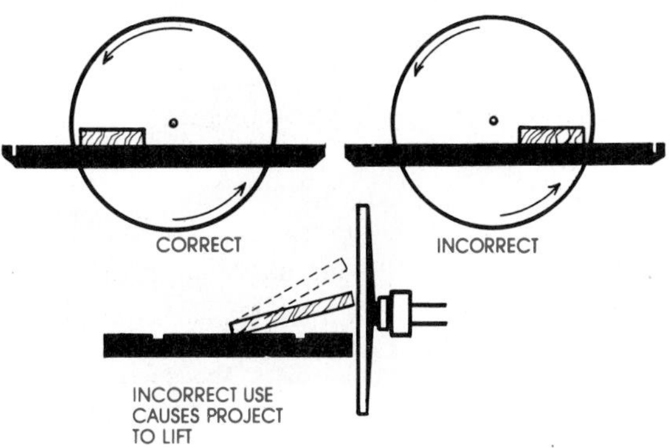

49-17(b). *Correct and incorrect ways to hold the work against the revolving disk.*

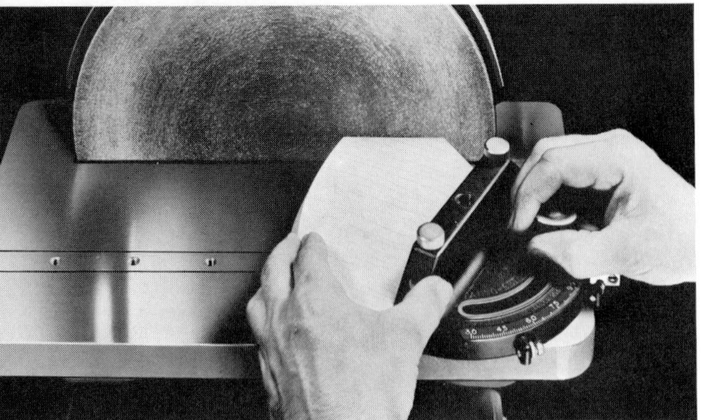

49-18. *Using a miter gauge for sanding.*

49-19. *The belt sander can be used either in vertical or horizontal position.*

49-20. *This type of belt sander can be used for many kinds of sanding operations.*

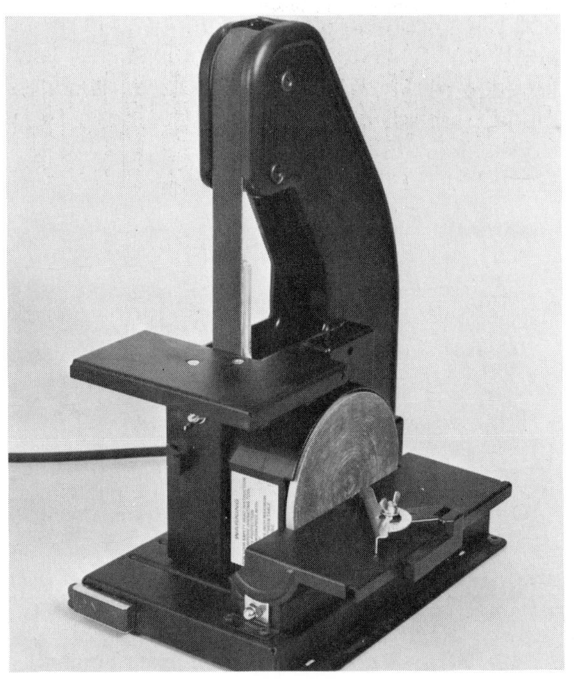

49-21. *A small disk belt sander.*

tal position. Fig. 49-19. The work should be pressed slightly but firmly against the belt. Excessive pressure should be avoided. Short stock should be held against the stop fence.

Remove the stop fence for sanding pieces that are longer than the table. To sand wide boards, remove the sanding disk (if it is a combination machine), the guard, and the belt-sander stop fence. Feed the work diagonally, using a small angle and fine belt to minimize the effects of cross-grain sanding.

By using the belt sander in a vertical position and mounting the disk-sanding table to the stop fence, all kinds of angle, edge, or end work can be done. A miter gauge should be used for such work as edging or beveling.

Inside curves are sanded on the end drum. The sanding-belt guard must be removed for this operation.

For beveling or angle sanding of long pieces, the belt sander fence attachment is required. The fence can be tilted from 0 to 45 degrees, left or right.

Another type of belt sander has a narrow belt that runs over three wheels. It is very useful for sanding recesses and other hard-to-get-at places. Fig. 49-20. Some narrow belt sanders also have a small disk sander. Fig. 49-21.

QUESTIONS

1. Do power tools require less or more skill than hand tools?
2. How is a jointer's size determined?
3. How can the jointer be used for face planing?
4. What is the purpose of the planer?
5. Name four uses of a circular saw.
6. Name three types of circular saw blades.
7. Describe the crosscutting operation.
8. Should a push stick be used for ripping? Explain how ripping is done.
9. What advantage does the radial-arm saw have over the circular saw? What kind of cutting can the radial-arm saw do?
10. How is a wood lathe's size indicated?
11. Describe the two kinds of turning.
12. What is the most common sander?
13. Tell how to use the belt sander.

ACTIVITIES

1. Across a sheet of paper, write the names of the power tools discussed in this chapter. Below the name of each tool, list its main uses. If possible, add pictures of each tool.
2. Select one of the tools discussed in this chapter. Prepare a safety checklist for using that tool.

LEARN THESE SAFETY RULES BEFORE USING PORTABLE POWER TOOLS

* Know your tools. Read the owner's manual or instructions carefully before using a tool. Learn the tool's correct application and its limitations.
* Ground all power tools, unless they are double insulated. If the tool is equipped with a three-prong plug, it should be plugged into a three-hole electrical outlet. If an adapter is used to connect the three-prong plug to a two-hole outlet, the adapter wire must be attached to a known ground. Never remove the third prong.
* If you need to use an extension cord, use one that has a suitable heavy-duty gauge (wire size) for its length and the ampere rating of the tool. Use a three-wire extension cord with three-prong plugs. Two-wire cords are suitable with double-insulated tools.
* Remove all keys and adjusting wrenches from a power tool before turning it on. If the tool has a guard, keep it in place and in working order.
* Disconnect a tool before changing accessories, such as blades, bits, or cutters. Never leave a tool running unattended. After you have disconnected the tool, make sure it has stopped running before you leave. Disconnect tools that are not in use.
* When disconnecting, never yank a tool by its cord. Do not carry a tool by its cord.
* Avoid accidental starting. Make sure the switch is in *off* position before plugging it in. Never carry a plugged-in tool with your finger on the switch.
* Use clamps or a vise to hold work when it's practical. It is safer than using your hand.
* Don't overreach. Maintain your footing and balance at all times when working with tools.
* Keep the work area clean and well lighted. Don't use power tools in a damp or wet location. If working outside with a power tool, wear rubber gloves and footwear.
* Wear proper apparel when working—no loose clothing or jewelry to get caught in moving parts. Use safety glasses or goggles with most tools.
* Keep other people at a safe distance from your work area.

Portable Power Tools

Portable power tools make woodworking jobs go faster and with greater accuracy. They are the ideal tools for work around the home. In a well-equipped shop these tools are used when stationary power machines are less convenient. The three most used portable tools are the electric drill, the router, and the finishing sander. Other common tools are the belt sander, saber saw, and portable circular saw.

A power tool should have a symbol that indicates it meets the standards of an independent testing agency, such as Underwriters' Laboratories. The tool should protect you from electrical shock by either of two safety systems:

- A tool with *external grounding* has a wire that runs from the housing through the power cord to a third prong on the power plug. When this prong is connected to a grounded three-hole electrical outlet, the grounding wire will carry any current that leaks past the electrical insulation of the tool.
- A *double insulated* tool has an extra layer of electrical insulation which eliminates the need for a three-prong plug and grounded outlet.

LEARN THESE SAFETY RULES BEFORE USING THE PORTABLE ELECTRIC DRILL

✻ Follow safety rules for all portable electric tools.

✻ Wear proper eye protection.

✻ Disconnect the tool from the power source before removing or installing drill bits or other tools.

✻ Make sure the drill bit is clamped securely in the chuck. Then remove the chuck key.

✻ Turn the chuck by hand to make sure the bit is in straight and doesn't wobble.

✻ Make sure the work is securely fastened. When clamping the work to a bench top, use a backup board.

✻ Locate the exact center of the hole to be drilled and mark it with an awl or center punch. This will help keep the drill from skipping around when it first contacts the workpiece.

✻ Apply steady, even pressure to the drill and let the drill do the work. With larger drills use the side handle.

✻ When the job is completed, disconnect the drill from the power source and remove the drill bit.

50-1. *This portable drill is cordless. It draws its power from a rechargeable battery pack in its handle.*

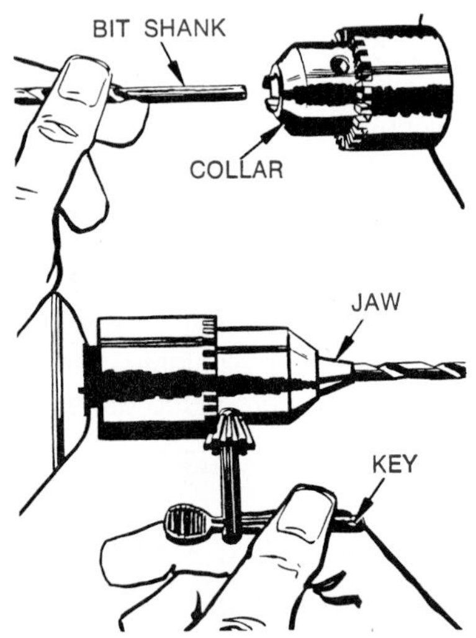

50-2. *Installing a twist drill in the chuck. Make sure the shank of the twist drill is in the jaws straight before tightening with the key.*

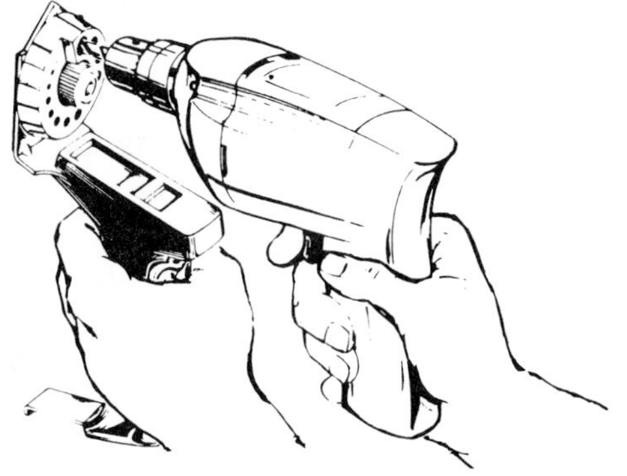

50-3. *Using a drill guide. Mark the location of the hole. Rotate the dial to the correct drill size. The guide will hold the drill straight so that the hole is drilled accurately.*

PORTABLE ELECTRIC DRILL

The portable electric drill is an excellent tool for drilling and boring holes and for many other uses. Fig. 50-1. It consists of a housing with a handle, a motor, and a chuck. The size of the electric drill is stated as the maximum size of bit the drill will hold. Most portable electric drills have a key-type chuck that will hold drill bits up to 1/4 inch or up to 3/8 inch.

For most jobs, a single-speed drill is adequate. However, a two-speed or variable-speed model is more suitable for drilling at slow speed or for use with accessories. A drill with both variable speed and reverse can be used to drive and remove screws.

Most drills have a pistol-grip handle. Some models also have a side handle so that the drill can be held with both hands for heavy work or for drilling in an unusual position. A trigger switch on the pistol-grip handle starts the drill. On variable-speed drills you can change the speed by varying the pressure on the trigger. The harder you press, the faster the speed.

To put a twist drill or a bit in the electric drill, first unplug the drill. Open the chuck and insert the shank of the twist drill or bit. Turn the outside of the chuck clockwise until the jaws close on the shank. Make sure the drill or bit is centered in the chuck. Then use a chuck key to tighten the jaws. Be sure to remove the chuck key before starting the drill. Fig. 50-2.

Using an Electric Hand Drill

1. Mark the location of the hole with an awl or center punch.
2. Hold the point of the drill over the place you want the hole.
3. Guide the drill with one hand on the housing or side handle. You can also use a drill guide. Fig. 50-3. Apply pressure with the other hand. The drill cuts a hole quickly; so be careful that it doesn't go in too far. If the revolving chuck touches the wood surface, it will mar the wood.
4. It is easy to break small bits in an electric hand drill. Hold the drill steady. Do not force it into the wood.

LEARN THESE SAFETY RULES BEFORE USING THE ROUTER

- **Follow general safety rules for all portable power tools.**
- **Wear proper eye protection.**
- **Be certain the power switch is off before connecting the plug.**
- **Make sure the work is rigidly clamped in the proper position and is free from obstructions.**
- **Check to see that the fence or guide is securely clamped.**
- **Hold the router firmly and against the work, using both hands.**
- **Keep the cutting pressure constant. Don't overload the router.**
- **Always lay the router down with the point away from you.**
- **When the job is completed, disconnect the router from the power source and remove the router bit.**

PORTABLE ROUTER

The portable router can do many cutting and shaping jobs. Fig. 50-4. It consists of a powerful motor mounted in an adjustable base. There is a collet chuck at the end of the motor shaft that can hold many different kinds of cutting tools. Some of the common router bits and cutters are shown in Fig. 50-5. To adjust for depth of cut, the router base is raised or lowered. In some routers the base screws onto the motor housing. In others it slides up and down.

The bit turns clockwise. Therefore, when cutting straight edges, move the router from left to right. When making circular cuts, move the router counterclockwise. Fig. 50-6. Routing can be done freehand or with a guide. Fig. 50-7. A guide is

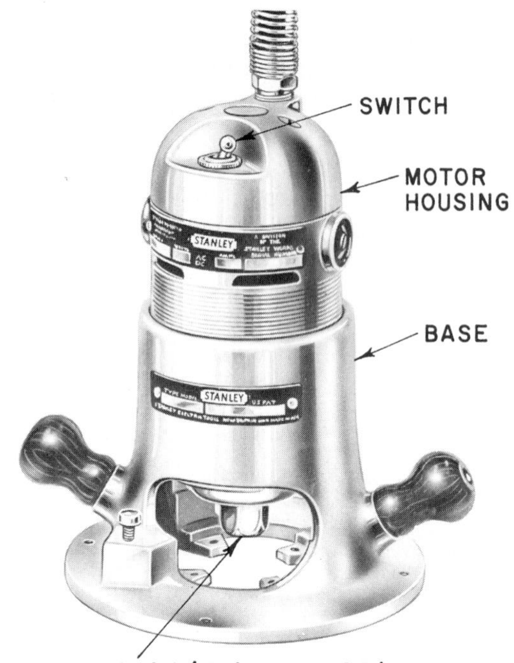

50-4. *Portable router.*

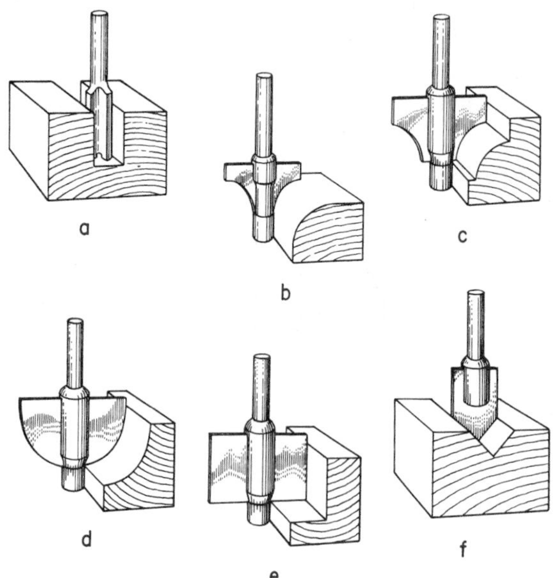

50-5. *A few of the common router bits: (a) Straight. (b) Rounding-over. (c) Beading. (d) Cove. (e) Rabbeting. (f) V grooving.*

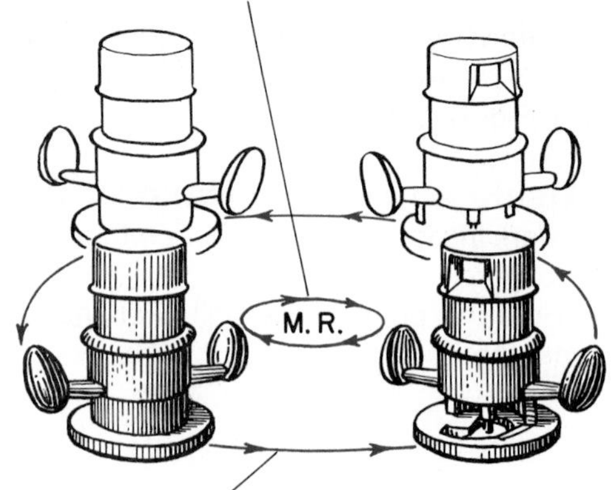

50-6. *Use the correct direction of feed when cutting with the router.*

used for making straight cuts, such as dadoes and grooves. Fig. 50-8. The width of the cut is determined by the bit. A wide cut can be made with a narrow bit by making two or more passes.

Using a Portable Router

SHAPING AN EDGE

By using a bit with a pilot on the end, the edge of stock can be shaped. The pilot extends from the bottom of the bit and guides it along the edge of the stock. Fig. 50-9.

1. Select the correct bit to match the shape of the edge you want.
2. To install the bit, unplug the router and lock the shaft. Loosen the nut or nuts. Insert the bit and tighten the chuck.
3. Adjust the depth of cut. Allow some stock to remain on the edge to serve as a guide for the pilot tip. Try the cutter on a scrap piece of wood of the same thickness as the finished piece.
4. Securely clamp the work to be routed.
5. Start the motor; hold the router firmly. Place the router base on the wood and move the router into the stock until the pilot edge touches the stock. Start the cut at one corner and work from left to right. Make the end grain cuts first. Feed the router slowly along each edge.

50-7. *Freehand routing. The router is moved and controlled by the operator.*

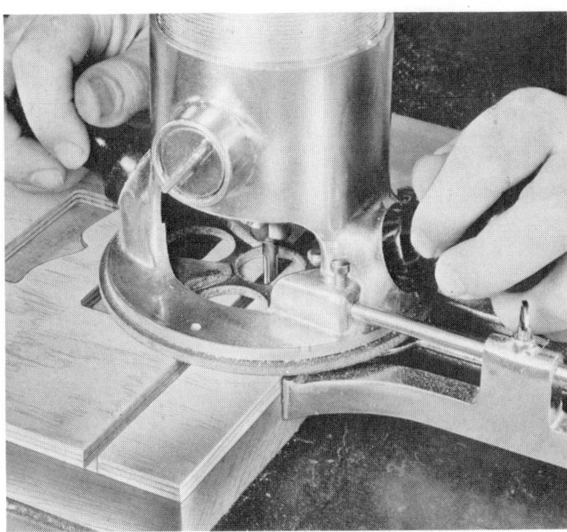

50-8. *Using a guide attachment for cutting a dado.*

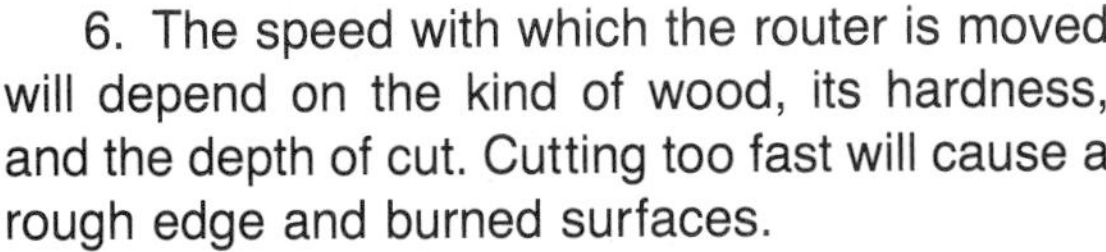

6. The speed with which the router is moved will depend on the kind of wood, its hardness, and the depth of cut. Cutting too fast will cause a rough edge and burned surfaces.

The Router as a Shaper

A shaper is the opposite of a router. You hold the router and move it into the workpiece. The shaper is a stationary tool mounted in a table, and you move the workpiece into it. To change a router to a shaper, then, you need to have a table for mounting the router. The router is mounted upside down on the table so that the cutter extends up through the tabletop.

GENERAL SUGGESTIONS

- Never work with stock less than 6″ wide without using safety devices (push stick and board to hold stock against the fence).
- Be sure the work is free of splits, checks and knots. The fast-spinning router bit could hurl a knot quite a distance. This can be dangerous, and the workpiece may be ruined.
- When you turn the router upside down in the shaper table, the rotation of the tool is reversed. The work now should be fed from right to left so that you work against the rotation of the cutter.

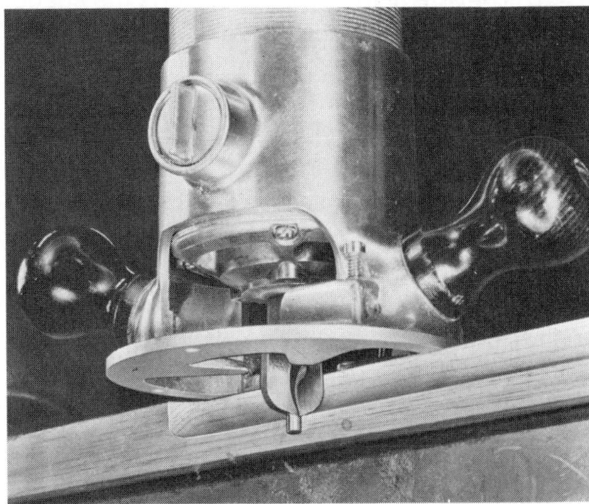

50-9. *The pilot on the end of the cutter controls the amount of cut. It rides on the edge and does no cutting.*

- When you feed work into the shaper, the cutter blade is hidden by the workpiece. Never permit your fingers to come within 3 inches of the cutter. Use a push stick for moving narrow work past the cutter.

LEARN THESE SAFETY RULES BEFORE USING THE PORTABLE SANDER

- **Follow general safety rules for all portable power tools.**
- **Never touch the edge of a moving belt, pad, or disk.**
- **Clamp small pieces securely in a vise or to the bench.**
- **Be sure the abrasive belt is installed with correct tension and is tracking correctly.**
- **Never place the sander on the bench when it is running.**
- **Hold the sander securely with both hands.**

FINISHING SANDER

Sanding wood before applying a finish is easier and faster when you use a power sander. Fig. 50-10. The size of the sanding pad and the speed and length of the sanding strokes tell the work capacity of a sander. You can find these specifications on the sander. Some finishing sanders have a self-contained dust collection bag.

Moderately priced finishing sanders usually have rotary motors and an orbital (circular) sanding action. More expensive models have both orbital and reciprocal (back-and-forth) sanding motions. Orbital action is better for rough sanding and reciprocal, or straight line, action is better for fine sanding. Fig. 50-11.

To take a worn abrasive sheet off the pad of a finishing sander and replace it with a new one, you must operate a special mechanism. On some models a lever opens and closes clamps at the front and back of the sanding pad. On others you use a special key or a screwdriver to loosen and tighten pad clamps. Still others have spring-loaded clamps that must be held open while an abrasive sheet is inserted. Fig. 50-12.

Using a Finishing Sander

1. Clip a sheet of abrasive paper to the pad. The sander should be unplugged while you do this.
2. Clamp the workpiece securely.
3. Turn on the power and let the sander reach full speed. Lower the pad onto the workpiece and move the sander back and forth slowly. Sand with the grain. Do not press down on the sander; the tool's weight and movement will do the work.
4. When you are finished, lift the sander off the workpiece before turning off the power. Wait for the sander to come to a full stop before setting it down.

PORTABLE BELT SANDER

Portable belt sanders are excellent for sanding assembled pieces. Fig. 50-13. The size of the machine is determined by the width and length of

50-10. *This cordless sander has a battery pack in its handle.*

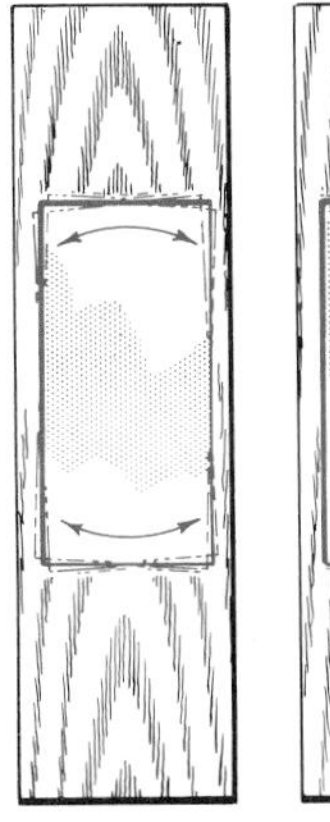

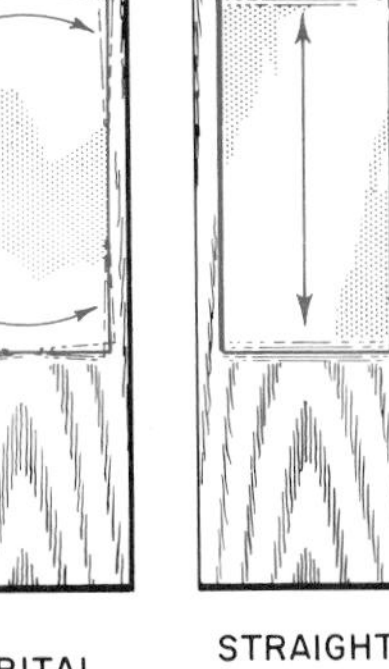

50-11. *Sanding motion of finishing sanders. On some machines two types of motion can be obtained by moving a switch.*

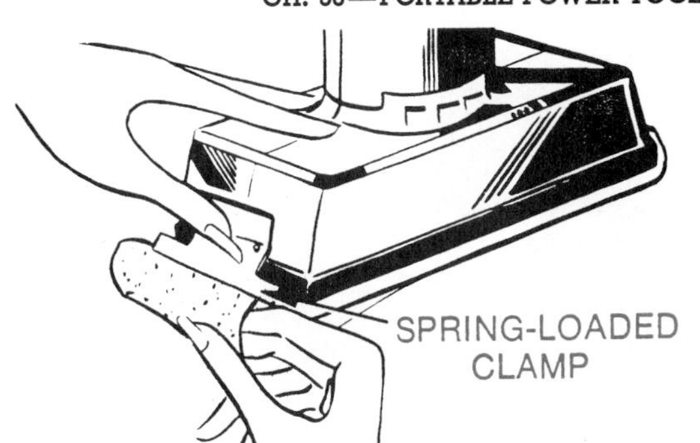

50-12. *Some finishing sanders have spring-loaded clamps to hold the abrasive paper on the sander.*

the belt. The most common sizes are 2″ × 21″, 3″ × 24″, 3″ × 27″, 4″ × 22″, and 4½″ × 26″. The belt should be installed so that the splice runs off the work. An arrow stamped on the back of each belt indicates the direction the belt should run. It is a simple job to replace a belt on most machines. Usually a clamp opens to release the tension on the belt. After a new belt is installed, it can be centered on the pulleys by turning the belt-tracking adjustment. The belt should never rub against the side of the machine. If the belt is a thick, soft one, then there must be extra clearance between the pulleys and the housing.

50-13. *A belt sander with dust bag.*

Using a Portable Belt Sander

1. Place the cord over your right shoulder out of the way. Hold the machine firmly with both hands. Turn on the power.

2. Lower the sander so that the heel touches the work first. Then move the sander back and forth in a straight line with the wood grain. Sanding is actually done *on the pull stroke.*

3. Never apply pressure to this machine since it cuts very rapidly. Do not allow the sander to stand in one place for any length of time as it will cut deep grooves in the wood. It is especially important to watch this when sanding plywood. Always machine slowly and evenly.

4. Cross sanding is sometimes done first to obtain a level surface. On woods such as fir, with both hard and soft grain, cross sanding should be done as much as possible.

5. To sand the edges of boards, allow the belt to extend beyond the edge a little. Be careful that the sander doesn't tilt or you will round the edges.

6. Always lift the sander from the surface before turning off the power. Let the sander come to a complete stop before setting it down.

LEARN THESE SAFETY RULES BEFORE USING THE SABER SAW

- **Follow general safety rules for all portable power tools.**
- **Make sure the switch is in the *off* position when connecting the tool.**
- **Be sure the work is properly clamped.**
- **Keep the cutting pressure constant. Don't force the cut or twist the tools.**
- **Hold the saw securely by the handles.**
- **When the job is complete, turn off the switch and allow the saw to come to a full stop before placing the saw on its side on the bench.**

SABER SAW

The saber (bayonet) saw has a long, slender blade for cutting either many-cornered or curved shapes in flat materials. Fig. 50-14. It cannot make long straight cuts as accurately and quickly as a circular saw. The simplest measure of the saw's work capacity is its maximum depth of cut in different materials. Common uses of the saber saw are shown in Fig. 50-15. The shoe (bottom part of the tool) consists of a base (skid), a cutting-angle adjustment, and a place to attach rip or circle guides. The base, or skid, provides stable support and should extend at least ¼ inch in front of the blade to prevent the saw from tipping forward as you guide it through the work. A rip guide for keeping the saw blade parallel with the edge of the work can be quickly attached, adjusted, or removed by turning screws. Fig. 50-16. Some designs can also be used as circle guides. The cutting-angle adjustment is a large, scaled hinge between the skid and the housing that allows precision angle cuts up to 45 degrees. The hinge is loosened by a lever, wing nut, screws, or small hex key. Then the base is tilted to the desired angle and the hinge is tightened.

The screws that hold a saw blade are loosened or tightened by either a screwdriver or a small hex key. The type of blade to use depends on the material being cut and the kind of cutting. Wood-cutting blades have 6 to 12 teeth per inch. Choose wide blades for straight cuts and narrow blades for curves. Fig. 50-17.

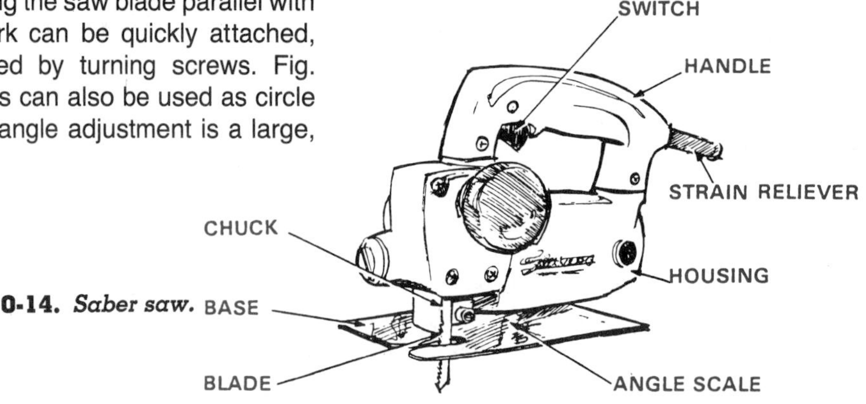

50-14. *Saber saw.*

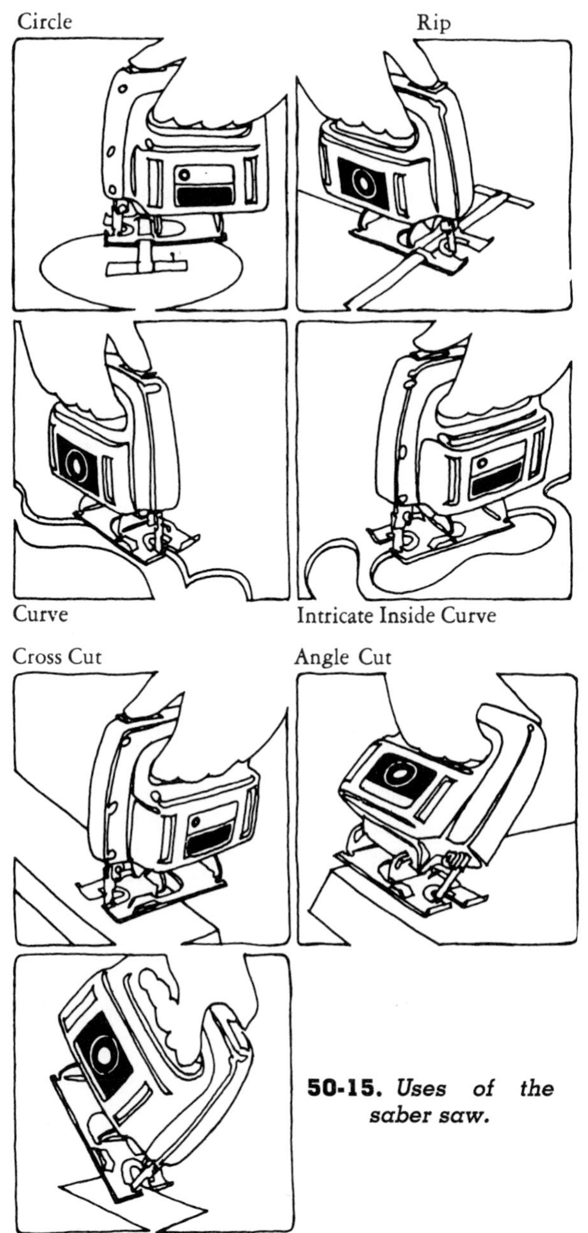

50-15. *Uses of the saber saw.*

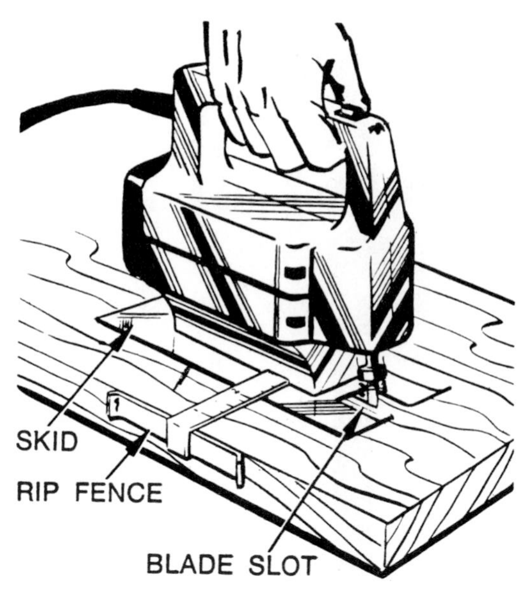

50-16. *Note the use of the rip fence to control the width of cut.*

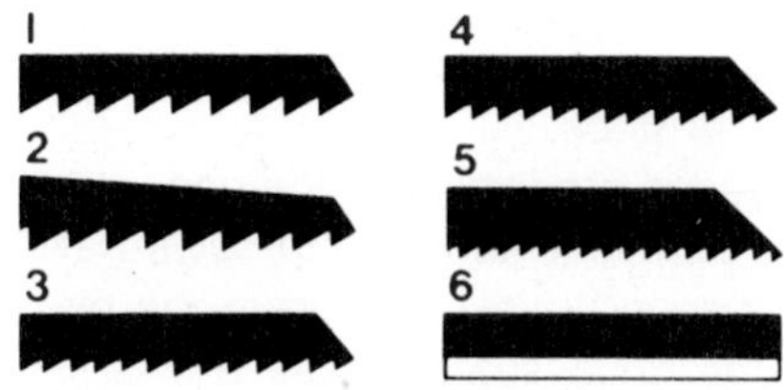

50-17. *Saber saw blades: (a) A 7-tooth blade for fast, rough cuts in wood. (2) An extra-long rough-cut blade for thick boards. (3) A 10-tooth blade for hardwood, plastics, etc. (4) A 10-tooth taper-ground blade for smooth cuts in plywood and veneers. (5) A 24-tooth hacksaw for metal. (6) A knife blade for rubber, leather, paper, and cardboard.*

Using the Saber Saw

1. Install the blade with the teeth facing *forward* and pointing *upward.* The cutting is done on the upstroke.

2. Clamp the work rigidly. If it vibrates, it will break the expensive blade. When clamping, be sure to leave space beneath the cutting line.

3. Start the motor and allow it to come up to full speed. Hold the saw firmly on the work; then move it along slowly. Do not force the cutting. Use only enough pressure to keep the saw moving at all times.

LEARN THESE SAFETY RULES BEFORE USING THE CIRCULAR SAW

* Follow general safety rules for all portable power tools.
* Use the saw only with your instructor present.
* Set the depth of the blade for the wood thickness. The maximum overdepth should be 1/8″.
* Be sure the saw teeth are cutting upward into the wood.
* Saw only to a straight line.
* Be sure that the guard operates properly.
* Before turning on the power, support the front of the saw on the wood to be cut.
* After completing the cut, let the blade come to a complete stop before removing the saw from the cut.

PORTABLE CIRCULAR SAW

To cut wooden building materials easily and quickly, you need a portable circular saw. Fig. 50-18. This saw is especially useful for cutting large panel stock.

The blades are similar to the ones used in the stationary circular saw. Some saws have a slip clutch or special washers where the blade fastens to the drive shaft. These are designed to prevent motor burnout if the saw blade sticks. They may also reduce the likelihood of kickback and loss of control.

In addition to enclosing the motor, electrical parts, and gears, the housing includes blade guards, a base, and cutting-depth and cutting-angle adjustments. Some models also have a rip guide. Fig. 50-19.

The blade guards include a stationary upper guard that covers the front, top, and back of the saw blade and a movable lower guard that covers the blade bottom when the saw is not in use. As you push a running saw into the work, this guard moves backwards and upwards into or outside the upper guard.

The base rests on the workpiece and holds the saw upright when it is operating.

The depth adjustment moves the base up and down. The angle adjustment tilts the base as much as 45 degrees. Fig. 50-20. The scale numbers should be easy to read, and the adjustment tilt lock knob should be easy to grasp and turn and should tighten securely.

A circular saw has a contoured handle at the top. Some models have a second handle at the side. The tool should be comfortable to hold and provide a clear view of the blade when the saw is in operating position.

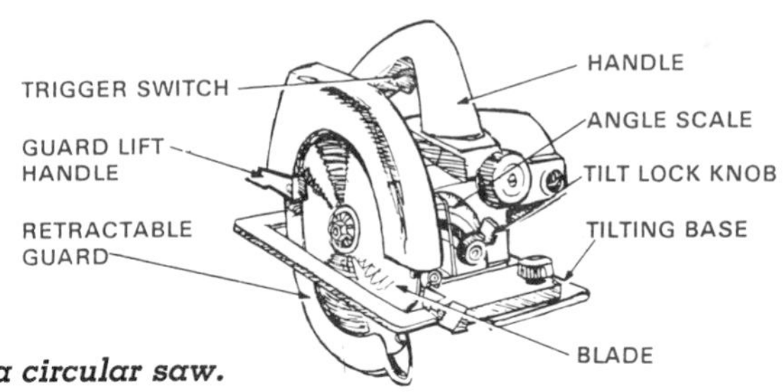

50-18. *Parts of a circular saw.*

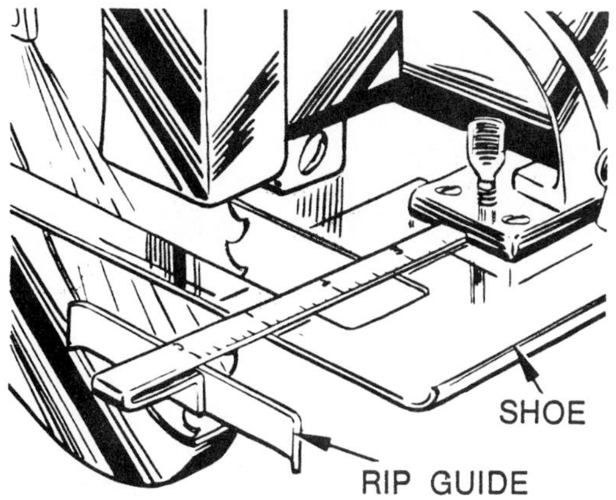

50-19. *The rip guide controls the width of cut. It is very difficult to make a straight cut with the circular saw if you don't use this guide.*

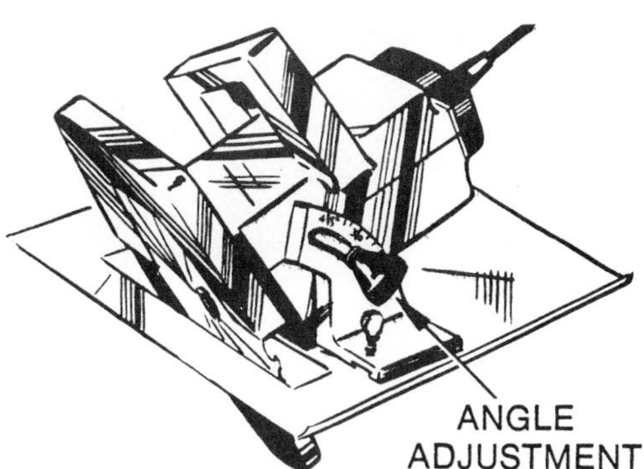

50-20. *An angle cut can be made when the saw is adjusted to the correct setting.*

Using a Portable Circular Saw

1. Clamp the stock to a bench or put it over sawhorses. The good side of the stock should be facing *down.* Make sure the layout line is clear of obstructions. For example, make sure you won't cut into the bench top. If you cut across a sawhorse, place a piece of scrap wood under the workpiece so that you don't cut the support.

2. Place the base of the saw on the stock with the blade in line with the layout line. The blade must not touch the stock.

3. Turn on the saw and allow it to come to full speed.

4. Slowly but steadily move the blade up to and then along the layout line until the cut is complete.

5. Allow the saw base to rest on the uncut stock and turn off the power. Do not remove the saw until the blade has come to a complete stop.

QUESTIONS

1. How is the size of a portable electric drill indicated?
2. What part of the drill holds the twist drill or bit?
3. Describe how to shape an edge with a portable router.
4. How can a router become a shaper?
5. What is the main use of a portable belt sander?
6. How should you determine what kind of blade to use in a saber saw?
7. Describe two kinds of blade guards used on the portable circular saw.

ACTIVITIES

1. Check a tool catalog or visit a local home improvement center. How many of the tools described in this chapter can you find? What do they cost?
2. Select one of the tools discussed in this chapter. Prepare a safety checklist for using that tool.

Lumbering

Lumber is one of the most useful products of the tree. The terms *forest products* and *lumber* mean the same thing to most people. If you ask anyone to name a tree product or something that means the same as wood, the answer is usually "lumber." However, as you will see in the next chapter, there are many forest products besides lumber.

About 60 percent of the nation's lumber comes from privately owned forest lands. The forest products industry supplies another 12 percent. Public lands—mostly national forests—give us the other 28 percent. Fig. 51-1.

HOW TIMBER IS HARVESTED

The harvesting of trees for lumber is called *logging.* Like any other industry, logging has its own language. You don't *cut* a tree, you *fell* it. And then you probably will *buck* it to log lengths. You'll go to work in a *crummy,* a small bus usually painted orange and almost always scarred inside and out by rough use.

Marking the Trees

Which trees to cut in a timber harvest is not decided by the people who cut them down. Trained foresters do this, and they supervise the harvest. Foresters mark the trees with a spray of white paint. They are careful to leave seed trees and young growing stock for future crops.

Felling the Trees

Trees selected for harvest are cut down by people called *fallers.* These people cut a notch in the side of the tree toward which the tree is to fall. They then use power saws to cut down the tree close to the ground. All limbs are removed, and the main stem is cut into equal lengths suitable for lumber. The fallers know what lengths to cut it and just how to get the most out of each tree.

In recent years, advanced equipment has been introduced to reduce time, labor, and waste. For example, the feller-buncher is a huge mobile machine big enough to grasp a tree up to a foot in diameter in its mechanical hands. It cuts the tree near the base, leaving a 6-inch stump. The feller-buncher then removes the limbs. Some models will cut the stem into log lengths and may even store the logs briefly in a holding rack.

Other machines actually do partial manufacturing right in the woods. Whole trees go in one end of the machine. Precision cut wood chips come out the other and are blown into waiting trucks. The chips are used to make pulp for papermaking.

Transporting the Logs to the Mill

Years ago, logs were moved to the nearest river or stream and left there through the winter. In spring, as the water rose, the logs were floated down the river to the mill. Today the logs may be dragged by machines to an open place in the woods.

In areas too rugged for this kind of machinery, and where trees grow larger, different logging approaches are used. In the Pacific Northwest and the Rocky Mountain states, cable yarding is the primary method.

In all cable systems, logs are dragged or carried by wire to a landing area or roadside. Some systems use stationary towers more than 100 feet tall. Others rely on smaller towers or cranes mounted on mobile, self-powered platforms. The reach of the cable can range from a

Forest Regions of the United States

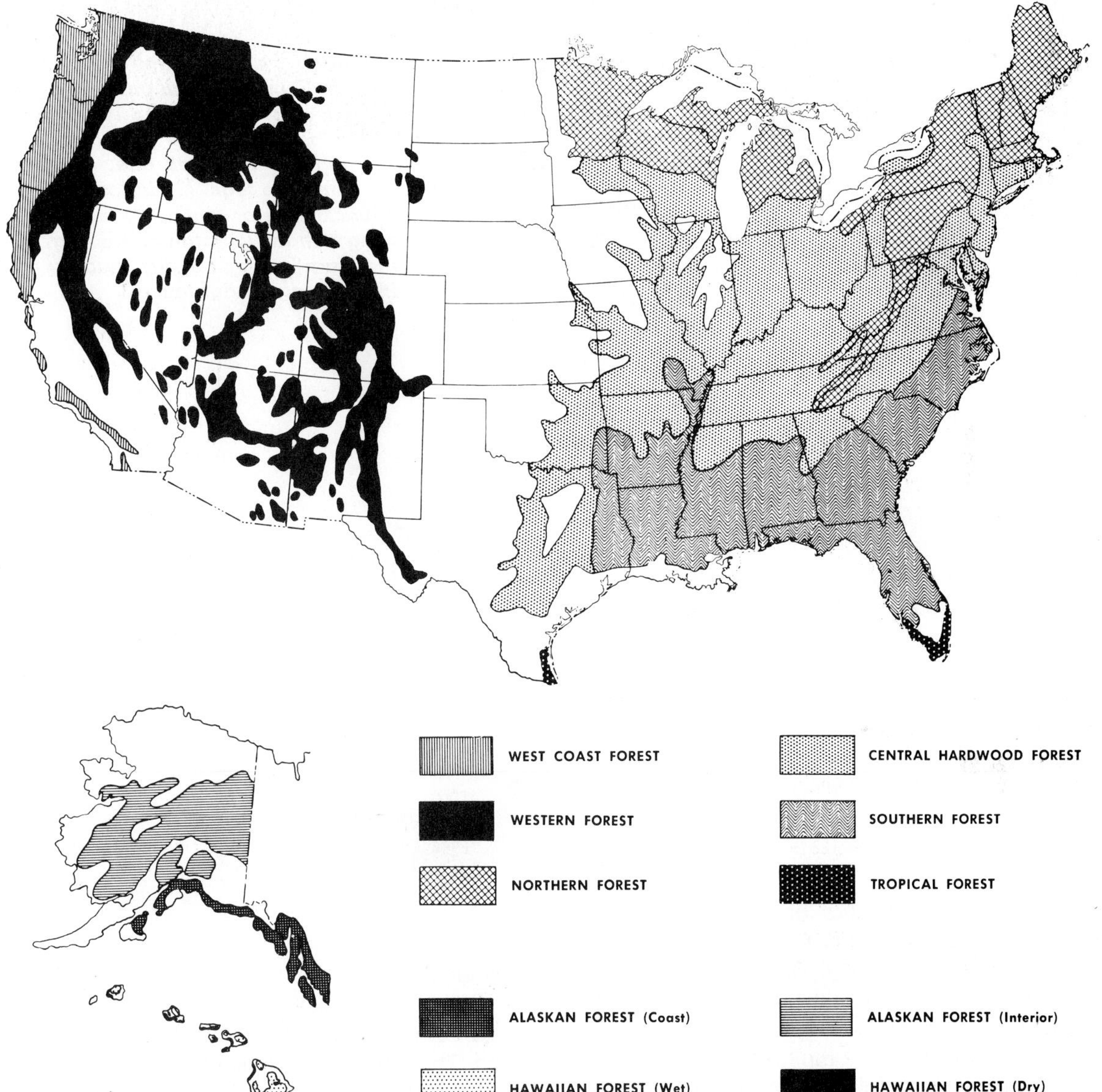

51-1. *This map shows areas of renewable natural wealth. The West Coast or Pacific forests are primarily Douglas fir. However, they also have western red cedar, spruce, and hemlock. The western forests include much of our softwood timber, primarily pine, although there are some hardwoods. The northern forests have such trees as hemlock, red spruce, white pine, and several kinds of hardwoods. The central hardwood forests include oak, cherry, birch, and many other kinds of hardwoods. In the southern forests are such softwoods as pine and cypress and many kinds of hardwoods. The tropical forests have ebony and palm trees. The coast regions of Alaska have primarily western hemlock and spruce, and the interior forests are heavy with white spruce and white birch. The Hawaiian forests include many softwoods and some unusual types such as monkey pod and koa.*

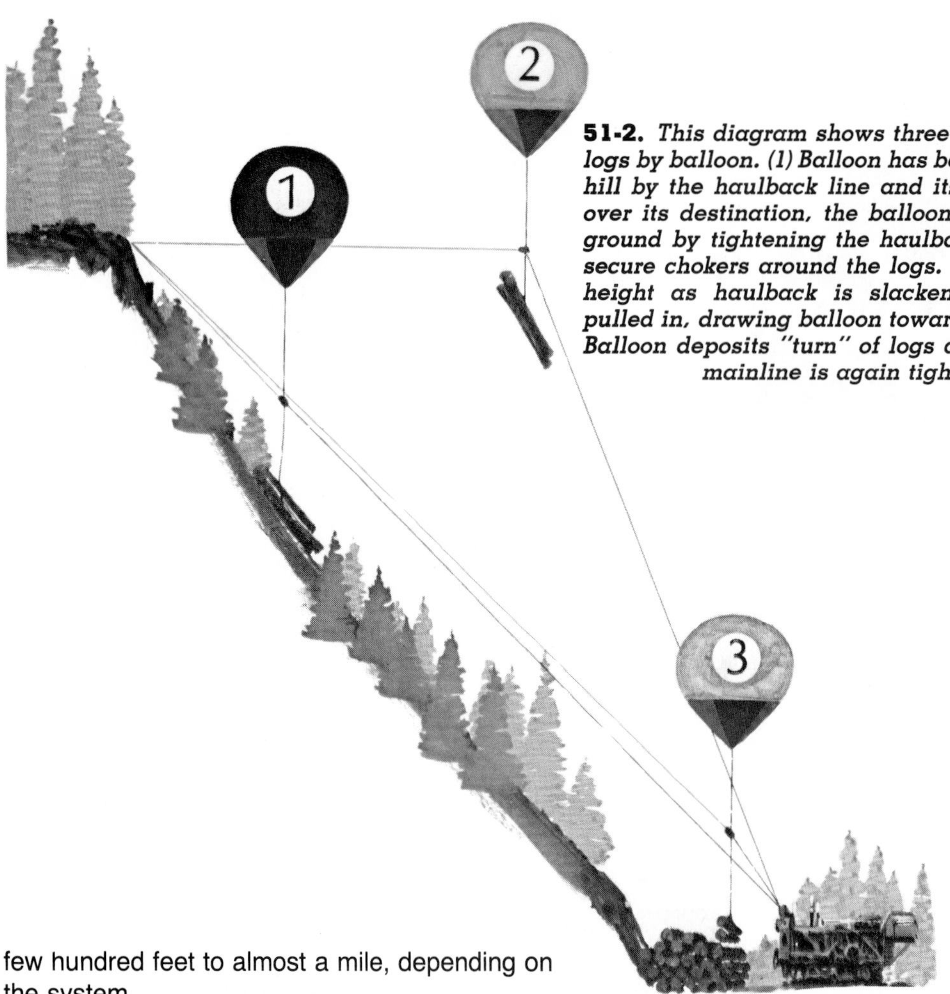

51-2. *This diagram shows three steps in hauling logs by balloon. (1) Balloon has been pulled up the hill by the haulback line and its own lift. When over its destination, the balloon is pulled to the ground by tightening the haulback line. Loggers secure chokers around the logs. (2) Balloon gains height as haulback is slackened. Mainline is pulled in, drawing balloon toward the landing. (3) Balloon deposits "turn" of logs at the landing as mainline is again tightened.*

few hundred feet to almost a mile, depending on the system.

Sometimes helicopters or giant helium-filled balloons are used to carry the logs to a roadside, river, or railway. Fig. 51-2. There they are loaded onto trucks, boats, or railroad cars which take them to the mill.

LOGS ARE PROCESSED

A modern lumber mill is a very complex factory. Fig. 51-3. It has a *control room* in which computers keep track of all of the operations.

When logs first arrive at the mill, they are *scaled* to check the species and quality as well as to estimate the amount of lumber that each log will produce. The logs are then stacked in a *log deck area* to await processing.

When the logs enter the mill, they go first to the *barking center* which strips the bark, dirt, and rocks from the logs. The waste wood is used as chips. The logs are then moved to the computerized *bucking station* where they are cut into the best lengths for use. From here the logs go to the *head rig* where large band saws cut them into big pieces of lumber.

The *chipper-canter,* controlled by the computer, makes sure that the maximum amount of lumber is obtained from the log. These operations are monitored at the *control console.* Then the lumber is *resawn* into desired sizes. The

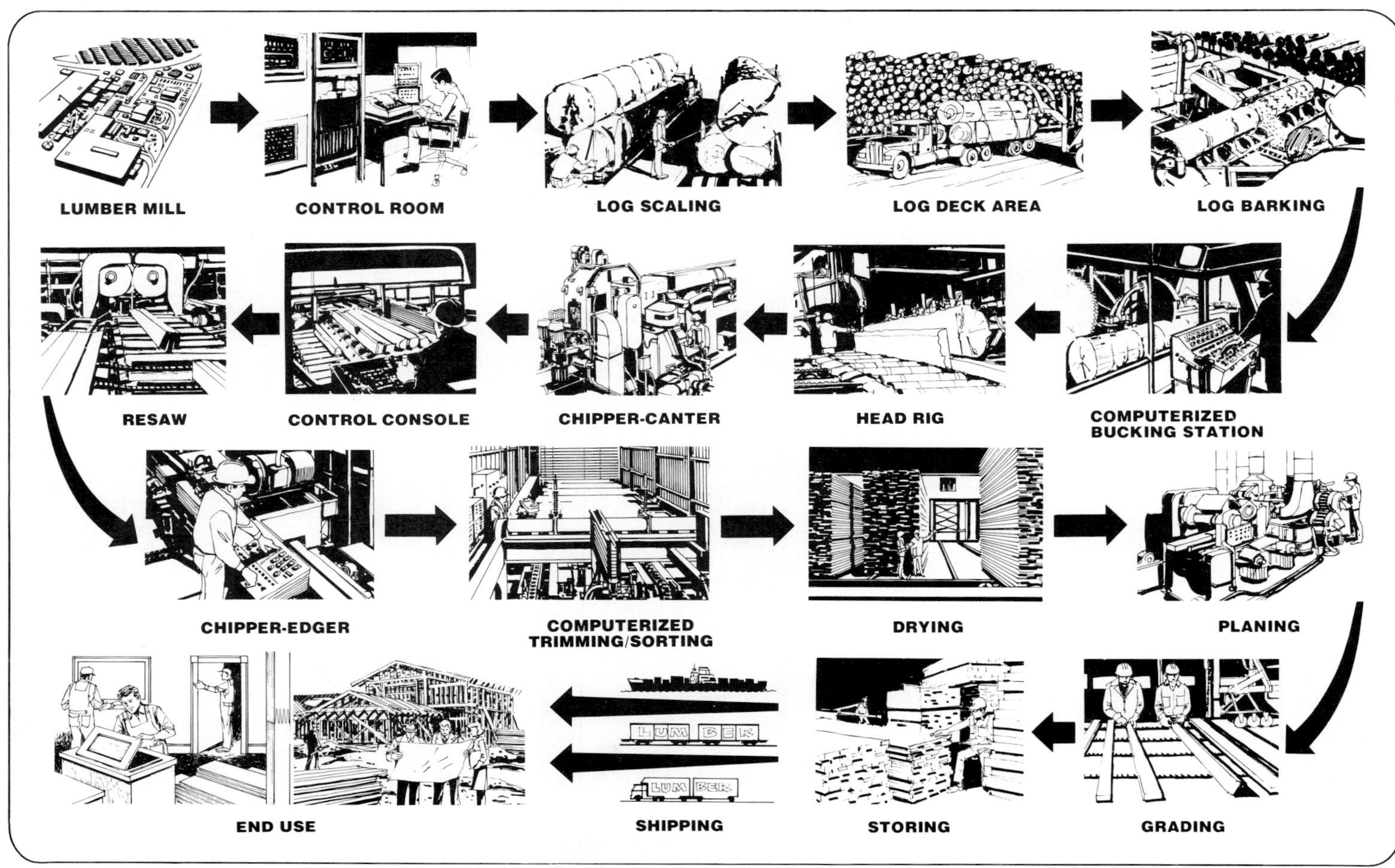

51-3. *This flow chart shows how lumber is manufactured.*

chipper-edger removes rough edges from the lumber. At the *trimming/sorting center* the lumber is cut to exact lengths. From here the lumber goes to large kilns where it is *dried.* The lumber is then *planed* to standard sizes. It is *graded* and *stored* to await *shipment.* The lumber is moved by truck, railroad, and ship all over the world for building houses and furniture and for thousands of other uses.

QUESTIONS

1. Who selects the trees to be cut?
2. What do fallers do?
3. How are logs taken to the mill?
4. How are logs processed?

ACTIVITIES

1. Lumber is important to our economy, but trees are important to our environment. Prepare a report about the lumber industry. What is being done to protect the environment? How are jobs affected?
2. The United States produces a lot of lumber, but lumber is also bought from other countries. Find out what kinds of wood are imported and where they come from.

Uses of Our Forest Products

As you can see from Fig. 52-1, we get many things from trees besides lumber. In recent years many more uses have been found for tree materials. There are about 10,000 different uses for wood and wood products. Some of the many products that come from trees are described here.

VENEER AND PLYWOOD

Veneer is a thin sheet of wood. Veneers of high-quality wood are sometimes used on furniture to cover less expensive wood or for decoration. There are three common ways of cutting veneer. Softwood veneer is rotary cut; that is, it is sliced off a log much as paper is unwound from a roll. Most hardwood veneers are made by cutting a log into thin sheets, either by flat slicing (same as plainsawing) or quartersawing.

Several sheets of veneer are glued together to make *plywood.* Fig. 52-2. Plywood is one of the most useful products of the tree. It is used in all kinds of home construction for floors, roofs, walls, and many other parts. It is also used to make furniture. There are three types of plywood:

- *Lumber-core plywood* has a thick middle layer of solid wood. This is the kind most often used for fine furniture. Fig. 52-3.
- *Veneer-core plywood* is made up of several thin layers of veneer. It can have 3, 5, 7, 9, or more layers, depending on the thickness. For

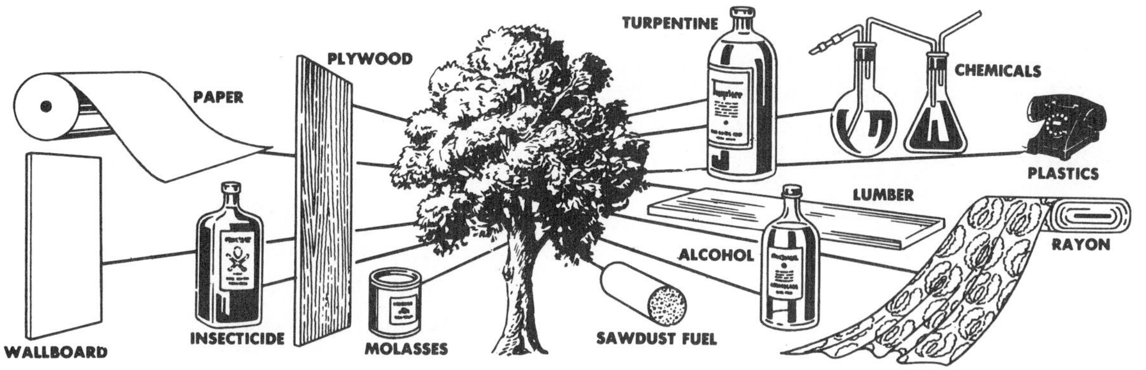

52-1. *Here you see some of the many things made from a tree.*

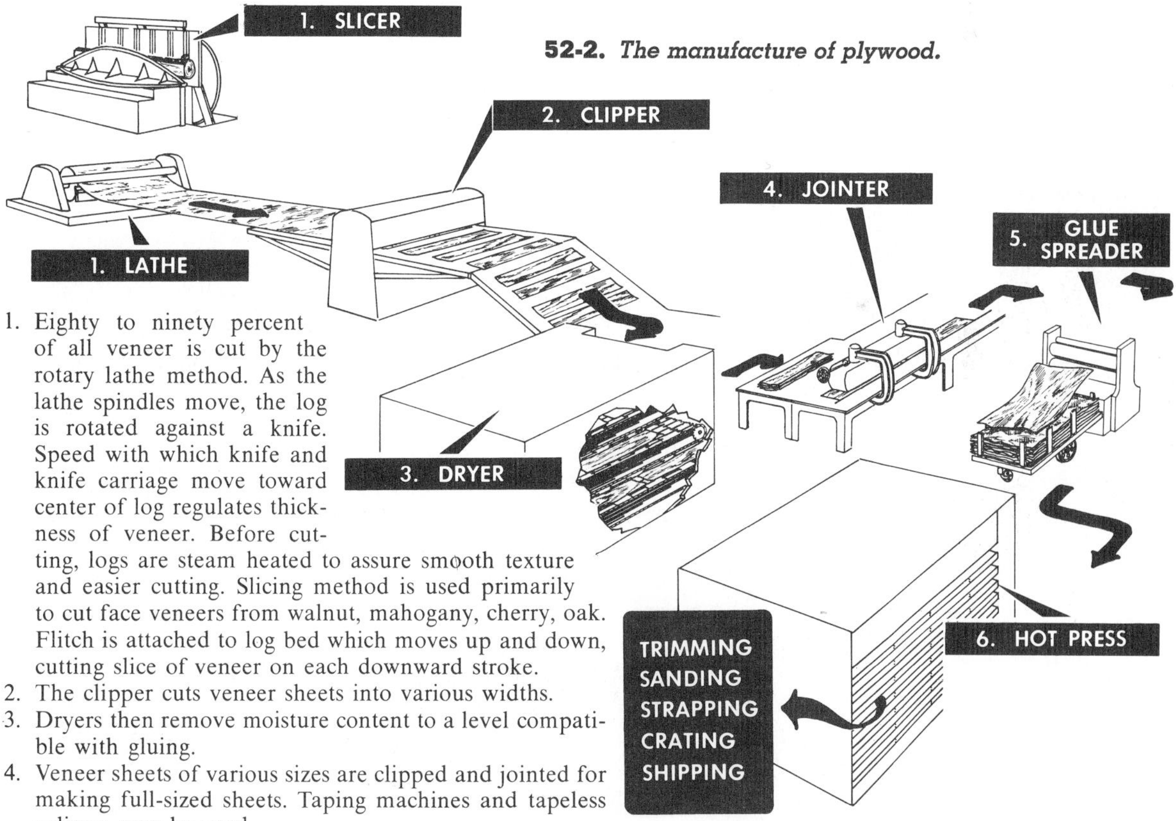

1. SLICER
2. CLIPPER
1. LATHE
3. DRYER
4. JOINTER
5. GLUE SPREADER
6. HOT PRESS
TRIMMING
SANDING
STRAPPING
CRATING
SHIPPING

52-2. *The manufacture of plywood.*

1. Eighty to ninety percent of all veneer is cut by the rotary lathe method. As the lathe spindles move, the log is rotated against a knife. Speed with which knife and knife carriage move toward center of log regulates thickness of veneer. Before cutting, logs are steam heated to assure smooth texture and easier cutting. Slicing method is used primarily to cut face veneers from walnut, mahogany, cherry, oak. Flitch is attached to log bed which moves up and down, cutting slice of veneer on each downward stroke.
2. The clipper cuts veneer sheets into various widths.
3. Dryers then remove moisture content to a level compatible with gluing.
4. Veneer sheets of various sizes are clipped and jointed for making full-sized sheets. Taping machines and tapeless splicers may be used.
5. Veneers are then coated with liquid glue, front and back, with a glue spreader.
6. Heat and pressure applied in the hot press bond the veneers into plywood famous for strength, beauty and versatility. Panels are trimmed, sanded and stacked for conditioning and inspection, after which they are ready for grading, strapping and shipping.

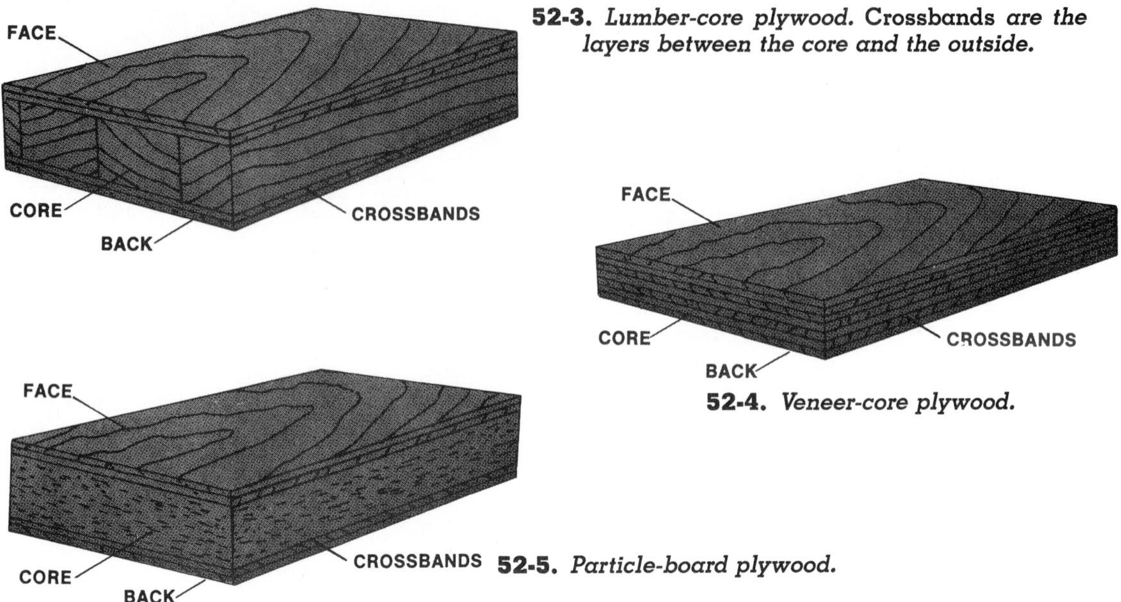

52-3. *Lumber-core plywood.* **Crossbands** *are the layers between the core and the outside.*

52-4. *Veneer-core plywood.*

52-5. *Particle-board plywood.*

1. Logs are conveyed from storage yards to huge chippers which reduce the wood to clean, uniformly sized chips.
2. The chips are then reduced to individual wood fibers by either the steam or the mechanical defibering processes.
3. Fibers are put through certain mechanical processes varying with the method of manufacture, and small amounts of chemicals may be added to enhance the resulting board properties.
4. The fibers are interlocked in the felter into a continuous mat and compressed by heavy rollers.
5. Lengths of mat, or "wetlap," are fed into multiple presses where heat and pressure produce the thin, hard, dry board sheets.
6. Leaving the press, moisture is added to the board in a humidifier to stabilize it to surrounding atmospheric conditions.
7. The board is trimmed to standard specified dimensions, wrapped in convenient packages, and readied for shipment.

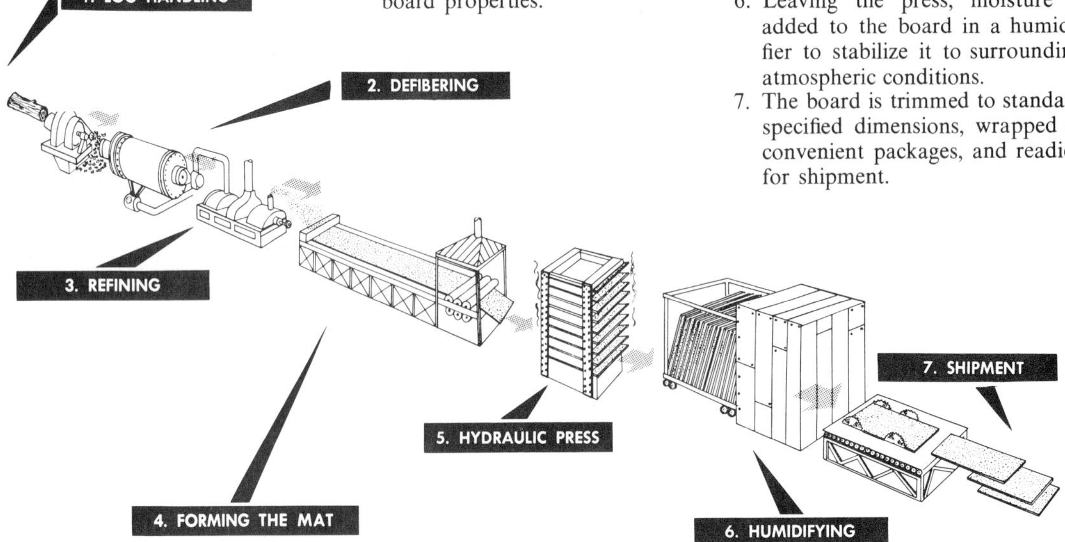

52-6. *The manufacture of hardboard.*

example, ¼-inch plywood may have either 3 or 5 layers. The more layers there are, the stiffer the plywood and the less likely to warp. Fig. 52-4.

- *Particle-board plywood* is made with a core of particle board. The other layers are veneer. This kind of plywood is often used in furniture construction. Fig. 52-5.

Plywood comes in standard 4′ × 8′ sheets. There are also smaller sheets such as 3′ × 8′, 4′ × 4′, and 4′ × 6′. There are many special kinds of plywood on which the surface has been decorated or treated in some way. These are usually used for wall paneling or for furniture.

HARDBOARD

Hardboard is made from wood which has been processed into fibers. Logs are cut into small wood chips which are reduced to fibers by steam or mechanical processes. These fibers are refined and then compressed under heat and pressure in giant presses to produce sturdy panels. Lignin (a chemical in wood) holds the fibers together. Fig. 52-6.

PARTICLE BOARD

Particle board is made by combining wood particles with an adhesive or other binder and then hot pressing them together into panels. Particle board is different from hardboard because the wood particles used for particle board are not broken down into fibers. Fig. 52-7. The

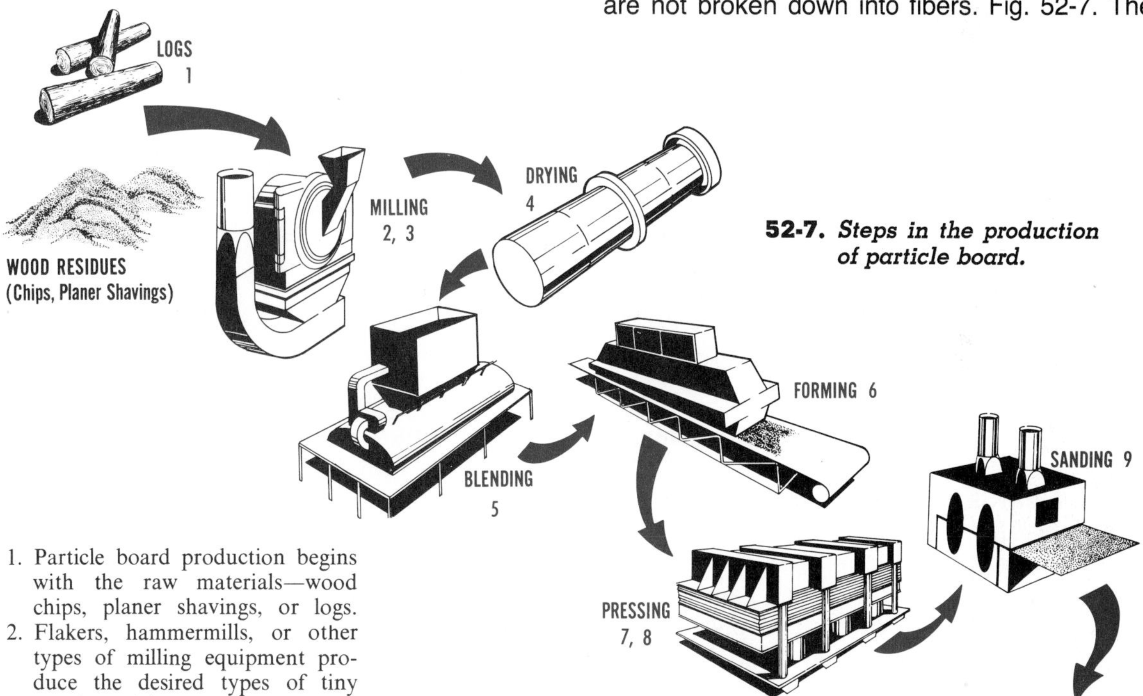

52-7. ***Steps in the production of particle board.***

1. Particle board production begins with the raw materials—wood chips, planer shavings, or logs.
2. Flakers, hammermills, or other types of milling equipment produce the desired types of tiny wood particles.
3. Screens classify the particles into the proper mixture of sizes.
4. Dryers remove excess moisture and uniformly control the moisture content to the desired level.
5. Resin binders and other chemicals are sprayed onto the wood particles at a controlled rate in a blending operation.
6. Forming machines deposit the treated particles onto belts or metal cauls forming mats.
7. Particle mats are consolidated and the binders are cured in heated hydraulic presses.
8. After pressing, boards are trimmed to the desired length and width.
9. Sanding in high-speed belt sanders produces the smooth surfaces and accurate thickness tolerances characteristic of particle boards.

properties of particle board can be changed by using different sizes and kinds of wood particles and different binders. Particle board is made in many sizes and thicknesses and is widely used as a core for plywood and for plastic laminates.

ENVIRONMENTAL PROBLEMS

There are many environmental problems relating to trees and the wood industry.

Clean Air

One of today's battles is the fight for clean air. Our natural atmosphere is mainly a mixture of the invisible, odorless, tasteless gases oxygen, nitrogen, and carbon dioxide. Air is polluted or robbed of its natural cleansing qualities in two basic ways: by addition of foreign substances and by changes in the proportionate makeup that diminish the supply of oxygen. Trees add to the oxygen supply. They consume carbon dioxide and release oxygen. Trees also filter out impurities.

Clean Water

Trees along lakes and river banks hold the soil so that it does not run off into the water during rainstorms. Soil that is carried by water runoff creates many problems downstream. By holding soil in place, trees are a very good barrier to erosion.

Clean Landscape

Landscape that is free of litter makes a more attractive and useful recreational area. The forest areas that are kept clean provide greater enjoyment for recreation.

Low Noise Level

The noise level in cities has increased greatly in the last few decades. Noise levels in a home can be reduced as much as 50% by the proper placement of trees and shrubs around the yard. Also, trees and shrubs planted along main highways through residential areas add beauty and control noise.

Conservation of Energy

Trees planted around a home screen out bright sunlight, reducing the electrical energy needed to keep the house cool in the summer.

QUESTIONS

1. Name five things other than lumber that can be made from trees.
2. What is the difference between veneer and plywood?
3. Name the three methods of cutting veneer.
4. Name the three kinds of plywood (according to the way they are made).
5. How does the number of layers affect the stiffness of plywood?
6. How do hardboard and particle board differ?
7. Name three problems relating to a clean environment.

ACTIVITIES

1. Prepare a report about paper products that are made with recycled paper.
2. Check the labels on clothing. Do any of them list rayon as one of the fibers?
3. Wood is used to make cellophane, charcoal, some plastics, and turpentine. Research one of these materials and write a report about how it is made.

Manufacturing

There are different kinds of industries. The ones that concern us most are *manufacturing* and *construction.* Both of these produce goods in large amounts through mass production. Fig. 53-1. This chapter discusses manufacturing. Construction is covered in the next chapter.

MAJOR CONCERNS

To know about manufacturing, you must know how a large industrial corporation works. These are the basic parts of all manufacturing industries:

- *Product.* A company is set up to make products that people need. These can be anything from pencils to furniture to houses. Fig. 53-2. Large industrial companies produce goods that are needed by millions of people. The tools and the machines you are now using in woodworking are products of industry. Many of you will someday work either directly or indirectly for a company that makes some kind of goods.
- *Management.* The most common way of organizing (setting up) a business is to create a corporation. People get a share (part) of a corporation by buying stock. The stockholders vote to choose a board of directors to head the corporation. This board of directors then hires management. Management includes the president, vice president, managers, and other officers. This group organizes and operates the company so that it will make a profit (earn money). Just how a corporation is organized depends on how big it is and what kinds of goods it will make. With good management, it is possible for a company to operate successfully and earn a profit. Poor management can result in the loss of money, and the corporation may go bankrupt (broke).
- *Capital.* Capital (money) that is raised by the sale of stocks and by borrowing is used to buy buildings, machines, tools, materials, and everything else needed to produce goods.
- *Personnel.* People with many kinds of skills are needed to make up the company's work force. People other than the management group are often called the labor force. This group includes skilled workers, laborers, machine operators, office and clerical workers, the sales force, technicians, and professionals such as engineers and researchers.

53-1. *Mass-producing cabinets for telephones. Notice the assembly line.*

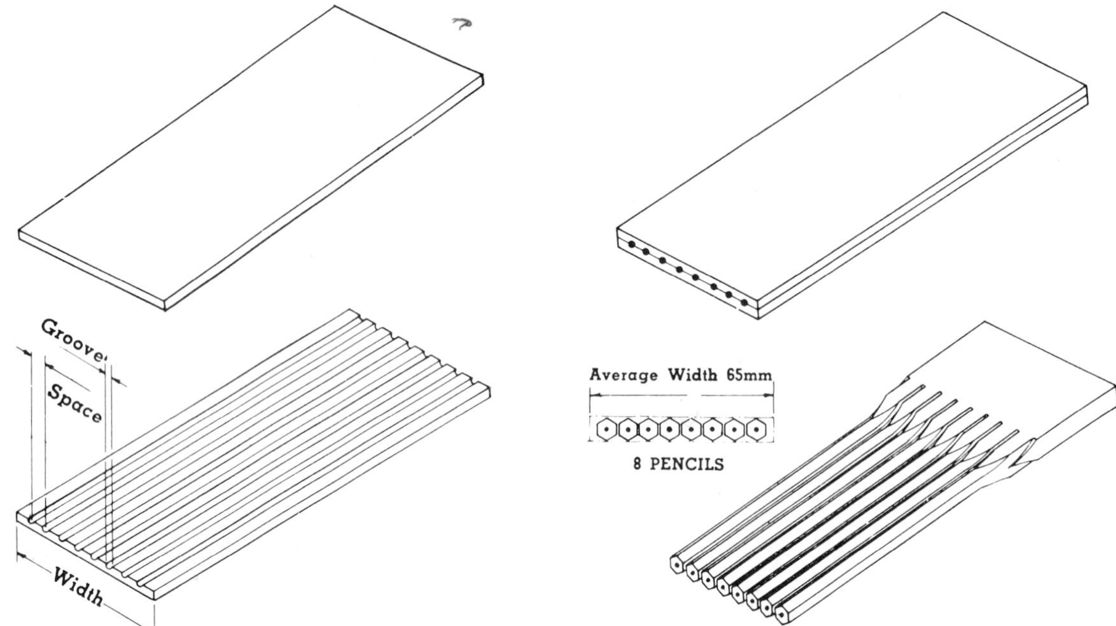

53-2. *Manufacture of pencils. The "leads" are a blend of materials in paste form. This paste is extruded (like toothpaste) in spaghetti-like strands. After drying, the leads are cut into 7" lengths. They are then sent to the woodworking department to be enclosed in wood. There cedar logs are sawed into small slats, each slightly longer than the length of the pencil but half the thickness and several pencils wide. Grooves are cut along the full length of each slat to a depth just one-half the thickness of the lead. Glue is applied to the wood, and a full length of lead is placed in each groove. A second slat, grooved and glued, is placed on top, and the two are pressed together to form a "lead sandwich." When thoroughly dry, this sandwich is fed through shaping machines that cut it apart into separate pencils, ready to be painted and stamped with the brand and quality. If an eraser is added, this is fastened to one end of the pencil with a metal* ferrule *(a ring of metal around a slender shaft).*

• *Raw materials.* Raw materials are the "ingredients" a company uses to make its products. The raw materials may be natural or processed. For example, a lumber mill's raw material is trees. Its finished product, lumber of various sizes, becomes the raw material for a furniture factory.

• *Research and development.* Research is done to find new knowledge and new materials. Both of these are needed for industrial progress. Research and development are also carried on all the time to make new products and improve old ones. Another type of research—market research—is carried out to find out what customers want.

• *Manufacturing engineering.* Manufacturing engineering, or production control, is concerned with all the problems that come up during the making of a product. People must decide what processes can be done on what machine. They must also decide what new tools and machines are needed, what changes in plant layout must be made, and how the industrial processes are to be carried out. They must determine if the company will make all the parts of the product or if the making of the parts will be "farmed out." This group is also concerned with material control and quality control, including testing and standards. The quality-control department must set up standards for testing the new materials, processes, and techniques. These people must make sure that products meet the standards of the manufacturer.

53-3(a). ***Cabinets for telephones are mass-produced. This worker is checking a part that has been glued on an electronic gluing machine.***

53-3(b). ***The finished cabinet. The telephone is stored inside.***

• *Manufacturing.* Products are manufactured by mass production methods. Mass production deals with the making of identical individual parts. It also deals with the assembly of those parts into a finished product. Fig. 53-3. All manufacturing operations can be divided into four major areas:

(1) *Cutting.* All materials must first be cut to size. This can be done in several ways, such as sawing, drilling, or turning.

(2) *Forming.* Forming is the way in which materials are reshaped. Some of the forming operations used most often are laminating and bending.

(3) *Finishing.* Finishing includes all the processes used to improve the appearance and to protect the product's parts. Finishing processes used in woodworking include painting, coloring, and coating.

(4) *Assembling.* Assembling means putting the parts together to make the finished product. Wooden parts can be assembled by using mechanical fasteners, such as wood screws, or by using adhesives.

All the major manufacturing processes can be done either by hand or by machine. Most of your experiences in this class will be in learning how to perform these processes. After assembly, products must be packaged for shipment.

• *Marketing.* Marketing deals with advertising, selling, distributing, and servicing products. Most products that we use are made many miles from where we live. Marketing informs us about the products and brings them to us.

• *Finance.* A large part of any corporation's personnel must deal with financial (money) matters. These include accounting, purchasing materials, paying labor, preparing budgets, collecting debts, and so on.

MASS PRODUCTION

Your class can set up a mass-production project. Fig. 53-4. Here are the major steps to follow:

Establish a Manufacturing Company

The class can decide whether to organize a corporation. A corporation is not necessary for mass-producing a product, especially if it is for class use alone. Perhaps the first class project will be concerned with manufacturing only enough products to allow each student to take one home. A formal company will not be needed for this. However, if a corporation is organized, experience will be gained in such areas as business, management, advertising, sales, and distribution. Your class must organize the company, sell stock, elect a board of directors, and "hire" the president and other management personnel.

Market Research

If the class decides to mass-produce an item for sale, market research must be done to find out the kinds of products that will sell best. A survey of your school or community will tell you what kinds of things people are willing to buy. Products such as games, cutting boards, or desk accessories would be good selections. Your class may decide to mass-produce products that will be given away, such as toys for needy children. Whether a product is to be sold or given away, you must decide what kind of product to build and how many. Figs. 53-5 and 53-6.

53-4. *Mass-producing a product involves ideas, materials, people, money, and many other aspects of business.*

Follow these rules when selecting a project to mass-produce in your class:

- Keep it simple. You'll soon find how complex even a simple project can be when it is mass-produced.
- As a member of the class, you should help in the project selection. Look in catalogs, stores, and magazines for ideas about what to make. Each member of the class should suggest a project. Then the class should narrow the suggestions down to the best five.
- If time permits, build a prototype of each of the five best ideas.
- When possible, make a market survey to find out if the product can be sold and at what price.
- Make sure the following are available:
  a. Tools and machines.
  b. The technology and time to make the jigs, fixtures, gauges, dies, and templates.
  c. The materials.
  d. The money.
  e. The time to complete the project.

Product Development and Engineering

After the product has been chosen, it is necessary to do the development work. This includes designing it, producing the drawings, and making a pilot model. Suppose, for example, that the class decides to produce a cutting board. The first thing to decide is what it will look like—what the design will be. Class members could suggest several different ideas. From these, one can be selected. Now the drafting class, operating as an

53-5. *Four prize-winning mass production projects (sponsored by Stanley Tools). Pine footstools were produced by a sixth-grade class and donated to Canadian students as a goodwill gesture. An eighth-grade class produced cutting boards in several designs. The gumball machine was manufactured by an eighth-grade class. The 20 team members produced 97 units that sold for $3.00 apiece. The logging truck was manufactured by a ninth-grade class. They donated 125 trucks to underprivileged children.*

engineering department, will make working drawings of the cutting board. Bills of materials and procedures lists must also be made. After the drawings are approved, prototypes (pilot models) must be built. Prototypes are needed:

- To discover any problems in construction.
- To develop a *flow process chart,* or *operation process chart,* for manufacturing. Fig. 53-7.
- To build the necessary templates, jigs, fixtures, and gauges.

These steps take a great deal of "lead time." Therefore your instructor may already have a product design for mass production, including all the necessary jigs, fixtures, and gauges.

Manufacturing Engineering, or "Tooling Up"

Before manufacturing can begin, a good many things must be done. This is called "tooling up" for production:

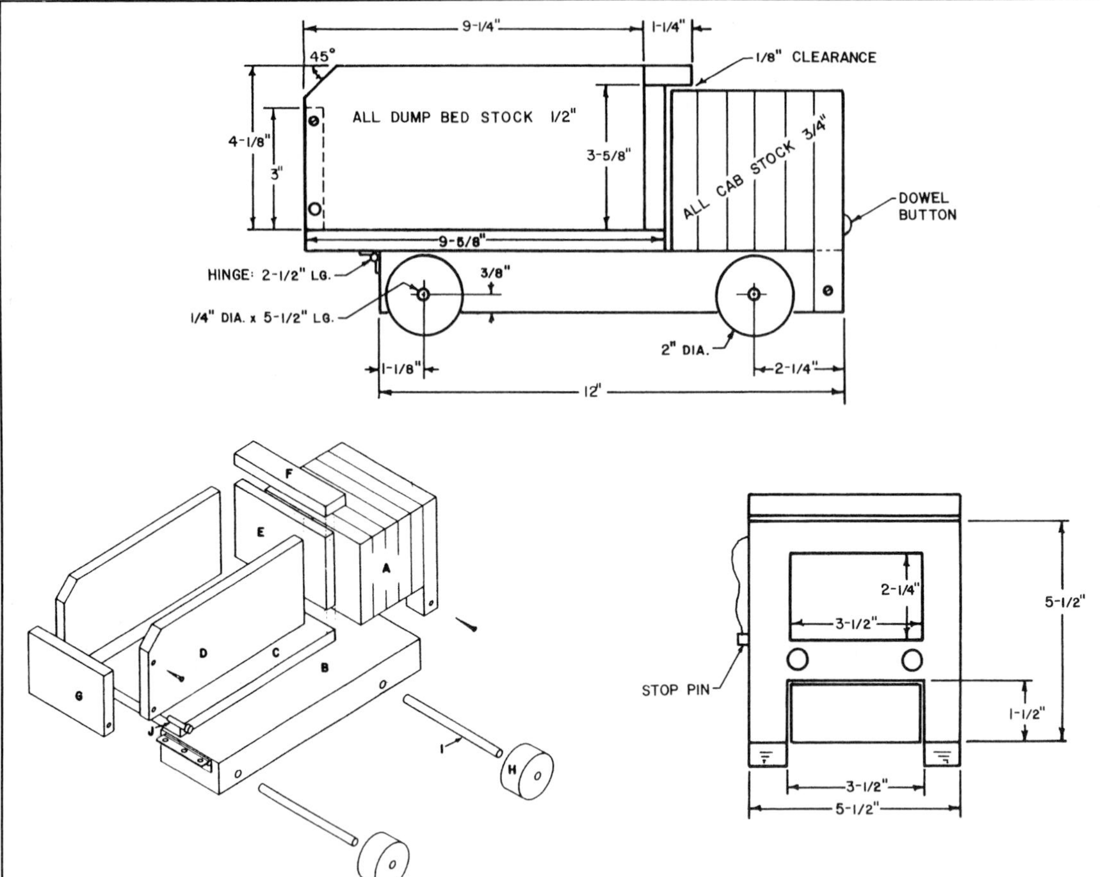

CONSTRUCTION PROCEDURES FOR TOY TRUCK

1. Cut cab, chassis, and wheel stock to rough dimensions.
2. Glue up cab, chassis, and wheels.
3. Cut ½″ stock for dump bed.
4. Assemble dump bed:
   a. Front to bottom.
   b. Sides to bottom.
   c. Headache board to front.
5. Countersink and fill nail holes.
6. Sand dump bed joints flush.
7. Machine cab to finish size.
8. Machine chassis to finish size.
9. Cut out wheels and disk-sand or turn round.
10. Drill:
    a. Axle hole in wheel.
    b. Axle hole in chassis.
    c. Screw holes in cab and tailgate.
    d. Stop pin hole in tailgate.
    e. Headlight holes.
    f. Hinge screw holes in chassis and dump bed.
11. Finish sand dump bed to chassis.
12. Finish sand cab to chassis.
13. Finish sand wheels and axles to chassis.
14. Glue dowel buttons in headlight holes.
15. Finish with urethane varnish.

BILL OF MATERIALS

No. Pieces	Description		Rough Size
1	A	Cab	5⅝″ × 5⅝″ × 4½″ deep
1	B	Chassis	1½″ × 3⅝″ × 12¼″
1	C	Dump Bed Bottom	½″ × 5½″ × 9⅝″
2	D	Dump Bed Sides	½″ × 4⅛″ × 9¼″
1	E	Dump Bed Front	½″ × 3⅝″ × 5½″
1	F	Headache Board	½″ × 1¼″ × 5½″
1	G	Tailgate	½″ × 3″ × 4⅝″
4	H	Wheels	1″ × 2⅛″ × 2⅛″
2	I	Axles	¼″ diameter × 5½″ long
1	J	Tailgate Stop Pin	⅜″ diameter × 1½″ long
2	K	Dowel Buttons	⅜″ inside dia.; ½″ outside dia.
4	L	Screws	2—1″ No. 3; 2—2″ No. 3
1	M	Hinge with Screws	¾″ × 2½″ long
20	N	Nails	1″ No. 18
	O	Glue	1 oz. (approx.)

53-6. *Plans for a toy truck similar to the one in Fig. 53-5. (Shopsmith, Inc.)*

- *Plant layout.* In your shop or laboratory, you will want to plan the best arrangement for manufacturing the product. Fig. 53-8.
- *Equipment.* Your class will have to use the tools and machines on hand. However, you can develop the necessary production devices, including the fixtures, jigs, gauges, dies, and templates.

A *fixture* is a device, usually fastened to a machine, to hold pieces in the right position for cutting or shaping. Fig. 53-9. A *jig* holds the part and guides the tool. Fig. 53-10. Sometimes jigs and fixtures are used interchangeably. A *gauge* is a device used to determine whether the part is the right size. Fig. 53-11 (page 280). A *die* is used to cut and form parts. A *template* is a pattern of wood or metal used to lay out duplicate parts, especially if they are irregular in shape. Fig. 53-12.

Obtaining Materials

By now you have decided how many items will be produced. You will have made a bill of materials for the product. Now the class must make sure that all these materials are available. It may be necessary to buy certain parts from other companies. For example, if desk sets with pens and penholders are to be made, the pens have to be bought.

Personnel

A basic idea in mass production is the division of labor among workers. You will need management personnel and production workers. Management personnel will include such persons as:

- President, vice president, secretary, and treasurer.
- Director or manager of production, sales manager, personnel director, and other managers.

53-7(a). *Five symbols used when making flow charts. You must learn these symbols so that you can read a flow chart.*

Flow Process Chart

Product Name Peg Puzzle Board			Flow Begins	Flow Ends	Date
Prepared By:		Section:		Approved By:	
Process Symbols And No. Used	Operations____ Inspections____ Transportations Delays____ Storages____				

Task No.	Process Symbols	Description of Task	Machine Required	Tooling Required
1	I-1	Inspect stock for possible defects	None	None
2	0-1	Layout lines for angle cut	None	Template
3	T-1	Transport to saw jig	Cart	Fixture
4	0-2	Cut stock on saw	Circular saw	Fixture
5	T-2	Move to the drilling jig	Cart	Drill jig
6	0-3	Drill the peg holes	Drill Press	Jig
7	I-2	Inspect the hole placement and depth	None	Gage
8	T-3	Transport to the sanding area	Cart	None
9	0-4	Sand all surfaces	Band sander	Fixture
10	I-3	Inspect for smoothness	None	Visual
11	T-4	Transport to the finishing area	Cart	None
12	0-5	Finish with oil	None	None
13	D-1	Drying time four hours	None	None
14	I-4	Final Inspection	None	Visual
15	S-1	Store	None	None

53-7(b). *A flow chart for the peg puzzle shown in Fig. 53-12. Note the numbers in the symbols. I-1 for example means inspection number 1.*

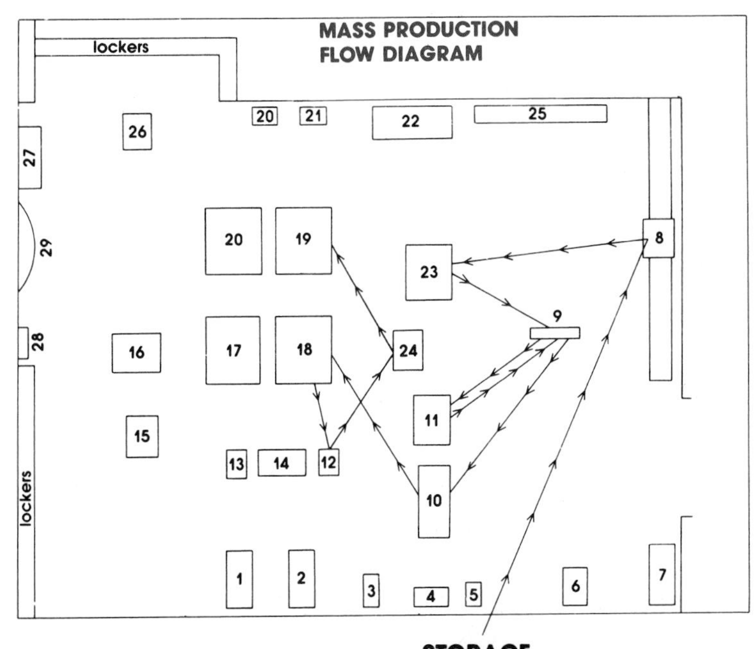

1. Wood Lathe
2. Wood Lathe
3. Jig Saw
4. Storage Cabinet
5. Grinding Wheel
6. Mortising Chisel
7. Bar Clamp Bench
8. Radial arm Saw
9. Jointer
10. Table Saw
11. Table Saw
12. Drill Press
13. Drill Press
14. Clamp Cabinet
15. Band Saw
16. Band Saw
17. Work Bench
18. Work Bench
19. Work Bench
20. Work Bench
21. Power Sander
22. Welding Table
23. Surface Planer
24. Shaper
25. Project Storage
26. Teachers Desk
27. Tool Cabinet
28. Safety Glass Storage
29. Sink

53-8. *A plant (shop) layout showing the flow of materials.*

53-9. *A fixture for cutting stock to length.*

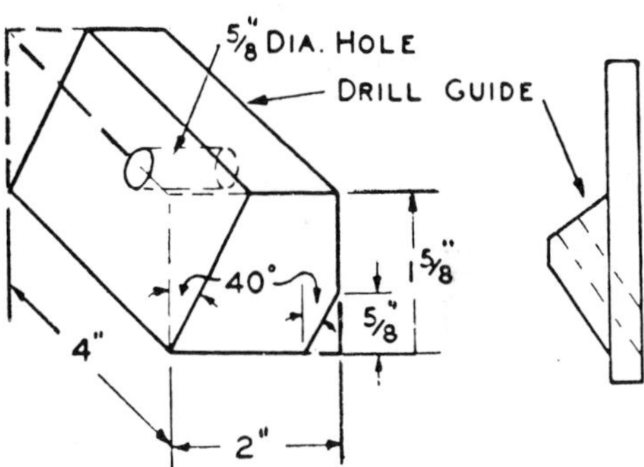

53-10(b). *A shop-made drill jig.*

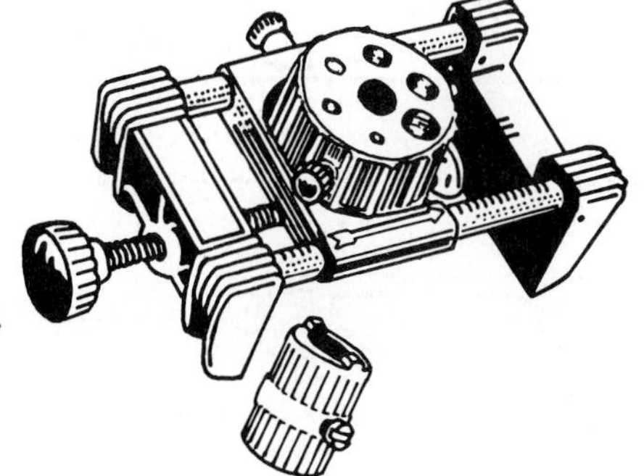

53-10(a). *An adjustable drill jig.*

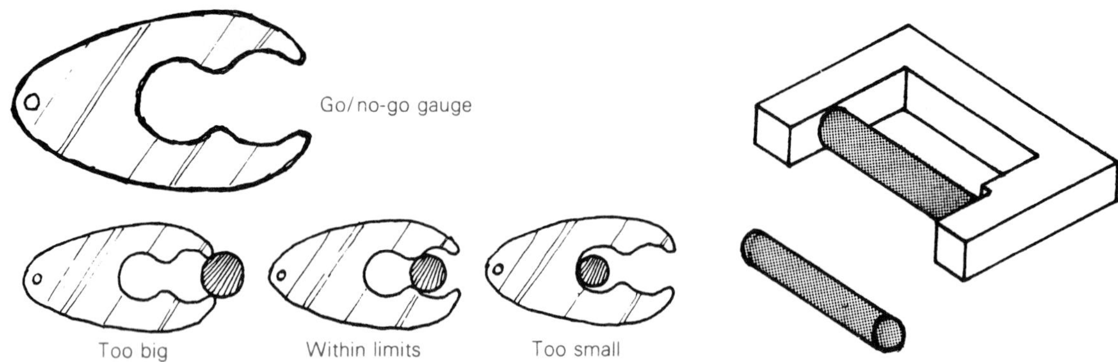

53-11. *Go/no-go gauges being used to check the diameter and length of a part.*

Production workers will include:

- A shop foreman or forewoman for each division.
- An assistant shop foreman or forewoman.
- Enough production workers for each work station to keep the production line going. For example, you might need three or four workers at each sanding station. However, only one might be needed at the drill press. Each person must know the job and be given the proper training for it.

Quality Control

All the parts and the final product must be made to certain standards. Otherwise the parts may not fit together, or the final product may not look good or work well. You should set up a quality-control program. The quality-control workers check the parts for such things as size, finish, and accuracy at each step as the parts are produced. The completed product must be checked during assembly and finishing.

Production Control

When you completed the plan sheet for making your own project, you had to list the steps in making the project. In industry this is called production control. This involves making flow charts and operation process charts for such

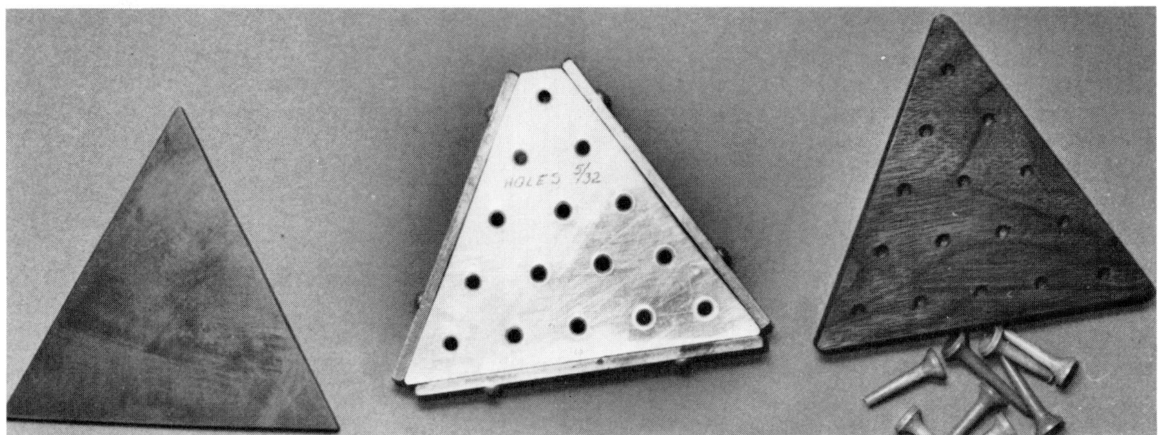

53-12(a). *A peg puzzle. Left to right: the hardboard template used to lay out the shape of the puzzle, the drill jig used when drilling the holes, and the finished product.*

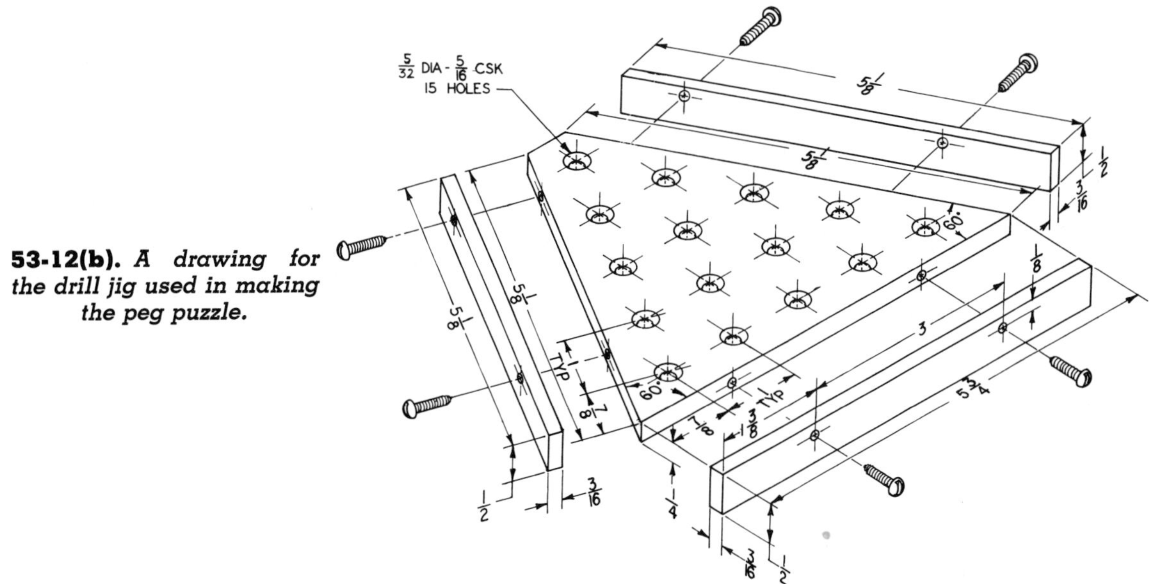

53-12(b). ***A drawing for the drill jig used in making the peg puzzle.***

things as materials, manufacturing, and inspection.

Manufacturing

You are now ready to manufacture the product. The shop has been organized. The equipment is available. The materials are ready, the workers have been trained, and the production devices have been made. The gauges for quality control are complete. The flow charts are made. Now the materials must be moved from the storage area to manufacturing. Then they go on to finishing and assembly and finally to inspection, packaging, and storage.

- *Material control and movement.* For efficient manufacturing, a method must be set up for moving raw materials and partly finished parts. In industry there are a number of methods. Small industries use stock carts and pallets. Larger industries use automatic conveyor systems. In your own school, shop carts will probably be best for moving the parts from one place to another.
- *Manufacturing processes.* All manufacturing processes can be divided into four basic types: cutting, forming, finishing, and assembling. All these processes are covered in this book. They might be done with hand or machine tools.
- *Inspection.* As the parts of the product are made, they must be inspected. They may be given a visual inspection and also inspected with gauges and measuring devices. Visual inspection may be needed for checking the quality of the finish and general appearance. Gauges and measuring devices are used to see if the parts are made to the correct size.

Business Activities

Business activities include the following:

- *Accounting.* Before, during, and after manufacture you need to keep careful cost records of the items produced. In industry there are four major cost factors: materials, labor, overhead, and profit. Cost of materials is quite easy to find out. This is done the same way as in making a bill of materials for an individual project. Labor costs are all the amounts paid to individuals to manage, manufacture, advertise, and sell the product. Overhead includes such things as the cost of the building, taxes, rents, equipment replacement, electricity, and heat and light. (Usually, a school class does not have to worry about overhead.)

You also need to keep track of sales and income. Manufacturing concerns cannot stay in business very long unless they make a profit. It is not necessary for your class to make a profit unless you have organized a corporation, sold

53-13(a). ***Here's a note box that might be a good mass-production project.***

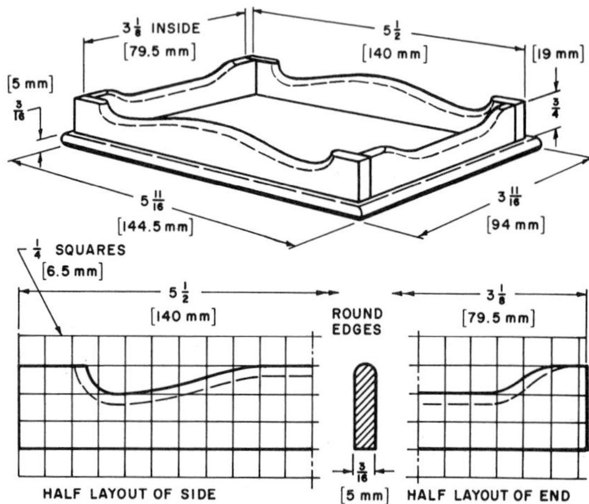

53-13(b). ***The drawing for the note box.***

stock, and hope to return a profit on each stockholder's investment.

- *Advertising and sales.* If your product is to be sold to the public, you must advertise and have a sales force.
- *Service.* Although your class may not need to be concerned with servicing the items you manufacture, this is important in industry. All products must be serviced either by the manufacturer or by the dealers who sell the products.

MASS-PRODUCTION PROJECT

There are many items your class could make as a mass-production project. A few ideas have already been mentioned. Figure 53-13 shows plans for another good project, a note box. You will find more project ideas in Chapter 57.

ITEMS NEEDED

Materials Needed per Box:

1 piece of wood 3⁄16 inch × ¾ inch × 17¾ inches (to allow for cutting).
1 piece of wood 3⁄16 × 3 11⁄16 inches × 5 11⁄16 inches.
20 No. 18 × ⅝″ wire brads.
Glue.
Sandpaper.
Plastic wood.
Finishing material.

Tools and Equipment:

Rule.
Try square.
Pencil.
Jigsaw.
Band saw.
Belt sander.
Circular saw (if available).
Crosscut saw or miter box saw.
Drill press or hand drill.
Claw hammers.
Drills.
Center punch.

Templates:

Pattern for sides.
Pattern for ends.

Fixtures and Jigs:

Jig for cutting sides and ends to length.
Jig for cutting irregular surfaces on sides.
Jig for cutting irregular surfaces on ends.
Fixture for sanding round edges of base.
Jig for drilling holes in sides for brads.
Jig for drilling holes in base for brads.
Fixture for assembling sides to ends.
Fixture for assembling base to sides and ends.

53-13(c). ***Items needed to mass-produce the note box.***

OPERATION PROCESS CHART

Stations	Activity	Equipment	Student Distribution
Foreman	Supervise production.	Flow charts and records.	1
1	Cut sides and ends to length.	Jigsaw or band saw and fixture.	2
2	Cut base to width and length.	Power saw (circular or band) and fixture.	2
3	Lay out irregular surfaces on sides and edges.	Template and pencil.	1
4	Cut irregular surfaces on sides and ends.	Jigsaw and fixture.	2
5	Round edges of base.	Sandpaper and fixture or belt sander and fixture.	2
6	Drill holes for nails in sides and ends.	Drill press, drill, and jig.	2
7	Assemble sides and ends.	Glue, claw hammer, and brads (fixture needed).	2
8	Fasten base to sides.	Glue, claw hammer, and brads (fixture needed).	2
9	Finish sand completed product.	Sandpaper	2
10	Apply wipe-on finish.	Wipe-on finish and rags.	2

53-13(d). *Operation process chart for the note box.*

QUESTIONS

1. What does manufacturing by mass production mean?
2. Describe a fixture.
3. What is a jig?
4. How are dies used?
5. What determines the amount of material needed for mass-producing a product?
6. Must machinery be moved around in a school shop in order to mass-produce a product? Explain.

ACTIVITIES

1. Will your class form a corporation to mass-produce a product? If so, prepare a report about what you expect to learn. What advantages might the corporation give you in manufacturing and distributing a product?
2. On a large sheet of paper, list the ten major concerns for a manufacturing company. Refer to this list as your class establishes its company. How will the company handle each concern?
3. List the four major areas of manufacturing and tell what your company will be doing in each area.

Construction

Where do *you* live? Nowadays there are so many places a person can live—one-family house, duplex or two-family house, condominium, apartment, houseboat, mobile home, and many others. Long ago, people had to build their own homes. Today, we have trained builders. Building houses and other living units is called *residential,* or *light* construction. Building bridges, roads, dams, commercial buildings and other large structures is called *commercial,* or *heavy,* construction. This chapter is about residential construction. Let's see how a typical house is built.

PLANNING A HOME

The kind of house built today depends on many things: its location, the number of people who will occupy it, amount of land available, climate, building materials, skill of the workers, and cost. You can see that building a house takes careful planning. Fig. 54-1.

Planning starts with an idea which the designer or architect puts down on paper in the form of drawings or plans called *blueprints.* These show what the house will look like, how big it will be, how many rooms it will have, the size of each room, and what materials will be used. The blueprint in Fig. 54-2 shows a *floor plan* for the first floor. A *land (plot) plan* is also needed to show the boundaries of the property and the exact spot on the land where the house will be built.

There are *elevation plans* which show what the house will look like from the front, back, and each side. Elevations for a one-story house are shown in Fig. 54-3.

The plans for the house also include a written list of all the materials to be used, including the built-in appliances to be installed, and the care with which the work will be done. This written list is called the *specifications,* or "specs."

THE JOB OF THE BUILDER

The builder is like the director of a play. He or she takes the plans and makes them work. The builder figures out how much the house will cost to build and what its selling price will be. The builder buys the best materials for the money and hires the best workers for the job. He or she makes sure that the natural environment, such as land and trees, is protected as the house is being built.

Just as the director of a play makes sure that each actor comes on stage at the right time, the builder makes sure that each kind of worker is on the job at the time he or she is needed. For example, it would be a waste of time and money to have the worker who puts on the roof waiting to work before the walls are built.

CLEARING THE LAND

First the land must be cleared with a bulldozer, which moves the topsoil into a big pile to be used after the house is built. Usually the builder makes a special effort to save trees and shrubs on the land.

Next, wood stakes are pounded into the earth to show where the corners of the house will be. Fig. 54-4. Then the backhoe or other equipment begins to dig the basement. (Instead of a basement, some houses have concrete slab foundations which rest right on the ground.)

The cement masons build low double walls (forms) of wood that run around the inside of the hole. These forms will hold the concrete for the

SOME TERMS USED IN CONSTRUCTION

batten	A thin, narrow piece of board used to cover vertical joints of plywood siding.
batter board	A temporary framework used to assist in locating corners when laying out a foundation.
blocking	Small wood pieces used between structural members to support panel edges.
bottom plate (sole plate)	The lowest horizontal member of a wall or partition which rests on the subflooring. Wall studs are nailed to the bottom plate.
chalk line (snap line)	A long spool-wound string encased in a container filled with chalk. Chalk-covered string is pulled from the case, pulled taut across a surface, lifted, and snapped directly downward so that it leaves a long, straight chalk mark.
collar beam	A horizontal tie beam in a gable roof, connecting two opposite rafters at a point considerably above the wall plate.
course	A continuous level row of construction units, as a layer of foundation block, shingles, or plywood panels, as in subflooring or roof sheathing (sheeting).
cripple	Any part of a frame which is cut less than full length, as in cripple studs under a window opening.
dimension lumber	Lumber 2 to 5 inches thick and up to 12 inches wide. Includes joists, rafters, studs, planks, girders, and posts.
doubling	To use two of the same framing members nailed together, such as studs or joists, to add strength to a building.
fascia	Horizontal board that is used as a facing.
fascia rafter	End rafter at the end of the rake.
footing	The concrete (usually) base for foundation walls, posts, chimneys, etc. The footing is wider than the member it supports, and it distributes the weight to the ground over a larger area to prevent settling.
gable	The triangular portion of the end wall of a house with a pitched roof.
gusset	A small piece of wood, plywood, or metal attached to corners or intersections of a frame to add stiffness and strength.
header	One or more pieces of framing lumber used around openings to support free ends of floor joists, studs, or rafters.

(Continued on next page)

54-1. ***It takes planning to build a home. These are some of the terms used in plans. They describe materials and procedures.***

SOME TERMS USED IN CONSTRUCTION (Continued)

in-line joint	A connection made by butting two pieces of lumber, such as floor joists, end-to-end and fastening them together by using an additional splice piece nailed on both sides of the joint.
joist	One of a series of parallel framing members used to support floor or ceiling loads. It is supported in turn by larger beams, girders, or bearing walls, or the foundation.
kiln dried	Wood seasoned in a humidity-and temperature-controlled oven to minimize shrinkage and warping.
o.c.	On center. A method of indicating the spacing of framing members by stating the measurement from the center of one member to the center of the next.
plumb bob	A weight attached to a line for testing perpendicular surfaces for trueness.
rafter	One of a series of structural members of a roof, designed to support roof loads.
rake	The overhanging part of a roof at a gable end.
ridge board	Central framing member at the peak, or ridge, of a roof. The roof rafters frame into it from each side.
setback	Placement of a building a specified distance from street or property lines to comply with building codes and restrictions.
sheathing (sheeting)	The structural covering on the outside surface of wall or roof framing.
siding	The finish covering on the outside walls of frame buildings.
sill (mudsill, sill plate)	The lowest framing member of a structure, resting on the foundation and supporting the floor system and the uprights of the frame.
soffit	Underside of a roof overhang.
span	The distance between supports of a structural member.
studs	Vertical members (usually 2 × 4's) making up the main framing of a wall.
subflooring	Bottom layer in a two-layer floor.
top plate	The uppermost horizontal member nailed to the wall studs. The top plate is usually doubled with end joints offset.
underlayment	Top layer in a two-layer floor. Provides a smooth base for carpet, tile, or sheet flooring.

Fig 54-1.

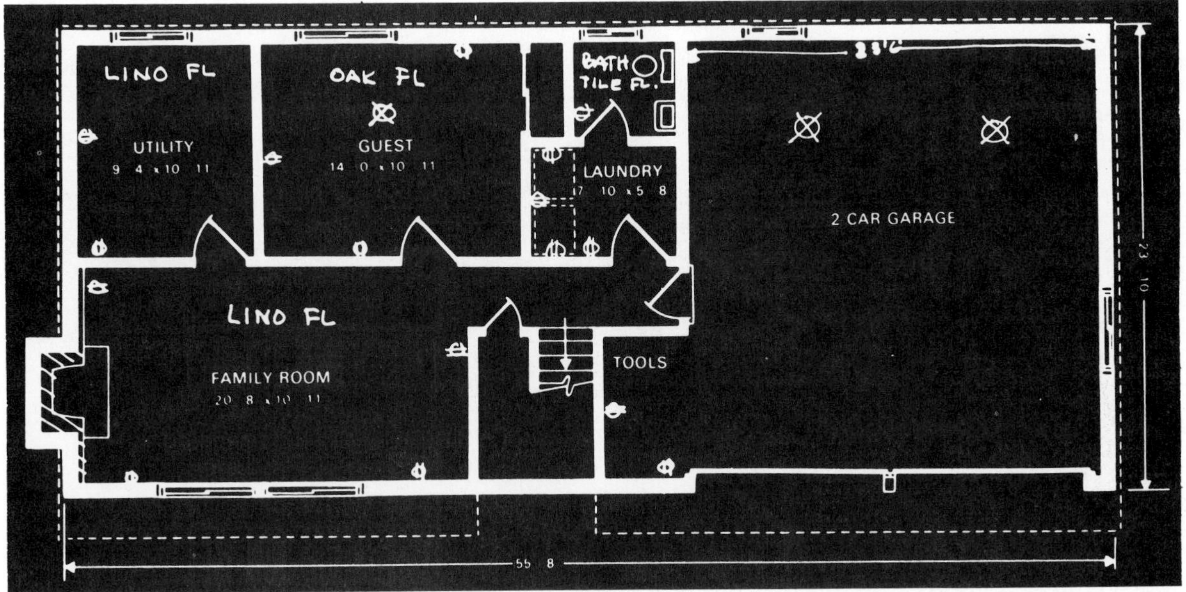

54-2. *Blueprints are necessary in planning a home. (A real blueprint has white lines on a blue background.)*

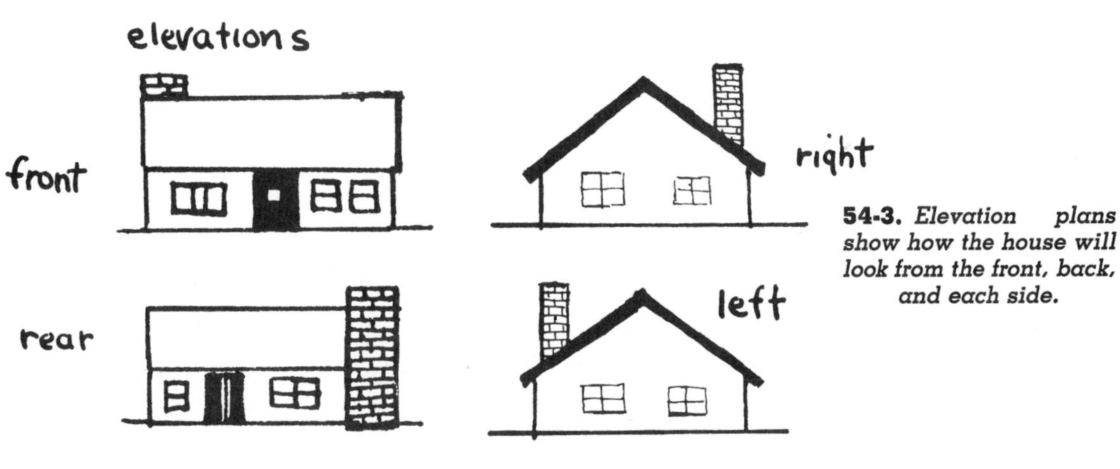

54-3. *Elevation plans show how the house will look from the front, back, and each side.*

54-4. *The corners of the house are marked with stakes.*

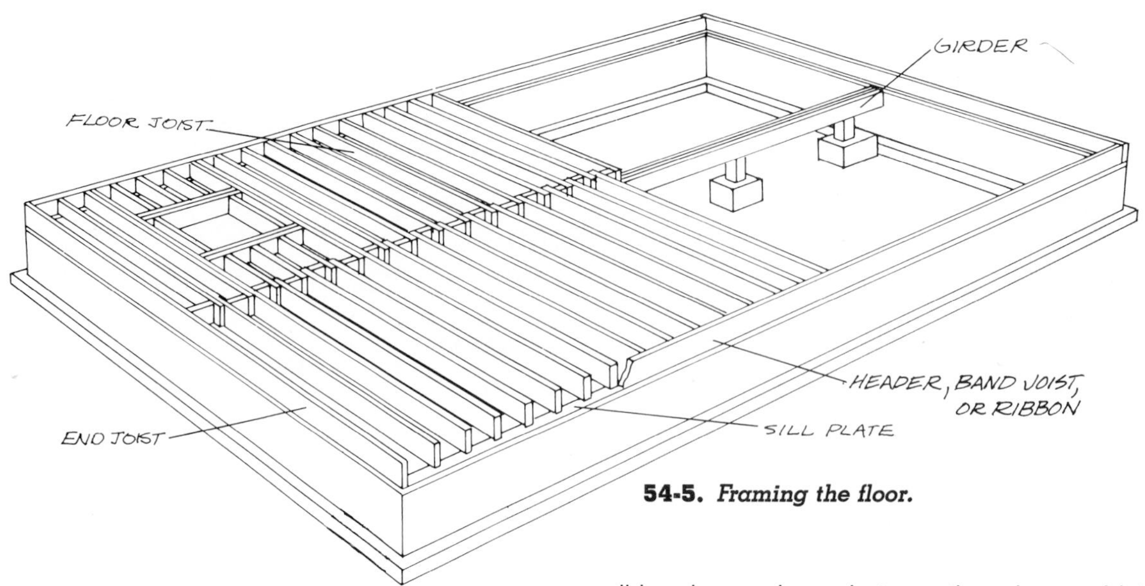

54-5. ***Framing the floor.***

footings for the house. The *footings* are at the bottom part of the foundation walls. The footings are wider than the foundation walls because they must support the weight of the house. Footings are like your own foot that must carry the weight of your body.

Concrete is cement mixed with water, sand, and gravel. The concrete arrives in huge mixer trucks ready to pour the foundation. The concrete slides down a long chute on the mixer and into the forms for the footings. When the concrete is dry, the wooden forms are removed.

The basement walls come next. Some houses have walls of poured concrete, but the house in this example will have concrete block walls. That's a job for the blocklayers. They work with mortar, which is a soft mixture of lime, cement,

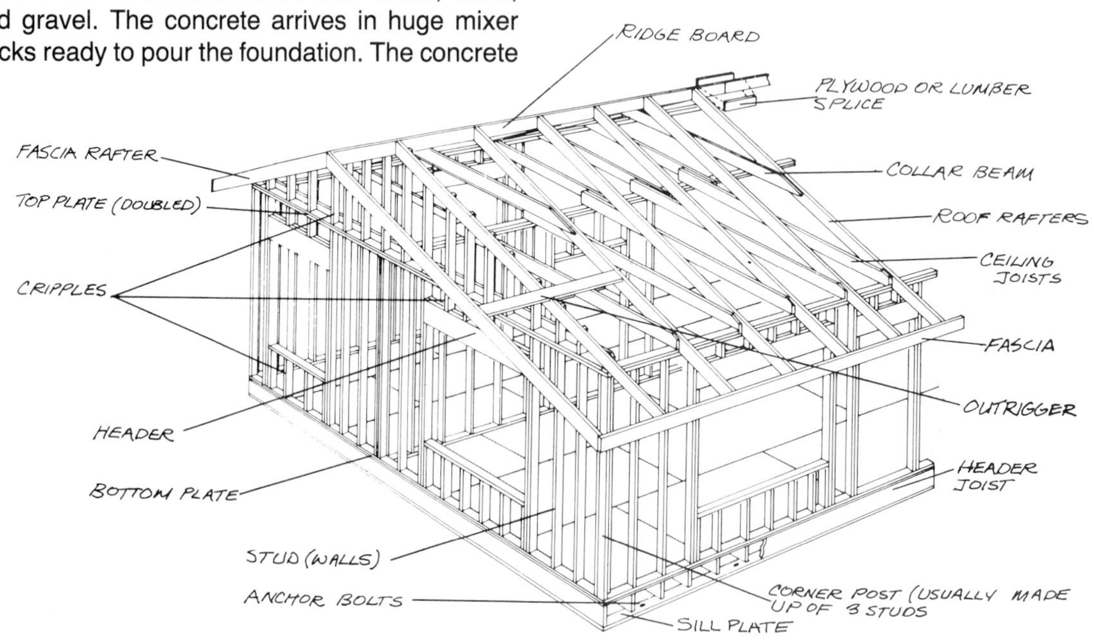

54-6. ***This shows the parts of a wooden frame.***

sand, and water. This will harden after it is spread between the blocks and will hold them together. The blocklayers trim the blocks to fit with a bricklayer's hammer.

The cement masons will return later to fill the hole for the basement floor with gravel, cover it with waterproof sheeting, and pour a concrete slab. They will set steel support posts in the middle of the floor. These posts, will support the weight of the middle of the house.

FRAMEWORK

First the carpenters put down the joists which support the floor. The *joists* are timbers placed across the foundation. Fig. 54-5. Then the rough floorboards are laid down at an angle. In most houses, plywood sheets are used instead of rough floorboards. Later, the regular floor will be laid on top of the rough subfloor. Two layers of flooring give the house a stronger floor.

Now the carpenters are ready to start the framework. Fig. 54-6. First they study the plans which show what sizes to cut the wood. As the carpenters start to build the framework, it looks like a row of fence posts about 16 inches apart. These posts are called *studs* or *two-by-fours.* A two-by-four is a piece of wood that actually measures 1½ inches by 3½ inches. At each corner, the carpenters nail together three studs, called *corner posts.* After the exterior walls of the house are framed, the carpenters start to frame in the different rooms.

Now it's time to build the roof. There are two ways to do this. The carpenters may nail joists across the top of the frame. They then put planks on top of the joists to stand on while they put up the rafters for the roof. The *rafters* are the sloped framing pieces that form the roof. Today, though, the carpenters usually use ready-made joist-and-rafter units, called *prefabricated trusses.* These look like triangles with braces.

By now the house is starting to take shape, but it's not a house yet. The builder must continue to check the blueprints.

CLOSING IN THE STRUCTURE

The next step is for the carpenters to close in the framework. They take large sheets of plywood or other sheeting material and nail them to the studs. Fig. 54-7.

Up on the roof, carpenters finish closing in the roof by covering the roof framework with large sheets of plywood.

THE ROOFERS

The roof of a house is very important. It must keep out rain, snow, and ice without leaking. The roofers must make it weathertight. They put waterproof roofing felt on the roof to seal all the cracks before installing shingles or tiles. They hang the gutters that catch rainwater and the leaders that direct it away from the house.

FINISHING THE EXTERIOR

For homes with a furnace or fireplace, there must be chimneys. These are built by the ma-

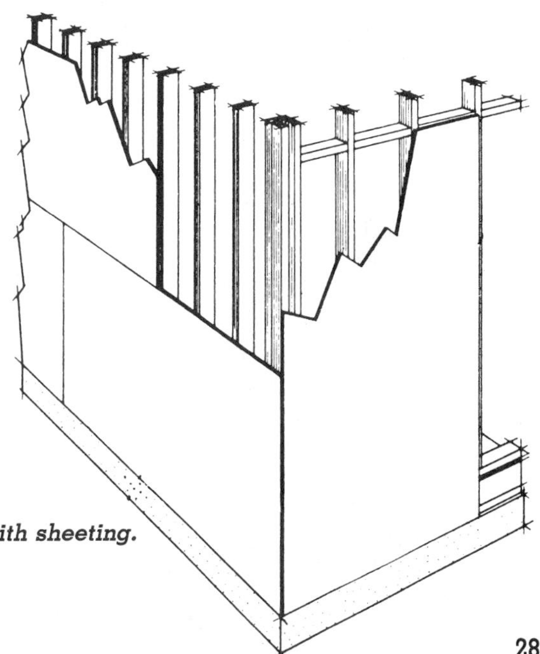

54-7. *The framework is enclosed with sheeting.*

sons. The plans tell them how big the chimney should be and what kind of fireplace is to be built. Everything must be built according to the "specs" so that the chimney will have the right amount of draft to carry smoke up into the air and not back into the house.

The outside of the house is finished by covering it with siding, shingles, brick, stone, or other materials.

DOORS AND WINDOWS

The carpenters install the doors and windows. They drill holes in the doors for the doorknobs and the locks. There are companies today that make prehung doors and windows that come complete from the factory with glass or screening. These are ready for the carpenters to install.

THE ELECTRICIAN

Now the house is ready for another member of the building team, the electrician. He or she must also follow the blueprints to see where all the wires will go, how many electrical outlets and light fixtures will be needed for each room, and where the light switches go. The electrician must look for many other things, such as instructions for the doorbell and outside lights. The electrical contract for a house is a big one.

The electrician drills holes in the foundation wall where the main circuit box will be. He or she uses a drill to make holes in the wooden joists and studs for the main electric cables. The electrician strings the wires that are to be connected to the light switches and the electrical outlet boxes. He or she uses wire cutters to cut the ropelike cables that carry electricity. The electrician trims the wires so that they can be connected. These wires will carry electric power where it is needed. The electrician must take care that these wires are properly connected.

THE PLUMBER

The plumber installs all the pipes that bring water and gas into the new house. Fig. 54-8. The pipes may be copper, galvanized iron, or plastic. He or she uses wrenches, drills, hammers, saws, blowtorches, adhesives, and threading machines. The plumber connects two sets of water pipes from the main water line. One set goes to the water heater and then to the places where the washing machine, dishwasher, sinks, showers, and tubs will be connected. This is the hot water line. The other set is the cold water line. This goes directly to the places where appliances such as the washing machine will be connected and also to the sinks, tubs, and toilets.

The plumber connects all the pipes from the main gas line that will go to such appliances as the stove, water heater, and clothes dryer. She or he connects the water heater and the furnace. The plumber connects the pipes that carry the waste water and sewage to the main sewer. He or she is responsible for making sure that all pipes are connected correctly, with no leaks.

THE PLASTERER

Next, the inside walls will be finished. But before the builder calls in the person who does that job, the sheet metal worker must put in the air ducts that will carry warm air from the furnace and cool air from the air conditioning system. Also, the carpenter must install the insulation.

54-8. *The plumber connects the pipes that carry gas and water into the house.*

54-9. *Molding gives a finished look to a room.*

There are many ways to finish inside walls. There is the plastered wall which goes on wet and dries to a hard finish. The most popular wall, however, is drywall. Drywall is made of gypsum board, fiberboard, and similar sheet materials. Drywall is easily put up with nails. The joints are then smoothed over with tape and a pastelike material called joint compound. Once this is done, drywall can either be painted or covered with wallcovering. Drywall is solid and soundproof. These walls are not expensive to put up and help to keep down building costs.

Drywall comes in large sheets 8 feet long and 4 feet wide. The drywall mechanic simply lines them up with the studs of the room and nails or glues them on. Then the spaces or joints between the drywall sections are covered with a special tape and joint compound to make the wall look smooth. The joint compound hardens to make a stiff, smooth joint.

INTERIOR TRIM

Carpenters return to the job now to nail down the regular floors on top of the rough flooring. Sometimes the regular floors are of smooth hardwood. In some rooms carpets will be laid over the rough flooring. Other rooms may have vinyl, wood tile, or other floorcoverings, but these jobs will be done by other workers.

Now the carpenters do all the interior trimming. They nail down the floor molding and install molding around doors, windows, and ceilings. Fig. 54-9. Molding gives a neat, finished look to the places where the walls, doors, floors, and ceilings meet. This completes the work of the carpenters.

OTHER JOBS

The electrician must connect the appliances and add the lighting fixtures and all of the switches.

The plumber must connect many different fixtures and appliances. He or she is responsible for the things which involve water, sewer, and gas service to the house.

The painter paints the house exterior. Inside the house, she or he paints the walls, ceilings, doors, trim, and door and window frames. Painting makes the house and rooms more attractive and also protects the surfaces it covers.

Painting is only one way to cover a wall. A wall may also be covered with paneling, tile, or wallcovering. Fig. 54-10. Wallcovering may be of paper, plastic, cloth, or other materials. Putting up wallcovering is the job of the paperhanger.

The paperhanger mixes the paste and measures the walls. Then she or he cuts the wallcovering to fit the walls. The paste is spread on the back of the wallcovering. (Some wall coverings come prepasted.) The wallcovering is applied to the wall and smoothed out. This job takes great

54-10. *Wallcovering is one way of decorating and protecting a wall.*

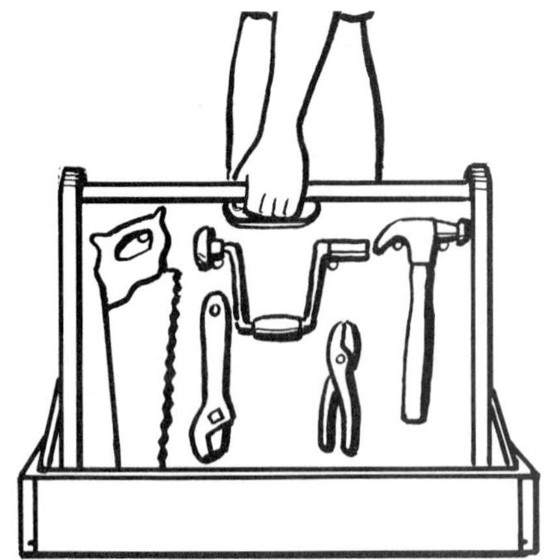

54-11(a). *Your tools will be where you need them when you need them, if you build this carry-all.*

care because the design on the wallcovering must match the design on the roll next to it.

There are a few more jobs to be done by the mason, such as outside steps, walks, or a patio. The mason builds the forms for the steps, mixes the concrete, pours it into the forms and then smooths it out. The mason is skilled in using poured concrete.

The mason builds the walks and the patio, sometimes with large smooth rocks and stones of different colors and interesting shapes. At other times, the mason uses poured concrete.

Next comes the driveway. This can be made of stones, gravel, concrete, or asphalt.

The carpenters, painters, paperhangers, masons, plasterers, electricians, plumbers, and all other workers have finished their work. The builder is still on the job. There is more work that needs to be done before the family can move in.

LANDSCAPING

The landscapers must smooth the ground around the house, making sure that it slopes away from the house so that rain will drain away and not under the foundation walls.

They push back the topsoil that was dug up when the land was first cleared. Then they plant grass seed or lay thick strips of grass sod. The landscaping contract usually includes the planting of some trees, bushes, or flowers to make the lot more attractive.

LEARNING ABOUT CARPENTRY

You have learned that people with many different skills are needed to complete a house or other wood building. In woodworking, your main interest will be in *carpentry.* There are many things you can build that will help you learn carpentry skills and techniques.

- Carpenters need such things as a tool box, miter box, and workbench. All of these can be built in class. Figs. 54-11 and 54-12.
- A variety of outdoor furniture can be built using dimension lumber like that used in framing a house. Fig. 54-13.
- You can build utility items such as mailboxes. Fig. 54-14.

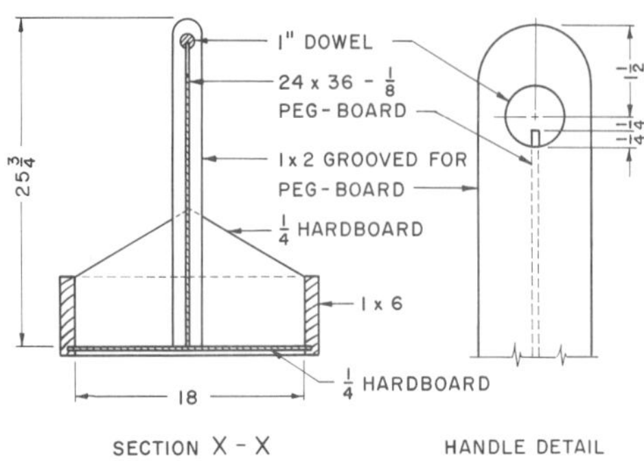

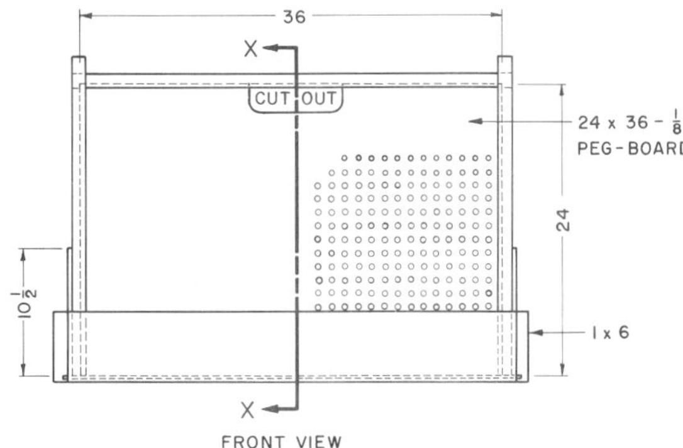

54-11(b). *These drawings show the information you need for building the carry-all.*

4½" WIDTH & 4½" LENGTH MAKE 45° CUTS
4½
3
3
3
12
¾
3
¾
4½
FIT PROJECTION INTO VISE.

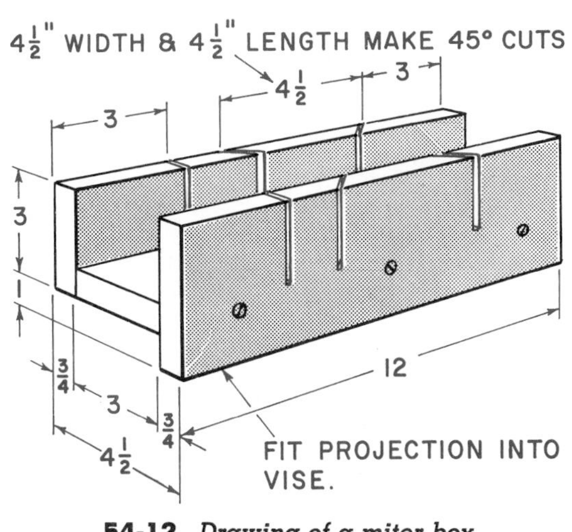

54-12. *Drawing of a miter box.*

- You can make a pet house of different designs and sizes for your dog or other pet. Figs. 54-15 and 54-16.
- A shed to be used for tool storage, a workshop, playhouse, or retreat shelter is a useful project. Fig. 54-17.
- You can build a scale model of a house following directions found in many carpentry books. The materials can be cut to scale, or a precut kit including the plans and materials can be ordered.

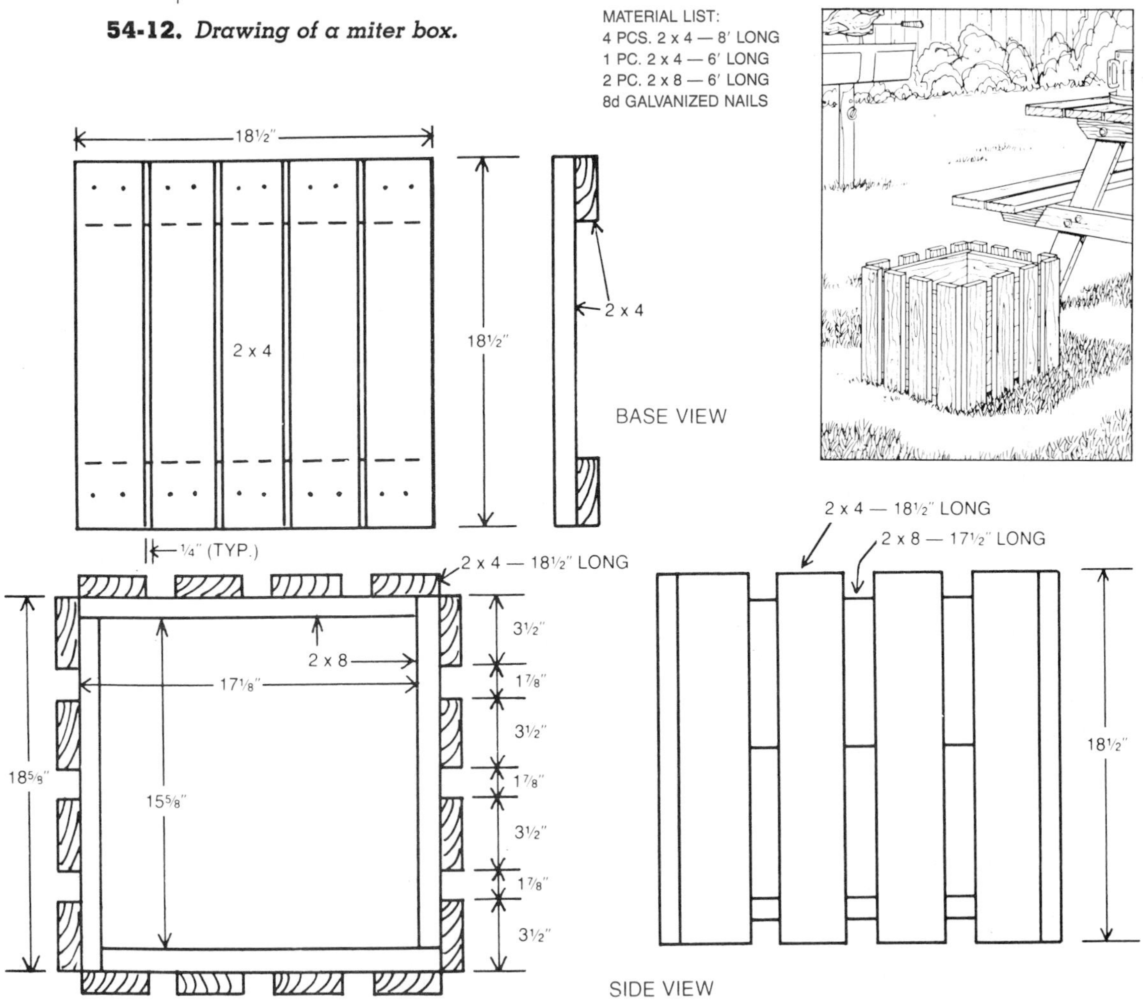

MATERIAL LIST:
4 PCS. 2 x 4 — 8′ LONG
1 PC. 2 x 4 — 6′ LONG
2 PC. 2 x 8 — 6′ LONG
8d GALVANIZED NAILS
18½″
2 x 4
18½″
2 x 4
BASE VIEW
¼″ (TYP.)
2 x 4 — 18½″ LONG
2 x 8
17⅛″
15⅝″
18⅝″
3½″
1⅞″
3½″
1⅞″
3½″
1⅞″
3½″
2 x 4 — 18½″ LONG
2 x 8 — 17½″ LONG
18½″
SIDE VIEW

54-13. *This outdoor wastebasket is built of dimension lumber.*

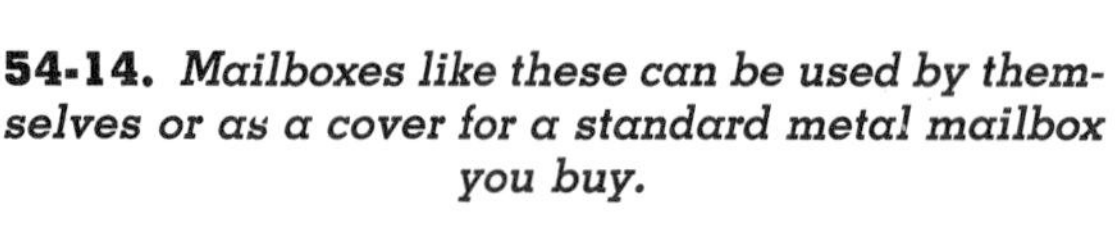

54-14. *Mailboxes like these can be used by themselves or as a cover for a standard metal mailbox you buy.*

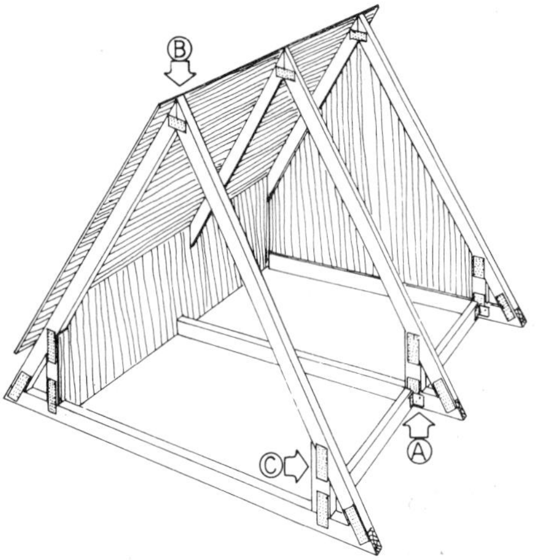

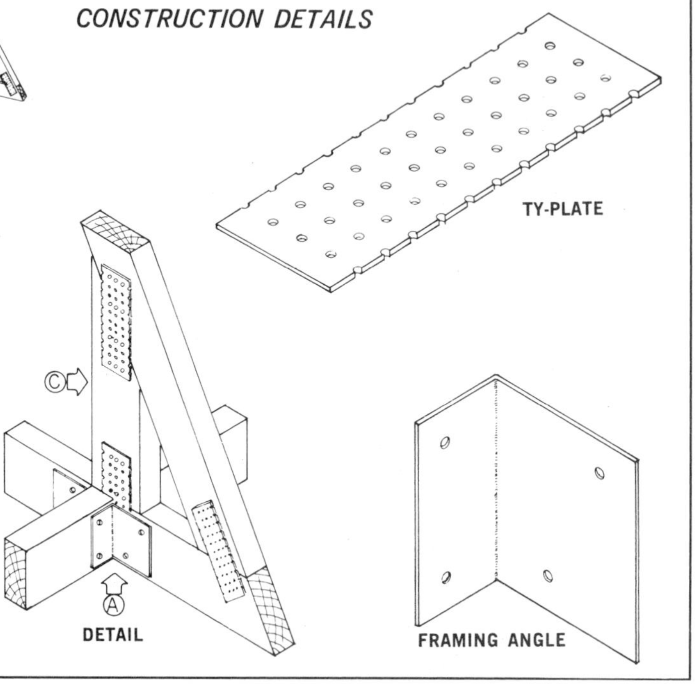

CONSTRUCTION DETAILS

TY-PLATE

DETAIL

FRAMING ANGLE

54-15. *This A-frame design can be built to any size. Metal framing angles are used at "A" and ty (nail-on) plates are used at A, B, and C. These angles and plates are standard metal products in house construction.*

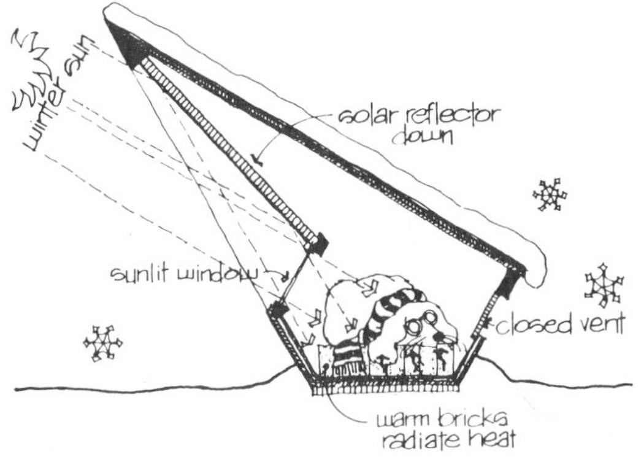

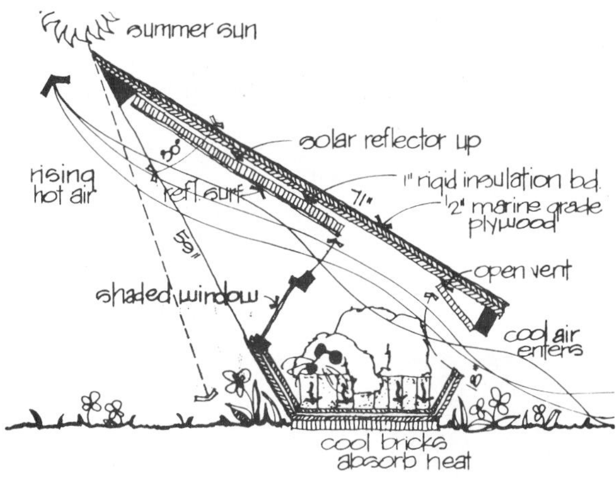

54-16. *Building this passive solar energy doghouse would challenge your carpentry skills.*

UTILITY OR LAWN SHED

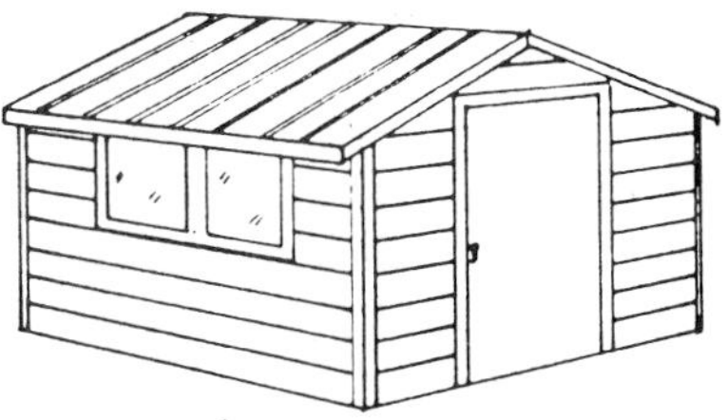

PLASTIC COVERED GREENHOUSE

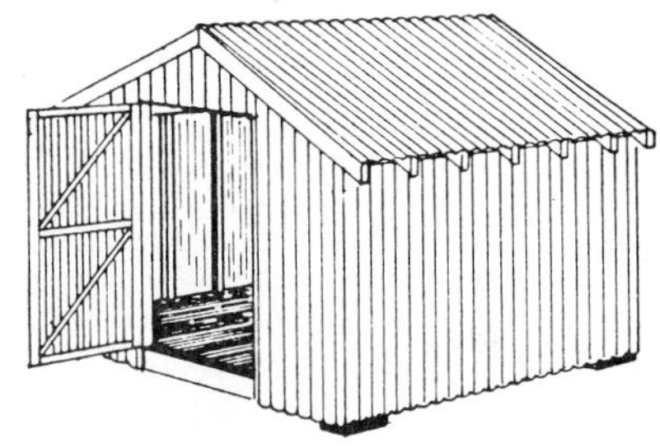

WORKSHOP OR TOOL SHED

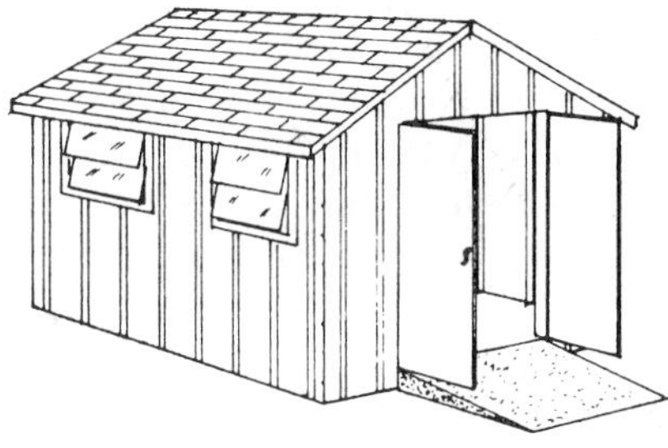

RECREATION OR RETREAT SHELTER

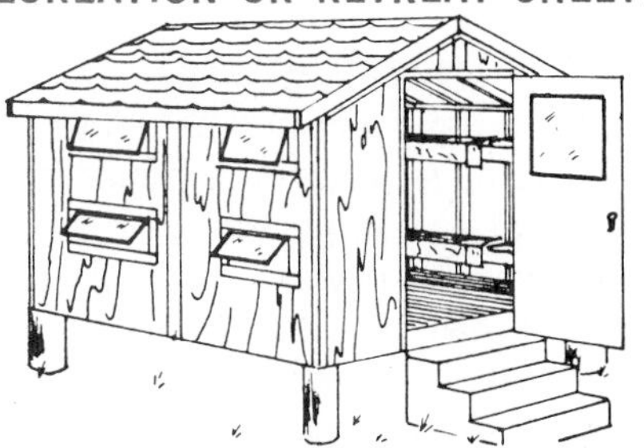

54-17. *A storage shed can be used for many purposes.*

QUESTIONS

1. Why are blueprints necessary?
2. What is the purpose of footings?
3. What is a two-by-four?
4. What kinds of materials are used to "close in" a house?
5. Name several workers who help to build the house after the carpenter has completed the exterior.

ACTIVITIES

1. In a newspaper or magazine, find a floor plan for a home. Tell what you like about it and what you would change.
2. Check real estate ads. What does a new home in your community cost?

CHAPTER 55 Careers

Many people earn their living by working on, around, or with woods. Today, well over two million people work in occupations directly or indirectly related to our forests and the use of lumber. Some work in the forests cutting trees (see Chapter 51); others use the lumber to build homes, boats, and other wood structures. Still others make furniture of wood. Many people find professional careers in woodworking, such as teaching woodwork. Here are some of the major occupations:

CARPENTERS

Most of you have watched carpenters build a house. If you have watched a house going up, you know that the carpenters use all kinds of hand tools, portable power tools, and woodworking machines. Also, you know that they do rough carpentry such as house framing, Fig. 55-1, and finished work such as building kitchen cabinets and built-ins. Would you be surprised to learn that carpenters are the largest group of skilled work-

55-1(a). *Carpenters put up the framing for a building.*

55-1(b). *Some buildings have metal frames.*

ers in the building trades? They are also the largest group of skilled workers in the United States. Well over one million people earn a living as a carpenter. Carpenters not only do the original building, but they also do repair and maintenance work in homes, stores, hotels, and other large buildings. All kinds of woodworking, such as building commercial buildings, are done by carpenters.

The tools used by carpenters are the same ones you have learned about in this course. Carpenters must know how to buy lumber and other building materials, how to plan a building or home, and how to read drawings and prints. They do all the things you have learned in making one of your woodworking projects. Carpenters work outdoors much of the time and must have the strength to handle heavy materials. They are among the better-paid skilled workers.

People become carpenters in one of two ways. Many take courses in carpentry in a school. Others learn the trade by becoming apprentices. An apprentice is a young person who works with an experienced carpenter, learning the skills of the trade, and then studies carpentry in school or on his/her own.

PATTERNMAKERS

Patternmakers are also skilled workers. They make the patterns for metal casting in a foundry. For example, a pattern was needed for casting the body of the plane you use in the shop. A patternmaker made that pattern.

Patternmakers are very skilled woodworkers who earn more money than carpenters.

BOATBUILDERS

If you live near water, especially large lakes or the ocean, you have seen boat builders at work. Here, too, is a specialized woodworker. The boatbuilder must thoroughly understand boat construction and must know how to select and shape woods properly for use in water.

OCCUPATIONS IN THE FURNITURE INDUSTRY

Many people earn a living in the furniture industry, but only a few of them are skilled. Most furniture workers run a single machine and do just one task or make one part. Fig. 55-2. Other people are furniture finishers who apply the finish to the wood furniture. Every big furniture store must employ a few skilled cabinetmakers and furniture finishers to repair broken or damaged furniture. Every furniture factory employs skilled cabinetmakers.

PROFESSIONS IN WOODWORKING

Many woodworking occupations require a college degree. Forestry, for example, is one such area. There are over 25,000 professional **foresters.** About 40 percent of them work in private industry, mostly for paper, lumber, and logging companies. The rest work for governments or universities or are self-employed. Foresters do many things. They mark timber, make rain surveys of the forest, do conservation work, and

55-2. *Many people who work in the furniture industry do one specific task. This woman is driving fasteners into a mirror frame.*

55-3. *Foresters must work outdoors much of the time. This young woman is checking trees to determine their rate of growth.*

55-4. *Woodworking teachers must know math and science as well as how to use tools and equipment.*

help protect forests from fire, disease, and insects. Fig. 55-3. A forester must have a four-year college degree.

There are about 70,000 **teachers of woodworking and carpentry**. Fig. 55-4. They must know how to use all types of hand and power tools. Their knowledge of the entire field must be complete. Your teacher can tell you more about this work.

There are people who work in **research** and **wood technology**. They must have a degree in chemistry or chemical engineering.

A very small number of people work as **furniture designers.** They plan and design the furniture built in factories.

Architects plan homes and other buildings. They must have a college degree and know much about woods and construction.

More information about careers in woodworking can be found in the latest editions of the *Occupational Outlook Handbook* and the *Dictionary of Occupational Titles*. Both of these government publications can be found in your library.

WOODWORKING AWAY FROM THE JOB

Even if you don't plan a career in woodworking, you will find many uses for the skills and knowledge gained in this course. Everyone who rents or owns a home needs to be handy with woodworking tools and machines to do simple repairs and remodeling. Do-it-yourselfers buy more power tools than all the carpenters and cabinetmakers combined.

You can also use your skills and knowledge in the most popular of all creative hobbies—making things of wood. People build everything from airplanes to zithers just for the fun of it. Fig. 55-5. It is a hobby that people become more interested in as they grow older. For example, the largest single group of subscribers to a famous woodworking magazine consists of physicians. Everyone needs both a career and a hobby, and woodworking is an ideal choice for either one.

55-5. ***This young man has a job with a large airplane manufacturer that builds huge passenger planes, mostly of metal. He is building his own amphibious plane, primarily with wood, as a hobby and to realize his dream of flying his own airplane.***

QUESTIONS

1. What is an apprentice?
2. Tell what a patternmaker does.
3. Are there many cabinetmakers in a furniture factory? Where else are they employed?
4. Tell about some of the professions in which a knowledge of wood is important.

ACTIVITIES

1. Check references such as the *Occupational Outlook Handbook* and the *Dictionary of Occupational Titles*. How many carpenters are there in the United States? What kind of training is needed for this career? What is the job outlook for carpenters?
2. Look in a newsstand or bookstore. Make a list of the woodworking magazines you see there.

CHAPTER 56 Technology in Woodwork

What do you think about when you hear the word *technology*—computers, solar panels, supersonic jets, space vehicles, and other present-day developments? These are all part of our high-tech world, but so are such things as a panel made of wood chips and adhesives, wood finishes of "super" chemicals, and electronic power tools, to name but a few. Fig. 56-1. Technology is often defined as the way people use available raw materials along with tools, machines, techniques, and systems to produce the products and services that make life easier and more pleasant. Technology requires the creative minds of people to develop these tools, machines, techniques, and systems that change the way things are made and done. Some people still think of woodworking as an old-fashioned craft, but it has changed dramatically due to technology. Many of the tools, machines, materials, and techniques we use today didn't exist a decade or two ago.

a

56-1. *This is a high-tech house not only because it has an active solar system (a), but also because the framework is covered with waferboard, an exterior bonded panel made of wafers of wood and waterproof resin that is stronger than plywood (b) and because it has a computer system that controls all the functions of the home such as heating, air conditioning, lighting, safety, security, and many other day-to-day activities (c).*

COMPUTERS

Today, computers play a big part in our lives. You know that they can do everything from playing games and figuring your math problems to doing tasks for government, business, and industry. There are many kinds of computer systems, from large "mainframes" that fill a room to small "microcomputers" that fit on a desk or even into a briefcase. Whatever its size and function, a computer system includes both hardware and software.

The *hardware* consists of:

- The computer itself—the brains of the system. Inside the computer are chips, tiny devices that contain electrical circuits. These chips store and process information, and they control the functions of the computer system.
- Peripherals—devices that are connected to the computer. Most peripherals serve as input/output devices. These enable people (or other computers) to communicate with the computer. For ex-

(continued on page 302)

b

c

HOW DOES A COMPUTER WORK?

The computer became possible when scientists and technologists developed a small electronic device about the size of a baby's thumbnail called the *chip* (or microchip). This chip is made primarily of silicon (from sand) and metal. It contains many, many electrical circuits that control the flow of electricity. The chip has only two conditions: low voltage, as when a dimmer switch has turned a light bulb all the way down, and high voltage, as it would be adjusted for full brilliance. We communicate with computers by translating numbers, letters, and symbols into a code of these electrical pulses. A high-voltage pulse is represented by the digit 1 and the low voltage by 0. Because the code is binary (uses only two numbers), these electrical pulses are called *bits,* for binary digits. You probably have studied the binary system in your math class. Most microcomputers digest information in chains of eight bits called *bytes.* For example, the number 3 would be 00000011, the number 7 would be 00000111, while a 15 would be 00001111. Inside the computer, the central processing unit (CPU), or "brain," manipulates millions of bits of data at about the speed of sound.

By itself, the CPU chip can't hold all the information it needs and creates as the computer is operating, so memory chips are needed. There are two kinds. One is the read-only memory (ROM) chip. This chip has permanent information stored on it during its manufacture. This memory is used for many routine directions the computer needs to function properly. The other is the random-access memory (RAM) chip. This contains the memory that the operator can temporarily store and retrieve as needed. The RAM is completely wiped out when the computer is turned off.

The chip operates like a light bulb that is turned all of the way to bright for a 1 or turned way down for a 0.

ample, a keyboard is an input device. You can use it to enter information into the computer. A printer is an output device. You use it to get a paper printout of the information stored in the computer. Some devices, such as monitors, disk drives, and modems handle both input and output. Fig. 56-2.

Software, or *programs,* give detailed instructions to the hardware on how to perform specific tasks. Most programs are recorded on magnetic disks (either floppy or hard). A disk is placed in a disk drive and the information on it is relayed to the computer. Fig. 56-3. Thousands of programs are available, and new ones are constantly being produced. Some examples for woodwork are programs for:

- Figuring board feet of lumber. Fig. 56-4.
- Controlling the kiln drying of wood.
- Designing homes and other buildings, including ways to make them more energy efficient.
- Estimating the cost of building a structure.
- Designing cabinets and other built-ins.
- Keeping a record (data base) of sources of materials, equipment, subcontractors, and other information needed in constructing a building.
- Completing all business procedures including accounting, billing, and record keeping.

56-2. *This computer system includes the central processing unit (CPU), the monitor, and the keyboard and mouse. Information is input using the keyboard or mouse. That information is then processed by the CPU, displayed on the monitor, and output on the printer.*

```
THE PROGRAM:
 10 REM SAVE AS "BD-FT"
 20 PRINTTAB(9)"*** BOARD FEET ***": PRINT:PRINT
 30 PRINTTAB(8)"DETERMINE BOARD FEET"
 40 PRINTTAB(5)"KNOWING THICKNESS T, WIDTH W"
 50 PRINTTAB(8)"AND LENGTH L, ALL"
 60 PRINTTAB(9)"GIVEN IN INCHES."
 70 PRINT
 80 PRINT"THICKNESS = ";:INPUT T
 90 IF T<=0 THEN GOTO 80
100 PRINT
110 PRINT"WIDTH = ";: INPUT W
120 IF W<=0 THEN GOTO 110
130 PRINT
140 PRINT"LENGTH = ";: INPUT L
150 IF L<=0 THEN GOTO 140
160 PRINT
170 LET B$ = "BOARD FEET = "
180 LET X = T*W*L/144
190 PRINT B$;" "X
200 END
```

56-4. *A simple program for figuring board feet in a single piece of lumber. This is written in BASIC, one of the most common languages used to "talk" to the computer.*

56-3. *Information can be stored in a variety of ways using computer technology. Shown here are several information storage disks. These include removable hard disks, as well as optical disks and floppy diskettes.*

• Operating routers and other production machines to produce all kinds of wood parts. For example, if a certain part for the back of a chair is needed, a program for that part is inserted in the computer. The computer instructs the router to shape the part. All that needs to be done by workers (or robots) is to load and unload the machine. A separate program is needed for each different design. For example, there may be one for a Traditional design and another for Early American. Fig. 56-5.

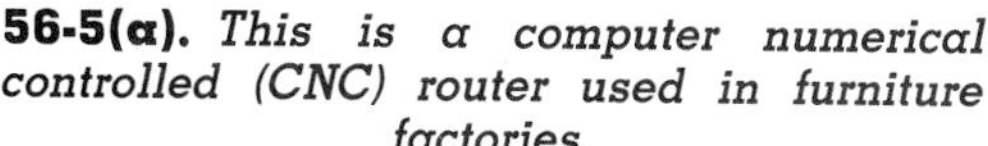

56-5(a). *This is a computer numerical controlled (CNC) router used in furniture factories.*

56-5(b). *A program was needed to machine the inserts for the backs of these chairs.*

56-6. *This computer-controlled router is designed to be used in schools to teach the fundamentals of the computer and how it controls a machine.*

CAD/CAM

As you've just read, computers can be used to control production machines. Fig. 56-6. Computers can also be used to design products. This application of computers is called computer-aided design or computer-aided drafting (CAD). In CAD, computer systems are used to create, store, and change drawings and related information.

Originally, CAD systems required large computers, but now there are numerous CAD systems that use microcomputers. In addition to the usual hardware (computer, keyboard, monitor, disk drive, and printer), a CAD system may include the following:

- A digitizing tablet and a stylus or puck. This is an input device. By moving the stylus or puck over the tablet's surface, you can draw figures which will appear on the monitor's screen. Fig. 56-7.
- A light pen. By touching the screen with this hand-held device, you can move a line, change a shape, or completely redesign the object. Fig. 56-8.
- A mouse. This is another input device that enables you to enter or change a drawing. Fig. 56-9.
- A plotter. This output device prints the drawing on paper. Fig. 56-10.

Like other programs, the software for CAD is stored on disks. Additional disks are used to store the drawings made on the CAD system.

Computer-aided drafting saves time and effort. Suppose, for example, you are designing a table. You create the working drawings for the table on the computer and then print them out with the plotter. But then you decide to change the dimensions of the top and the design of the legs. Do you have to start all over? No. With CAD, you can call up the existing drawing on the computer, enter your changes, and direct the plotter to print out the new version of the table.

The designs created on a CAD system can be relayed to the production line, where other computers, numerical control machines, and robots produce the product. This use of computers to design and produce products is called CAD/CAM (computer-aided drafting/computer-aided manufacturing). In the future, most factories will probably operate in this highly automated way.

56-7. *While the keyboard is used to input text, the mouse is commonly used to select menu commands and to create graphic designs.*

56-8. *This engineer is using a light pen to redesign a product.*

56-10. *This plotter produces drawings on paper or film from the design on the computer screen. Shown here is a plot plan for construction.*

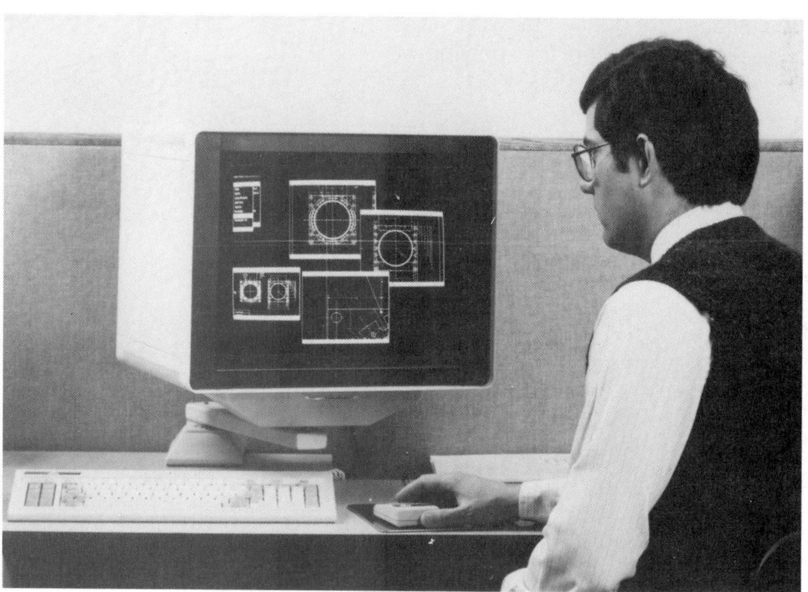

56-9. *This person is using a mouse to change the design on the screen.*

ROBOTS

A *robot* is an automatic machine controlled by a computer. It differs from other automatic machines (like those in a plant where bottles are filled, capped, and labeled) because those machines can do one job and one job only. By contrast, a robot can be programmed and reprogrammed to do many different jobs. The robot can be made part of a total manufacturing system that includes other high-tech equipment like automatic material carriers, computer inspection points, and computer controlled machine tools.

The most common uses for robots in furniture factories are to move heavy material, load and unload machines, and apply finish to furniture. Fig. 56-11. The most common type of industrial robot is a pillar (stand) mounted, multijointed arm that moves on commands from a computer. Fig. 56-12. The robot is the most practical solution to the following problems:

- Hazardous work such as welding, spraying, and handling toxic materials.
- Monotonous work and/or repetitive work which the human worker finds tedious and boring.
- Precision work in which the robot repeats each operation precisely and identically each time. The robot is totally consistent in quality of work it produces. This makes it the ideal tool for applying finishes.

Most robots lack visual or touch senses. They follow blindly a preprogrammed series of motions and are no faster than a human worker. Unless the workpiece arrives at the exact location at the correct time, the robot will fail to do the job properly. Newer robots with vision devices and other sensors can recognize defects and adjust to handling misfed or misaligned parts on an assembly line.

56-12. *A pillar-mounted robot. Note the ways the arm can move.*

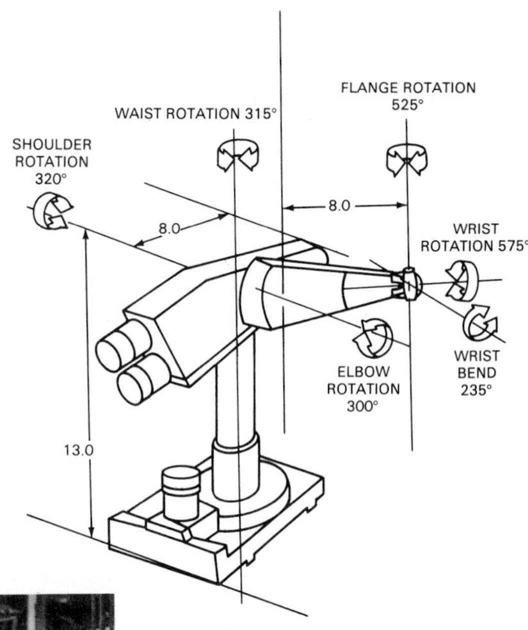

56-11. *This robot is being used to move heavy sheets of material in a furniture factory.*

LASERS

The laser is a device that amplifies and strengthens light and then concentrates it into a very small area. Fig. 56-13. It is one of our greatest scientific discoveries and has changed the way many processes are done in industry. It is also one of the key elements in the Star Wars defense plan. The term *laser* stands for *l*ight *a*mplification by *s*timulated *e*mission of *r*adiation. The way a laser beam operates can be compared with the way a magnifying glass operates when it is used to direct the rays of the sun to start a fire—the intense heat from the small beam of light ignites the wood. Lasers can produce heat of over 7500° F.

Because the laser ray can be concentrated on such a small spot, it can be used for various manufacturing processes such as cutting, drilling, etching, and welding. All plastics, rubber, cork, and wood can be cut with the laser beam to very precise specifications. Fig. 56-14.

Etching can be done on all kinds of materials. Next time you visit an office supply store, look at the desk accessories of hardwood (such as mahogany and walnut) that have a design on them. See and feel the very finely etched pictures on the surface that were cut with a laser beam. Fig. 56-15.

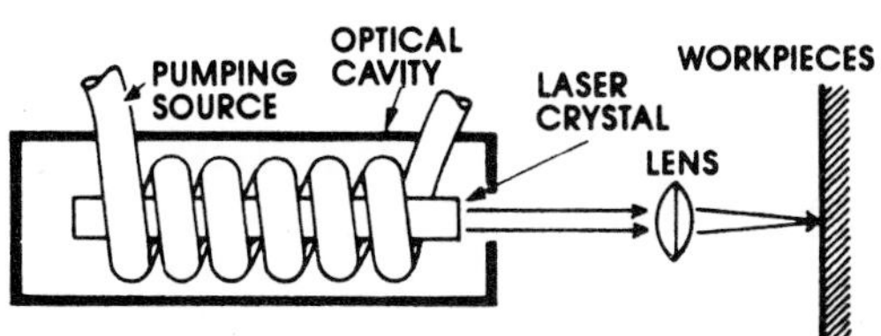

56-13. *The ruby laser is one of several kinds of lasers. It consists of a ruby rod (laser crystal) surrounded by a coiled flash lamp that serves as a pumping source. The ends of the ruby rod are flat and parallel. One end is completely coated with reflective materials. The other end is only partially coated. Each time the flash lamp is set off, it excites atoms in the ruby rod. These atoms give off light that is concentrated through a focusing lens into a very precise beam.*

The laser can also be used to make precision measurements. One example is the laser transit. The traditional transit is a mechanical sighting device for surveying. It is used to establish the lot

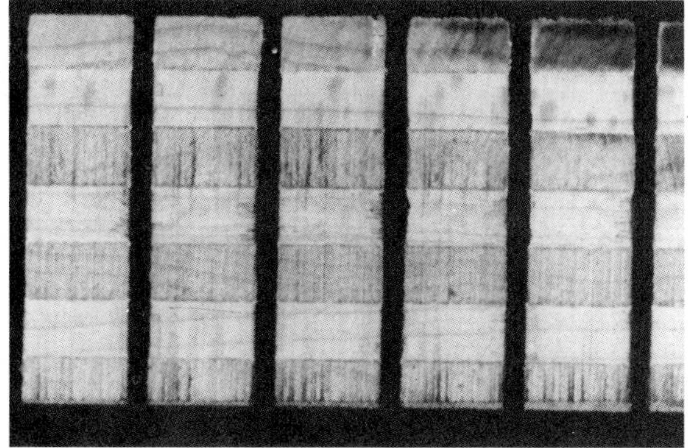

56-14. *A laser beam was used to make these clean cuts through plywood.*

56-15. *A laser beam was used to etch these fine line designs on pen holders.*

lines, measure variation in the surface of land, and establish height locations on existing structures. With the traditional instrument, two people are needed, one to hold the measuring rod and another to sight through the transit level. With a laser transit, only one person is needed. Fig. 56-16. The person sets up the electro-beam level that automatically levels itself. The person then goes to the location where the measurements are to be made. He or she moves a detector up or down to determine the correct reading. The electro-beam level, which contains a laser, sends out safe, strong, precise beams of invisible light that reflect off the detector. One or more detectors can be used to complete in hours a surveying task that might have taken days with the traditional instrument.

56-16. *This is a laser transit. On the right is a close-up of the self-leveling unit that contains the laser along with a measuring rod on which is mounted an electronic detector. On the left, a worker is using the electronic detector to locate the 4-foot mark on a pole that is part of a new building. The electronic laser beam tells the worker when the detector is at the correct height.*

ELECTRONIC POWER TOOLS

On traditional woodworking machines, power may be supplied to the cutting tool at a single constant speed, using a belt and pulleys (Fig. 49-6), gears (Fig. 50-1), or direct drive (Fig. 50-4). On some machines, such as the scroll saw, power is supplied at four or more different speeds by changing the belt on step pulleys. Fig. 48-7. On still others, variable speeds are possible within a limited range by using a belt on adjustable pulleys. Fig. 48-1. All of these methods are a compromise because different kinds and thicknesses of material need different cutting speeds with adequate power to do the job. The high-tech solution is to design machines that contain a microprocessor (see the Glossary) so that a wide range of speeds and power is available to cut many kinds and thicknesses of material. Fig. 56-17. These electronic machines maintain the same cutting speed regardless of load. If you use a traditional portable router to cut very hard wood like oak and you feed the tool too fast, the machine will first "labor" and then slow down and sometimes stop completely. In the process, the wood is burned and the cut is very rough and irregular. With electronic machine tools, the exact setting can be made so the tool will handle the cutting with ease. These tools also electronically monitor the feed rate and signal when they are operating too slow or fast.

AIRLESS SPRAYING

With a standard spray gun, the finishing material is first converted into millions of tiny droplets. These droplets are then forced towards the product by means of air pressure. Many of the droplets either miss the product completely or strike the surface and bounce back into the air, producing a "fog." With airless spraying, the fluid is released under high pressure through a very small hole in the spray gun. This allows the softer spray to reach the recesses and cavities of the product without producing the fog associated with air spraying. Fig. 56-18.

56-17. *Three electronic portable power tools. Each contains a microprocessor.*

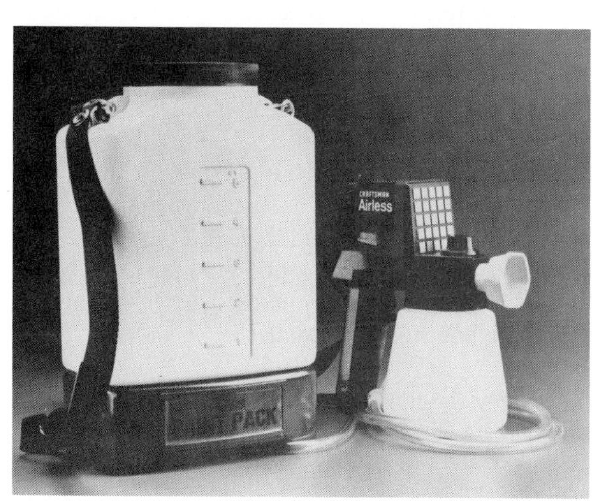

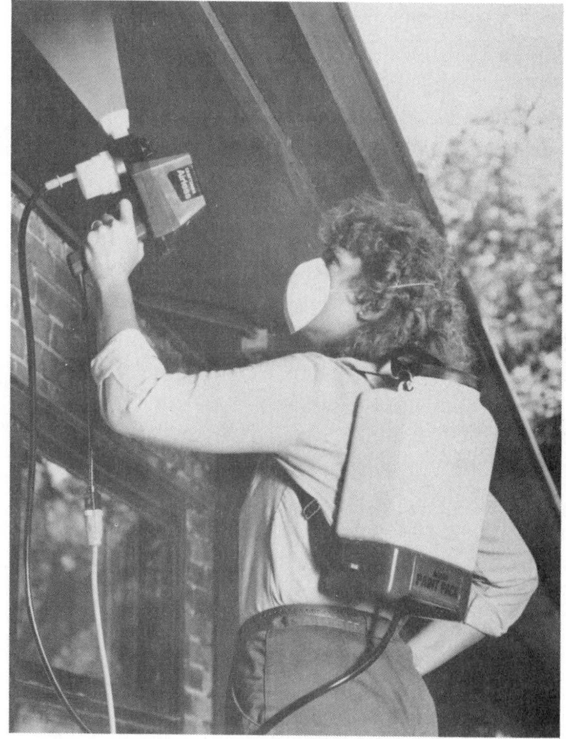

56-18. *An airless spray unit can be used for all kinds of finishing operations. This type of unit saves finishing materials and is more efficient.*

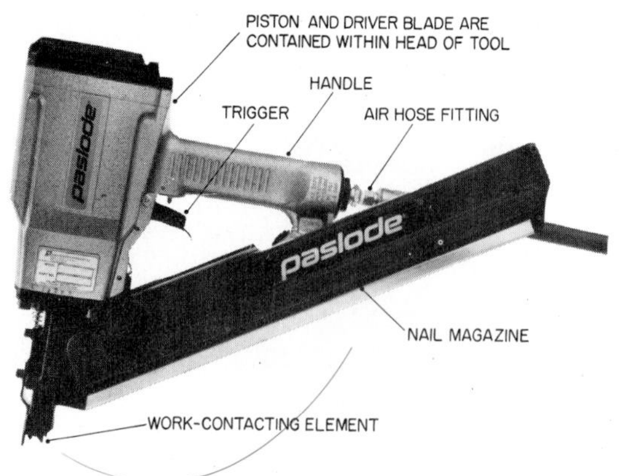

56-19. *The parts of a pneumatic strip nailer. This one has an angled nail magazine.*

PNEUMATIC NAILERS

Pneumatic nailers are also called nailers or air-nailers. They come in a variety of sizes because they must fit the type of nail being driven. For example, a nailer designed to drive 16d nails will not be able to drive brads. When choosing a nailer for a particular job, first determine the type and size of nail needed. Then find a nailer that will drive that nail. Finally, find a compressor to suit the chosen nailer.

There are two basic types of nailers:

• Strip-fed nailers. These nailers hold a row of nails in a spring-loaded magazine. The magazine can either be angled away from the nose of the tool or not. Fig. 56-19.

• Coil-fed nailers. These tools are shorter than strip nailers because they hold the nails in a coil behind the head of the tool.

Most nailers and staplers work on the same basic principles. Air under high pressure is fed to the tool through a high-pressure hose linked to a compressor.The head (and sometimes the handle) of a nailer holds a charge of compressed air. When the trigger is pulled, this air is released against a piston in the head of the tool. This piston is attached to a driver blade. When the piston is forced downward by the compressed air, it pushes the driver blade, which strikes a fastener. The fastener is then driven into the wood at high speed. After a fastener has been driven, pressurized air forces the piston back into place, pulling the driver blade with it. The spring-loaded magazine pushes another fastener into place. The tool is then ready to fire again.

Some nailers are equipped with a pressure relief safety valve. This will prevent damage to the nailer if the air pressure reaches a level that is higher than the tool can handle.

Operating a Nailer

All nailers and staplers employ a two-step firing sequence. This is an important safety feature. The trigger must be pulled *and* the nose of the tool must be pressed against the workpiece before the tool will fire. The trigger will not work otherwise. This helps to prevent the tool from being fired accidentally.

A nailer is typically held in one hand and pressed firmly against the workpiece. Because of the striking force of the driver blade, the nailer will recoil somewhat. With practice, you will be able to prevent this recoil from marring the wood being nailed.

There is another reason for practice-firing a nailer when first using it. The nosepiece sometimes obscures the exact position of the nail. This can make it difficult to place the nail exactly where it is needed. This is more important when doing finish work such as nailing trim.Some nailers exhaust air through a plate in the top of the nailer. This plate can be adjusted so that exhaust air does not blow into the face of the operator.

Most nailers operate on about 80 psi to 120 psi. The operating pressure appropriate for the tool is found in the owner's manual.

NO-COMPRESSOR NAILERS

The majority of air nailers are operated with air supplied by an air compressor. A relatively new type of nailer is considerably different. The force that pushes the driver blade into the fastener is supplied by a very small internal combustion engine located in the head of the tool. A special butane fuel, supplied by the manufacturer in disposable canisters, is injected into a chamber above the piston.

Because the tool is entirely self-contained, hoses and a compressor are not required. This makes the nailer particularly useful in remote locations, or in places where air hoses and a compressor would be awkward to use. Fig. 56-20.

PNEUMATIC STAPLERS

Pneumatic staplers are very similar to nailers, both in the way they work and in the way they are used. These tools are used primarily for installing sheathing, subflooring, and roofing. However, they can also be used to fasten framing, trim, and wood flooring.

Operating a Stapler

Staplers, like nailers, incorporate a two-step firing sequence as a safety feature. This requires that the stapler be held against the workpiece before the trigger will operate.

Staples should be driven flush with the surface of the wood. They should not be countersunk because this reduces the effective thickness of the wood. To avoid overdriving a staple, the crown of the staple should be kept perpendicular to the grain of the wood.

56-20. *This framing nailer is powered by a small internal-combustion engine located in the head of the tool. It does not require a compressor or hoses, which makes it very portable.*

QUESTIONS

1. Give a simple definition of technology.
2. What are input/output devices? Give examples.
3. What is a chip?
4. Define software.
5. Describe two kinds of programs used in woodwork.
6. Define CAD. Name three input devices that can be used to change the graphics on a screen.
7. What is a robot? How does it differ from a traditional automatic machine?
8. What is a laser?
9. Name some industrial uses for the laser.
10. What high-tech device is found in electronic power tools?

ACTIVITIES

1. Does your school offer instruction in CAD? If so, find out what hardware and software are being used. How might CAD be used in a woodworking class?
2. Select one of the devices discussed in this chapter, such as lasers or robots. Research and write a report about how industry uses the device.

CHAPTER 57

Suggested Ideas in Woodwork

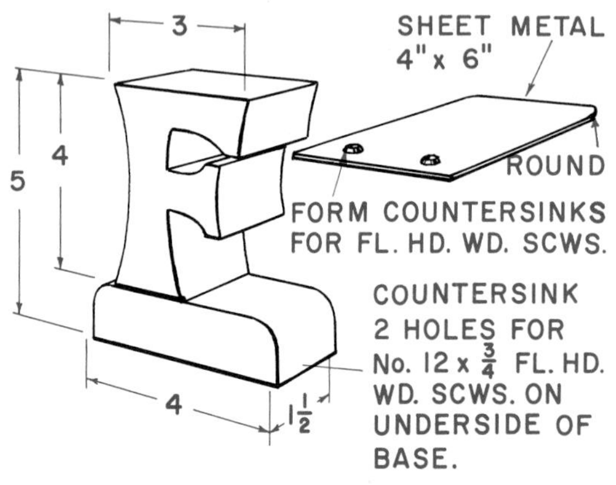

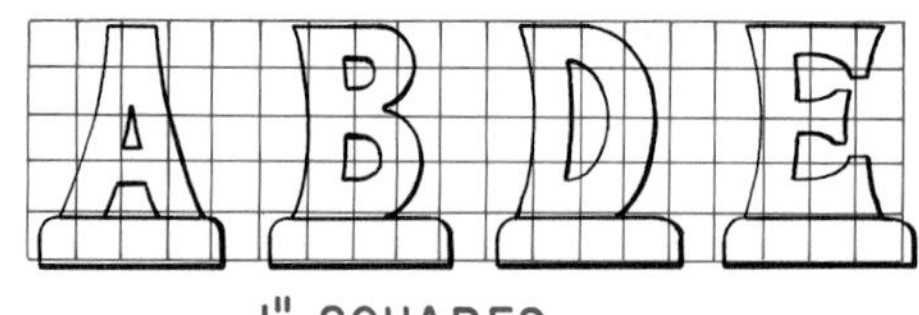

INITIAL BOOKENDS: You can design these large initial bookends. One end could be your first initial and the other could be the initial of your last name.

DACHSHUND TIE RACK: This project can be cut out with a coping saw or jigsaw. The rack can be made in the shape of a long bone. To give character to your dog, shape the eyes, ears, and tail with a gouge, or paint these marks on. Pine would be a good choice of wood.

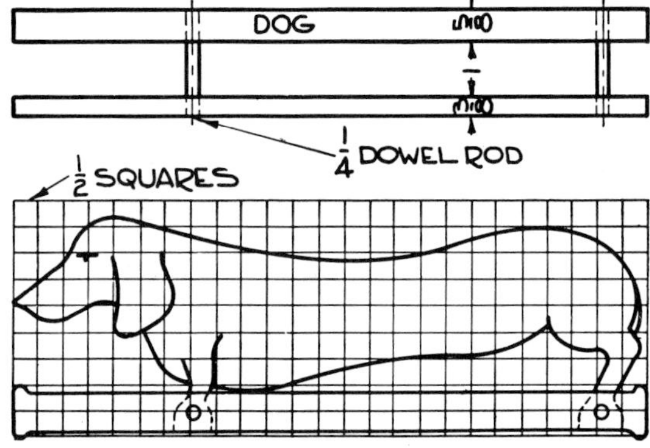

BUTLER TRAY: Here's a handy way to carry food and beverages. Use cabinet grade plywood for the tray board; hardwood for handles and edge strips. (Dremel)

BILL OF MATERIALS
(In inches, finished dimensions)

A	Tray board (1)	½″ × 13¾″ × 20″
B	Side handles (2)	¾″ × 3″ × 16½″
C	Edge strips (2)	⅜″ × 1¼″ × 20″
D	Brass screws (16)	#8 × 2″ Flathead
E	Plugs (16)	⅜″

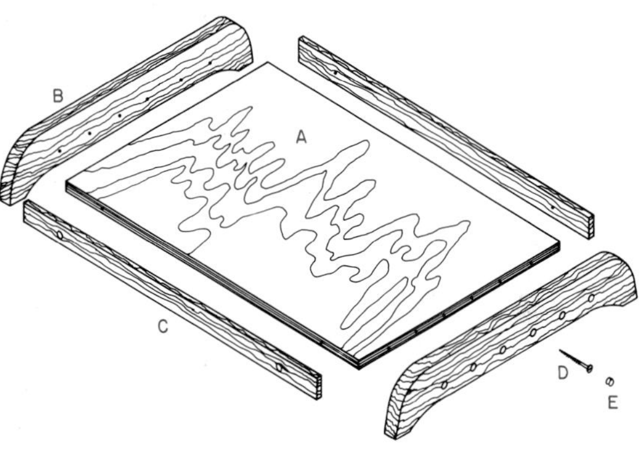

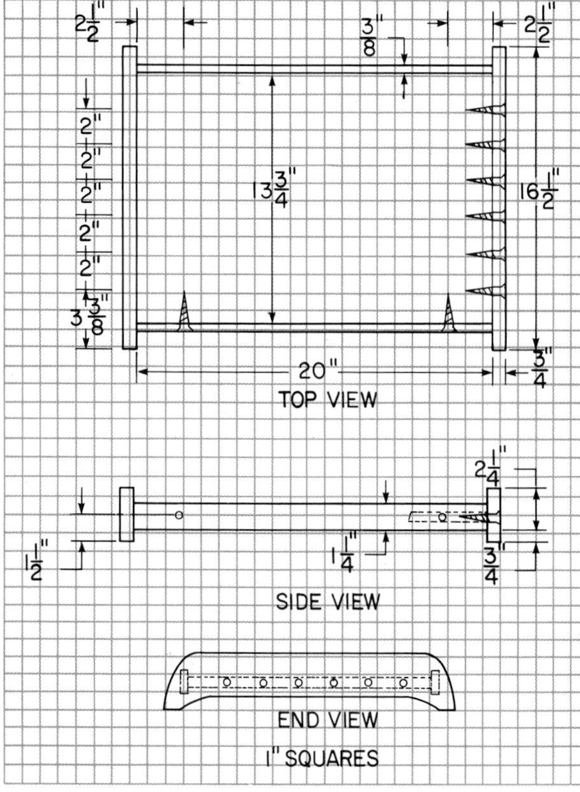

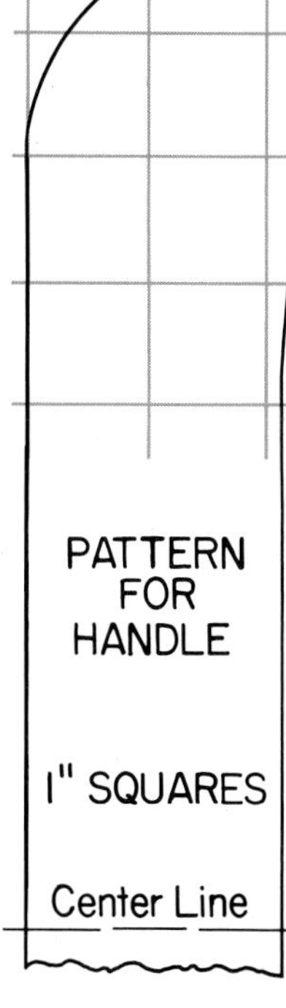

ENLARGE THIS PATTERN AND LAY OUT SHAPE OF HANDLES. (REVERSE FOR OPPOSITE HANDLE END.)

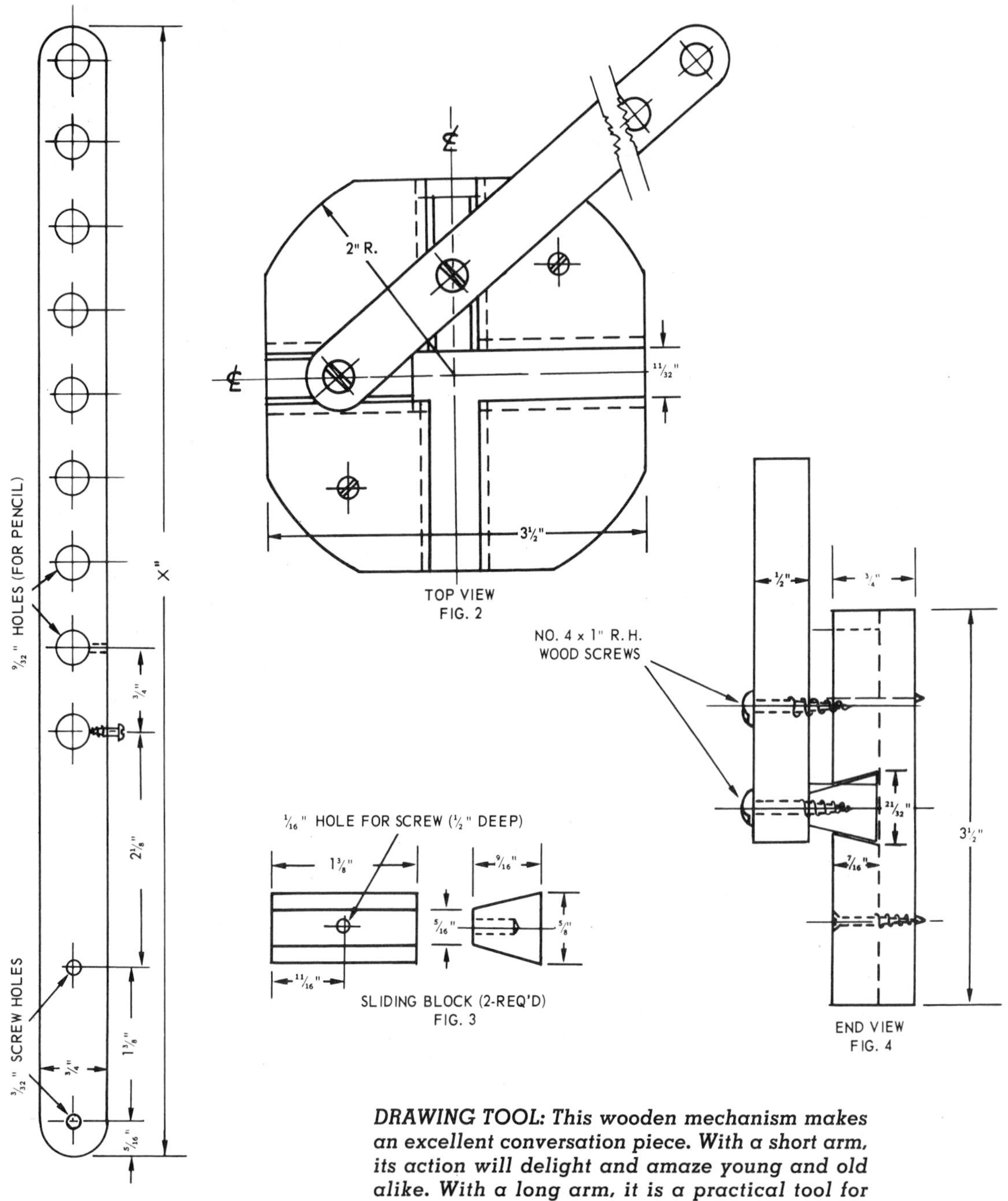

PENCIL ARM DETAILS
FIG. 1

TOP VIEW
FIG. 2

SLIDING BLOCK (2-REQ'D)
FIG. 3

END VIEW
FIG. 4

***DRAWING TOOL:** This wooden mechanism makes an excellent conversation piece. With a short arm, its action will delight and amaze young and old alike. With a long arm, it is a practical tool for drawing ellipses.*

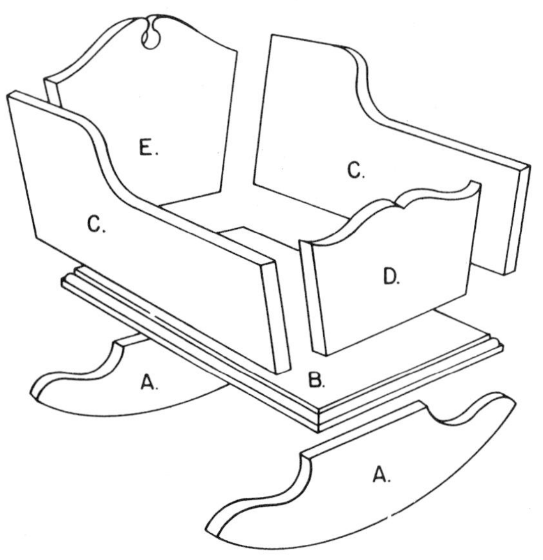

BILL OF MATERIALS (In inches, finished dimensions)		
A	Rockers (2)	3/4″ × 4″ × 18″
B	Bottom (1)	3/4″ × 11″ × 20″
C	Sides (2)	3/4″ × 8″ × 19″
D	Footboard (1)	3/4″ × 5 1/4″ × 10 1/4″
E	Headboard (1)	3/4″ × 10 1/4″ × 11 1/4″
	Flathead screws (6)	#10 × 1 1/2″

DOLL CRADLE: Pine would be a good choice of wood for this cradle. A color picture of the cradle is shown on page 4. (Shopsmith)

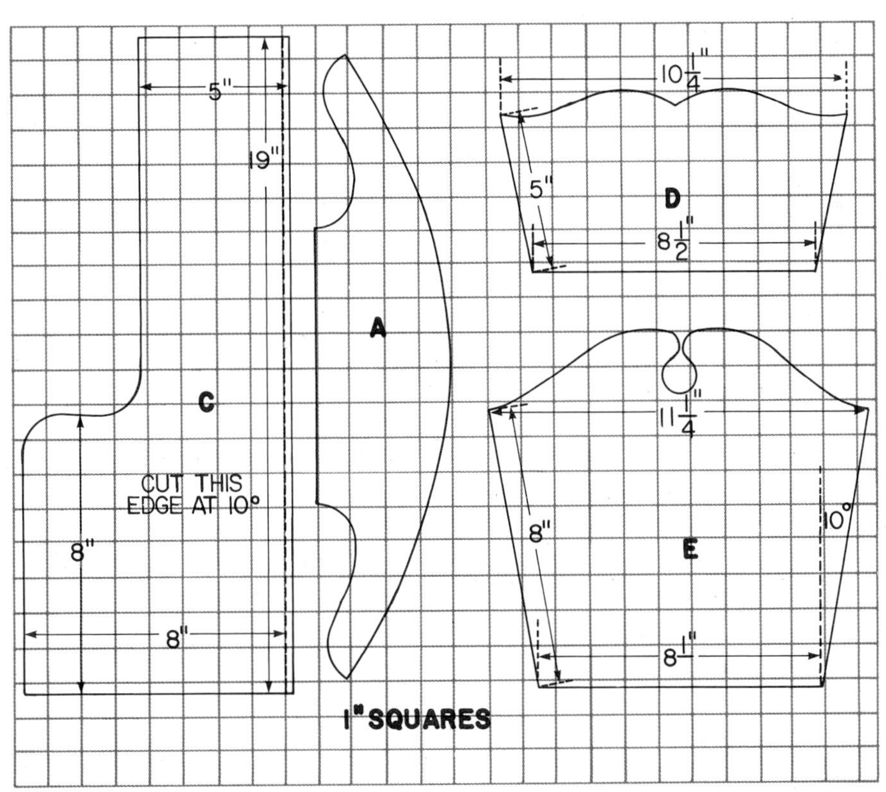

DESKTOP BOOKSHELF: *Keep books handy with this simple-to-build, adjustable book rack. It's a sturdy, useful organizer for desk top, kitchen counter, or workbench. (Shopsmith)*

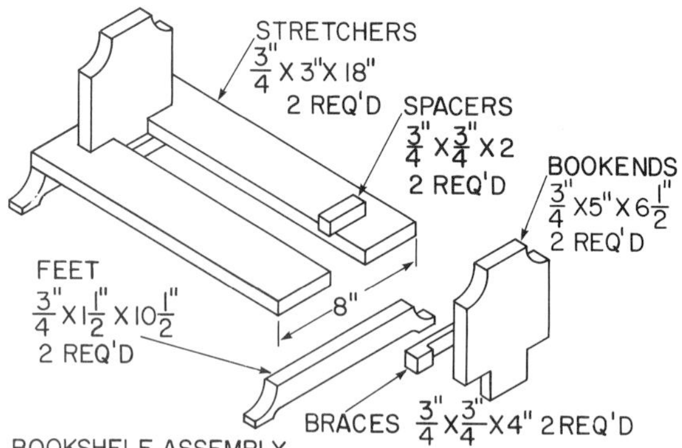

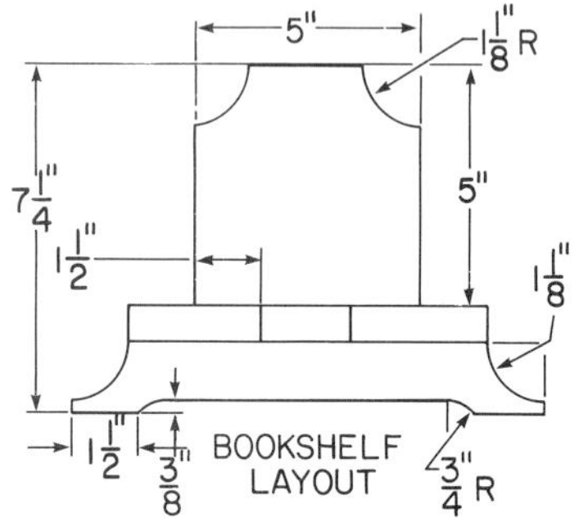

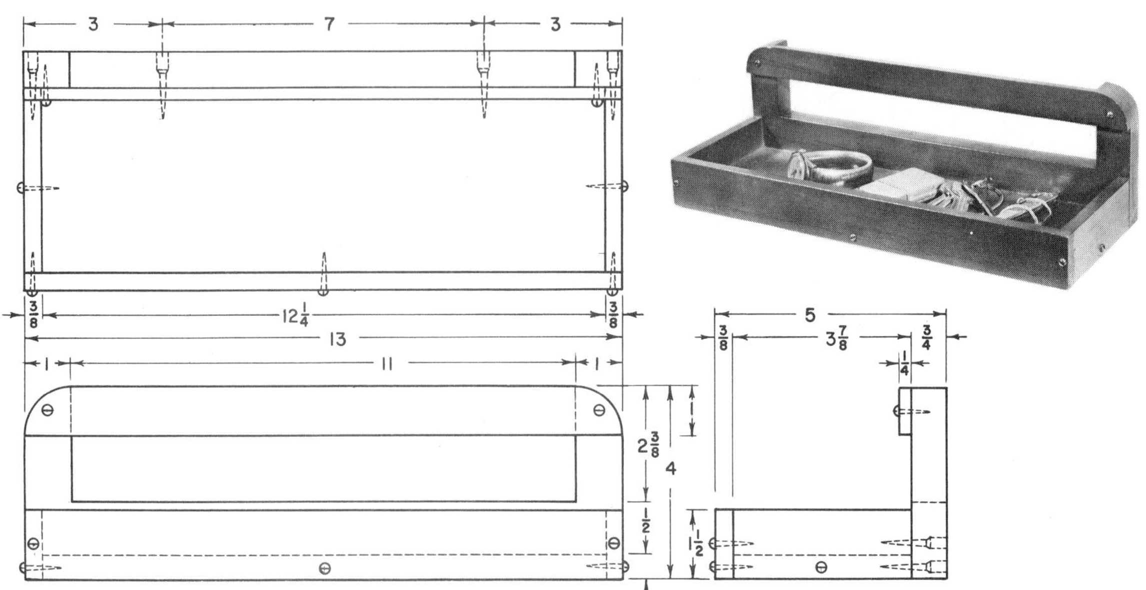

***ODDS-AND-ENDS HOLDER:** A good place to put all the "junk" you have in your pockets. You can fasten the holder to the wall or place it on a chest or dresser.*

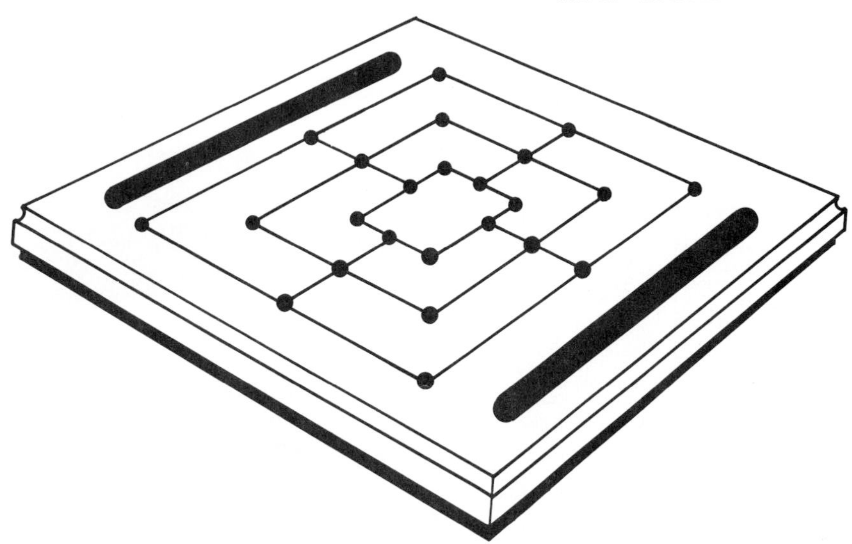

NINE MEN'S MORRIS: In this classic game, two players try to capture each other's marbles. To make the board, use a core box router bit mounted in a drill press to bore the holes. You'll need 18 marbles in two different colors for playing pieces.

RULES

To begin, players take turns placing one marble at a time on the board. A player who makes a mill (places three of his or her marbles in a row) can take one of the opponent's marbles off the board. A marble cannot be taken out of a mill unless no other marble is available. Captured marbles are "dead" for the rest of the game.

When all marbles have been placed, players take turns moving their marbles to try making mills. A marble can be moved only into an adjoining free space. Players may open their existing mills and reclose them on the next turn. The game ends when one player has only two marbles left or when one player has made it impossible for the other to move.

Variation: When one player is down to three marbles, he or she may hop to any free space on the board rather than move only to adjoining spaces.

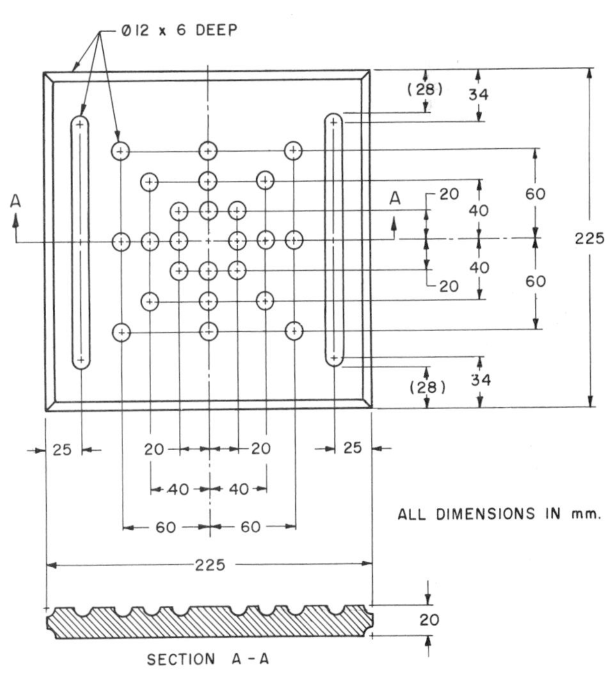

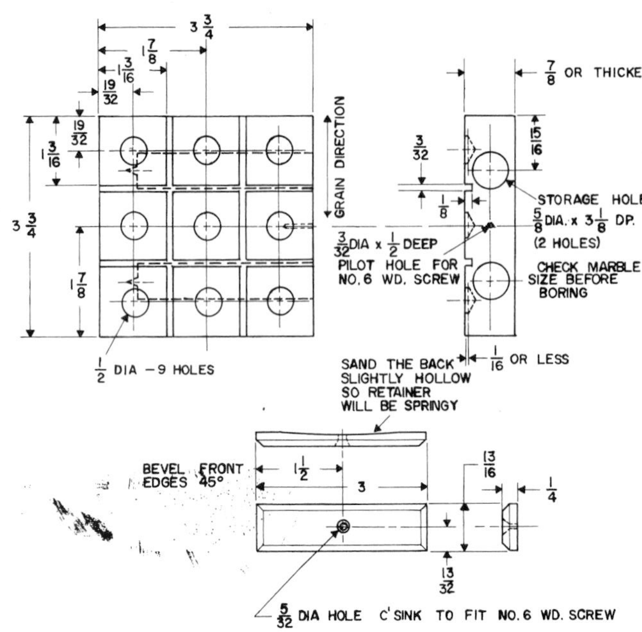

TICK-TACK-TOE: This is a game for two players. Each player uses a different color of marbles, five for each player. The object is to get three marbles of one color in a row (horizontally, vertically, or diagonally). The players alternate turns until all of the marbles have been played.

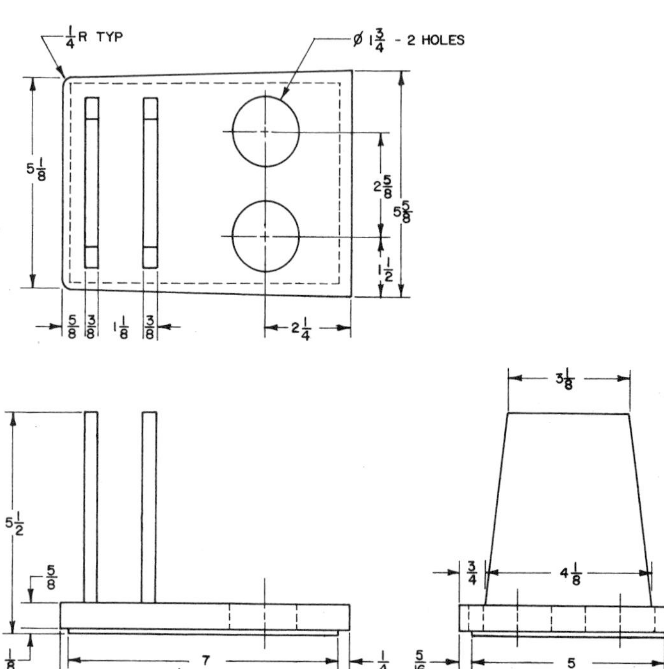

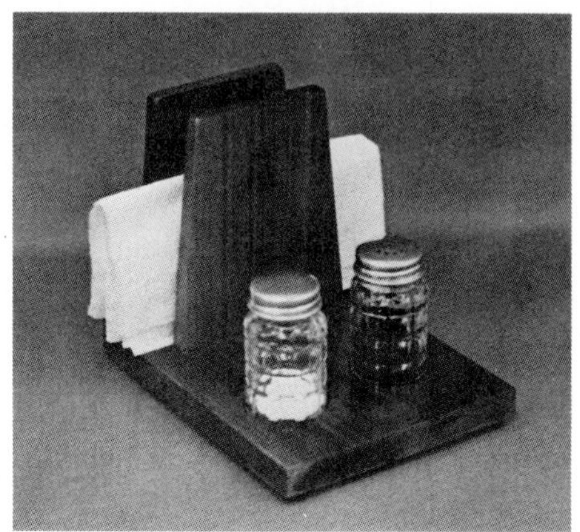

SALT-PEPPER-NAPKIN HOLDER: This project would make a good gift.

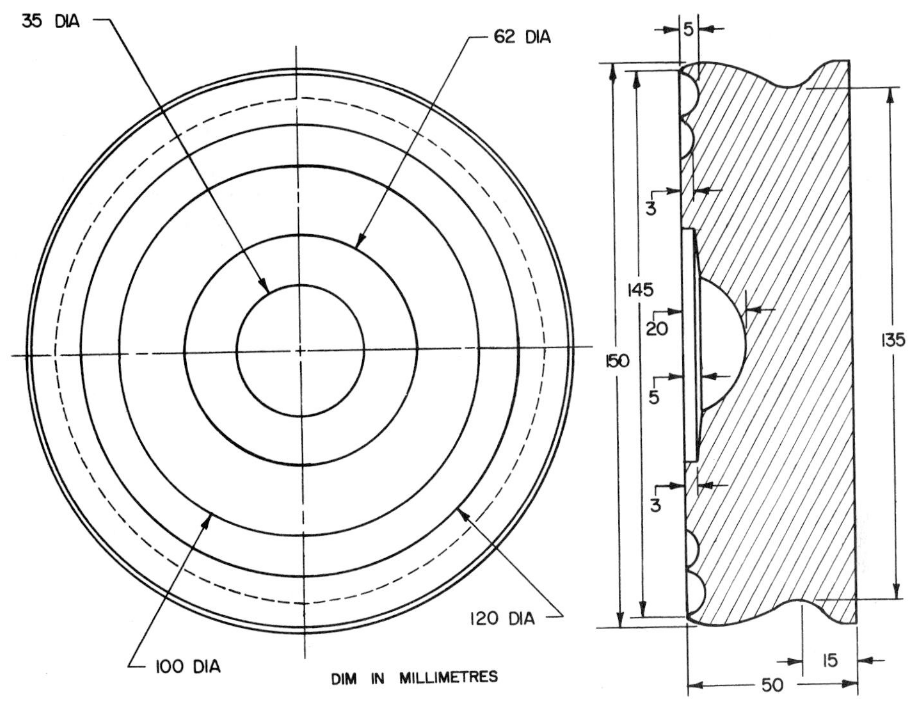

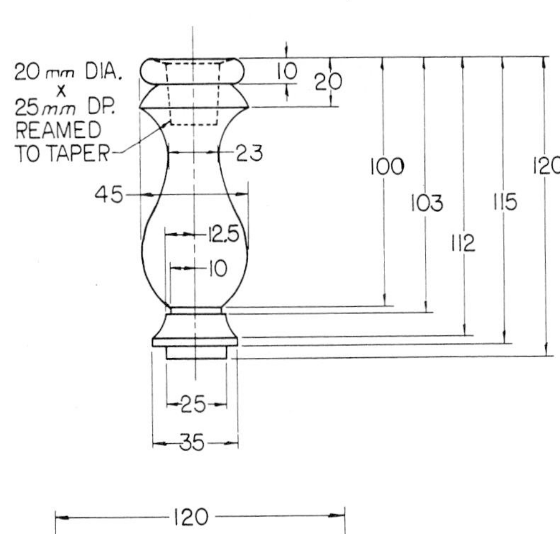

CANDLEHOLDERS: *Here are two designs with metric dimensions. This is a good way to learn to use the metric system.*

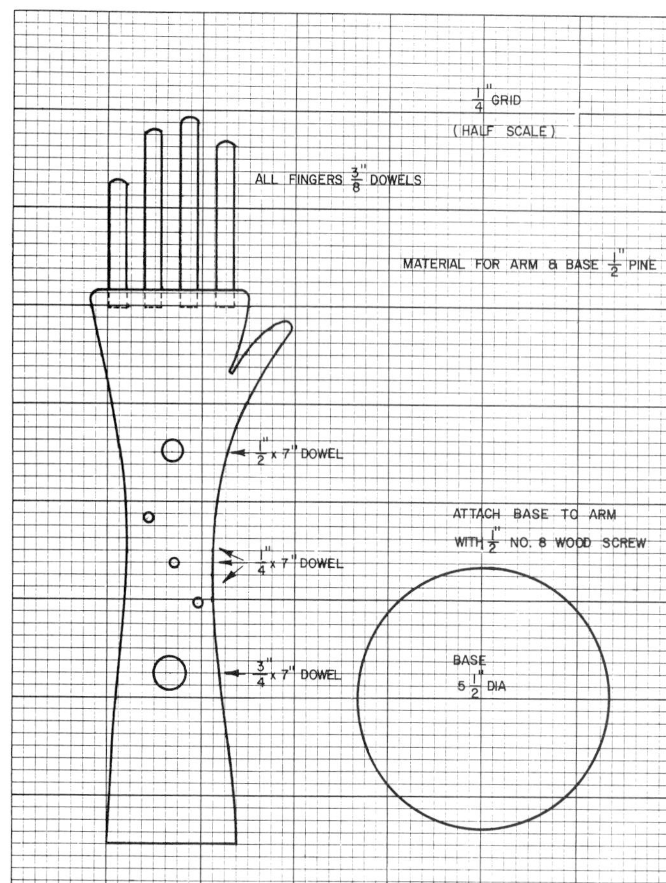

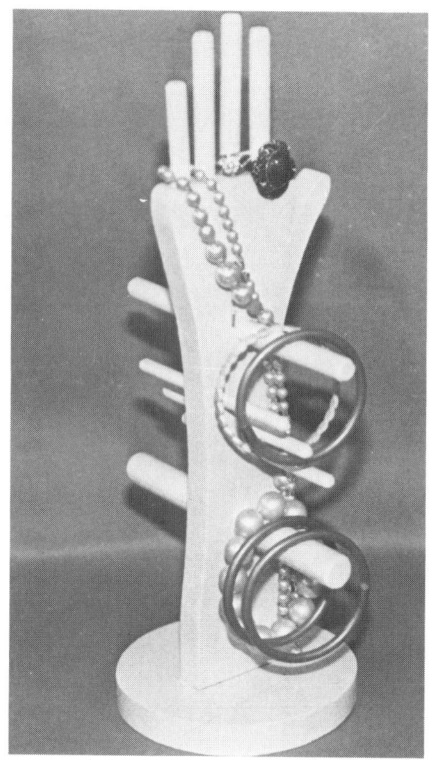

***JEWELRY HOLDER:** This is a clever design for holding all kinds of jewelry, including rings, bracelets, and necklaces.*

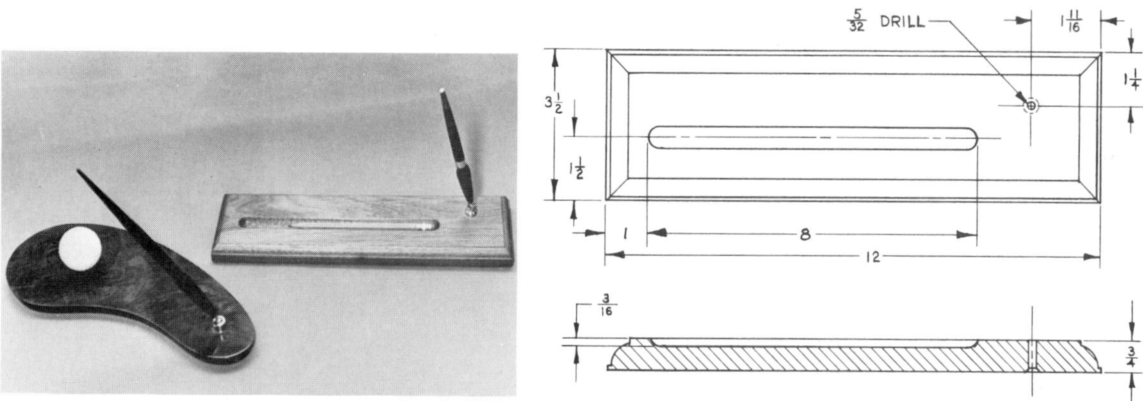

***PENHOLDERS:** Two different designs for penholders. The one on the right has a slot for a pencil. This design gives you good experience in using hand tools, squaring up a board, and decorating edges with a router. The penholder on the left is a free-form design with space for adding a personal touch, such as a ball for a golfer.*

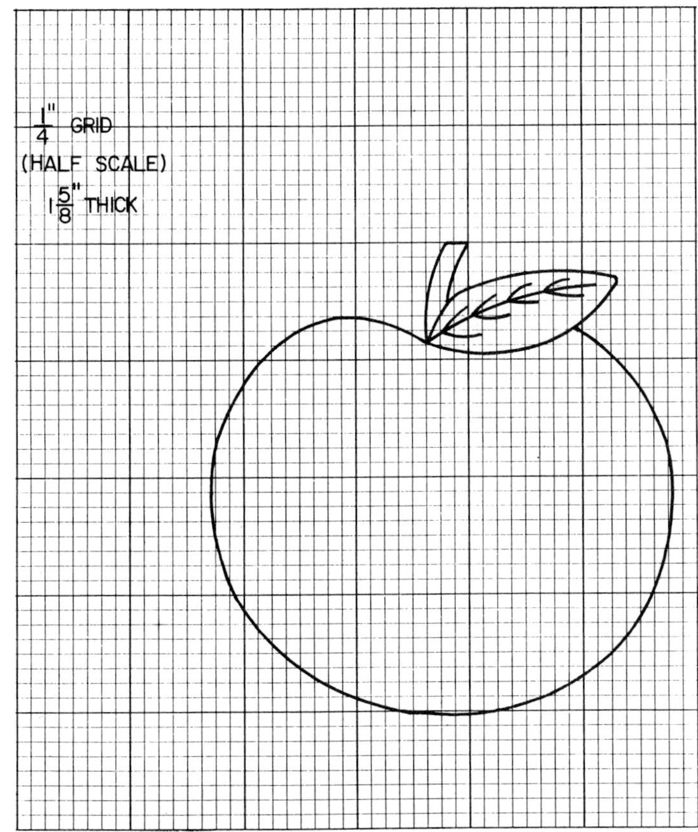

APPLE-SHAPED CUTTING BOARD: This cutting board is thick and sturdy.

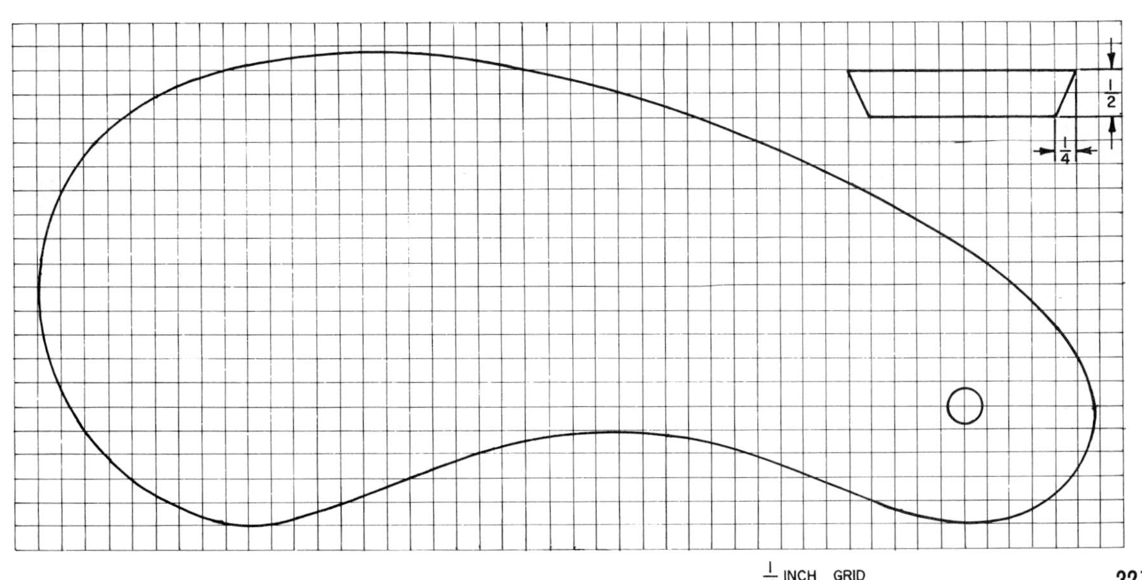

$\frac{1}{4}$ INCH GRID

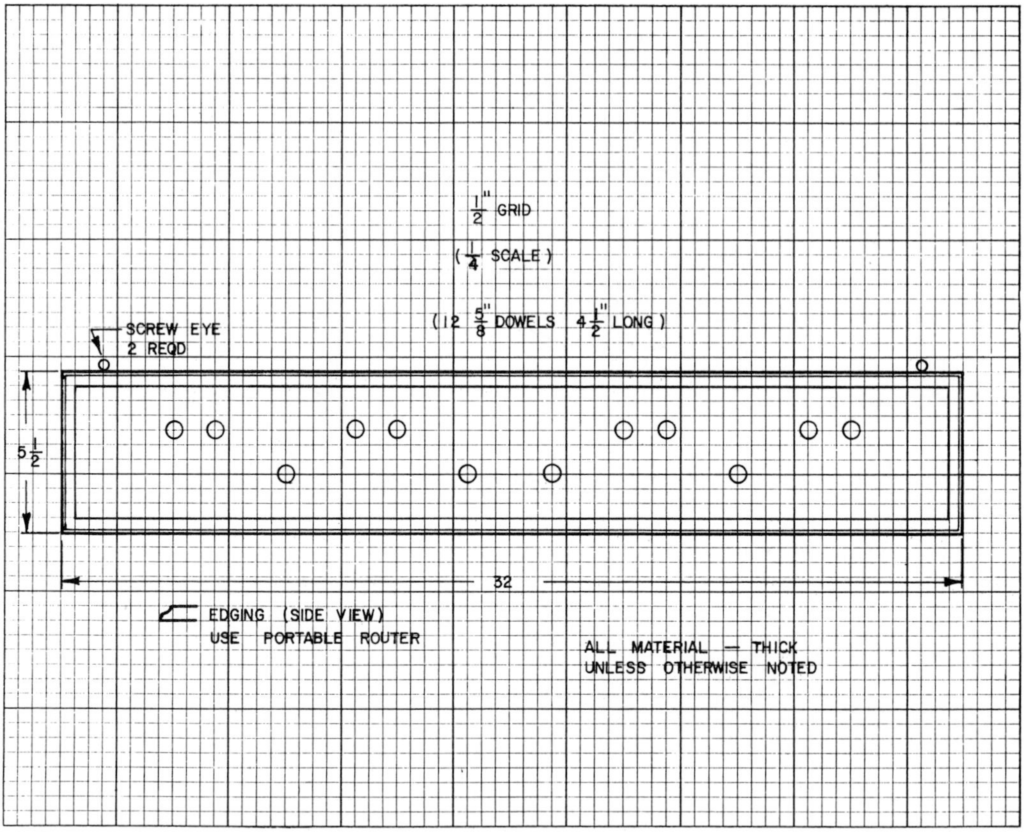

$\frac{1}{2}$" GRID

($\frac{1}{4}$ SCALE)

(12 $\frac{5}{8}$" DOWELS 4 $\frac{1}{2}$" LONG)

SCREW EYE
2 REQD

5 $\frac{1}{2}$

32

EDGING (SIDE VIEW)
USE PORTABLE ROUTER

ALL MATERIAL — THICK
UNLESS OTHERWISE NOTED

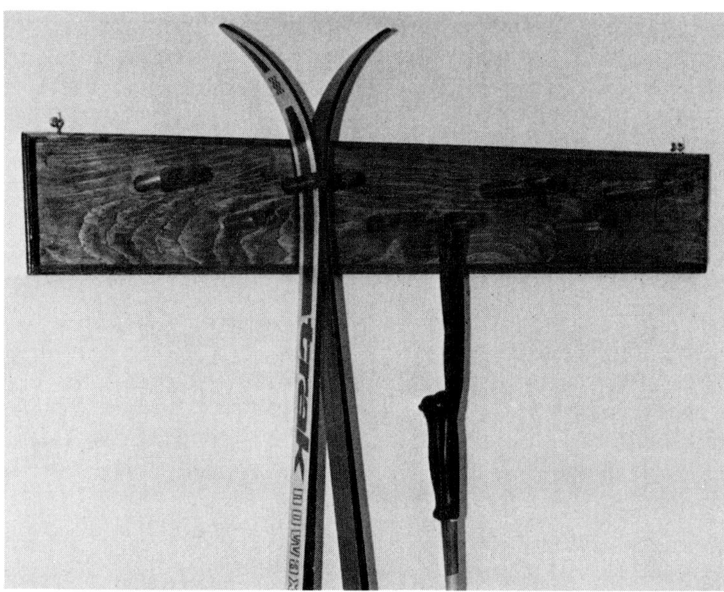

***SKI RACK:** This ski rack is designed for four sets of skis and poles. It could also be used to hold two sets of skis and poles plus two pairs of ski boots.*

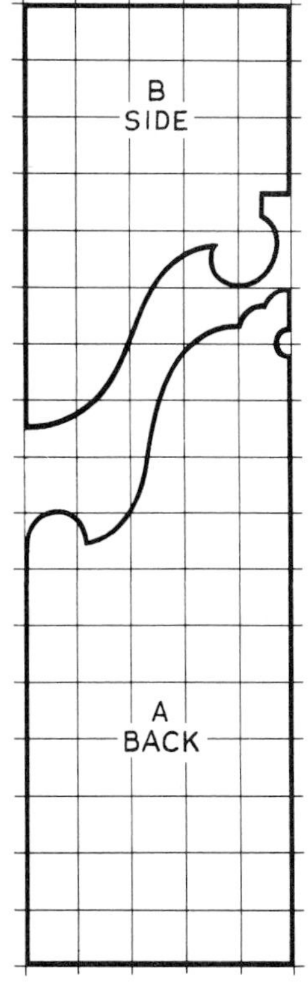

WALL BOX: This project can be hung on the wall to provide a place to show off a treasured piece of china. It can be made of ½" plywood or solid wood in any size you want.

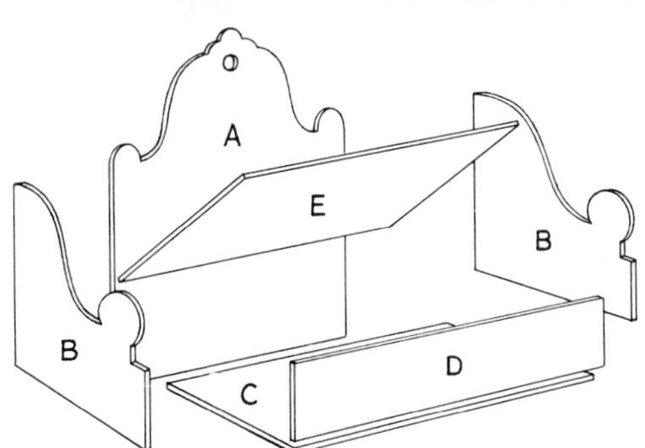

PENCIL HOLDER: This one-piece pen and pencil holder is easy to make.

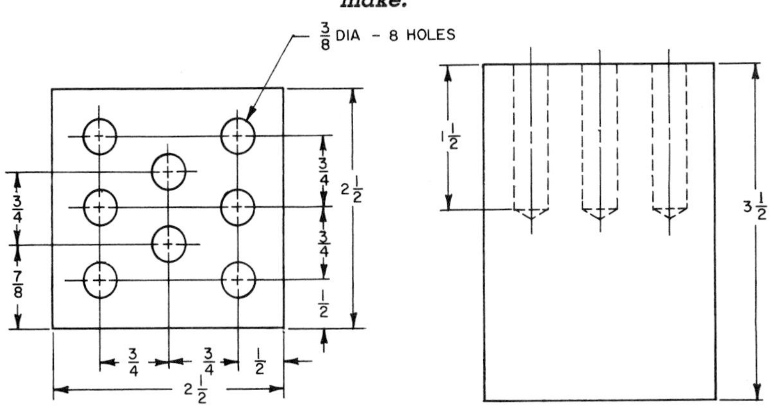

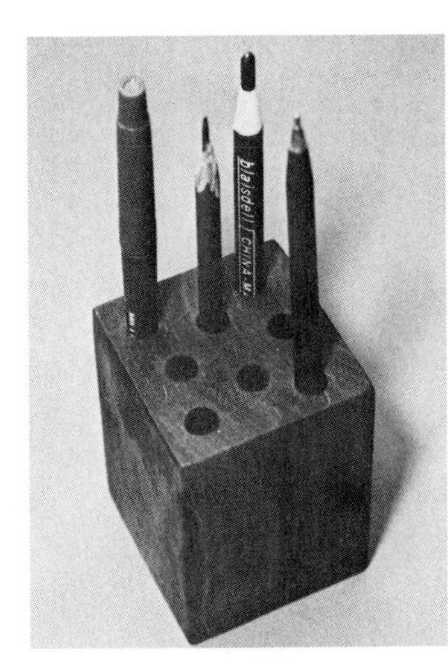

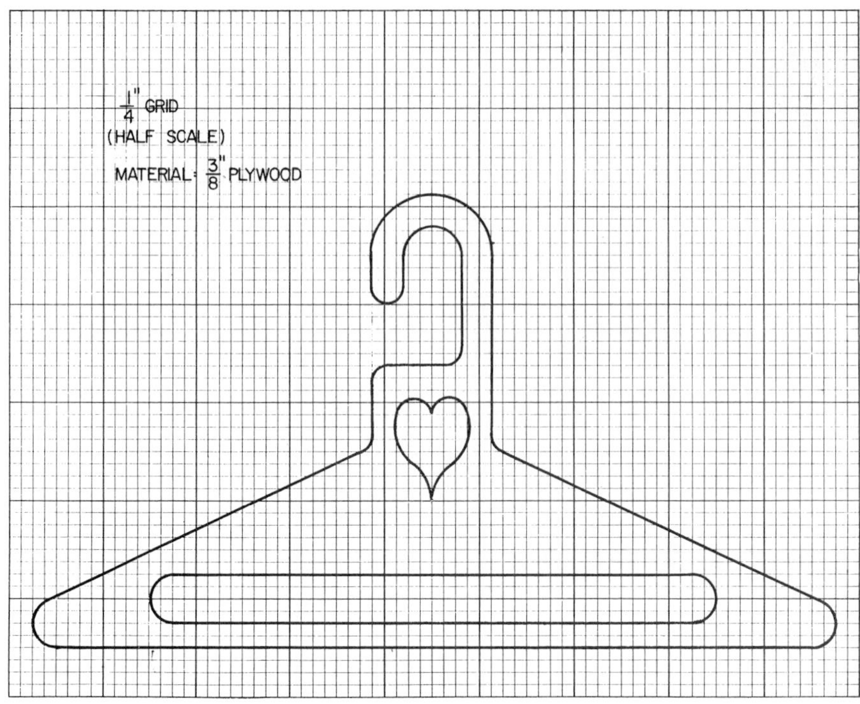

TOYS: Wooden toys are popular and fun to make. Plans are given here for the airplane and for the rabbit puzzle. You could also design your own puzzle using any simple shape. (Shopsmith)

BILL OF MATERIALS FOR AIRPLANE
(In inches, finished dimensions)

A	Fuselage Sides (2)	12″ × 3½″ × ¾″
B	Vertical Stabilizer	13½″ × 6½″ × ¾″
C	Horizontal Stabilizers (2)	4⅜″ × 4⅛″ × ¾″
D	Top Wing	14″ × 4″ × ¾″
E	Bottom Wing	14″ × 3½″ × ¾″
F	Wing Struts (4)	6½″ × ⅜″ dia.
G	Cowling	¾″ × 3½″ dia.
H	Propeller	6″ × 1⅜″ × ½″
I	Pivot	2½″ × ⅜″ dia.
J	Keeper	½″ × 1″ dia.
K	Landing Struts (2)	2½″ × 1″ dia.
L	Axle	4¾″ × ⅜″ dia.
M	Wheels	¾″ × 1¾″ dia.

***HANGER:** This clothes hanger made of plywood adds a touch of class to your closet.*

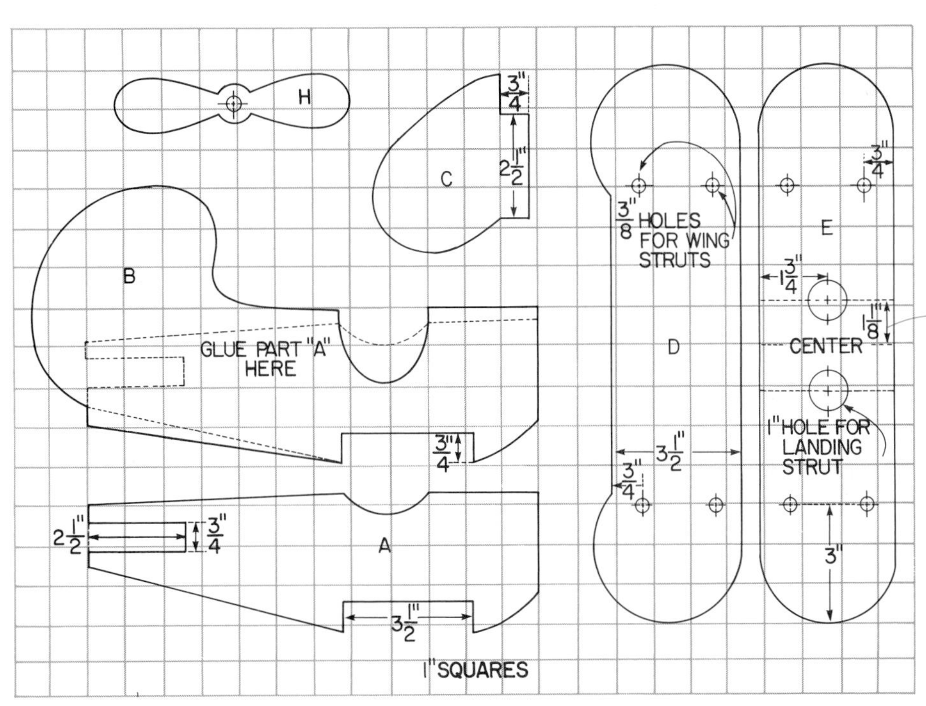

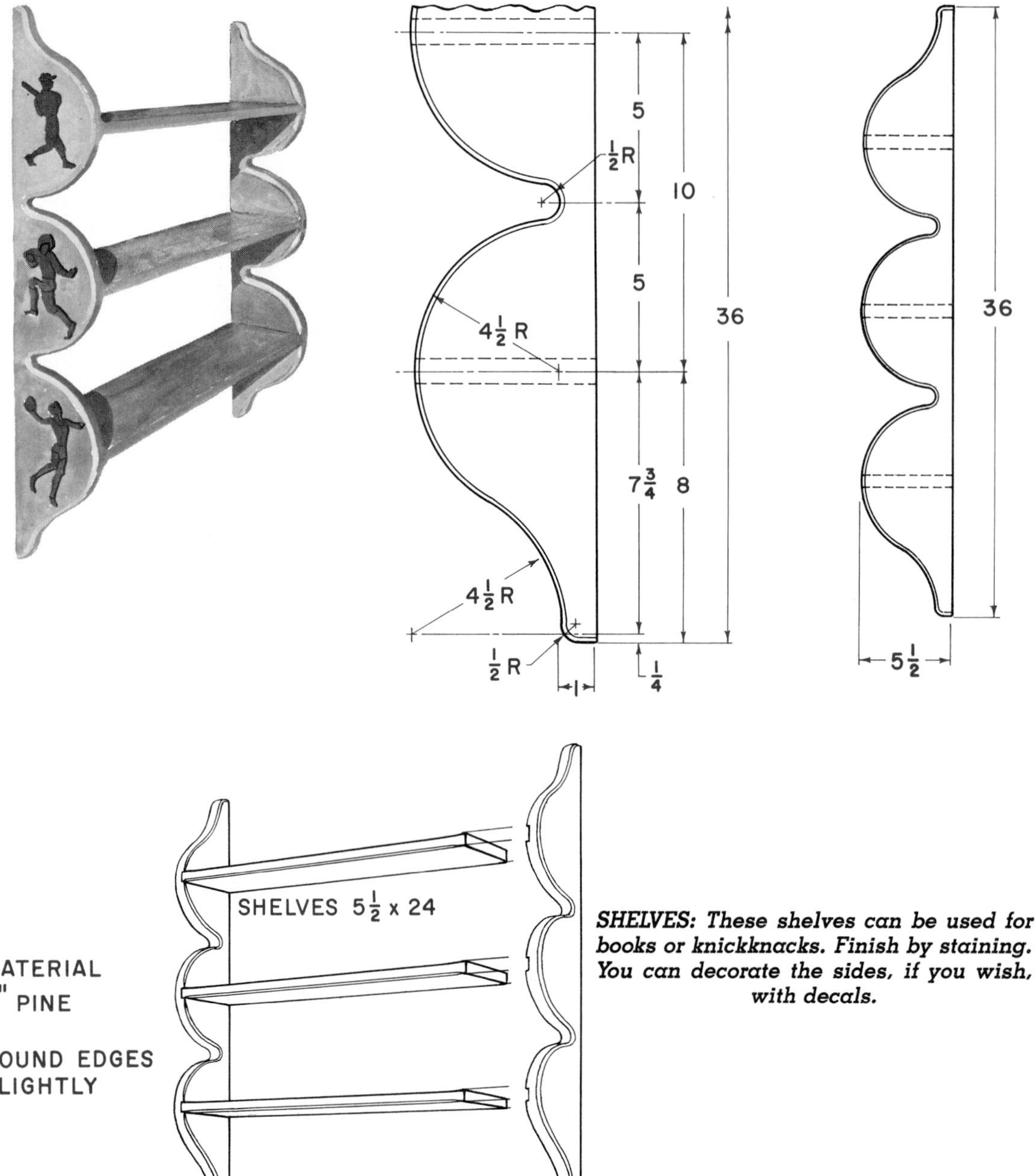

SHELVES: *These shelves can be used for books or knickknacks. Finish by staining. You can decorate the sides, if you wish, with decals.*

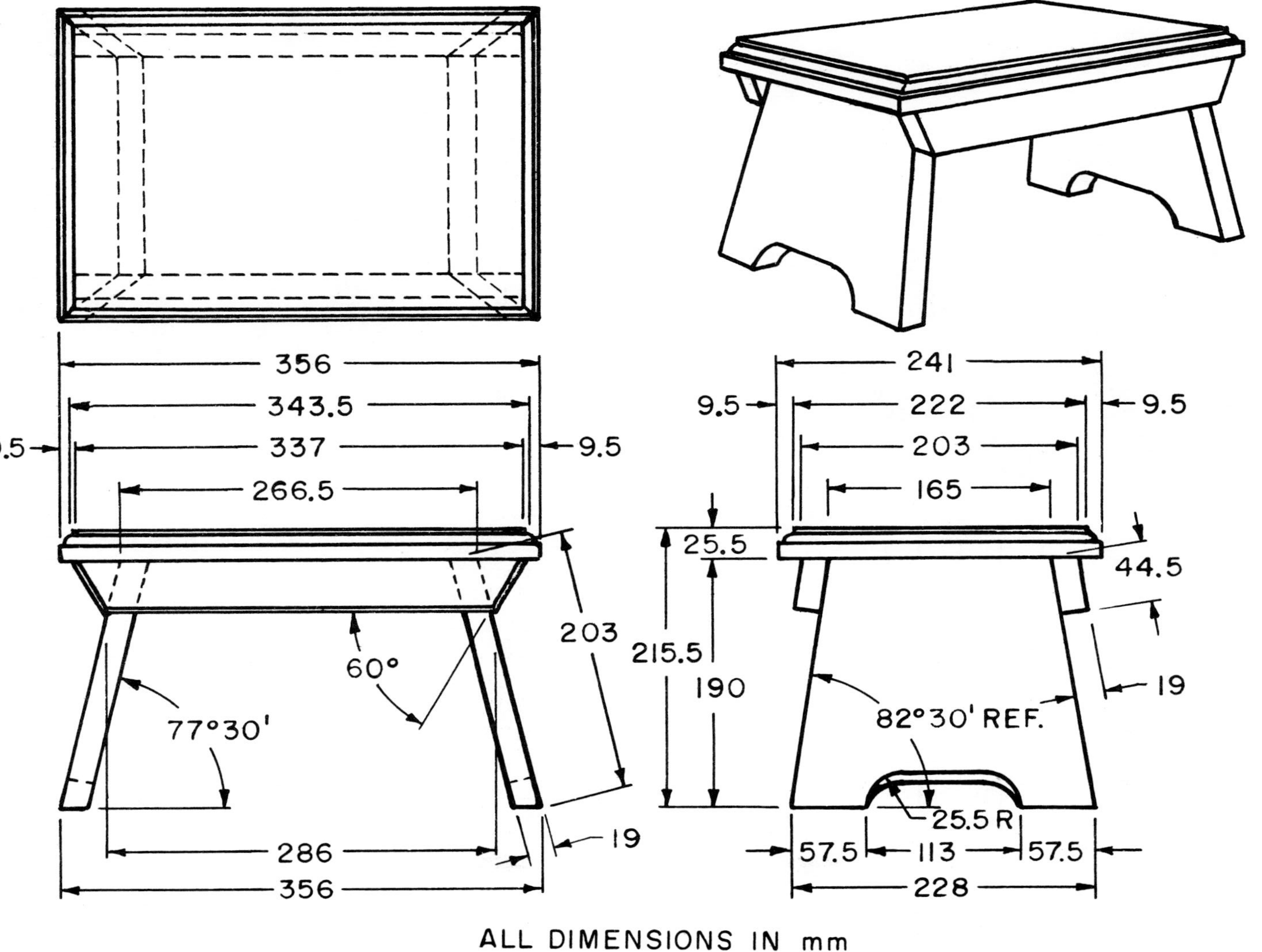

FOOTSTOOL: A good footstool is a useful addition to any home.

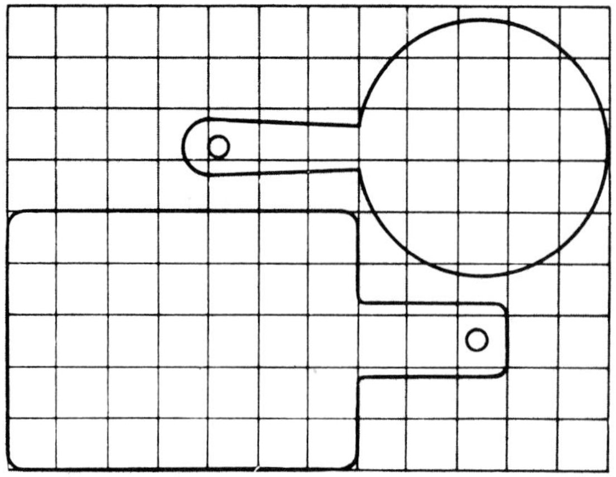

CUTTING BOARDS AND SERVING PADDLES: These are useful when cutting food or serving snacks.

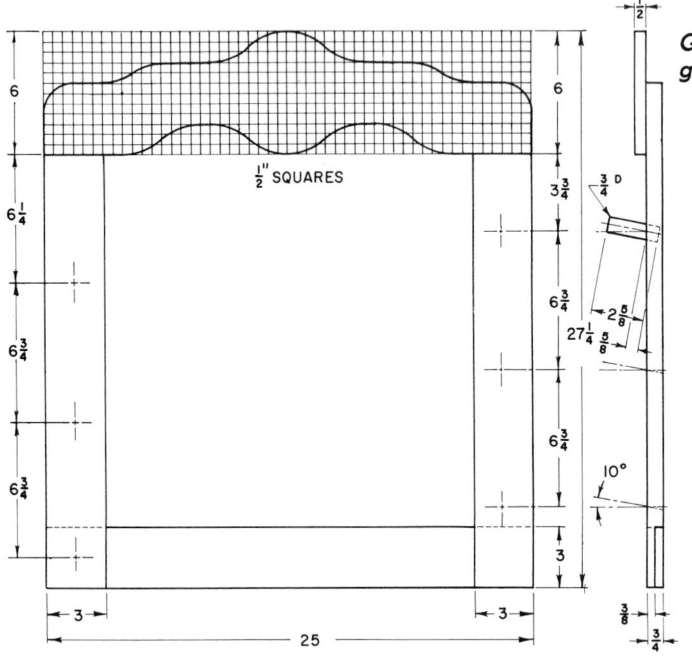

GUN RACK: This is a very simple gun rack that will hold real or toy guns.

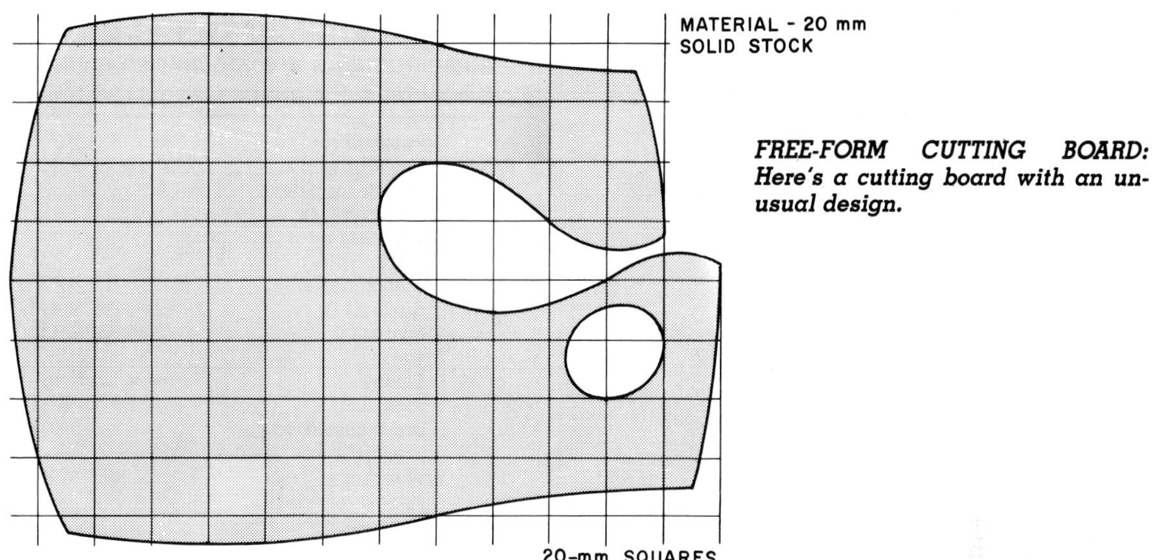

FREE-FORM CUTTING BOARD: Here's a cutting board with an unusual design.

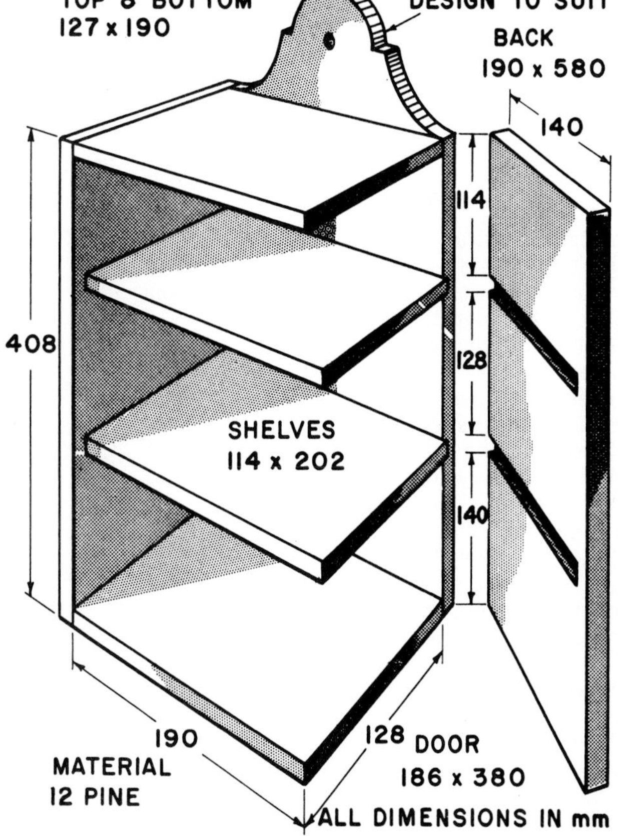

SHELF: Drawing for a shelf using metric measurements only.

***KITCHEN TOOLS & RACK:** Wooden utensils are attractive and will not conduct heat or scratch cooking pots or china. Shown here are a pasta sizer, pasta pick-up, flipper, tongs, spatula, and stirring spoon. (Dremel)*

BILL OF MATERIALS
Measurements are for blank shapes.
See drawings for shapes and proportions.

A	Pasta sizer (1)	⅜″ × 3″ × 10⅜″
B	Pasta pick-up (1)	⅝″ × 1¾″ × 13¼″
	Dowels for pick-up	
	¼″ × 1⅞″ (4)	
	¼″ × 2″ (4)	
	¼″ × 2¼″ (2)	
C	Stirring spoon (1)	¾″ × 2″ × 12¼″
D	Spatula (1)	½″ × 1⅝″ × 12¼″
E	Flipper (1)	¾″ × 1¾″ × 11″
F	Tongs	
	Blades (2)	5/32″ × ¾″ × 13¾″
	Wedge (1)	9/16″ × 1″ × 3½″
	Brass escutcheon pins (6)	½″
G	Wall rack (1)	¾″ × 4½″ × 19½″
	Hanger dowels (9)	¼″ × 2⅜″
	Brass roundhead screws (2)	#12 × 2
	Waterproof glue	

TIPS

1. For the **pasta sizer,** you may want to experiment with holes cut in cardboard to determine which sizes best fit your needs. Generally, a 1¼″ hole would hold enough uncooked spaghetti for two adults.
2. For the **pasta pick-up,** drill the dowel holes ¼″ deep. Glue and insert the precut dowels so that the longest ones are in the middle and the shortest are at the ends. This will give the utensil a convex profile to match the contour of a pot or bowl.
3. It is not necessary to carve a thin lip on the **stirring spoon.** A solid-edged lip will give best results.
4. After shaping the **spatula,** use a sander to create a knife edge, but be careful not to make it too thin.
5. Make the curved profile of the **flipper** by removing wood from underneath the handle area and from above the flipper area, as shown in the drawing.
6. For the **tongs,** use glue and escutcheon pins to fasten the wedge piece to the tong blades. Do one side at a time.
7. After final sanding, use a finish approved for use in contact with food, such as "salad bowl finish" or light mineral oil.
8. Clean the utensils in hot soapy water. Do not soak them or put them in a dishwasher.

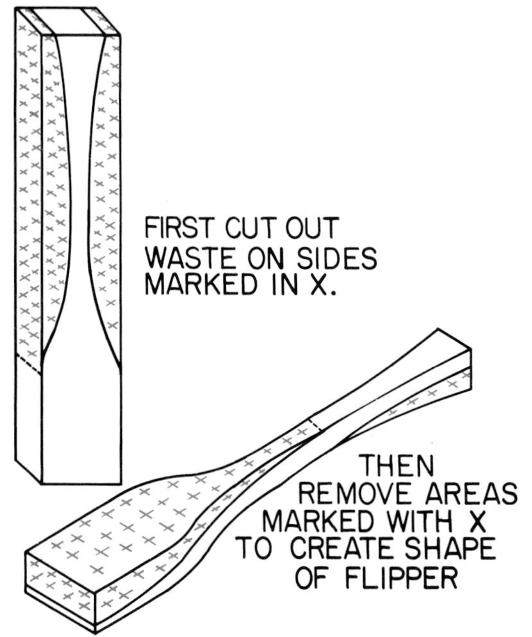

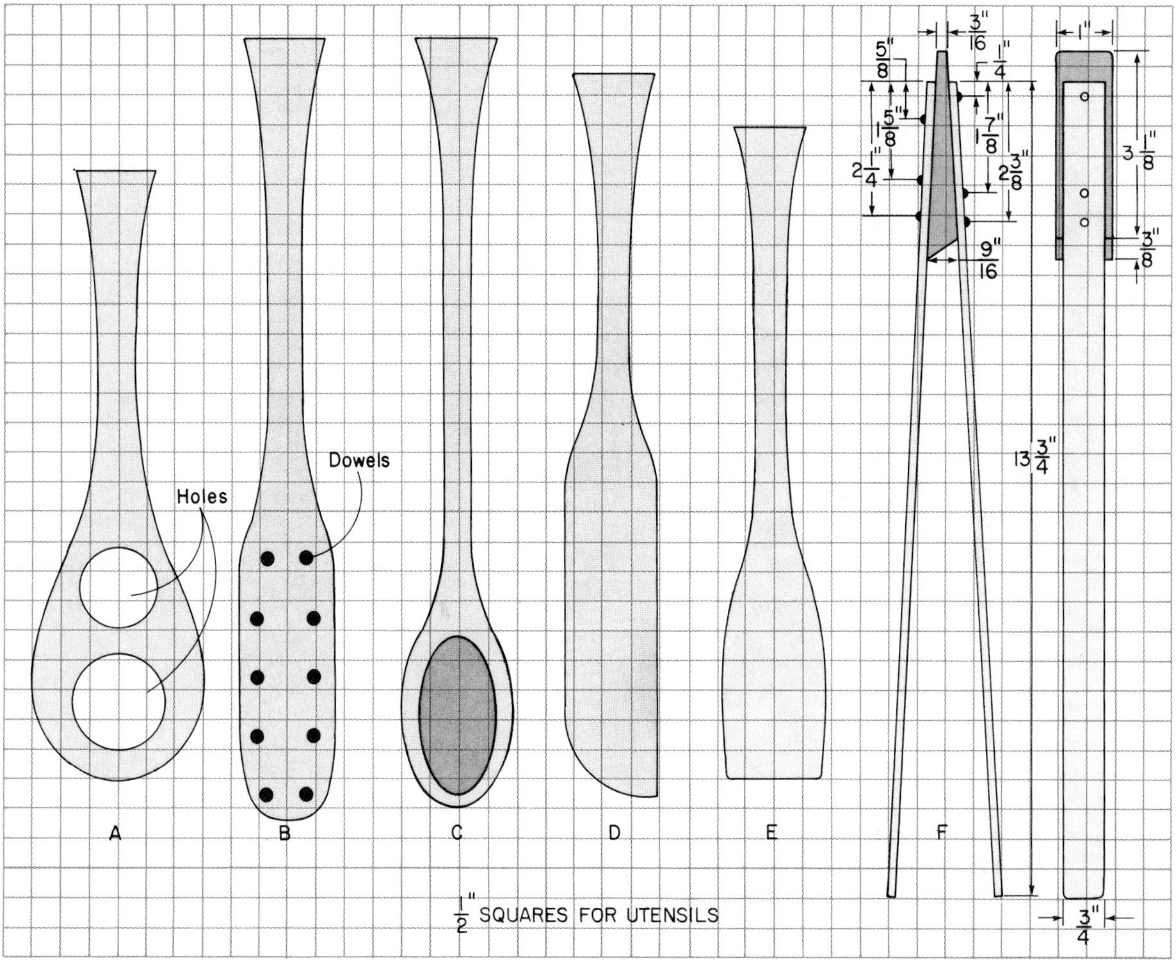

Holes
Dowels
A
B
C
D
E
F
5/8"
3/16"
1/4"
1 5/8"
1 7/8"
2 1/4"
2 3/8"
9/16"
13 3/4"
1"
3 1/8"
3/8"
3/4"
1/2" SQUARES FOR UTENSILS

1" SQUARES FOR WALL RACK
19 1/2"
4"
5/8"
3/4"
2 1/2"
2"
3/4"
1"
1 1/2"
Screw Holes
7/8"
1 1/8"
2"
2 1/2"
17"
Front View
4 1/2"
2"
3/4"
Side View

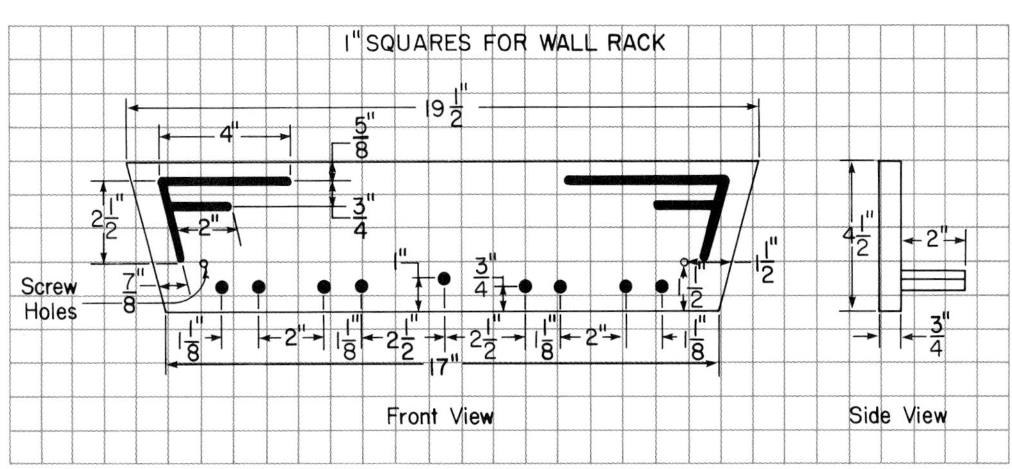

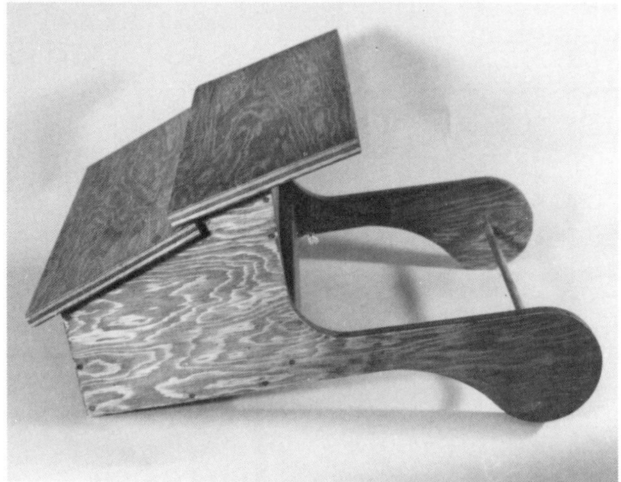

BIRD FEEDER: This bird feeder will turn on its support. Make it of exterior plywood and apply a coat of nontoxic wood preservative.

DIMENSIONS IN mm

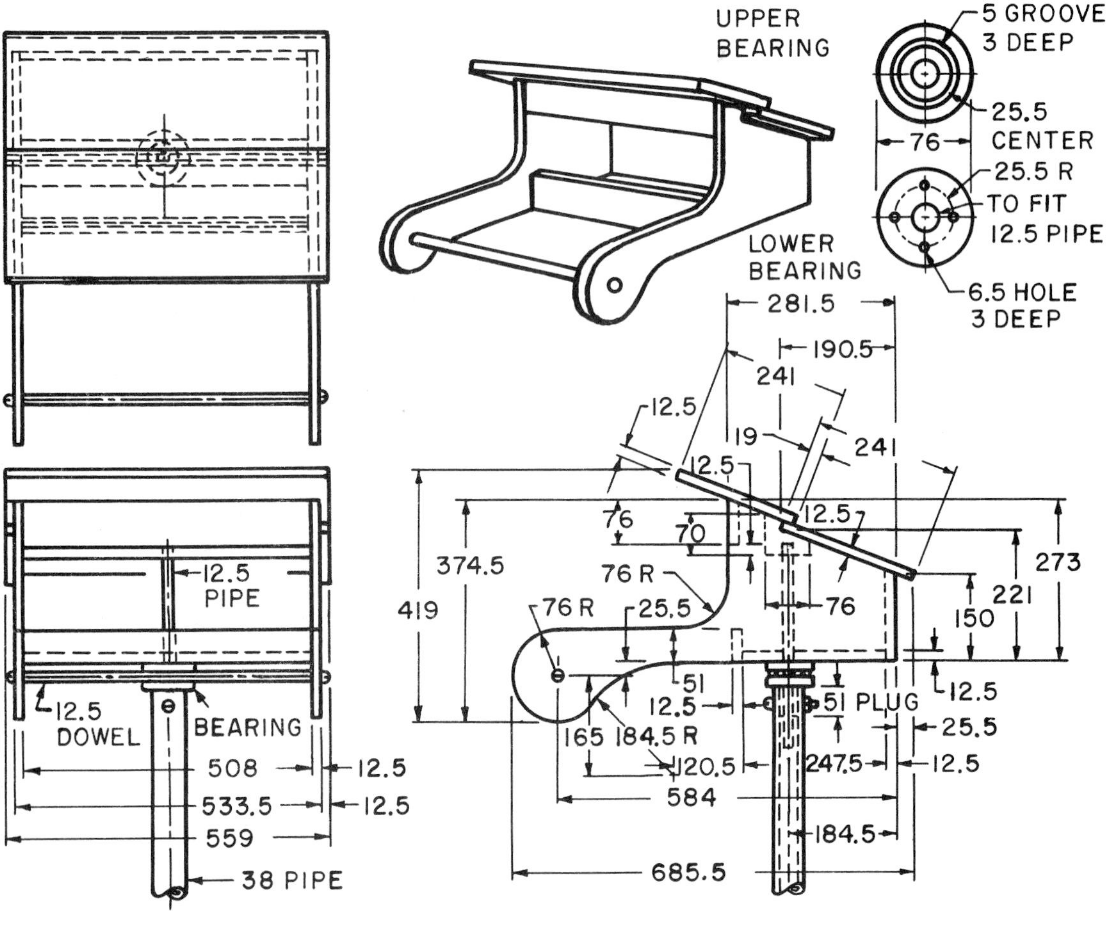

UPPER BEARING
5 GROOVE 3 DEEP
25.5 CENTER
76
25.5 R
TO FIT 12.5 PIPE
6.5 HOLE 3 DEEP
LOWER BEARING
281.5
190.5
241
12.5
19
241
12.5
12.5
76
70
374.5
419
76 R
76 R
25.5
76
273
221
150
12.5 PIPE
12.5 DOWEL
BEARING
51
12.5
51 PLUG
12.5
25.5
165
184.5 R
120.5
247.5
12.5
508
12.5
533.5
12.5
559
584
184.5
685.5
38 PIPE

ROBIN SHELTER: This shelter is made of 13-mm (½") cypress or redwood. It can be used as a bird feeder. Finish the shelter with two coats of brown stain.

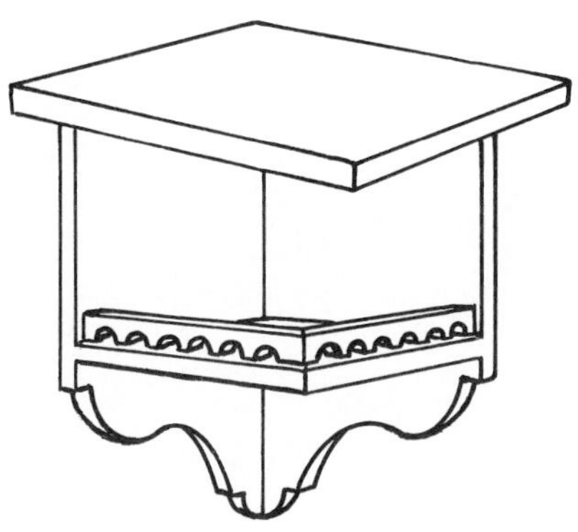

PERSPECTIVE VIEW

ROBIN SHELTER
ALL MATERIAL 13 THICK
ALL DIMENSIONS IN mm

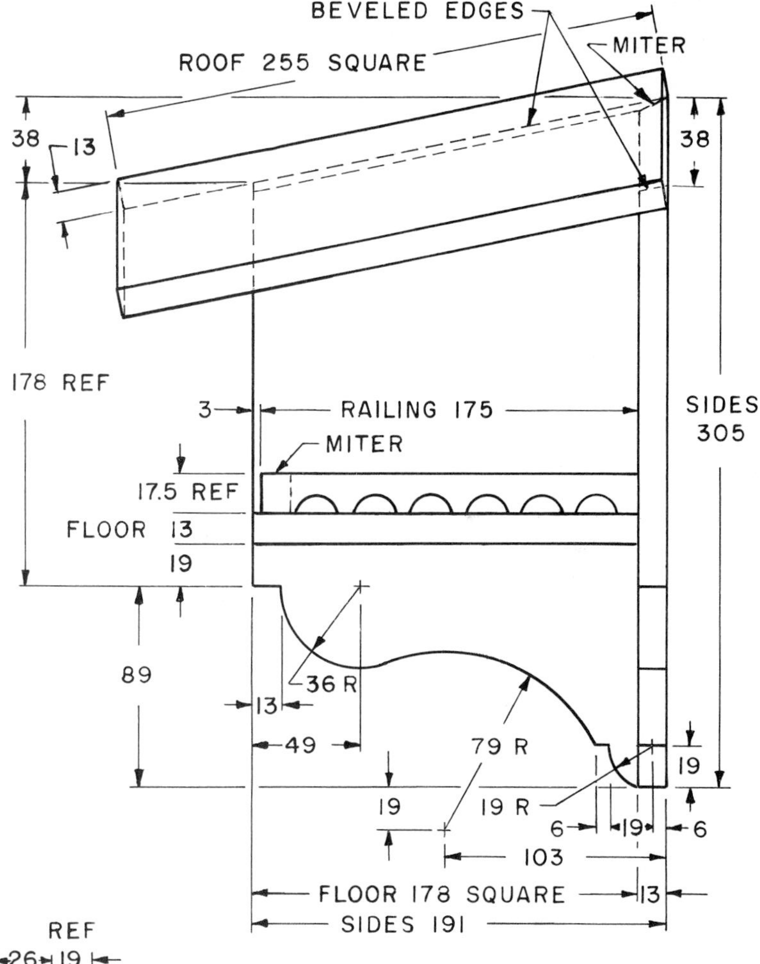

RAILING

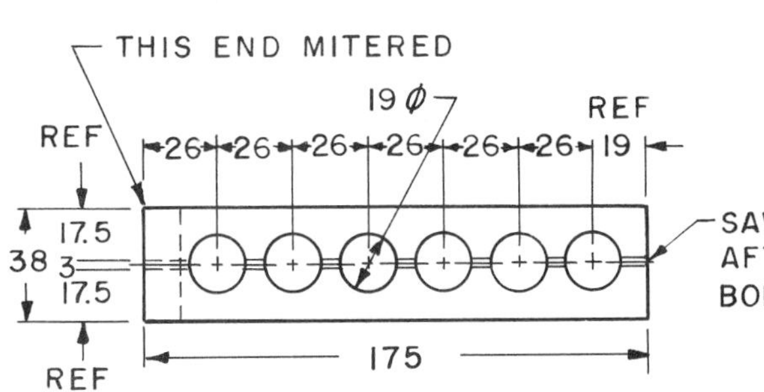

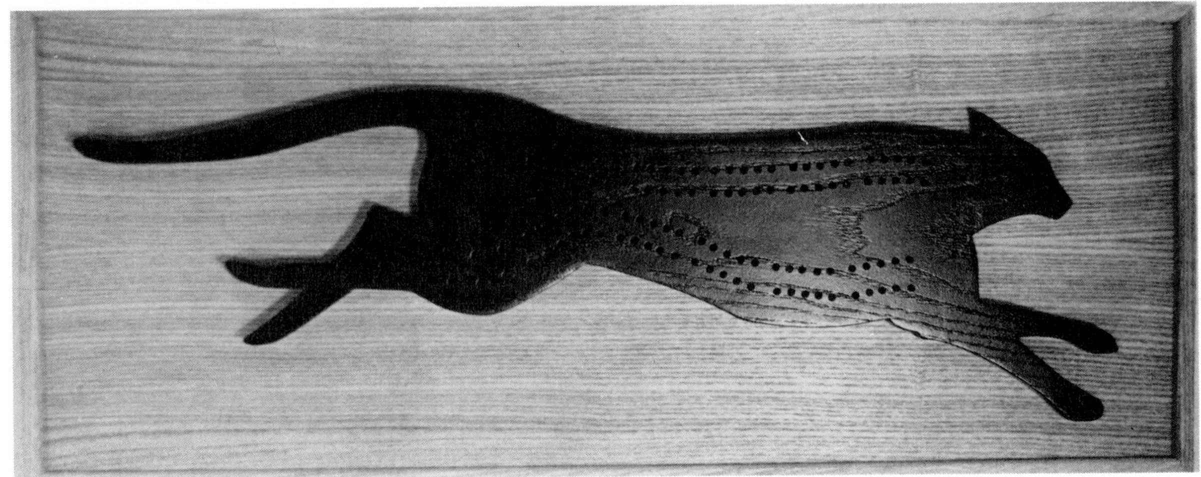

CRIBBAGE BOARD: This board is designed to be hung on the wall when not in use. For the frame, use a hardwood. Select a matching veneer plywood for the panel. The leopard can be made out of any solid hardwood. For contrast, you may want to stain or paint the leopard before gluing it to the panel. Instead of a leopard, consider other designs, such as the ones shown below. (Dremel)

BILL OF MATERIALS
(In inches, finished dimensions)

Frame sides (2)	5⁄16″ × 1″ × 8⅜″
Frame top (1)	5⁄16″ × 1″ × 21″
Frame bottom (1)	5⁄16″ × 1″ × 21″
Panel (1)	¼″ × 8″ × 20⅝″
Leopard (1)	½″ × 6″ × 19″
Pegs (4)	⅛″ dia. dowels × 1¼″

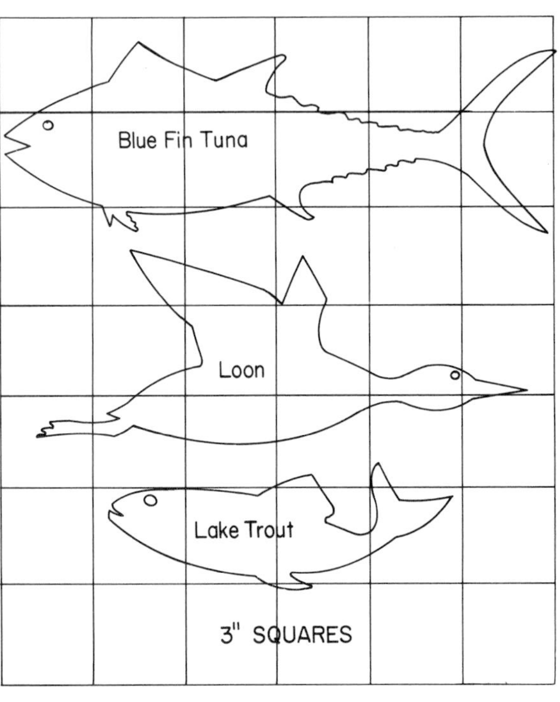

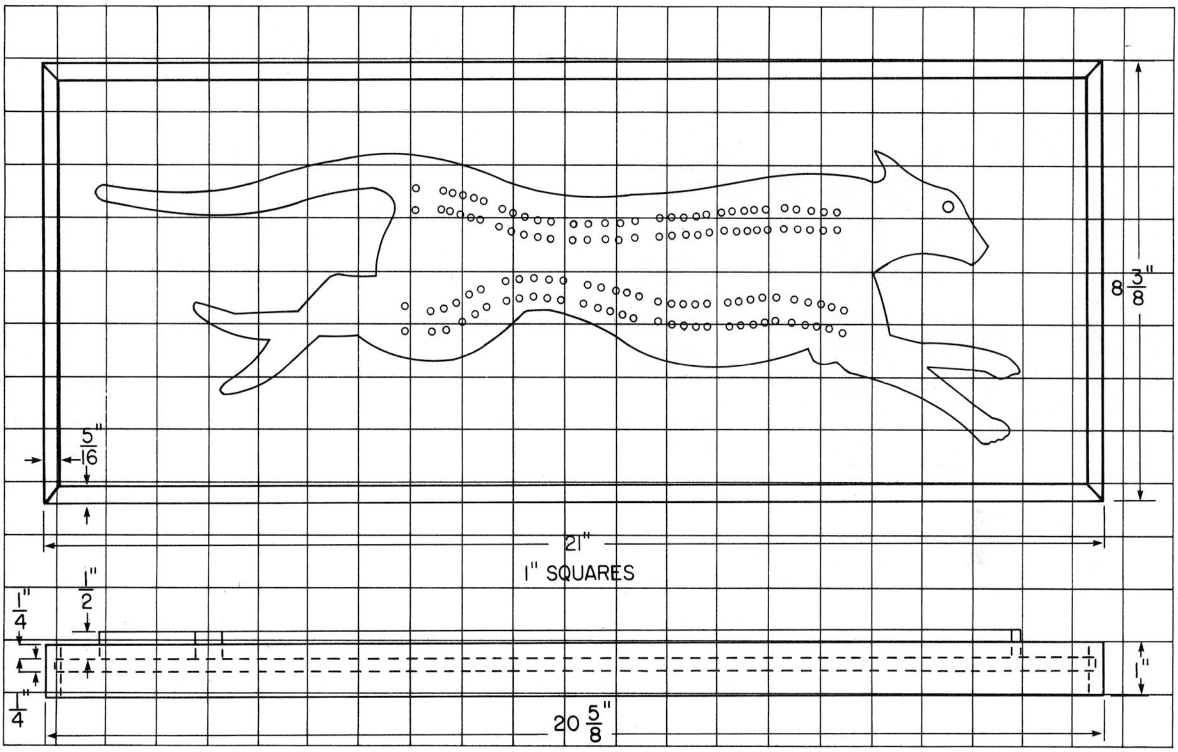

1" SQUARES

CONSTRUCTION CHECKLIST

1. Cut all pieces to dimensions as described in the bill of materials.
2. Cut grooves on the inside of the frame pieces.
3. Cut miter corners on all frame pieces.
4. Sand to smoothness the inside faces of all frame pieces and the flat surfaces of the panel.
5. Glue and assemble the frame and panel. Do not apply glue to the shorter side frame grooves.
6. Cut out leopard, and sand to smoothness.
7. Drill out all peg holes in leopard.
8. Glue leopard to panel.
9. Make cribbage pegs.
10. Finish.

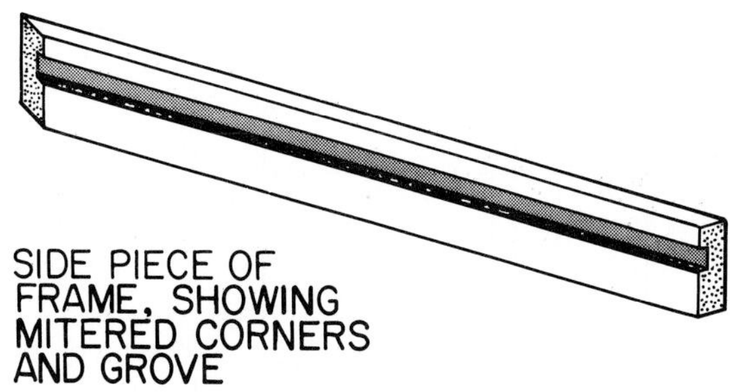

SIDE PIECE OF FRAME, SHOWING MITERED CORNERS AND GROVE

TABLE: This small occasional table can be made of any hardwood. The top can be built of plywood or solid glued-up stock.

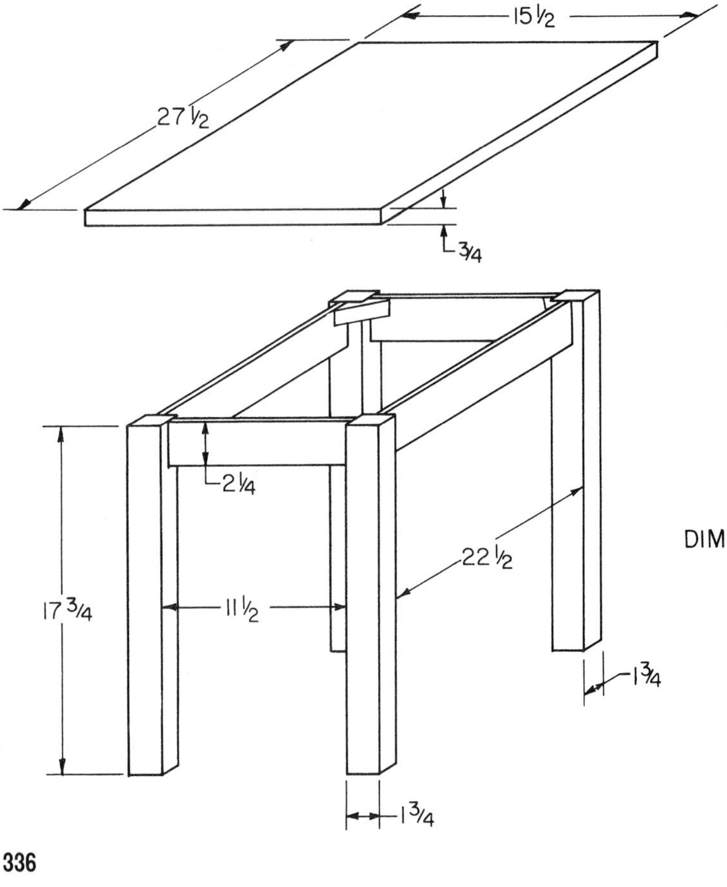

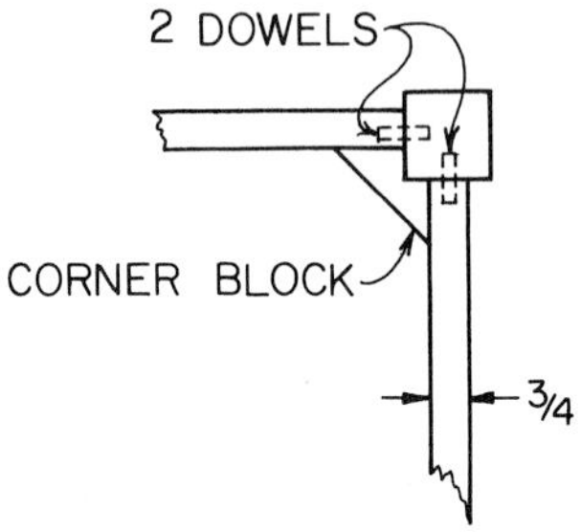

15 1/2
27 1/2
3/4
2 DOWELS
CORNER BLOCK
3/4
2 1/4
17 3/4
11 1/2
22 1/2
1 3/4
1 3/4

DIMENSIONS IN INCHES

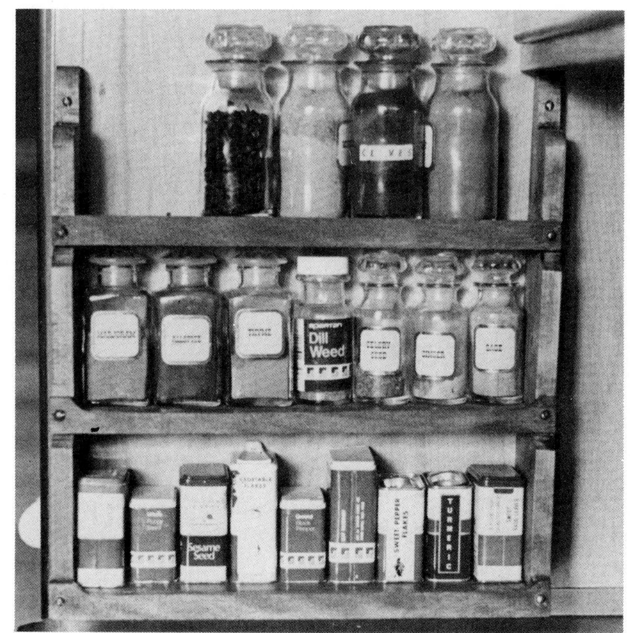

SPICE RACK: This rack will hold different sizes and shapes of bottles and metal containers. It would be a great gift for someone who likes to cook.

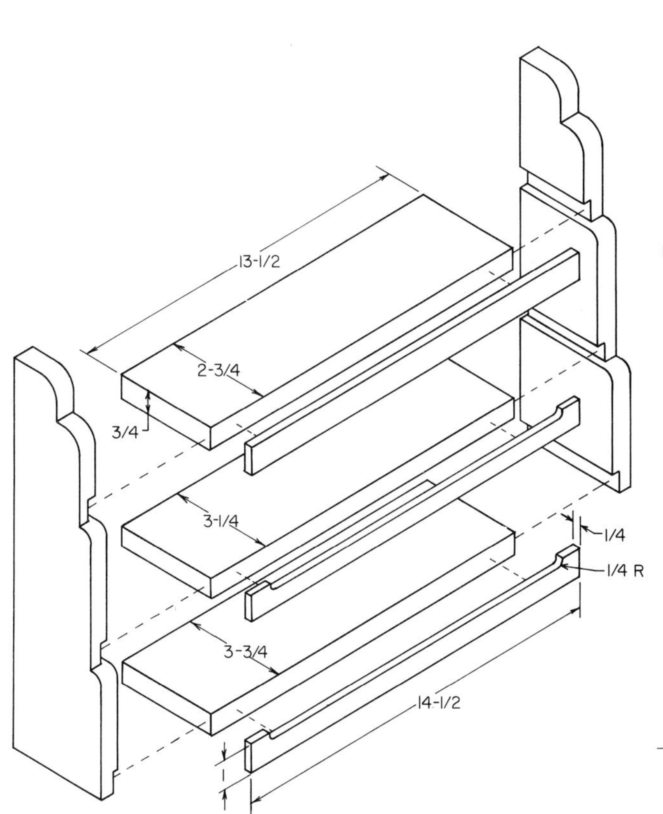

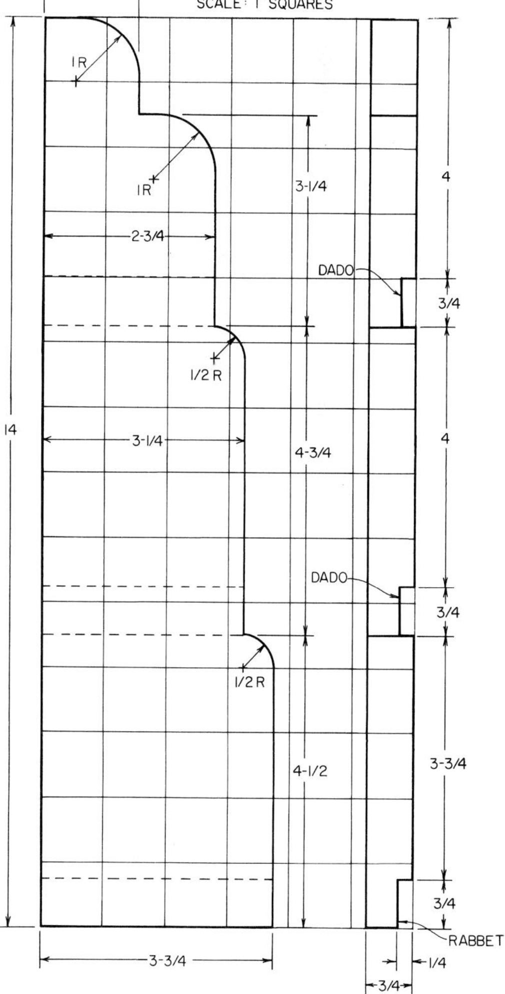

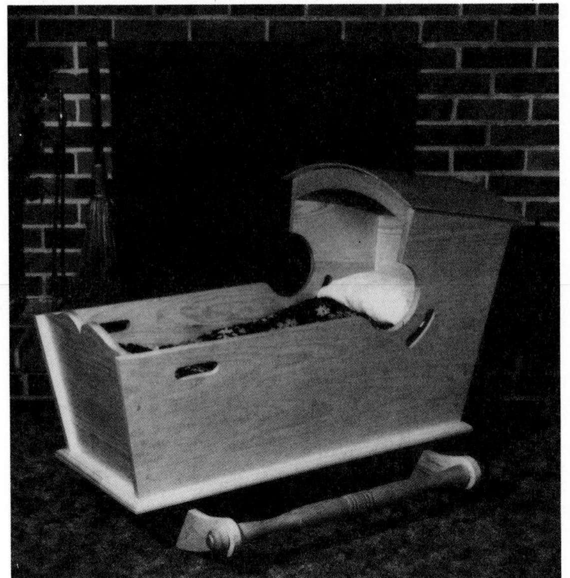

BILL OF MATERIALS
(In inches, finished dimensions)

A	Side (2)	¾″ × 21½″ × 40″
B	Headboard (1)	¾″ × 18″ × 23¼″
C	Footboard (1)	¾″ × 13″ × 15″
D	Base (1)	¾″ × 15½″ × 36″
E	Canopy support (1)	¾″ × 4″ × 18″
F	Canopy center piece (12)	¼″ × 1¼″ × 14″
G	Canopy edge piece (2)	¼″ × 3″ × 14″
H	Rocker (2)	¾″ × 5½″ × 28″
J	Treadle bar (2)	1¾″ dia. × 26″
K	End cap (4)	1¾″ dia. × 1⅜″

CHILD'S CRADLE: A full-color photo appears on p. 9. (Shopsmith)

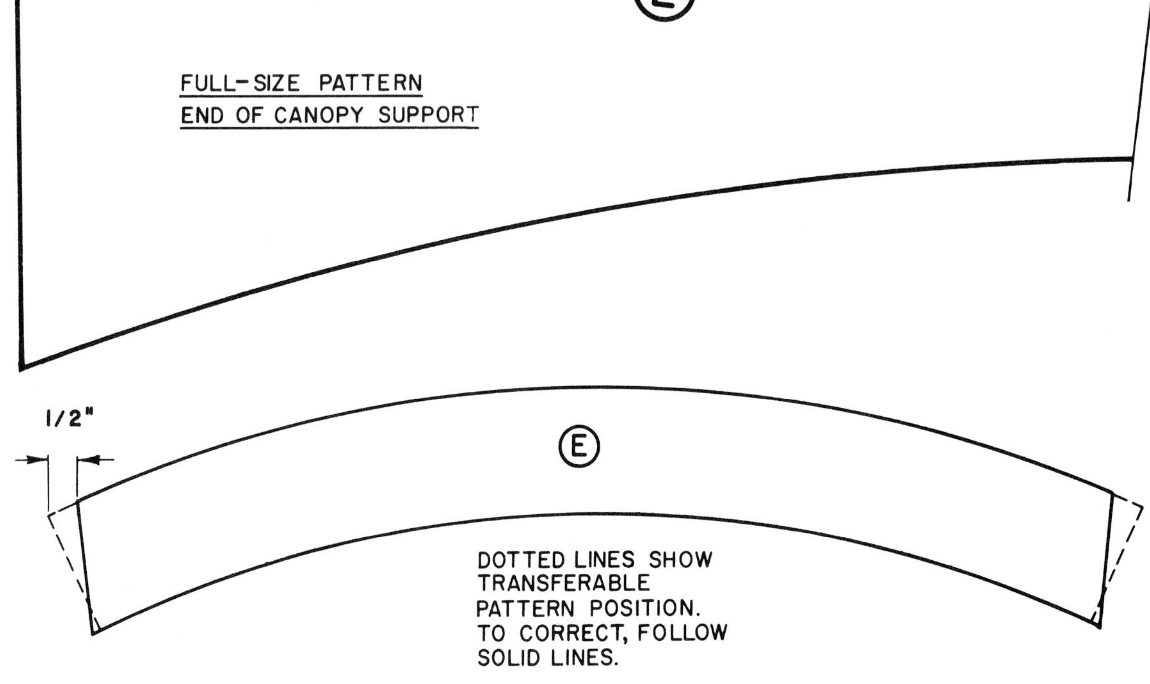

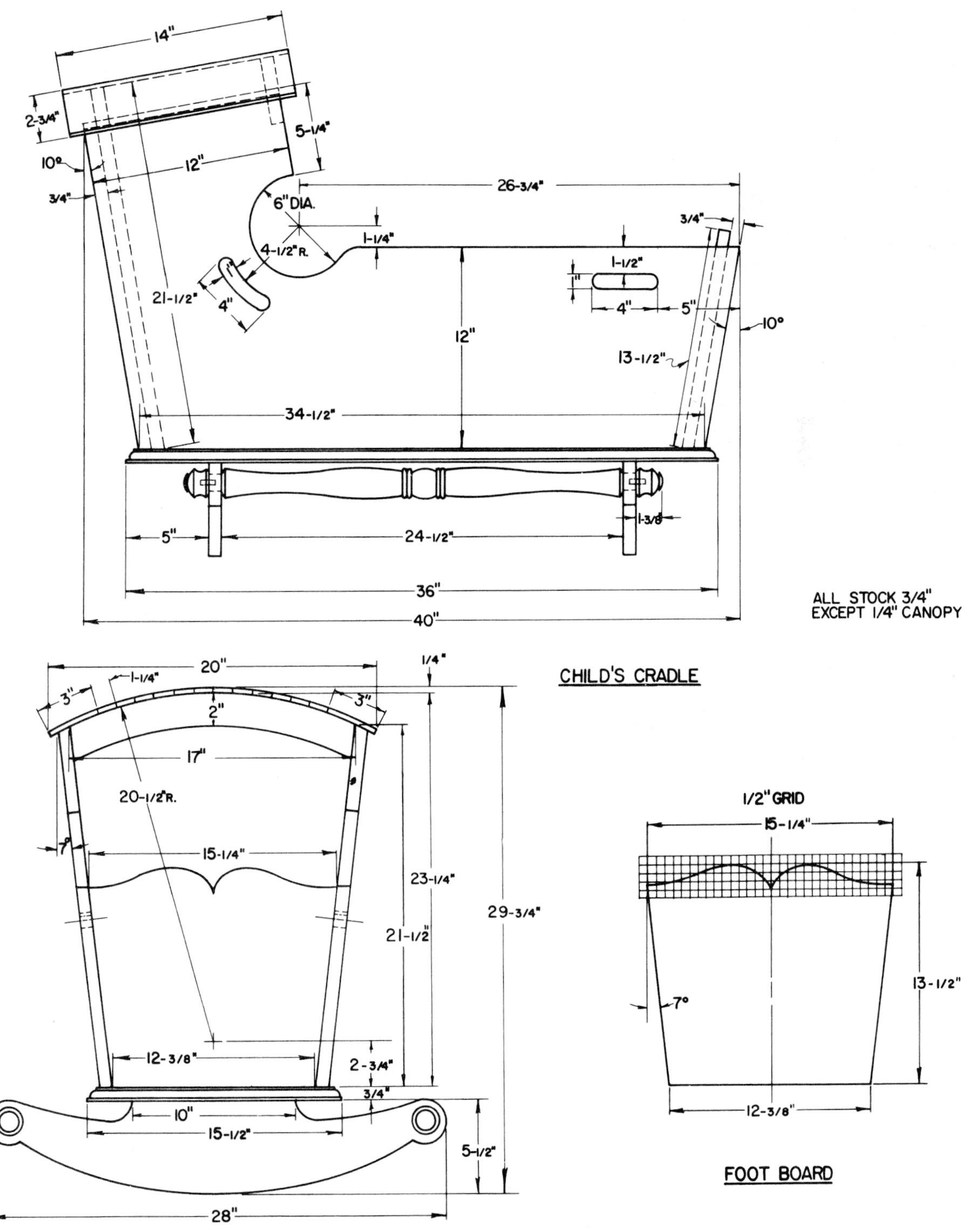
14"
2-3/4"
5-1/4"
10°
12"
3/4"
26-3/4"
6" DIA.
1-1/4"
4-1/2" R.
1"
4"
21-1/2"
3/4"
1-1/2"
1"
4"
5"
10°
12"
13-1/2"
34-1/2"
5"
24-1/2"
1-3/8"
36"
40"
ALL STOCK 3/4"
EXCEPT 1/4" CANOPY
20"
1-1/4"
1/4"
3"
3"
2"
17"
20-1/2" R.
7°
15-1/4"
23-1/4"
29-3/4"
21-1/2"
12-3/8"
2-3/4"
3/4"
10"
15-1/2"
5-1/2"
28"
CHILD'S CRADLE
1/2" GRID
15-1/4"
7°
13-1/2"
12-3/8"
FOOT BOARD

CANDLE HOLDER: Tall candles can be stored in the upper part; short candles and matches in the lower.

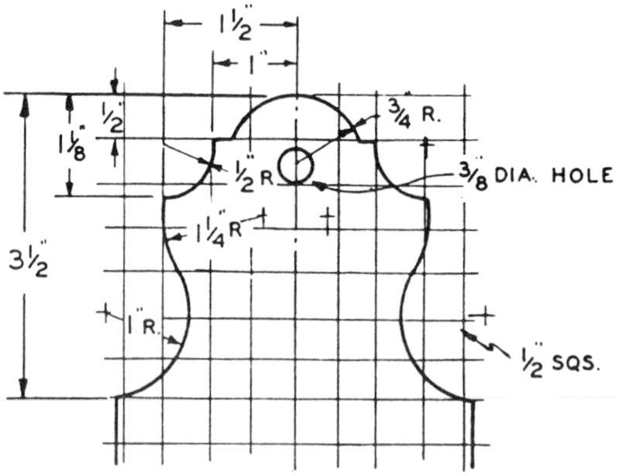

BACK PANEL DETAIL

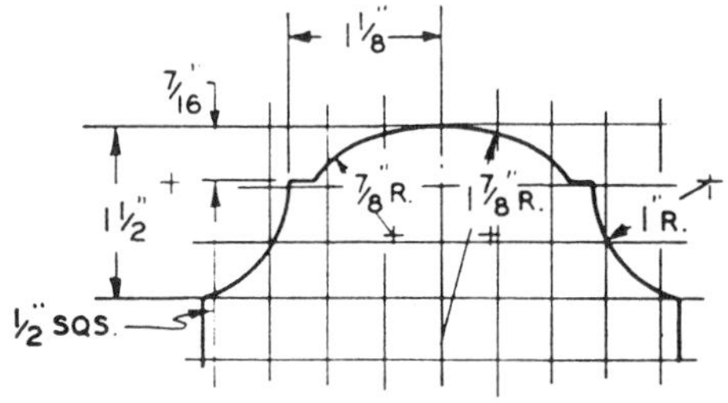

FRONT PANEL DETAIL

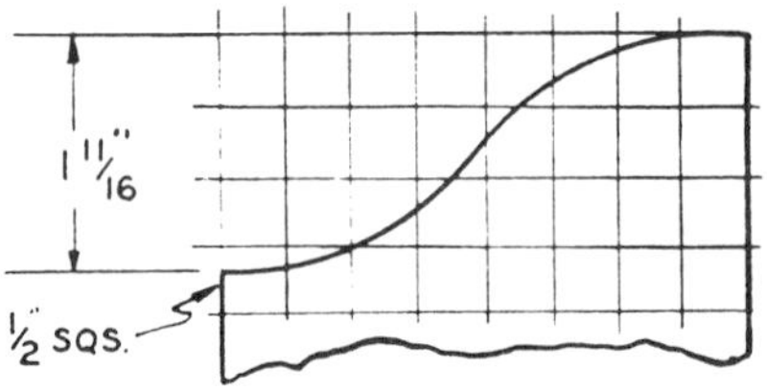

SIDE PANEL DETAIL

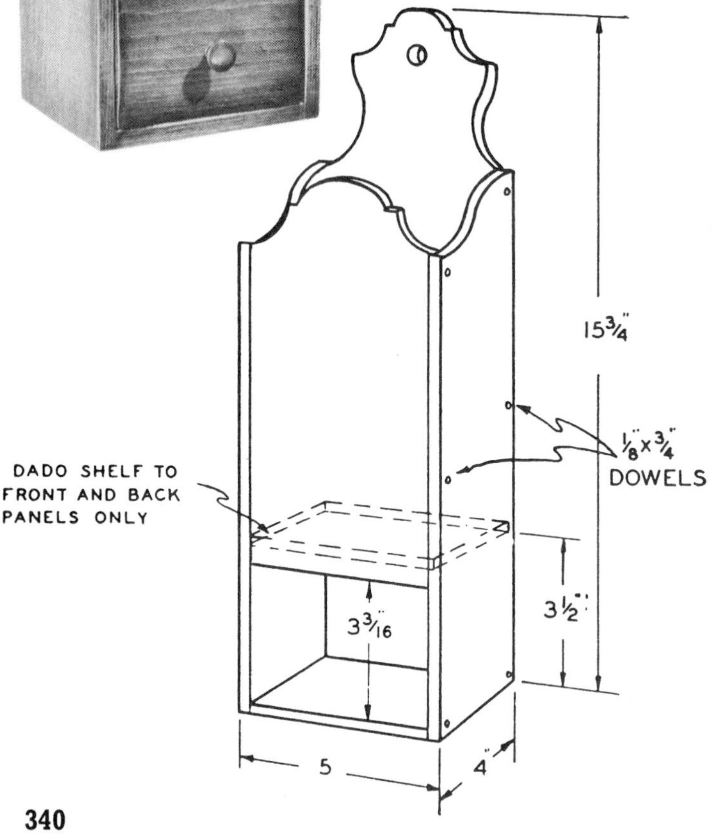

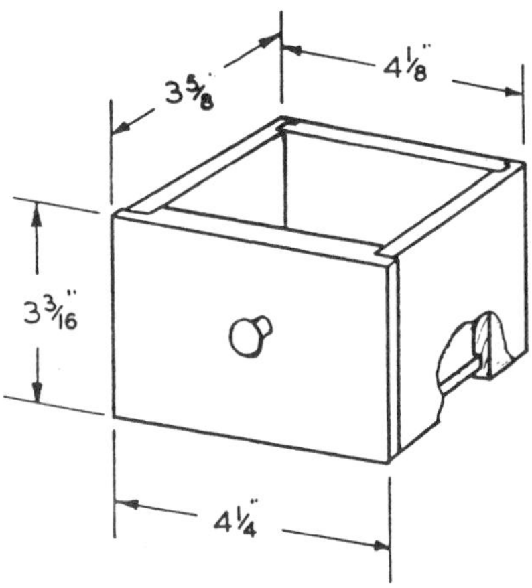

DADO SHELF TO FRONT AND BACK PANELS ONLY

1/8" x 3/4" DOWELS

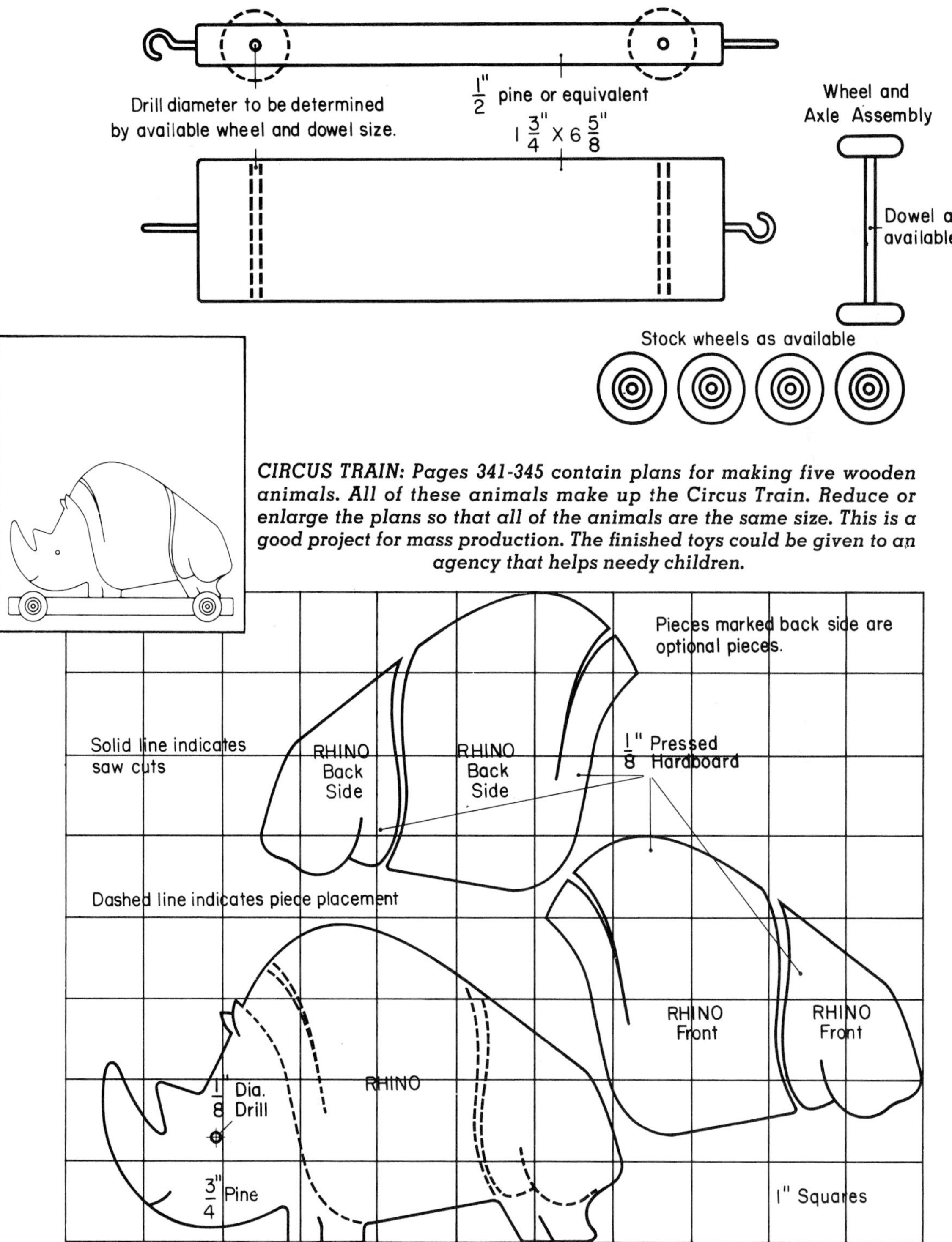

CIRCUS TRAIN: Pages 341-345 contain plans for making five wooden animals. All of these animals make up the Circus Train. Reduce or enlarge the plans so that all of the animals are the same size. This is a good project for mass production. The finished toys could be given to an agency that helps needy children.

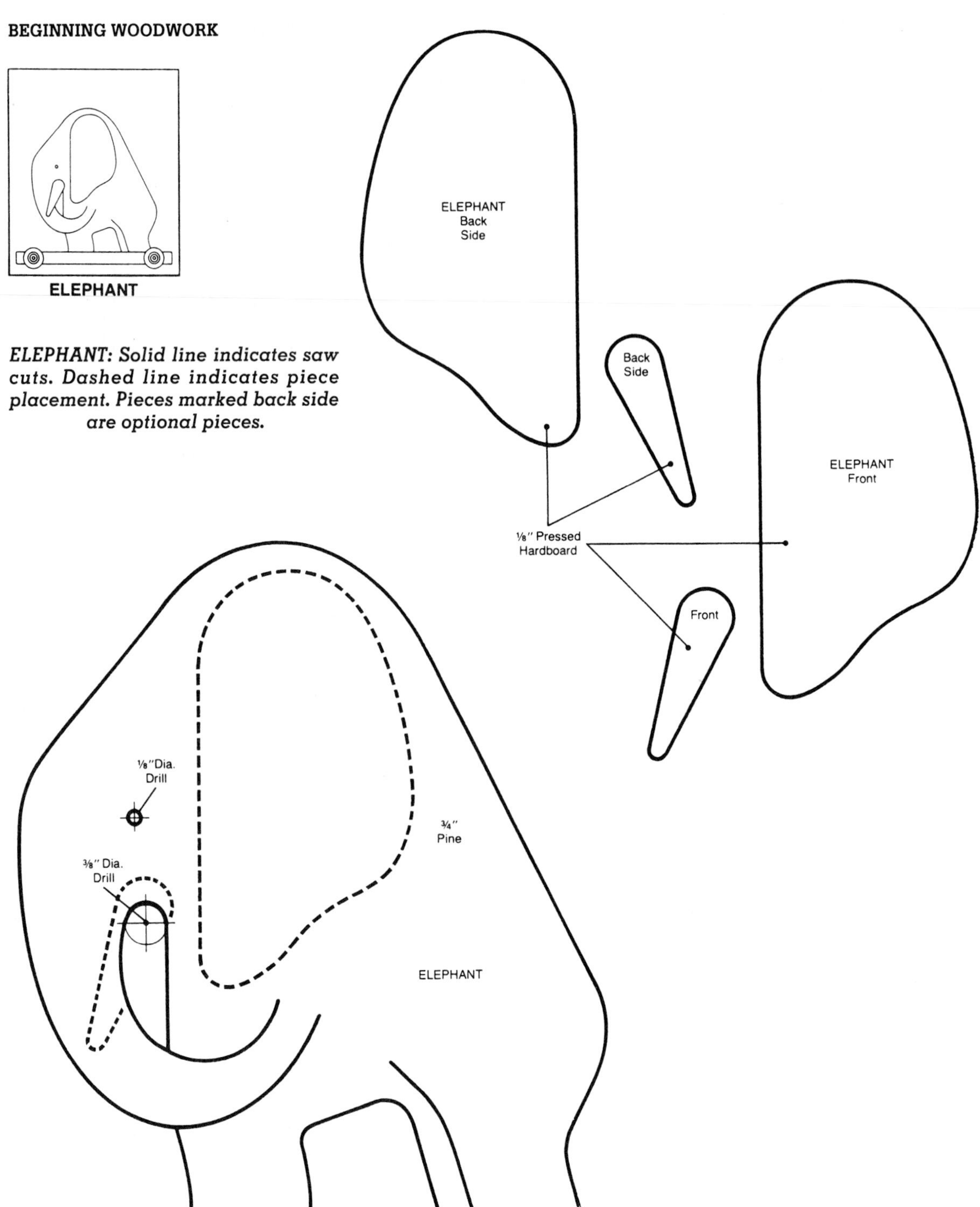

ELEPHANT: Solid line indicates saw cuts. Dashed line indicates piece placement. Pieces marked back side are optional pieces.

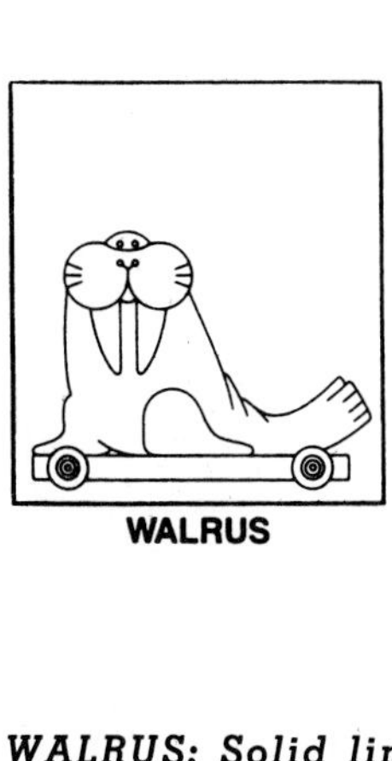

WALRUS: Solid line indicates saw cuts. Dashed line indicates piece placement. Pieces marked back side are optional pieces.

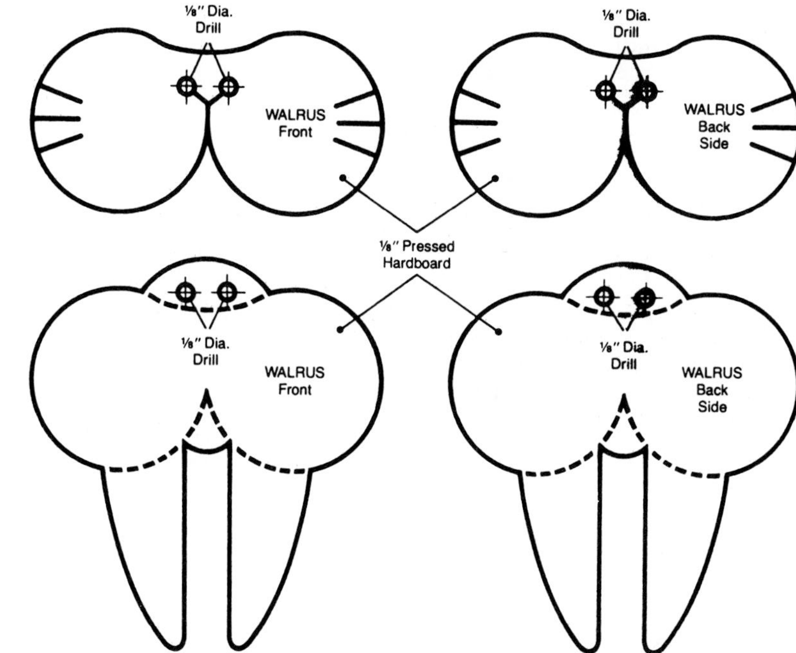

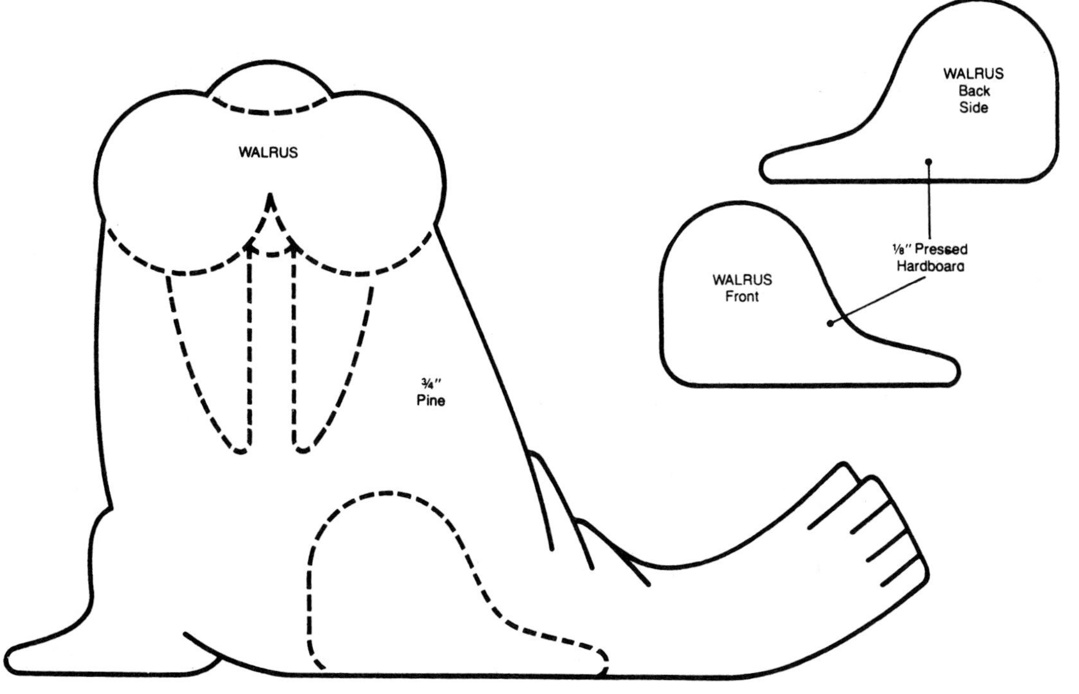

***APES:** Solid line indicates saw cuts. Dashed line indicates piece placement.*

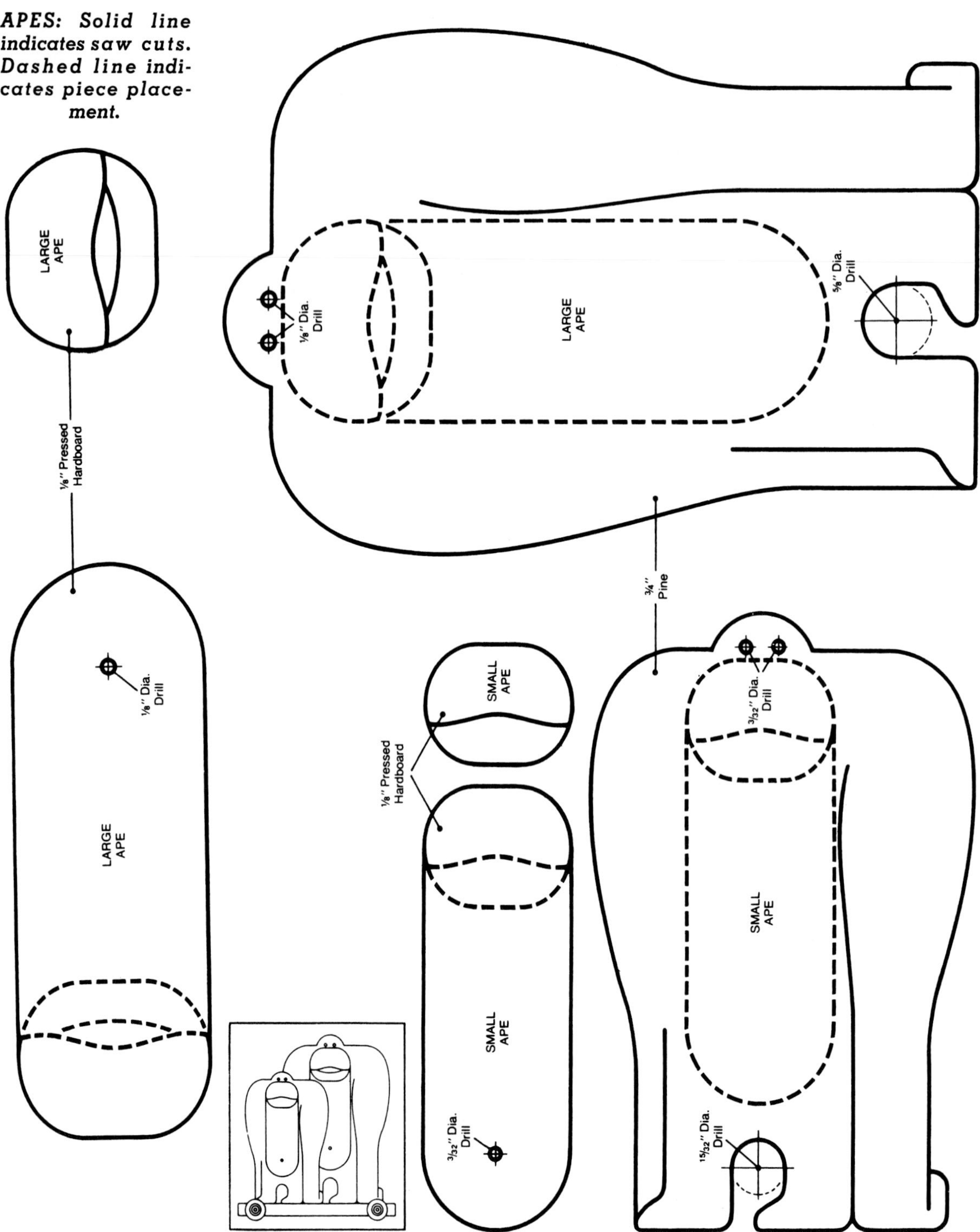

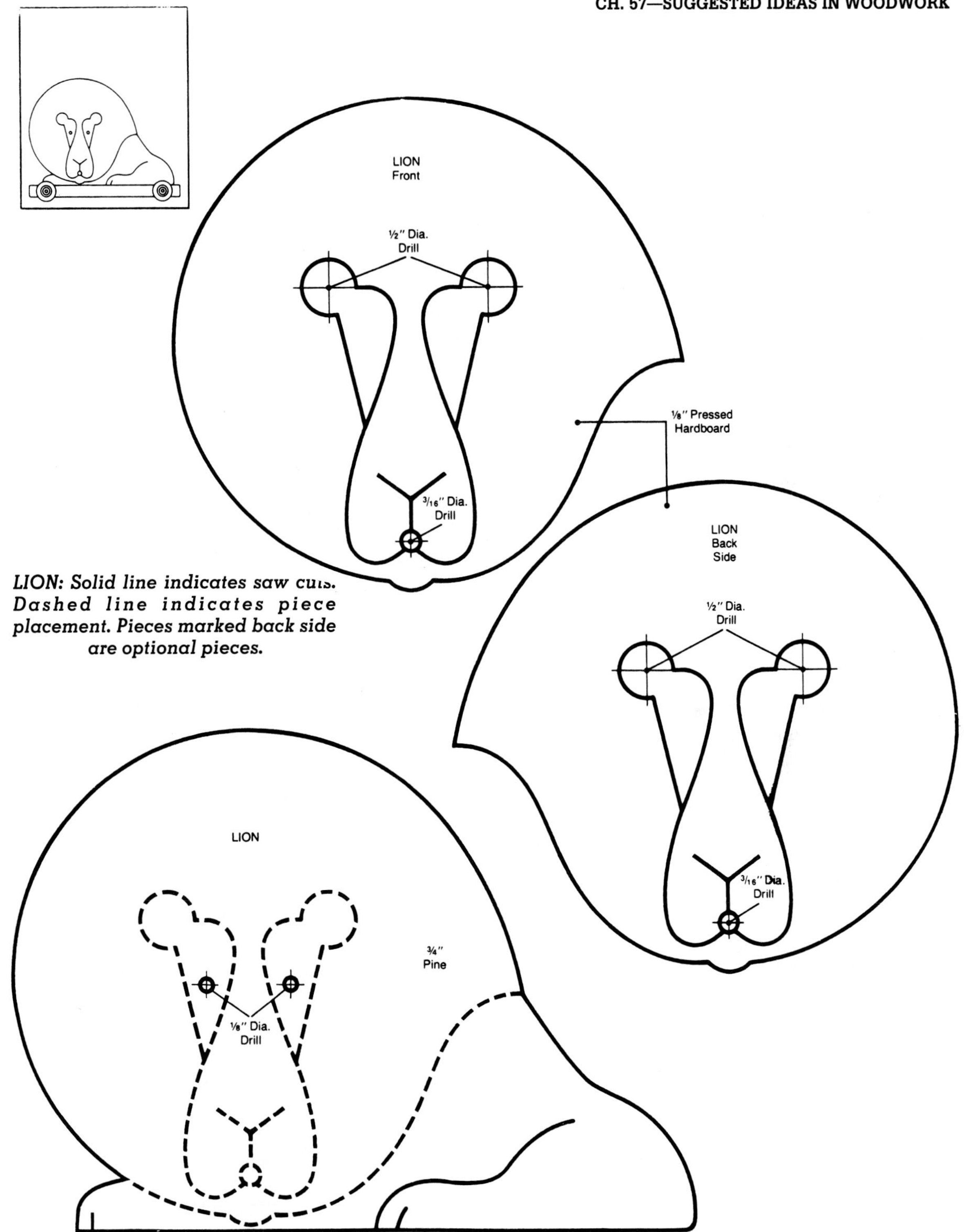

LION: Solid line indicates saw cuts. Dashed line indicates piece placement. Pieces marked back side are optional pieces.

THE TRACTOR ("SEMI"): This toy includes in miniature many of the features of the tractor part of a tractor-trailer. (Shopsmith.)

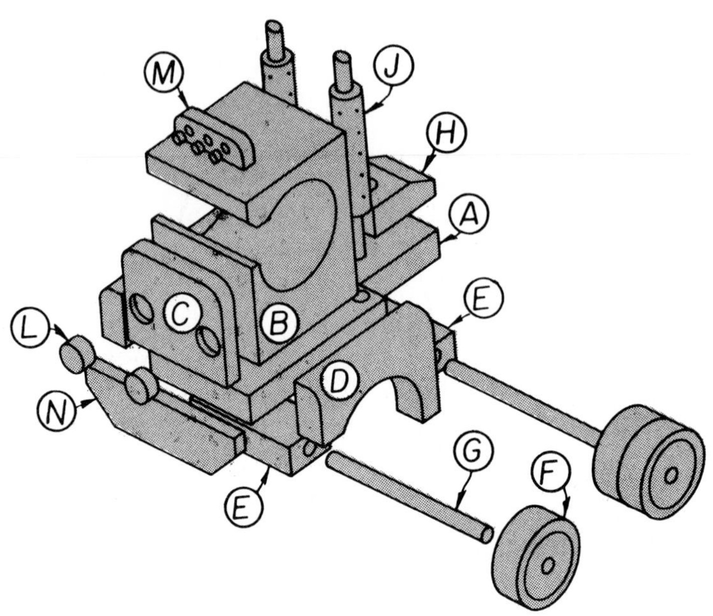

BILL OF MATERIALS
(In inches, finished dimensions)

A	Base	¾″ × 3″ × 7″
B	Cab	3″ × 3¼″ × 4¼″
C	Grill	⅜″ × 2½″ × 3″
D	Fenders (2)	¾″ × 2½″ × 3½″
E	Front carriage	¾″ × 1¼″ × 3″
	Rear carriage	¾″ × 1¼″ × 2″
F	Wheels (6)	2″ dia. × ¾″
G	Axles (2)	¼″ dia. × 4⅝″
H	Hitch	¾″ × 1½″ × 2″
J	Exhaust stacks (2)	¾″ dia. × 5¼″
K	Steering wheel	1¼″ dia. × ¼″
	Steering wheel shaft	¼″ dia. × 2½″
L	Headlights (2)	¾″ dia. × ½″
M	Cab light block	⅜″ × ½″ × 2″
	Cab lights (3)	¼″ dia. × ½″
N	Front bumper	¼″ × 1¼″ × 4½″

PROCEDURE

1. Cut all parts to size.
2. Saw and drum sand the circular window.
3. Drill the ¼-inch hole for the steering wheel shaft (K).
4. Use a 2½-inch hole saw or bandsaw to cut the circular outline of the fenders (D).
5. Round the top and front outside edges with a disc or belt sander. **Caution:** there's a left and right fender — and they're *not* interchangeable.
6. Make and assemble wheels (F), axles (G) and carriage (E).
7. Cut and drill hitch (H).
8. Turn exhaust stacks (J) from ¾-inch dowel.
9. Drill ⅛-inch "ventilation" holes in them for detail.
10. Drill holes in cab light block (M) and use ¼-inch dowels for lights.
11. Shape the front bumper (N).
12. Round all sharp edges. Assemble and glue all parts together.

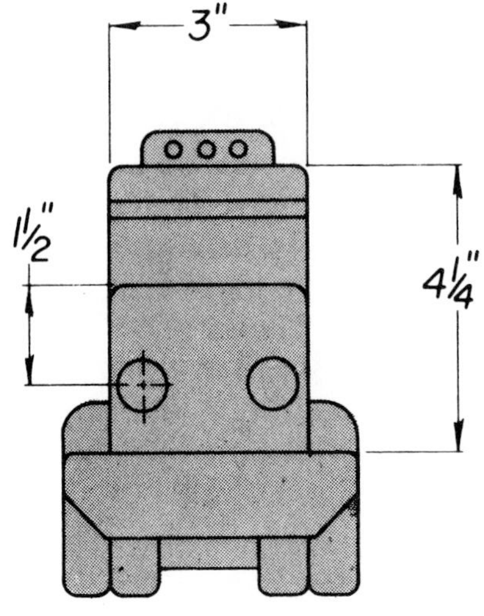
3"
1½"
4¼"

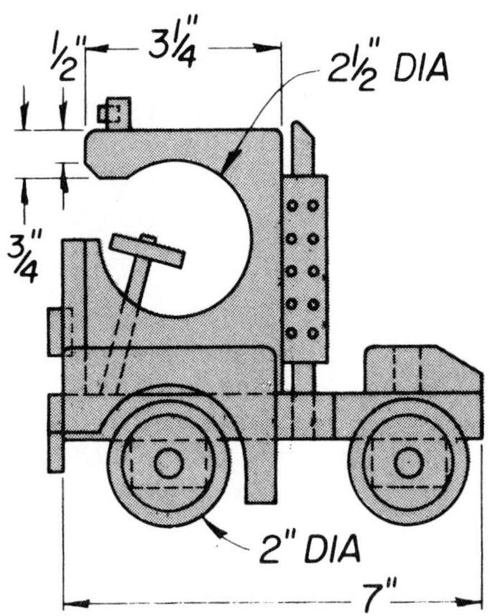
½"
3¼"
2½" DIA
¾"
2" DIA
7"

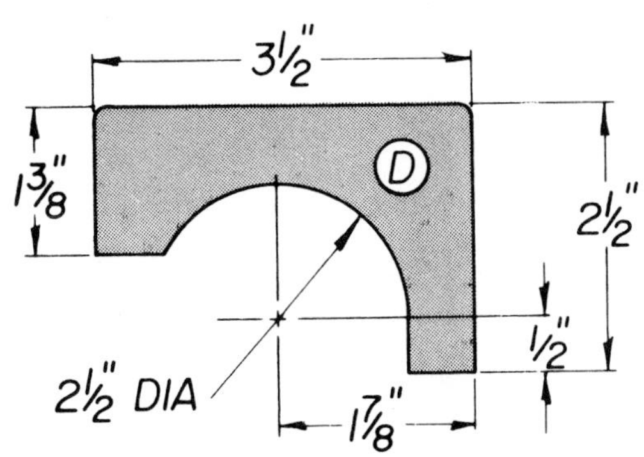
3½"
1⅜"
D
2½"
½"
2½" DIA
1⅞"

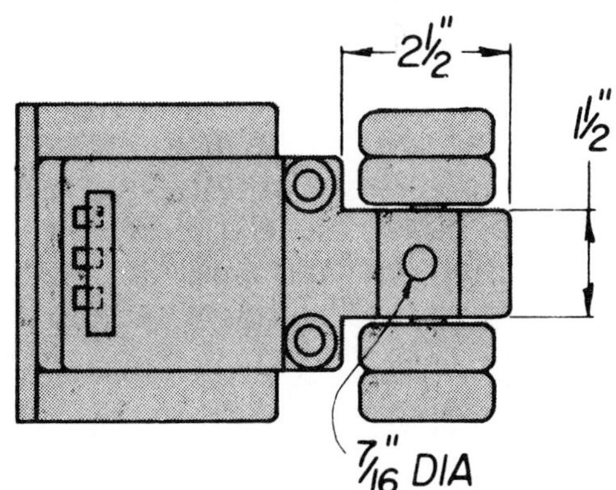
2½"
1½"
7/16" DIA

ROCKING PLANE: This plane makes an attractive toy for a child. (Shopsmith.)

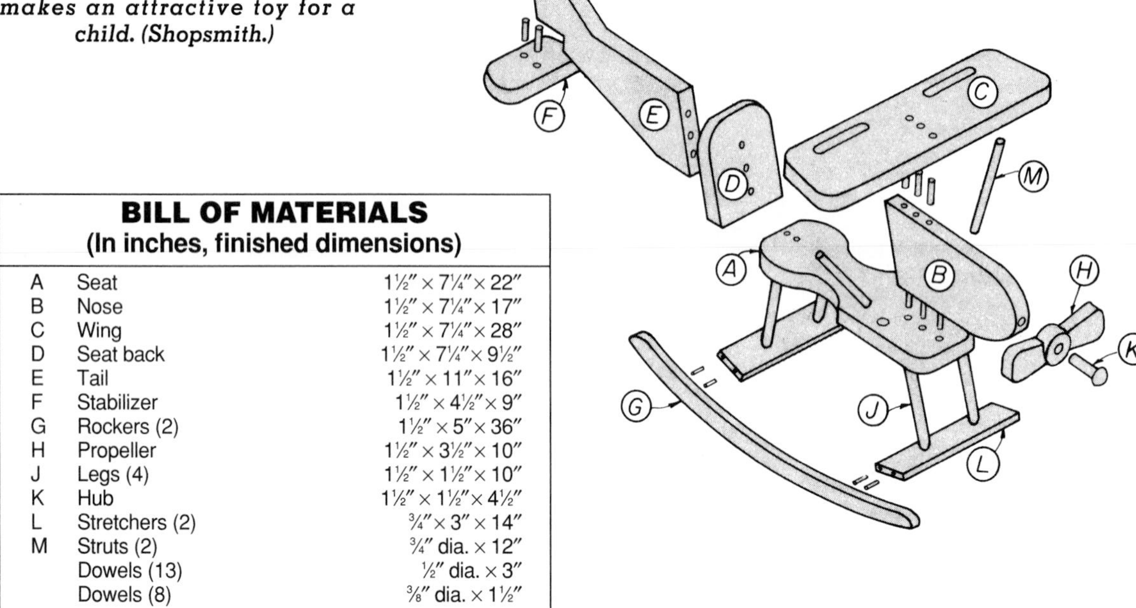

BILL OF MATERIALS
(In inches, finished dimensions)

A	Seat	1½″ × 7¼″ × 22″
B	Nose	1½″ × 7¼″ × 17″
C	Wing	1½″ × 7¼″ × 28″
D	Seat back	1½″ × 7¼″ × 9½″
E	Tail	1½″ × 11″ × 16″
F	Stabilizer	1½″ × 4½″ × 9″
G	Rockers (2)	1½″ × 5″ × 36″
H	Propeller	1½″ × 3½″ × 10″
J	Legs (4)	1½″ × 1½″ × 10″
K	Hub	1½″ × 1½″ × 4½″
L	Stretchers (2)	¾″ × 3″ × 14″
M	Struts (2)	¾″ dia. × 12″
	Dowels (13)	½″ dia. × 3″
	Dowels (8)	⅜″ dia. × 1½″

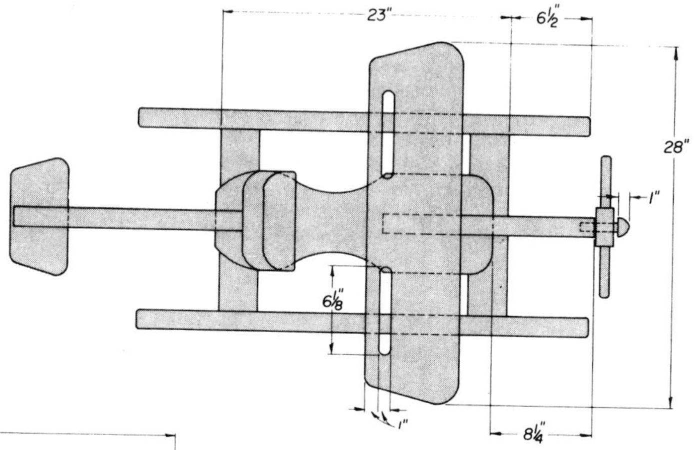

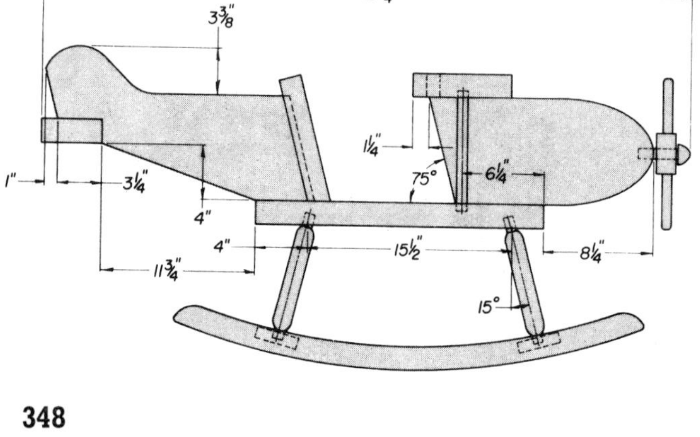

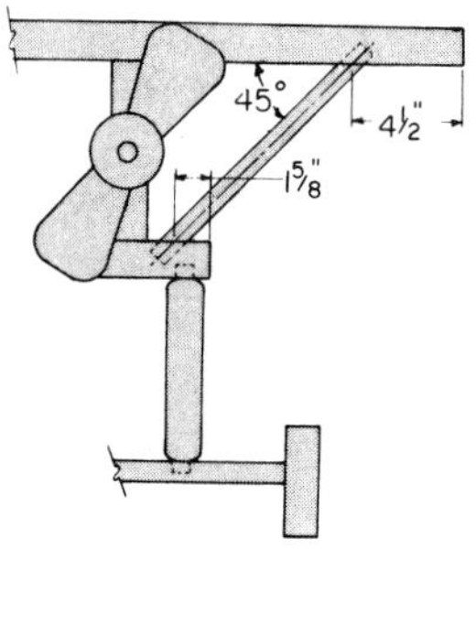

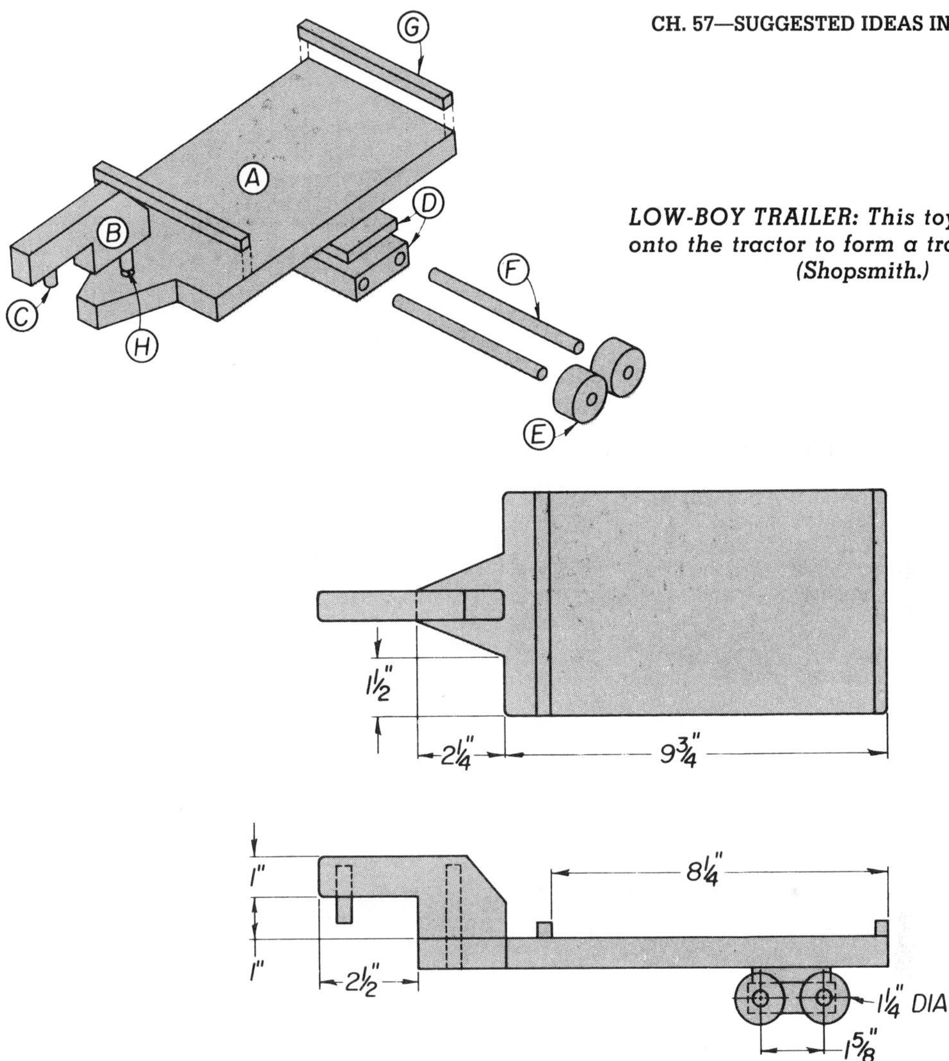

LOW-BOY TRAILER: This toy trailer fits onto the tractor to form a tractor-trailer. (Shopsmith.)

PROCEDURE

1. Cut all parts to size.
2. Drill the two axle holes in the carriage (D) and glue the two pieces together.
3. Make and assemble wheels (E), axles (F), and carriage (D).
4. Cut coupling arm (B) to shape. Glue this on the floor (A).
5. After glue has set, reinforce this butt joint with a flush-set ⅜-inch dowel.
6. Round all sharp edges.
7. Assemble and glue all parts together.

BILL OF MATERIALS
(In inches, finished dimensions)

A	Floor	¾" × 5¾" × 12"
B	Coupling arm	¾" × 2" × 4¾"
C	Coupling pin	⅜" dia. × 1⅝"
D	Carriage (2 pcs.)	¾" × 2¼" × 3¾"
		⅜" × 2" × 3½"
E	Wheels (4)	1¼" dia. × ¾"
F	Axles (2)	¼" dia. × 5¼"
G	Stops (2)	⅜" × ⅜" × 5½"
H	Dowel	⅜" dia. × 2⅝"

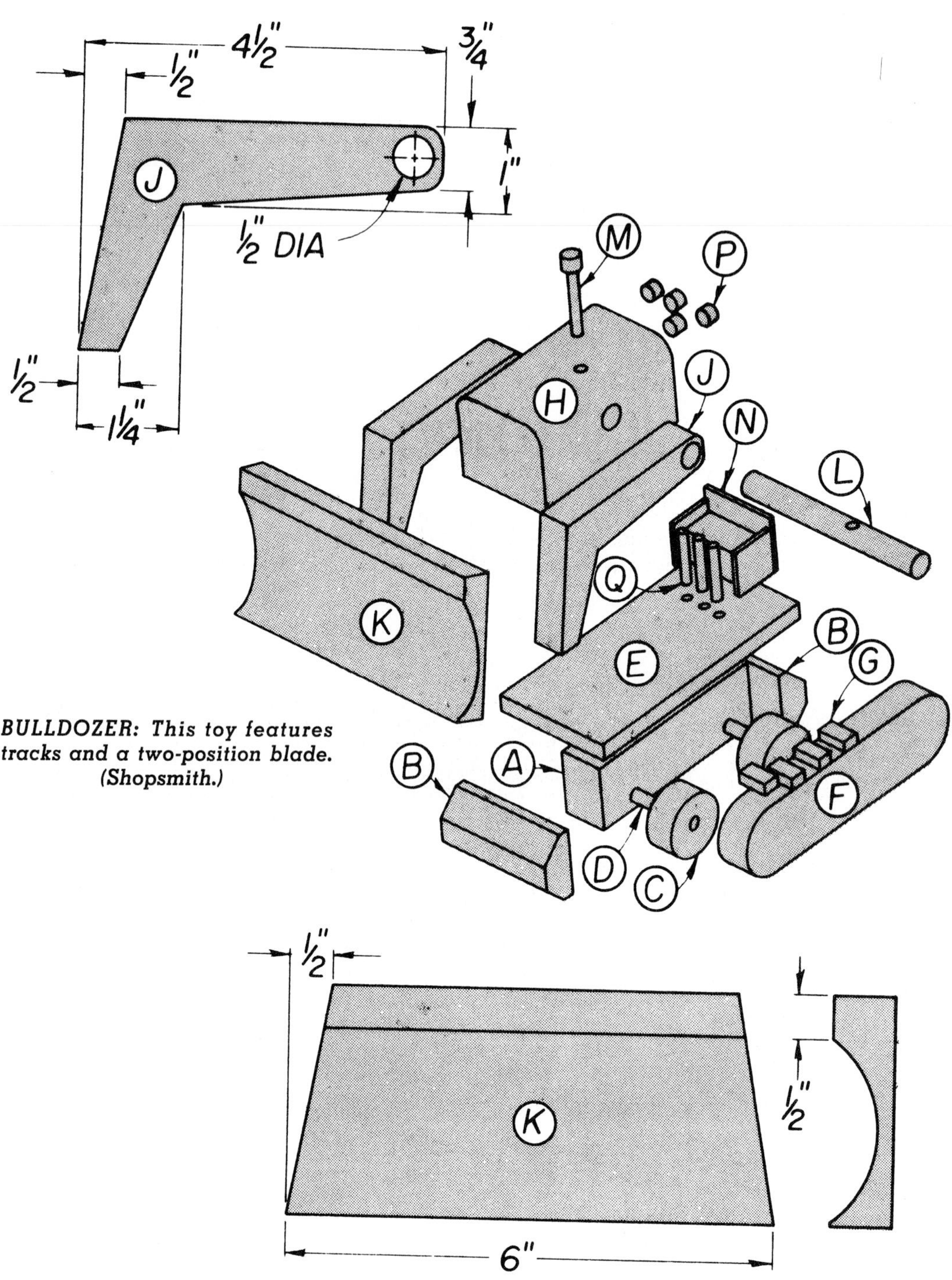

BULLDOZER: This toy features tracks and a two-position blade. (Shopsmith.)

PROCEDURE

The blade is held off the ground by the exhaust stack engaging a hole in the blade axle. The builder must watch that the chassis center beam (A) and the chassis end beams (B) are cut exactly to size in the Bill of Materials. This provides adequate clearance for the wheels when the tracks are glued to the chassis.

1. Start by cutting all parts to size according to the Bill of Materials.
2. Drill axle holes in (A). Glue parts (B) to (A). Install wheels.
3. Glue track lugs (G) onto track blocks (F) starting on the top and bottom center and working towards the ends. Use a spare lug as a spacer. For lugs glued on the rounded ends, wrap sandpaper over a large dowel to sand a concave surface for better adhesion.
4. Drill hole for the blade axle (L).
5. Insert blade axle and drill ¼-inch dia. hole for the exhaust stack (M). This hole goes through the blade axle.
6. Remove the blade axle and redrill the ¼-inch dia. hole to 5⁄16-inch dia.
7. Drill dashboard holes for the gauges and insert gauges (P).
8. Blade (K) has a concave face. This shape can be achieved using the belt sander or the drum sander. Assemble blade (K), blade axle (L), blade supports (J), and engine (H).
9. All parts of this toy are held together with glue only. Be sure to round all sharp edges of the toy.

BILL OF MATERIALS
(In inches, finished dimensions)

A	Chassis center beam	1″ × 1½″ × 4¼″
B	Chassis end beams (2)	¾″ × 1½″ × 2¾″
C	Wheels (4)	1¼″ dia. × ¾″
D	Axles (2)	¼″ dia. × 2⅝″
E	Chassis platform	¼″ × 2¾″ × 5¾″
F	Track blocks (2)	¾″ × 1½″ × 6″
G	Track lugs (36)	⅜″ × 3⁄16″ × ¾″
H	Engine	2″ × 2¼″ × 3¾″
J	Blade supports (2)	¾″ × 2¾″ × 4½″
K	Blade	¾″ × 2¾″ × 6″
L	Blade axle	½″ dia. × 4″
M	Exhaust stack (2 pcs.)	¼″ dia. × 2″
		½″ dia. × ½″
N	Seat	¾″ × ¾″ × 1½″
	Seat sides (2)	⅛″ × 1″ × 1¼″
	Seat back	⅛″ × 1¼″ × 1½″
P	Gauges (4)	⅜″ dia. × ½″
Q	Control levers (3)	⅛″ dia. × 1¼″

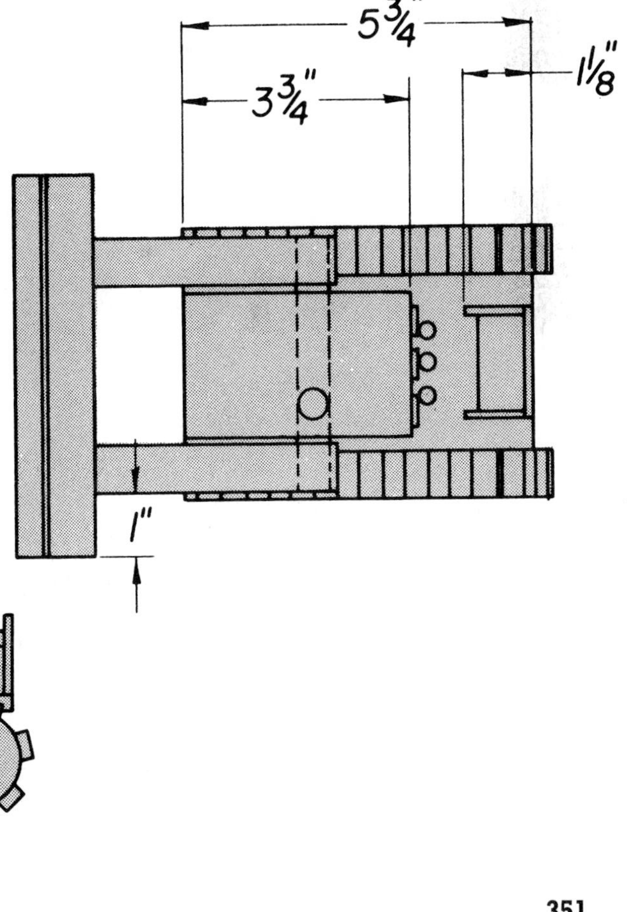

MYSTERY BOX: This box has a sliding top. (Shopsmith.)

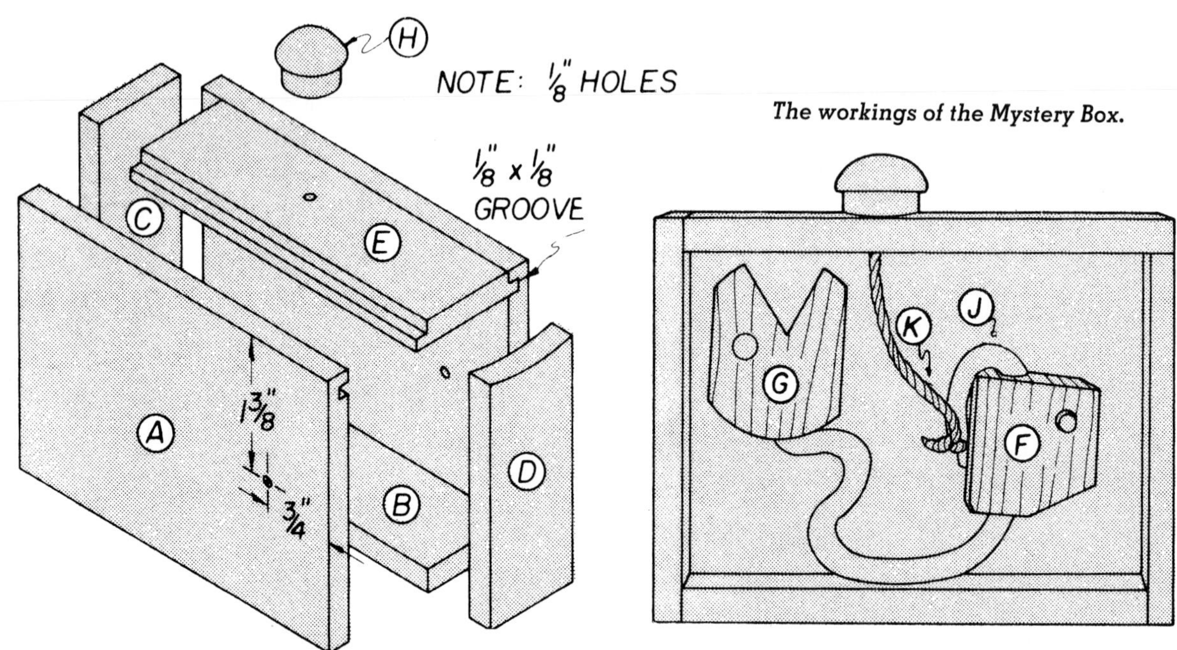

The workings of the Mystery Box.

PROCEDURE

1. Cut all pieces to size. Resaw stock on the bandsaw or use ¼-inch plywood. Cut out the pivot (F) and head (G).
2. Make the grooves in the sides (A) for the sliding top (E) on the table saw.
3. Cut the rabbets in the top (E). Cut arc in front (D) for string.
4. Drill holes in the sides (A) for the steel pivot rod and in the pivot (F) and head (G).
5. Assemble with glue the front (D), back (C), and bottom (B) to one of the sides (A).
6. Decorate the head and assemble the remaining parts according to Fig. 1.

BILL OF MATERIALS
(In inches, finished dimensions)

A	Sides	¼" × 2¾" × 3¾"
B	Bottom	¼" × 1" × 3¼"
C	Back	¼" × 1" × 2¾"
D	Front	¼" × 1" × 2½"
E	Top	¼" × 1¼" × 3½"
F	Pivot	¾" × ¾" × 1"
G	Head	¾" × 1" × 1⅛"
H	Dowel button	
J	5" 10 ga. Wire	
K	4" String	

MISCELLANEOUS

2 #10 Flat washers
⅛"× 1¼" Steel rod

WALL TRIVET: Made of wood, this is a purely decorative trivet, requiring careful work with a jigsaw. You might want to use the completed trivet as an attractive wall decoration.

***BUFFALO:** Buffalo were once abundant on the Great Plains. Now, after facing extinction, buffalo herds can be found in certain parks. This rustic wood carving captures the character of this animal.*

PROCEDURE

The block size will be 1½ inches thick, 3½ inches high, ½ inch wide, with grain running vertical.

1. Trace pattern on to block.
2. Saw between legs (to save whittling).
3. Drill holes for tail and horns.
4. Start whittling on outside shoulders, as this is the widest portion.
5. Follow the different sketches and proceed to form the rest of the buffalo.
6. Finish the dark brown stain. Do not paint the horns. Add the eyes and nostrils with black ink.

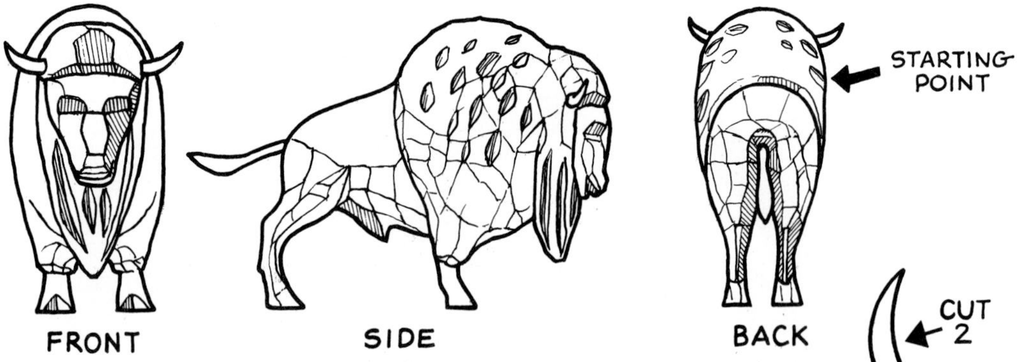

STARTING POINT

FRONT

SIDE

BACK

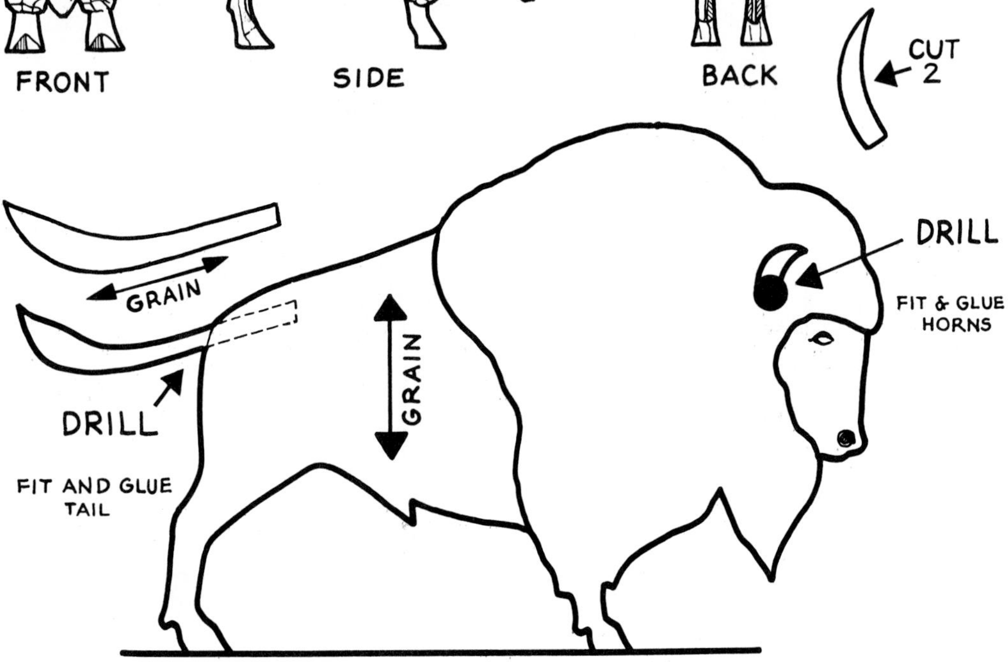

CUT 2

GRAIN

DRILL

FIT AND GLUE TAIL

GRAIN

DRILL

FIT & GLUE HORNS

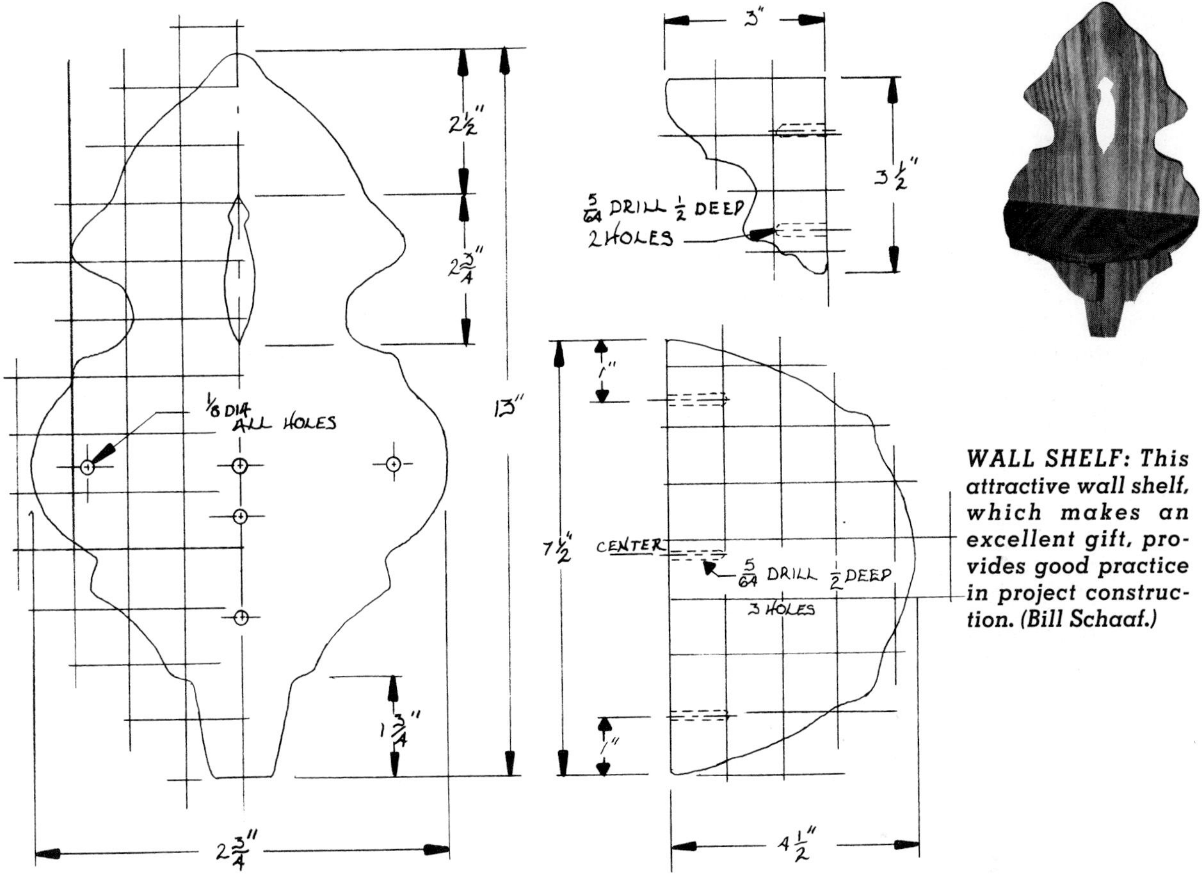

WALL SHELF: This attractive wall shelf, which makes an excellent gift, provides good practice in project construction. (Bill Schaaf.)

PROCEDURE

1. Process stock to ⅜ inches × 8 inches × 20 inches (square ends).
2. Locate vertical center line.
3. Lay out patterns on stock.
4. Locate horizontal centerline on backboard.
5. Rough-cut back, shelf, and brace.
6. Remove excess waste.
7. Locate five holes on center lines:
   One hole 3 inches left of center hole.
   One hole 3 inches right of center hole.
   One hole 1 inch down from center hole.
   One hole 3 inches down from center hole.
8. Cut exterior shape to exact pattern.
9. Drill ¼-inch hole through interior curved design.
10. Cut interior curved design. File, sand, and smooth all curved edges.
11. Drill five ⅛-inch holes through the backboard.
12. Countersink all holes for #4 × ⅞ inch flathead screws.
13. Locate holes on shelf. Drill 5/64-inch holes in shelf. Attach shelf to back.
14. Locate holes for brace. Drill 5/64-inch holes in brace. Attach brace to back.
15. Disassemble.
16. Final sand.
17. Stain if desired and apply finish.
18. Reassemble.

***PLANTER:** This planter has a removable bottom, allowing easy changing of the soil.*

BILL OF MATERIALS
(In inches, finished dimensions)

Cut from 1 pc. — 2″ × 8″ × 10′
2 pcs 2″ × 8″ × 4′ — 3″ Lg. sides
2 pcs 2″ × 8″ × 7⅞″ — Lg. ends

1 pc 1″ × 6″ × 3′ — 8 15/16″ Lg. cut from 1 pc 1″ × 6″ × 4′

1 pc ½″ ϕ × 9″ Lg. Wood Dowel

8 pcs #10 × 3″ Lg. Rd. Hd. Wood Screws

NOTE: 16 to 20 penny galvanized nails may be used in place of screws if desired.

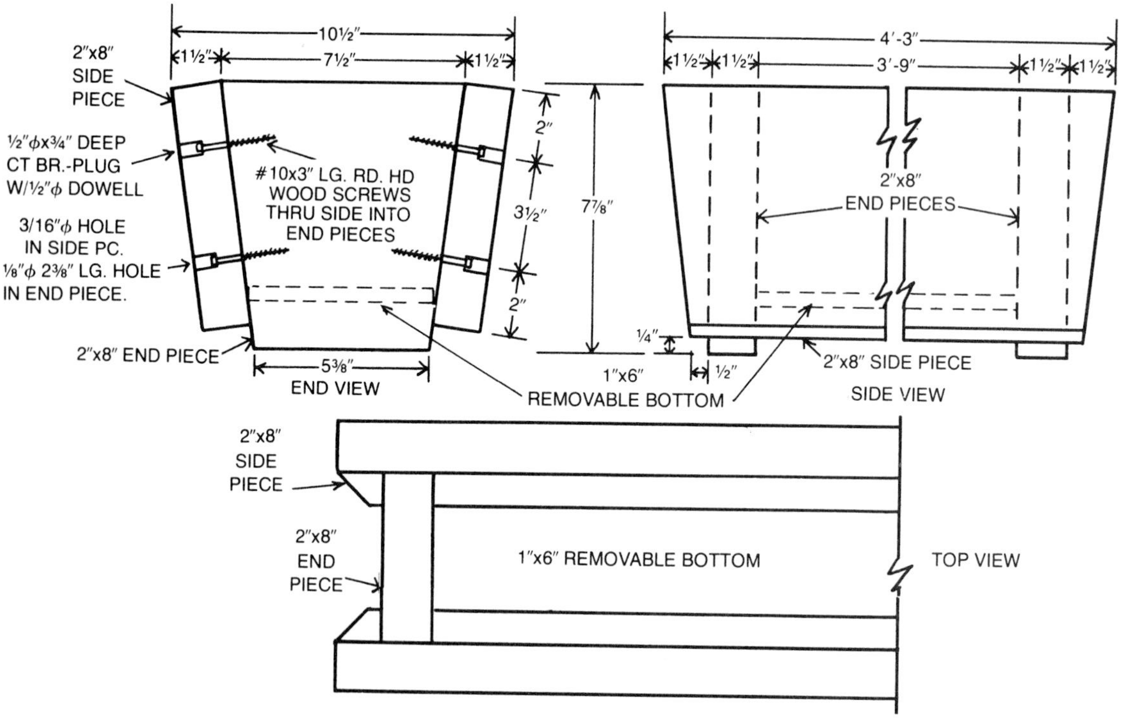

10½″
1½″ 7½″ 1½″
2″x8″ SIDE PIECE
½″ϕx¾″ DEEP CT BR.-PLUG W/½″ϕ DOWELL
3/16″ϕ HOLE IN SIDE PC.
⅛″ϕ 2⅜″ LG. HOLE IN END PIECE.
#10x3″ LG. RD. HD WOOD SCREWS THRU SIDE INTO END PIECES
2″ 3½″ 2″ 7⅞″
2″x8″ END PIECE
5⅜″
END VIEW

4′-3″
1½″ 1½″ 3′-9″ 1½″ 1½″
2″x8″ END PIECES
¼″
1″x6″ ½″
REMOVABLE BOTTOM
2″x8″ SIDE PIECE
SIDE VIEW

2″x8″ SIDE PIECE
2″x8″ END PIECE
1″x6″ REMOVABLE BOTTOM
TOP VIEW

MAGAZINE RACK: This rack can be built using standard-sized dowels and scrap lumber left from other projects. (Shopsmith.)

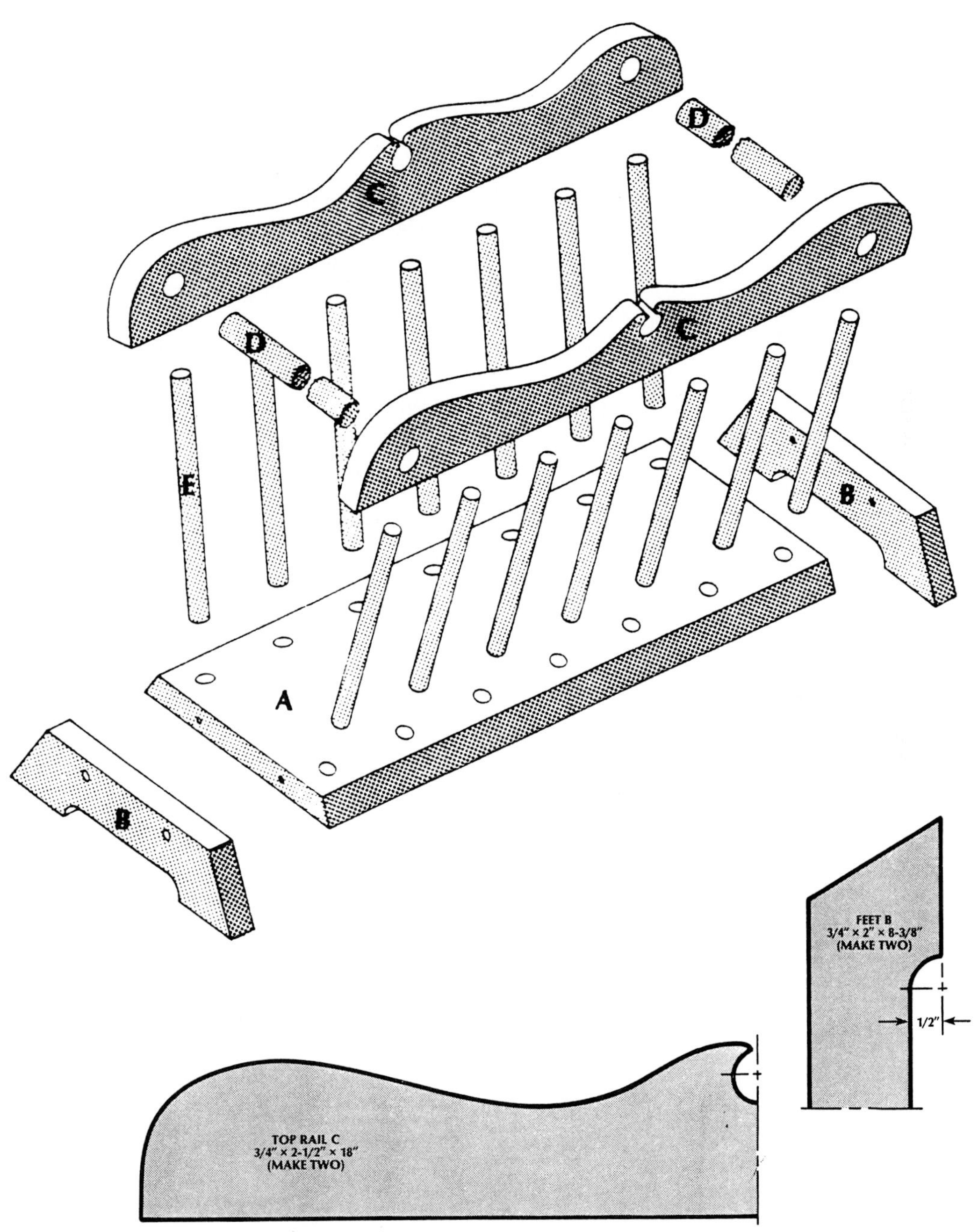

BILL OF MATERIALS
(In inches, finished dimensions)

A	Base	¾″ × 7″ × 16½″
B	Feet (2)	¾″ × 2″ × 8⅜″
C	Rails (2)	¾″ × 2½″ × 18″
D	Braces (2)	¾″ dia. × 9¾″ dowels
E	Columns (14)	½″ dia. × 10½″ dowels
	Flathead wood screws	#8 × 1½″
	Wood glue	

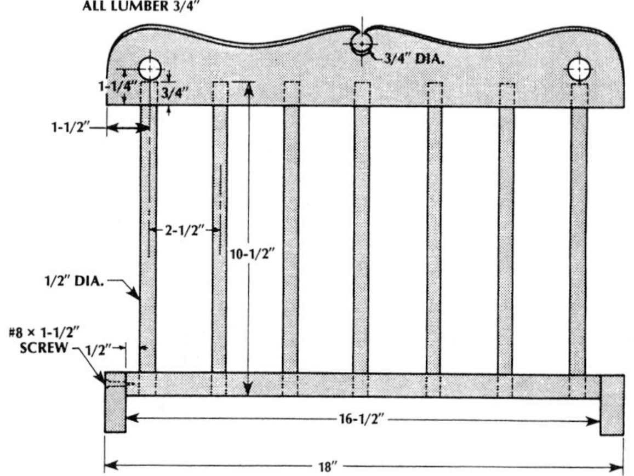

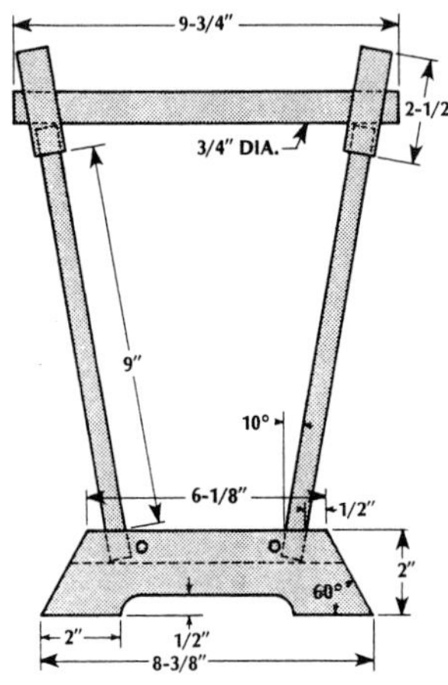

PROCEDURE

What better place to store your periodicals than in this inexpensive magazine rack? Using standard size hardwood dowels and scrap wood left over from other projects, you can build it in no time at all.

1. Sand all stock with 100-grit paper to remove mill marks.
2. Mark the location of all holes to be drilled. The fourteen ½-inch diameter column holes in the base (A) and the four ¾-inch diameter brace holes in the rails (C) must be drilled at 10° angles.
3. Change the drill press table back to 90° to drill the fourteen ½-inch diameter column holes and the ¾-inch diameter decorative holes in the top rails.
4. Using the patterns provided, cut the contours of the top rails and the feet (B).
5. With a handsaw or table saw, cut a 60° bevel on the edges of the base and the ends of the feet. Make sure the pieces are exactly the same width and the same angle where they join.
6. Cut the braces (D) and columns (E) to length, making sure to knock off any burrs on the ends.
7. To assemble, first attach the feet to the base using glue and #8 × 1½-inch flathead wood screws. Countersink the screws.
8. To complete the rack assembly, use glue to fasten the ends of the columns and braces. Be sure to wipe off any excess glue immediately with a damp rag.
9. Using a sanding block to round over all sharp edges, including the protruding ends of the braces, and to smooth the joints between the base and legs.
10. Stain the rack with an Early American stain. Natural oil is recommended for the finish.

TOY CHEST: This toy chest provides storage room for toys and games. (Shopsmith.)

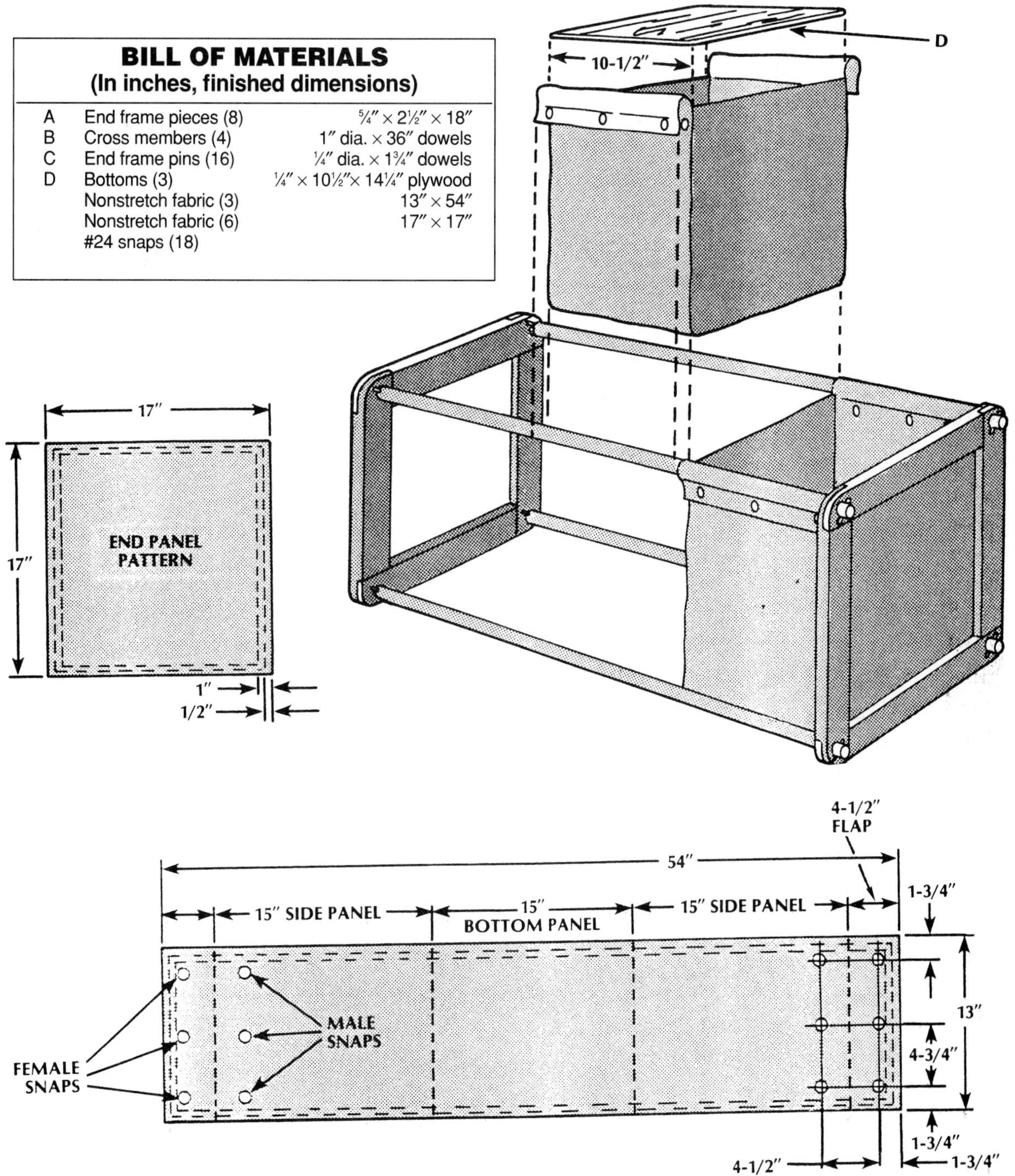

BILL OF MATERIALS
(In inches, finished dimensions)

A	End frame pieces (8)	5/4″ × 2½″ × 18″
B	Cross members (4)	1″ dia. × 36″ dowels
C	End frame pins (16)	¼″ dia. × 1¾″ dowels
D	Bottoms (3)	¼″ × 10½″ × 14¼″ plywood
	Nonstretch fabric (3)	13″ × 54″
	Nonstretch fabric (6)	17″ × 17″
	#24 snaps (18)	

BOTTOM AND SIDE PANEL PATTERN

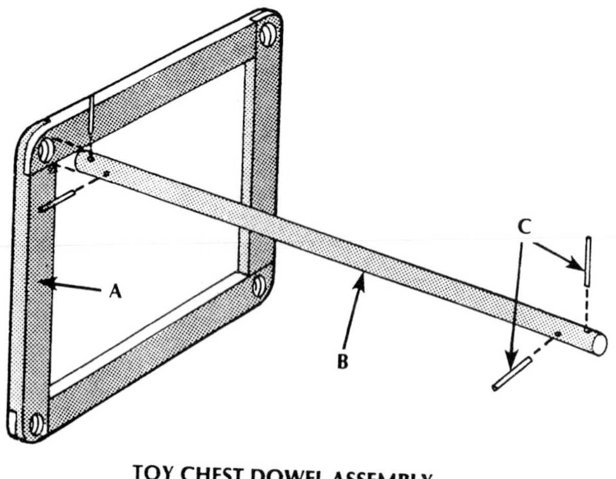

TOY CHEST DOWEL ASSEMBLY

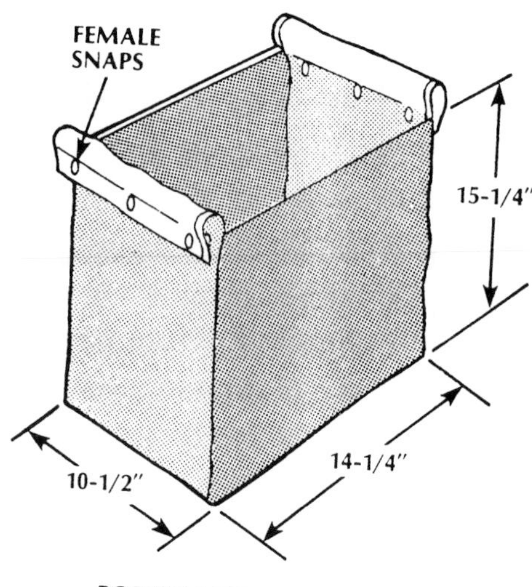

POUCH ASSEMBLY

PROCEDURE

1. Cut all of the parts to size using the dimensions given.

2. Cut half laps on both ends of all end frame pieces (A). Alternate the half laps by cutting one on the top of each piece and the other on the bottom as shown.

3. Glue and clamp the end frames together. Cut a 1-inch radius at the corners and a ¼-inch radius on all edges. Sand and drill 1 inch diameter holes as shown.

4. Draw two lines lengthwise and 90° apart on each of the cross members (B). Along one of the lines on each cross member, measure in ½ inch from each end and mark. Along the other line, measure in 1⅞-inches from each end and mark.

5. Drill a ¼-inch diameter hole all the way through the cross members at each of the marks. These holes are needed to accommodate the end frame pins (C).

6. Chamfer the ends of the cross members and end frame pins; then sand.

7. Smooth the edges of the bottoms (D); then sand.

8. Cut the fabric for the bottom and side panels to size. Draw a fold line 1 inch in from the edges of each piece. Do the same with the fabric for the end panels.

9. Fold one edge of the end panels over to the 1-inch line. Then fold it over again to create a ½-inch hem. Pin and sew. This will form the top edge of the end panels.

10. Pin the end and side panels together for each pouch. Sew the pieces together, being sure to leave a ½-inch hem. The finished flaps should be 3½ inches long.

11. Fold the pouches right side out to measure the locations for the snaps. Holding the snaps in position, use a nail to punch three holes through the flap and side. Fasten three snap sets in the holes. Then repeat the procedure for all the flaps.

12. Insert the cross members through the holes in the end frames. Secure with end frame pins.

13. Attach the pouches by wrapping the flaps around the cross members and snapping them shut.

14. Finally, set the bottoms into the pouches.

15. Finish as desired.

CHILD'S DESK: This child's desk features supports that allow for a dual-position top. (Shopsmith.)

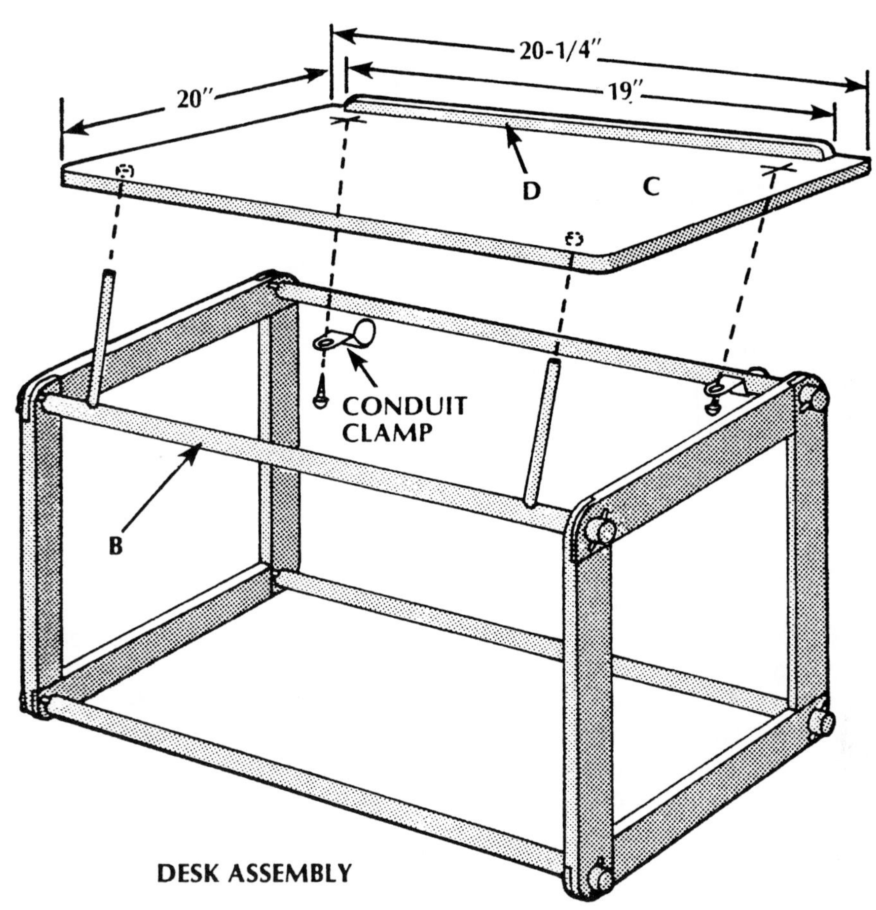

	BILL OF MATERIALS (In inches, finished dimensions)	
A	End frame pieces (8)	5/4″ × 2½″ × 18″
B	Cross members (4)	1″ dia. × 24″ dowels
C	Top	¾″ × 20″ × 20¼″ particleboard
D	Pencil holder	¾″ × 1″ × 19″ particleboard
E	End frame pins (16)	¼″ dia. × 1¾″ dowels
F	Top supports (2)	½″ dia. × 7¾″ dowels
	Conduit clamps and screws (2)	
	Wood glue	

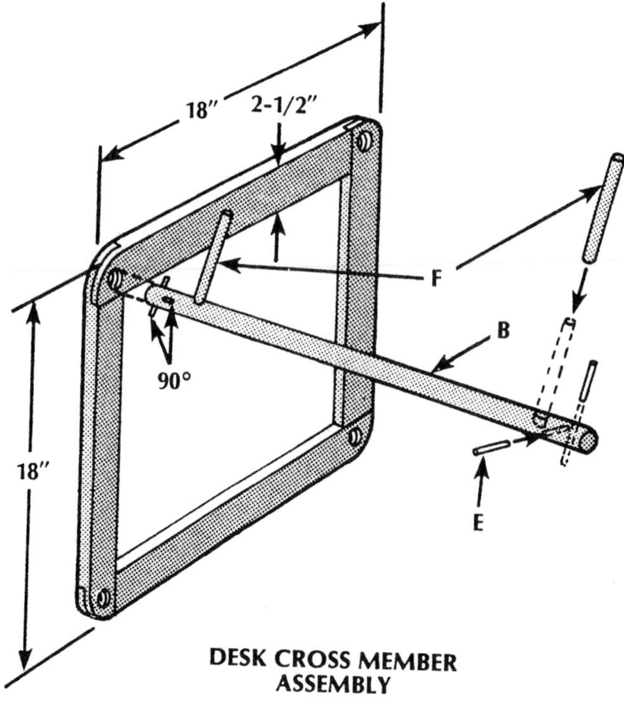

DESK CROSS MEMBER ASSEMBLY

PROCEDURE

1. Begin by cutting all parts to size according to the dimensions given.

2. Cut half laps on both ends of all end frame pieces (A). Alternate the half laps by cutting one on the top of each piece and the other on the bottom as shown.

3. Glue and clamp the end frames together. Cut a 1-inch radius at the corners and a ¼-inch radius on all edges. Sand and drill 1-inch diameter holes as shown.

4. Draw two lines lengthwise and 90° apart on each of the cross members (B). Along one of the lines on each cross member measure in ½ inch from each end and mark. Along the other line measure in 1⅞ inch from each end and mark.

5. Drill a ¼ inch diameter hole all the way through the cross members at each of the marks. These holes are needed to accommodate the end frame pins (E).

6. On one of the cross members, measure in 4¼ inches from both ends of one line and mark. At these marks drill ½-inch diameter × ¾-inch deep holes to accommodate the top supports.

7. Chamfer both ends of the cross members and end frame pins, and one end of each top support. Sand all pieces.

8. On the back side of the top (C), drill two 9/16-inch diameter × ¼-inch deep holes to accommodate the top supports and two ⅛-inch diameter × ½-inch deep holes to accommodate the conduit clamps.

9. Cut a 1-inch radius on the corners of the top, and a ¼-inch radius around all edges. Sand the top.

10. Cut a 1 inch radius on both ends of the pencil holder (D), then glue it in place on the top.

11. Insert the cross members through the holes in the end frames and secure with the end frame pins.

12. Glue the top supports into the holes in the cross member.

13. Place the top over the frame and secure with conduit clamps and screws as shown.

14. Finish the desk as desired.

DESK STOOL: This stool is sturdy enough to withstand playtime abuse. However, it is light enough for a child to move. (Shopsmith.)

BILL OF MATERIALS
(In inches, finished dimensions)

A	End frame pieces (8)	5/4″ × 2½″ × 12″
B	Cross members (4)	1″ dia. × 12″ dowels
C	End frame pins (16)	¼″ dia. × 1¾″ dowels
	Nonstretch seat fabric	10″ × 24½″

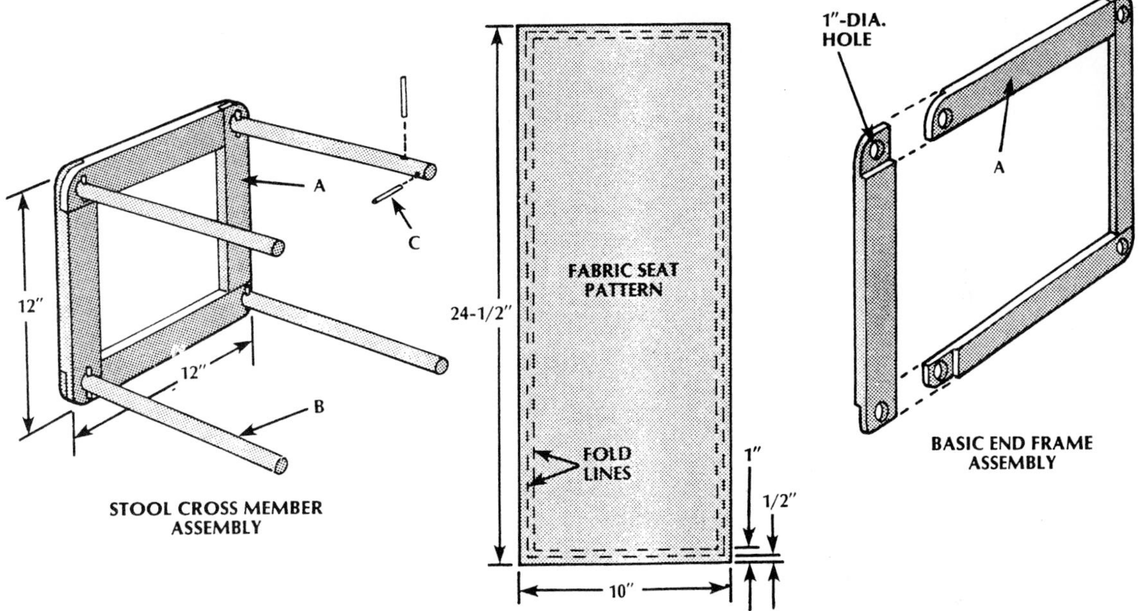

PROCEDURE

1. Cut all of the parts to size according to the dimensions provided.

2. Cut half laps on both ends of all end frame pieces (A). Alternate the half laps by cutting one on the top of each piece and the other on the bottom as shown.

3. Glue and clamp the end frames together. Cut a 1-inch radius at the corners and a ¼-inch radius on all edges. Sand and drill 1-inch diameter holes as shown.

4. Draw two lines lengthwise and 90° apart on each of the cross members (B). Along one of the lines on each cross member measure in ½ inch from each end and mark. Along the other line measure in 1⅞ inches from each end and mark.

5. Drill a ¼-inch diameter hole all the way through the cross members at each of the marks. These holes are needed to accommodate the end frame pins (C).

6. Chamfer the ends of the cross members and end frame pins; then sand.

7. Do any finishing now; it can dry while the seat cover is being made.

8. After cutting the seat fabric to size, draw a fold line 1 inch from the edge of the fabric. Fold over all edges to the line. Then fold again to form a ½-inch hem around the perimeter of the seat. Pin and sew.

9. Bring the two 8-inch sewn ends together, overlapping them ¼ inch. Again pin and sew.

10. Insert the cross members through the holes in one of the end frames and secure with end frame pins.

11. Slip the seat cover over the cross members, then insert the cross members through the holes in the other end frame. Secure with end frame pins.

GAVEL: Making this gavel will provide practice in wood turning on the lathe and making careful measurements. (Bill Schaaf.)

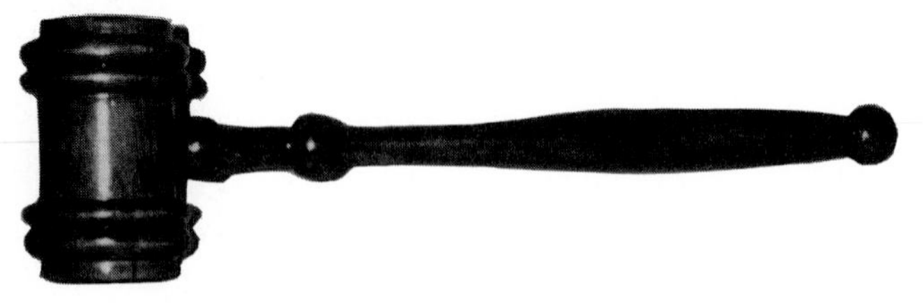

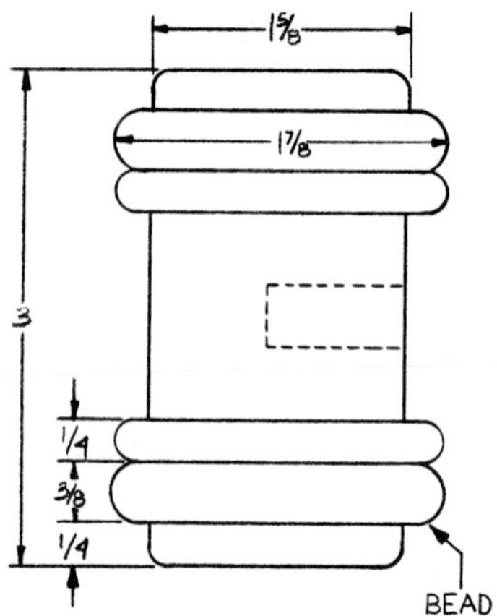

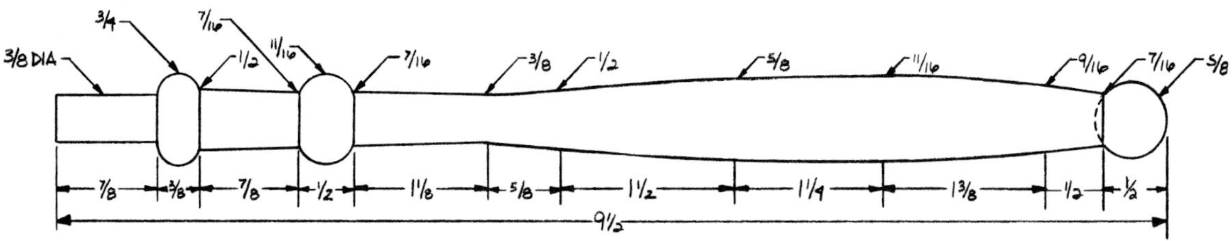

PROCEDURE

1. Obtain walnut stock.
2. Locate center points on the end of each piece. Mark with awl.
3. Crosscut one end of each piece. Mark other end at center.
4. Head procedure:
   - A. Turn to $1\frac{15}{16}$ inch (allows $\frac{1}{16}$ inch for sanding).
   - B. Part 3-inch head from length of stock with parting tool.
   - C. Locate and mark beads and flat areas.
   - D. Turn center and end areas to $1\frac{5}{8}$ inches. (Use small skew.)
   - E. Part each pair of beads with small skew held on edge.
   - F. Mark center of each bead.
   - G. Round all beads, using center line as reference.
   - H. Check measurements. Round over ends.
   - I. Sand 80, 120, 220.
5. Handle procedure:
   - A. Turn stock to $\frac{13}{16}$ inch.
   - B. Part $9\frac{1}{2}$-inch handle from length of stock.
   - C. Mark points of measurement.
   - D. Turn larger areas first. Turn smaller areas last.
   - E. Check all measurements.
   - F. Sand 80, 120, 220.
6. Cut head and handle from waste stock. Use V-block and miter gauge on band saw.
7. Locate point on head to mount handle.
   - A. Secure stock in V-block or vice on drill press.
   - B. Drill $\frac{1}{8}$-inch pilot hole followed by $\frac{3}{8}$-inch hole for handle.
8. Clean excess glue.
9. Final sand (with grain).
10. Apply finish.

LETTER RACK: This letter rack serves as an organizer for mail received and mail to be sent out.

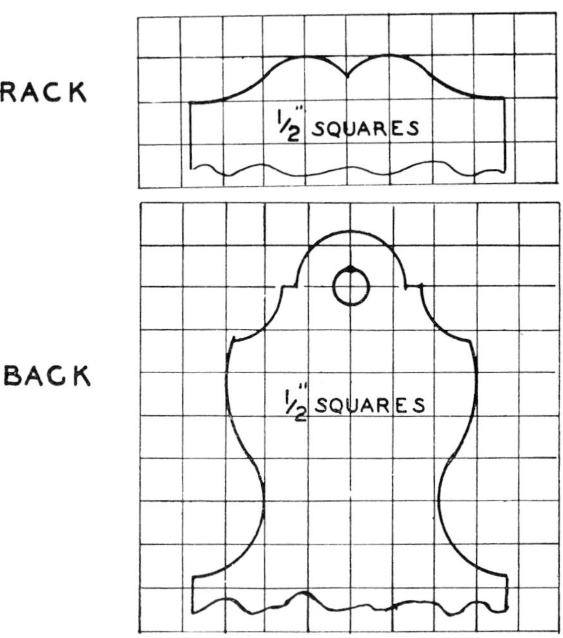

5/16 DRILL

15°

3/8"

1 1/4"

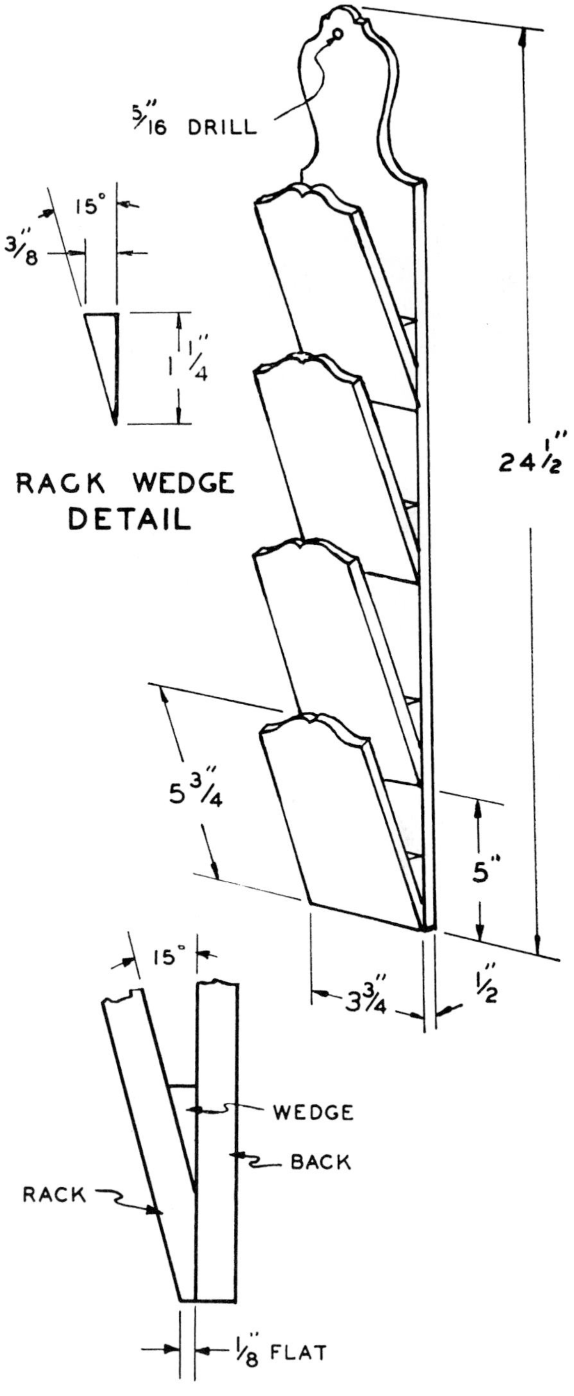

RACK WEDGE DETAIL

24 1/2"

5 3/4"

5"

3 3/4"

1/2"

15°

WEDGE

BACK

RACK

1/8" FLAT

BOTTOM RACK DETAIL

BILL OF MATERIALS
(In inches, finished dimensions)

STOCK: Knotty Pine

Part	Dimensions
Back (1)	½" × 3¾" × 24½"
Racks (4)	⅜" × 3¾" × 5¾"
Wedges (4)	⅜" × 1¼" × 3¾"

PROCEDURE

1. Lay out the design of the backboard and racks on paper. Trace the stock and cut on a jig saw. Drill the hole for hanging.
2. Cut the bevels in bottom end of racks by tilting circular saw blade 15° and using the fence as a guide.
3. The rack wedges should be made with grain running vertically. They can be cut on a band saw or circular saw from a single piece of 3¾-inch wide stock.
4. Assemble with glue and brads.
5. Sand well, giving the piece a worn appearance by rounding the edges. Apply a finish.

CHESSBOARD: Constructing this attractive chessboard provides an excellent opportunity to practice a variety of woodworking skills. (Bill Schaaf.)

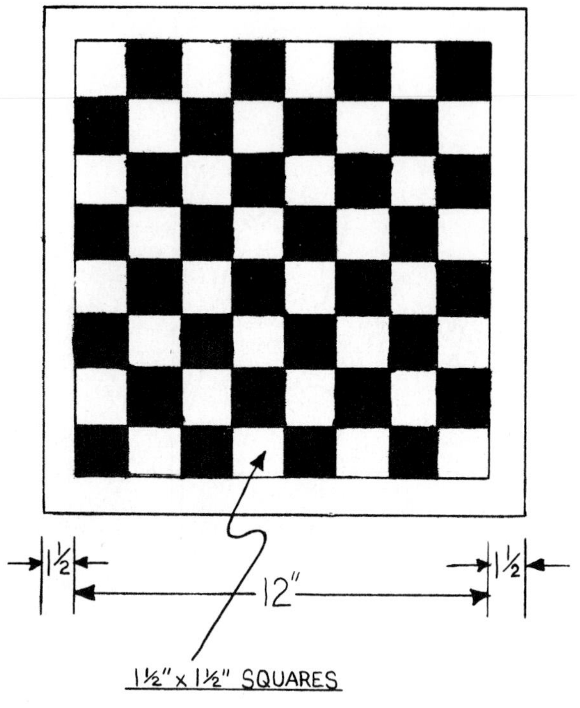

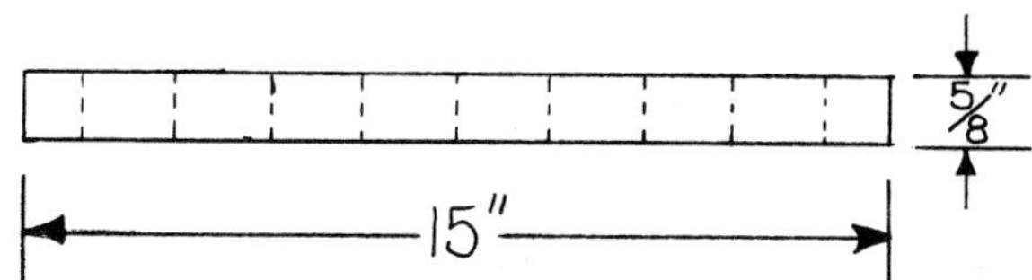

PROCEDURE

1. Join and square all eight chessboard strips. Rip to 1½-inch width.
2. Glue the eight strips together alternating colors.
3. Square one end of the chessboard, using a radial-arm saw.
4. Crosscut the chessboard into eight 1½-inch strips. Use a table saw.
5. Glue alternating strips together, two at a time. You will need three bar clamps.
6. Glue the three remaining joints together the next day.
7. Scrape glue.
8. Surface both faces of the chessboard. Use a wide-belt sander. Leave the maximum thickness possible.
9. Check for square (12 inches × 12 inches). Trim as necessary.

BORDER PROCEDURE

1. Square and joint the remaining boards. Rip to 1½-inch width.
2. Cut one end of each of two boards at 45° angle.
3. Put mitered ends together. Check (with framing square) for 90° angle. (Make necessary adjustments if not square.)
4. Cut the other two ends at 45° angles. Then place these strips at opposite ends of the chessboard.
5. Trim to exact length. Then glue.
6. After the first border pieces are glued, cut the ends of the other two borders at 45° angles. Fit as needed.
7. Glue these two borders in place. Remember to put glue on the miter joints.
8. Scrape glue.
9. Surface the chessboard.
10. Sand (by hand) and router edge.
11. Finish.

Glossary

This glossary defines terms commonly used in woodworking.

Abrasives. Substances rubbed on wood to smooth it before or between applications of finish coats. Flint, garnet, aluminum oxide, and silicon carbide are common abrasives.

Adhesive. A material capable of holding other materials together by surface attachment. Glues, cements, pastes, and mucilage are some common adhesives.

Air-dried lumber. Lumber that has been dried by storage in yards or sheds. In the United States, the minimum moisture content of thoroughly air-dried lumber is 12 to 15 percent. The average is higher.

Auger bit. A tool used to bore holes in wood.

Awl. A pointed tool used for marking locations of nails or screws.

Backsaw. A handsaw with extra metal on the top of the blade to keep it stiff.

Band saw. A saw blade fixed together in one big loop. It runs on *revolving* (turning) wheels. This is also the name of the power saw using this blade.

Bar clamp. See *Cabinet clamp*.

Bark. Outer layer of a tree. It is made up a thin, inner, living part (phloem) and a corky, outer part which is dry, dead tissue.

BASIC. (Beginner's All-purpose Symbolic Instruction Code). A simplified, algebra-like computer programming language. Most microcomputers use some form of BASIC.

Beam. A long, heavy piece of lumber. When used in construction it is usually supported at the ends. In turn, it supports a load that is laid across it.

Belt sander. A motor-driven portable machine that uses an endless sanding belt.

Bench hook. A board with cleats (blocks) on each end. It is used for holding other boards on the workbench.

Bench rule. A stiff piece of wood or metal marked in centimetres and millimetres, and/or inches and fractions of inches.

Benzine. A liquid obtained from petroleum. Used in dyeing, painting, and as a cleansing agent.

Bevel. An angular surface across an edge of a piece of stock.

Binary. Having two possible states. The 0 corresponds to the "off" or low-voltage state, and the 1 to the "on" or high-voltage state of the electronic circuitry.

Biscuit. An oval-shaped piece of compressed beech used to strengthen joints.

Bit. Abbreviation for binary digit, one of the two numbers — 0 and 1 — used to convert computer data into machine language. A bit is expressed by a high or low electrical voltage. It is the smallest unit of information a computer uses.

Bleaching. A method of lightening the color of wood by application of chemicals.

Block plane. A small hand plane. It is generally used for planing end grains.

Board. Lumber less than 2″ thick.

Board foot. A board 1-foot square and 1-inch thick, or the equivalent of this size.

Boiled linseed oil. Linseed oil to which enough lead, manganese, or cobalt salts have been added to make the oil harden more rapidly when spread in thin coatings.

Booting. Transferring a disk operating system program from its storage on a disk to a computer's memory. It is necessary to boot a disk to begin using its other programs.

Boring. The process of cutting a round hole in wood.

Bow. (Rhymes with low.) The distortion in a board that is no longer flat lengthwise, but has remained flat across its faces.

Box nail. A thin nail with a point on one end and a flattened head on the other.

Butt joint. A joint made by fastening together the ends or edges of two pieces of wood. It forms a 90-degree angle.

Byte. A group of eight bits used to specify a letter, number, or symbol.

C clamp. A clamp with a shape like the letter C.

Cabinet clamp. A clamp with a long bar and two adjustable clamping jaws. It is also called a *bar clamp*.

CAD (Computer-Aided Design). Using a computer to assist in the creation or changing of a design.

Caliper. A tool used to measure the diameter of cylindrical (round and long) work.

CAM (Computer-Aided Manufacturing). Using computer technology to plan, manage, and control the operations of a manufacturing plant.

Cambium. A thin layer of tissue between the bark and the wood of a tree. It subdivides to form new wood and bark cells.

Carpenter. A person who works with wood to build houses and commercial buildings.

Casein Glue. An adhesive substance composed of casein (the curd of milk), lime, and sodium salt. It comes as dry powder to which water is added.

Casing nail. A heavy nail with a small, conical head that can be set below the wood surface. It is used for installing doors, windows, and trim.

Cathode ray tube (CRT). The video screen that displays data and graphics.

Centimetre. One one-hundredth (0.01) of a metre.

Central Processing Unit (CPU). The part of the computer that controls its overall operation. The CPU carries out instructions given to the computer. In a microcomputer, the CPU is contained on a single chip called a microprocessor.

Chamfer. A beveled surface cut on the corner of a piece of wood.

Chip (microchip). A small piece of silicon that is a total semiconductor device. It contains microminiaturized electronic circuits.

Chisel. A woodworking tool with a wedge-shaped cutting edge.

Circular saw. See *Table saw.*

Clamp. A device that hold things together, often used to hold pieces of wood together while glue on them dries.

Claw hammer. A hammer with a claw for pulling nails from wood.

Clinching. Bending over the pointed ends of nails that stick through a board. Clinching makes nails hold more securely.

CNC (Computer Numerical Control). Using a computer in a numerical control unit to control some or all of the operations of a machine tool.

Cold-setting resin glue. A resin-base glue that comes in powder form and is mixed with water.

Combination square. A tool with a blade and a handle used for checking squareness, levelness, plumb, and miters. It is also used for measuring and marking distances. Some have a level and scriber in the handle.

Common nails. Flathead nails ranging in size from 2d to 60d. They have a larger diameter than finishing nails and are used mainly in rough carpentry.

Compass saw. A 12- or 14-inch saw with a tapered blade used to cut gentle curves and internal cuts. It is larger than a keyhole saw.

Computer. An electronic machine that stores information, manipulates data, and solves problems.

Conifer. Cone-bearing. (See *Softwood.*)

Coniferous. A class of tree with needlelike leaves that stay on the tree all year. These trees do not shed their leaves annually. Coniferous trees produce softwood.

Coping saw. A narrow saw blade about 165 millimetres long (6½ inches) held in a steel bow frame with pins. It is used for cutting curves.

Core (plywood). The center of the panel. It may be either veneer or lumber.

Corner block. A large triangular piece of wood or metal used for adding strength at the corners of frames or where legs and rails join.

Corrugated fasteners. Small, rippled, rectangular pieces of steel used to reinforce joints and make repairs.

Counterbore. A bit that drills a shallow hole for recessing a screw head.

Counterboring. Enlarging a hole so that the head of a screw or bolt inserted in it can be completely covered.

Countersink. To make one end of a hole larger for a flat- or an oval-head screw so that the screw head can be flat with the board.

Countersink bit. A tool for countersinking.

Countersinking. Removing stock around the end of a hole so heads of screws or bolts can be brought flush with the surface.

Crossband. Layers of wood placed with grains at right angles to minimize shrinking and swelling. Also, in plywood of three or more plies, a layer of veneer whose grain direction is at right angles to that of the face plies.

Crosscut saw. A saw for cutting across the grain.

Cursor. A marker on a CRT used to show the next point at which a character will appear. The cursor can be moved by the computer user.

Customary system. A measuring system used in the United States and formerly used in other English-speaking countries. It is based on traditional measurement units. Also called the *English,* or *Imperial, system.*

Dado. A rectangular groove across grain in a board.

Dado joint. A joint made by fitting the end of one board into a groove in another board.

Data base. The collection of information stored in a computer.

Deciduous. A class of tree with broad leaves that are shed in the fall and winter. Deciduous trees produce hardwood.

Decimal system. A numerical system that divides units into subunits divisible by ten.

Deft. A semigloss, clear, interior wood finish.

Depth gage. A gage that allows for boring to a desired depth with an auger.

Digitizer. A tablet-like device with a stylus or puck that transforms information and graphics into a form that can be processed by the computer.

Dimension line. In a drawing, a line that shows the dimensions or distances between lines. It has an arrowhead at one or both ends and is broken in the center.

Disk. A circular plate with a magnetic coating. It is used to store computer programs and data. Both rigid (hard) and flexible (floppy) disks are available. Disk drives for microcomputers usually use floppy disks.

Disk drive. A device that reads from, or writes to, magnetic disks.

Dividers. A two-legged tool used for a variety of purposes including laying out an arc or circle, scribing, and stepping off measurements. On some types, one leg can be removed and replaced with a pencil. (This is sometimes called a *pencil compass.*)

Double-cut file. A file with teeth cut in two directions so that they cross each other.

Dovetail joint. A joint in which one piece has dovetail-shaped pins or tenons that fit into corresponding holes on the other piece.

Dovetail saw. A small, fine backsaw used for making smooth joint cuts.

Dowel. A small, wooden pin used to strengthen a joint. Also, in foundry work, a pin placed between the sections of parted patterns or core boxes to locate and hold them in position.

Dowel pin. A long, round wooden pin used as a fastener. It is also used to make joints stronger or to line up boards.

Drill. A tool that bores holes.

Drilling. The process of cutting holes in wood with a drill bit.

Dual dimensioning. A method of drawing in which dimensions are shown in both customary and metric measurements.

Edge-grained. See *Grain.*

Edge joint. A joint in which wood pieces are joined edge to edge. It is commonly used in panel construction.

Enamel. A kind of paint in which the vehicle is a drying oil or combination of drying oil and resin. It dries to an even, hard finish. Usually it leaves a glossy surface, but the addition of a flatting agent can reduce the glossiness.

Escutcheon nails. Small brass nails with round heads used for their decorative quality.

Expansive bit. A wood-boring bit with an adjustable cutter for drilling holes of different diameters. This bit is designed to cut holes larger than 25 millimetres (1 inch) in diameter.

Expansion bit. A bit having its cutters arranged to allow radius adjustment so that one tool can bore holes of different diameters.

Extension line. In a drawing or sketch, a line that extends out from the outline. It provides two lines between which measurements or dimensions can be shown.

Face veneer. The veneer sheet on the front side of a plywood panel. It is usually of better quality than the other layers of the panel.

F.A.S. Grade of lumber. The abbreviation stands for "firsts and seconds."

Fence. An adjustable metal guide bar. For example, a fence is mounted on the top of a circular saw table as a guide for ripping.

File. A hard steel blade with cutting ridges. Files come in various shapes, sizes, and cuts. They are used to shape and smooth wood or metal.

Filler (wood). A heavily pigmented preparation used for filling and leveling off the pores in open-grained woods.

Finish. The process of adding stains, filler, and other materials to protect and beautify the surface of wood.

Finishing nail. The finest of all nails. It is used for fine cabinetmaking and finish carpentry.

Flat-grained. See *Grain.*

Foerstner bit. A wood-boring tool without a feed screw. It is used to bore holes to any depth without breaking through the wood.

Foundation. The part of a building or wall that supports the superstructure.

Framing. The rough structure of a building, including interior and exterior walls, floor, roof, and ceilings.

Framing square. A large steel square used by carpenters. It contains guides and scales for determining angles on rafters and other processes of carpentry. It is used to measure, to square lines, and to test large surfaces for wind.

Glue. An adhesive, commonly used in joining wood parts. (See also *Casein glue, Cold-setting resin glue.*)

Glue joint. A joint held together with glue.

Gouge. A woodcutting chisel that has a concave (hollow) cutting edge with either an inside or an outside bevel. Gouges are used on a lathe for grooving, and for shaping edges.

Grain. The direction, size, arrangement, appearance, or quality of the fibers in wood or lumber.

Green. Freshly sawed lumber, or lumber that has had no intentional drying; unseasoned.

Groove. A long, hollow channel, cut by a tool, into which a piece fits or in which it works. Carpenters have given special names to certain forms of grooves, such as dadoes and housings. A *dado* is a rectangular groove cut against the grain the full width of the piece. A *housing* is a groove cut at any angle with the grain and partway across the piece. Housings are used for framing stair risers and treads.

Half-lap joint. A lap joint used to connect two pieces end to end in a straight line.

Hand drill. A tool designed to hold a drill bit. It is operated with a crank on a handle.

Handsaw. A flat crosscut or ripsaw blade with a handle on one end.

Handscrew clamp. A clamp made of two parallel jaws and two screws.

Hard copy. A printout on paper.

Hardboard. A wood board produced by converting wood chips into wood fiber, which is then formed into panels under heat and pressure.

Hardware. The physical equipment of the computer system.

Hardwood. In forestry, the wood of trees that have broad leaves, in contrast to the wood of cone-bearing trees, which is called softwood. In this sense the term has no reference to the actual hardness of the wood.

Header. In framing, a piece of timber, usually a short joist, that supports tail beams and is framed between trimmer joists; the piece of stud or finish over an opening; a lintel.

Heartwood. In a tree, the wood extending from the pith to the sapwood, the cells of which no longer help in the life processes of the tree. Heartwood may be infiltrated with gums, resins, and other materials that usually make it darker and more decay-resistant than sapwood.

Hone. A special stone used for whetting sharpening tools. To whet a tool edge.

Input. Information fed into a computer or into its storage devices.

Jack plane. A general utility plane. It is used for roughing a board to approximate size.

Jig. A special device that holds or guides a tool.

Jigsaw. A power-drive saw that operates with an up-and-down cutting motion. It has an open-throat frame that holds a narrow, thin, short saw blade.

Joint. The junction of two pieces, as of wood or veneer.

Jointer plane. A long-bed machine tool plane. It is used to true edges (make them exactly smooth and at 90 degrees to each other).

Jointing. (1) Smoothing and straightening the edge of a board. A jointer is a machine which does this automatically. (2) Grinding or filing the teeth or knives of power tools to the correct height. Circular saws are jointed so that there are no high or low teeth. Knives of planers and jointers are jointed so that each knife makes the same depth of cut as all others.

Joist. One of a series of parallel beams that support floor and ceiling loads and that are supported in turn by larger beams, girders, or bearing walls.

Kerf. The cut made by a saw.

Key. A small piece of wood inserted in one or both parts of a joint to hold it firmly together.

Kiln drying. Artificial drying of lumber in a specially designed furnace or heated chamber called a kiln.

Knot. A hard, irregular lump that occurs at the point where a branch grows out from the trunk or a large limb of a tree. As a knot appears on the sawed surface it is merely a section of the entire knot, its shape depending on the direction of the cut.

Lacquer. A varnish-type solution used for finishing wood, metal, porcelain, and similar materials. Lacquers dry quickly and leave a tough, durable, flexible, lightweight film. They should not be used over oil-base paints because they contain solvents that will cut such paints. There are several types of lacquers. Cellulose lacquers have a base of nitrocellulose or pyroxyline; others have a resin base.

Laminate. To glue wood in layers. Plywood is an example. The laminated unit is stronger than the original wood itself.

Lap joint. A joint made by putting *one* board *on top of the other* (overlapping). Dadoes are cut in each, usually half the thickness of the board, so that the joint will fit smoothly.

Laser (Light Amplification by Stimulated Emission of Radiation). (1) A machine that produces a very narrow and intense beam of light that can be focused onto a very small spot. (2) A high-intensity beam of light that is emitted over a narrow frequency range and that can be directed with high precision.

Lathe. A power-driven machine used for spindle and faceplate turning.

Layout. A full-sized drawing showing arrangement and structural features.

Level. A term describing the position of a line or plane that is parallel to the surface of still water; also, an instrument or tool used in testing for horizontal and vertical surfaces, and in determining differences of elevation.

Light pen. A tiny photocell mounted in a plastic tube. It is held against the cathode ray tube (screen) to change the nature of the display.

Linseed oil. A yellowish drying oil obtained from flaxseed, widely used as a vehicle for lead-based paints. It is soluble in ether, benzene, and turpentine.

Lumber. The product of the saw and planing mill not further manufactured than by sawing, resawing, passing lengthwise through a standard planing machine, crosscutting to length and matching.

Board. Yard lumber less than 2 inches thick and 1 inch or more wide.

Dimension. Lumber at least 2 inches thick but less than 5 inches thick, and 2 inches or more wide. Includes joists, rafters, studding, planks, and small timbers.

Dressed size. The dimension of lumber after shrinking from its size when green and being surfaced with a planing machine. Usually this size is ⅜ inch or ½ inch less than the nominal or rough size. For example, a 2 inch by 4 inch stud actually measures 1½ inches by 3½ inches, under American lumber standards for softwood lumber.

Lumber core plywood. A plywood in which the core is not veneer, but strips of lumber bonded together.

Machine language. The actual language used by the computer when it performs operations. Machine language is usually a binary code.

Magnetic disk. See *Disk*.

Mainframe. A large computer, as distinguished from a minicomputer or a microcomputer. Mainframes are large units that are usually kept in a climate-controlled room.

Mallet. A wooden or fiber hammer. It is used to drive wood chisels.

Marking gauge. A tool for marking lines parallel to the edge of a board.

Memory chip. A semiconductor device that stores information in the form of electrical charges.

Metre stick. A rule one metre long (approximately 39.27 inches). A metre is the basic SI metric unit for measuring length.

Metric system. A measuring system based on natural units of 10.

Microcomputer. A small, portable computer whose basic element is a microprocessor consisting of a single integrated circuit.

Microprocessor. An integrated circuit in one chip that provides functions equal to those contained in the CPU of a computer. A microprocessor interprets and carries out instructions. It usually can do arithmetic and has some memory. It is a CPU on a chip or a computer system designed around such a device. This device is also used to control various functions on cars, machine tools, appliances, and many other products.

Miter. The joint formed by two abutting pieces meeting at an angle.

Miter box. A tool that looks like a box and has slots cut in the sides at 45-degree and 90-degree angles. The slots guide a saw in cutting edges for miter joints.

Miter joint. A joint made by fastening together two pieces of wood whose ends have been cut at angles. Usually, the cut on the end of each board is at 45 degrees. Thus, when the boards go together the joint is a right angle (90 degrees).

Mortise. The hole that is to receive a tenon; or any hole cut into or through a piece by a chisel or mortiser. It is generally of rectangular shape.

Mortise-and-tenon joint. A joint made by fitting a tenon or projecting tongue of one piece into a mortise or hole in another piece.

Mouse. A device that a user moves over the surface of a graphics tablet. Its position is recorded by a computer. The mouse is used to record or change the position of text or illustrations on a computer display screen.

Nail set. A short steel rod with one end tapered and slightly cupped to fit a nail head. It is used to set a finishing nail below the surface of the wood.

Natural finish. A transparent finish, usually a drying oil, sealer, or varnish, applied to wood for the purpose of protection against soiling or weathering. Such a finish should not seriously change the original color of the wood or obscure its grain pattern.

Numerical control (N/C). A system for directing the work of machines by means of tapes or cards. These store instructions and give them to the machines at the proper time.

Object line. In a drawing, a line that represents edges or surfaces that can be seen.

Oblique drawing. A pictorial drawing in which one side of the object shown appears close to the viewer. The other sides are slanted away.

Oil paint. A paint in which the vehicle is oil.

Oil stain. An oil-base stain. It is used to color wood surfaces.

Oil varnish. A varnish consisting of a hard resin combined with a drying oil and a drier thinned with a volatile solvent. After application, the solvent dries first by evaporation, then the oil dries by oxidation.

Oilstone. A smooth abrasive stone used for sharpening tools.

OSHA. The Occupational Safety and Health Administration.

Output. Information sent out by a computer or its storage devices.

Paint. A color or pigment mixed with oil and other ingredients.

Panel. (1) A large, thin board or sheet of lumber, plywood, or other material. (2) A thin board with all its edges inserted in a groove of a surrounding frame of thick material.

Particle board. A board composed of wood chips held together with adhesive.

Paste filler. A thick wood filler made of ground silicon, linseed oil, coloring, turpentine, and a drier.

Penetrating finish. One of several types of oil finishes that sink into the wood instead of laying on top of it like paint.

Penny. A term used to note the size of a nail (abbreviated with a small d). A 2d nail is the smallest, and 60d the largest.

Perspective drawing. A pictorial drawing showing an object as it appears to the eye.

Phillips head. A term referring to screws with crossed slots in their heads and compatible screwdrivers.

Phillips-head screw. A wood screw with a cross-shaped slot. It may have a flat, round, or oval head.

Pictorial drawing. A type of drawing that looks like a photograph.

Pilot hole. A hole drilled to receive the body of a workscrew.

Plain sawn lumber. The cheapest and most economical way to cut hardwood. The log is squared and cut lengthwise from one end to the other.

Plan (of a building). The representation of a horizontal section of a building, showing such parts as walls, doors, windows, stairs, chimneys, and columns.

Plane. A hand tool for smoothing or shaping boards.

Plane iron. The cutting blade of a plane.

Plastic wood. Puttylike plastic that can be colored and used to plug holes in wood.

Plate. Another name for *biscuit*.

Plate joiner. A portable power tool used to cut the slots in the adjoining pieces of wood to install biscuits.

Plotter. An output device with an automatically controlled pen or pens which print on paper the design displayed on the computer screen.

Plumb. Exactly perpendicular; vertical.

Ply. A term used to denote a layer or thickness, as of building or roofing paper, or a layer of wood in plywood.

Plywood. A wood product made by fastening together layers of veneer, or a combination of veneer layers with a lumber core. The layers are joined with an adhesive. Adjoining plies are usually laid with grains ar right angles to each other. An odd number of plies are usually used.

Primer. The first coat of paint in a job that consists of two or more coats; also the paint used for such a coat.

Printer. A computer output device that prints characters one at a time or one line at a time on paper.

Program. A set of instructions, arranged in order, telling the computer to do a certain task or solve a problem.

Pumice. An extremely light, spongy, or porous material used in powder form to smooth and polish surfaces.

Push drill. A drilling tool for wood. It is also called an *automatic drill.*

Push stick. A wooden stick used to push and guide a narrow board through a woodworking machine.

Quartersawed. See *Grain.*

Rabbet (noun). A groove cut on the edge or face of a board. The edge of another board fits into the groove to make a rabbet joint.

Rabbet (verb). To cut a rabbet in a board; to join two edges in a rabbet joint.

Rafter. One of a series of structural members of a roof, designed to support roof loads. The rafters of a flat roof are sometimes called roof joists.

Random-Access Memory (RAM). A type of memory that holds information that can be stored or retrieved independently. Its contents are held only as long as the computer stays on.

Read-Only Memory (ROM). A memory chip in which information is permanently stored during the manufacturing process.

Relief cuts. Cuts made on a piece of wood so that a band saw can cut a sharp curve.

Resaw. To saw a board the lengthwise (long way). It is done to reduce the thickness of boards, planks, or slabs by cutting them into two or more thinner pieces.

Resawing. Sawing lumber again after the first sawing; specifically, sawing into boards or dimension lumber.

Ridge board. The board placed on edge at the ridge of the roof to support the upper ends of the rafters.

Rip. To saw or split lumber with the grain.

Ripping. Sawing wood along the grain.

Ripsaw. A saw for cutting wood with the grain.

Robot. A reprogrammable device designed to move materials, parts, and tools. It also refers to a specialized device used for doing a variety of tasks.

Roof. The covering or upper part of a building.

Rotary cutting. A way of cutting veneer from a log. The log is fastened in a large lathe. A sharp knife cuts the veneer in much the same way as paper is unwrapped from a roll.

R.P.M. (rpm). Revolutions per minute.

Router plane. A place used to surface the bottom of grooves or other recesses.

Saber saw. Another name for the portable electric jigsaw.

Sanding. Rubbing sandpaper or similar abrasive over a surface before applying a finish.

Sapwood. The living wood, usually of a pale color, near the outside of the tree. Under most conditions the sapwood is more susceptible to decay than heartwood.

Scale. A short measurement used as a proportionate part of a larger dimension. For example, the scale of a drawing may be expressed as ¼″ = 1′.

Scraper. A flat blade for smoothing wood surfaces.

Screw. A tapered, round, metal shaft with a point on one end, a slotted head on the other, and a continuous spiral rib.

Screwdriver. A rod of steel flattened on one end to fit a screwhead slot.

Scribe. To mark a line with the point of an awl or knife.

Scroll saw. See *Jigsaw.*

Semigloss paint or enamel. A paint or enamel made so that its coating, when dry, has some luster but is not very glossy.

Shank hole. A hole drilled large enough to put in the shank of a screw.

Shellac. A preparation made by dissolving lac in alcohol. It is used commonly in the finishing of wood. Lac is a resinous substance secreted by a tropical insect.

Slip stone. A small, wedge-shaped oilstone. It is used principally for whetting turning tools.

Smooth plane. A small, lightweight bench plane used primarily for short pieces and final planing.

Soft copy. Output that is not in printed form, such as a display on a video screen.

Software. A program or set of programs used to direct the operation of a computer.

Softwood. One of the botanical groups of trees that, in most cases, have needlelike or scalelike growths rather than broad leaves. (These trees are known as conifers.) The term *softwood* also applies to the wood produced by such trees. In this sense it has no reference to the actual softness of the wood.

Solvent. A liquid in which things can be dissolved. Also, more loosely, a liquid in which tiny particles of a substance can be dispersed in suspension, without actually dissolving. Solvents commonly used in wood finishing are turpentine, alcohol, and petroleum and coal-tar distillates. The solvent in a finishing material usually evaporates, leaving the pigment or other necessary ingredients dry on the finished surface.

Spline. A thin strip of wood used to reinforce joints. Also known as a "feather" or "tongue."

Spline joint. A butt joint strengthened by cutting a groove in each member and inserting a thin wood strip (spline) in the groove to connect the two.

Spring clamp. A clamp that looks and works like a large clothespin.

Springwood (early wood). The portion of a tree's wood that is formed during the early part of the season's growth, as indicated by the annual growth rings. It is usually less dense and weaker than summerwood.

Square (noun). A plane figure with four equal sides and four right angles. The opposite sides of a square are parallel. A square is also the name of a tool. See *Framing square* and *Try square.*

Square (verb). To plane all faces and edges of a board to make them flat, smooth, and at right angles to each other.

Stop chamfer. A chamfer that does not extend the whole length of a board.

Stud. One of a series of slender wood or metal structural members placed as supporting elements in walls and partitions.

Summerwood (late wood). The portion of wood that is formed after the springwood formation has ceased. It is usually denser and stronger than springwood.

Surface (noun). A face of a board. The outside of an object.

Surface (verb). The act of making a board smooth with a plane or a joiner.

Table saw. A power-driven saw built into a table or frame. Also called a *circular saw.*

Taper. A gradual and uniform decrease in size, as of a round or rectangular piece or hole.

Template. A full-sized pattern from which structural layouts are made. They may be made of paper, cardboard, plywood, or metal.

Thinner. A volatile liquid added to finishing material to make it flow more easily and smoothly.

Tint. A color produced by adding white pigment or paint to a colored pigment or paint, with the amount of white being greater than the amount of colored pigment.

Toenailing. To drive a nail so that it enters the first surface diagonally and usually penetrates the second member at a slant also.

Tongue. A projecting rib cut on the edge of a board that fits a corresponding groove on the edge of another board; also the narrow or short side of a steel square.

Try square. A measuring device used to test squareness and to lay off right angles.

Turpentine. A paint, enamel, and varnish thinner. Most turpentine comes from the slash and longleaf pines.

Twist drill. A drill with two spiral grooves extending along its usable length.

Undercoat. A coating applied prior to the final or top coat of a paint job.

Varnish. A thickened preparation of drying oil, or resin and drying oil. When applied to a surface it leaves a hard, glossy, transparent coating. It may also be mixed with pigments to make enamels. Clear varnish is a slightly yellow, semitransparent liquid.

Veneer. A thin layer or sheet of wood; usually one that has beauty or value and is intended to be overlaid on an inferior surface. Rotary-cut veneer is veneer cut in a lathe that rotates a log against a knife. Sawed veneer is veneer produced by sawing. Sliced veneer is veneer that is sliced off a log, bolt, or flitch with a knife.

Vise. A clamp with two jaws and a device to tighten them. A vice holds boards for working.

Warp. A variation from a true or plane surface, as in a piece of lumber. Warp includes bow, crook, cup, twist, and any combination thereof.

Whet. To sharpen the cutting edge of a tool by rubbing it on an oilstone.

Wood filler. A mixture of ground silex and linseed oil, japan drier, or turpentine. It is used for filling pores of open-grained wood.

Workability. The ease with which wood can be smoothly cut and shaped with hand or machine tools.

Working drawing. A drawing that contains all the views, dimensions, and instructions needed to make a project.

Working face. The flat surface of a board that has been planed smooth and flat. It is then used as a basis for squaring the other surfaces.

Zigzag rule. A folding rule made in short pieces. Zigzag rules come in lengths from 610 millimetres to 3 metres (2 to 10 feet). The name suggests the way the rule opens and closes.

Index